D1767696

ESSENTIALS OF PSYCHOLOGICAL TESTING

Lee J. Cronbach
Stanford University, Professor Emeritus

ESSENTIALS OF PSYCHOLOGICAL TESTING

FOURTH EDITION

1817

HARPER & ROW, PUBLISHERS, New York
Cambridge, Philadelphia, San Francisco,
London, Mexico City, São Paulo, Sydney

Sponsoring Editor: George A. Middendorf
Production Manager: Willie Lane
Compositor: ComCom Division of Haddon Craftsmen, Inc.
Printer and Binder: R. R. Donnelley & Sons Company
Art Studio: Vantage Art, Inc.
Cover Design: Aurora Graphics

Essentials of Psychological Testing, Fourth Edition

Copyright © 1984 by Harper & Row, Publishers, Inc.

All rights reserved. Printed in the United States of America. No part of this book may be used or reproduced in any manner whatsoever without written permission, except in the case of brief quotations embodied in critical articles and reviews. For information address Harper & Row, Publishers, Inc., 10 East 53d Street, New York, NY 10022.

Library of Congress Cataloging in Publication Data

Cronbach, Lee Joseph, 1916-
  Essentials of psychological testing.

  Bibliography: p.
  Includes index.
  1. Psychological tests. I. Title. [DNLM: 1. Intelligence tests.
2. Personality tests. BF 431 C947e]
BF176.C76   1984   150'.28'7   83-22613
ISBN 0-06-041419-7

HARPER INTERNATIONAL EDITION
ISBN: 0-06-350249-6

Contents

List of Figures *xiii*
List of Tables *xvii*
Preface xix

Part I **Basic Concepts**

Chapter 1 Who Uses Tests? And for What Purposes? *3*
Testing and Social Policy *4*
How the Testing Enterprise Has Evolved *10*
Purchasing Tests *13*
　Sources of Information 13
　Who May Obtain Tests? 15
Decisions for Which Tests Are Used *19*
　Classification 20
　Promoting Self-understanding 22
　Program Evaluation 23
　Scientific Inquiry 24

Chapter 2 Varieties of Tests and Test Interpretations *26*
What Is a Test? *26*
Classification of Procedures *28*
　Tests of Maximum Performance 29
　Tests of Typical Performance 32
Generating Tests by Computer *35*
　Item Banks 36
　Automated Administration 37
　Simulating Personal Interaction 40
Psychometric vs. Impressionistic Testing *41*
Inferences, Short and Long *44*
　Traits, States, and Acts 45

Chapter 3 Administering Tests *49*
Two Specimen Tests *50*

    Mechanical Comprehension Test   *50*
    Block Design   *52*
Procedure for Test Administration   *54*
    Giving Directions   *56*
    Judgments Left to the Examiner   *58*
    Policies Regarding Guessing   *61*
    Providing for Physical Handicaps   *62*
Testing as a Social Relationship   *63*
    Recognizing Needs of the Examinee   *64*
    Characteristics of the Tester   *66*
    How Testers Distort Results   *67*
Motivation of the Test Taker   *69*
Preparing the Test Taker for the Test   *73*
    The Contract with the Test Taker   *74*
    Coaching and Test Sophistication   *78*

Chapter 4   Scoring   *81*
Scoring Procedures   *81*
Interpretation of Scores   *83*
    Raw Scores   *83*
    Criterion Reference and Domain Reference   *87*
    Setting Standards   *91*
Statistical Aspects of Scores   *93*
    Percentiles   *93*
    Standard Scores   *98*
    The Normal Distribution   *102*
    Comparison of Systems   *104*
    Profiles   *105*
Norms   *106*
    Characteristics of Useful Norms   *106*
    What the Manual Should Report   *110*
    Differentiation of Norms   *111*
    Norms by Calibration   *114*
Unidimensional Scaling   *116*

Chapter 5   Validation   *121*
The Need for Critical Scrutiny of Tests   *121*
    Sources of Information and Criticism   *123*
Overview of Methods of Inquiry   *125*
    Introduction to Criterion-oriented Validation   *126*
    Introduction to Content Validation   *131*
    Construct Validation: Explaining Test Scores and Their Relations   *131*
Validation Against a Criterion: A Closer Look   *134*
    The Criterion   *134*
    Correlation and Regression Coefficients   *136*

Interpreting Correlations 140
Validity in Classification 140
Content Validation: A Closer Look 145
Selection of Content 145
Task Format 146
Statistical Properties of Items 147
More on Construct Validation 149
Inquiries Contributing to Explanation 150
Validation as Persuasive Argument 154

Chapter 6 How to Judge Tests 158
Conceptions of Error of Measurement 158
True-Score Theory 159
Generalizability Theory 161
Estimating How Large Errors Are 164
Simple Correlational Studies 164
Estimation from a Two-Way Score Table 166
Internal-Consistency Formulas 169
Interpreting Findings 172
Range of the Group: Effects on the Coefficient 172
Relation to the Number of Observations 174
Effects of Error on Correlations 176
Accuracy for Particular Individuals 177
Further Considerations in Choosing Tests 181
Evaluating a Test 184

Part II **Tests of Ability** 189

Chapter 7 General Ability: Appraisal Methods 191
The Emergence of Mental Testing 192
Measurement Before Binet 192
Binet Defines Intelligence 194
Developments in the United States 196
Appreciating the Diversity of Abilities 199
Score Scales of Mental Tests 202
Description of Two Individual Tests 205
Wechsler Test Materials and Procedure 205
The Stanford-Binet of 1960 214
Illustrative Group Tests 216
A Homogeneous Test: Matrices 217
The Cognitive Abilities Test 219
Notes on Additional Tests 222
New Individual Tests 222
Conventional Group Tests 224

    Tests for Admission to Advanced Education   226
    Tests for Ages 3 to 6   227
Tests in Infancy   231

Chapter 8   General Ability as a Construct   *234*
Consistency and Change in Scores   235
    Error of Measurement   235
    Changes with Age   237
    Predictive Correlations   242
How Unitary is General Ability?   250
    Consistency Across Tasks   250
    Fluid and Crystallized Abilities   252
Specialized Hypotheses About General Abilities   258
    "Adaptive Behavior"   258
    Ability to Learn   259
    Divergent Thinking   261
    Physiological Hypotheses   263

Chapter 9   Components in Intellectual Performance   *269*
Individual Styles   270
Information Processing   275
    Piaget's Account of Intellectual Development   275
    Modeling Thought Processes   277
    Analysis of Components   281
Sorting Tests by Factor Analysis   283
    How Factor Analysis Is Carried out   284
    Alternative Pictures of the Makeup of CogAT   287
    Factor Hierarchies   289
    Results in the Thurstone Tradition   292
    Guilford's "Structure of Intellect"   295
    Possibilities in Microanalysis   298
Multifactor Profiles in Guidance   300
    Representative Guidance Batteries   301
    Spatial and Mechanical Abilities   306
    Limitations on Interpretation of Profiles   310

Chapter 10   Interpreting and Fostering Individual Development   *316*
How Nature and Nurture Combine   316
    The Continuity of Development   317
    What Kinship Correlations Do Not Mean   318
Cultural Factors   321
    Studies of American Ethnic Groups   321
    How Culture Channels Motivation   323
    Modification of Test Procedure   324
    Cultural Shaping of Profiles   327

CONTENTS

Cultural Loading of Ability Tests *330*
Intervention to Modify Abilities *334*
Testing and Educational Differentiation *338*
   Decisions About Learners with Handicaps *340*
   Fitting Instruction to the Child *342*
   Evaluation of Assignment Schemes *345*
Achievement Tests in Educational Management *347*
   The Role of Objectives *348*
   Standard Tests *351*
   An Advanced Placement Test *354*
   Constructed-Response vs. Choice-Response *357*

Chapter 11 Personnel Selection *358*
Developing a Selection Procedure *359*
   Job Analysis *360*
   Choice of Tests for Tryout *362*
   Experimental Trial *363*
   The Criterion *365*
   Translating Predictions into Decisions *369*
Two Examples *373*
   Selecting Power-Plant Operators *373*
   An Aptitude Test for Programmers *375*
What Level of Validity Is Acceptable? *380*
Fairness in Selection *383*
   Some History and Law *383*
   Psychometric Issues *386*
Issues of Test Bias in Review *391*
Adjusting Validity Coefficients *394*
Predictor Composites *395*
   Linear Regression *395*
   Crossvalidation *397*
   Classification Decisions *398*
Validity Generalization *400*
Patterns and Configurations *402*
   Nonlinear Rules *403*
Prediction by Human Judges *405*

Part III. Measures of Typical Performance *409*

Chapter 12 Interest Inventories *411*
Dimensionalizing Interests *414*
Construction of Inventories *418*
   Decisions in Instrument Development *418*
   How Techniques Have Been Combined *423*

Interest Measures in Counseling   424
  Broadening the Client's Horizon   425
  Correlates of Scores   428
Interpreting Criterion Keys   432
  What Does It Mean to Be "Similar to" a Diverse Group?   432
  Technical Issues   434
Erasing Sex Differences   438

Chapter 13   General Problems in Studying Personality   441
The Range of Inquiries   442
Types of Data   444
  Alternatives to Self-report   444
  Should Methods Agree?   446
Ethical Issues   450
  Respecting the Dignity of the Persons Tested   451
  How Permissible Is Deception?   452
  Limits on Scientific Inquiry   453
Conceptualizations of Individuality   454
  Trait Measures as Samples   455
  How Many Dimensions Should Be Distinguished?   460
  Inferences About Internal Characteristics   464
  Responses as Signs   465
Self-description: Report of Typical Behavior?   467
  Limitations of Inventory Responses   469
  Coping with Biases and Distortions   472

Chapter 14   Personality Measurement Through Self-report   475
Specimen Instruments   475
  Simple Evaluative Scales   475
  Multiscore Descriptions   481
  Computerized Interpretation   487
  A Listing of Inventories   488
Validity for Evaluating Disorders   491
  Screening   491
  Classification   494
  Forecasting Response to Treatment   495
Predictions in the General Population   496
  Occupational Predictions   496
  Educational Predictions   498
Structure of the Individual   502

Chapter 15   Judgments and Systematic Observations   508
Ratings by Supervisors and Professional Observers   508
  Sources of Error   509
  Improvement of Ratings   512

Collecting Information from Acquaintances and Associates *520*
 Mothers' Reports on Children *520*
 Peer Ratings *524*
Participants' Reports on Settings *527*
Observation of Behavior *529*
 The Situational Context *529*
 The Schedule for Sampling *530*
 Observer Error and Its Reduction *533*

Chapter 16 Inferences from Performance *537*
Psychometric Measures *538*
 Problems of Design and Validity *545*
Two Stylistic Tests *547*
 The Bender Gestalt *548*
 Inkblot Tests *553*
Thematic Tests *556*
 The TAT and Its Meaning *556*
 Correlates of Responses *559*
Integrative Assessment *561*
 History of Assessment Programs *562*
 Specialized Tests for Organizational Behavior *563*
 Validity, Past and Present *566*
Toward an Ecological View *571*

References *575*

Appendix A Sources Listing Specialized Tests and Measuring Devices *606*

Appendix B Selected Publishers and Test Distributors *608*

Index **611**

Figures

1.1 Illustrative catalog entry *14*
1.2 Embedded figures *15*
1.3 Purchaser's qualification statement *18*
1.4 Expansion of opportunity through classification *21*

2.1 Two of the Porteus mazes *30*
2.2 Complex Coordination Test *31*
2.3 Scheme for generating true-false items by computer *37*

3.1 Mechanical comprehension items *51*
3.2 Block Design materials *53*
3.3 Student anxiety on days with and without course examinations *71*
3.4 Maze performance with and without ego involvement *72*

4.1 Part of Ayres's scale for scoring handwriting *82*
4.2 Scoring rules for a Social Reasoning item *84*
4.3 Expectancy charts for aircraft-armorer trainees *90*
4.4 Determining percentile equivalents *94*
4.5 Raw-score distribution and distribution of percentile equivalents *96*
4.6 The normal distribution *103*
4.7 DAT profile of Robert Finchley *105*
4.8 Stages in scaling test items *117*

5.1 Scatter diagram for Test 1 and criterion C *137*
5.2 Scatter diagrams yielding large and small coefficients *140*
5.3 Validity coefficients in groups of wide and narrow range *141*
5.4 Possible findings in an experiment on pupil classification *144*
5.5 Considerations supporting validity argument for a selection program *156*
5.6 Item from a test for fire fighters *157*

6.1 Test and retest scores on pitch discrimination *178*
6.2 Distribution for three tests given to the same group *179*

7.1 Alpha scores of Army personnel, by rank *198*
7.2 Alpha scores of Army personnel, by level of education *199*
7.3 Wechsler performance tasks *208*
7.4 Profiles based on general and differentiated norms *210*
7.5 Matrix items at three levels of difficulty *218*
7.6 Cognitive Abilities tasks *219*
7.7 Class listing of CogAT scores for fifth-graders *221*
7.8 Items from two CIRCUS tasks *229*
7.9 Experience table for a screening test *230*

8.1 Trends over time in general ability *238*
8.2 Stanford-Binet correlations from age to age *239*

8.3 Test standings of three children from age 2 to 18   *240*
8.4 Educational and occupational histories of 97 boys   *245*
8.5 Validity with which college marks are predicted   *247*
8.6 Score portraits of three job applicants   *249*
8.7 Spectrum of general abilities   *253*
8.8 Overlap of CogAT standings with achievement standings   *255*

9.1 Two styles of response to a paper-folding item   *272*
9.2 Choice format for Block-Design task   *273*
9.3 Successive stages in command of bead-chain tasks   *278*
9.4 Actions making up bead-chain performance: preoperational level   *279*
9.5 Actions making up bead-chain performance: operational level   *280*
9.6 Two plots of CogAT factor loadings   *288*
9.7 Hierarchical scheme representing relations among abilities   *290*
9.8 A two-dimensional mapping of diverse tests   *291*
9.9 Three diagrams requiring closure   *292*
9.10 Guilford's categories for test tasks   *296*
9.11 Items representing subtests of the DAT   *302*
9.12 Two GATB profiles for a student engineer   *311*

10.1 Learning curves for pups of four breeds   *319*
10.2 Block-design responses accepted by non-Western subjects   *325*
10.3 Complex Coordination variance on early and late trials   *326*
10.4 Findings in an experiment on compensatory education   *335*
10.5 Proposed steps in evaluating a pupil referred for possible assignment to special education   *343*
10.6 Items from tests of specific objectives in ability to analyze language   *353*
10.7 Multiple-choice questions on European history   *355*

11.1 Apparent test validity under experimental and operational conditions   *365*
11.2 Predictive validity with three sets of criteria   *366*
11.3 Engineering grades plotted against aptitude scores   *370*
11.4 Success in engineering as a function of test score   *371*
11.5 Diagramming task for prospective programmers   *378*
11.6 Benefit from a selection program   *382*
11.7 Prediction within sexes from two aptitude measures   *387*
11.8 Change in work force with increase in minority hiring   *388*
11.9 Possible nonlinear relations of outcome to test score   *403*
11.10 Expected outcome as a function of two predictors   *404*
11.11 Relation among trait ratings and hiring recommendations of two industrial interviewers   *408*

12.1 Themes in the *RIASEC* system   *414*
12.2 A map of the world of work   *416*
12.3 Direct and norm-referenced profiles   *421*
12.4 Interest profile of Mary Thomas   *426*
12.5 Comparison of two criterion-keying techniques   *436*
12.6 Mean scores of librarians compared with norm groups   *439*

13.1 Data reflecting personalities of first-grade girls   *448*
13.2 Sources of variation in student behavior   *459*
13.3 Ordered array of personality traits   *461*
13.4 "Self-confidence" scores of students playing two roles   *472*

14.1 PSI profile of a rebellious adolescent girl   *480*
14.2 JPI profile of a 22-year-old male student   *482*
14.3 Outcomes when teacher style corresponds to student personality   *500*
14.4 Meaning systems of the two Eves   *504*

15.1 Descriptive graphic rating scales   *513*
15.2 An employee-rating scale anchored in behavior   *515*
15.3 A pupil-rating scale anchored in behavior   *516*
15.4 How students and teachers perceive classrooms   *528*

16.1 Standardized arrangement for observing mother and child   *539*
16.2 Stylistic differences in maze performance   *541*
16.3 Bender-Gestalt patterns to be copied   *549*
16.4 David's Bender reproductions   *550*
16.5 Thematic pictures to measure reactions of parachutists   *560*
16.6 Stages in assessment and in criterion development   *568*

Tables

2.1 Behavioral and impressionistic assessment compared *47*

4.1 Experience table for drafting courses *90*
4.2 Tenth-grade norms for DAT Mechanical Reasoning *98*
4.3 Determining standard scores *100*
4.4 Block Design norms *100*
4.5 Standard-score systems *101*

5.1 Criterion-oriented validation: Elements in a direct inquiry *128*
5.2 Illustrative reports on TMC validity, 1969 *130*
5.3 Illustrative reports on TMC validity, 1980 *130*
5.4 Content-oriented validation: Elements in a direct inquiry *132*
5.5 Data on ten salespersons *136*
5.6 Rated innovativeness correlated with ability and personality measures *142*
5.7 Correlations of tests similar in form or in content *146*
5.8 Kinds of evidence offered to TMC interpreters *151*

6.1 Analysis for five observations of typing speed *167*
6.2 Illustrative reliability calculations *170*
6.3 What error means under several procedures *173*
6.4 Effect on error of making additional observations *174*
6.5 Effect on validity of making additional observations *176*
6.6 A form for evaluating tests *185*
6.7 Evaluation form for TMC *186*

7.1 Subtests of Wechsler scales for various ages *206*
7.2 Wechsler verbal tasks at three levels *207*
7.3 Mercer's three assessment models *212*
7.4 Representative tasks from the Stanford-Binet *215*
7.5 Practical consequences of selective admissions *227*

8.1 Measurement error of WISC-R *236*
8.2 Independence in adulthood of persons who scored low on mental tests in childhood *243*
8.3 Correlations of school marks with Wechsler scores *243*
8.4 Correlations among WISC-R subscores *250*
8.5 Stability and consistency for convergent and divergent abilities *262*
8.6 Approximate intercorrelations for subtests of K-ABC *267*

9.1 Intercorrelations of four measures for adult workers *284*
9.2 Factor loadings of four tests *285*
9.3 Intercorrelations of six ability tests *286*
9.4 Factor analysis of CogAT *288*

9.5 A CogAT analysis with correlated factors *289*
9.6 Notes on the Kit of Factor-Referenced Cognitive Tests *294*
9.7 Symbolic Classification tests: Median intercorrelations for "operation" subcategories *297*
9.8 Correlations within the DAT *303*
9.9 DAT correlations with course marks 9 months later *303*
9.10 Correlations between DAT and GATB *306*
9.11 Grade-11 scores predicted from grade-5 tests *314*
9.12 Stability of GATB scores *314*

10.1 Average IQ in four demographic groups *322*
10.2 Black-white differences on WISC-R subtests *332*
10.3 Responses of students classified by home background *333*
10.4 Dialog to orient a child to an easy matrix item *337*

11.1 Validity coefficients for CPAB *379*
11.2 Test bias against minorities: Some questions and answers *392*
11.3 Validity data and combining weights in military classification *396*
11.4 Mean validity coefficients in two categories of clerical job *401*

12.1 Construction patterns of selected inventories *413*
12.2 Interest categories of the USES *417*
12.3 Raw scores and normed scores as predictors for college women *422*
12.4 How Engineer(f) scoring weights were established *434*
12.5 How Engineer(m) scoring weights were established *435*
12.6 Responses to items in three time periods *437*

13.1 Correlations of ratings in a multitrait-multimethod design *447*
13.2 Description of a Cattell factor *463*

14.1 Convergent correlations for JPI scores *481*
14.2 Reputations and self-descriptions associated with MMPI scores of college women *486*
14.3 Success of a cut score in distinguishing mental patients *493*

15.1 Intercorrelations of ratings on power-plant operators *510*
15.2 Characteristics associated with creativity in women mathematicians *519*
15.3 Hierarchical mapping of problem behavior in children *522*

16.1 Physiological response of parachutists to thematic pictures *561*
16.2 Correlation of criterion rankings with assessments of marketing managers *569*

Preface

This book is intended for three audiences: professionals in testing, other professionals who encounter test scores and score reports in their work, and citizens. And, of course, it is addressed to students who will be playing these roles. Testing specialists are concerned with constructing, selecting, giving, and interpreting tests. The second audience spreads over many professions. Physicians and teachers receive reports from psychological examinations; lawyers argue cases in which tests supply important evidence and cases where tests themselves are the focus of dispute; business executives pass judgment on plans for employee selection; science educators have to decide whether unsatisfactory test results imply that the curriculum should be changed; and many kinds of research teams work with behavioral data. Thirdly, tests and test findings affect the lives of citizens and their social institutions. Therefore, citizens properly make up the jury when controversies about the role of tests in social management arise.

When a first version of this book appeared in 1949, a reviewer spoke of it as "impatiently contemporary." He was right—there was much news to tell. The 1940s had seen brilliant applications of testing in military classification and in analysis of breakdowns and emotional disorders. Professionals had come to recognize the role of social backgrounds in the developing of abilities. They had come to prefer multiscore aptitude profiles to single scores, and tests intended to produce meaningful profiles had appeared. The Minnesota Multiphasic had rocketed to stardom in evaluating neuropsychiatric casualties, and observations in standardized stress situations had enabled the Office of Strategic Services to evaluate fitness for exotic responsibilities. The innovations have not fulfilled the hopes of those days, but they revolutionized thinking about assessment.

I trust that this fourth edition can also be called contemporary. It is not "impatient," though; we have come to realize that human institutions change gradually and that technical advances can generate social problems as well as relieve them. In the 1970s, the push for broader distribution of opportunity has stimulated psychologists to reconsider all the consequences of test use. Through educational classification and employment selection, tests help determine who gains affluence and influence. Tests used in program evaluation affect the fortunes and the efficiency of social services. Reacting thoughtfully to criticisms of test use, the profession has begun to reverse some practices, the most notable advances of the 1970s being the greater flow of information about tests to those affected by them. In some instances, after considering the alternatives, professional consensus supports a traditional practice; and, of course, the profession is sharply divided regarding some issues. Most of my professional activity since 1970 has been on this policy frontier.

"Contemporary" does not mean topical and transient. The ideas of the 1940s remain important; indeed, an astonishing number of awards given recently for scientific or professional contributions in psychology honored work founded on advances in measurement made in the 1940s and the early 1950s. The 1981 award to Anne Anastasi makes this an appropriate time to salute her as a competitor. The emphasis in successive editions of her text differs from mine, but her interpretations of research and her insistence on professional probity are admirable.

Current topics fit into a historical perspective. The fresh analytic methods of Sternberg, for example, connect with those of Piaget and with the ideas of Binet before him. And the issues in the *Bakke* case trace back to Jefferson. The 1950s and the 1960s were periods of consolidation. To name but two examples, the Test Standards of 1954 and J. McV. Hunt's *Intelligence and experience* (1961) integrated, elaborated, and dramatized professional perceptions that had been scattered and inarticulate. The 1970s were a period of challenge and disestablishment.

Now the time has come for consolidation at a higher level. A current synopsis should take advantage of the criticisms, explain what resolutions are currently accepted and why, clarify the basis on which emerging techniques and practices are to be judged, and point out promising lines for further development. When such matters are addressed, there is again much news! The aim of this book is to present lessons of experience and theory and to highlight the values that enter into decisions. Undergraduate and advanced students, lay people and professionals will take different things from the book. Each of them, I hope, will become an informed participant in policy formation, and—within the limits of an introductory exposure—an astute user of test information.

I am indebted to many investigators and to staff members of agencies that produce tests for information, including unpublished data. I owe much to opportunities for exchange of views with students and with senior colleagues, notably, in the latter case, as a member of a multidisciplinary Committee on Ability Tests (Wigdor & Garner, 1982). Goldine Gleser, Richard Snow, and J. Thomas Hastings head the very long list of others from whom I have learned. More and more I appreciate how indispensable to work of this kind are librarians and secretaries. Claire Russell, in particular, performed wonders to move this and other work toward completion. My thanks to one and all.

LEE J. CRONBACH

PART I
BASIC CONCEPTS

1
Who Uses Tests? And for What Purposes?

Tests of abilities and other personal characteristics play a large role in modern life, contributing to countless decisions that shape individuals' upbringing, schooling, and careers. Tests direct attention to the talented; they issue an early warning and constructive hints regarding individuals who will need special help. Almost never does, or should, a test score by itself determine what is to be done. In working up a case report on an adult, for example, the clinical psychologist may consider—alongside the test scores—the past and present family history, the educational and employment history, the medical record, feelings expressed in an interview, and opinions elicited from the person's acquaintances.

Tests have been much criticized because misconceptions and misapplications have led to some decisions that, in hindsight, we see as unwise or unjust. Professional leaders had bad ideas as well as good ones in older days, and some of today's "best" ideas will surely be rejected in a wiser future. It is this corrective process, however, that sets testing apart from other sources of information about persons and institutions. *Tests are almost unique in being reproducible and explicit.* Since the validity of interpretations and decision rules can be checked out, information from tests is more likely to be steadily improved than is appraisal of other kinds.

In this book, the concept of "test" encompasses Socratic questioning of a student, an apparatus in which a pigeon obtains a grain of rice by pecking at the brighter of two light spots, and a round-robin chess tournament. The book will concentrate, however, on tasks designed to be presented in the same way to many persons in many places. These "standardized" tests are important in themselves, and they are especially suitable for textbook treatment because research on them accumulates. Most of the concepts used to analyze these tests apply to unstandardized tests.

One main topic is ability tests. The book also takes up systematic observation of children, teachers, industrial workers, and so forth; questionnaires about beliefs, feelings, and behavior; and probes searching out motives of which an individual may be unaware.

Test interpretation will receive more attention here than test construction, and particular tests will be described primarily as illustrations. The book will discuss the kinds of tests used in schools, mental health clinics, counseling centers, industry, and military settings. Tests used in research are also considered. How does a certain new drug affect mood and alertness? How does the makeup of a group affect its teamwork? At what age does a child become able to "see things through the eyes of another person"? In a developing country, how do new attitudes about work styles and social institutions spread? And so on. Beyond psychology and education, tests contribute to research in fields as diverse as anthropology, economics, and genetics.

TESTING AND SOCIAL POLICY

The book discusses public policy and public debates, as well as test technique and scientific findings. Month after month, disputes about tests and test results make headlines. You may recall some of the controversies. Did the negative evaluation of Head Start in the late 1960s give a true picture? Has the ability of the pool of college applicants been declining from decade to decade—and, if so, who is to blame? Do services that coach for the Law School Admission Test give an unfair advantage to applicants who can afford time and money for the coaching? Can a medical school properly put an applicant of minority origin ahead of a nonminority applicant with a higher test score? Although such specific topics fade into history, the basic conflicts recur. Recent controversies have echoed controversies dating back to the beginnings of modern testing (Cronbach, 1975b; Haney, in Glaser & Bond, 1981). The same misunderstandings about tests and the same value conflicts surface again and again.

There are two sides to most of the issues. For example, some children have profited from being placed in a class for the "educable mentally retarded (EMR),"[1] and some have not. At times unsound testing or bad interpretations

---

[1] Abbreviations such as EMR are convenient and are much used by professionals. Nearly every such abbreviation appears either in the subject index—perhaps under the subject listing, as in "Educationally mentally retarded (EMR)" or under "Tests and techniques: Embedded Figures Test (EFT)," for example. Abbreviations used for publishers are listed in Appendix B.

of tests have assigned children to the retarded category who did not belong there. On the other hand, as Lambert points out (in Glaser & Bond, 1981), *the majority* of children whose failure in schoolwork leads teachers to suspect retardation are saved from the EMR class by the positive evidence of the psychological examination.

Public controversy deals in stereotypes, never in subtleties. The Luddites can smash up a device, but to improve a system requires calm study. So, following the advice of a professional study committee, the same California legislature that voted in 1972 to outlaw group [mental] testing by local districts instituted a new, carefully safeguarded, statewide test of mental ability for first-graders, these data being needed as a base line in evaluations of reading instruction that the legislature desired. On the advice of the same committee, a statewide mental test in grades 6 and 10 that had no proper function was canceled. Sound policy is not *for* tests or *against* tests; what matters is how tests are used. But what the public hears is endless angry clamor from extremists who see no good in any test, or no evil.

Reformers' hopes for tests. "Testing has been politicized in recent years," some professionals complain. But testing of abilities has always been *intended* as an impartial way to perform a political function—that of determining who gets what. In complexly organized societies, some positions inevitably carry more responsibility and influence than others; ambitious individuals seek those posts, and each subcommunity with a special interest seeks to place its friends in them. Power and privilege, responsibility and reward are allocated by formal and informal processes.

Broadly speaking, it is through connections or through competence that individuals move into rewarding roles. Inheritance of a family firm, an uncle's influence at city hall, the acquaintances a poor youth makes at a rich kids' university—these are among the forms of advancement-through-connections. Coming up with a slogan that captures customers, handling a football well enough to attract big-league scouts, listening carefully enough to citizens that one's next campaign speech addresses their concerns—*that* is moving ahead through competence. A society can give great scope to connections or little. Shifting that balance is the aim of many a reform movement.

Those who want to match responsibility to competence have repeatedly advocated testing as a superior way to distribute opportunities. Proposing reforms for education in Virginia, Thomas Jefferson said that the state should start everyone off with a few years of education close to home. Then a traveling examiner should choose, each year, "the boy of best genius"; if his parents were poor, he would be sent forward to a regional grammar school at state expense.[2] After his two years there, another test would select who

---

[2]The gender here is Jefferson's. In the remainder of this book, I adopt a convention that will annoy some readers until they come to appreciate its virtues. Such gender-equalizing devices as "he or she" and speaking only in plurals are awkward, and in psychology they can blur meanings. Therefore, I arbitrarily shall use female nouns and pronouns when referring to a tester or investigator (other than an identified male). Except where special emphasis on both sexes is required or where I am speaking of an identified female, I assign males to all other roles—test taker, a person who engages the tester's services, and so forth. At times I change pronouns within direct quotations to conform to this style.

should continue. Ultimately half of these would be subsidized to study at college, the less excellent being left to find posts (very likely as schoolmasters). Since children of wealthier parents could attend these same schools at their own expense, Jefferson's plan struck only a feeble blow against privilege. But its intent was to bring forward a "natural aristocracy" of virtue and talent, to displace a "tinsel aristocracy" founded on wealth and birth (quoted from a letter to John Adams, October 28, 1813).

Civil-service systems were intended to place public business in the hands of qualified workers rather than of applicants with powerful patrons. Perhaps the high point among meritocratic proposals was the one John Stuart Mill made to the British in 1861. Mill wanted to extend voting rights from property owners to all ranks of society, but he placed a premium on competence. The first necessity, as he saw it, was universal education. For the sake of what we would now call pluralism, Mill wanted numerous private local schools rather than a state system. State funds would help poor parents pay for tuition—not unlike some proposals current today in the United States. Achievement tests should be given annually to make certain that every child was being properly schooled; if the child failed the test, the parent (!) would be fined (Mill, 1977, vol. 20, pp. 302ff. [1859]).

In voting, every adult male was to have one vote, but, to qualify, he would have to pass a test of reading, writing, and arithmetic. Mill also thought that extra votes should be given to those whose opinions deserved greater weight, so he proposed giving the banker more votes than the tradesman. For equity, though, there had to be a harder test (optional) by which the tradesman might prove himself the mental equal of the banker and so gain a banker's number of votes (Mill, 1977, vol. 19, pp. 323ff. [1859]).

Tests have helped to extend educational opportunity. The prestigious American colleges of the East had little need for entrance examinations in the days when they drew their applicants mostly from nearby academies. Knowing the curricula and standards of those schools, the colleges could judge the credentials supplied by the academies. When in the 1920s they sought applicants from the entire nation, the colleges found transcripts from distant high schools hard to interpret. Tests in school subjects, they felt, would be a poor basis for comparing students when course content differed from school to school. To permit fairer comparisons, they established the Scholastic Aptitude Test.

Ability pretests came into the lower schools for a similar reason. Prior to 1900 the schools had been Procrustean. Students kept up with their class or were told to repeat the grade; those with poor records left school early.

Once the schools had accepted the challenge of providing 12 years of education to as many youngsters as possible and of keeping children with classmates of their own age, it became necessary to choose a level and pace of instruction to fit the students. Ability grouping, assignment of some children to "special" education, and allocation of high school students into precollege, commercial, and technical courses of study were all part of this attempt. Tests were a favored basis for such decisions because they seemed blind to sex, to color, and to family origins. John Gardner's comment (1961, p. 48) recaptures some of the thinking of those times:

> An acquaintance of mine who recently visited a provincial school in France reported, "The teacher seemed to find it impossible to separate his judgment of a pupil's intelligence from his judgment of the pupil's cleanliness, good manners, neatness of dress and precision of speech. Needless to say, his students from the upper and upper middle social classes excelled in these qualities." Before the rise of objective tests American teachers were susceptible—at least in some degree—to the same social distortion of judgment. Against this background, modern methods of mental measurement hit the educational system like a fresh breeze. The tests couldn't see whether the youngster was in rags or in tweeds, and they couldn't hear the accents of the slum. The tests revealed intellectual gifts at every level of the population.

Employers, the armed services, schools, and mental hospitals all employ tests to keep their institutions running smoothly. But do not be misled by the fact that the largest sales of tests are for such essentially conservative, stabilizing purposes. Tests can also serve—indeed, are sometimes of great value to —the reformer. The pioneering tests of Galton, a hundred years ago, advanced the idea that one's place should depend on competence and not on family position. The same hope animates the pioneers devising educational activities today for children who do not prosper under the usual instruction (Scarr, in Glaser & Bond, 1981). Tests call administrators' attention to schools where children from an impoverished background do less well than similar children elsewhere. When a school's approach works, tests can provide convincing evidence of the achievement and encourage other schools to adopt similar practices.

Over and over, evidence from tests has challenged familiar practices and ideas. The very first use of behavioral measures to study character (see p. 542) found that traditional "character-building" programs did not immunize youngsters against the temptation to cheat and steal. By this standard, both the Boy Scout organization and the Sunday school failed. A little later, the origins of hostility, distrust, and bigotry were studied. It turned out that many of the bigots were prosperous citizens, respected and chosen for responsibility in social organizations. The tests disclosed inner fears and feelings of inadequacy that were in sharp contrast to acquaintances' image of these persons as secure and trustworthy adults (Adorno *et al.*, 1950).

Critics' discontent. Responsibility and opportunity are not distributed as critics of society would wish. Evaluating the criticisms fits properly into later chapters (see also Wigdor & Garner, 1982), but here I note three main complaints.

Matching opportunity to competence, some say, is exaggerated into winner-take-all competition. Everyone agrees that persons who are assigned responsibilities should be competent to carry them and, if given an opportunity, should be capable of making good use of it. Above the level of adequacy, however, should small differences in apparent competence determine who gets the opportunity (to become a physician, for example)?

Second, it is said that evidence of competence collected at one age is allowed to predetermine the person's remote future. So much the worse, if the competence measured is irrelevant to the later responsibility for which it serves as gatekeeper. A famous example is the now abandoned practice of making moderate competence in Latin a prerequisite for admission to American medical schools.

Third, and most basically political, is discontent because youngsters born into favorable circumstances tend to do better in the educational system and to reach higher-level occupations. They also score higher on ability tests. One humanist (Barzun, 1959, p. 142) explained the connection this way:

> There is no mystery about it: the child who is familiar with books, ideas, conversation—the ways and means of the intellectual life—before he begins school, indeed, before he begins consciously to think, has a marked advantage. He is at home in the House of Intellect just as the stableboy is at home among horses, or the child of actors on the stage.

If less educated parents or those from a certain subculture are not equipping the child with the competence the school builds on, then matching opportunity to competence may be perpetuating a social hierarchy.

A society must sort. Specialized roles have to be filled. So individuals *should* follow somewhat different paths in order to accumulate training and experience relevant to this or that role. But for which roles should sorting replace open access? Should especially rich opportunity be given to those whose homes have done least for them? At what ages should selection and self-selection into lines of concentration (and levels of intellectual demand) take place? What evidence about individuals should enter these routing decisions? And, once the evidence is in hand, what policies should govern the sorting?

No policy applying to all opportunities can ever be found. Even with regard to a single specialty, there is bound to be disagreement. Among those shaping policy for admission to pediatrics, for example, some will emphasize scientific competence; others will give priority to skill in developing positive emotional relationships.

Each generation has to think afresh about basic principles—about the meaning of "equal opportunity," for example. Members of the new generation may think differently from their elders because fresh knowledge has emerged or priorities have shifted. To understand and evaluate old practices and new proposals, we must give some attention to legal decisions about testing practice, to the laws that impose tests on schools and students in the name of "accountability," and even to the moth-eaten arguments about the inheritance of abilities (Glaser & Bond, 1981: Heller *et al.,* 1982).

A reader might reasonably ask about my biases. I am critical of many practices in testing; on the other hand, I could not write this book if I opposed testing. Individuals ought to develop understanding of themselves, and institutions have to reach decisions; tests, I think, can help. So I shall be pointing out how suitable tests can be helpful and warning against questionable practices.

One further preliminary remark: The words *bias* and *fairness* score points in debate, but make poor terms for scholarly analysis. *Bias* can refer to a deliberate effort to harm an individual or group, to a completely honest misinterpretation, or to a sound interpretation that the speaker dislikes. The meaning of *fairness* changes from year to year in legal circles, and in some reviews of testing practice even the Supreme Court splits down the middle. To foster calm consideration of specific questions, I shall avoid the words *fairness* and *bias* where I can. I take up the pertinent research and value questions at many places in the book, looking at challenges to tests in connection with specific uses and interpretations. (For example, many threads of argument regarding ability tests are gathered together in Chapter 11, p. 391.)

1. *What do these terms mean to you?*
   a. *equality among citizens*
   b. *equality of opportunity*
   c. *elitism*
   d. *merit system*
2. *Some courts have screened prospective jurors by testing their verbal comprehension and reasoning. What can be said for and against such a procedure?*
3. *The licensing examination for drivers is applied mechanically without taking facts about the person's background and past opportunities into account. Is it proper to be so "objective" when the person's quality of life and earning power are at stake?*
4. *It is conceivable that by 2033 women, blacks, and other identifiable groups in the United States will have the same range of education and occupational responsibility as any other group and will have wage rates to match. Assume that the sorting processes (not necessarily based on "tests") are appropriate to the various responsibilities. What objections to* that *society would be likely to come from an egalitarian?*
5. *Michael Young (1958, pp. 25–26) mocks the ideal of utilizing talent by projecting an actual British study into the future:*

> Some years earlier [John Doe had calculated that ability] of at least forty per cent of the nation's children was then

being denied expression. . . . It was not until much later, however, that Professor Marlow was, on a body of cogent assumptions, able to estimate the wastage in the U.K. as having been equal to about thirty-eight megaunits per annum in the forties, falling to about thirty-three in the sixties, to about eighteen by the nineties and to 5.2 megas in the 2020s. This is said to be the irreducible minimum, or in technical terms the Marlow Line, beyond which social efficiency cannot further be improved. But after all that has happened in the past century, who can safely predict what further progress may still be possible? Nor is the basis of these calculations yet altogether satisfactory.

What economic (or other) circumstances would make it vital to reduce a nation's "wastage" to a minimum? How might the effort impair quality of life? Can that damage be avoided?

HOW THE TESTING ENTERPRISE HAS EVOLVED

Testing had informal, even casual beginnings. A psychologist or physician wanted to observe some type of motor, intellectual, or emotional behavior and chose a stimulus or task that gave a good opportunity for observation. As she mentioned her findings to others, they copied the technique in their own clinics and laboratories. Soon there was a small market for equipment (tachistoscopes for studying flash perception, formboards for testing perception and reasoning, etc.). Around 1910 a few books were written, each describing one investigator's procedures.

The 1920s saw the publication of tests in editions of hundreds of thousands of copies. This bespoke the enthusiasm for testing in schools that followed the mass testing of recruits in World War I. To psychologists of those days, the great advantage of published tests was the norms they provided. Until norms were available, the clinician's basis for identifying especially strong and weak performance was limited to her own experience. The school administrator likewise found it advantageous to give tests other school systems were using; then the local averages could be compared with experience elsewhere (D. Resnick, in Wigdor & Garner, II, 1982).

What is still called "test publishing" was that and nothing more in those days. A psychologist who had prepared a test printed copies for general sale, perhaps through a firm selling apparatus to psychology laboratories. As the demand for tests grew, some textbook publishers began to handle tests, and some firms specializing in school tests or industrial tests were established. Until about 1945, the typical test was developed by an author or team of authors who completed the test and offered it to the publisher. The publisher assisted in the final stages of research and in editing the test manual, but the main scientific responsibility was the author's.

Testing was largely decentralized. Every institution—college, business, clinic, or whatever—planned and administered its own program. Each school system was free to adopt tests or not and to choose whichever ones it preferred. Counseling agencies purchased different tests, and sometimes each psychologist within the agency chose the tests she preferred. This decentralization encouraged publication of tests in great number and great variety. With published tests available, the industrial psychologist no longer thought it necessary to make up new tests for her own factory. Even a great national agency such as the Veterans' Administration relies on published tests for its clinics and counseling services.

The beginnings of centralization came slowly. Specialists at the state university might develop an "every-pupil" test to be given in the lower grades throughout the State, so that local officials could compare the local score range with that of other schools teaching much the same curriculum. In the 1920s a cooperative agency of colleges commissioned L. L. Thurstone to test linguistic and quantitative aptitudes of high school seniors. The aim was guidance rather than selection; a secondary use was to tell college officials and faculties how student intake varied from college to college. As I have mentioned, the College Entrance Examination Board introduced the now ubiquitous Scholastic Aptitude Test. To serve employers who were ill-equipped to develop tests, the United States Employment Service developed entry tests for various occupations.

A wave of expansion occurred after 1945—in clinical psychology, in vocational guidance, in selection for schools and jobs, and ultimately in policy-oriented surveys. Centralization proceeded apace. The Educational Testing Service *(ETS)* was formed in 1948 by combining smaller agencies that had served special groups of schools. It became a facility for developing tests for admission, for regular testing of student accomplishment, and for specialized studies—for example, on the effect of "Sesame Street" on children's development. Commercial publishers of tests merged into larger units, and some became subsidiaries of giant corporations like IBM (Holmen & Docter, 1972).

The desire for technically refined tests, whose development requires concentrated effort and large resources, was one of the reasons for centralization. The burden is especially great when a test must be prepared for just one season of use. The Law School Admission Test, for example, must be given several times per year to accommodate applicants. A new form is needed for each testing. The effort is enormous: item writing; tryout of items and review of the resulting data; assembly, printing, delivery, and administration of the final test; scoring; reporting of scores to those tested and to the schools of their choice; plus follow-up research to profit from the year's experience. Similarly extensive effort is required when Congress calls for an evaluative study of, for example, federally supported bilingual education. The necessary test development is most often done by an organization that has built up an experienced staff for such research. Other centralized activities include testing within the Department of Defense to support classification of recruits into specialties, industrywide personnel testing, and statewide tests for high school graduation.

For many purposes, tests are still chosen by individual psychologists or by local service agencies. For the most popular types of tests, the market is larger and more competitive than ever. The publisher of an established test fights to keep it prominent, and the publisher of a new one must make a major effort to break in. The publishing of tests is now a publishing enterprise in name only. To accept a test that some professor or clinician assembled in her spare time, almost as a hobby, and make it available to interested purchasers —that is traditional publishing. For a staff of professionals to identify a kind of instrument that could be sold, to design and construct the instrument (perhaps with help from teachers or clinicians outside the staff), to carry out some years of research before releasing the test, to attract customers by displaying the test at professional meetings, to arrange seminars to train interpreters, to provide a scoring-and-reporting service—all this is test production.

Centralization brings benefits. There has been steady improvement in the technical aspects of testing with the growth of qualified staffs. Modern scoring equipment and computer processing produce prompt reports and make possible instructive analyses of data from hundreds of localities. The developer who has amassed information in that way can offer excellent advice to users. Firms handling mass-market tests vie to provide supplementary services.

Centralization is an enemy of diversity. Some tests become prominent while worthy competitors go out of print. Large firms are understandably reluctant to invest in a test that will have a small market, and a small firm cannot afford to develop an extensive research base. The surest way to find a large market is to bring out a test that resembles the popular ones. Just as large automobile manufacturers compete by bringing out cars that have much the same specifications, so the testing industry puts most of its effort into a few tried and true designs. The huge markets of every-pupil testing and admissions testing in higher education are well served. For those uses where tests must be selected to fit the individual or to answer a question that concerns rather few users, the need is usually filled, if at all, by a "cottage industry." Even in the main product line, there is a regrettable tendency to keep old titles and designs in production, with minor improvements when modern ideas suggest radically different designs. An industry with a large investment cannot move far ahead of its customers. Only if the next generation of test purchasers understands the possibilities in uncommon types of tests will someone be enterprising enough to supply them.

PURCHASING TESTS

Sources of Information

Someone who wants to examine tests that might serve her particular purpose must first survey the tests available in order to identify likely candidates. Books such as this cannot begin to list the many tests in each category; even a specialized book on, for example, disorders of speech is unlikely to be exhaustive. Moreover, no book can keep up with new tests.

Probably the best starting point for a survey is *Tests in Print* and *Mental Measurements Yearbooks (MMY)*. Their latest editions are dated 1974 and 1978, respectively; new editions are being prepared by the Buros Institute for Mental Measurement at the University of Nebraska, with *Tests in Print* due to appear in 1983. Another resource for those who do much testing is the periodical *News on Tests* and the companion *Tests on Microfiche* (both from ETS). *News on Tests* lists all new tests that come to the attention of the staff and also cites books and test reviews. *Tests on Microfiche,* which can be consulted in many university libraries, lists unpublished tests (most of them developed as part of research projects). An investigator interested in such a test can obtain a copy and negotiate for the right to use it.

Specialized listings of tests, with or without critical evaluations or comparisons, are produced from time to time. These vary in quality, some being shaped by the tastes of the compiler and some bringing together the judgments of many experts. Some of these references are located in Appendix A.

Another way to locate tests is to obtain catalogs from the larger test publishers and from those that specialize in the user's field of application. An exhaustive list of publishers appears in the *MMY*. My Appendix B lists some publishers that persons who do much testing should know about. Many publishers are referred to in the text by shortened names or initials; Appendix B breaks this code. Publishers not listed in the appendix are not referred to by code; their addresses can almost always be found in the *MMY*.

Catalogs vary considerably in the amount of detail they provide and in the amount of advertising prose and artwork with which they embellish the facts. Figure 1.1 reproduces information reported for the Embedded Figures Test (EFT), a test having a specialized market. (CEFT is a form of EFT for children.)

Note the entry for a "sample set" of the Group EFT; an equivalent term is "specimen set." Ordinarily, such a package includes a copy of the test questions and the basic manual. Professionals using many tests collect specimen sets and supplementary technical manuals. Most universities maintain collections that can be examined by persons with a professional need-to-know. The files are not openly available; this policy keeps persons who might be tested from learning about the questions in advance.

The embedded figures task (Fig. 1.2; also called hidden figures) has been

Embedded Figures Test (b)
Herman A. Witkin

The test, designed originally for research in cognitive functioning and cognitive styles, has been used extensively in assessment studies which relate performance on the EFT to analytic ability in other tasks, social behavior, body concept, preferred defense merchanisms, etc.

The test is available in alternate forms, useful for test-retest situations. Each requires subjects to find simple geometric figures in each of 12 complex colored designs. For individual administration to older children, adolescents, and adults. Requires a stopwatch.

Time: No limit. Either form usually requires 10 to 45 minutes.

> Test Kit (card sets, stylus, 50 recording sheets): $12.75
> Card Sets: Forms A & B (including Simple Figures and Practice Items): $6.50
> Stylus: $1.00
> Recording Sheets: Pad of 50—$5.00
> Manual: See below

Group Embedded Figures Test (b)
Philip K. Oltman, Evelyn Raskin, & Herman A. Witkin

A 25-item embedded figures test in a 32-page booklet, the GEFT is designed for group administrations. Correlations suggest it may be an acceptable substitute for the individual EFT. Subjects find one of eight simple figures in the 18 complex designs, marking them in pencil. Requires stop watch.

Time: 20 minutes.

> Sample Set manual not included): $1.50
> Extra Scoring Key: $1.00; Manual: See Below
> Test Booklets (expendable): Pkg of 25-$14.00

Manual for the Embedded Figures Tests (b)
Herman A. Witkin, Philip K. Oltman, Evelyn Raskin, & Stephen A. Karp

The 32-page manual contains directions for administration and scoring, plus normative, reliability and validity data for three tests in the series—the EFT, CEFT, and GEFT. In addition it contains a masterful essay on the conceptual basis for the tests, including a thorough summary of the variety of psychological problems that have been studied with the EFT technique. 131 references. $5.00

Figure 1.1. Illustrative catalog entry. Typography modified and information on quantity discounts removed. The code (b) indicates that the purchaser must have completed courses in testing or have equivalent training.
Reproduced by permission from the 1983 catalog of Consulting Psychologists Press.

prominent in research. In discussing findings from tests of this general type, I shall refer to EFT without distinguishing which version of the test was employed in particular studies. There is some risk in this device because a shift in technique—even as simple as changing the time limit—can alter what

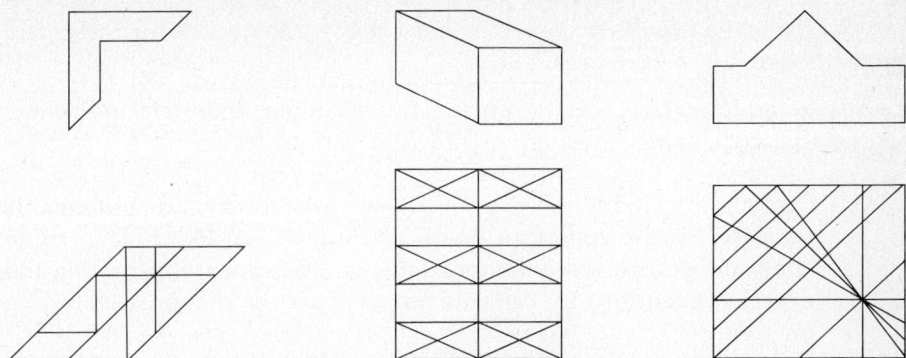

Figure 1.2. Embedded figures.

a test measures. Findings from forms of embedded figures tests have not varied conspicuously, however.

Before deciding to adopt a test for some use, one should study its manual and any relevant research summary. Whereas the catalog description is a few paragraphs long, the manual offers several pages of information on the purposes for which the test is best suited, methods of administering it, and its limitations. Sometimes the research summary is placed in a technical handbook.

A publisher's releases cannot keep up with all important developments relating to a test, and there is no surefire way to track them down. To keep informed, psychologists read journals, attend conventions, search *Psychological Abstracts,* and, on occasion, direct specific questions to the publisher or test author. On EFT, the principal research information is found in the author Witkin's reports on his theory of development and performance.

Who May Obtain Tests?

In the hands of persons with inadequate training, tests can do harm. Untrained users may administer a test incorrectly. They may place undue reliance on inaccurate measurements, and they may misunderstand what the test measures and reach unsound conclusions. It is, therefore, important for the user to confine herself to tests that she can handle properly.

To see the implications of this remark, consider industrial personnel testing. To a manager, it may appear simple to give a printed reasoning test, score it with a punched-out key, tabulate the scores, and hire applicants with top scores. A personnel psychologist, however, knows that applicants of middling ability are better bets for some routine jobs than applicants who score very high but are likely to become bored and quit. She knows that a general mental test may not measure the abilities most important in a factory job and that even experts make errors when they try to guess which tests will predict success in a given job.

Levels of qualification. Let us pursue this example. Industrial personnel workers in the United States are qualified at various levels:

- Diploma in industrial-organizational psychology. A diploma is awarded by the American Board of Professional Psychology to an applicant who possesses (among other qualifications) the training and experience required for carrying out all phases of an industrial testing program.[3]
- Doctoral degree in personnel psychology. A psychologist at this level (who may have been trained in a university department of psychology, education, or business management) should be able to plan a selection procedure and verify its soundness by research. If she has limited experience, she may need to consult a better-qualified person, especially in planning the program. Numerous consulting firms provide assistance in planning.
- Limited specialized training. Workers who have training in personnel methods equivalent to a master's degree can carry out specialized functions within a general plan. They can administer complicated tests, collect data on the performance of employees, and make some decisions about individuals. A psychologist can train an intelligent assistant to perform such functions under supervision.
- Intelligent workers without psychological training. A person without psychological training can learn to administer many group tests, take charge of the scoring of objective tests, and apply mechanical rules for reducing the list of applicants to a list of finalists.
- Ordinary clerical workers. These workers should be used only for routine scoring under competent supervision and for assisting in test administration.

When tests are used in a vocational counseling service, a school testing program, or a diagnostic service in a mental hospital, we would observe similarly varied roles are to be played. There is need for some routine handling of tests and test data, for responsible supervision, and for high-level planning of the total program. A testing program involves far more than a package of tests and a stopwatch.

Some tests can be administered and interpreted by responsible persons who have no specialized training. Other tests serving the same general purpose can be used only by well-qualified psychologists. For example, two tests that might have some value in selecting prospects for training as junior executives are the Concept Mastery Test and the Thematic Apperception Test (TAT). The former is a difficult test of word knowledge. The directions for

---

[3]The board also grants diplomas in clinical psychology, in school psychology, and in counseling.

administering and scoring procedure are simple enough for a high school graduate to follow. An employer with no psychological training can easily understand the results. To administer and interpret the TAT, a person must have graduate training in the psychology of personality and should have supervised experience with the TAT itself. It is used to investigate the motives of the test taker and his feelings about other persons. Serious errors would result if the test were interpreted by anyone save a cautious and able psychologist.

Test distribution. At one time, detailed rules to control test sales were laid down by professional associations. Tests that are difficult to interpret were restricted to well-trained practitioners. For several reasons, one being a desire to keep professional codes brief, there is no longer an explicit code for distribution. The American Psychological Association's ethics code of 1981 stops with general admonitions: Avoid misuse of tests, and try to prevent misuse by others.

Self-restriction is a professional obligation. Responsibility to restrict test distribution that once rested with publishers has been shifted increasingly to prospective purchasers. The theme is well represented by this advice from the American Personnel and Guidance Association (1978, p. 6): "Select tests that are within the level of skills of administration and interpretation possessed by the practitioner." Figure 1.3 is part of a sheet to be filled out by individuals obtaining tests from one distributor; it embodies a part of the important APA Test Standards (p. 124).

Such statements recognize that different qualifications apply at each level of test administration and interpretation and that being a trained psychologist does not automatically qualify one to handle all types of psychological tests. Being expert in personnel selection or in the analysis of poor readers does not necessarily qualify one for other test applications. Being a psychiatrist, social worker, teacher, or school administrator does not by itself imply readiness to use personality tests or even to make sound use of standardized achievement tests. Persons other than the tester come into the picture. An excellent procedure may be hard to explain to nonprofessionals; in some circumstances, the psychologist should select a simpler, though less accurate, test.

Publishers once made a considerable effort to screen purchasers. In 1967, however, the Federal Trade Commission accused them of restraint of trade, and they signed a consent decree that reduced their control. (The FTC [according to Holmen & Docter, 1972] was responding to complaints from business consultants wanting to test job applicants for client firms on a mail-order basis—a practice not favored by testing specialists.) Today publishers commonly fill without question official purchase orders from schools, colleges, and government agencies. A business firm may have to show that it has professionals as staff members or consultants. The individual purchaser may be asked to supply information on his or her pro-

___

Professional duties involving use of psychological tests

___

Membership in professional organizations ☐ APA ☐ AERA ☐ APGA

___

The following excerpts from the "Standards for Educational and Psychological Tests" ©1974 by American Psychological Association relate to qualifications for test users:

A test user, for the purposes of these standards, is one who chooses tests, interprets scores, or makes decisions based on test scores. He is not necessarily the person who administers the test following standard instructions or who does routine scoring. Within this definition, the basic user qualifications (an elementary knowledge of the literature relating to a particular test or test use) apply particularly when tests are used for decisions, and such uses require additional technical qualifications as well. A recurring phrase in discussions about testing is "the legitimate uses of a test." One cannot competently judge whether his intended use is among those that are "legitimate" (however defined) without the technical skill and knowledge necessary to evaluate the validity of various types of inferences.

G1. A test user should have a general knowledge of measurement principles and of the limitations of test interpretations. Essential

G1.1. A test user should know his own qualifications and how well they match the qualifications required for the uses of specific tests. Essential

G2. A test user should know and understand the literature relevant to the tests he uses and the testing problems with which he deals. Very Desirable

G3. One who has the responsibility for decisions about individuals or policies that are based on test results should have an understanding of psychological or educational measurement and of validation and other test research. Essential

G3.1. The principal test users within an organization should make every effort to be sure that all those in the organization who are charged with responsibilities related to test use and interpretation (e.g., test administrators) have received training appropriate to those responsibilities. Essential

G3.1.1. A test user should have sufficient technical knowledge to be prepared to evaluate claims made in a test manual. Very Desirable

G3.2. Anyone administering a test for decision-making purposes should be competent to administer that test or class of tests. If not qualified, he should seek the necessary training regardless of his educational attainments. Essential

G4. Test users should seek to avoid bias in test selection, administration, and interpretation; they should try to avoid even the appearance of discriminatory practice. Essential

G5. Institutional test users should establish procedures for periodic internal review of test use. Essential

___

I certify that I and/or other persons who may use the test materials being purchased by me "have a general knowledge of measurement or principles and of the limitations of test interpretations," as called for in the APA *Standards for Educational and Psychological Tests*, and that I/we are qualified to use and interpret the results of the tests being purchased as recommended in the APA Standards.

I further certify that:
- Tests will be kept in a secure place at all times.
- Tests will be administered only as directed in the manual.
- The confidential nature of the tests and results of testing will be adhered to.

___

Signature   Date

___

Figure 1.3. Purchaser's qualification statement.
This form is reproduced by permission of CTB/McGraw-Hill, Monterey, CA 93940. The extracts from the Test Standards are copyright © 1974 by the American Psychological Association. Reprinted by permission.

fessional training (Figure 1.3). A professor's endorsement is requested on orders from students. This control, though less than strict (Oles & Davis, 1977), tends to keep tests out of the hands of prospective examinees.

An entirely different kind of control is imposed on many selection devices. In the usual major program of selection—one for medical schools, for example—the test is under tight security. The testing organization hires someone in each test site to receive the materials and administer the test according to prescribed procedures on the announced date and then immediately return all materials to the producer. Copies of past examinations may be distributed to inform prospective applicants and the faculty member or employer who interprets test scores. Items released in this manner may be used again, sparingly sprinkled into forms of the next several years.

Security is less than perfect. Many a college has been shaken by the discovery that final exam questions for some course have leaked to a fraction of the class. The agency that prepares and administers a licensing test for real estate brokers sued a coaching school for damages after the test questions showed up in that school's curriculum. The damage was real because applicants who do not have illicit help suffer and because replacing the leaked questions is costly.

6. *An employer without psychological training decides to buy personality tests and use them on applicants. What is gained by refusing to sell the tests, in view of the fact that without them he will base judgments entirely on superficial impressions gained through an interview?*
7. *Psychologists do not favor distributing tests to people who wish to assess their own (or their children's) aptitudes or personality characteristics. Why?*

DECISIONS FOR WHICH TESTS ARE USED

A personnel manager decides whom to hire; a teacher decides whether a pupil is ready to take up long division; a physician decides how a patient should be treated. For every such decision made about the person by others, he makes dozens for himself. He decides to try for an A in chemistry or to settle for a B, to go to the community college or to take a job, to seek work as a salesperson or as a taxi driver. Even ten-year-olds are making significant decisions. The child who sees himself as capable of excellence will spend long hours at the workbench or the piano bench; the child who expects little of himself turns to pastimes.

Every decision rests on a forecast. A test tells about some difference among people's performances at this moment. That fact would not be worth knowing if one could not then predict something about the adequacy of a later performance.

Consider a test of visual recognition. We flash a row of letters on the screen for an instant, and the person reports what he has seen. Some people recognize four letters; others grasp seven in the same brief interval. This difference is intriguing, but it is unimportant until it can be related to other behavior. The applied psychologist sees that this task possibly has something in common with airplane recognition and with perception in reading. She investigates whether the flash-recognition test will predict success in these practical activities. If so, it can assist the armed forces to select lookouts or help the primary grade teacher to plan reading instruction.

A clinician might use the flash technique to see whether a person has special difficulty in perceiving emotionally toned words like *guilt* and *fail-*

ure, that being a possible indicator of emotional conflict. Such a test is useful only if the unusual score indicates probable deviant behavior or serious emotional upset at some time in the future. The significance of the clinical test is that it predicts behavior that should be forestalled or forecasts whether a certain treatment method will bring improvement. If perception of emotionally toned words is a sensitive indicator, it may serve as a way to check on the person's progress; finding that the abnormal reaction has faded carries a predictive message.

The scientific investigator may not care about practical applications, but she too must have tests that predict. Flashing letters on the screen is a good laboratory procedure because, if conditions are not altered, today's test predicts tomorrow's score. If the score changes when the experimenter changes the illumination, we know that the change resulted from the illumination and not from chance variation. The experimenter, therefore, can study systematically how flash perception is related to illumination.

It is convenient to distinguish four uses of tests:

Classification.
Promoting self-understanding.
Evaluation and modification of treatments or programs.
Scientific inquiry.

(The categories overlap, and some uses of tests are hard to squeeze into these rubrics.) The first and second uses have to do primarily with decisions about the particular persons tested; the third and fourth refer to the search for more general knowledge and policies. The first and third are most often a part of the operations of an institution. Enhancing self-understanding, on the other hand, serves the individual first and institutions only incidentally.

8. *Demonstrate that prediction is intended in each of the following situations:*
   a. *A supervisor is asked to rate probationary workers on quality of work.*
   b. *Airlines require a periodic physical examination of pilots.*
   c. *A psychologist investigates whether students are more "liberal" in their attitudes toward arms control after two years of college study.*
   d. *A teacher gives James a grade of C in algebra and Harry a grade of A.*
9. *Having spent three weeks on the Civil War, its antecedents and consequences, a history teacher gives an examination. Her plan is to turn next to a new topic: economic issues from 1880 to 1910. Which of the uses listed above could her test have?*

Classification

Classification takes place whenever a person is assigned to one category rather than another (and treated accordingly). The assignment may have long-term consequences or may be for the short term, easily reversible. The choice may be between two categories or among ten; treatment options may even be so flexible that there is a different assignment for every individual. A whole string of terms, all emphasizing particular aspects of the decision process, refer to varieties of classification: selection, certification, screening, placement, and diagnosis.

We speak of *selection* when some persons are rejected or left in their initial category. The term is most often applied to admission of students, hiring of employees, and picking individuals for an advanced responsibility (executives, officers, etc.). The emphasis is on the in/out character of the options. *Screening* ordinarily refers to a quick survey to locate individuals who may need or be eligible for special treatment. Screening pupils to locate possible hearing disorders is an example; so is a "talent search." A closer case study follows the screening.

Certification also has an in/out character: the person who passes a bar examination is allowed to practice, and the one who does not must study further. The test for a driver's license has a certifying function (and so do most educational examinations that mark the end of training). Everybody could, in principle, pass the certifying examination whereas in selection or screening it is usual to pick out only a fraction of those examined.

Placement is a sorting process that provides different levels of service for different persons: inpatient versus outpatient status, advanced English versus remedial English.

Figure 1.4 brings out a fundamental difference between classification and simple selection (Brogden, 1951). Suppose we are filling two kinds of jobs and that the average applicant is marginally acceptable in each job. If Test A is equally relevant to both jobs, we can accept applicants who score average and above, but Test A gives no basis for deciding which job is better for an applicant. If Test B is relevant to Job 1 and Test C is relevant to Job 2, we can divide the applicant pool as shown in panel ii. The tests are providing information on a difference within the person as well as on differences

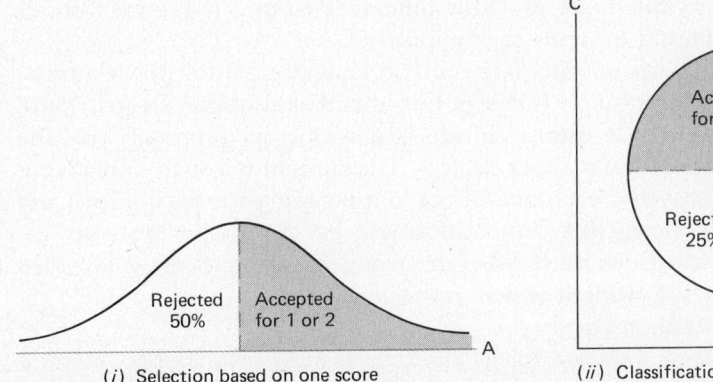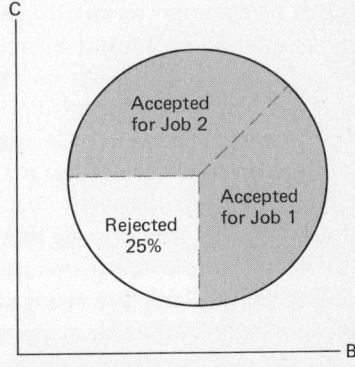

Figure 1.4. Expansion of opportunity through classification.

between persons. This permits use of a larger fraction of a manpower pool or reduction in recruiting costs or raising the standard of acceptance. A similar opportunity arises for an educational institution if it can select applicants into particular curricula (that is, classifies) instead of selecting generally superior students. As we shall see, however, predictors that give useful differential information have been hard to find.

Diagnosis usually refers to an examination conducted because of personal distress, inadequate performance, or inappropriate behavior. In school, mapping what a pupil has and has not learned is also referred to as diagnosis. Diagnosis is much more than an attempt to label the case. How a shortcoming is conceptualized strongly influences the treatment plan. The succinct label—"learning disability," for example—has a certain place in summary statistics for administrative purposes and for certain kinds of research. But a proper diagnosis is as much concerned with the situations the person copes with as with his failures. Anyone planning treatment should ask the tester to provide an account, as elaborate as the data warrant, of the examinee's behavioral characteristics, concerns, and desires—and the implications of these for treatment.

10. *Is there any logical difference between selection and screening? between classification and diagnosis?*
11. *Is there any occasion for "diagnosis" of persons who are functioning adequately?*

Promoting Self-understanding

There may have been a day when the counselor saw herself as an authority who was to sort out the facts about the client and tell him what career lines he should follow or what other actions he should take. As the profession matured, counselors realized that decisions of this kind are for the client to make. The counselor acts as a teacher, helping the person to perceive his full range of options, to anticipate probable outcomes, and to judge for himself how satisfied he would be with each choice.

A similar emphasis on self-determination has come into college admissions. A national commission (College Entrance Examination Board, 1970) emphasized that entrance into a college is a reciprocal process. Both the student and the college are making choices. The student needs to know what colleges to consider, what each one offers to a person with his abilities and interests, and how strong the competition will be. Admission tests are installed because institutions must make decisions, but the process is lopsided unless the prospective student is well informed when he takes up one offer of admission rather than another.

From early years a person forms and revises impressions of his competence, interests, and traits. There is a generalized self-concept—"I'm OK"—and an endless string of differentiated perceptions—"My oral reports get by without criticism if I keep them short and simple." Tests are only one among the many sources that contribute to these impressions, but tests often take on special weight because the scores are definite. Significance is added by such reference points as the "perfect" score, the "passing" score, and the group average.

Information about the self is stored up and integrated into an impression that affects actions year after year. A descriptive portrait gives more help with the ever-changing questions than does a score or a simple categorization. For instance, a test battery plus other facts might classify a student as a promising engineer, and this would lead him to enroll in engineering. A description would report in addition the assets and liabilities that distinguish this student from other prospective engineers. He is especially interested in aviation; he has a rather immature and uncooperative attitude toward superiors; he works energetically in short bursts with no long-range scheduling. All these facts, brought to consciousness, help the student to choose situations where he is likely to perform well, to regulate his conduct, and, in time, to overcome some limitations.

Program Evaluation

Modern educational testing is ordinarily dated from the efforts of the reformer Joseph Mayer Rice, who in the 1890s was attacking "the spelling grind" and other traditional teaching practices. Rice persuaded schools in many communities to administer the same spelling test. Schools spending more time on spelling drills did not finish with higher average scores; the time, said Rice, could be better spent on more enriching lessons. Rice's purpose in testing was to evaluate a school policy, not to judge individual students, teachers, or even school districts.

In discussions of program evaluation, *program* ordinarily refers to a plan for rendering service of a particular kind. Thus, there are evaluations of job-training programs, of welfare programs, and of campaigns to encourage behavior that reduces the likelihood of a heart attack. The program may be national or local. The scale is small when a chemistry teacher's end-of-year test indicates which topics should be given extra attention next time round. The scale is large when a federal agency commissions an evaluator to determine how well day-care programs around the nation function and what effects seem to follow from differences in the child-to-staff ratio and other features.

Evaluations feed into controversies—controversies about how much money to spend on particular services, about how efficient agencies are, and about the proper approach to crime, unemployment, family disorganization, or teen-age pregnancy. It is increasingly recognized that evaluation ought to advance the thinking of the entire policy-shaping community and not merely of those who head the program (Cronbach *et al.*, 1980). The evaluation supplies facts, but the facts mean different things to persons holding different social values and having different interests at stake. Some citizens, for example, would be enthusiastic about any training program that reduces the ranks of the unemployed; but a critic who notes that the graduates mostly enter dead-end jobs is likely to call the program, as it stands, a near failure. This illustrates the importance of asking wide-ranging questions rather than settling for one or two measures of outcome.

Some evaluations are close to pure science, but nothing value-laden can be purely scientific. A controlled experiment can establish whether a tranquilizer elevates mood and can identify physiological or behavioral side effects. If the findings are positive, how freely to administer the drug remains an issue. *One Flew over the Cuckoo's Nest,* you will recall, attacked the mental hospital's reliance on tranquilizers just because the tranquilizers succeeded so well in making patients "manageable" and thereby dehumanized them.

Scientific Inquiry

The functions of testing considered so far have to do directly with practical affairs. Tests also play a large role in science, for example in checking on a hypothesis such as, "The change of perceptual span with change in illumination is greater when a person is under stress." Tests provide a more objective and dependable basis for evaluating hypotheses than rough impressions do, and measurement is essential to arriving at a numerical relationship.

Sometimes a scientific investigator uses tests published for practical purposes, but a test invented to fit the experiment will often work better. In one study, for example, the experimenter played sound recordings of words backwards in order to study how people learn to recognize strange stimuli. Such a task, just because it is novel, makes a good experimental test.

The diversity of test functions implies that tests of many types are needed and that no one test is likely to serve the several purposes equally well. Chapter 2 will offer a rapid survey of the variety of test contents and procedures and of contrasting methods of using tests.

> **12.** *Rice found that schools providing more drill did not have better average scores in spelling. Can his finding be explained in any way except by the conclusion that drill does not work?*
>
> **13.** *A program aimed to reduce teen-age pregnancies will surely be the subject of political controversy. Does this political sensitivity influence the conduct of its evaluation? Or can the evaluator view her task as straightforward factual inquiry down to the point where the results are released? (This example is relevant to testers because an evaluator would want to assess concepts and attitudes, not merely to count pregnancies.)*
>
> **14.** *Show that a college-level reading test might be used for any of the four functions listed earlier.*
>
> **15.** *Classify each of the following with respect to the four categories of test use. More than one use may be pertinent.*

a. An instructor rides with a pilot at the end of his training, and fills out a checklist to show which maneuvers he performed correctly.
b. A psychologist compares the average vocabulary size of only children with that of children from larger families of similar social background.
c. Students sign up for a series of "behavior modification" sessions intended to increase their assertiveness. They keep a log of incidents in which they hear a statement (in class or in conversation) with which they disagree, and they record in the log whether they responded and how. The log is kept during the first week and the last week of the training.
d. A representative sample of high school seniors in Colorado are tested on their understanding of the Bill of Rights.
e. A medical clinic places a device in its lobby that enables each visitor to take his own blood pressure. A booklet explaining the readings is provided.

2
Varieties of Tests and Test Interpretations

WHAT IS A TEST?

There is no fully satisfactory definition for *test*. The word usually calls to mind a procedure in which a standard series of questions is presented, and the subject gives written or oral answers. But the road test for a driver's license is a test having neither questions nor answers, and the procedure varies from one examiner to the next. The task set for the driver cannot be standardized since the traffic through which drivers are asked to maneuver will vary from one hour to another. Perhaps the following definition is broad enough to cover the procedures with which this book will be concerned: A test is a systematic procedure for observing behavior and describing it with the aid of numerical scales or fixed categories. A numerical scale is used when a person is described as having 20/100 vision; a category system is used when he is said to have red-green color blindness. The test is "systematic" in the sense that information of the same kind is collected from one person after another. This definition embraces questionnaires for obtaining reports on personality, procedures for observing social behavior, apparatus tests measuring coordination, and even systematic records of output on a production line.

Many terms are used to characterize tests. The meaning of *pencil-and-paper test, apparatus test, oral test,* and so forth should be obvious. Although all tests call for performance of some sort, the name *performance test* is usually applied to a task requiring a nonverbal response. Among the performance tests that have been used for various purposes are repairing a piece of electronic apparatus, drawing a picture of a man, stringing beads, and "inventing" a hatrack when given two long sticks and a C-clamp.

Group tests differ from *individual* tests in that the former permit many subjects to be tested at once. Group tests can be given to a single individual if that is desirable. Many individual tests require careful oral questioning or observation of reactions. Some individual tests can be modified and simplified to permit group administration. An example is the inkblot test of personality. In the individual form, the test taker looks at a card bearing an inkblot and tells what he thinks the blot looks like. He is questioned about each response until the tester is sure just what the person sees. A group form of the test may use printed booklets or may project the blots onto a screen. The test taker writes his responses, and individual questioning is omitted. Information is less complete, but the cost of testing is reduced.

The concept of standardized testing procedures dates back to 1900. In those days every laboratory had its own method of measuring memory span, reaction time, and so on, and it was difficult to compare results. It was difficult also for school officials to judge how well pupils were learning to spell when every teacher used a different test. A test is considered to be *standardized* when the tester's words and acts, the apparatus, and the scoring have been fixed so that the scores collected at different times and places are fully comparable. If the standardization is fully effective, every tester "gives the same test." Professional tests vary in the completeness with which they are standardized.

Tests vary also in objectivity. If a test is objective, every observer or judge seeing a performance arrives at precisely the same report. To do this, each one must pay attention to the same aspects of the performance, record her observations to eliminate errors of recall and score the record by the same rules. Objectivity may be judged by comparing the final scores assigned by independent observers. The more subjective the procedure, the less the judges agree.

Tests in which the respondent selects the best answer (e.g., true-false, multiple-choice) are "objective" in the sense that scorers agree fully. In contrast, an ordinary essay test allows room for great disagreement among scorers. By careful instructions to the observer or scorer, free-response tests and observations can be made fairly objective. Tables of norms tell what scores are earned by representative subjects. Tests having norms are sometimes called "standardized tests." I am not using the word in that sense, because I wish to emphasize standardization *of procedure*. A test may have a table of norms even though its procedures are not clearly specified, and a test with well-standardized procedures may not have norms. Obviously, collecting norms is not profitable until procedures are standardized. (Much is written nowadays about the contrast between "norm-referenced" and "criterion-referenced" testing. These terms do not designate types of tests; they refer to interpretations, as Chapter 4 will explain.)

1. *Judge each of these statements true or false and defend your answer:*
   T a. *Batting averages are* objectively *determined.*
   T b. *The 220-yard low hurdle race is a* standardized *test.*
   F c. *A teacher has each member of the class read the same article in a current magazine. Time is called at the end of three minutes, and each pupil marks the place where he is reading. He then counts the number of words read and computes his reading rate in words-per-minute. This score is compared with a table of average reading speeds for typical magazine articles. This test is highly* objective.
   F d. *The test described in* c *is* standardized.
2. *Psychological tests often start from very crude procedures. Psychologist X thinks that she obtains useful information by laying a sheet of paper on the table at arm's length from the test taker and asking him to touch with his pencil exactly in the center of a circle printed on the paper. The person is told to withdraw his hand and repeat the movement, as rapidly and accurately as possible, until told to stop. Psychologist X gives the man a mark from 1 to 10 on each of the following qualities: speed, carefulness, and persistence.*
   a. *What changes would improve the objectivity of the test?*
   b. *What aspects of the procedure would need to be taken into account in standardizing the test?*
3. *Industrial morale surveys often use questions made up by the plant personnel office or its consultants. What advantages and disadvantages would there be in using the same standardized questions in many companies?*
4. *Block Design (see Figure 3.2, p. 53) is one of the most popular testing procedures. The person constructs a pattern from colored blocks to match a printed sample. The test is chiefly used in child guidance, clinical diagnosis, and measurement of general ability of persons who do poorly on verbal tests. It is also used for research on frustration and on cultural differences. Many versions of the test (different items, different scoring rules, etc.) are used in different clinics and different countries. What are possible advantages and disadvantages of this diversity?*

CLASSIFICATION OF PROCEDURES

For convenience, this book sorts procedures into two broad classes, the first being those that seek to measure *maximum* performance. These serve when we wish to know how well the person performs when asked to do his best. From this we infer "ability." Procedures in the second category seek to appraise *typical* response, that is, what the person most often does or feels—in a recurring specific situation or in a broad class of situations.

The second category includes techniques for examining personality, habits, interests, and character. "Shy," "interested in art," and "anxious when in disagreement with a superior" describe the individual's typical behavior. "Behavior," here, may refer to overt actions such as remaining silent in a social group or to thoughts and feelings that can be directly observed only by the person or to the statements the person makes. Martin may typically *act* as if interested in his spouse's anecdotes about her day at the office and might typically *say* he is interested, though he is not. Both are within the realm of typical responses. (But to make her believe—*that* is ability!)

Typical behavior and ability are not truly separable. Martin demonstrates the ability to play the role of interested listener and a willingness to make that effort. Suppose that Philip appears to be interested in his spouse's anecdotes about half the time. What does this mean? Perhaps Philip is genuinely interested in half the stories. Perhaps he is consistently lacking in interest, but capable of simulating interest and motivated half the time to put up a good show. A person's record on typing tests establishes that his ability has reached some level; if he does not push himself, the test does not display his maximum. Maximum performance (ability) is a convenient fiction. The concept helps in organizing my discussion, but observing the maximum is no easier than locating the end of the rainbow.

5. *"An ability test is one on which the person cannot earn a better score than he deserves; on questions about emotional adjustment and social attitudes the person can give responses that make a good impression even if the responses are false." Does this distinction match the distinction between maximum performance and typical behavior?*
6. *Typing rates vary from one trial to another. Can the rate reached on the person's best trial be taken as a true record of "ability"?*

Tests of Maximum Performance

The distinguishing feature of a test of ability is that the test taker is encouraged to earn the best score he can. The goal of the tester should be to bring out the person's best possible performance (within the rules), and this means that the examinee must want to do well and must understand what is considered a good performance. If he is to show at his best, directions need to be clear and explicit, even to the extent of explaining how various sorts of errors will be penalized.

Test directions almost never tell the subject how to approach the task; style of performance falls under the head of typical behavior. The Porteus maze (Figure 2.1) is an observation technique in which the tester looks for evidence of planning and foresight, as well as being an ability test scored for speed and correctness.

Some ability tests pose familiar tasks; others require the person to do something unfamiliar. In the Complex Coordination Test (Figure 2.2), a per-

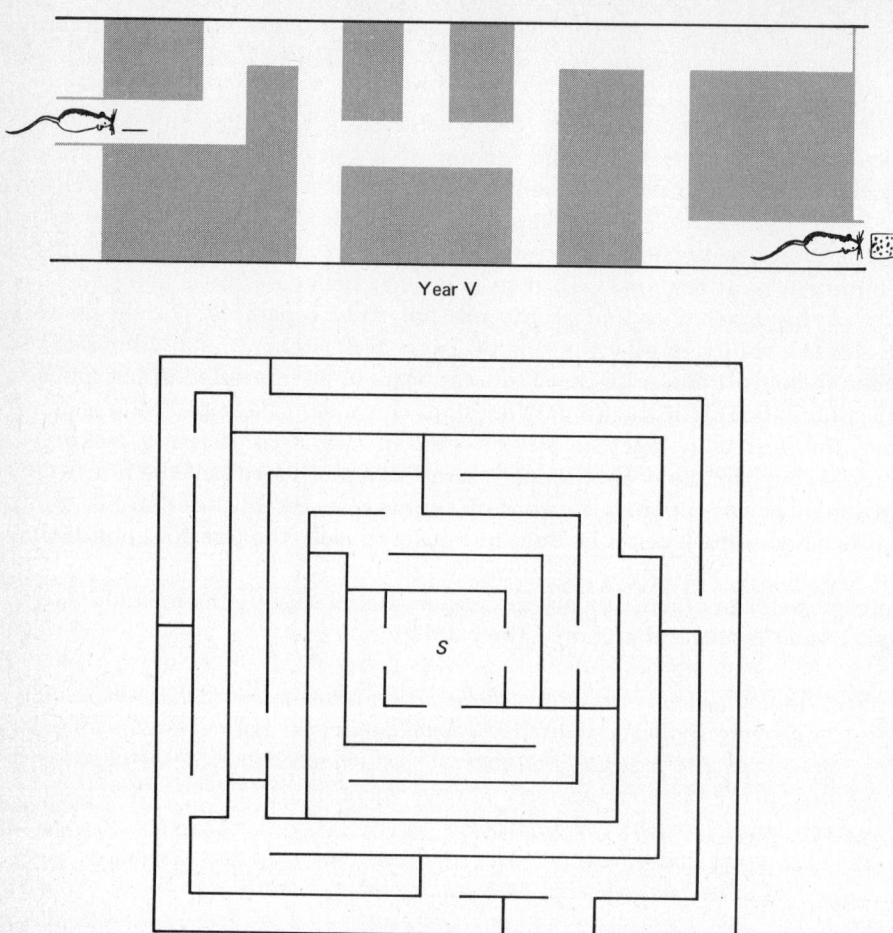

Figure 2.1. Two of the Porteus mazes. The test taker is to trace the shortest path through the maze. A trial is scored as a failure whenever his pencil enters a blind alley. He is then given further trials on the same maze. When he gets one maze correct, he goes on to a more difficult one, continuing until he fails several trials on a maze.

These mazes are copyright © 1933, 1953, 1955 The Psychological Corporation and reproduced by permission.

son who has never flown a plane operates a "stick" and "rudder bar." Flashing lights signal for certain movements; prompt, coordinated responses earn a high score. Other things being equal, a person superior on this test will more quickly master the skills of flying.

One large group of tests includes EFT and mazes, and also tests of verbal reasoning; I refer to these as measures of *general mental ability*. This term refers to a set of abilities valuable in almost any type of thinking. Tests of this sort are often called "intelligence tests," but test interpretation is sounder if we

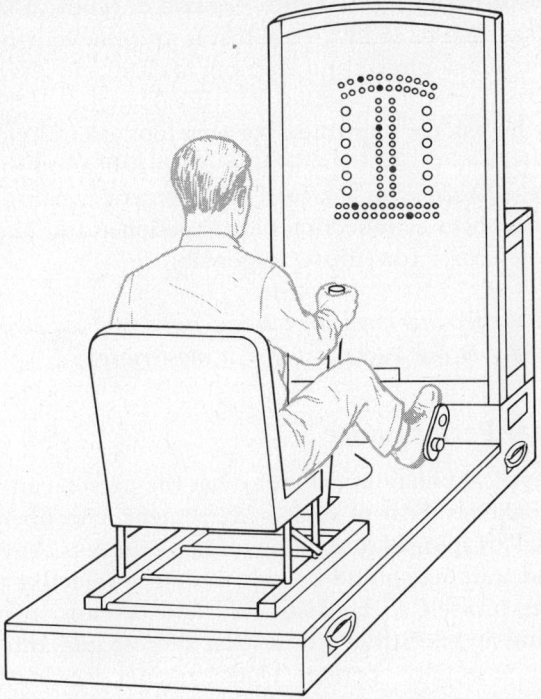

Figure 2.2. Complex coordination test.

avoid the myths that cling round the word *intelligence.* Alongside general abilities are those pertinent to a limited range of tasks: mechanical comprehension, sense of pitch, finger dexterity, and so on.

Performance on a task important in its own right gives evidence of proficiency or competence. One can measure proficiency in speaking French, in "hot-line" counseling, in fixing a faucet. The narrower term *achievement test* refers to a test covering something that the school presumably has taught directly—reading, for example, or knowledge of the solar system. A "mastery test" is an achievement test on a limited topic or skill, designed to establish whether a student has command of that material. The term *minimum competency* came into use in the 1970s. Critics of the schools had complained that many high school graduates were not adequately literate and employable. A test used to identify such students (either as an early warning or as a final hurdle prior to graduation) came to be known as a minimum competency test.

An *aptitude* test is one intended to predict success in some occupation or training course—there are tests of engineering aptitude, musical aptitude, aptitude for algebra, and so on. These tests are not distinct in form. A test of engineering aptitude may include sections measuring general mental ability, mechanical and spatial reasoning, and proficiency in mathematics.

The achievement/aptitude contrast is one of point of view, more than of test content (see also p. 254ff.). Any test is an achievement test inasmuch as it is a report on development and learning to date; and it is an aptitude test inasmuch as it says something about the future. Flaugher (1978) suggests that many of those who ask for "aptitude" testing look on individual differences in abilities as fixed and count on selection or classification to match persons to responsibilities. Those who ask for "achievement" testing, he says, think of individual differences as reflecting past experience and hope that training can equip the low scorer for future responsibility.

7. *It was said earlier that prediction enters into every decision. Would this statement apply to the teacher's use of a mastery test?*

Tests of Typical Performance

Inquiries about typical behavior ask not what the person can do but what he does or feels or believes. Fear of snakes, agreement with liberal policies, and so on are "internal" responses, but behavior none the less. Any inspector with proper vision and training should be able to detect defective parts. The poor inspector permits himself to be distracted and careless in run-of-the-mill duty. Those hiring an executive whose past success guarantees ability wish also to know *how* he usually operates. Does he supervise closely, down to the last detail? Or does he outline a general task and turn his subordinates loose? Is he equally concerned with production, human problems, and finances? Does he prefer long-range planning or quick adaptation? Knowing his pattern helps to place him properly in the organization.

To most questions on typical performance, no particular response can be singled out as "good." There is nothing good or bad about interest in engineering. Likewise, we cannot say that a certain degree of dominance is best; the world offers roles congenial to persons all along the scale.

Information on habits has predictive value; what a person does once he is likely to do again. Most psychologists would deny, however, that a person's observed habits *are* his personality. A person does not always act as he did on past occasions. We do not wish to regard exceptional reactions as capricious and unexplainable. Therefore, we assume that the responses are generated by a consistent "personality structure" or belief system that is sensitive to situational differences. The structure has to be inferred from observations of behavior and reports on acts, opinions, and fantasies.

In the weeks before Prince Charles's wedding, the British press pursued every last scrap of information on the princess-to-be. She had taught kindergarten, and a reporter tracked down one of her pupils to ask, "What was she like?" Said the tot, "I don't know. She never told me." Most psychologists are in the position of the child—90 per cent of the information collected on personality, interests, and attitudes comes from subjects' reports. Nearly all the other psychologists are in the position of the reporter, relying on second-hand impressions. Direct and systematic observation by the psychologist and her aides is comparatively uncommon—but potentially a superior source of data.

Observations. Standardized observation requires that each subject be placed in essentially the same situation. Personality may be observed during a mental test, during a group discussion, or when the person is challenged to walk along a two-by-four while blindfolded. Special tasks—performance tests of personality—have been devised to provide a good opportunity for observation.

The standardized observation enables us to compare persons who are not normally seen in similar circumstances. Moreover, it elicits responses that could be seen only occasionally in everyday life; for example, it examines reactions to frustration. The person commences a task and is prevented in some way from attaining the goal. His reactions give insight into his emotional control. In one study, preschool children were given the opportunity to play with ordinary, reasonably interesting toys. Then they were allowed into an adjoining room with extremely attractive toys. After a period of play in this room, they were herded back into the first room, and a wire screen was placed between them and the attractive toys. The children reacted in many ways: pounding on the fence, regressing to simple play with rocks, trying to pry under the fence, or going off to take a pretended nap. In general, games after frustration were less mature and less constructive than before.

If an observation is to be typical, the subject must not know what is being observed. The observer may be concealed, or the person may be led to believe that he is being tested on one characteristic while something else is observed. When reaction to frustration is being studied, the test taker may be told that his mental ability is being tested. When he is frustrated by difficult questions, his responses are little disguised.

Typical behavior may also be observed in samples taken "in the field." Children on the playground reveal a good deal about their habits and personality; so do noncoms leading platoons and workers in the office. Field observations may use elaborate videotaping or tallying procedures or may consist merely of impressionistic judgments. The baseball batting average summarizes systematically recorded field observations. The industrial supervisor's merit ratings are also based on observation, but the judgments are almost completely unsystematic.

When the tester proposes to disguise her purpose or to observe without the target's knowledge, ethical questions arise. Ethical principles worked out for the conduct of research have implications also for testing (American Psychological Association, 1973; in brief, 1981).

"Invasion of privacy" is being more and more strictly interpreted; practices considered normal in one decade are judged inadvisable in the next. Every psychology laboratory has a half-silvered mirror that enables an observer to look into the interview room or play room without herself being seen. In times past, the subject would not have been told about the observer. Today a common practice is to show the subject (or the parent if the subject is a young child) the observer's station and the view through the mirror, explaining casually that the arrangement is intended to eliminate distraction. Once absorbed in a task and especially on repeat visits, the subject is not likely to remain mindful of the mirror. Another fair practice is to give a generalized indication: "We'll be observing how you interact with your child from time to time when you are at the center, even when we do not tell you that we are keeping a record. Sometimes the observations will help us to make suggestions to you. Of course, if you do not wish to be observed, you should tell us. And if, on a particular day, something happens that you don't want in the file, you can ask us to tear up any record and we will."

Candor ought not be pressed beyond the limits of common sense. The speech clinician does not say, "I'm going to count how many times you stammer"; the child psychologist does not tell the mother, "I'm going to count the times when you seem uncertain of yourself."

Self-report. A person knows a great deal about his own behavior. Questionnaires—often called "inventories"—are used to obtain self-descriptions. There are study-habit inventories, interest inventories, social-attitude inventories, and so on.

Honesty is crucial if a self-report is to be taken as a picture of typical behavior, yet any self-report is distorted to some degree. It is now agreed that a questionnaire title should avoid the word *test* in order to avoid the impression that (say) dominance is directly measured. Little is implied by "Smythe Survey of Social Reactions." If an old instrument originally became popular under the name "Smythe Dominance-Submission Test," the publisher is understandably reluctant to alter the name; for this reason, a few prominent inventories are still called "tests."

Whereas the traditional inventory asks generalized questions—"Are you a heavy drinker?"—another approach asks the person to observe his own behavior at a particular time. The person can be asked to record *each evening* his alcohol intake for the day, perhaps along with a note on the circumstances under which he took each drink. The virtue of "self-monitoring" is the definiteness of the information. The procedure is highly intrusive and is likely to alter the behavior itself—an advantage when the recording reinforces a therapeutic process and a disadvantage when one is trying to investigate typical behavior.

8. *Classify each of the following as a test of ability, a self-report, an observation in a standardized situation, or an observation in an unstandardized situation:*
    a. *An interviewer from the Gallup poll asks a citizen how he will vote in a coming election.*
    b. *A television producer wishes to know what program features appeal to different types of listeners. She presents a show to a small audience, who*

press signal buttons to indicate whether they enjoy or dislike what they are seeing at each moment.
   c. *A test of "vocational aptitude" asks how well the counselee likes such activities as selling, woodworking, and chess.*
   d. *A spelling test is given to applicants for a clerical job.*
   e. *Inspectors in plain clothes ride buses to determine whether operators are obeying the company rules.*
   f. *During a maze test, the examiner watches for evidence of self-confidence or its absence.*
   g. *Students are told about a proposal to limit population growth in a suburb by giving few permits for new sewer connections. They are asked to say what the town council should do and to give reasons to support the choice.*
   h. *An inspector in a stocking factory is supposed to detect all stockings with knitting faults. As a check on efficiency, at certain times a number of faulty stockings that have been marked with fluorescent dye are mixed into the batch for inspection. The dye is invisible to the worker, but by turning an ultraviolet lamp onto the stockings after inspection the supervisor can readily locate any faulty stockings the inspector missed.*
9. *Classify each of the following tests, using as many of the descriptive terms discussed in the text as are clearly applicable.*
   a. *The Study of Values consists of printed questions, such as*

   In your opinion, can a man who works in business all week best spend Sunday in
   1. trying to educate himself by reading serious books
   2. trying to win at golf, or racing
   3. going to an orchestral concert
   4. hearing a really good sermon

   The respondent checks whichever answer he prefers. A numerical key counts up how important "aesthetic," "religious," and other values are for him.
   b. *In a certain "mechanical aptitude" test, the person marks illustrations of tools and other objects to show which go together (e.g., hammer and anvil).*
   c. *A Picture Arrangement Test item presents four pictures that, arranged in the correct order, tell a story in the manner of a cartoon strip (see Figure 7.3). Each picture is on a separate card. The cards are presented in a random arrangement and the test taker arranges them to make an intelligible story.*

GENERATING TESTS BY COMPUTER

The computer plays many roles behind the testing scene and can do a star turn as tester. The topic is introduced here because the computer is changing our ideas of what tests can and should be. Because of its consistency, the computer carries standardization to an extreme, yet it can achieve standardized measurement while presenting different questions (and personalized feedback) to every test taker.

Item Banks

The most familiar kind of test is an organized whole—a printed booklet filled with questions. A file of items ("item bank") allows compilation of tests to order. A school can, for example, ask a publisher for a social studies test on topics stressed in its curriculum. Any number of equivalent tests can be made up by selecting every set of items according to the same plan. Information on the difficulty of items in tryout groups provides a basis for comparing individuals or groups who respond to new compilations of items. Computers do much more than store the information. A computer can sort out items, produce tests that meet specifications of a school system, direct the printer that produces test copies, and—once the students have taken the test—prepare a report comparing them with samples to whom the items have been given previously.

The federal government once planned to have much of civil service testing on computers (Urry, 1977). The plans were shelved before completion, apparently not because feasibility and cost were in question. The fact that the computer can generate a fresh test for every person is its prime attraction for the civil service. Month after month, applicants for the same kind of job come in for testing, and questions leak when a test is used over and over. A human staff can assemble no more than a few test forms for each job. With numerous items on a computer tape, the computer can assemble a form for every applicant.

The advantage becomes considerably greater when the test covers problems a computer can solve. Would-be customs officers might be asked to compute the duty to be paid on a shipment of assorted imports according to a complex rate schedule. That task can be framed in a general way. For each examinee, the computer can arbitrarily alter the rates, rules, or makeup of the shipment. Facing that kind of test, the candidate has as his only option learning to apply rate schedules. He gains nothing from finding out just what rules a friend had to apply last week.

Millman and Outlaw (1978) have suggested how classroom teachers using the computer can prepare innumerable forms of an instructional test. Figure 2.3 illustrates a generator of true-false items, a program that can be applied to one bit of content after another. The teacher feeds 30 sets of content elements (the bracketed terms) into the computer. The elements in the example come from a course in vocational agriculture. Any one set can be linked in 32 combinations, each a grammatical sentence that can be judged true or false. (In the figure, the rule at 180 limits the set to 8 of the 32 combinations; bulls may be paired with cows and not other species.)

At the start of the week, the teacher could stock up on tests over that week's lessons. A common test may be given to the whole class, then dis-

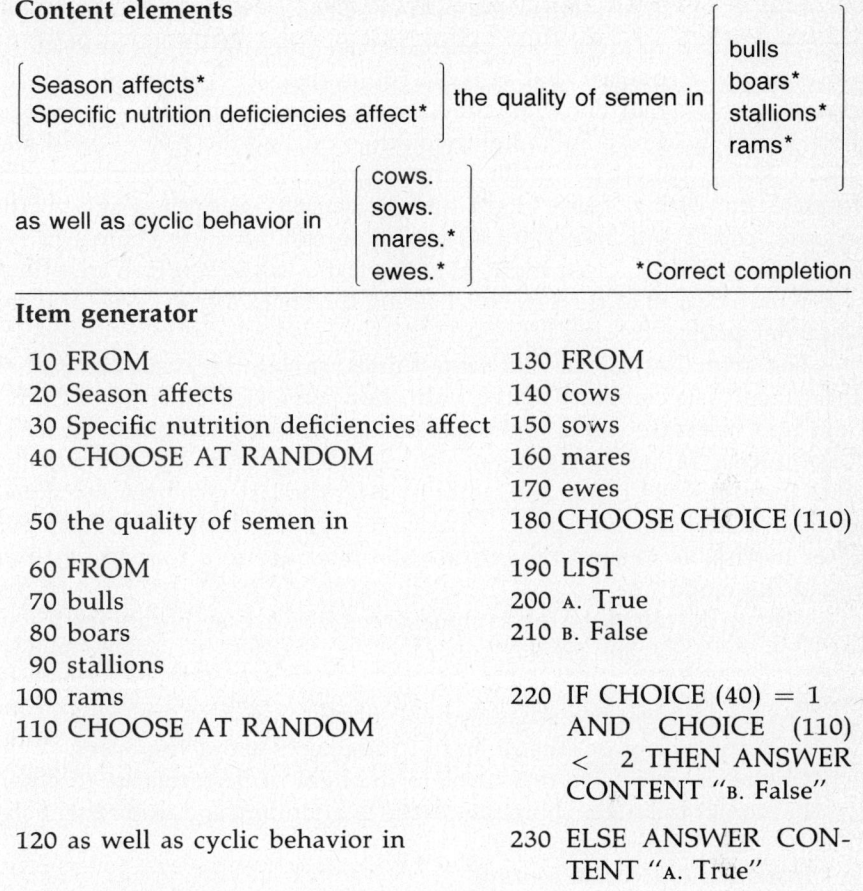

Figure 2.3. Scheme for generating true-false items by computer.
Source: Millman & Outlaw, 1977; slightly edited.

cussed and followed by a new form. Alternatively, copies may be put on a shelf; each student can test himself when and as often as he chooses. The content elements the teacher prepared are saved on cards or tape for use with future classes.

Automated Administration

Computers are good at giving structured tests directly to individuals—an audiometric test, for example. In diagnosing hearing disorders and in fitting hearing aids, the tester adjusts pure tones upward and downward in volume to determine the least volume the person can hear. A human tester would direct the subject to press a key when he hears the tone in his headset. She would set the frequency dial at (say) 800 cycles, set the volume dial at a middling level (say, 5), and press for 0.5 second the key that delivers the tone. The subject would respond, a light would go on, and the tester would mark a record sheet. More trials at the same frequency—without further audible directions but with a "ready" light—might use settings 4 (eliciting a positive response, coded $+$), 3 ($+$), 0 ($-$; a trial to test for false claims), 2 ($-$), 3 ($-$), 2 ($-$), 3 ($+$), ... At some point the tester would settle on an estimate (somewhere near 3) of the person's hearing threshold at 800 cycles and shift to another pitch.

The computer can do the same things, saving the costly time of the professional. The computer delivers directions on a visual display or from an audio tape, resets the signal without error, and times signals precisely. Unlike a knob turner, it can set signals at values of 3.1 or 3.05. The computer can locate the threshold faster and, seconds after the last response, can display the final audiogram and print a permanent record. Satellite transmission makes it possible to send the information instantly to a specialist halfway around the world.

Among the talents of the computer seen in this example are the following:

Precise adherence to schedules and plans.
Delicate control of stimuli and of judgments about responses.
Choice of successive test items in the light of performance to date.
Immunity to fatigue, boredom, lapse of attention, and inadvertent scoring error.
Instant and accurate scoring.
Legible records in several forms, with multiple copies and distant transmission.

For the test taker, interacting with the computer can be fascinating. A study in which reasoning problems were presented to college students either by a computer or by a human tester led to the following observations (E. S. Johnson & R. F. Baker, 1972, p. 31; for a formal report, see Johnson & Baker, 1973):

[C]omputer-run subjects are more apt to pause for long periods of time without typing anything into the computer. Human-run subjects may feel under some pressure to keep behaving even at the risk of doing something wrong. Computer-run subjects have been heard (through the semi-soundproofed walls of their cubicles) to shout for joy, curse, bang the walls, and sing, certainly modes of expression which a typical subject avoids in the presence of an experimenter.

It might be thought that the computer is adapted only to literate and emotionally stable subjects. But preschool children and mental patients respond well to automated displays. The computer's patience is inexhaustible. If the deteriorated schizophrenic does not make a move for four hours, the display simply waits. If the distractible child can only be captured for testing by four preliminary sessions with animated cartoons, the computer provides them without fidgeting.

These long-drawn-out procedures are not expensive even when a full-size computer is used. The computer is called on only when a response is made. While "waiting," it spreads its time—a millisecond here, a millisecond there—among the subjects who *are* responding, perhaps on terminals in distant places. Microcomputers now are in many counseling centers, clinics, and schools for on-line testing or for scoring alone. It may soon be possible to buy or lease a software package for administering this or that test on the same microcomputer that does bookkeeping for the practitioner. Presenting a prepackaged test on a computer terminal, however, is a trivial use of computer capabilities.

Adaptive testing. Not much use has been made of the computer's ability to choose suitable test items in the light of previous successes and failures. This is called sequential or adaptive or tailored testing. Audiometric testers have always chosen test stimuli in the light of previous responses. It was sensible to present signals at levels 2 and 3 once the respondent detected signals of strength 4; if a person made errors at 4, slightly louder signals would be appropriate. The computer can follow elaborate rules in choosing items and can easily compare persons who took different items.

Adjusting difficulty so that the examinee works mostly on items that are neither too hard for him nor too easy might improve motivation. Also it is easy for the computer to indicate instantly whether an answer is right or wrong, and that might heighten motivation. An illustrative finding: Without instant feedback, blacks in an inner-city high school omitted many items and got lower scores than white classmates. When the computer provided feedback after each item, blacks omitted few items and overtook the white students (Betz, 1975; for other studies, see Betz & Weiss, 1976a, 1976b; Prestwood & Weiss, 1978). It would be a mistake to generalize; what encourages one person disturbs another.

Computer-assisted instruction embodies many features of adaptive testing. When the student logs onto the terminal today, the computer recalls not only yesterday's level of performance but the tasks on which the student was least adequate; today's exercises are chosen accordingly. The exercises themselves serve as a test. Hence the computer's record becomes an up-to-the-minute multidimensional description of the individual, more differentiated than an ordinary test offers and more accurate than a teacher's perceptions. There are similar possibilities in speech therapy, career exploration, and other developmental activities.

Simulating Personal Interaction

The computer can simulate a human interviewer remarkably well. One application is in career counseling (p. 425). Another is in testing and teaching medical diagnosis; for state-of-the-art examples, see Clancey *et al.* (1979). As an example for lay readers, I quote from a student's interaction with an older, simpler program (Swets & Feurzig, 1965). Every response of the computer is rule-generated; the student draws responses from a standard, rather long list. Student remarks appear here in capitals.

Begin the physical examination as soon as you are ready.
PHYSICAL EXAM?
Fine. What in particular would you like to know?
CHEST EXAM?
It is common practice in the medical profession to begin an examination by checking the patient's general appearance.
GENERAL APPEARANCE?
Acutely prostrated, lying in bed on his right side. Looks acutely ill, sweaty, apprehensive, but alert. Paroxysmal cough, bringing up a little rusty streaked sputum. Breathing with difficulty.
EENT EXAM?
Check all of the vital signs first!
TEMPERATURE?
103.
BLOOD PRESSURE?
150/84.

At a later stage, after laboratory tests have been ordered and reported on, the student attempts a diagnosis:

PULMONARY INFARCTION.
There's no question of the need to account for this possibility. . . . But rule it out, won't you, on the basis of the history of shaking chills, high temperature, and somewhat excessive WBC.
ACUTE PYELONEPHRITIS.
Very good. You should think of acute pyelonephritis. It's consistent with many of your patient's signs and symptoms—but not all. Wouldn't you want some signs of dysuria to support this diagnosis? And what about the respiratory symptoms in the history and findings? You'd better reevaluate the evidence.
FRIEDLANDER PNEUMONIA.
A wise thought—but off the mark. You don't have the usual Friedlander pneumonia gelatinous type sputum nor the Klebsiella organism—do you? Hold off on this diagnosis for awhile.[1]

[1] Copyright © 1965 by the American Association for the Advancement of Science. Reprinted by permission.

Varieties of Tests and Test Interpretations 41

10. *It would be possible to put an audiometric test on a sound tape. The tape would, let us say, speak the item number, then present a tone or a silent period; the respondent would check items during which he hears a tone. What are the advantages and disadvantages of this procedure? Compare with the procedures described in the text for*
  a. *the human tester*
  b. *the computer*

PSYCHOMETRIC VS. IMPRESSIONISTIC TESTING

Psychometric testing sums up performance in numbers. Its ideal is expressed in two famous old pronouncements:

If a thing exists, it exists in some amount.
If it exists in some amount, it can be measured.

Note the assumption that the psychologist is concerned with "things," with elements or traits that somehow "exist." All people are considered to possess the same traits (e.g., assertiveness or mechanical comprehension), but in different amounts. This view of psychological investigation takes its cue from physical science, which identifies common aspects of dissimilar objects. Numbers representing abstract dimensions—weight, velocity, and intensity of energy of a certain wavelength—serve to describe rocks and rockets, candles and fireflies. Behavioral assessment, which is discussed later, is similar in its specificity but avoids general trait concepts, preferring to count acts in a narrow category.

A less quantitative style of assessment, which is referred to in this text as "impressionistic," strives for comprehensive description. Impressionistic psychologists trust the sensitive observer who picks up cues by any available means and reports a total impression. Studying one trait or act at a time is, they say, no substitute for considering the person as a whole. The impressionist is not satisfied with knowing the magnitude of an ability. She asks how the person expresses his ability, what kinds of errors he makes, and why.

To evaluate a person's background, a psychometric tester would present a checklist covering experiences that many people have (for example, "Were you a Boy Scout or Girl Scout patrol leader?"). She would count the items checked to get scores for, say, "interest in sports" and "leadership experience." The impressionist, on the other hand, would perhaps set no more definite task than "Please write your life story in 2500 words." She would note what the individual considers important to report and also his emotional tone. The free response gives unsystematic information but covers matters the checklist ignores.

The measurer must fall back upon judgment when she applies score information in teaching, therapy, or supervision of employees. The portraitist cannot afford to ignore facts the psychometric approach provides. The styles differ with respect to definiteness of tasks, control of response, objectivity of recording, scoring and combination of data to reach decisions, and validation of interpretations. In pointing out these features of the psychometric style, I neither recommend them for all purposes nor do I imply that all psychometric testing has these features. Most procedures are psychometric in some respects and impressionistic in others. The more exceptional the person under study or the more unprecedented the decision to be made, the greater the reliance on judgment must be.

Definiteness of task. The task set may be definite or vague. The writer of a biographical essay is free to employ any style and bring in any content. Not so when he is asked to check off his activities on a printed list.

A task is said to be *structured* when everyone interprets it in much the same way. The more latitude allowed, the less structure. Of special interest are projective techniques, which ask the person to interpret a stimulus that has no obvious meaning. For instance, he may be told to report what he sees in an inkblot. If he asks how many ideas to report, whether to use the same portion of the blot in two ideas, or any other such question, he is told, "That's up to you." Structuring obtains a definite answer to a question formulated in advance. The less structured technique elicits more diverse responses; the responses suggest questions to the psychologist as well as answers.

Constructed response vs. response choice. The test taker may be asked to construct a response orally or in writing or to manipulate objects. An interviewer might ask, "Are you at ease in social gatherings?" and wait for a reply. The psychometric tester provides alternatives such as ALWAYS, OFTEN, SOMETIMES, NEVER. A series-completion item (7 5 8 6 9 . . .) may be open-ended or supplied with answer choices.

The choice format makes scoring easy, but the behavior displayed is less rich. Even on a number-series item, differences can appear. One person says, "Seven" directly; another hesitantly says, "Well, it might be seven. I guess that's right." Psychologists who prefer free response value the supplementary observations. Teachers tend to prefer free response as evidence of the student's command of ideas and skills. The English teacher prefers to judge a student from a sample of free writing rather than from tests in which he merely identifies errors. The mathematics teacher wants students to solve problems, not merely to select the best of several alternatives. I leave to Chapter 10 the evidence on the degree to which the two types of test overlap, as well as the considerations in choosing between them.

Analysis of performance. Psychometric testing concerns itself with the tangible product of the performance—the answer given, the block tower constructed, or the essay written—and only rarely with the process. When a psychometric tester does pay attention to the process, she arms herself with a record sheet for tabulating what she sees. And she selects in advance the particular aspects of the person's style that she will record. Formulating in advance just what variables the observer will attend to is an unacceptable restriction to the impressionistic psychologist. She prefers to form an impression as to what is significant in each examinee's behavior as she watches him at work. Consequently, she favors tasks that people approach differently. Numerical scores are pivotal in psychometric interpretations whereas the impressionist may translate a test performance into a character description without ever counting up a score.

When a decision is to be made, one can apply some formal rule to the various facts in the record or can combine them impressionistically. For example, one teacher assigns course marks by averaging the tests. Another relies on overall impressions: This student is "doing B work even if he did slump at the end" whereas that one is "not really as good as his tests suggest." The psychometric tester prefers impersonal rigor; the impressionist prefers flexibility.

Critical validation. Finally, we come to validation. Psychometric testers place their trust in interpretations made by a rule derived statistically from previous groups; they distrust more subjective, individualized interpretations. A psychometric tester accompanies every numerical score with a warning regarding the error of measurement and would like to attach an index of uncertainty to every prediction. The impressionist is less concerned with formal validation. If no two cases are alike, interpretations are not repeated, and experience tables cannot be cumulated. Validating qualitative interpretations and "portraits" is much more difficult than validating numerical predictions. In effect, it requires validating the interpreter.

In the impressionistic style, the interpreter must be an artist, sensitive to observe and skillful to convey impressions. Some psychologists are presumably better judges of personality than others. The psychometric method seeks procedures that everyone can use equally well. The objective test is a camera pointed in a fixed direction; every competent photographer should get the same picture with it. Thus, psychometric testing aims to reduce measurement to a technical procedure. To the extent that it succeeds, it reduces the need for a "wise" professional psychologist.

The psychometric and impressionistic approaches differ most sharply on the issue of confidence in the psychologist. Advocates of rigor regard the tester as an erratic instrument whose unregulated interpretations entangle truth with speculation. Impressionists view the observer as a sensitive and even indispensable instrument. The impressionist does not deny the danger of bias and error. She, however, is unwilling to ignore the person's background and present situation—and the meanings he gives to them—as a standard formula for scoring does.

11. *"Psychometric testing trusts the judgment of the test constructor, where it is unwilling to trust the tester as observer." Is this a defensible statement?*
12. *Distinguish between* structured *and* standardized.

13. *In what respects are the following procedures unstructured?*
   a. *In the Ayres handwriting test, pupils are told to write the Gettysburg Address neatly, doing as much as they can in a fixed time.*
   b. *In a test of mental development, the child is told to "draw the best man you can."*
   c. *In a recorded pitch-discrimination test, the subject hears two tones and responds* H, L, *or* N, *accordingly as the second tone appears higher than, lower than, or no different from the first.*

INFERENCES, SHORT AND LONG

Some interpreters are willing—and some reluctant—to make inferences regarding future circumstances. For some purposes, the tester need scarcely look beyond the time and place of observation. A child makes no errors such as "The cows is" in today's composition; this fact might be extended no further than "This week he is handling singular-plural constructions correctly." Bold long-reach inference is illustrated when a fond mother, noting that her child often sings a tune correctly upon first hearing it, says, "He has a real aptitude for music." That generalizes over a broad class of tasks, over many years to come.

The most conservative approach to inference is to assume that the person will in the future be what he has been in the past (or, allowing for growth, will hold his high or low rank among his fellows). An assessment of competence in a practical task or role is likely to be valid for a long time to come (McClelland, 1973; Wernimont & Campbell, 1968). In the absence of a physical decline, even competence that fades through disuse can be recaptured with renewed practice. Habits also are more likely to persist than to change. A driver's record of accidents and traffic citations is a sound basis for inference by the insurance company or the firm hiring drivers. The chief business of the helping professions, however, is to bring about change. For the persons they serve, conservative predictions are inherently pessimistic or limiting. The professional must make longer inferences to help the person set goals for change and to judge what assistance will help him most.

Long inference is usual in impressionistic interpretation; it tries to suggest how the person will respond to changing conditions. Some psychometric interpretations also have a long reach, as when certain errors made in copying geometric drawings are identified (probabilistically) with a particular kind of brain damage or when earthbound tests are used to select persons for training as astronauts.

An observation can be a mere historical statement: "Today Sam took $4\frac{1}{2}$ minutes to type 200 words." But facts are recorded with broader questions in view. As a minimum, that performance is regarded as representing Sam at this point in training. It is a sample of this day's, or this week's, work. If the tester is conducting research on fatigue, and this score comes on the fifth piece of copy Sam typed during a single session, the score sums up performance at this moment; the investigator does not regard the score as representative even of the session. Still, the investigator is assuming that the decline in performance that accompanied fatigue today represents what would be found on other days. All tests, then, are samples.

Sometimes the behavior sampled is of no direct interest; rather, it is taken as a sign or indicator of other behavior or inner states. The maze test is of interest as a sign, not as a sample. No animal and no person ever runs a maze except as a psychological test. The number of trials required to learn the maze is taken as an indicator of a broader ability. It is far more difficult to study learning in the natural ecology than in the test situation, and rates of learning something with which some learners are already partly familiar would be harder to interpret than rates on the unfamiliar, artificial task.

Traits, States, and Acts

Psychologists investigate both "trait anxiety" and "state anxiety." The intensity of anxious feelings (the person's present state) shifts from day to day. The person's trait level is usually conceived as an average or typical state; if so, it reflects in part the person's social environment. Typing rate fluctuates; that is to say, the performance is statelike. "Ability" refers not to typical performance but to something more like "typical performance under excellent conditions."

Concepts such as "anxiety" and "ability" are constructs (*"con-* structs"), that is, terms that attempt to describe how actions or thoughts are organized. Construct interpretations evolve. In former days it was assumed that the maze score indicates "intelligence pure and simple." That idea had to be revised. The notion that a certain carefully bred strain of rats had superior "intelligence" broke down; so did the construct "aptitude for maze learning." The research justified only a conclusion of this sort: "This strain has aptitude for learning elevated mazes when kept hungry and given food at the goal box" (p. 317f.).

A broad construct is required when inference reaches out to diverse situations. "Musical talent" is a more convenient dimension than "talent for stringed instruments." That, in turn, is handier but less definitive than "dexterity in rapid finger movements" and "pitch discrimination." The broad construct is neither true nor false; it is adequate for some purposes and inadequate for others.

Constructs that go deeper into the psyche are obviously bolder hypotheses. (Compare "Is unable to accept his own hostile impulses" with "Response to challenging questions is cool, formal, polite.") The deeper interpretation rests on a complex theory about the wellsprings of behavior, and few such theories have been well substantiated. How appropriate it is to offer a somewhat speculative, somewhat artistic analysis-in-depth has been disputed for decades. Only two morals need be drawn at this point. Those who stick to literal reports of acts leave to others the burden of interpretation; those others might (or might not) be better served if the psychologist had offered an interpretation. Those who offer imaginative hypotheses as if they were scientific reports lead their clients into quicksand.

Since the days when phrenology was exposed as fallacious, psychologists have been trying to get away from the notion that traits are objects, comparable to the pituitary gland and the X chromosome. We find it natural to speak of "shyness." But shyness is not an entity; the word is a summary of responses. To say that a person is shy means only that, in many situations, the person has exhibited actions associated with that construct.

Placing a person on a scale or tallying up actions merges diverse acts and glosses over the texture of behavior. A person may be shy at parties and not in debate, with strangers and not with acquaintances, with females and not with males. The shyness may be wholly internal; the person confides feelings to a counselor that everyday associates know nothing of. The inhibition and withdrawal of another "shy" person is open for all to see.

The behaviorist, disliking "trait" language, still has to categorize situations and acts. In assessing how messages regarding heart disease affect eating, she could ask each subject to record daily food intake on a checklist. One entry would be "eggs." Would it not be better to ask whether the eggs are boiled or fried? And, if fried, whether in lard or safflower oil? The finer categories fit the information more closely to the problem. Even so concrete a measurement, then, is framed by constructs ("high cholesterol," "polyunsaturated"). The fineness of categories will depend on the purpose of an inquiry, but categories there must be.

Behavioral assessment. Psychologists in the behavioristic tradition minimize reference to mental states, categories of disorder, and global traits of personality. When a person with emotional distress seeks assistance, a psychologist of this school tries to pin down the *kinds* of situation the client typically has trouble coping with or that arouse unpleasant feelings. Yet behaviorists may measure fairly general traits. Thus, one scale reports on "positive assertiveness," "negative assertiveness," and "self-denial"; the first of these scores summarizes the person's report that he does (or does not) often express affection, approval, and agreement (Galassi *et al.,* 1974).

In planning treatment, in evaluating progress, and in assessing alternative treatment methods, behaviorists have as much occasion to test as other applied psychologists. Indeed, tests play a special role in their work because the client learns to regulate himself by keeping track of his responses. He is taught, for example, to note whether he does speak up each time he does not concur with something his spouse says. Behaviorists avoid the word *test* because of its association with broad traits and differences among individuals. They are concerned with the frequency of significant acts in context and with changes in the person's use of them. Whether a person is sufficiently assertive is to be judged by that person's ideals and by the demands of his world. The "norms" for assertiveness are, at most, no more than background for such judgments.

"Behavioral assessment" refers to practices that fit into behavior modification and other situationally oriented applications. Its proponents sharply distinguish behavioral assessment from the assessment that describes forces internal to the person ("dynamics"). Ciminero (in Ciminero *et al.*, 1977) has summed up main differences between behavioral assessment and impressionistic assessment (Table 2.1). As a preamble, he quotes Mischel (1968, p. 10): "In behavioral analysis the emphasis is on what a person *does* rather than on inferences about what attributes he *has* more globally." What the person does in a defined situation can be described in a simple count of actions on several occasions. To say "what the person is like" requires the psychologist to go beyond counts of actions to descriptive language and, beyond that, to imaginative construction of an explanation.

As row 1 of the table notes, dynamic interpreters seek to explain behavior in terms of prior events and the traces they have left in the person's perceptions, fears, goals, and so on. Behaviorists feel no need to probe into the origins of a response pattern; they search out current circumstances that trigger the response. Row 2 likewise refers to the behaviorists' attempt to avoid inference. The data they use are closely matched to the clients' difficulties—no inkblot tests for them. The same point reappears in row 7: behavioral treatment bears directly on the acts that are to be retrained (and not on attempts to develop the client's "insight" or to resolve his internal conflicts). When one is trying to increase self-assertion, the repeated tallying-up of acts

Table 2.1 *Behavioral and impressionistic assessment compared*

	Behavioral assessment	*Impressionistic assessment*
Assumptions:		
1. Personality concept	Behavior explained in terms of [present] environment	Behavior explained in terms of underlying causes
2. "Test" interpretation	Behavior as sample	Behavior as sign
3. Situations sampled	Varied and specific	Limited and ambiguous
Primary functions:		
4.	Description in behavioral-analytic terms	Description in psychodynamic terms
5.	Treatment selection	Diagnostic labeling
6.	Treatment evaluation	
Practical aspects:		
7. Relation to treatment	Direct	Indirect
8. Time of assessment	Continuous with treatment	Prior to treatment

SOURCE: Adapted from Ciminero, in Ciminero *et al.*, 1977, p. 4. Reprinted by permission of the publisher, John Wiley & Sons, Inc.

of self-assertion is a test that matches the "lessons." The same kind of record is made week after week. Row 8 contrasts such monitoring with a conventional practice: making a formal assessment only at the time the treatment plan is developed. (But dynamic therapies also embody continual assessment and evaluation.)

Rows 4, 5, and 6 refer once more to the concreteness of the behavioral analysis—where does the trouble occur? when?—and the linkage of that analysis to the treatment. Traditional abnormal psychology no doubt has taken diagnostic labels too seriously. But traditional assessment *is* carried out for the purpose of guiding treatment, and a good case workup by no means stops with labeling.

14. *In which of these respects would you expect behavior analysts to follow the tradition of psychometric measurement?*
    a. *Expressing numerically the strength of a response tendency.*
    b. *Grouping within one category or score two kinds of behavior, such as submissiveness and shyness, that tend to be found together.*
    c. *Specifying a definite kind of task or situation in which to collect data on many persons.*
15. *What testing, if any, would play a part in a behavior analyst's approach to a 10-year-old who has made poor progress in learning to read?*
16. *"Comprehends what he reads" is a broad construct. What narrower constructs might describe distinct types of comprehension?*
17. *Anastasi (1982, p. 488) notes that the behaviorist uses constructs when speaking even of something as definite as "fear of dogs." She says that the boundaries of the construct have to be checked so that generalization is not too broad. How would one check the boundaries? Would they be similar for all persons distressed by dogs?*

3
Administering Tests

The tester's first responsibility is to choose a test that fits the test taker. It is gross malpractice to give an ability test on which the person is likely to do badly for irrelevant reasons. The maze test, for example, should be given only to persons possessing normal control of their hand movements. Similarly, a vocational-interest questionnaire designed for college students should not be applied to 14-year-olds in a nonacademic program—at least not without verifying that they understand the questions.

A misleading score is worse than none at all, and if a suitable test cannot be found, the proper report is "no score could be obtained." Even when someone engages the tester to give a specific test, the tester ought to judge independently whether the test is suitable. The same is to be said of the research assistant told to collect data on a group of uncooperative drug users. Choking off the flow of bad data is no small part of the job.

If data are to be interpreted in the light of accumulated experience with the same test, the tester must follow the standard procedures. But the tester is obligated to give the examinee a full chance to display his ability, and standard procedures may not fit. The tester will not necessarily realize in advance that a test is unsuitable, but she should remain alert to indications of invalid response. When standard procedure will lead to invalid conclusions, she will often be wise to change the procedure. Her report must emphasize that the test was nonstandard.

Some tests are sufficiently simple for any adult to give; a few are so subtle that months of special training are recommended. Considerable skill is required when the tester is to question the examinee orally and to use follow-up questions when the first answer is unclear.

TWO SPECIMEN TESTS

This chapter gives a general introduction to test administration. It cannot, of course, make the reader into a skilled tester; that comes with practice. To illustrate this chapter and several later ones, the Bennett Mechanical Comprehension Test and the Block Design test are described now in some detail. These tests are important in themselves, but are brought in here to illustrate general principles.

Mechanical Comprehension Test

The Mechanical Comprehension Test, originated by George K. Bennett, is widely used for employee selection. The Mechanical Reasoning section of the Differential Aptitude Test (DAT) battery for high school guidance is a member of the same family. Illustrative data and research findings will be drawn from the DAT and on current and past editions of the Bennett test. I shall let TMC refer to any form of the Bennett or DAT.

The manual for one version begins with this description of purpose:[1]

> Forms S and T of the *Bennett Mechanical Comprehension Test* . . . measure the ability to perceive and understand the relationship of physical forces and mechanical elements in practical situations. This type of aptitude is important for a wide variety of jobs and for engineering training, as well as for many trade school courses.
>
> . . . .
>
> Mechanical comprehension may be regarded as one aspect of intelligence, if intelligence is broadly defined. The person who scores high in this trait tends to learn readily the principles of operation and repair of complex devices. Like other aptitude tests, the *Bennett Mechanical Comprehension Test* is influenced by environmental factors, but not to an extent that introduces important difficulties in interpretation. Care has been taken to present items in terms of simple, frequently encountered mechanisms that do not resemble textbook illustrations or require special knowledge.

The items reproduced in Figure 3.1 are presented to orient the person before the test proper begins. More than 17 aspects of machines appear in

---
[1]Quoted material in this section reproduced by permission of The Psychological Corporation.

Administering Tests

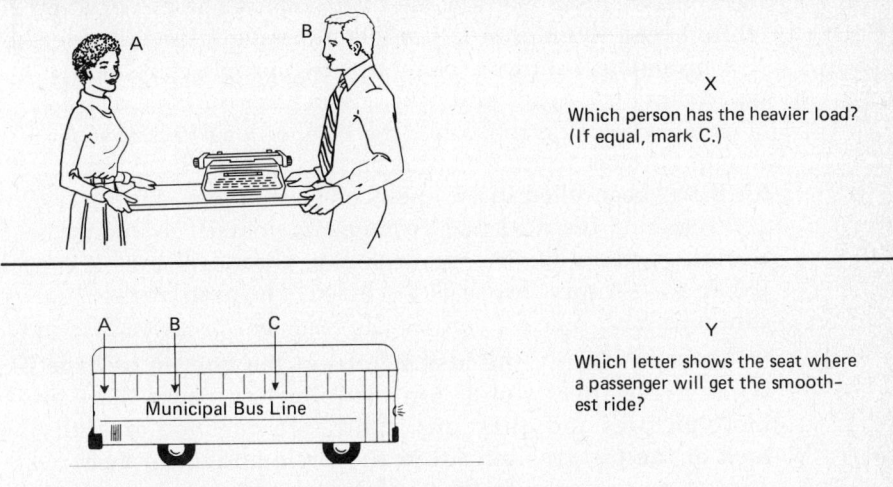

Figure 3.1. Mechanical comprehension items. Sample item X from Forms U and V of the DAT Mechanical Reasoning Test.
Copyright © 1972. 1980, 1982 by The Psychological Corporation.
Sample item Y from Forms S and T of the Bennett Mechanical Comprehension Test.
Copyright 1940, renewed 1967; 1941, renewed 1969; 1942, renewed 1969; © 1967, 1968 by The Psychological Corporation. Both items reproduced by permission.

items of Forms S and T; each form has 8 items on hydraulics, 5 on pulleys, 3 on electricity, and so forth. The distribution of content reflects not only the authors' judgments about importance but also their success in devising items that were appropriately challenging, and that depended more on reasoning than on specific technical knowledge.

The manual carries the following directions to the tester:

Seat the examinees in a well-lighted, adequately ventilated room. There should be enough desk or table space to accommodate a test booklet and answer sheet for each person. Chairs with tablet arms should be avoided if possible. Each examinee should have two well-sharpened pencils, and the examiner or proctors should have a spare supply.

Distribute answer sheets first and then the test booklets. Speaking clearly and loudly enough for everyone to hear, say:

"Please do not open the test booklet until I tell you to. You will do all your writing on the answer sheet only. (Examiner holds up answer sheet.) **Now look at your answer sheet.**

[Instructions to fill in name and other information follow.] . . .

**"Open your test booklet to Page 2 and fold back the rest of the booklet. Read silently the directions at the top of Page 2 while I read them aloud. 'Look at Example X on this page.'

Example X shows a picture of two people carrying a typewriter on a board and asks, *Which person has the heavier load? (If equal, mark C.)* Person B has the heavier load because the weight is closer to him than to person A. Therefore, the circle for B has been filled in on line X of your answer sheet.

Now do the next one, Example Y, yourself. Mark the correct space on line Y of your answer sheet."

[After a time, this answer is discussed. The examiner continues:]

"Now read silently the instructions at the bottom of Page 2 while I read them aloud. 'On the following pages there are more pictures and questions. Read each question carefully, look at the picture, and fill in the circle under the best answer on the answer sheet. Make sure that your marks are heavy and black. Erase completely any answer you wish to change. Do not make any marks in this booklet.' "

After the instructions have been read, say:

"You will have thirty minutes for the entire test. . . . Are there any questions? If you have any questions, you must ask them now because we cannot allow questions after the test has begun."

During the ensuing thirty minutes walk about quietly, checking whether the examinees are marking the answer sheets properly. If any of the examinees finish before the end of the test period, collect their answer sheets and test booklets and dismiss them quietly. At the end of thirty minutes, say:

"This is the end of the test. Please give me your answer sheets and test booklets."

Block Design

In Block Design, the examinee is to construct prescribed designs out of colored 1-inch cubes. S. C. Kohs's Block Design test was one of many mental tests invented during the 1920s, when applied psychology first came into prominence. As schools began to hire psychologists to examine children, demand arose for standardized collections of tests. A psychologist acting as editor collected tests by various authors; improved the directions, materials, and scoring procedures; and applied the whole set to many children to obtain norms for each age. The block-design task was chosen for many of these collections, as it measures nonverbal reasoning over a wide range of difficulty. Revision and restandardization have continued down to the present day. The modification may alter the items or the directions or change the procedure radically (pp. 62, 273, 324).

Administering Tests

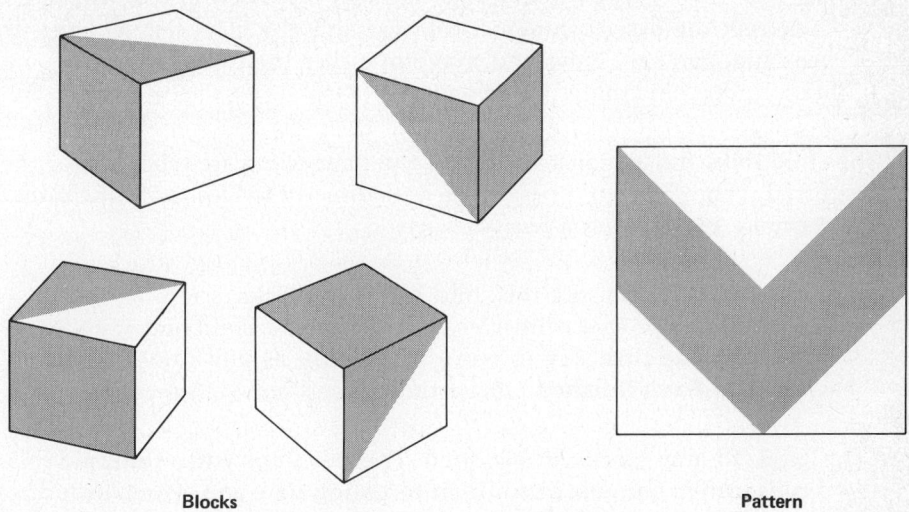

Blocks   **Pattern**

Figure 3.2. Block Design materials.
Pattern copyright © 1940, 1955, 1976, 1981 by The Psychological Corporation and reproduced by permission.

I shall describe the version used in WISC-R, the Wechsler Intelligence Scale for Children—Revised (Wechsler, 1974, pp. 84–88). Red-and-white blocks and cards (Figure 3.2) are used. Children of age 8 and above start with Design 3, and try Designs 1 and 2 if they fail on Design 3. Designs 1 and 2 are presented as block models to be copied; for Designs 3 to 11, the child is to match the pattern on a card. The directions are detailed. For example, the examiner is told to make sure that the child is seated squarely with the table and is told to place the model slightly to the child's left if the child is right-handed and to the right otherwise. The blocks are laid out irregularly before the child, but the rules specify, for example, that when four blocks are used, only one of them is to have its red-and-white surface facing up.

The general procedure is to lay out the pattern and the required number of blocks, time the performance, and allow credit if a correct copy is made in the specified time. If the child does not perform adequately on Design 3, he is allowed a second trial before moving back to Design 1. On Designs 4 to 11, only one trial is allowed, and a quick success earns a bonus. The specific directions to the tester are as follows, when the test begins with Design 3:[2]

> DESIGN 3. Take four blocks in hand and say, **See these blocks? They are all alike. On some sides they are all red; on some, all white; and on some, half red and half white.** Turn the blocks to show the different sides. Then say, **They can be put together to make a design like the one you see on the card. Watch me.**

[2]Copyright © 1974 by the Psychological Corporation. Reprinted by permission.

Construct the design slowly. Then scramble the blocks, give them to the child, and say, **Now you make one like the card. Go ahead.** Start timing, and allow 45 seconds.

If the child fails, the demonstration and the scrambling are repeated for the second trial. When the child passes, he goes directly to Design 4. The directions continue in part as follows:

DESIGNS 4–11. Be sure the child has four blocks; scramble the blocks. Place the card with Design 4 before the child and say, **"Now make one like this. Try to work as quickly as you can. Tell me when you have finished."** Start timing, and allow 45 seconds.

At Design 9, all nine blocks are required. The test stops when the child fails on two consecutive designs. In addition to noting time and errors, including errors the subject spontaneously corrects, the tester watches for any revealing remark, any emotional reaction or blocking, and any unusual method of attacking the task. Some children deal with the pattern as a whole, and some consider each tiny section in turn. Some give up when they face difficulty, some become erratic and make the same error repeatedly, and others show increased interest under the greater challenge.

1. *If TMC were administered individually, could profitable observations be made?*
2. *Can you think of any questions a subject might ask that the directions do not cover?*
3. *What techniques are used in Block Design to give the child a full opportunity to understand what is wanted?*
4. *What style of work will earn the highest score on Block Design as Wechsler scores it? Is it appropriate to reward that style?*
5. *The manual is not regarded as sufficient to prepare one to give the Wechsler test. The tester learns by observing an experienced tester and discussing procedures with her. What do you think you could learn about giving Block Design that the manual did not specify?*

PROCEDURE FOR TEST ADMINISTRATION

The importance of uniform procedure is especially obvious in the great competitive testing programs for scholarship awards and college admissions. On seven weekends, forms of the Scholastic Aptitude Test are given in over 1000 centers. At 9 A.M. on a particular Saturday in January, the seal is broken on the test package in each center: in Bronxville and Berkeley and Kodiak, in

Berne and Beirut and Kodaikanal. The completed papers pour into the scoring center, and reports go out to the candidates and the colleges they are applying to. A boy in Beirut may be in competition with one in Berkeley for admission to the same college, and the selection procedure is unfair unless the two are tested in an identical manner.

To obtain meaningful results, the tester must become thoroughly familiar with the test. Even a simple test presents stumbling blocks; most will be avoided if the tester studies the manual in advance. But carelessness can produce spectacular errors. At a time when the adequacy of an all-volunteer army was a focus of public debate, the Pentagon asked its staff to find out how many recruits fell below borderline ability. The staff defined the borderline by testing a sample of qualified soldiers; scores toward the lower end of that group were accepted as a standard of adequacy. Unfortunately, whoever tested these soldiers cut the testing time short by mistake. Recruits who reached the same score level in the full working time were far less able than the soldiers who had reached it under time pressure. The Pentagon report said that few recruits were below the borderline score; if its logic had been applied to properly collected scores, six times as many recruits would have been counted as substandard. (Whether standards should be set on the basis of score distributions is another issue. See pp. 91–93.)

The physical setting for the test matters: Does the examinee have a convenient place to write? Sufficient space to spread out materials? A position from which directions can be heard and demonstrations seen? Very large rooms are bad for group testing unless proctors are provided. In the large room, a person may hesitate to ask a question about unclear directions that he would raise before a smaller audience. A proctor can come to his seat and answer his question.

Occasionally, it is necessary to test a person at an unfavorable time, as when psychological examinations must be given to an accused person prior to his trial. College freshmen may be tested in the midst of a hectic week of establishing new friends and living arrangements. Military classification tests have been given to soldiers just after induction when they lack sleep, are recovering from a farewell party, or feel ill from inoculations. In one study soldiers who took a second form of such a test after becoming stabilized in army routines raised their scores, on the average, by the amount that separated prospective noncoms from prospective officers (Duncan, 1947).

Data can often be improved by spacing tests. Alert examinees are more likely to give their best than examinees who are weary. But equally good results *can* be produced at any hour of the day if the examinees want to do well. Fatigue apparently affects effort rather than the ability one can summon up.

With school beginners and other young children, it is necessary to be especially mindful of the child's readiness for testing. The setting for the test, the persons present, and the task demands may all be strange. Not surprisingly, then, scores collected in the first week of school experience can run quite a bit lower than those obtained two weeks later. Likewise, the tester who becomes acquainted with a child over several sessions of non-test activities elicits higher scores at the end of the period than a strange tester would. The recommendations are obvious: wait until the child is at ease; retest when a low score has important consequences. In evaluation of early education, pretest-posttest differences are inflated if pretests are given before children are accustomed to the setting.

Giving Directions

With reasonably mature and cooperative examinees who expect to do as the tester requests, group testing is essentially a problem in command. Efficiency is to be maintained without interfering with the opportunity of individuals to ask questions. One person should be in charge, standing in front of the group where she can see all members. She will find helpful the adage "Never give an order unless you expect it to be obeyed." False starts, preliminary attempts to call the group to order while latecomers are finding seats, and ineffectual rapping for attention are counterproductive. The tester should have full attention before she starts to explain.

Directions should be given simply, clearly, and singly. A complex instruction such as "Take your booklet, turn it face down, and then write your name on the answer sheet" will lead to confusion. Much better: "Take your booklet." (Hold up a sample. Check to be sure everyone has his booklet.) "Turn it face down." (Demonstrate. Wait until everyone has done so.) "Now take your answer sheet." (Exhibit a sample, and wait for compliance.) "Write your name on the first line, last name first."

Formal commands—firm, audible, polite—are effective. Too military a manner, however, may enhance the "inhuman" character of the test situation. Both control and rapport can be achieved if the examiner is friendly and patient and is informal when formal control is not called for. After establishing control, for example, she may relax her "command manner" and make informal comments about the test and its purpose; this does not interfere with resuming formal control for the test proper.

There is no point in adhering to a testing schedule if that schedule will give false information. Emergencies arise that prevent uniform testing. Thus, occasionally, an examinee becomes ill. It should be possible to provide for a makeup test later.

The purpose of standardizing is to obtain a measurement comparable to measurements made at other times. Administering tests by tape recorder has advantages for many tests. The tape says the right words, and it times the test accurately. Taped administration can present the same test in many languages and dialects. See also pages 37–40 on computerized testing.

The standard directions usually invite the examinee to ask questions after the directions have been read. In the answering of these questions, adding ideas not expressed in the directions makes the testing nonstandard. The directions are part of the test situation; in some tests the way the examinee follows the set directions is intended to influence the score.

The most troublesome questions concern matters about which the standard directions are silent. Here are two examples: "How much is taken off for a wrong answer?" "If I find a hard question, should I skip it and go on, or should I answer every question as I go?" The published directions were evidently not adequate if they ignored these topics. When the tester refuses to add advice on guessing, some examinees will guess, and some will not. Sometimes the tester will decide to supplement the directions; when she does so, she is in effect creating a new test, and the norms no longer apply.

Directions should be complete and free from ambiguity (except where —for the sake of observing the examinee's preferred style—a test is deliberately left unstructured). A test for aviators illustrates the crucial importance of defining the task. In making a check on ability to execute a maneuver, testers found it necessary to tell the pilot exactly how the performance would be scored. When they did not, one pilot kept attention on maintaining altitude perfectly; a pilot of equal ability who concentrated on the plane's heading earned a different score.

The psychometric tester tries to standardize the state of examinees, eliminating individual differences in every characteristic save whatever the test seeks to measure. To clarify this, consider the physiological measure of basal metabolism rate (BMR). A doctor who wants a BMR measure requires the patient to fast for 8 hours before the test because the digestive process uses oxygen. For the test itself, a measure of oxygen intake and carbon dioxide exhaled, it is necessary to reduce bodily activity to a minimum by putting the person into bed. Every examinee is, in effect, reduced to an artificial "standard condition" that almost never occurs in real life. The person's day-to-day metabolism rate is not much like his BMR since the former is raised by his eating and movement.

Most psychological tests are similarly designed to extract one purified variable from the total life activity. In setting the stage for a test, the psychologist tries to bring all examinees to a "standard state" of motivation, expectation, and interpretation of the task.

No matter how standardized and long-established a task, the test taker may give it a meaning wholly his own. Pour water from one jar to a narrower one; the water level is now higher. Has the amount changed? Children around the world have answered this Piagetian question, correctly or incorrectly. When a Pakistani 5-year-old said, "Yes"—an "immature" response—the tester was not surprised. The tester *was* surprised when the child amplified by touching a dusty finger to the bottom of the original jar and bringing up a droplet the pouring had left behind (Berland, 1981). Only the individual tester has a good chance to learn what question the test taker is really considering.

Judgments Left to the Examiner

The tester who likes people will develop many techniques for establishing rapport. The person who proceeds coldly and "scientifically" to administer the test, without convincing the test taker that she regards him as important, will get only limited cooperation. Evidence of poor rapport includes inattention during directions, giving up before time is called, restlessness, or complaining about the test items.

What Terman and Merrill (1973, pp. 47 ff.) said regarding the Stanford-Binet test is applicable to most individual tests.

> The accepted practice is to limit changes in test order to *practical* requirements of testing. Thus, it is sometimes advisable, in order to secure the child's effort when a certain type of test (such as repeating digits or drawing) is found to arouse resistance, to shift temporarily to a more agreeable task. When the subject is at his ease again, it is usually possible to return to the troublesome task with better success.
>
> To elicit the subject's best efforts . . . [is] the *sine qua non* of good testing, but the means by which these ends are accomplished are so varied as to defy specific formulation. The address which puts one child at ease with a strange adult may belittle or even antagonize another.
>
> Keeping the subject encouraged . . . can be accomplished in many subtle, friendly ways; by an understanding smile, a spontaneous exclamation of approval, an appreciative comment, or just the quiet understanding between equals that carries assurance and appreciation. . . . In general it is effective to praise frequently and generously, but if this is done in too lavish and stilted a fashion it is likely to defeat its own purpose. Expressions of commendation should be varied and should fit naturally into the conversation. The examiner should remember that he is giving approval for effort rather than for success on a particular response.
>
> Under no circumstances should the examiner permit himself to show dissatisfaction with a response, though he may smilingly refuse to accept a flippant answer obviously intended to "test the limits." With younger children, especially, praise should not be limited to tests on which the child has done well. Young children are characteristically uncritical and are often enormously pleased with very inferior responses. In praising poor responses of older subjects, the examiner should remember that the purpose of the commendation is to insure confidence and not to reconcile the subject to an inferior level of response. In the case of a failure that is embarrassingly evident to the subject himself, the examiner may take occasion to point out that he doesn't expect the subject to be

able to do all these things, or he may interject, *"That was a good try!"*
. . .

[T]he examiner should [not drag] out responses by too much urging and cross-questioning. To do so robs the response of significance and discourages spontaneous effort. While the examiner must be on his guard against mistaking exceptional timidity for inability to respond, he must also be able to recognize the silence of incapacity or the genuineness of an *"I don't know"* from the child who knows when he knows not![3]

Sometimes credit is allowed only when a task is done in (say) 2 minutes, but the directions do not tell the examiner to stop the subject at that time. The tester must decide whether to let the person work after he has passed the credit limit. Art comes into play; no rules can prescribe how to minimize the frustration that attends an unsuccessful trial. Success on one problem has an encouraging effect during the next, but the effect of failure depends on the tester. In the tester's eyes, the subject failed when he did not complete the task within the time limit. Allowed to continue without interruption, the subject may finish the task and be encouraged by that. Another subject, even with extra time, may not solve the problem. If he is becoming confused and upset, to let him continue might leave him more discouraged. The tester should observe carefully and choose whatever course seems likely to have the best effect.

It is the duty of the tester to obtain the best record the subject can produce by his own efforts—without aid. The tester must learn to suppress direct and indirect hints. Unintended help can be given even by facial expression. The person taking a test is always concerned to know how well he is doing and watches the examiner for indications that he is doing right. Suppose the task is this: "Repeat backward, 2–7–5–1–4." He may begin "4–1–7 . . ."; if the examiner, on hearing the "7," permits her expression to change, the subject may take the hint and catch the mistake. The examiner must maintain a completely unrevealing expression while at the same time silently assuring the examinee of her interest in what he says.

For exceptional cases the tester has no alternative save to throw away the rule book. Shapiro (1957) tells of the 7-year-old who was uncooperative and at times aggressive toward the tester. The first session was wasted; the girl simply would not do the test. The second session started equally unhappily. Finally the psychologist slammed one of the playroom toys against the wall. Said the child, smiling at last, "Do it again." After a bit of routine cooperation—the child fetching toy and the psychologist smashing it against the wall—they were pals; in due time, the girl settled down to take the test and scored in the normal range.

Not only in exceptional cases but also in routine testing, the tester ought

---

[3]Reprinted by permission of the Riverside Publishing Company.

to write down a brief account of the procedures. Even when all goes smoothly, the tester should record an impression of the apparent confidence, cooperation, and level of tension of the person or persons tested. Such a record may shed light on discrepancies among data collected at different times.

6. *An employment office gives all applicants a reasoning test when their applications are filed. One man takes the test, together with several friends, and the group leave together. Ten minutes later he returns, greatly agitated: "Was I supposed to turn over the last page? I thought I had finished when I got to the bottom of page 9, so I looked back over my answers. I had plenty of time, and I'm sure I could have done well on the last page—my friends say the questions there were easy." What should be done in this case, if at the bottom of page 9 the booklet carried the printed statement "Go on to the next page?"*

7. *In testing a group of college freshmen to obtain information for use in guidance, the examiner finds that a student newly arrived from Latin America is having great difficulty following directions because of unfamiliarity with English. The student asks many questions, requests repetitions, and seems unable to comprehend what is desired. What should the examiner do?*

8. *In the course of a clinical analysis of a preschool child who is believed to be poorly adjusted, tests are requested. The psychometrist finds the child negativistic. After cooperating reluctantly on two tests, the child becomes inattentive and careless on the third. Assuming that the test results are needed as soon as possible, what should the tester do?*

9. *In the Hand-Tool Dexterity Test, nuts and bolts are to be mounted in a frame as fast as possible, with the aid of two wrenches. Somewhat more than 200 words of directions tell how to do the task. Before giving the directions, the manual says this to the examiner: "The essence of the examination procedure is to measure the ability of the examinee to perform the manual tasks required; ability to understand directions is not part of the intended measurement. Accordingly, the examiner should feel free to supplement the following directions in any reasonable way to improve the examinee's understanding of the task."*
    a. *What can be said for and against this departure from standardization?*
    b. *What would be an "unreasonable" way to supplement the directions?*

10. *In the Metropolitan Achievement test for elementary grades, the pupil has the option of checking* DON'T KNOW *rather than an answer option. This response, of course, receives no credit. The test developer argues that this option encourages an honest attitude in test taking.*
    a. *Why is the practice open to question?*
    b. *Not uncommonly, teachers giving this test warn their classes against marking* DON'T KNOW *(because it cannot help their scores; Horne & Garty, 1981). Who, if anyone, suffers from this violation of standard procedure?*

Policies Regarding Guessing

Over and over the tester is asked, "Should I guess when I am not sure?" Whatever advice the test directions give, some room for judgment remains. The discussion that follows is intended to clarify the guessing problem for the tester and test developer. It should not influence procedure in giving a standard test, as supplementary advice is against the rules.

For the moment, suppose that questions fall into two categories: those whose answer the respondent knows and those he cannot answer. Choice response gives the ignorant person a chance to pick the correct response. On true-false items, guesses will succeed half the time by chance alone. One common scoring formula assumes that every wrong choice represents an unlucky guess. The number of lucky guesses is supposed to be proportional to the number of wrong responses, and credit is subtracted accordingly. The final score on a true-false test is then "number of items right minus number marked wrong." The penalty is the number of items thought to have been marked correctly by guessing.

With n choices per item, the probability of a correct guess is $1/n$ and that of an unlucky guess is $(n-1)/n$. For every $(n-1)$ incorrect guesses, there will be one correct guess, on the average. Hence the usual formula is "rights minus wrongs/$(n-1)$." On a 50-item test with 3 choices per item, a person who gets 36 right and 10 wrong receives a score of 31 ($= 36 - 10/2$). The formula attempts to wipe out the advantage of those who take more chances.

Unfortunately, the formula does not neutralize all the risk taker's advantage. Items do not divide into those the respondent knows perfectly and those he does not know at all. There are items he knows fairly well but is not positive of, and others where he has hazy knowledge. Perhaps he can eliminate one or two choices as implausible. A person who "guesses" intelligently on 10 five-choice items can expect to get perhaps 4 items right, not 2. Four right answers would give a formula score of $2\frac{1}{2}$ points. Since he would score zero on those items if he did not guess, the score is raised by willingness to gamble.

From the point of view of the tester, tendency to guess is an uncontrolled variable that interferes with measurement. The systematic advantage of the guesser is eliminated if the test manual directs everyone to guess, but guessing increases chance variation. It is usual now to warn only against wild guessing, for example:

> Because of the way the test is scored, haphazard or random guessing for questions you know nothing about is unlikely to change your score. When you know that one or more choices can be eliminated, guessing from among the remaining choices should be to your advantage.[4]

[4]From *Taking the SAT*, 1981, p. 4.

Techniques have been invented in which the test taker bets on his degree of certainty. The simplest method is to ask the person to mark, not the right answer, but every choice he can rule out. Consider:

The capital of Chile is   A. Valparaiso   B. Buenos Aires   C. Santiago.

The child who knows a little about Latin America gains some credit by rejecting B, without having to guess between A and C. This sensible procedure has had little use.

An alternative that requires some technology but that irons out differences in confidence and willingness to take a chance is an "answer until correct" rule. The respondent pulls a tab or marks chemically sensitive paper; answers are precoded so that he learns at once that the choice is right or wrong. If it is wrong he makes further choices until he succeeds. As we saw in connection with computerized testing, immediate feedback increases the motivation of many persons. Logically, that ought to improve a measure of ability.

11. *Compute scores for each of the following persons by the usual correction formula:*

   Test 1, true-false.   A has 20 right, 6 wrong, 7 omitted.
   B has 22 right, 8 wrong, 3 omitted.

   Test 2, 3-choice.   C has 15 right, 6 wrong, 4 omitted.
   D has 18 right, 3 wrong, 4 omitted.

   Test 3, 5-choice.   E has 20 right, 6 wrong, 9 omitted.
   F has 6 right, 6 wrong, 23 omitted.

12. *Earlier forms of TMC were scored by a correction formula; in Forms S and T, the score is the count of right answers. What kinds of evidence would justify this simplified scoring?*
13. *Should test directions tell what scoring formula will be used?*
14. *When scores are "corrected for guessing," some person may receive a negative score. What does this mean? Is he less able than a person scoring zero?*
15. *Some instructors advocate scoring achievement tests by formulas that penalize "bluffing" heavily, such as "number right minus twice number wrong." What is the probable effect on validity of measurement?*

Providing for Physical Handicaps

It is now federal policy to provide all possible opportunity to the handicapped, but conventional testing can only be a barrier to them. Clinical testers have been able to allow for disabilities by altering procedures (recognizing that, with nonstandard procedure, the scores do not have their ordinary significance). Clinical testers can call on a number of tests specially designed for one or another handicap—for example, a Block Design test in which textured surfaces replace the usual colors (Dauterman & Suinn, 1966). Conventional group tests can be adapted. Testing time can be extended. Print can be enlarged, tests can be printed in Braille, or questions can be read aloud. The person with a motor handicap can dictate answers. Directions in sign language can be filmed. These alterations are already in use in some testing for college admission and employment. Handicapped candidates, however, have often been discouraged by the prospect of having to pass the tests, not realizing the options available to them (Ragosta, 1980).

To adapt a test to a particular handicap, many distinctive arrangements are required. It is pointless to try to equate handicapped college applicants with usual candidates. To develop norms for each category of handicapped examinees would be impracticable and probably pointless. A person who is average within his category may be a better or worse candidate than the person who is average in the general population. To study just what each altered test measures and how well it predicts success in various training programs (themselves suitable only when adapted to each handicap) is an inexhaustible task. Often the best solution is to exempt the handicapped person from the usual test and rely on evidence from a job tryout. For recommendations on appropriate testing and test interpretation for the handicapped, see Sherman and Robinson, 1982.

16. *If sighted persons take the textured version of Block Design, will they rank as they did on the version with colored patterns? Do the two tests measure the same thing?*

TESTING AS A SOCIAL RELATIONSHIP

The tester has been accustomed to think of herself as an unemotional, impartial task setter. The traditional language suggests that the psychologist, like an engineer, is "measuring an object" with a technical tool. But the tester's "object" is a person. The traditional recommendations that the tester be encouraging and help the person to understand the value of the test barely touch the sociopsychological complexities of testing.

What Schafer (1954, p. 6) has said about clinical testing applies in some degree to every test that may affect the person's opportunities or self-esteem:

> The clinical testing situation has a complex psychological structure. It is not an impersonal getting-together of two people in order that one, with the help of a little "rapport," may obtain some "objective" test responses from the other. The psychiatric patient is in some acute or chronic life crisis. He cannot but bring many hopes, fears, assumptions, demands and expectations into the test situation. He cannot but respond intensely to certain real as well as fantasied attributes of that situation. Being human and having to make a living—facts often ignored—the tester too brings hopes, fears,

assumptions, demands and expectations into the test situation. She too responds personally and often intensely to what goes on—in reality and in fantasy—in that situation, however well she may conceal her personal response from the patient, from herself, and from her colleagues.

Recognizing Needs of the Examinee

The person coming for an individual test almost invariably is in difficulties. He may have been referred by some authority who has control over his fate; if so, the tester may be simply another authority to fear or rebel against. One might expect cooperation when the client is self-referred, but his objectives can conflict with the tester's. The test taker may have doubts regarding his adequacy that he is attempting to suppress. It is commonplace to discover, behind a college student's self-referral for remedial reading or vocational counseling, a problem of sexual adjustment or conflict with parents. The student, focusing his attention and that of the psychologist on a lesser problem, is using unconscious sleight of hand to conceal the problem he does not want to face. None of us is willing to expose himself completely or to learn the whole truth about himself, yet the tester is commissioned to penetrate. Often the clinical examiner must try to learn about sexual attitudes, hostilities, feelings of inadequacy, or wishes the patient is ashamed of. Even when the testing has a limited aim, the patient may believe that the test will expose intimate desires and anxieties. Conversely, a patient concerned about himself may believe that the test is too insensitive to bring his difficulties fully to the attention of the therapist; then the clinician must try to allow for exaggeration of symptoms.

Giving a test individually, one establishes a relationship that can bring emotions close to the surface. Joseph Matarazzo (1972, pp. 494 ff.) tells what happened in his assessment of a 41-year-old male, who had applied for a post as executive vice-president. The man had a record of vigor, productivity, and success; he had taken over as head of the family business when his father died two years earlier. Although the man spoke confidently and cheerfully in the intake interview, the tests suggested serious disturbance (see p. 271).

Matarazzo continues, speaking of himself in the third person:

> [T]he psychologist, having established the element of mutual trust and respect so critical and necessary in executive assessment . . . shared with this young executive his findings of numerous assets but also his concern that all was not as well with him currently as it had been in the past. This was the stimulus for a flood of tears and the shared statement, *in confidence,* that he had not recovered from his father's unexpected and precipitous death two years earlier. In view of the immediate clinical demand, various elements of this frank, depressive episode were explored in this initial session; and the suggestion was offered that psychotherapy might provide some relief

for his by now openly discussed personal suffering. He accepted the idea and arrangements were made. Discussion then returned to his candidacy for the position of Executive Vice President and the client volunteered that he had entertained this idea more as "flight" from his current, unendurable situation than in terms of any effectiveness he might bring to the challenge.

The man asked what report would be made to the hiring firm. The answer was that if the client thought himself unready for the stress of the position, he should withdraw, which would make it inappropriate for the psychologist to report. The client was referred to therapy and continued in it, but the story ends with his suicide two years later.

Schafer recommends that the social situation itself be considered an important way of understanding the person and that his strategies, demands, and resistances be taken into account in the interpretation. Schafer's view is summarized in this paragraph (1954, pp. 72–73):

> The ideal of objectivity requires that we recognize as much as possible what is going on in the situation we are studying. It requires in particular that we remember the tester and her patient are both human and alive and therefore inevitably interacting in the test situation. True, the further we move away from mechanized interpretation or comparison of formal scores and averages, the more subjective variables we may introduce into the interpretive process. . . . But while we thereby increase the likelihood of personalized interpretation and variation among testers, we are at the same time in a position to enrich our understanding and our test reports significantly.

Schafer calls for impressionistic interpretation. Those who reject Schafer's recommendation must find their own solution to the problems of interpersonal dynamics. Even a strictly poker-faced administration of an individual mental test can be an hour-long stress situation, every moment of which involves emotional interaction between tester and test taker.

17. *Does a formal and impersonal attitude toward all test takers standardize the testing relationship?*
18. *In an "agility" test used by the British Armed Forces at one time, each soldier was tested separately while his squad of perhaps 20 others watched. The task called for running back and forth along a cross-shaped pattern, transferring rings from one post to another.*
    a. *What effect on score would be expected from being tested in a group rather than without an audience?*
    b. *What effect would be expected as a result of announcing each person's score at the end of his trial—to be applauded if good?*

c. What advantage or disadvantage would a person have who came last in the group?
19. An anthropologist, giving psychological tests to Eskimos for purposes of crosscultural research, tells how the participation of subjects was obtained: "... not because they knew me or had any investment in my procedure, but because I had a tenuous identification with another white member of this community.... In one such community, the Public Health nurse ... simply stepped outside her house and waited in ambush, so to speak, for some prospect as the Eskimos walked down the path... beside her house. Such subjects were told in a kindly, but peremptory, fashion that he or she was to do whatever I asked" (C. Preston, 1964).
a. Does this method of recruiting have any effect on the interpretation of Preston's Eskimo records on mental tests and personality measures?
b. Is your answer to question **a** modified by learning that two of the Eskimos thought the study was intended to locate persons who should be locked up in a mental hospital?

Characteristics of the Tester

A remarkable amount of research has tried to find out which styles or tester characteristics raise scores on ability tests and by how much. Does it matter if the tester is familiar to the child? Does frequent encouragement help? What about the sex of the tester? Warmth and chattiness? Age? Her anxiety? And so on. (For bibliographies, see Lutey & Copeland, in Reynolds & Gutkin, 1982; and Sattler, 1974, pp. 31, 60 ff., and 1981, pp. 93, 361ff.)

Studies typically report that the variable under study neither raised nor lowered scores by much on the average, and successive reports of average differences contradict each other. One reason that studies add up to no rules or generalizations is that averages are beside the point. Test takers react to what the examiner does and to immediate circumstances.

The recurrent question about the match of tester to test taker in ethnicity or race is a serious one. I shall not dwell on the obvious—if one person does not fully understand the other's speech, the testing will be invalid. But Western psychologists, turning to pantomime, have had considerable success in giving maze tests and the like in isolated tribes whose language they could not speak. Language is not an impassable barrier. No doubt, children having better command of Spanish than English should be tested in Spanish (unless the intent is to measure, specifically, performance in English). At school ages, however, many children from Hispanic homes in the United States speak English better than Spanish (Jensen, 1980, p. 606). For testing urban blacks, it has been suggested that Black English be used. The evidence, however, is that blacks are not handicapped by testing in Standard English (Quay, 1974). Sometimes they are handicapped when the tester uses Black English, perhaps because of local variations. On average, black children do not score higher when the tester is black rather than white; here again, the differences found in controlled studies are inconsistent and usually small (Jensen, 1980, pp. 596ff.; Sattler, 1970, 1974, 1981). Let us put aside the pessimistic (and racist!) hypothesis that you cannot relate to another person unless your skins have the same color. And let us put aside attempts to generalize as if blacks (or Hispanics or any such category of persons) are uniform.

A social relationship is constructed by the parties. The conventional style of testing may elicit little response from a test taker who considers the tester an alien and a threat. The tester, of whatever social and family origins, must discover a style that reaches persons from a different background or disqualify herself.

Labov's memorable story (1970) carries its own moral. Interviewers collected speech samples from Harlem 8-year-olds in school, using a friendly but dignified technique. Rarely did the boys produce full sentences or elaborate their ideas; one-word responses were the norm. Formal interviews in a boy's home sometimes did no better, so an informal approach was tried. The interviewer brought in one of the boy's friends, got down on the floor with the two youngsters, dumped out a bag of potato chips, and started a conversation. A few taboo words were tossed in as an "Anything goes" signal. The boy whose speech was rated immature on the basis of the formal interviews now burst into expansive, fluent speech.

How Testers Distort Results

The history of science records numerous instances of self-delusion by trained observers. Many of the errors are self-serving—slanted not to gain material rewards but to satisfy needs of the observer or to confirm her beliefs or desires.

Testers seek emotional satisfactions. A tester chooses the profession because it satisfies her needs. The tester, for example, may be one who, feeling inadequate in social relations, can obtain reassurance from seemingly objective instruments. The overly "objective" tester may be quick to detect difficulties that can be treated unemotionally (limited vocabulary, for example), but overlook emotional needs. The tester who seeks emotional response may be too lenient. The competitive tester may be too eager to find weaknesses. A prison psychologist (D. P. Wilson, 1951) trained selected convicts to test new inmates; he had to supervise constantly to prevent their making procedural errors that would reduce the subject's score and so magnify their own superiority.

Rosenthal (1966) has recounted historical incidents of bias due to preconceptions and experimental demonstrations of it. Here are a few examples:

- In studies of telepathy a respondent attempts to guess what symbol a "transmitter" is concentrating on at a given moment. A recorder writes down the guesses alongside the true signal. Recording errors

made by those who believe in telepathy run 2 to 1 in the direction favoring telepathy; errors made by disbelievers tilt the other way.
- Laboratory technicians counting blood cells through a microscope take check readings on the same slide. They agree more closely than they would if proper procedure were followed. Evidently discrepant readings are suppressed.
- Student experimenters are told (untruthfully) that the rats they are to run have been genetically selected for brightness. These rats learn a maze faster than those run by experimenters who are told that they are running a dull strain. (Is it possible that teachers who are told that their students are bright teach them more? See pp. 342–344.)
- Student testers are led to think that college students normally give a sizable number of responses to an inkblot. They get about 50 per cent more responses than other testers led to expect few responses.

Distortion of test results in evaluation is a danger. Suppose that *you* have designed a new method of teaching mechanical comprehension and want to prove its excellence. To an experimental set of trainees you give Form S of the Bennett as a pretest and Form T as a posttest. You can almost guarantee a positive finding if, when pretesting, you tell the trainees that the scores "don't count," run through the directions fast, and perhaps misread your watch, shortening the working time. The opposite tactic can raise the pretest scores of a control group or posttest scores of the experimentals.

Some errors are deliberate, but "motivated error" can be unintentional. Standard procedure cannot prevent subtle influences on scores when the tester expects the pretty little girl in the starched dress to do well or when the tester's social conscience demands that her black examinees show up well. The more the tester knows of her own personality, of her preferences for different types of subject, and of the biases she brings to test interpretation, the greater the chance that she can meet each situation properly.

Medical research adopts the double-blind technique to guard against self-delusion. Half the patients are given a neutral substance (placebo). All doses are coded and look the same. Neither doctor nor patient nor laboratory technician knows which patients are receiving the drug. Psychologists and educators cannot arrange complete blinding. But tests can be given by outsiders who do not know which persons have been receiving treatment. And all papers—from pretests, posttests, experimentals, and controls—can be intermixed randomly before scoring begins.

Biased testing is especially likely when the scores will bring benefit or blame to the person charged with collecting the data. Teachers whose futures depend on the test scores their classes earn are quite likely to help the children in illegitimate ways (Horne & Garty, 1981). It is easy to nudge children toward the keyed responses. ("Are you *sure* you want to erase that?")

In recent years some legislators have desired to provide extra money to schools where the educational need is greatest. When they propose to define "need" by average start-of-year test scores of student bodies, the lawmakers come close to inviting fraud. In one city, teachers were told that *they* should fill out the answer sheet for any student whose native language was not English, making enough errors to produce a failing score. "We need a zero score to satisfy federal and state funding requirements," said the director of the school testing department (*San Francisco Examiner,* October 19, 1980). It is impractical to have agents of the central government give the tests everywhere. It is unrealistic to expect the school staff to elicit a student's best performance when his *worst* performance will bring money to the school. (A proposal to base financial aid on an end-of-year test would have another fault. If two schools with equal budgets take in equally unprepared students, the one that produces higher posttest scores will be judged less "needy," will get no extra funds next year, and so will be penalized for having done a superior job.)

20. *In what way could sympathy and love for children bias a tester? What parts of the testing process would be affected by this bias?*
21. *Can the "superior performance" of rats whose experimenters think they are bright be attributed to any causes other than error in recording or error in procedure?*
22. *What acts or judgments of the tester—short of gross error—might modify the scores earned*
    a. *in an individually administered vocabulary test?*
    b. *in a group-administered vocabulary test?*
    c. *in an individual story-completion test in which the responses are tape-recorded and later scored, by persons other than the tester, for aggression and hostility themes.*

MOTIVATION OF THE TEST TAKER

In the weighing of a truckload of wheat, there is no problem of motivation. Likewise, in weighing a person, when we put him on the scale, we get a good measure no matter how he feels about the operation. In a psychological test the subject places himself on the scale, and unless he cares about the result, he cannot be measured.

The ability tester is like the industrial manager who wants a high rate of production. Effort and productivity depend on the reward the person foresees. The most direct reward for good test performance is being hired for a job or being given a desirable assignment. Equally powerful and more universally available as a source of motivation is the desire to maintain self-respect and the respect of others. Effort is stimulated also by sheer interest in the task, by the habit of obeying authority, and by the friendliness of the tester. The generalized encouragement recommended by Terman and Merrill is expected to have an effect. Ability-test scores are not readily altered by simple incentives such as prizes, pep talks, and a monetary payment after the test to reward a good score (Lutey & Copeland, in Reynolds & Gutkin, 1982). However, when the test task is convincingly presented as important in its own right, scores tend to improve (Flanagan, 1955; B. W. Hall *et al.*, 1974). In the same vein we saw (p. 39) that providing immediate knowledge as to whether each answer is right or wrong improves scores. This is not a matter of special incentives but of leading the person to regard the task seriously. (See also p. 336.)

Not every subject wants to do well. The accident victim seeking compensation or the worker applying for a disability pension may deliberately exaggerate his difficulties or attempt to mimic the test performance of an aphasic (for example). The tester may recognize such malingering because fakers do not mimic disorders accurately, but she is left with an uninterpretable test record (Heaton & Heaton, McMahon & Satz, both in Filskov & Boll, 1982).

Attitudes toward oneself and toward task performance have a profound influence on response to tests and to school assignments. The typical schoolchild has learned to work hard because he obtains praise, tangible rewards, and special opportunities when he achieves. But maximum motivation may not be optimum motivation. The test taker's very desire to do well may interfere with performance. A tense performer overlooks errors that he would correct otherwise. In psychomotor tests, tension leads to poor coordination and erratic movements. In a verbal test, the respondent may guard against criticisms of his answers by being overcritical of himself. In clinical tests, anxious patients find fault with their own answers or elaborate obsessively, spoiling answers that would have received credit.

For many children tests become stressful. College students seek counseling because they believe that their anxiety is lowering their examination marks. Although much is said about detriment from anxiety, it is also true that mild anxiety can heighten performance.

Research on test anxiety has been conducted with questionnaires; the Test Anxiety Scale of Sarason, in its successive versions, has perhaps been used most often (I. G. Sarason, 1980, p. 9). Items refer to typical or average behavior—for example, "I freeze up on intelligence tests." Such a measure of "trait anxiety" gives no picture of day-to-day, test-to-test changes in state.

Day-to-day fluctuations in state are illustrated in Figure 3.3. Self-descriptions were collected (by means of a simple adjective checklist) on 77 consecutive days from student nurses taking the same classes and the same exams. Anxiety built up as crucial examinations approached, tending to peak on the evenings after examinations.

Items on detrimental anxiety fall into two groups. There are "emotionality" items such as "I have an upset, uneasy feeling before taking a final examination." And there are "worry" items, such as "Thinking about the grade I may get in a course interferes with my thinking and my performance on tests" (Spielberger *et al.*, 1978). The worry component is the one that

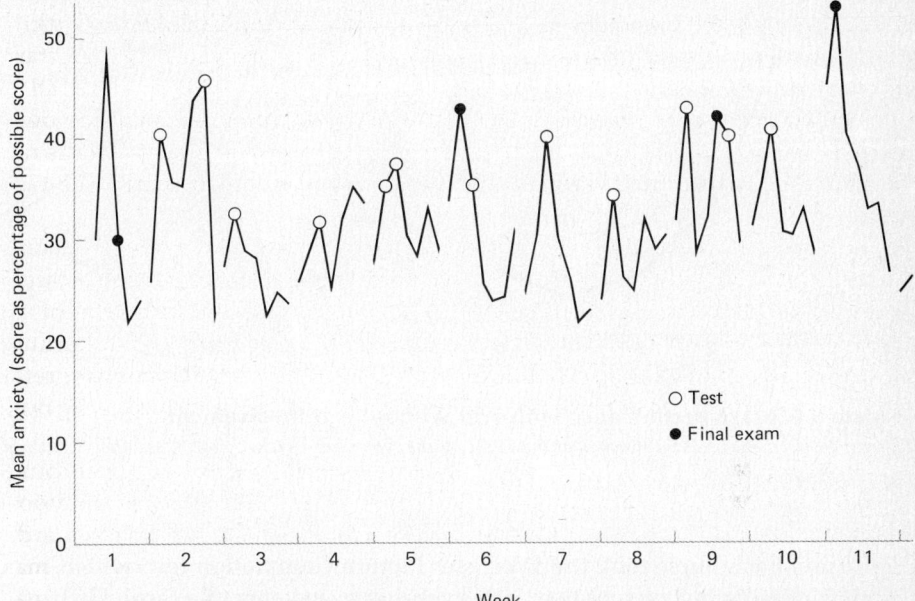

Figure 3.3. Student anxiety on days with and without course examinations. On 77 evenings, students checked a list of adjectives to describe "how you feel now—today." Open dots represent the average score on the evening of the testing day (i.e., after the test). In each week save Week 1, the first point is for Sunday evening.
Source: Based on a figure in the manual for the Multiple Affect Adjective Check List and data supplied by M. Zuckerman. See Zuckerman, 1976.

correlates with low grades. One cannot be confident as to the direction of causation here; poor learning may be the source of weak test performance, from which anxiety follows.

Detrimental effects may be increased by tactics the tester uses to increase effort. S. Sarason and his associates (1952) ran an experiment on Yale freshmen with high and low anxiety (HA and LA groups, respectively). During a maze test, half the students received "ego-involving" (EI) instructions: this was an intelligence test and would be used to assist in interpreting freshman entrance tests. The NEI ("not ego-involved") group was told that the examiner was standardizing the maze task and that no attention would be paid to individual scores. Error scores are shown in Figure 3.4. The NEI groups had intermediate scores, there being little difference between the HA–NEI and LA–NEI subgroups. Among students who said that they do not become anxious about tests (left panel), EI instructions raised scores a little. Anxious subjects performed much worse when threatened by the emphasis on doing well than they did under emotionally neutral conditions.

How anxious and defensive reactions interfere was shown by Wiener (1957). "Trustful" and "distrustful" student nurses were selected by a ques-

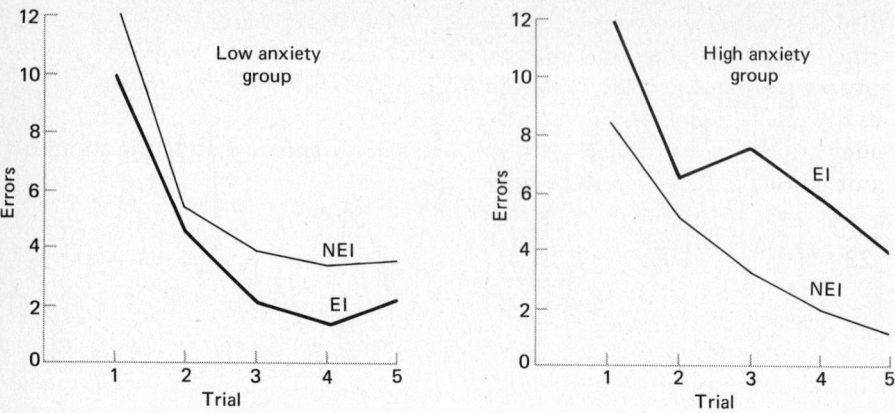

Figure 3.4. Maze performance with and without ego involvement.
Source: Sarason et al., 1952. Copyright © 1952 by the American Psychological Association. Adapted by permission.

tionnaire. Each nurse took the Wechsler Picture Completion test, which asks what is missing in a picture (e.g., one eyebrow in a sketch of a face). Distrustful subjects were inclined to deny that anything was missing when the answer did not come to them immediately. Likewise, on Similarities ("How are *praise* and *punishment* alike?") the distrustful students were more inclined to deny that the words were alike. Distrustful students averaged 2.7 suspicious comments on the two tests compared to 0.9 for the trustful students. In Wiener's words: "People who say, 'There is nothing missing in that picture!' are responding to internal needs rather than to the testing situation." Sometimes reducing threat elicits superior performance. I. G. Sarason (1978) gave an examination to a small college class in the usual manner and then offered a no-risk retest. Students were promised that whichever score was higher, test or retest, would be kept for the record, the other being discarded. On average, scores went up on the second test. More important, the gain averaged around 3 points out of 50 for students low in test anxiety and around 10 points for those with high (trait) anxiety scores. The study deserves to be repeated with better controls and with measures of *state* anxiety (p. 45). Perhaps the change in group climate made as much difference as the direct response of individuals to the instructor's generosity.

A striking example of the effect of anxiety is the case of the young reserve officer, eager to serve in time of war, who failed his physical examination twice. The importance of passing made him emotional—and the emotion brought his blood pressure over the acceptable limit. A series of "reconditioning" treatments made it possible for him to take the test calmly. The accumulated research on counseling and reconditioning procedures (Benjamin *et al.,* 1981; I. G. Sarason, 1980; Spielberger *et al.,* 1976; G. Tryon, 1980) indicates that it is easy enough to change reported anxiety—mere suggestion will do that much. Training in relaxation and reconditioning appear to go further in reducing emotionality, but academic performance seems to improve only when the therapy is combined with training in study skills. Tryon sees the greatest promise in reducing the "worry" component by training the student to focus on the task and to push self-oriented, distracting thoughts about consequences of failure out of his mind.

23. *Hebb and Williams (1946) devised a test to measure the learning ability of rats. The test consists of a set of mazes to be run, the performance being called a success when a direct path to the food box is taken on the second trial on each maze. What problems of motivation would need to be considered in administering this test?*
24. *In individual testing, many strongly motivated students hesitate to answer when having difficulty. According to Johnson and Baker (1973), this hesitancy is reduced when a test is given by computer. Suggest an explanation.*

PREPARING THE TEST TAKER FOR THE TEST

Even where test scores are to guide decisions by others, the examinee can be made a part of the tester's team. The tester can honestly indicate the purpose of testing and portray the test as an opportunity for the person to find out about himself just as the physician tells the patient what medicine is being given and what results are to be expected from it. If sound measurement is to the respondent's advantage and he knows it, he will have little motive to provide an untruthful picture.

For tests that act as gatekeepers, such as tests for selection or certification, it is increasingly common to orient the examinee in advance. The publisher may offer an explanatory booklet that describes the test content, displays representative items, and advises on efficient work procedures. The armed services, for example, offer a test through high schools. Chiefly, the test collects information for recruiters, but it also assists the school in its vocational counseling. A movie that dramatizes the importance of test information in career choice is available for the school to show. Students and parents must sign a consent form in advance of the test; the movie encourages them to agree, and it should increase students' readiness for the tests.

In 1979, New York State mandated public release of the questions from college entrance tests after they have been administered. Test developers objected to having to assemble entirely new questions each time the test is offered. This is costly, and for some kinds of tests fresh items would be hard to invent. Two justifications of the requirement were offered: releasing the tests has educational value because students will study the items missed;

second, release enables students to verify the scoring and the answer key itself (Bersoff, in Glaser & Bond, 1981).

The first fruits of the law were news stories demonstrating that among hundreds of thousands of college applicants, one of them manages at a certain moment to reason more subtly than test developers did; occasionally, a response keyed as wrong has a logical defense. Releasing items seems to invite endless wrangles over items that call for subtle judgment. Such threats could drive out tasks where judgment enters, shifting test questions toward recall of indisputable facts and sending candidates on a spree of memorization.

The Contract with the Test Taker

Members of all professions are expected, in the 1980s, to be far more open in their relations with those served than was formerly the case. Professional codes have always avowed that the professional acts to advance the interests of the client and the public; the new theme is that people can judge what serves their interests better than the professional can. Consequently, professional standards are changing. Testing practice has been affected by new laws and recommendations on such themes as privacy, informed consent, limits of experimentation on humans, and freedom of information. The details of changing regulations are less important than principles.

The tester enters into a contract with the person tested. In former days the understanding was left vague. The tester is now expected to be frank and explicit in her agreement with the client (or, in the case of a young child or disturbed adult, with the client's representative). The tester is often a go-between—between a college and an applicant or between a court and a prisoner, for example. The tester has responsibilities in both directions, and she should try to make sure that these opposite numbers have mutually consistent expectations. If the tester promises that persons in certain specific responsible posts—and no one else—will see the client's scores, the tester ought to assure herself that the institution to which she reports will adopt and enforce that degree of confidentiality.

Opinion has not stabilized regarding the principles presented in the list that follows. Representatives of client interests press for ever-increasing restraints on testing. Professionals accept many of the restraints but believe that the trend can go too far. They point to risks of inhibiting research, of impairing the quality of decisions, and of increasing their cost. The principles that follow are derived from policy statements of the American Personnel and Guidance Association (1978) and the American Psychological Association (1981) and from the discussions of a national committee on ability testing (Wigdor & Garner, 1982). See also London and Bray (1980). The sources do not cover precisely the same points, but they are in harmony. Some main principles are the following:

- The record of test performance is the property of the person tested. Individual scores should not be supplied to any person or agency

without the examinee's authorization save where it is necessary to warn someone of physical danger or where an authority with acknowledged jurisdiction commissioned the testing. An initial authorization is established when the tester—in obtaining consent for the testing—explains why the test is given. The examinee should be told what will be done with the test results: who will see them, what decisions may be affected by them, and how long they will be kept on file.
- Scores that will have an important effect on the person's future should be reported to him in understandable form. Exceptions are warranted where the person is immature, or disclosure would be unsettling, or special training is required to understand the report. If the tester considers it inadvisable to report to the test taker, it should be possible for a qualified representative of the person to obtain the information so as to verify the reasonableness of the conclusions.
- A procedure for challenging a test report should be available and the test taker should be informed of the procedure. A score found to be seriously invalid should be removed from the record.
- In educational and employment testing, a score from two years back is out of date. It is useful—if at all—only as a benchmark against which to judge current performance. Old scores should not be retained except in research files. This principle would not apply in some clinical practice, where a long-term history of ups and downs in test performance is likely to shed light on a current decision.
- Records in research files should be coded so that users of the files cannot identify test scores with individuals. Identified files should be secured so that no one sees a case record without specific authorization from the responsible professional.

Such principles are not easily put into practice; and costs of a well-intentioned procedure have to be weighed against benefits. Take scoring errors as an example. When a person's opportunity hinges on a score, he should have a way to question its accuracy even though the likelihood of error is small. Just as a patient can obtain a second opinion when his physician recommends a surgical operation, parents can reasonably ask for an independent review after the school psychologist has appraised their child. The principle of openness has its limits, though.

When two members of a union were passed over for promotion, the union sued on their behalf. It claimed for itself the right to rescore the promotion tests of these workers and the ones who were promoted in order to confirm whether its clients had done as poorly as the company said. The company objected particularly to releasing test papers of successful candidates without their consent, but security of the test was also a concern. The risk that the questions and answers might be leaked to future candidates outweighs the risk of a scoring error, said the U.S. Supreme Court—by a vote of 5 to 4 (*Detroit Edison Co.* v. *N.L.R.B.*, 99 S. Ct 1123, 1979; Roskind, 1980).

Third-party ombudsman arrangements will evidently be necessary in conflicts over scoring and test reports.

Citizens are rightly uneasy about files containing information that could someday be dragged out by an adversary. Research files can be subpoenaed. For example, social scientists who had interviewed recipients of public welfare were unable to deny access to supposedly confidential files when a prosecutor suspected some recipients of fraud. Similar conflict could arise in a suit alleging medical or educational malpractice. Safeguards for confidentiality can be devised. Once individual identification is erased, the files no longer can serve a prosecutor.

Replacing an individual's name with a code number in a research file is simple, but there is a hidden cost. Ten or 20 years later it may be scientifically important to trace the subsequent development of those persons. Conversely, it could be important to look back at the early history of those who, at age 30, display some unusual excellence or defect. A number of devices for protecting research values without endangering privacy have been suggested (Boruch & Cecil, 1979; see p. 454 for one device).

Policies for testing by employers and schools have received more attention than policies for clinical testers. Clinical psychologists have generally seen their responsibility to persons they treat as requiring confidentiality like that between physician and patient. But medical confidentiality is now under question, and psychological records will surely be no more protected than medical records. With regard to health records, a reporter for *Science* had this to say (Holden, 1977):

> There is general agreement now that citizens should know what is in their files and who has them, and should have say in the use to which they are put. But there is considerable disagreement among various factions over the proper balance between an individual's right to privacy and society's need for information to keep insurance costs down, guard against fraud, pursue criminal justice, and conduct epidemiological research.[5]

This same demand for information about psychological services arises, especially when they are covered by third-party payments.

What tests are given and how they are reported is likely to change as more reports are opened to examinees. Testers will avoid words having strong emotional connotations, such as *mental retardation* and *neurotic*. They will be tempted to muffle a serious finding in phrases to which no one could object. "Face valid" tests—for example, asking the person to follow realistic directions—will become more popular. On the one hand, the quality and richness of test information can be expected to decline; on the other hand,

---

[5]Copyright © 1977 by the American Association for the Advancement of Science. Reprinted by permission.

the emerging policies will reduce misuse, misunderstanding, and harmful labeling.

25. *One member of Congress pressed (unsuccessfully) for the rule that a patient's file could be examined only with his explicit consent. Those familiar with health research said that this would make the files available for research on the effectiveness of treatment so unrepresentative as to be worthless (Holden, 1977). What rights and values are in conflict here? Consider particularly files of persons treated for behavioral or emotional disturbances.*
26. *On a mathematical reasoning test, a student planning to go to graduate school earns a score that is about average for seniors in scientific fields. He does much better on another form of the test 6 months later, ranking in the upper quarter. Should he have the right to specify that only the second score be transmitted when he applies to graduate schools? (Would you give the same answer if his first score had been the higher one?)*
27. *What explanation would you give the test taker in each of the following cases?*
    a. *College freshmen are to be tested to determine which ones may fail because of reading deficiency.*
    b. *At the end of a course in industrial relations for supervisors, an examination on judgment in grievance cases is to be given.*
28. *How could a "cooperative" point of view in testing be adopted:*
    a. *By a school principal who wishes to find out how well each eighth-grade class is mastering written English?*
    b. *By a veteran's counselor who must approve the plan of a handicapped veteran to go to college and prepare for dentistry?*
    c. *By a consulting psychologist who is asked by a social agency to diagnose and report on a potential delinquent?*
29. *The first principle listed earlier—"the record is the property of the person tested"—is stated strongly enough to be debatable. Consider these applications:*
    a. *Should a law school supply, to the prospective employer of a graduate the person's score on a test given at the time of admission? The student's grade record?*
    b. *A school psychologist evaluating an emotionally disturbed child employs a sentence-completion test with items such as*

    When I can't answer a question the teacher asks, I . . . .
    My parents . . . .

    When the psychologist recommends that the child be placed in a residential school, should the parents be allowed to see the child's responses?
    c. *A teacher in grade 9 asks students, midway in the year, to write autobiographical essays. Should copies of those essays be available to other teachers?*

d. *Should the advanced calculus teacher have access to a student's grades in lower-level math courses?*

Coaching and Test Sophistication

Test-wiseness. Sophisticated test takers have many tricks (cataloged by Millman *et al.,* 1965). In general, it is sensible to work through a test rapidly, making a quick judgment or even a guess, then returning to reconsider answers in the time that remains. That is far better than methodically finishing each question in turn. Paying careful attention to directions—for example, to what is said about the scoring rule—is advisable. Responding when not completely certain of the answer choice is advisable. And so on.

Another set of techniques depends on "psyching out" the test constructor or capitalizing on her mistakes. When he sees two essentially similar alternatives in a choice-response item, the test-wise student knows that both are probably incorrect. He also has observed that, in a true-false test, "always" appears mostly in false statements. Allowing test-wiseness to operate lowers test validity because the wise students rank higher than they would on the basis of content knowledge alone. By providing sound directions and editing carefully, the test maker can reduce this influence. Pacing and guessing remain in the student's hands. As they go through school, all students should gradually be informed about effective test-taking strategies. (But teachers probably give as much bad advice as good: "Take your time, and don't guess.") Sarnacki (1979) reviews much research on test-wiseness—even reporting on a test of test-wiseness.

Intensive coaching. Bulletin boards on every campus are papered over with ads for coaching schools serving applicants for business school, law school, medical school, you name it. High school juniors aspiring to selective colleges crowd into coaching schools, and some high schools allocate class time to preparing for college aptitude tests. Your nearest drugstore may have a rack of do-it-yourself coaching guides for civil service tests as well as for admissions tests.

Similarly, when administrators impose achievement tests to judge how well particular schools or teachers are doing, it is not uncommon for teachers to set the regular course of study aside while preparing students specifically for the test. One group of educational innovators, distressed because experimental teaching methods they had confidence in were not raising standard test scores, added lessons in test taking to the experimental treatment, so that any actual gains in reading would be sure to show. As an outgrowth, a series of "minitests" has been marketed to prepare classes to show up well on the next standard achievement test given for administrative purposes.

After much dispute regarding the effectiveness of coaching, a consensus has emerged about the facts—if not about the propriety of coaching (Anastasi, in Glaser & Bond, 1981). The controversy and the research have centered on the Scholastic Aptitude Test (SAT). Until recently, the College Entrance Examination Board advised students that coaching is a poor investment; experimental comparisons of coached and uncoached groups were said to show little advantage for those coached. The Federal Trade Commission (FTC) took the reasoning a step further: if this is true, it said, coaching schools defraud the consumer and should be prosecuted. When it collected evidence, the FTC was surprised to discover that one school was producing notable score increases (and two were not). The comparison was ambiguous because self-selection accounted for some of the superiority of coached applicants. The combined evidence to date, however, including studies with equated groups, has generated the following conclusions (Messick, 1980; Pike, 1978; Slack & Porter, 1980).

Coaching programs differ in character, and their effects depend on the student's prior preparation and motivation. The mere opportunity to take a test twice will have some effect, especially if the students originally had little idea what to expect. A few hours of orientation, hints about test taking, and practice can add, on average, 8 to 10 points on the SAT scale. (That average includes some persons whose scores rose 20 points or more and some whose scores declined a bit; luck plays a part.) The 20-point gains begin to seem important when we learn that, in the typical selective college, just 30 points separate the average accepted applicant from the best of the applicants told to go elsewhere. This question remains: Do a 20-point benefit for a few students and a smaller benefit for others warrant their investment of time?

The payoff mounts as the coaching changes from a quick brushup to an intensive course. When they truly taught mathematics—21 hours of classwork and 21 hours of homework—Evans and Pike (1973) produced an average gain of 16 points in the SAT Mathematics score. In the FTC study, a 40-hour course plus homework produced gains of 20 to 30 points on both the Verbal and Mathematics tests. So instruction in the abilities crucial to test performance and presumably to much college work has an appreciable effect. On the other hand, Messick and Jungeblut (1981) warn of diminishing returns. Their estimate of the hours of student effort required to produce specified score increases is as follows:

For a gain of	10	20	30	40	points
in the Verbal score:	12	57	260	1185	hours
in the Mathematics score:	8	19	45	107	hours

The current College Board advice reviews these facts and says that only the applicant and his parents can decide whether intensive preparation "is worth the time, effort, and money."

The major complaint about coaching is its possible social inequity. Students with time and money for a substantial coaching course are more likely to get into the colleges they prefer than students who get no coaching.

The fair procedure, some people say, is to make coaching available to every student in high school who wants to attend a selective college. But then the tail of testing wags the instructional dog: what is pushed out of the student's school schedule may be more significant than the test-oriented instruction. The verdict of a national policy committee was put in these words: "[T]here may be considerable advantage to explicitly preparing students for an examination *if the examination tests abilities and knowledge that are educationally worthwhile*" (Wigdor & Garner, 1982).

If coaching specific to a test is prevalent, something is wrong with the system. In a society in which life at the top is much better than the life of the majority *and* one make-or-break decision takes away a young person's chance for high status, the tests that influence the decision take on an all-too-rational importance. It is the system that is irrational. There are many kinds of talent, and these talents emerge over the years, so there is no one right age at which to sort people out. In some nations a young man has to complete the academic course to escape a life as hoe wielder. Parents become abnormally sensitive to news that certain high schools come out ahead in college admissions, that certain lower schools get the most graduates past an earlier test hurdle and into these prestige high schools, and even that certain kindergartens increase the child's chances in life. Coaching for the kindergarten entrance examination follows! Since private tutoring is costly, the overselective system gives an advantage to children of the prosperous.

30. *In some college residence halls, students build up files of the examinations they have taken. From the point of view of the professor teaching the course year after year, do these files increase or decrease the validity of measurement?*
31. *It is evidently easier to improve scores on the Mathematics section of SAT than the Verbal section. What might account for this?*
32. *What changes in insight and motivation are likely to take place during a 5-hour coaching course?*
33. *Does the evidence on susceptibility to coaching cast doubt on the validity of SAT as an indicator of readiness for college work?*
34. *What implications do the investigations of coaching have for those who use mental tests to select scholarship winners?*
35. *In Japan a young person's career opportunities depend very much on capturing one of the limited number of openings in a good university. Vacancies are filled on the basis of entrance examinations and school records. Magazines bearing such titles as* **Student Days, Examiners' Circle,** *and* **Period of Diligent Study** *have large circulations. These magazines deal with topics of interest to candidates including information about typical test materials (though the actual test questions are of course guarded). Would such magazines increase or decrease the validity of the tests?*

4 Scoring

SCORING PROCEDURES

Any student who has tried to understand why he received a low score on some essay examination must realize how difficult it is to define a good answer and to assign proper partial credit. Starch and Elliott (1912, 1913) provided famous evidence. They took a pupil's English composition to a convention of teachers and asked volunteers to grade it on a percentage scale. The grades ranged from 50 to 98. *This* disagreement could perhaps be tolerated because the judgment of a composition is inherently subjective. To drive home their point, Starch and Elliott had volunteers grade a geometry paper. Scores ranged from 28 to 92, presumably because some scorers gave credit for neatness, partial solutions, and so on.

One way to systematize scoring is to develop rules for judgment that all scorers will follow. The other possibility is to tell the subject to choose among fixed alternatives; once the answer key is determined, scoring requires no judgment.

The test taker constructs a response in recall tests and essay tests, Block Design and other tests of complex problem solving, and most tests of job performance. Scoring is judgmental, but procedures that increase agreement among scorers have been devised. A classic example is Ayres's guide for scoring pupil handwriting (Figure 4.1). The guide displays specimens representing various levels of quality; to determine the score, the teacher locates the sample most similar to the pupil's writing. Product-rating scales can be developed for judging quality of sewing, shopwork, and so on. Guides can show the approved scoring of representative verbal answers and of behavioral observations.

Figure 4.2 is part of the guide for the Social Reasoning Test of the British Ability Scales. The directions go on to describe how a credit of 5 can be earned with a response that rises to the level of stating a general principle. The manual gives further illustrations of the scoring of actual responses of children between 8 and 11. Certain Social Reasoning responses are said to represent greater maturity of thought and, therefore, deserve greater credit. The scoring rules embody the theory of Piaget and Kohlberg that maturing children become increasingly able to see a situation through the eyes of others.

A choice-response test comes with a list of answers to be given credit. For scoring by hand, these are often displayed in a key that can be laid over or alongside the respondent's answers for easy comparison.

Most technical scoring devices use scanners. Each mark on the answer sheet is translated into an electrical impulse that can be matched against the keyed answer. "Optical" scanners use photocells; another type relies on the fact that pencil marks conduct electrical current. Each type of scanner requires its own answer sheet, so the scoring procedure should be considered when test materials are purchased. The examinee who erases carelessly or who makes stray marks sends false signals. Therefore, clerks should inspect papers and make some erasures. The test giver should emphasize filling the printed spaces with solid black marks.

Especially suited to short questionnaires is a punch-out card. To indicate each answer, the respondent presses a spot on the card with a pointed object. A machine "reads" the holes so created and feeds the information into a computer. Free responses can later be coded for similar automated handling.

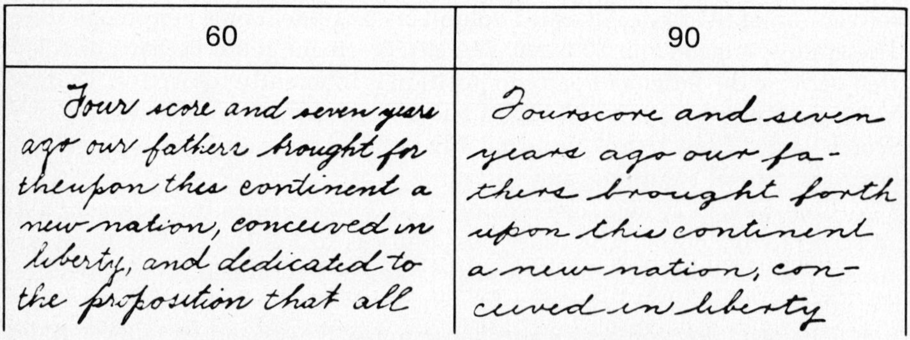

60	90
Four score and seven years ago our fathers brought for theupon this continent a new nation, conceived in liberty, and dedicated to the proposition that all	*Fourscore and seven years ago our fathers brought forth upon this continent a new nation, conceived in liberty*

Figure 4.1. Part of Ayres's scale for scoring handwriting.
Reproduced by permission of the present publisher, the University of Iowa Press.

Scoring can be built directly into the testing procedure. The apparatus for the Complex Coordination test (p. 220) can note response times and errors and feed the data into a computer memory. Automated scoring is an integral part of any test given by computer.

Scoring by machine is rapid, accurate, and economical. Moreover, a computer can print out score rosters and graphic score reports for individuals and file the information for research. Even tests given on a modest scale are scored by computer. Papers from just one class may be graded by the computer; the instructor obtains not only the scores but also informative statistics. Computer scoring programs for many published tests report multiple scores for each person and add verbal interpretation. (See p. 487.)

Nearly all booklets of test questions sold commercially are designed to be used many times, separate sheets being provided for responses. Some purchasers have printed their own answer sheets to save money. Such answer sheets are ordinarily not suited for machine scoring, which requires a certain quality of paper and precisely located printing. Moreover, it is shortsighted to save money on answer sheets. The publisher's charges cover costs of research on further development and revision of the test, costs of new tests in preparation, and a financial return to author and publisher. (When a test is administered at a computer terminal, no answer sheet is used. The usual licensing arrangement specifies a fee to be paid for each person given the test.)

1. *The question "Why should people wash their clothing?" is used to test adults' comprehension of common situations. Prepare a set of standards for judging correctness of answers. Make your rules so clear that scorers would be able to agree in scoring new answers.*
2. *Use Figure 4.2 to score the following responses to item 2 of the Social Reasoning Test. (These are taken from the BAS manual.)*
   a. *They wanted one because they are selfish—so they took his to be mean.*
   b. *It was a new teddy.*
   c. *John feels sorry he ain't got no toy to play with. He will tell his mum and she'll come back and tell them to get another one.*

INTERPRETATION OF SCORES

Raw Scores

The direct count or measure of performance is called the *raw score*. This may be the number of questions the person answered, the time he required, a count of right answers plus bonuses for fast work and minus penalties for errors, or some similar number.

Raw scores can easily be misinterpreted. Willie's report card shows a 75 in arithmetic and a 90 in spelling. His parents can be counted on to praise the latter and disapprove the former. Willie might quite properly protest, "But

---

SCORING CRITERIA

All the answers given in the examples following this section are complete—it will be apparent that with a more extended response they could merit a higher score, but in these cases this was not forthcoming.

Conversely, a few responses are over-extended; having completed a response the child has produced irrelevancies subsequently, but should not be penalized for this. . . .

Score 0—Pre-reasoning
The child is unable to comprehend what is required, or to provide a relevant response. . . .

Score 1—Immediate Consequences
The child now responds relevantly, but only in terms of **immediate reactions or consequences,** often talking about the punishment or reward which one person in the item will get, or how he will feel. This may be shown by references to getting into trouble, being punished, being good or naughty, without further elaboration, being injured or breaking things. . . .

Score 2—Partial Evaluation
The child has now progressed to a broader grasp of **one side of the problem only.**
This may be expressed either as value judgements about stealing, keeping promises etc., statements of simple rules about behaviour, or practical solutions for solving the problem from one angle only. What is **not** apparent is a real view of both sides of the problem; one person is seen as being in the right or as being wrong. . . .

Score 3—Full Evaluation
An attempt is made to find reasons and explanations for the actions of **both parties.**
Some stereotyped judgements may be given, but unlike the Stage 2 response, an attempt is made to see both or all sides of the problem. However, the Stage 3 child is still immersed in the rights and wrongs of the particular problem . . .

Figure 4.2. Scoring rules for a Social Reasoning item.
Source: Elliott et al., Manual 3 of the British Ability Scales, 1978. Reproduced by permission of NFER-Nelson Publishing Company, Ltd.

SCORING

> Joe did not have many toys, but he had a teddy bear he loved very much. One day some older children took his teddy bear and burned it. They said it didn't matter. What do you think? . . . . Why? . . . .
>
> *Note for scoring:*
>   *Most responses focus either on Joe's having no more toys—a one point score unless further elaborated; or on Joe having loved his teddy—usually a two point score.*
>
>
> **Score 0**   That's a good story.
>
>   He cried—my dad's name is Joe.
>
>
> **Score 1**   If he likes his teddy so much he shouldn't make friends with other children.
>
>   His mum smacked him—because he lost his teddy bear.
>
>   Did matter—they'll get into trouble.
>
>   Does matter—the boys will get told off and Joe will be sad.
>
>
> **Score 2**   It did matter—they are thieves.
>
>   They shouldn't have burned it—they are naughty for taking other people's things.
>
>   It did matter—Joe loved it very much and did not have other toys.
>
>
> **Score 3**   If he was a baby it did matter, but if he was a grown up boy it didn't matter—grown up boys don't have teddy bears.
>
>   It did matter to Joe because he cared for it—it didn't matter to the boys because they were cruel.
>
>   It mattered to him—perhaps they didn't know how much it meant to him.

you should see what the other kids get in arithmetic. Lots of them get 60 and 65." The parents, who know a good grade when they see one, refuse to be sidetracked by such irrelevance. But what do Willie's grades mean? It might appear that he has mastered three-fourths of the course work in arithmetic, and nine-tenths in spelling. Willie objects to that, too. "I learned all my combinations, but the teacher doesn't ask much about those. The tests are full of word problems, and we only studied them a little." Willie evidently passes 75 per cent of the questions asked, but since the questions may be easy or hard, the percentage itself is meaningless to his parents. We cannot compare Willie with his sister Sue, whose teacher in another grade gives easier tests. It could be, too, that Willie's shining 90 in spelling is misleading, if the spelling tests are restricted to the words assigned for study.

Physical measuring scales generally have a true zero and equal units along the scale; this permits us to say, for example, that one boy is twice as tall as another or has attained 60 per cent of his probable adult height. We cannot make statements like this about psychological measures. Suppose that Willie scored 10 per cent in spelling. Would this mean that he knows only one-tenth of the words he should? No, for the teacher probably did not ask about easy words that Willie was sure to know. Even a score of zero on the test would not mean zero ability to spell. The difference between Willie with a score of zero and the model pupil who earns 100 is perhaps a difference in ability to spell only 20 words out of an active vocabulary of several thousand —if those 20 constituted the test.

The same argument applies to tests of reasoning. A raw score of 80 may appear to represent ability twice as great as a raw score of 40. The test does not include the problems everyone can solve, however; if people were tested on every possible problem calling for reasoning, the true ratio might be 140 to 180 or 1040 to 1080. Even an infant, looking toward the door when he hears a parent's footstep, shows some ability to reason. Absolute zero in any ability is "just no ability at all."

Differences in raw scores do not ordinarily represent "true" distances between individuals. Suppose, on DAT Mechanical Reasoning Form V, Adam gets 53 points, Bill gets 56, and Charles gets 59. The raw-score differences are equal. Is Charles truly as different from Bill as Bill is from Adam? We cannot be sure, since the score difference depends on the items used. Adding difficult items to the test would give Charles a chance to lengthen his lead. "Equal differences" is a meaningful phrase only after some practical criterion pins down a scale of values. Different standards lead to different comparisons. On the DAT, the three raw scores are equally spaced. The probabilities of passing a college engineering course almost certainly are not equally spaced; they might be something like 0.0, 0.0, and 0.56. The boys' most likely freshman grade averages may be D, C+, and B—. And their respective probabilities of later success in a demanding engineering firm may be 0.0001, 0.05, and 0.5. "Equal intervals" on one scale are unequal on another.

3. Decide whether an absolute zero exists for each of the following variables and, where possible, define it. (Where the zero level of the trait cannot be defined, it is sometimes possible to define the opposite extreme of perfection.)
   a. Height of a person.
   b. Ability to discriminate between the pitches of tones.
   c. Speed of tapping.
   d. Gregariousness, seeking the companionship of others.
   e. Rifle aiming.
4. If a different set of test questions were used in arithmetic, would Willie's raw score change? His rank?
5. Amelia, a college freshman, seeking guidance on her academic plans, takes four tests of ability. Scores could be presented in four ways. Interpret separately each row of scores.

	Vocabulary	Verbal reasoning	Nonverbal reasoning	Mechanical comprehension
Raw score	116	32	44	48
Percent of possible points	77	73	80	71
Points above average	24	10	20	0
Rank among 260 freshman	104	113	161	136

6. Is it sensible for a school to fix a numerical standard for assigning course marks on the basis of test averages? (For example: 93–100 = A, 85–92 = B, etc.)
7. Some instructors "grade on the curve," assigning As to a fixed proportion of the pupils, Bs to another proportion, and so on. Is there any logical basis for fixing these percentages?
8. Two runners train for the mile. One, between his junior and senior years, reduces his time from 4 min. 56 sec. to 4 min. 44 sec. The other starts with a time of 5 min. 56 sec. What time must he achieve for us to say that he has made as much improvement as the first runner?

Criterion Reference and Domain Reference

To understand a score, we must bring in information about the task or the performance of other persons or both. A norm-referenced report tells where the person stands among others who took the test. A domain-referenced report tells what level of difficulty a person can cope with in a specified kind of task. The test content is usually a sample of that domain. A criterion-referenced report views the score as a sign that the person can or cannot be expected to satisfy some practically significant requirement. Here are examples.

- Norm reference. "James did better in solving these linear equations than 80 per cent of representative algebra students tested at this stage of training."
- Domain reference. "James's score indicates that he is able to solve about two-thirds of all one-variable linear equations of this complexity."
- Criterion reference. "Students who have reached James's level on linear equations usually succeed in the subsequent unit on simultaneous equations without special help or extra time" (that is, James is ready to move ahead).

Almost any test could be given all three types of interpretation. Arguing for or against one kind of interpretation is pointless; the question is, Which kind is relevant to a particular use?

Many writers include both sample and sign interpretations within the term *criterion-referenced,* but I believe that criterion reference ought to be identified with interpretation as a sign (p. 45). An expectancy statement refers to behavior in a situation *unlike* the test. For example, "A student with this vocabulary score who enters training as an accountant has a 4-to-1 chance of completing the course." A reading test might be interpreted by printing out a list of books the child can be expected to understand. It is logical to associate such interpretation with criterion reference because a "criterion," in validation research, is the target of a statistical forecast (p. 126 ff.).

An interpretation is domain-referenced when the test is interpreted as a sample and the subject's level of performance on content *like* that in the test is estimated. The interpreter has an obligation to identify unequivocally the domain of tasks to which a content interpretation refers (Nitko, 1980). Unfortunately, many a test developer who identifies the domain vaguely nonetheless speaks of her test, fashionably, as criterion-referenced.

Current enthusiasm for criterion reference and domain reference is chiefly a reaction against a competitive, comparative emphasis in education. The pupil who improves considerably in reading during the school year, for example, receives little encouragement if test interpretation focuses on the fact that he is somewhat below average at the start of the year and at the end. Pioneer psychological testers thought that their main task was to highlight individual differences. Therefore, they rarely worked out either a criterion-referenced or domain-referenced interpretation. Producers of educational tests for large-scale use emphasized norms, in part because this feature is lacking in local, teacher-made tests. Many of today's achievement tests do offer information to assist in translating scores into statements about skills mastered.

Enthusiasm for norm reference remains high in much testing for guidance. I would say, however, that there is little point in telling a student that (for example) many people have greater interest in science than he does; the question ought to be, does he like scientific activities well enough to find such a career satisfying? Chapter 12 will explain why many colleagues disagree with me and call for norm-referenced interest profiles. The end of this chapter and a section of Chapter 9 will also discuss norm reference.

Content scales. Interpretation in terms of content requires clearly defined levels of difficulty, as in "reads material from the news columns of *The New York Times* at the rate of 280 words per minute, when told to be able to summarize it." (To say only "reads 280 words per minute" means much less.) Interpretations could refer to easier and harder materials or to other reading purposes; they may describe the materials in terms of a formal index of "readability."

The most direct way to give meaning to a raw score is to display the content of the test, but a summary report cannot do this. Nor can a long test readily be inspected. A reasonable substitute is to display specimen tasks. Ten representative items could appear on the report sheet with this statement: "Julia's raw score is 17. Persons with that raw score can, on the average, solve 6 of these 10 problems." For a reading test, one could display paragraphs ordered from easy to difficult, stating, for example, that "a test score of 93 implies ability to comprehend paragraphs up to and including level f."

Interpretation on a content scale is not sensible unless the content is significant in its own right. We are little interested in knowing what complexity of block design a person can assemble successfully; the task is not significant in the world at large. When the content is significant in itself, we can often bring an established standard to bear. The teacher may say, for example, that no one will be allowed to take up the study of shorthand until his typing speed reaches 50 words per minute.

Experience tables. To equip herself for interpretation in terms of expectancies—that is, criterion reference—the tester obtains information regarding a large number of persons who have taken the test and whose later success in some undertaking can be observed. The results can be formed into an experience table such as Table 4.1. The expectancy for a person taking the test is inferred from the record of success among persons who earlier earned the same score.

Table 4.1 is intended to assist counselors in interpreting a version of the Armed Services Vocational Aptitude Battery. Test scores and grades were recorded in 25 widely dispersed high schools. (A tabulation for the counselor's own high school would be more meaningful because course demands and grading standards differ from school to school. The counselor can prepare local experience tables wherever a sufficient number of student records accumulate.)

The battery included 13 subtests. Arithmetic and form-perception tasks were most related to success in drafting. The counselor advising a student would add those two subtest scores and direct the student's attention to the row of the table that corresponds to his total. If his score is 25, the table indicates that he has two chances out of three of earning at least a C. The table

Table 4.1. *Experience table for drafting courses*

Aptitude score[a]	Probability of earning a grade at least as high as			
	D	C	B	A
41–50	99	92	62	21
31–40	98	82	42	10
21–30	94	66	25	4
11–20	85	47	12	1
1–10	71	29	5	<1

[a]Composite of Arithmetic Reasoning and Space Perception.
SOURCE: Adapted from G. L. Bower and J. R. Lewis, 1975, p. 9.

gives a more complete, more definite picture than any other system of norms can offer, especially when tables are available for many of the courses the student is considering.

Note that norms enter this criterion-referenced interpretation. Likewise, in an earlier example, norms were used to translate Julia's mathematics score of 17 into the statement that she could probably pass 6 out of 10 specimen items. This is a paradox of current terminology. A "norm-referenced" interpretation is one that *stops* with a comparative statement.

An experience chart, though less precise than a table, shows trends dramatically. Figure 4.3 presents charts for three tests; the dexterity test is a much less accurate predictor than the other two.

9. *Which of these reports is (are) referenced against a criterion? Against a domain? Against a norm group?*

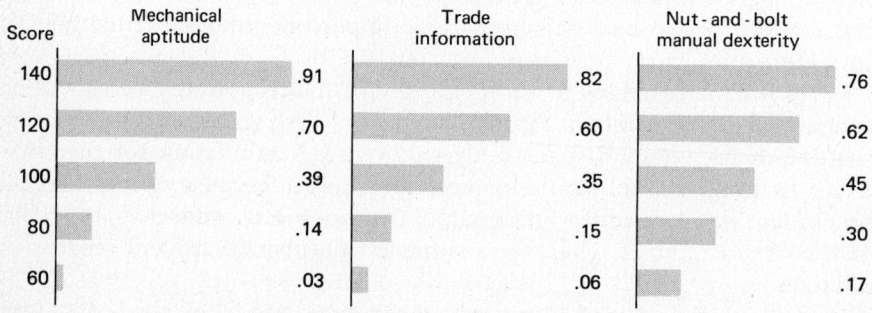

Figure 4.3. Expectancy charts for aircraft-armorer trainees. These three charts represent validity coefficients of 0.5, 0.45, and 0.25, respectively. Such coefficients will be explained in Chapter 5.
Source: Personnel classification tests, 1946.

a. *A vision test is reported in such terms as "at a 12-inch distance, can read 10-point, or larger, type."*
b. *A measure of "dental age" is obtained by comparing a child's teeth to a chart showing what teeth are ordinarily present at age 5, at age 6, and so on.*
c. *Six children out of 30 name Barbara as "a good person to play with."*

10. For each of these decisions, would you prefer a report that is criterion-referenced, domain-referenced, or norm-referenced?
    a. *Susana's teacher wants to know the maturity of Susana's interests as a basis for selecting literature for her to read.*
    b. *A student reports many symptoms of anxiety, and the counselor wishes to decide whether this degree of anxiety is unusual.*
    c. *A school wants to provide intensive exercise for every student whose physical fitness is poor.*
    d. *Ruby transfers from another school. The counselor wants to know whether her ability in Spanish is good enough for her to enroll in an advanced section.*
    e. *When a student's spelling is poor enough to be of concern, the school wishes to make a report to her parents.*
11. *Experience tables prepared for local use are clearly meaningful. Can experience tables profitably be included in test manuals in view of the fact that probability of success in a job or in a course of study depends on local conditions?*
12. *Prior to training, a prospective aircraft armorer earns these scores: Mechanical Aptitude, 120; Trade Information, 140; Nut-and-Bolt Test, 100. Interpret, using Figure 4.3.*

Setting Standards

In some applications of tests, decision rules can be highly flexible. Whether a student enters a course where he has one chance in three of a poor grade is usually regarded as something for him to decide. Candidates for admission to a college may be rejected forthright if the odds against survival are high, and those who seem certain to do well may be admitted without hesitation. In midscale, the admissions committee will take into account not only facts unique to the individual but also a preference for diversity in the student body considered as a whole (see Chapter 11). At the classroom level, a decision that James is ready to go on to simultaneous equations and Jerry is not will be based on a rule this teacher has worked out by experience. If the standard is too lenient, no harm is done because James can be sent back to review the basics when and if the decision proves to have been too optimistic.

It is in certification that the setting of standards is critical. In certification it is usual to apply cutoff scores "blindly" (because individualized judgment would invite charges of favoritism). The safeguard for the individual is the opportunity to take the test again, without prejudice. The number of candidates allowed to pass the bar exam is not constrained by a quota of places to be filled (as is the case in admitting students and hiring employees). Likewise, the score defined as a qualification for high school graduation can be raised or lowered as those in authority choose.

The setting of standards has three aspects: empirical (i.e., based on experience), political, and judgmental. One might, over time, trace the success of young persons in getting and holding jobs, for example, and prepare an experience table relating that success to scores on the competency test. This would provide some basis for locating the region of the score scale where the risk of unemployability is substantial. Any such follow-up study with respect to lawyers or drivers or any other certified group uses an incomplete criterion; so it should not be the sole basis for the decision rule.

Some political pressures are for higher standards and some are for lower standards. Employers would like schools to set tough standards; then their graduates could be hired with confidence. With regard to professional certification, persons already certified have many motives for raising standards—some high-minded and some selfish. To candidates, an increase in standards reduces opportunity. Furthermore, high standards may entail social costs. The cost of remedial work for students who do not meet the standard is more or less proportional to the number failed. There is a subtler cost if the resources put into reading and arithmetic squeeze civics, art, or economics from the student's course of study. Also, the handicap faced by the student who leaves school without a diploma must be considered, for raising standards increases the number of dropouts. Obviously, weighing up benefits, costs, risks, and political palatability comes down to an exercise of judgment.

Technical procedures may improve content-referenced judgments. If a committee is asked to pinpoint a passing threshold on the score scale, the decision is bound to be an arbitrary compromise. No defense can be offered for a norm-referenced cutoff—"Let's set it so that 10 per cent fail." The old "70 is a passing mark" leaves the candidate at the mercy of the item writers. Requesting judgments at the item level makes better use of reviewers' expertise. Committees of judges and lawyers could review a bar exam. Teachers, employers, parents, and recent graduates could review a high school proficiency test. The instructions given reviewers are subtle, but they come down to this: "Should *every* high school graduate in our state pass this item?" This process, repeated with all the items, identifies items that the great majority of borderline performers should pass and also the difficult or irrelevant items where the judges do not regard an error as a clear sign of incompetence.

Such information can be used in two ways. First, it can be used to eliminate from the item pool the items judged to be unreasonably hard or unimportant. Second, statistical procedures can determine what score on the total test implies that the student has reached the level defined by the judges. Calibration methods described later in this chapter can reduce or eliminate the need for fresh judgments when further item sets are developed.

Scoring

Procedures of this kind are still undergoing development. The various procedures that seem logical do not necessarily reach a common conclusion. B. J. Andrews and J. T. Hecht (1976) applied two well-regarded techniques to the same test. Technique 1 put the cut score at 46 per cent correct; Technique 2, at 69 per cent. Thirty-seven per cent of typical candidates would fail by the first standard; 93 per cent (!), by the second. Relevant references are Jaeger *et al.*, 1980; Messick, 1975; and Nedelsky, 1954. See also page 407 on "policy-capturing" research.

13. *If judges of items are told how many students a proposed standard is likely to fail, they usually modify their recommendation in the direction of leniency. Assuming that their original judgment was conscientious, what is to be said for and against allowing this stage of revision?*
14. *One device is to set the diploma requirement by giving the test to "successful" adults living in the school district and choosing the cut score that would pass (say) 90 per cent of them. What is to be said for and against this plan?*

STATISTICAL ASPECTS OF SCORES

Now statistical concepts that enter norm-referenced interpretations (and much other analysis) will be considered. The end of the chapter returns to domain reference and Chapter 5 returns to criterion reference.

Percentiles

It is difficult to compare scores from tests of different lengths unless raw scores are changed to a common scale. The easiest form of comparison is ranking: "Person A stands third out of 40 on Test A, tenth on Test B." Ranks depend on the number of persons in the group. If we wish to examine change in standing from one occasion to another we have difficulty because the size of the group changes. To avoid such difficulties, ranks are changed to percentile scores. A *percentile score* is the rank expressed in percentage terms. Writers use various terms: percentile score, percentile rank, percentile, centile—all have the same meaning.

A percentile rank tells what proportion of the group falls below this person. Case A ranks third; below him are 37 persons. We arbitrarily divide case A (and all persons tied with him, if any) between the two groups. Assuming no ties, $2\frac{1}{2}$ cases are above him and $37\frac{1}{2}$ below. Since $37\frac{1}{2}$ is 94 per cent of 40, the percentile score is 94.

By this method of computation, the person exactly in the middle of the group is at the 50th percentile; "at the median," we say. The *median* can be thought of as the performance of a "typical" person.

A graphic procedure is advantageous. It smooths out irregularities in the sample and so gives a better estimate of what may be expected when further groups are tested. Figure 4.4 demonstrates this method, using Bennett TMC scores for hypothetical job applicants.

Raw scores and percentiles are distributed differently. In Figure 4.5 the distribution of raw scores is high at the center and tapers away at each end. To prepare the lower part of Figure 4.5, I changed each raw score to its percentile equivalent and tallied the number of persons in each part of the percentile scale. This distribution is nearly rectangular. The percentile con-

1. Begin with the raw scores (these are scores of 75 job applicants on Bennett Form S).

```
54  42  35  51  50  66  36  47  21  40  58
32  48  66  35  25  45  41  49  46  40  51
48  57  31  53  50  38  53  52  58  28  45
51  49  42  41  45  60  24  46  50  56  38
48  38  41  44  57  41  37  17  49  64  41
47  28  49  22  55  52  43  59  43  25  25
33  51  54  61  26  43  56  43  40
```

Highest score = 66; lowest score = 17; range = 49.

2. Identify the highest score and the lowest score. If there is a wide range, choose a class interval of 1, 2, 5, 10, 20, etc., and divide the range into classes of equal width. Fifteen or more classes are desirable.

A class interval of 5 will be used. (A smaller interval, such as 2, would be preferable but would be inconvenient in this computing guide.)

Scores	Tallies	Frequency (f)	Cumulative frequency	Cumulative percent
65–70	//	2	75	100
60–64	///	3	73	97
55–59	ℍℍ ///	8	70	93
50–54	ℍℍ ℍℍ ///	13	62	83
45–49	ℍℍ ℍℍ ////	14	49	65
40–44	ℍℍ ℍℍ ℍℍ /	16	35	47
35–39	ℍℍ /	6	19	25
30–34	///	3	13	17
25–29	ℍℍ /	6	10[a]	13
20–24	///	3	4	5[b]
15–19	/	1	1	1
		75 N	0	0

3. Tally the number of cases having each score.

4. Write the number of tallies in the Frequency (f) column. Add this column to get N, the number of cases.

[a] 10 cases fall below 29.5; 13 below 34.5; etc.

[b] 5 per cent of the cases fall below 24.5; 5 is the cumulative percentage corresponding to a raw score of 24.5.

5. Begin at the bottom of the column and add frequencies one at a time to determine the cumulative frequency, the number of cases below each division point.

6. Divide the cumulative frequencies by N to determine cumulative percentages.

Figure 4.4. Determining percentile equivalents.

Scoring

version spreads apart persons near the middle of the raw-score distribution. Thus a large percentile difference near the median can arise from a small difference in performance. Persons with extreme raw scores are squeezed together by the percentile scale. The difference between the 90th and the 99th percentiles may be as great as the difference between a 5-minute and a 4-minute mile. To take this into account, profile forms space out the 95, 90, and 80 percentile points, crowd 60, 50, and 40 together, and spread out 20, 10, and 5. For an example, see Figure 4.7.

7. Plot cumulative percentage against score (chart below). (In practice, a large sheet of graph paper would be used. Panel 8 assumes that ordinary graph paper is used; a special "probability paper" makes it easier to fit this kind of curve.)

8. Draw the smooth curve that best fits the points plotted.

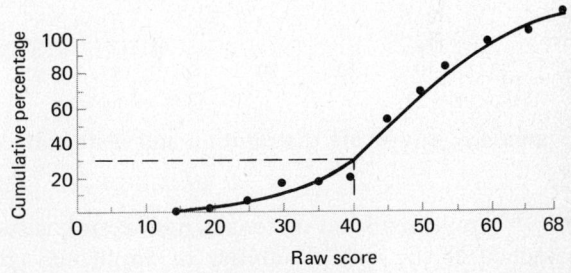

9. Determine the percentile equivalent of a score by reading from the curve. (The lines on the chart show how one finds that the percentile equivalent of a raw score of 40 is 29).

Percentile equivalents

Raw	%ile	Raw	%ile	Raw	%ile
20	2	35	18	50	64
21	3	36	20	51	68
22	3	37	22	52	72
23	4	38	24	53	75
24	5	39	27	54	78
25	5	40	29	55	81

Figure 4.4. *(continued)*

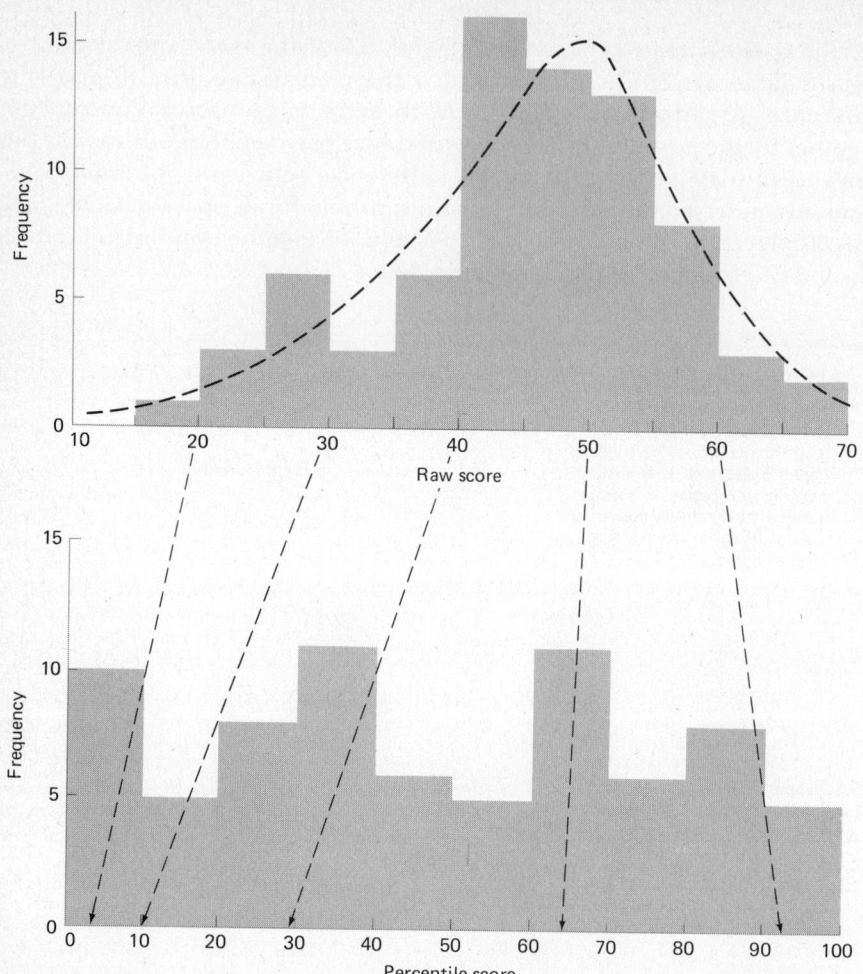

Figure 4.5. Raw-score distribution and distribution of percentile equivalents.

Norms are a kind of census figure, and as such they provide a frame of reference. If the median ability of applicants coming to the firm is much below that of the general norm group, the employer should reexamine his or her recruiting procedures. It appears that he or she is not attracting a full share of able applicants. The fact that, among students entering a course, the median score in reading is much below that of the norm group is a fact important for the teacher to consider in planning instruction.

Norms are basic to comparisons across tests. Norms on a test battery enable one to say that a student is at the median in mechanical comprehension, around the 80th percentile in verbal abilities, and at the 20th percentile in numerical ability. Interpretations across tests are treacherous, however (see p. 105 f.).

SCORING

Percentile scores from two tests cannot be compared unless the groups on which the conversions are based are similar. Where one test bases norms on students or job applicants, another gives norms for workers actually hired. According to the 1980 TMC norms, a white male who scores 50 stands at the 70th percentile among white male applicants to a union training program for apprentices in the construction trades and at the 5th percentile among applicants for mechanical jobs in an aviation company. Whenever norms are used, the group they represent must be kept in mind.

In the 1980 Bennett norms, the user finds a collection of percentile conversions permitting her to compare an examinee with reference groups in a dozen industrial settings. (Two were mentioned in the preceding paragraph.) The norm tables for some settings separate cases by sex or minority status. The DAT version of TMC is provided with norms for fall and spring testing in grades 8 through 12; Table 4.2 reproduces a fraction of the information. This format is more convenient than that at the end of Figure 4.4 if a manual presents, on one page, the norms for several subtests.

15. *Estimate Amelia's percentile score in each of the four tests she took (question 5, p. 87).*
16. *Interpret the following record of ability test scores for one person, where all scores are percentile scores based on a random sample of adults: Verbal, 54; Number, 46; Spatial, 87; Reasoning, 40.*
17. *Why does the table of TMC norms begin at 1 and stop at 99, instead of ranging from 0 to 100? (A raw score of 70 is perfect.)*
18. *Scores usually change when a test is repeated because of chance errors of measurement. If each of the following persons changes 2 points up or down in raw score on TMC, how much would the percentile score change?*
    a. *A tenth-grade boy with a percentile score of 55 on the first test.*
    b. *A tenth-grade boy at the 10th percentile on the first test.*
19. *The norms on the Abstract Reasoning test of DAT are almost identical for boys and girls in grade 10. The median is close to 32 for each sex. Suppose that both Ralph and Rosemary score 34 on Abstract Reasoning and 45 on Mechanical Reasoning. The norms suggest that Rosemary is "better" on MR than AR, and that Ralph is "worse." Explain the contradiction.*
20. *The following scores are the times, in seconds, required by a group of persons to construct an easy block design. Prepare a table of percentile equivalents for this group:*

```
52  34  41  42  46  45  27  48  35  35  38  29  54  36  33  30
48  39  44  36  36  34  51  40  30  33  37  41  56  32  48  35
37  28  28  45  31  39  31  27  35  36  34  42  38  33  33  31
39  28  36  33  37  36  34  54  34  32  33  38
```

Table 4.2. *Tenth-grade norms for DAT Mechanical Reasoning*

Percentile	Corresponding Raw Score	
	Males (N = 6150+)	Females (N = 6250+)
99	66–70	61–70
97	64–65	58–60
95	62–63	56–57
90	61	53–55
85	59–60	51–52
80	58	49–50
75	56–57	48
70	55	46–47
65	54	45
60	53	43–44
55	51–52	42
50	50	40–41
45	48–49	39
40	47	38
35	45–46	36–37
30	43–44	35
25	41–42	33–34
20	39–40	31–32
15	36–38	29–30
10	31–35	26–28
5	27–30	23–25
3	24–26	20–22
1	0–23	0–19
Mean	48.7	40.9
s.d.	10.8	10.1

SOURCE: Administrator's Handbook for the Differential Aptitude Tests (DAT), 1982, p. 21. Reprinted by permission of The Psychological Corporation.

21. *According to the table prepared in question 20, how much difference in seconds does a difference of 10 percentile points represent?*

Standard Scores

Mean and standard deviation. The second common way to summarize performance of a group is to use the mean and standard deviation. The mean $(\bar{X})$ is the arithmetical average obtained when we add all scores and divide by the number of scores. The standard deviation (s.d.) describes the spread of scores.

The standard deviation is a kind of average of the departures of scores from the group mean. We might determine how far each person is from the mean and average (ignoring the direction of deviation). Instead of doing this, we square each deviation and average the squares. This average is called the variance of the distribution. The standard deviation is the square root of the variance.

The procedure can be illustrated simply. Consider five scores whose sum is 50 (mean = 10). We have

Scores	9	16	4	10	11	
Deviations	−1	6	−6	0	1	Sum = 0
Squares	1	36	36	0	1	Sum = 74

Dividing 74 by 5 gives a variance of 14.8 and a standard deviation of 3.85.[1] The larger the range of scores, the larger the s.d. tends to be. Here the range is 4 to 16—12 points—and the s.d. equals about one-third of the range. But the range is most often 5 or 6 times the s.d. (see Table 4.2). The s.d. rather than the range is used to describe the spread of scores because it is more stable from one sample to another.

Conversion scales. A "standard score" scale based on the mean and standard deviation serves the same purpose as the percentile scale. A standard score reports how many standard deviations above or below the mean the person is. The scores introduced in Figure 4.4 and Figure 4.5 had a mean of approximately 44 and a standard deviation near 11. Then a raw score of 55 is one s.d. above the mean and the standard score is +1. A standard score of −1.8 would be 1.8 s.d. below the mean. The corresponding raw score is 44 − (1.8)11 or approximately 24.

Table 4.3 shows how to convert raw scores to a standard-score scale with a mean of zero and with each s.d. above the mean counted as one unit. I speak of this as a "zero ± one" scale, referring to the numbers assigned the mean and s.d., respectively. This z conversion, important in statistical work, is not often used in test reports.

Test scores are more often placed on a 50 ± 10 scale—one with the mean at 50 and the s.d. equal to 10 points. That makes it possible to express every score as a positive whole number. As Table 4.3 indicates, converted scores are derived from the 0 ± 1 scale. Changing from raw scores to standard scores of this kind does not alter the form of the distribution.

Wechsler Block Design norms are in standard-score form, as Table 4.4 illustrates. The range of converted scores is from 1 to 19, because Wechsler chose a 10 ± 3 scale. That is, he set the mean equal to a standard score of 10 and counted each s.d. above or below the mean as 3 standard-score points. (The manual refers to these standard scores as "scaled scores.")

Other values for converting the mean and s.d. can be chosen. Table 4.5

---

[1] In modern statistical practice, it is usual to divide by $N-1$, not N, though this makes little difference when N is large. An explanation of the preference for $N-1$ can be found in texts on statistics.

$$74 \div 4 = 18.5 \text{ (variance)} \qquad \sqrt{18.5} = 4.3 \text{ (s.d.)}$$

Table 4.3. *Determining standard scores*

1. Begin with the raw scores to be converted.	Assume mean = 44, s.d. = 11
2. To obtain z scores, express each raw score as a deviation from the mean. Divide by the s.d. $$z \text{ score} = \frac{\text{raw score} - \text{mean}}{\text{standard deviation}}$$	For raw score 60: $$z = \frac{60 - 44}{11} = \frac{16}{11} = 1.5$$ For raw score 25: $$z = \frac{25 - 44}{11} = \frac{-19}{11} = -1.7$$
3. To obtain scores on 50 ± 10 scale, multiply each z score by 10 and add to 50: $$50 \times \frac{10 \text{ (raw score} - \text{mean)}}{\text{standard deviation}}$$	For raw score 60, $z = 1.5$. $$50 \times 10 (1.5) = 65$$ For raw score 25, $z = -1.7$. $$50 \times 10 (-1.7) = 33$$

summarizes several standard-score systems. Confusion results from the plethora of scales. In my opinion, test developers should use the system with mean 50 and s.d. 10 unless there are strong reasons for adopting a less familiar scale. (IQs and scores that simulate IQs with a 100 ± 15 scale are peculiarly open to misinterpretation; see p. 203.) Where a single-digit code is preferred, the stanine ("stay-nine") scale is recommended.

The scale used for the Scholastic Aptitude Test (SAT) is so often encountered that its peculiarities need to be explained. The scale began as a 500 ± 100 scale, based on the distribution of college applicants in 1941. In theory, today's conversion table assigns the score of 500 to whatever score on today's test would have been earned by the average 1941 applicant, this being determined by special test-equating methods (Angoff, 1971). A college that has learned to expect good performance from applicants with an SAT-V score of 600 can make that same interpretation year after year since the level of ability required to earn that score does not shift with the changing distribution of applicant ability. The scale does *not* represent standard scores for today's applicants. Because the SAT is now used in less-select colleges and because a larger segment of the population is now applying to college, recent averages

Table 4.4 *Block Design norms*

Scaled score	1	2	3	4	5	6	7	8	9
Raw score	0	1	2	3–8	9–15	16–20	21–23	24–27	28–31
Scaled score	10	11	12	13	14	15	16	17	18	19
Raw score	32–35	36–38	39–41	42–44	45	46–48	49	—	50	51

SOURCE: Manual for the Wechsler Adult Intelligence Scale—Revised, p. 144. Copyright © 1981 by The Psychological Corporation, New York, N.Y. All rights reserved. Reproduced by permission.
Note: Standard-score equivalents of raw scores for the Block Design test, ages 20–24; a 10 ± 3 scale is used.

Table 4.5 Standard-Score Systems

Mean set equal to	s.d. set equal to	Standard score corresponding to 1 s.d. above mean	Standard score corresponding to 2 s.d. below mean	Name of system, remarks
0	1	1	−2	z scores, prominent in mathematical theory of testing
5	2	7	1	Stanine scores
10	3	13	4	Scaled scores for Wechsler subtests
50	10	60	30	Most widely used system
50	21.06	71	8	Normal-curve equivalent (NCE); mandated for certain evaluation reports from schools to the Federal government
100	15 or 16	115 or 116	70 or 68	The usual scale for IQ
100	20	120	60	Used for aptitude tests of U.S. Employment Service

have been around 430 for V and around 470 for M. (Perhaps, also, changes in teaching and in student effort during high school have lowered the performance of applicants who are demographically comparable to the 1941 group; see College Entrance Examination Board, 1977).

Age and grade scales. This is as good a place as any to mention—and condemn—the popular but fallacious conversions known as "age equivalents" and "grade equivalents." Whatever score the average 7-year-old earns is converted to an "age-equivalent" score of 7; thus a 5-year-old or a 10-year-old may have a converted score of 7.0. Whatever score the average fifth-grader earns at the start of the school year is converted to 5.0 on the "grade-equivalent" scale; an eighth-grader who makes the same score is said to be performing at the fifth-grade level. Whereas the standard score compares the pupil with a group of which he is a member, these scales compare him with groups he may not belong to.

Grade equivalents generate such misleading statements as "The average Mexican-American child entering the seventh grade here is two grades behind the Anglo children in performance." The child's converted score of 5.0, however, may not be far below that of the Anglos in his class. Perhaps a third of the entering seventh-graders of Anglo extraction are also "2 years behind." The progress made in one year varies from one school subject to another. According to national norms for the Iowa Test of Basic Skills (ITBS), the middle two-thirds of entering seventh-graders range from 5.0 to 9.4 in language usage, that is, from the fifth-grade to the ninth-grade level. The reason is not that the ablest seventh-graders have mastered the curriculum in language for the next two grades. They "equal" the average ninth-graders because the average pupil, ordinarily coming from a home where elegant usage is not prized, is still making many commonplace errors in grade 9. The seventh-graders whose usage is good would not do so well if tested specifically on rules of usage that ninth-graders study.

Professional opinion is critical of grade conversions; standard scores or percentiles or content reference serve better. Too often, laypersons expect every class or even every individual to be "at grade level" and to advance one grade-equivalent unit each year. Because abler classes make greater progress, a low-scoring class would have to progress *faster* than average classes in order to show "one year of gain" on the test norms. This puts an unfair demand on weaker pupils and their teacher. (Age conversions are also likely to be misinterpreted; see p. 204).

22. a. *Compute the mean and standard deviation for the Block Design scores given in problem 20.*
    b. *How does the mean compare with the median computed previously?*
    c. *What is the approximate percentile rank for a score 2 s.d. above the mean in this distribution?*
23. *Wechsler fixes the mean IQ at 100 and the s.d. at 15. Express on a 50 ± 10 scale the following IQs: 100, 85, 130, 140.*
24. *Show the relation between raw scores and standard scores in Table 4.4, in the manner of Figure 4.5.*
25. *An argument for single-digit scales such as that of the Wechsler subtests and the stanine is that providing a second digit would convey an impression of precision that is unwarranted. Acknowledging that errors of measurement are often much larger than 20 points on the SAT scale, what argument can be given* for *reporting SAT scores at 10-point intervals?*
26. *The middle two-thirds of entering seventh-graders range from 5.6 to 8.7 on the grade-equivalent scale for ITBS mathematics. This range is less than for language. Suggest an explanation.*

The Normal Distribution

The frequency distribution shown at the top of Figure 4.5 is jagged, but if more cases were added and smaller class intervals were used, it would become relatively smooth. A likely shape for that smooth distribution is the curve shown in the top portion of Figure 4.5; the curve was obtained by smoothing, as in Step 8 in Figure 4.4. This distribution is not perfectly symmetrical, but it tails off on both sides. Most score distributions have this general character. It is sometimes advantageous to convert the score scale so that every test has the same distribution form, that of the normal probability curve.

The normal curve (Figure 4.6) is symmetric; the distance from the mean to the point on the shoulder that separates the convex, hill-like portion from the concave tail equals the s.d.

Many biological measures such as heights of American men fall into a

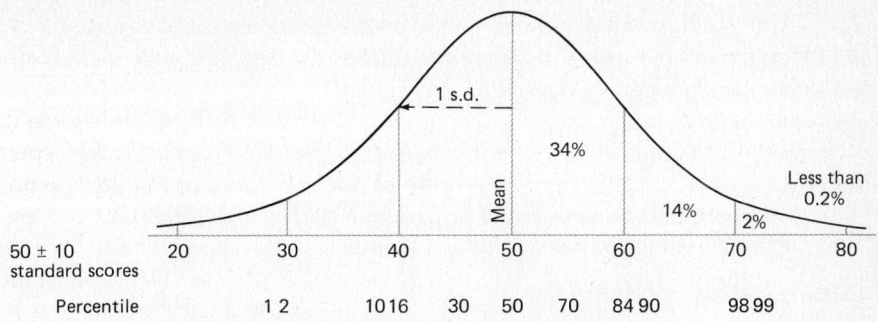

Figure 4.6. The normal distribution.

nearly normal distribution, perhaps because chance combinations of chromosomes determine much of the variation. Score distributions of many psychological tests are also approximately normal. Early investigators thought it a natural law that abilities are normally distributed. Most scientists now consider such a statement meaningless since the shape of the distribution depends on the scale of measurement and the experiences of the population, as well as on biological variation. By selecting items, the test developer can change the shape of the score distribution, flattening the central hump, producing two humps, and so on.

If a normal distribution is sliced into bands of equal width, a fixed percentage of the cases falls in each band. As Figure 4.6 shows, about two-thirds of the cases fall between -1 s.d. and $+1$ s.d. Since 99.6 per cent of the cases fall between $+3$ s.d. and -3 s.d., the range of test scores is somewhere near 6 standard deviations (less, when the group is small). These facts enable us to reconstruct roughly the score distribution when told its mean and s.d.

Assuming a normal distribution, one can quickly convert standard scores to percentiles and vice versa. Below the mean are 50 per cent of the cases. Below $+1$ s.d. are $50 + 34$ or 84 per cent of the cases; hence a standard score of 60 (on the 50 ± 10 scale) corresponds to the 84th percentile. Most test specialists probably would say that the use of normal curves in test scaling is a convenience; it does not assume any "normal distribution of behavior" in nature. A minority view is represented by Jensen's belief (1980, p. 95) that "mental ability is normally distributed in the population." He argues that the compounding of multiple causes, genetic and environmental, would be expected to create a normal distribution.

27. *What percentile rank corresponds to a score 2 s.d. above the mean? To a score 1 s.d. below the mean?*
28. *Translate the following percentile scores into approximate standard scores on a 50 ± 10 scale if the distribution is like Figure 4.6: 5, 40, 85.*

29. *Using the standard deviations and percentile norms reported in Table 4.2, and the facts in Figure 4.6, determine whether the boys' and girls' distributions for Mechanical Reasoning are normal.*
30. *Scores on the Medical College Admissions Test (MCAT) are reported on an 8 ± 2.5 scale; only whole numbers are reported. Assuming a normal distribution, what is the likely range of MCAT scores in the applicant population? What score would fall nearest to the 80th percentile?*

Comparison of Systems

If norms are to be used and data for a suitable reference group are available, which system of scores is preferable?

The percentile score has these advantages; it is readily understood, which makes it especially satisfactory for reporting to persons without statistical training; it is easily computed; it can be interpreted exactly regardless of the distribution shape. The disadvantages of the percentile score are these: it magnifies differences near the mean that may not be important, and it reduces the apparent size of large and practically important differences in the tails of the distribution. Also, it is often less appropriate for statistical analysis.

The advantages of standard scores are these: differences in standard score are proportional to differences in raw score; use of standard scores in averages and correlations gives the same result as would come from use of the raw scores. The disadvantages: standard scores cannot be interpreted readily when distributions are skewed, and they are unfamiliar to untrained persons. Nonspecialists can learn to interpret standard-score scales. High school teachers and parents quite comfortably discuss Pete's SAT of 550 alongside his 66 on a 50 ± 10 scale from some other test.

Some test developers normalize scores. *Normalized scores* are obtained by stretching a distribution to make it nearly normal. Normalized scores are a compromise. They spread out cases in both tails of the distribution and yet can be readily translated into percentiles. The DAT profile form shown in Figure 4.7 illustrates typical current practice. Percentiles are plotted, but the spacing corresponds to normalized scores (converted to a 50 ± 10 scale).

31. *A teacher wishes to convert scores on class examinations so that the record book will show at a glance how well a person is doing and she can average all tests equally in the final grade. Should she use raw, percentile, or standard scores?*
32. *A high school gives a reading test to all ninth-graders. The results are to be listed and supplied to all teachers for their use in planning instruction. Should the report be in terms of raw scores, standard scores, percentiles, or a content-referenced scale?*
33. *What disadvantage might normalized standard scores have? (Consider, as an example, a measure of reaction time that will be used in clinical diagnosis.)*

Scoring

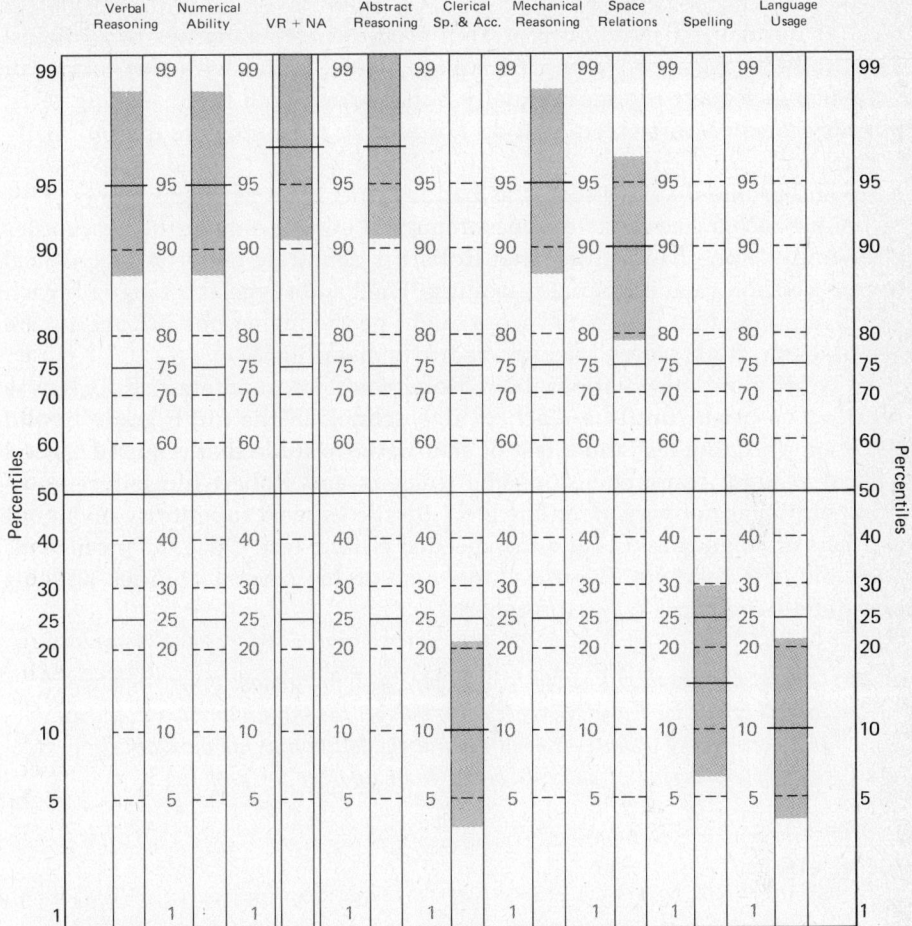

Figure 4.7. DAT profile of Robert Finchley.
The profile information is taken from Counseling from Profiles, *Copyright 1951, © 1977. The report form is copyright © 1972, 1973, 1982 by The Psychological Corporation, New York, N.Y. All rights reserved. Reproduced by permission.*

Profiles

Derived scores make it possible to compare standing on one test with standing on another, but profile interpretation must be circumspect. Equal percentiles do not mean equally good performance. If almost everyone can count and almost no one can carry a tune, the 50th percentile on the former means good performance and the 50th percentile on the latter is poor. *It is logically impossible to "equate" tests that measure distinct variables.* Failure to recognize this leads to errors that will be discussed in Chapters 8 and 10.

Profiles play a large role in guidance. The Differential Aptitude battery contains eight tests including TMC. After raw scores are changed to percentiles (or normalized standard scores), a profile charts standings in all fields. The profile in Figure 4.7 compares a high school junior with the norms for junior boys. Robert is almost equally outstanding in all the reasoning tests, but his scores on three tests that do not require reasoning are exceptionally low.

The profile displays scores as bands rather than as single points. This technique recognizes errors of measurement. Looking only at the percentiles of 95 and 90, one might think that Robert is definitely better in mechanical comprehension than in spatial reasoning. The band suggests a range for each score, implying that the spatial score might be the higher one if Robert were tested again. Both scores are expected to remain high.

A bit more information about Robert will be of interest. Robert was regarded as bright until he reached high school. In the ninth grade he did badly on a reading test and a test of scholastic aptitude that required a good deal of reading comprehension. His teachers and Robert himself came to think of him as not very able. The DAT profile showed superiority on all but the tests of language skills and the speeded clerical test. Once the profile was available, the teachers "were talking . . . of his several abilities and his identified handicaps," says the report.

34. *Rearrange the DAT subtests of Figure 4.7 in random order, and sketch a new profile for Robert Finchley. Do you get the same impression regarding the consistency of his performance and the location of his peak abilities? Is any one ordering of subtests better than another for profiling?*

NORMS

Characteristics of Useful Norms

Some testers attach too much importance to norms in selecting tests and in interpreting scores. Norms are unimportant when the tester intends to identify individual differences within a group or is concerned with absolute performance. Norms are of almost no use when the employment manager has to hire the 10 most promising applicants or knows from actual trial that most persons with scores of 72 or better on Test A make satisfactory punch-press operators.

Whereas the employer compares an applicant with a local standard, a student being counseled needs to judge himself in relation to the population he will compete with when he leaves school. Students move from the high school to trade schools, universities, and jobs in supermarkets; they move from village to city, from South to North. As no one can foresee which subcommunities students will drift into, the comparison must be with the whole population or with broad subcategories.

The norms for the DAT version of TMC come from a systematic national sample of students. The manual devotes about 3000 words plus two tables to describing the sample and its selection. The following paragraphs give some impression of the care that goes into modern sampling.

The starting place was a directory of all public school districts enrolling 300 or more students. Sorting by size and by socioeconomic level gave 32 categories of public schools; a list of Roman Catholic school systems was added. Districts chosen at random from the 33 lists were invited to give the tests. Any district that declined to participate was replaced from the same list. (Refusals were comparatively frequent among wealthy school districts and urban school districts.)

In small districts, every student in grades 8 through 12 was tested; in districts of intermediate size, a sample from every school was drawn; in very large districts testing was carried out in a sample of schools. The scores were weighted to adjust for departures of the actual sample from the sampling plan and for new census data that became available as the study proceeded. A norm table for Catholic schools was prepared. Further tables were compiled for less systematic samples of students in vocational high schools and in a few institutions of higher education.

What matters in norming a test is not the number of scores compiled but the match of the sample to an appropriate population. Applicant pools, clinic intakes, and school districts can differ markedly. The number of these aggregates in the sample is more significant than the number of persons. It was wise, in norming DAT, to test a fraction of each student body in order to cover more student bodies within about the same budget.

Even with substantial effort and a sampling plan that looks good on paper, things go awry. When two standardized tests are given side-by-side in several fifth-grade classes, the percentile scores (and standard scores) may run higher on one test than the other. This can occur when the sampling plans differed or a plan was not followed strictly. Among achievement tests, at least, the test whose converted scores "run high" has a certain market advantage. Teachers prefer a test that makes their students look good.

Norms play a prominent role when educational programs are evaluated with standardized tests. The school officials and the public may be content if the end-of-year performance of the pupils matches the national average and will be dissatisfied if the local pupils fall short. Communities differ, however, and no means of allowing for those differences is completely satisfactory. Many publishers prepare norms by categories of schools, as with the DAT norms for Catholic schools. A school using the California Achievement Tests *(CTB)* has the option of describing the makeup of its student body. When scoring the papers from this student body, the computer then uses information from the publisher's national standardization sample to say how the local average on each subtest compares with that of the schools having similar student bodies.

Norms are not "standards." A common mistake is to assume that all ninth-graders should reach the ninth-grade norm. This is, of course, a fallacy; 50 per cent of the standardizing sample fell below the norm. Conversely, the teacher whose class reaches the average has no cause for complacency. The norms show what schools are doing at present. It is highly unlikely that schools are doing so well that the national average represents what could be attained with the best of teaching.

Test norms become obsolete. On general mental tests, for example, adults score higher on the average than adults did a decade or two ago. These changes may be attributed to an increasing level of education or other social changes.

Test format matters. Marking in the test booklet may give a different score range from one obtained by using a separate answer sheet, and scores may be higher with one form of answer sheet than another. It is essential that norms be verified when a test is altered. For a "structural visualization" test, a circular disk was cut into pieces of irregular shape for the test taker to reassemble. Originally, this test was made of heavy aluminum. After some years, the manufacturer changed to wood. For one group of subjects, the mean time on the wooden test was 182 seconds, compared to 140 seconds on the metal version (J. W. Wilson & K. E. Carpenter, 1948). The norms collected on the original test no longer applied.

Whenever she can, the test interpreter should prepare norms for the local groups with which she deals. A high school counselor could profitably use information about the score distribution for all boys in her high school, for boys in the shop curriculum, for boys who later attend the local college, and for workers in certain large local industries.

35. *A test intended for Grade 1 provides norms by age, in the form of a "School Ability Index" (SAI), a standard score on a 100 ± 16 scale. A perfect score on the test is converted to an SAI of 150 if the child's age is 5 years 10 months and to an SAI of 137 if the age is 7 years 10 months. Is it reasonable to suppose that the upper limit of ability drops in this period? Can you explain the anomaly? (Hint: The manual says that a child reaching a top score should be given the next, more difficult test in the series.)*

36. *The U.S. Employment Service has a test for statistical typists. It required norms for employed statistical typists so as to compare persons considering such work with employees in the field. To obtain norms, state employment services in a large number of the states were asked to test employed typists. Consider the following aspects of the sampling plan.*
    a. *Would you take an equal number of cases from each cooperating state, take whatever number each one could conveniently provide, or what?*
    b. *What restrictions would you place on the work experience of persons admitted to the sample?*

c. Would you prevent the agencies from testing government typists, whom they could locate relatively easily?

37. The chart displays a portion of the profile for an interest questionnaire. A person scores high on Dominant Leadership, for example, by saying he would like a job where he gives orders. Interpret the several scores. You need to know that the raw score is the number of positive responses out of a possible 17 in each scale, that percentiles are based on students and young adults, and that Jackson chose a 30 $\pm$ 10 standard-score scale based on the two sexes together. The subject is a 25-year-old male artist (unsuccessful) who had dropped out of engineering school.

38. Would this subject's profile look the same if the male percentiles were converted to standard scores and plotted? What can be said for or against Jackson's use of a mixed-sex group as the basis for the profile?

39. The following information about Walter Zordaky is taken from *Counseling from Profiles, 1977*, pp. 92–93. All the tests mentioned would be classified as general-ability or academic-aptitude tests, except for the California Achievement Tests. Do the tests present a consistent picture? What is a reasonable summary of Walter's scores?

   a. Grade 12. Cooperative School and College Ability Tests (SCAT). Percentiles. Verbal, 8; Quantitative, 55.

   Differential Aptitude Tests (DAT). Percentile bands. Verbal Reasoning, 6–29; Numerical Ability, 6–29.

   b. Grade 10. California Test of Mental Maturity (CTMM). IQs. Language, 104; Non-Language, 96.

   c. Grade 8. California Achievement Tests. Grade equivalents. Reading Vocabulary, 5.9; Reading Comprehension, 7.9; Mathematics Computation, 8.8; Mathematics Concepts and Problems, 7.1.

	Raw score	Percentile M	Percentile F	Standard score (Average) 10–55
Dominant leadership	7	74	51	xxxxxxxxxxxxxxxxxxxxxxxxx
Job security	12	89	83	xxxxxxxxxxxxxxxxxxxxxxxxxxxxxxxxx
Stamina	10	59	47	xxxxxxxxxxxxxxxxxxxxx
Accountability	13	71	62	xxxxxxxxxxxxxxxxxxxxxxxxxxx

Source: From the Jackson Vocational Interest Survey (JVIS) Manual, 1977, p. 27.

40. *Administration of a conventional test on a computer terminal could affect the applicability of the norms. What kinds of test characteristics make this more likely?*

What the Manual Should Report

Norms presented in the test manual should refer to defined and clearly described populations. These populations should be groups to whom users of the test will ordinarily wish to compare the persons tested. The test manual should report whether scores vary for groups differing in age, sex, and training.

Although current norms for widely sold tests are much better than those of 1950, the following complaints from that date are of more than historical interest; they apply to tests recently published.

> Legitimate and illegitimate general norms abound in current test manuals. People-in-general norms are legitimate only if they are based upon careful field studies with appropriate controls of regional, socioeconomic, educational, and other factors—and even then only if the sampling is carefully described so that the test user may be fully aware of its inevitable limitations and deficiencies. . . . [M]any alleged general norms reported in test manuals are not backed even by an honest effort to secure representative samples of people-in-general. Even tens or hundreds of thousands of cases can fall woefully short of defining people-in-general. Inspection of test manuals will show (or would show if information about the norms were given completely) that many such massed norms are merely collections of all the scores that opportunity has permitted the author or publisher to gather easily. Lumping together all the samples secured more by chance than by plan makes for impressively large numbers; but while seeming to simplify interpretation, the norms may dim or actually distort the counseling, employment, or diagnostic significance of a score.
>
> With or without a plan, everyone of course obtains data where and how he can. Since the standardization of a test is always dependent on the cooperation of educators, psychologists and personnel men, the foregoing comments are not a plea for the rejection of available samples but for their correct labeling. If a manual shows "general" norms for a vocabulary test based on a sample two-thirds of which consists of women office workers, one can properly raise his test-wise eyebrows. There is no reason to accept such norms as a good generalization of adult—or even of employed-adult—vocabulary. It is better to set up norms on the occupationally homogeneous two-thirds of the group and frankly

call them norms on female office workers. Adding a few more miscellaneous cases does not make the sample a truly general one [Seashore & Ricks, 1950].

Reliance on the cases that come to hand is illustrated in the manual of a modern questionnaire on stress, intended for research and for clinical appraisals. The norms are based on "2588 males in middle- or upper-echelon jobs who were employed in ten large corporations in the San Francisco Bay and Burbank areas of California and ranged in age from 48 to 65." The occupational level is also described (e.g., 1195 of the cases were "managerial"). In addition to the general group, score statistics are reported for 35 samples as exotic as "Faculty of private university in Oklahoma" and "Random sample of the male European population of Auckland, New Zealand." I leave the reader to decide how well these descriptions would satisfy Seashore and Ricks.

If the manual describes the norm sample adequately, the user can judge the norms by these questions:

- Does the standard group consist of the sort of person with whom my examinee(s) should be compared?
- Is the sample representative of this population?
- Does the sample include enough cases?
- Is the sample appropriately subdivided?

41. *Suppose you wished to collect norms for the stress questionnaire to assist clinical users. You believe that you can obtain a grant from the National Institutes of Health, but you recognize that the larger the budget, the less chance there is of getting the grant. What population or populations would you try to represent? Would you pay the persons whose help you solicit? How much? How many cases? How would you locate them and win their consent?*

Differentiation of Norms

A truly perplexing question, for test maker and test user alike, is whether to focus on a broad or a narrow comparison group. Norms are often subdivided to allow comparison with reference groups of similar age and sex and type of community. An astonishing number of other background factors correlate with scores.

Tests of comprehension of English and Spanish among Hispanics in the United States will serve as an example. Performance could be judged without reference to norms or with reference to the scores in a child's own class. But comparison with norms is sometimes inescapable, for example, in establishing that a child is eligible for special services or that a research sample is representative of the relevant school population. What norms would be helpful? Should children of Puerto Rican background be kept separate from Cubans? Should Florida norms be used in Florida or national norms? Should a Texas community use general norms for children of Mexican background —or should it separate those whose families have lived in Texas for years from those who just crossed the border? And should separate norms be prepared according to the parents' command of English?

Asking sufficiently complex questions is hard enough. Answering all of them is nearly impossible. But a tester ought to understand the compromises and trade-offs. A parable may make the difficulty clearer. Henry Crumpet tells Dr. Good that he isn't sleeping well—four hours a night, on average, Henry complains. She would like to give Henry reassurance or to work on his problem *if* his sleep is abnormal. Dr. Good's computer console can call up norms for any broad or narrow population she defines. (Too good to be true, but in a parable anything goes.) Henry is remarkably short on sleep, compared to norms for Americans, for 40-year-old males, for 40-year-old American executives. He is "below normal." Indeed? Why stop there? The interview puts Henry in a more specific category: His wife is threatening to leave him; he suspects that his boss will soon fire him; he is drinking quite a lot. When Dr. Good asks the computer about hard-drinking 40-year-old males threatened with divorce and unemployment, the message changes. Four hours of sleep *is* their norm. If Dr. Good took norms seriously, her message would be something like, "I'm sad about your nonmedical problems, Henry, but fortunately you can be contented with your sleeping performance. It exactly fits a person like you." Scores that seem "normal" in a population that is in trouble are symptoms of present trouble and indicators of greater future trouble. (If nothing else, Henry will drink more to get to sleep.)

Overadjustment can erase the message of the test. If schools in some region are coping miserably with newly arrived immigrants, to compare a child with the performance of that region's recent immigrants only papers over the defect. If adolescent females in Midwestern schools know vastly less about gears and levers than boys, only an ostrich would dismiss the fact as "normal."

The most elaborate scheme of differentiated norms is that for Mercer's System of Multicultural Pluralistic Assessment (SOMPA). As part of the case workup, the child's background is summed up in indices for family size, family structure, socioeconomic status (SES), and urban acculturation. The child's ability test is interpreted in the light of what children of the same background and ethnic origin do. As Mercer's manual says, "We have as many norms as there are various combinations of the sociocultural scores, and the child's performance is compared only with the performance that would be expected from the same sociocultural background. Thus, we have an assessment model based on pluralistic norms."

Mercer accomplishes this by the technique of multiple regression (p. 395). Test scores and indices from a sample are fed into the computer. Out comes a formula such as this one developed on 520 Hispanic children: Add together

—0.38 times the family size index
0.27 times the SES index
0.08 times the Urban Acculturation index.

That (plus a constant) predicts the verbal IQ of the Hispanic child. Family structure did not enter this formula because, among Hispanics, that index did not correlate with the test. Mercer subtracts from the score the child earns the score the formula predicts for him and transforms this deviation into a 100 ± 15 standard score, which she labels "Estimated Learning Potential" (ELP).

Mercer's procedure is daring, and its logic can be questioned (Reschly, in Reynolds & Gutkin, 1982). Mercer's transformation puts the average of any socially defined subgroup very close to 100. A superior ELP, then, reports that the child is outdoing others *in similar circumstances.* If 50-year-olds were given a medical examination, converting the evidence relevant to life expectancy by Mercer's technique would produce an "Estimated Living Potential." The urban poor would average out at 100, and so would the well-to-do, who on average are in much better physical condition. If insurance companies are willing to sell life insurance without an extra premium to anyone scoring above 80, the urban poor can afford more life insurance than if premiums are matched to actual risk. That is the sort of equity that Mercer seeks to attain by judging children against their own group. "Pluralistic" norms are a two-edged sword. Reporting a Living Potential score of 100 ("just average") to the person assessed implies "no need to be concerned"; that has bad consequences when the person belongs to a group whose typical health habits are detrimental. Mercer's well-motivated scheme has not yet been subjected to the critical discussion it should receive. Chapter 7 treats SOMPA further.

Differentiated norms subtract out whatever part of the score can be predicted from other information, and therein lies a paradox. Should the formula maker do a very good job of prediction and hence make a radical adjustment? Or should she stop with a poor predictor? If the prediction is accurate, adjustment removes most of the information; the part that remains is largely attributable to random errors of measurement. If prediction is inaccurate, the adjustment adds bonuses or penalties to erase group differences and does nothing else. Mercer adjusts Performance scores of Hispanics using a predictor that correlates only 0.2 with the score.

To illustrate the overkill that comes with *excellent* prediction I turn to another source. The California State Department of Education wants to report how well schools are doing. Since scores in wealthy suburban districts come out ahead in an unadjusted ranking of score means, each district is compared with "similar" districts. The district reading score in grade 6 is adjusted to iron out differences predictable from the percentage of pupils who are bilingual, the percentage whose families are receiving welfare aid, and the average of achievement tests in grade 3. (The rationale for including the last of these factors is that the sixth-grade data ought primarily to tell what the school has been doing for these pupils *lately.*)

The estimates correlate 0.85 with the districts' sixth-grade averages in reading (California Assessment Program, 1977). Differences among districts, unfortunately, are unstable; unadjusted reading averages correlate only 0.66 from one year to the next. This means that the departure of the school's average from the prediction is largely due to minor fluctuations in student-body membership or, at most, to a temporary dip or spurt in student performance. Being dominated by transient fluctuations, this year's adjusted score gives a misleading picture of the school's efficiency relative to other schools with the same background.

42. *The USES Interest Inventory is used with adolescents who are acquainting themselves with career options and (usually in state employment offices) with adult workers seeking new positions. The norms were collected by asking employment services in 28 states (unnamed) to collect specified quotas of cases proportional to the state's population. The aggregate 6530 cases divided evenly between in school and out; included 2876 males; and included 231 Orientals, 92 American Indians, 999 Hispanics, 1788 blacks, and 3420 "nonminority." All cases were combined in the norms except that some norms are split along sex lines.*
   a. *What further information would help the user judge the adequacy of the norms?*
   b. *How well does the norm group seem to fit the population on whom the test will be used?*
   c. *Would norms for subpopulations other than the two sexes be useful?*

Norms by Calibration

Instead of collecting a fresh representative sample for a new test, developers nowadays are likely to tie the new test to a test for which recent norms are available. The calibration process is like the procedure makers of aneroid barometers use when they mark the dials to agree with an accurate mercury barometer. Such a technique has been used with the Scholastic Aptitude Test from 1941 to date; the linkup is made by including a subset of common items in tests for consecutive years. As was explained earlier, this equating enables a faculty to gain experience with what an SAT score of 600 means even though that score is based on new items each year. Many technical refinements can be brought to calibration (Angoff, in R. L. Thorndike, 1971), and the methods are still imperfect (Slinde & Linn, 1977); but explanation of equipercentile conversion will demonstrate the basic approach.

Suppose that high school norms for the Bennett TMC are wanted, and it is accepted that the DAT norms for *its* TMC are adequately representative of current students. A few hundred persons would be given both tests; it is not essential that they be a representative norm group, but they ought to come from several schools. They should include males and females and the pertinent range of grade levels. The raw scores on each test can be expressed as percentiles within this group; as the maximum score on DAT is 70 points and the maximum on the Bennett is 68, the two could not match perfectly. Suppose we have these numbers:

Percentile in equating sample	10	25	50	75	90
DAT *raw score*	30	41	50	56	64
Bennett *raw score*	28	38	47	53	61

We conclude that a DAT score of 64 is just as hard to attain as a Bennett score of 61. Similarly, all along the same scale, we can map a Bennett raw score into a DAT score and look that up in the tables of DAT grade-by-sex norms. Calibration methods can piggyback new tests on old ones until the original norms go out of date. They are comparatively inexpensive and are one good way to equate tests; unidimensional scaling, the topic of the next section, is an alternative.

Matching-up of tests at the same level is called "horizontal equating." The same technique can be used for reporting elementary and advanced levels of a test on a common scale; that is "vertical equating." Achievement tests are, of course, geared to the grades in which they are given, but schools would like to compare a student's performance in grade 4 with his performance when he took an easier test in grade 3. It is necessary to test a sample for whom both forms are reasonably appropriate—classes tested early in grade 4, for example. A score of 20 out of 30 on the easy test falls at the same percentile point as a score of, say, 12 on the harder test. These matched points can be converted to some arbitrary common scale. (The grade-equivalent scale is often used, but its surplus meanings are a source of trouble.) If such a scale is built up over the range from the primary-grade test to the test for grade 9, the school or the research worker can trace the development of each student even though the level of the test changes with each administration.

A noteworthy application of calibration was the Anchor Test Study (Jaeger, 1973; Loret *et al.*, 1974), which tied seven prominent reading tests to the same scale. The federal government wanted this conversion so that evaluation reports from schools that had given different tests could be interpreted together. Part of the Metropolitan Achievement Test was chosen as anchor, and fresh norms for it were established. A sample of children took the tests under investigation, no child taking more than two tests; the sample was carefully constructed and the subsamples were counterbalanced.

UNIDIMENSIONAL SCALING

In a "pure" measuring procedure, all the tasks or questions would measure the same dimension. One way to find out how many grams object X weighs is to put it on the left pan of a balance and put objects of known weight—200 g., 250 g., and so on—on the right pan. Each of these is like a test item. Object X "passes" the item when the left pan goes down; the test continues until we reach an object heavy enough to pull down the right side of the balance. The test procedure is unidimensional because the items all measure weight. Familiar though such an example is, "measure the same thing" is a subtle notion.

A set of items is "unidimensional" if their order of difficulty is the same for everyone in a population of interest. Memory for digits has the property: if you can remember strings of eight digits, you can also remember shorter strings. (Some irregularity has to be accepted. You won't be consistent on successive trials. And it is easier to remember "5–4–3–2–1–1–2–3–4–5" than "7–2–1–9–4–1".)

The main ideas of "unidimensional scaling" are introduced here without a precise account of assumptions or computations. These techniques are becoming increasingly prominent in test construction and score reporting. Many of the new tests mentioned in this book employ the techniques in some way. The procedures not only check a set of items for purity but locate the test taker on a special kind of scale.

Figure 4.8*(i)* summarizes information from a (hypothetical) trial of four items. Ability increases from left to right; the ability scale used in this first analysis is perhaps a crude raw score. All along the scale, item *a* is easier than item *b*, *b* is easier than *c*, and *c* easier than *d* (if we disregard sampling fluctuations). This permits us to argue that the items all reflect the same characteristic, that the set is unidimensional.

To go further with scaling, the test maker represents each set of *P*'s by a smooth curve panel *(ii)*. These "item characteristic curves" differ in steepness. The test maker now imposes a rule: The steepness ought to be the same for all items (to the extent possible). To achieve this, she stretches the A scale wherever curves rise steeply and shrinks it where slopes are gradual. This makes the curves nearly parallel panel *(iii)*. Then she places numbers on the new scale. The size of the numbers is arbitrary, but they must be spaced evenly along the line.

Performance can be described in terms of these new "scale values." The person's scale value is the level where his probability of passing items is 50 out of 100 (after adjustment for guessing, when choice items are scaled). When the person takes the four items represented in the figure and passes just one of them, we infer that his ability most likely lies in the range 21.3–22.6. A longer test locates the person's scale position more precisely.

The preceding paragraph gives a rough idea of the scaling method

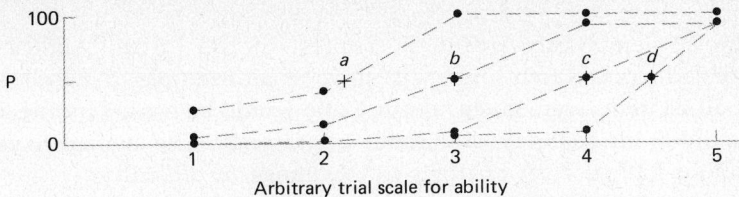

(i) Proportion passing four items at each score level

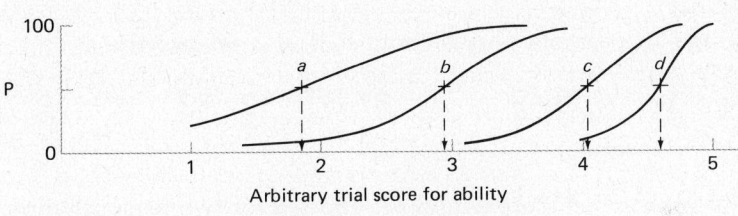

(ii) Smoothed item characteristic curves

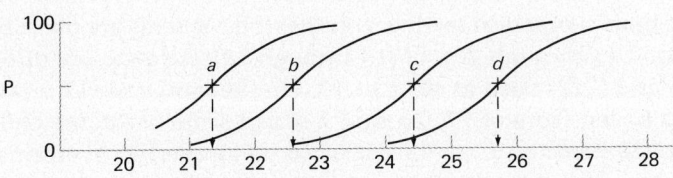

Scale established by Rasch procedures

(iii) Characteristic curves with uniform slope

Figure 4.8. Stages in scaling test items.

developed by Gunnar Rasch (1980); for a precise but introductory account, see M. J. Allen and W. Yen (1979) or Hambleton (1979). Others have developed alternative procedures. This line of effort is known as "latent trait theory" or "item response theory" (Lord, 1980).

In Rasch scaling, an item is assigned the "scale value" where its characteristic curve crosses the $P = 0.50$ level. The curves for some items are much less steep than the curves for typical items. These items are candidates for discard as not belonging to the scale. Perhaps, like the ugly duckling, they belong to a different family, or perhaps they are strongly affected by error of measurement. Another basis for locating suspect items is to repeat the scaling processes on males and females separately or on members of two cultures or on pupils in a high grade and a lower grade. If the item scale values based on different populations do not correspond, at least some items violate the definition of unidimensionality. (On item analysis, see pp. 147 f., 333)

The 28-item Basic Arithmetic subtest of the British Ability Scales (BAS), scaled along Rasch lines, will serve as an example of Rasch conversions. If all 28 items were given, about 5 or 6 would be passed by the average British child at his birthday, and about 14 at age 10. The average 8-year-old passes about half of a set of items in this range of difficulty:

$$\begin{array}{ccc} 14 & 5 & 33 \\ +87 & -2 & -15 \end{array}$$

The average 10-year-old passes about half of a set like these:

$$3\overline{)9} \qquad \begin{array}{c} 87 \\ \times 14 \end{array} \qquad 12\overline{)72}$$

The same scaled score would be reported for two persons who pass the same items though one is 6 years old and the other is 12. Raw scores 6 and 14 on the 28-item test are mapped into scaled scores 38 and 65, respectively. (Percentiles and standard-scores conversions are also provided.)

To save time in practical testing, subsets of BAS items are used: B (items 1 through 12), C (1 through 20), D (13 through 28). A raw score of 6 on the easy scales B and C is scaled at close to 40. On the hard scale D, a raw score of 6 implies a scaled score of 77. To earn a scaled score of 98, the child must pass 19 out of 20 items on C, or 11 out of 16 on D. (Perfect performance on B is recorded only as a scaled score "over 70.") This technique makes it possible, in principle, to string simple counting, arithmetic, computation, quadratic equations, and calculus together on one scale. (BAS stops with division of decimals.)

The comments that follow are not specific to any system of analysis. Remarks on the value of the methods must be mixed with warnings (e.g., Slinde & Linn, 1977); enthusiasts have claimed almost magical qualities for scales constructed in this way.

Applications. Scaling techniques allow single items to be calibrated. In panel *(iii)* of Figure 4.8, item 1 is "located" at a scale position of 1.4. If a test developer includes new items in a trial along with items already scaled, the scale value for each new item can be identified. Items so scaled are stored in item banks. New test forms can be constructed to measure any dimension or mixture of dimensions at any desired level of difficulty. The information on the items makes it possible to convert raw scores on the new test to scale values. If the population has not changed much, old norms for scale values apply to the new test.

Scaling is useful in "adaptive testing" (p. 39) because it can place on the same score scale persons who were presented with different item sets. Instead of counting right and wrong answers, the computer estimates the difficulty level (on a very long test) at which the person's success rate would be 50 per cent. These methods of statistical inference (Lord, 1980) can be applied to packaged tests as well as computerized tests, and scoring services for some tests provide this option. For most packaged tests, the complexly derived scores tell essentially the same story that ordinary raw scores do. The complex scoring is likely to give better information with short tests and with students who guess on many items (Thissen, 1976).

The scaling methods are especially compatible with domain-referenced interpretations. A standard such as "70 per cent is a passing mark" fluctuates with the difficulty of the test. Policy makers can perhaps agree as to the level of task difficulty where an adequate performer would pass on 70 per cent of his trials. That level of difficulty can be translated into a scale value, which becomes a permanent standard applicable to new sets of items.

Cautions. Rasch scales need not be truly uniform in content, as the Arithmetic subtest illustrates. A scale of weight measures weight, and nothing else, for any object properly placed on the balance. The BAS score measures competence in arithmetic—and effort and carefulness. It stretches over many subskills. A child can be confused about decimals when he has command of improper fractions, and vice versa. Growth in arithmetic is not simply acquiring more of "the same thing." As a matter of fact, tasks from entirely different domains can come out "unidimensional" in the usual scaling procedure if one kind of task is easy and the other hard. Despite the distinct content, the order of difficulty is the same for everyone.

Although they are not norms, the scales are dependent on a reference group. They are derived from persons having particular histories. The scale values of items, hence those reported for test takers, could change if scaling were carried out on a distinctly different population. It is incorrect to suggest, as some writers have, that the scale numbers are independent of culture, education, age, and so forth. Whether the initial scale fits another group depends on the groups and on the test content.

Finally, the numerical scale has "equal units" in only a limited sense. In making the characteristic curves equally steep all along the scale, the scalers apply an approach that goes back a century and a half. Gustav Fechner, one of the first experimenters in psychology, wanted to measure the *apparent* loudness of sounds—the psychological dimension as distinct from the physical energy. Let us assume, he said, that judgments that are equally hard to make represent equal differences in loudness. So he presented tone pairs such as X and Y or Y and Z. If signal X is called louder than signal Y on 80 per cent of the X/Y trials, and Y is called louder than Z on 60 per cent of the Y/Z trials, then on the psychological scale Y must be closer to Z than to X. Scales based on this principle are not like the physical scales that allow simple equations to express laws (e.g., "force is proportional to the length of the lever arm"). Suppose Gina moved from 40 on a Rasch scale to 50 during grade 3 and then to 57 during grade 4. There is no justification for saying that Gina "grew faster" during grade 3. (L. V. Jones, in R. L. Thorndike, 1971, explains why psychological scales have this limitation.)

43. *Would the order of difficulty for Basic Arithmetic items be the same for American school children as for the British standardization group?*
44. *What might cause the scale values of fixed items to change from one generation to another? Of the following tests, which would be most likely to change in this respect: Block Design, Porteus maze, or TMC?*
45. *Would it mean anything to say, "John is as heavy as he is tall"?*
46. *Which of these can be given meaning without reference to how other persons perform?*
    a. *Belle is better at the backstroke than the crawl.*
    b. *Max speaks Italian better than French.*
    c. *Math is easier for Perry than foreign languages.*
    d. *John is better in Basic Arithmetic than in Vocabulary.*

5
Validation

We have already examined some of the qualities that make a test suitable or unsuitable. Chapter 1 urged the user to select tests that she is competent to give and interpret. Chapters 3 and 4 considered such topics as clarity of directions, convenience of scoring, objectivity, and appropriateness of norms. In this chapter we come to the most important quality: validity. But let us begin with some comments on judging tests—which is the theme of Chapters 5 and 6 taken together.

THE NEED FOR CRITICAL SCRUTINY OF TESTS

"What is the best test of general mental ability?" "What is the best test of reading comprehension?" "What is the best measure of anxiety?" Industrial, clinical, and school psychologists ask questions in that form; so do classroom teachers, sociologists, program evaluators, and psychologists pursuing research questions. Regardless of the trait to be measured, the test that best serves one of these questioners will not be the best for most of the others. Not even a narrow question—"What is the best measure of mechanical comprehension for selecting industrial trainees?"—has a universal answer.

The person choosing a test[1] faces a confusing array of options: long tests and short tests, famous tests and unfamiliar tests, old tests and new, ordinary tests and novel ones. One test distributor offers 25 instruments for assessing general mental ability or scholastic aptitude and 15 devices for appraising personality. Buros's 1978 *Yearbook* listed about 1000 tests that were new since the 1972 edition or had been revised or supplemented by significant new information.

No test maker can put all desirable qualities into one test. A design feature that improves the test in one respect generally sacrifices some other quality. Some tests measure good readers validly but not poor readers; some give precise answers but require much time; some estimate overall ability well enough, but do little to analyze strengths and weaknesses.

A test is selected for a particular situation and purpose. What tests are pertinent for a psychological examination of a child entering first grade? That depends on what alternative instructional plans the school is prepared to follow. Which test of skill in English usage is suitable for surveying a high school class? Those teachers for whom clarity of expression is important will be discontented with a test requiring only that the student choose between grammatically correct and incorrect expressions.

Those who are not professional testers should know what questions to ask about the suitability of tests and testing practices. In arriving at recommendations regarding a juvenile offender, for example, the clinical psychologist may be overenthusiastic about the procedures in which she is expert and may draw too forceful a conclusion. The youth advocate should be ready to ask pointed questions, and so should the judge reviewing the case.

Sometimes it makes sense not to act as the psychologist recommends. A counselee may, for example, be able to consider facts not available to a tester. Yet giving great weight to supplementary impressions and little weight to observations that are objective and relevant spoils more decisions than it helps. When the user of test information knows how to judge a test, she can also judge whether other impressions are substantial enough to deserve comparable weight.

The reputation of a test is not an adequate indicator of its merit. New tests are produced, new uses of tests are discovered, and some old uses are discredited. Modern test development is usually self-critical, and the quality of tests and test information has improved. Nonetheless, there are bad tests and bad testing practices. Moreover, test titles, advertising, and manuals can mislead. Consumers and those affected by tests have to remain alert.

In the 1970s, for example, the Armed Services persuaded high schools throughout the nation to give their vocational aptitude test to a million students a year. The test scores helped recruiters locate talented prospects and were also valuable in the school's guidance efforts—at least that was the plan. When in 1977 the test came under professional review, it was seen to be badly

---

[1]The logic of choosing a test applies also to the choice of any other procedure or source of information: interviews, ratings, informal observation, and so on.

constructed. Worse, it offered wildly inappropriate suggestions regarding the careers the student with certain score patterns should consider. In this instance, because members of Congress showed concern, the test promoters quickly corrected the gravest faults in the interpretative materials. Still, the test supplied to schools in 1982 was unchanged from 1977. In contrast, the counterpart test used *within* the Armed Services had been overhauled; in particular, certain subtests considered to be invalid had been discarded! (For a fuller story, see Cronbach, 1979.)

1. *Improving a test in one way weakens it in another. What advantage and what disadvantage come from each of the following changes?*
   a. *Lengthening a test.*
   b. *Making it interesting to children.*
   c. *Making it more diagnostic of strong and weak points.*
   d. *Giving it as an individual test instead of as a group test.*
2. *This is a letter received by a psychologist from an industrial personnel manager hiring office and factory workers. How would you answer it on the basis of the preceding paragraphs, knowing that the tests mentioned are representative of their type?*

   . . . Just now we are planning to use the following tests: Wonderlic intelligence and Minnesota Multiphasic Personality Inventory and aptitude tests related to our openings, such as the Bennett test. Does this seem to be a well-balanced testing schedule for industry? Are there tests that you think preferable to these?
3. *It has been suggested that the American Psychological Association award a seal of approval to all well-prepared psychological tests. Discuss the advantages and disadvantages of such a system. Would this plan eliminate the need for critical judgment by users?*
4. *Would your answer to question 3 be the same if it referred to the National Council on Measurement in Education and to tests of school learning?*

Sources of Information and Criticism

Some limitations of tests reflect only the fact that no one test can do everything, but some reflect lack of self-criticism by the developer or user. Fortunately, a great deal of information is available on most published tests.

The test manual. The manual, together perhaps with a technical handbook, is ordinarily the principal source of information. A firm or a public authority making a test for its own use rarely distributes a manual, but the agency ought to assemble the kinds of data that would go into a manual for such a test. The data can aid in quality control and in examining the fairness of decisions based on the test. That information should be open to a concerned outsider.

Materials provided by a publisher supply directions for test administration and scoring, summarize research findings, and may give specific advice regarding use of scores in teaching, counseling, or other practice. It is not easy to make a report clear and comprehensive. The more research there is, the harder the task of summary. A test manual should be clear enough that any qualified user can comprehend it—and clear enough that the reader who is not qualified will realize that fact.

Test reviews. Test construction and reporting were much improved by the efforts of the late Professor O. K. Buros, who began to release critical reviews of tests in 1934. Nearly all tests currently marketed in English-speaking countries are reviewed in this continuing series. Each test is examined independently by two or more specialists; they suggest proper uses of the test and draw attention to any questionable claims in the manual. Test reviews also appear in many journals, for example, *Journal of Educational Measurement, Measurement and Evaluation in Guidance,* and *Professional Psychology* and in journals dealing with reading, pediatrics, and other specialties.

It remains for the purchaser to exercise considerable judgment, especially when reviewers disagree. A test that has faults is not necessarily a bad choice. Even when a particular test has been given thorough and balanced review, its appropriateness depends on the local purpose to be served. Often that purpose will be served better by making cautious use of the test scores than by relying wholly on nontest information.

Test standards. A profession develops through exchange of opinions and experiences at its meetings and in its journals, stimulated in part by the reactions of the publics it serves. Codes of practice are prepared by study groups, exposed for criticism, and ultimately endorsed by the governing body of a professional association.

The major document of this character, the *Test Standards,* has gone through three editions. A major revision is scheduled to appear in 1984. The *Standards* cover psychological and educational tests in general use. The *Standards* are not geared to tests having only a local use, such as those a teacher prepares. The American Psychological Association, the American Educational Research Association, and the National Council on Measurement in Education developed (1974) the *Standards* jointly, but for brevity they are often referred to as the "APA Standards." Division 14 of APA, whose members specialize in industrial psychology, prepared *Principles for Personnel Testing* (Division 14, 1980).

No one has laid down general rules about test *quality.* What is called for is information and evidence. It is sensible to request, for example, that the size and composition of any norm group be reported. The user who wants norms has to judge whether the norm sample is relevant to her situation. Appropriately, the *Standards* do not say that every norming sample should reach a specified size. To impose a fixed demand on every test developer would increase the cost of tests and would discourage the development of special-purpose tests whose market is likely to be small. The philosophy of the draft 1984 *Standards* is that an economical shortcut is acceptable when the departure from ideal procedures probably will do no serious harm or injustice to persons tested.

Material in Figure 1.3 (p. 18) was taken from the 18 pages of the 1974 *Standards* devoted to "use of tests." There are six sections on responsibilities of the test producer: Dissemination of information (3 pp.), Aids for interpretation (5 pp.), Directions for administration and scoring (5 pp.), Norms and scales (5 pp.), Validity (17 pp.), and Reliability and measurement error (7 pp.).

The standards labeled "Essential" are broad. They set forth practices that were usual and accepted by testing specialists at the time the edition of the *Standards* was published. New standards are added in each revision, and sometimes an old one is liberalized or discarded. From 1954 through 1974 some standards were labeled "Very desirable" and "Desirable," as in Figure 1.3. These encouraged practices whose cost or inconvenience made universal adoption unlikely. The weaker classification was also given to statements about which professional opinion was not unanimous. (An example is the recommendation that scores not be translated into mental ages or grade equivalents; see pp. 101 and 204). For the 1984 revision, the code will be rephrased, and a principle may be classified differently in such distinct areas of application as school guidance and examination of delinquents for a court.

The *Standards* were produced originally as an educational aid for the profession rather than as formal regulations. They discourage hucksterism, but the only "enforcement" is that an association could censure or expel a member for unethical practice. The *Standards* and the Division 14 *Principles* took on more weight during the 1970s when legal guidelines and court decisions relied on them (Bersoff, in Glaser & Bond, 1981; Novick, in Wigdor & Garner, II, 1982). The *Standards* are now used by bureaucrats and judges to call particular test applications proper or improper (and the interpretations sometimes have reached beyond the professional consensus).

OVERVIEW OF METHODS OF INQUIRY

Obviously, no aspect of a test is more important than validity: the soundness and relevance of a proposed interpretation of scores. No matter how satisfactory a test is in other respects, if it is wrongly interpreted it is worthless in that time and place. Only as abbreviation is it legitimate to speak of "the validity of a test"; a test relevant to one decision may have no value for another. So users must ask, "How valid is this test for the decision to be made?" or "How valid are the interpretations I am making of the scores?"

Psychologists have given specific names to dozens of "kinds" of validation—that is, lines of argument to verify the soundness of an interpretation. Three of the terms—criterion-oriented (predictive), content, and construct validation—are used so frequently that anyone concerned with tests should become familiar with them.

I begin with examples of the classical, separate usage of the terms:

- When the U.S. Navy is assigning sailors to a course on ships' engines, it seeks those who will finish the course successfully. Its personnel psychologists try out the TMC, comparing it against a measure of success in the course, a *criterion*.
- When a school system is testing how well its high school seniors understand American government, the test ought to cover the *content* that district officials consider important. The testing officer has to satisfy herself of the content validity of the items singly and as a set.
- The score on a test of "introversion" claims to describe an aspect of the person's behavior or feelings. To evaluate the truthfulness of a description, we must first pin down its intended meaning. How (according to the interpreter's theory) do "introverts" act in social situations? What incentives do they respond to? How do they handle emotional stress? Once meanings have been spelled out in this way, we can check out whether persons who score high on the test act as the theory says they will. Terms entering explanations—such as "introversion"—are constructs; hence this is *construct* validation.

It might appear that criterion validation is for aptitude tests, content validation for educational tests, and construct validation for personality tests, but that generalization is false. The *Test Standards* were organized around these three terms in the 1950s. Unfortunately, they came to be seen as "something of a holy trinity representing three different roads to psychometric salvation" (Guion, 1980, p. 386).

The end goal of validation is explanation and understanding. Therefore, the profession is coming around to the view that *all* validation is construct validation (Cronbach, 1980b; Messick, 1975; for a dissent, see Ebel, in Reynolds & Gutkin, 1982). Content- and criterion-based arguments develop parts of the story. With almost any test it makes sense to join all three kinds of inquiry in building an explanation. The three distinct terms do no more than spotlight aspects of the inquiry.

5. *Some early writers said, "A test is valid if it measures what it purports to measure." How does this statement differ from today's conception, as sketched in the preceding paragraphs?*

Introduction to Criterion-oriented Validation

Tests obviously are used predictively in vocational guidance, in hiring, and in educational admissions. A diagnosis also ought to have predictive value;

VALIDATION

there is no point in labeling a difficulty if the label does not imply a treatment likely to bring improvement. Validity of predictions is checked by follow-up. To produce the experience table exhibited on page 90, the psychologist ranked trainees on the test. Later she recorded course marks and compared them with the ranking given by the test.

The rating or mark is a common criterion. Aptitude tests are validated against marks earned in school. Industrial predictors are validated against ratings by supervisors. These ratings are not entirely satisfactory as criteria. The judge may not know the facts about the person. Often a rating reflects the personal relation between worker and supervisor rather than the quality of the work. When a test fails to predict a rating, it is hard to say whether this is the fault of the test or of the rating. A measure is a "criterion" only when an audience accepts it as important and relevant. Before an investigator adopts a criterion, she should take a hard look at its dependability, freedom from bias, and credibility.

Table 5.1 outlines the follow-up study; it is a summary-in-advance of later pages. The left column lists what the investigator looks at. She has to look into a certain situation. She seeks an adequate criterion. And so on. An actual plan falls short of the ideal as the examples will show. Departures from the ideal put the interpreter of the evidence on the defensive. Indirect reasoning becomes critical.

Illustrative follow-up studies. Example 1 in the table investigates a test to screen applicants to a law school. The study develops an experience table. After conferring with the investigator about it, the committee that sets admission policy will decide whether to require future applicants to take the test and how much weight to put on the score.

The experience table tells the history in this school in this year. The rather typical study described in Example 1 does not provide a final answer even to factual questions. The reported relations may not hold in this same school next year if the curriculum or grading standards change. The history would not be perfectly duplicated in another school. The direct evidence is on the first-year grade average, not on "success in law school" or "promise as a lawyer." Moreover, the experience table is not based on representative *applicants.* In the year the data were collected, applicants the admissions committee saw as unpromising were not admitted. No one knows how many of them would have made acceptable records.

Example 2 outlines a follow-up study for an achievement test. If this test works well, the investigator should be able to suggest a passing standard that would certify workers expected to be adequate or better on the job. Workers below the standard could be retrained and retested. Again we have an unrepresentative sample because the firm cannot afford to send a badly qualified employee to serve customers.

Concurrent studies. The follow-up in Example 1 spanned one year. Sometimes, instead, the test and criterion measurements are separated by a short

Table 5.1. *Criterion-oriented validation: Elements in a direct inquiry*

Element (in ideal study)	Examples of Realistic Practice	
	Example 1. Law-school Admissions	Example 2. Certifying Proficiency of Graduates
Situation that concerns the test user	Law school A has an established curriculum. Applicants outnumber places. Faculty desires to admit students likely to do well.	Manufacturer Z trains workers to maintain equipment. After training, they work out of local offices, repairing most breakdowns but calling experts from headquarters when necessary. It is costly to send an underqualified worker to the field.
Criterion; accepted as adequate by client and investigator	Course grades received during the first year of law school are averaged.	Regional supervisor rates employees in the field after examining a log of service rendered and related information.
Elapsed time; accepted as adequate	Confining attention to the first year produces an early report.	Ratings at end of first six months are to be used.
Sample; accepted as representative of those about whom decisions will be made hereafter	The aptitude test under investigation is given to all entering students in 1980. They are not actually representative of 1980 applicants.	The proficiency test is given to all persons completing the course in January through June of 1980. The workers— no matter what their scores— are sent to the field unless the instructor has rated them seriously deficient in performance.
Test; data are collected as they will be when predictions are made "for keeps."	Testing is conducted during the first week of school; student attitude may not match that of applicants.	The test is given at the end of training. Each trainee's errors are discussed with him.

interval or none. Strictly speaking, this is "concurrent" validation, but in most contexts it does no harm to stretch the term *predictive* to cover such data.

A concurrent study is fully logical when a test is proposed as a substitute for a more expensive procedure. The developer hopes that the test indicates what the expensive procedure would say about the person at this time. The soundest way to survey mental health in a community would be to have an experienced clinician interview every member of the sample and rate the degree of adjustment of each one. It is far more practicable to print up a list

VALIDATION

of questions, have members of the sample respond YES or NO, and score the responses. Do these scores tell the story the professional ratings would? To check this out, one would apply both procedures to perhaps 30 persons, perhaps in the same week. Crosstabulation would show the degree of agreement.

Sometimes the concurrent study is a preliminary to a long-term follow-up, and sometimes it is a substitute. Thus Z Company might give its proposed proficiency test to workers already in the field. If performance ratings on these workers are in line with their test scores, that encourages the use of the test at the end of training. But the argument is indirect. Possibly superior test scores reflect what the more alert workers learned on the job. If so, some high-rated workers probably would have seemed inadequate if tested as they left school. The concurrent study departs from the logic suggested by the first column of Table 5.1. The study leaves room for uncertainty.

When E. K. Strong produced his interest questionnaire to help adolescents choose careers, concurrent studies were appropriate. To find out if the score profile of a 20-year-old really predicts what work he will enjoy as an adult, Strong would have had to collect the profiles and then put himself on hold for 20 years while the criterion ripened. Strong, therefore, offered as evidence of validity the fact that questionnaires answered in middle age distinguished men or women in one occupation from those in another. For example, the scores of doctors on Strong's Physician scale averaged much higher than those of nondoctors. The purpose of the test, however, is not to find out which middle-aged person is a doctor; it is to find out if a young person will in later years be satisfied with that career. If the direction of interest at 40 is usually the same as at 20, then the concurrent validation on older persons is indirect evidence that the test predicts. Until follow-up evidence came in, users of the Strong questionnaire had to assume that a person's interests remain much the same from age 20 to age 40. Strong did accumulate evidence by following some persons for 20 years or more and ultimately verified his long-term predictions.

Illustrative results for TMC. The 1969 manual for TMC gave information from criterion-related studies. Approximately 30 findings were listed, and attention was drawn to sources reporting additional studies. Table 5.2 presents a handful of the results to show what a manual offers. For the moment, simply regard the values of r as numbers on a 0-to-1 scale that show how well the test forecasts the criterion. These results are given in the manual not to answer users' specific questions but to illustrate typical findings. The manual urges the user to make her own local follow-up study.

A fuller story, based on better research, is offered in the 1980 supplement to the manual. The contrast between Tables 5.2 and 5.3 is a striking example of the steady improvement in research on tests and the reporting of it. In 1969 most of the criteria in the manual were judgmental, not direct measurements. (Attendance and conduct, for example, probably influence the

Table 5.2. *Illustrative reports on TMC validity, 1969*

Group	N	Criterion	r
Aircraft engine factory; foremen	208	Performance ratings	0.55
Naval aviation cadets (no flight experience)	1187	Success in flight training	0.30
Technical school machine shop; students	67	Shop marks[a]	0.48
Automobile company; apprentices in skilled trades	662	Rating of job knowledge	0.21
	634	Grade in shop arithmetic	0.12

[a] The test was given early in grade 9. The criterion was marks given for performance in grade 11.
SOURCE: Manual for Forms S and T of the Bennett Mechanical Comprehension Test, 1969, pp. 8–10.

Table 5.3. *Illustrative reports on TMC validity, 1980*

Group (with mean and s.d. on TMC)	N	Criterion	r
Coal producer; inexperienced miners (50.9; 8.1)	178	Combined rating and ranking	0.23
Southern chemical plant; operators (45.1; 7.0)	87	Rating on reaction to emergency	0.36
		Rating on safety rules	0.21
		Rating on job knowledge	0.39
Southern chemical plant; operators (48.0; 7.5)	136	Test on job knowledge	0.63
Steel producer; apprentice millwrights and mechanics (50.0; 6.8)	30	Average course grades	0.54
Utility company; technician trainees (39.6; 9.7)	83	Time needed to complete training modules	−0.52

SOURCE: Manual supplement for Forms S and T of the Bennett Mechanical Comprehension Test, 1980, pp. 6–7.

grades a shop teacher gives to adolescents.) In the chemical plant, one analysis took a direct measure of job knowledge as a criterion—and the correlations went up! In the utility company, training time provided another behavioral criterion. The recent report gives detail not reproduced here—in particular, the proportion of males and of whites in nearly every group is stated.

Both reports have limitations. Some samples are as small as 30 cases, making the evidence thin. For only one study are readers told how much time elapsed between test and criterion measurement. Nor are they told how much more select the subjects were than the original applicant pool. Why that is important will be explained later.

Despite the departures from ideal design and reporting, the information

Validation

warrants the conclusion that, in many kinds of technical work, TMC has a worthwhile relation to success.

6. *Four TMC coefficients for operators in a chemical plant are reported. What reasons can you suggest for the variation among them?*
7. *Can you make a general statement about the type of job or criterion for which TMC gives comparatively accurate predictions?*

Introduction to Content Validation

Scrutiny of content is especially important in a test that certifies competence or that is used to evaluate an educational or therapeutic service. Those delivering a service try to develop competence of a certain kind or to encourage certain attitudes or to cause people to act differently. A final test, then, ought to assess *those* characteristics, not something else. Table 5.4 outlines examples of two kinds. Example 1 illustrates how careful task definition and sampling support the content validity of a measure of typical behavior. This argument is direct.

Example 2 returns to the test of maintenance skills of Table 5.1. If the examination is a good "work sample," then the graduate of the maintenance course demonstrates that he can do the job when he passes the test. To judge content validity, the investigator compares the test content with that of job duties. There will be some mismatch; how much this impairs the usefulness of the test is a matter for judgment. Identification of the pertinent domain and obtaining agreement on it are as critical in content validation as the choice of criterion is in predictive validation.

8. *The pencil-paper portion of the licensing examination for drivers has a different mix of content in different states. What questions would you ask to evaluate which of the examinations have superior content validity?*
9. *What questions would you ask to evaluate the content validity of the behind-the-wheel portion of the test for drivers?*

Construct Validation: Explaining Test Scores and Their Relations

The test developer and test user seek to understand why some persons score high and some score low and why performance on a test does (or does not) correspond to everyday behavior. Explanations have practical consequences: improvement in the test, change in the way it is used, modification of the requirements of a job or an instructional program, and hints for designing new tests. For example, evidence that vocabulary and reading ability predict how much fire fighters learn during training should prompt the question: "Did the training program make unnecessary verbal demands?" If so, perhaps

Table 5.4. *Content-oriented validation: Elements in a direct inquiry*

Element and Investigator's Role	Examples of Realistic Practice	
	Example 1. Observing Teachers	*Example 2. Certifying Proficiency of Graduates*
Situation that concerns the test user	A workshop for teachers encourages them to use certain kinds of reinforcement. The success of the workshop is to be judged from follow-up observations of teaching.	Manufacturer Z trains workers to maintain equipment. After training, they work out of local offices, repairing most breakdowns but calling experts from headquarters when necessary. It is costly to send an underqualified worker to the field.
Domain of content; specified by investigator, accepted by client	Workshop director tells investigator what actions he is encouraging. Investigator defines categories and prepares a guide so observers can classify each classroom episode. She also prepares a briefer version to serve as record sheet.	Psychologist obtains record of all service calls encountered by the newly trained workers and summarizes the types of malfunction they have dealt with over a 3-month period. Supervisors and experienced workers indicate what action they would recommend in the situation described.
Domain of occasions; specified by investigator, accepted by client	Investigator suggests, and workshop director agrees, that behavior is to be observed only during classwork in reading and arithmetic and that the data will be collected during a 4-week period, 2 months after the workshop.	
Sampling of observations: Investigator's plan guarantees adequate sample; *or* sampling is unsystematic; the distribution of content, occasions, etc., is judged against the domain.	Investigator lays out schedule so that each teacher is visited on randomly chosen days and so that at scheduled moments the teacher's next act of reinforcement is recorded.	Psychologist had (earlier) prepared test tasks from the outline of the training program with the advice of the instructors. The psychologist classifies the tasks of the proficiency test and points out how the tasks or the answers given credit differ from practice in the field.

the training can be modified so that aspirants with limited verbal ability can master the job. This would benefit them, would benefit the service by increasing the supply of suitable applicants, and would benefit society by reducing the number of "unemployables."

Every test is to some degree impure and unlikely to measure exactly what its name implies. Identifying impurities is one part of the process of explanation. Kent (1937, p. 423) spoke of the difficulty the school psychologist faces in evaluating scores of a youngster who has made little progress in reading:

> A composite test which contains reading matter . . . discriminates against the subject whose inability to read is due to any cause other than mental retardation. A test which calls for oral response discriminates very seriously against the child who by reason of speech defect or impediment is unable to make himself understood. It is little more than a farce to use a timed test or a test containing timed items for a psychotic subject whose mental processes are pathologically slowed up. What we measure by the test may be significant, but it is something quite other than what the test is intended to measure.

The tests Kent criticized would probably correlate with criteria of school success and would probably be judged to sample significant adaptive performances. Sooner or later every tester has to go behind the experience table and behind the test content, to say what processes seem to account for the responses observed.

Explaining test scores is much like any scientific reasoning—a back-and-forth exchange between curiosity, speculation, collection of evidence, and critical review of possible interpretations of the evidence. A theory is built out of constructs, each one a category invented to describe apparently similar events, objects, situations, or persons (p. 45). Observations of behavior are summarized in terms of constructs: "the family of sales jobs," "small-group instruction," "aggressive acts," "encoding," "manic-depressive," "knowledge of the number system," and "divergent thinking." *Construct* comes from *construe*; a construct is a way of construing—organizing—what has been observed.

The theory used in explaining test scores, though sometimes close to everyday thinking, is hard-won knowledge going well beyond the obvious. It was and is obvious that "memory" counts in college work, and memory for strings of numbers is a traditional test of memory. Yet grade averages have almost no correlation with how long a digit string each student can recall. Today's interpretation of memory emphasizes how ideas are organized. The fact that digit strings are unorganized explains the lack of correlation with college learning.

To speak of "aptitude for sales jobs" implies that the several jobs given this label have similar requirements. This kind of interpretation is likely to be only partly correct; research has to determine just which jobs belong in the category. If sales jobs prove to be diverse, the research will have to suggest finer job categories.

The originator of a test sets out to measure a loosely defined trait. The tentative conception of it suggests a kind of item to try. Samuel Kohs, inventor of Block Design, had a hunch that breaking patterns into elements is a key aspect of reasoning. Therefore, he presented the complete design on a card; asking the test taker to match single blocks would not test what Kohs was after. The inventor's working hypotheses are challenged, first when surprises come up in the data and later when other investigators disagree with his interpretations. Sometimes additional studies can settle the disagreement. Sometimes two or more alternatives are accepted as possibilities to keep in mind. Today there are psychologists who regard Block Design as a measure of "abstract" reasoning ability and others who see it as testing a specialized ability to think about geometric forms.

This lengthy—indeed, endless—process of revising hypotheses is referred to succinctly as construct validation. As the preceding examples show, it is a matter of asking tough questions about the test content and its correlates. For such a free-ranging program of analysis there is no simple or ideal design.

VALIDATION AGAINST A CRITERION: A CLOSER LOOK

The Criterion

To consider predictive studies in more detail, I turn to another example. A wholesale hardware firm hires salespersons. Test scores can be put on file as persons apply for jobs, during a period of several months. Ideally, these scores will not be allowed to influence hiring. That gives us a chance to find out how well persons all along the score scale do on the job.

The hardest part of predictive validation is getting suitable criterion data. The outcome that interests the firm is how much each employee sells. Perhaps "amount sold during the first 6 months" will be suggested as a numerical index of success. If the 6-month record does not really represent "selling success," the test has not been given a fair trial. Look at the weaknesses of the suggested criterion. Although "amount sold" appears to be a fair basis for judging success, some of the salespersons were assigned more desirable territory than others; the sales do not reflect ability alone. Suppose we control this by comparing the sales record with the average sales in past years in the same territory. We still have not allowed, for example, for poor crops in one region that make business bad. Another limitation is that sales alone may not be what is wanted from the firm's representative. High pressure selling may build up sales on a first trip, but overselling can eventually harm the firm's business. Note also that the study is limited to the wholesale hardware business. Additional predictive studies will be wanted if the test is considered for hiring sellers of insurance or machine tools. (Some psychologists believe that a test valid in one situation can be counted on to work in another. In Chapter 11 this belief in "validity generalization" is examined further.)

10. *Criticize each of the following criteria:*
    a. *Number of accidents a driver has per year as an index of driver safety.*
    b. *Number of accidents a driver has per thousand miles as an index of driver safety.*
11. *A study-habits inventory asks such questions as "Do you daydream when you should be studying?" What criterion would you use to determine how well the inventory evaluates study habits?*
12. *Criticize the procedure indicated in the following report of a study of success of students who graduated from a teachers' college:*

    The correlation between all thirty of the predictor variables and the school superintendents' ratings was only 0.17, but that between the variables and marks earned during four years of college was 0.79. Since college marks were predictable on the basis of the thirty variables and the superintendents' ratings were not, the marks were substituted for the ratings as a criterion of success.

13. *How long a time should elapse between test and criterion measurement when*
    a. *the U.S. Employment Service wishes to determine which job seekers have had enough experience to be referred to contractors who have vacancies for electricians?*
    b. *a pencil-paper test is proposed for identifying students entering junior high school who have emotional difficulties and should be singled out for counseling?*
14. *Which of the following describes concurrent validation, and which describes predictive validation? In which instances would some other time interval between measurement and collection of criterion data be more informative?*
    a. *A new employment test is found to correlate 0.9 with a clerical test that has been used for some time as a predictor of job success.*
    b. *A manual for a test of mental ability reports correlations with high school course marks assigned one month later.*
    c. *A correlation is calculated to determine how well a certain test distinguishes patients who have been diagnosed as schizophrenic from those diagnosed as brain-damaged.*
    d. *School records of delinquents and nondelinquents in high school are searched to learn what data recorded during the elementary grades correlate with present delinquent status.*

15. *Present employees take a test in a concurrent validation. Would their attitude toward the test be the same as the attitude of job applicants?*

Correlation and Regression Coefficients

Correlation coefficients and regression coefficients tell how closely two variables correspond. A correlation of a test score with a criterion measure (such as we saw in Tables 5.2 and 5.3) is called a validity coefficient. Other correlations answer questions such as the following: Do the ranks of these persons today agree with their ranks a year ago? Are people who become anxious over tests also more anxious in social situations? As neither measure is a "criterion," neither correlation is called a validity coefficient. I shall not explain how to compute coefficients; here the important topic is interpretation. This chapter only introduces the topic. More will be said in almost every later chapter.

Let us work through an artificial illustration. Ten salespersons took three tests when they came on the job; criterion information was obtained later (Table 5.5). The table records the criterion in units of $10,000; so 25 implies sales of $250,000.

Inspection tells something about validity. As raw scores are hard to scan, the data have been translated into ranks—not a necessary part of the analysis. Man E, the poorest salesman, ranked low on Test 1, high on Test 2, and middling on 3. Woman I, middling on the criterion, ranked high on Test 2 and low on Tests 1 and 3. Before reading ahead, study the ranks to form an impression of the validity of each test for the purpose of this firm.

If high test scores go with high criterion scores, the correlation coefficient is positive. For Test 1 and criterion C, the correlation r_{1C} is 0.77. The two variables correspond imperfectly; persons H and I in particular pulled the correlation down from 1.0.

Table 5.5. *Data on ten salespersons*

Salesperson	Sex	Test Score			Criterion Measure C	Criterion Rank	Test Rank		
		1	2	3			1	2	3
A	F	30	45	34	25	6	4	7	7
B	M	34	64	35	38	2	2	3	5½
C	M	32	32	35	30	4	3	9	5½
D	F	42	52	31	40	1	1	5	9
E	M	20	74	36	7	10	9	1	4
F	M	24	50	40	10	9	7	6	1
G	F	27	53	37	22	7	5	4	3
H	F	25	36	30	35	3	6	8	10
I	F	22	71	32	28	5	8	2	8
J	M	16	28	39	12	8	10	10	2

The correlation coefficient between Test 1 and Test 2 is defined as the average of $z_1 z_1$, the product of the z-scores for each person. You will recall from Chapter 4 that z scores have an s.d. of 1. This means that the sum of $z_1 z_1$ is 1, and a score correlates perfectly "with itself." It would be possible to get the correlation between any two variables by converting them to z scores, forming products, and averaging. Other procedures are more common in practice. Correlations in research reports are usually calculated to two decimal places; in this book, to avoid a false appearance of precision, I shall generally round to the nearest 0.05.

A coefficient close to zero says that the test does not predict the criterion. The value of -0.05 for r_{2c} implies that Test 2 does not predict. If high test scores go with low criterion scores, the coefficient is negative. Thus, if $r_{3c} = -0.75$, you may wonder how it happens that a low score on Test 3 goes with good job performance. This is most likely with a variable like time-to-completion, which assigns a large number to a poor performance.

We conclude that Tests 1 and 3 are good predictors for this firm; Test 2 is not. There is only a moderate relation between Tests 1 and 3: $r = 0.45$. As these two tests look at somewhat distinct aspects of performance, both together might be useful in picking employees.

It is always advisable to look at a plot, which can be prepared either by

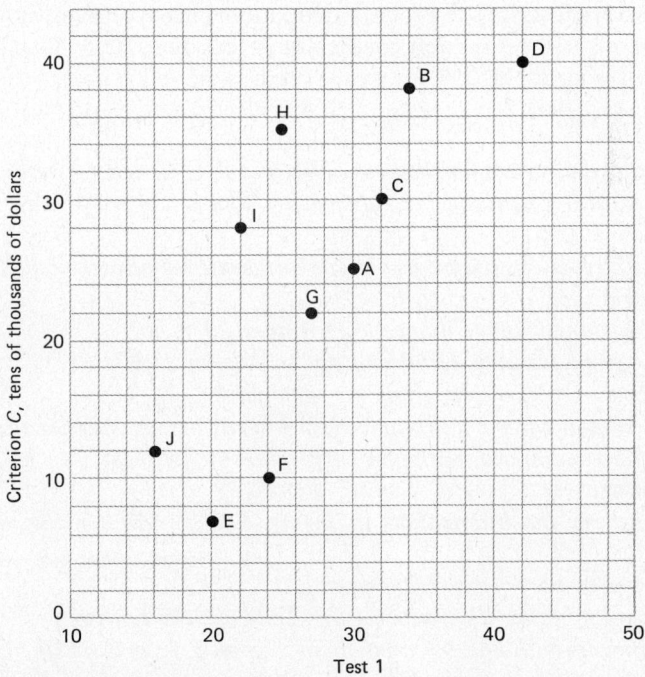

Figure 5.1. Scatter diagram for Test 1 and criterion C.

hand or by computer. This so-called "scatter diagram" adds meaning to the numerical index. Figure 5.1 plots scores 1 and C. The predictor is placed on the horizontal scale. Woman A is plotted above 30 on that scale and opposite 25 on the vertical scale. The trend is easily seen: as score 1 rises, C tends to rise. Even though the coefficient reaches 0.75, prediction is inaccurate; F and H are nearly equal on the test, but their sales differ by $25,000.

The artificially regular scatter diagrams in Figure 5.2 give a sense of the meaning of coefficients of various sizes. When $r = 1.0$, one variable is predicted perfectly from the other. With $r = 0.6$, prediction is approximate; in Figure 5.2, people who stand at 8 on X average near 7 on Y, but they spread from 3 to 9.

The trend line in each diagram is known as the Y-on-X regression. When there are many data points, we can slice up the X scale and find the average Y in each column. When plotted, these averages ordinarily fall along a straight line or a curve. The line that best fits the points is the regression line. The stronger the relation of outcome to test score, the steeper its slope. The higher the correlation, the closer the individual data points cling to the regression line. (A similar line, through the *row* averages, is the X-on-Y regression.)

The regression coefficient tells how steep the trend line is. The correlation coefficient is actually the regression coefficient calculated from standard scores; correlations are comparatively simple to report and read. The raw-score regression describes the relationship more clearly, however. For the data on salespersons, the regression coefficient is just over 1000. That is, expected sales go up by about $1000 for every additional score point on Test 1.

16. *Would the correlation between Test 1 and Criterion C be increased or decreased if J had sold twice as much? (Think it through with the aid of Figure 5.1.)*
17. *How large a correlation would you anticipate between the following pairs of variables?*
    a. *Age and annual income of men aged 20 to 50.*
    b. *Age in January 1980 and age in March 1990.*
    c. *Scores on two tests given the same week.*
    d. *Annual income and number of children among married urban men.*
    e. *Maximum and minimum temperature in Wichita, day by day for a year.*
18. *Transform the information in Figure 4.3 (p. 90) for the mechanical aptitude test into a scatter diagram. (The criterion has only two values, average-or-above, and below-average.)*
19. *Prepare a scatter diagram relating Test 3 to the criterion.*
20. *Beginning with the information in Figure 5.2, prepare an "experience table" similar to Table 4.1, corresponding to each of the following values of r: 0.9, 0.4, 0.2.*

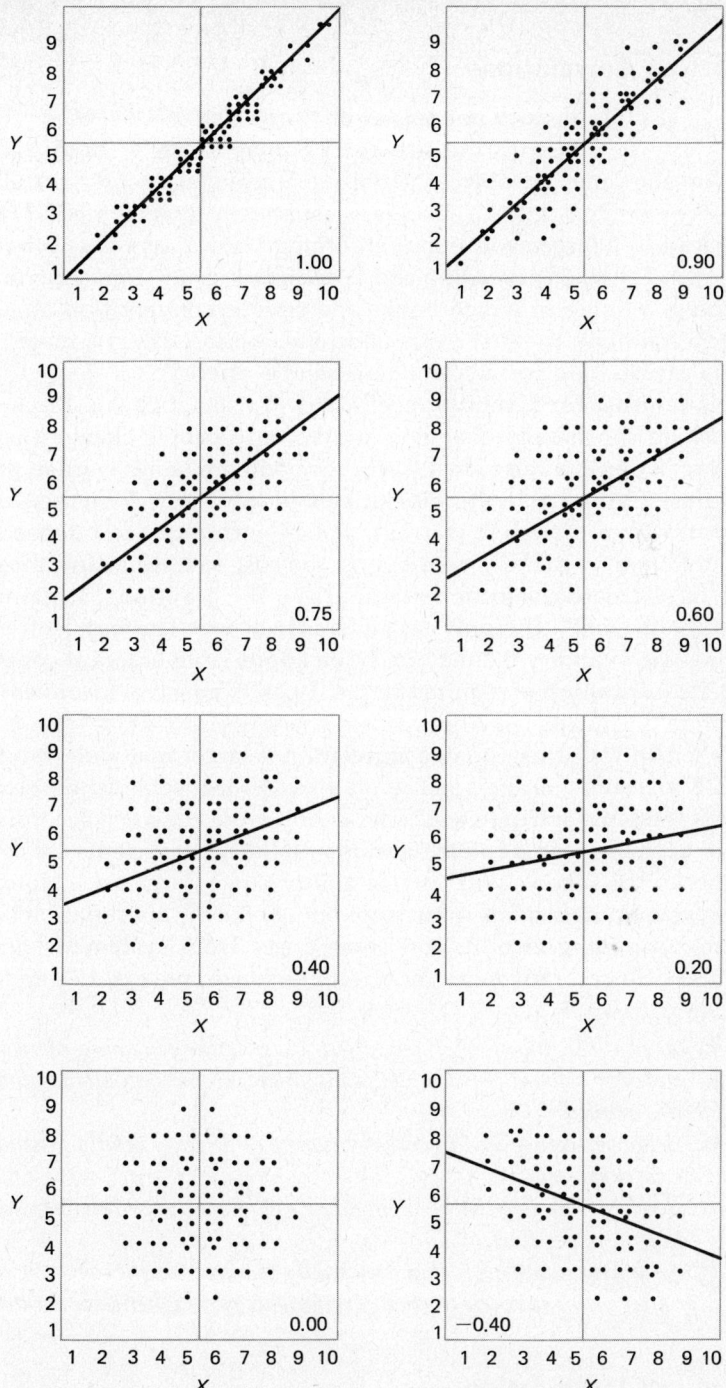

Figure 5.2. Scatter diagrams yielding large and small coefficients. The decimal in the corner is the correlation coefficient.

Interpreting Correlations

When r_{AB} is high, it does not follow that one variable "causes" the other. A may cause or influence the size of B, B may cause A, or A and B may depend on the same variable or variables. Vocabulary scores correlate with reading scores. Does good vocabulary cause one to read well? Does good reading lead to a larger vocabulary? Common sense says yes to both questions. Beyond that, both reading and vocabulary result from superior mental functioning, a home in which books and serious conversation abound, and superior teaching in the first years of school. Almost always, more than one plausible explanation for a correlation can be offered.

It is unusual for a validity coefficient to rise above 0.6. Because social situations are continually changing and because people change themselves, perfect prediction is a false ideal. Long ago, William James warned psychologists against trying to "write biographies in advance." Whether a validity coefficient is large enough to warrant prediction from the test depends on the benefit obtained by making predictions, the cost of testing, and the cost and validity of alternative selection methods. To the question, "What is a good validity coefficient?", the only sensible answer is, "The best you can get." Predicting with validity 0.2 may make an appreciable practical contribution. A greater contribution is required to justify an expensive, inconvenient procedure than an inexpensive one.

Other things being equal, a correlation is larger in a wide-range group. Figure 5.3 presents validity coefficients from 94 law schools whose students had taken the same aptitude test. The schools were classified according to the spread of aptitude scores among entrants. Validity coefficients are considerably higher in the schools with a wide ability range (large s.d.). Note also the variation among coefficients in each column. Some of this variation is statistical noise ("sampling error"), and some arises from systematic differences among the colleges. (For more on effects of range, see pp. 172 and 394.)

21. *What possible causal relations might underlie the following correlations?*
    a. *Between amount of education and annual income of adults (assume that r is positive).*
    b. *Between average intelligence of children and size of family (assume that r is negative).*
    c. *Between Sunday-school attendance and honesty of behavior (assume that r is positive).*
22. *Why, among law schools that are equally selective, might some schools find year after year that their predictive coefficients run higher than the average?*

Validity in Classification

Every classification implies a prediction of the form "Treatment A will work out better for this individual than Treatment B." Diagnosis is designed to

VALIDATION

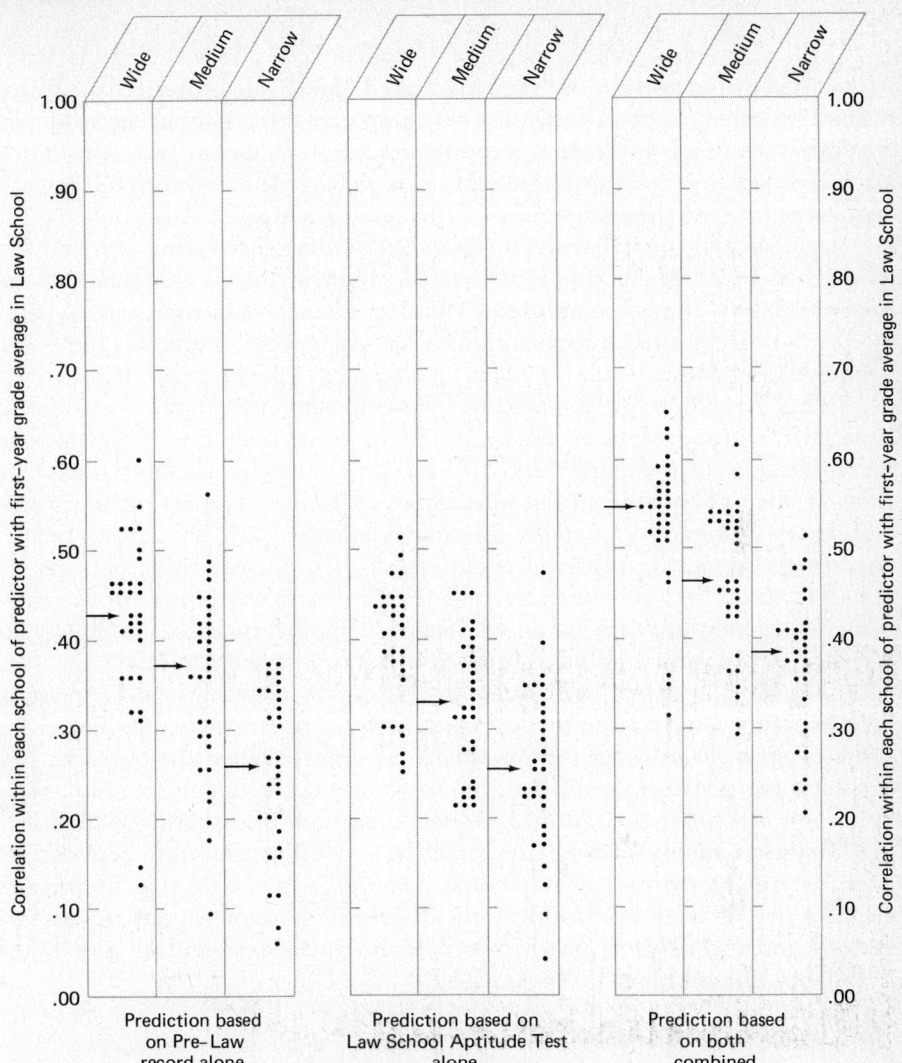

Figure 5.3. Validity coefficients in groups of wide and narrow range.
Source: Adapted from Schrader & Pitcher, 1969.

guide choice of therapeutic or educational treatment. Extending the word *treatment* slightly, we can speak of guidance into career lines and assignment to military specialties as choices of treatment. Sometimes the number of alternative treatments is large, as in working out an individualized educational plan. In effect, a prediction has to be made for each treatment, and the predictions have to be compared. For comparison, outcomes from the treatments must somehow be mapped onto a common criterion scale.

An example of predicting how circumstances affect success is Forehand's (1968) comparison of "group centered" and "rule centered" organizations. He sorted agencies into the two categories after asking, for example, whether friendship between a superior and a subordinate was considered normal or was avoided for the sake of impartiality. He asked the staff in each agency to rate the innovativeness of the agency manager. Also, he gave the managers several tests; Table 5.6 presents the more interesting correlations. (Names of variables are simplified here, and personality scores that showed negligible correlations are omitted.) With only 60 cases in each group, Forehand's data are limited; supporting findings come from Andrews (1967) and Schneider (1978).

The data show an interaction between personality and organization type. In the group-centered organizations, the managers rated highest tend to be intellectually superior and to be discontented when constrained by rules. In the rigid organizations, managers indifferent to others' feelings generate more change. Bright and autonomous persons, then, should be encouraged to go into group-centered organizations. Dull, conforming persons are expected to do no worse than average (by Forehand's criterion) in the rule-centered agency and are better off there. This information, obviously, is relevant to vocational guidance and to making job assignments.

Attempts to match individuals to treatments or settings call for a study of interaction. So do attempts to explain why a treatment works better for some persons (or in some settings) than for others. When the outcome-on-predictor regression slope differs from treatment to treatment, we speak of an *aptitude-treatment interaction.* Although questions about interaction are central to psychological theory and testing practice and although some provocative findings are summarized in this book, it is well to say here that findings to support use of tests in classification, diagnosis, placement, and so on, are limited and inconsistent. With regard to instruction, Cronbach and Snow (1981, pp. vii, 492) had this to say:

Table 5.6. *Rated innovativeness correlated with ability and personality measures*

Predictor	Group-centered Organizations	Rule-centered Organizations
General mental ability	0.45	0
Fluency of ideas	0.3	−0.15
Willingness to defer to others[a]	−0.4	−0.1
Preference for ordered, predictable situations[a]	−0.35	0
Desire to respond to others' feelings[a]	0.2	−0.35
Desire for close personal relationships[a]	0	−0.1

[a]Self-report, on the Edwards Personal Preference Schedule.
SOURCE: Forehand, 1968, p. 71.

No aptitude-treatment interactions are so well confirmed that they can be used directly as guides to instruction. . . . Aptitude-treatment interactions exist. To assert the opposite is to assert that whichever educational procedure is best for Johnny is best for everyone else in Johnny's school. Even the most commonplace adaptation of instruction, such as choosing different books for more and less capable readers of a given age, rests on an assumption of ATI that it seems foolish to challenge. It becomes clear that the problem of characterizing, understanding, and using . . . interactions poses the major challenge to educational and psychological science today.

Frederiksen *et al.* (1972) say almost the same thing in the context of industrial-organizational psychology, and the perplexities of personality research are exhibited by dozens of authors in Magnusson and Endler (1977) and Pervin and Lewis (1978).

To carry out adequate research is exceedingly difficult. Most studies like Forehand's try to make sense of relations in existing groups. A strict experiment with controlled assignment is required to produce directly interpretable results, and even experimental trials encounter many difficulties (Cronbach, 1982a). Here again, it is useful to describe an ideal design.

How might we validate a classification policy in a school? Suppose—to oversimplify what teachers do—that entering first-graders are sorted on the basis of Text X. Pupils whose scores imply "readiness" are started immediately on instruction in reading (Treatment A). The others are given developmental experiences and are started on actual reading only when the teacher considers them ready (Treatment B). In due time outcomes are assessed, and regression lines are determined. From a logical standpoint we would prefer to send equivalent groups into the two treatments, but it would be unethical to send excellent students into a "slow" treatment and vice versa. A sound compromise is to put low scorers into B and high scorers into A, but to divide those near the borderline strictly at random. (In the figure, dotted lines project the findings of such a study into the region where no observations were made.)

The school's assignment is justified if regressions take the form shown in panel i of Figure 5.4. This pattern of crossing regressions is called a *disordinal interaction*. (In this chart it appears that the trial borderline was set a bit low.)

When the regressions do not cross (panel ii of Fig. 5.4), the same treatment averages out best for children at all score levels. Such an *ordinal interaction* is of theoretical interest and can be practically important. Classification might be justified in some circumstances where the A regression is above the B regression at all levels of Test X. Examples:

- Treatment B for reading works better on some second criterion, such as tension among those who do poorly if introduced prematurely to reading.

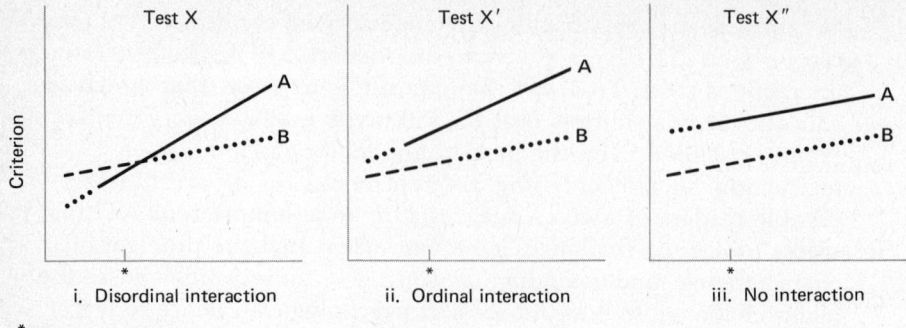

*Indicates trial borderline.

Figure 5.4. Possible findings in an experiment on pupil classification.

- Psychotherapeutic Treatment A is more expensive than B.
- Facilities for giving Treatment A are limited.

Demonstrating a test-criterion correlation is not enough to validate use of the test for classification. Test X" predicts outcome, yet it is useless for classification. No interaction appears in panel iii.

23. *"Figure 3.4, on test anxiety, describes an interaction."* Defend that statement.
24. *In Figure 1.4, the outcome variable is not displayed graphically. Sketch a* **three**-*dimensional figure to show the regression of outcome on aptitude. What predictor shows the strongest interaction (largest difference in regression slopes)?*
25. *Consider the hypothesis that the sex of the examiner interacts with the confidence of a child to affect the score on Block Design. Sketch panels like those in Figure 5.4 (with confidence as the horizontal axis and Block Design as the vertical axis and one line for each sex). What testing practice would be recommended if evidence on the question took the form of panel i? Panel ii? Panel iii?*
26. *In the* **Larry P. v. Riles** *decision, the judge ruled against the use of mental tests on the ground that no one had demonstrated the validity of low scores for placement in special classes. If a psychologist were to try to demonstrate criterion-related validity of such a test for special-class placement, how should the study be designed? (Two side remarks: Court opinions on pupil classification are divided at this time; see Bersoff, in Reynolds & Gutkin, 1982, or Sherman & Robinson, 1982, pp. 87–91. And the issues are too complex to be settled by purely statistical findings.)*

CONTENT VALIDATION: A CLOSER LOOK

Content validity is improved when the test is carefully planned. Making a sound plan requires insight into what the test is intended to measure.

Selection of Content

Ideally, the test developer defines the domain appropriately and represents it fairly in the test. The definition ought to cover the following:

> The appropriate range of tasks, stimuli, or situations.
> The kinds of response the observer or scorer is to count.
> The statement that tells the test taker what he is to do.

Altering any of these can change the test significantly. It is impossible to defend one definition of a variable as universally appropriate. In measuring reading for some purposes, one would confine the selections to text material; for other purposes, one would want the selections to range over fiction, newspapers, or instruction manuals or a combination of these. If the definition is made clear, the prospective user can decide whether the test aims at the target she has in mind.

The best guarantee of representativeness is to map out subdivisions of the domain and collect the desired number of items for each subdivision. In a reading test, for example, this prevents such faults as an overemphasis on content from economics or selection of a set of passages that is too easy.

To sample content from a clearly defined domain is a pleasing and logical ideal, but test construction is rarely so simple. Most often the test constructor has some general idea of the behavior to be observed but cannot give a neat definition. Can an investigator measuring sociability of preschool children catalog the situations in which sociable behavior arises? Can another investigator characterize unambiguously the whole set of human-relations problems a supervisor should be able to deal with? Can a third test developer truly define the domain of situations in which scientific reasoning is to be shown by a science student? Obviously not. Examining content validity, therefore, requires judging whether each item bears on what the tester wants to measure. Two further judgments are required: Did the test items overemphasize any subtopic? Did any feature of the test that was not part of the intended "content" have much effect on scores? (Examples are pictures that are hard to read, pressure for rapid work, and obscure directions.) The test *user* has to make these judgments though it is, of course, desirable for the test author to tell how the content was chosen. In the end, it is the user's intent that counts.

Content validity plays an important role in judging the soundness of a school examination. In general, the test should cover what some evaluating authority *wanted* the school to teach. Decision makers are likely to have different ideas as to what content is important. A test on, say, geography distributes its content over particular topics and skills. A teacher might be satisfied to judge its validity by comparing the test outline with the outline of the course he has been giving. The State Board of Education might have in mind a substantially different domain—maybe a broader one, maybe a more conventional one. The test that has a high degree of content validity in the eyes of the teacher will not be so satisfactory to the board and vice versa. One resolution of the difficulty is to prepare a broad test that covers what any of the parties regards as important and to report the achievement on each subset of the content separately.

A test that affects the fate of individuals nonetheless encounters objections—no matter how worthwhile the content—if the teacher did not devote time to that content. Reviewing a Florida examination required for high school graduation, a court approved the content as such, but refused to allow enforcement of the requirement until the state could prove that all the items were covered in each student's course of study (*Debra P.* v. *Turlington,* 644 F.2d. 397 [1981]). The court held that the diploma is a constitutional right of any student who has faithfully done the work set before him or her.

Task Format

The form of the task can be as important as the substance. Validity of a measure of factual knowledge suffers, for instance, if the person who knows a fact loses credit because of reading difficulties. The Navy Mechanical Knowledge Test contained four types of items: mechanical facts, tested verbally; mechanical facts, tested pictorially; electrical facts, tested verbally; and electrical facts, tested pictorially. Similar content produced lower correlations than similar form (Table 5.7). In other words, the form of the items largely

Table 5.7. *Correlations of tests similar in form or in content*

Tests similar in form	
Verbal tests: mechanical vs. electrical	0.8
Pictorial tests: mechanical vs. electrical	0.85
Tests similar in content	
Mechanical: verbal vs. pictorial	0.7
Electrical: verbal vs. pictorial	0.75
Tests different in form and content	
Mechanical verbal vs. electrical pictorial	0.65
Electrical verbal vs. mechanical pictorial	0.6

SOURCE: Conrad, 1944. All correlations are adjusted, to estimate the relations between perfectly reliable tests.

determined the score. Another study provides even stronger evidence that the verbal element in tests may be undesirable. Training of U.S. Navy gunners had been validly evaluated by scores made in operating the guns. As an economical substitute, verbal and pictorial tests were developed. Identical information was tested in the two forms, the same question being asked in words alone or by means of pictures supplemented by words. Questions dealt with parts of the gun, duties of the crew, appearance of tracers when the gun was properly aimed, and so on. The pictorial test had a correlation of 0.9 with instructors' marks based on gun operation whereas the validity of the verbal test was only 0.6. The verbal test was in large measure a reading test; it correlated 0.6 with a U.S. Navy reading test whereas the picture test correlated only 0.25 with reading (Training Aids Section, 1945).

Speed is relevant and important in tests of typing attainment or reading facility or arithmetic for cashiers. Speed is irrelevant when we wish to know how large a pupil's vocabulary is, how much science he knows, or how penetrating his reasoning can be.

Many popular testing techniques allow response styles to affect scores. A response style (or set) is a habit or a momentary attitude causing the subject to earn a different score from the one he would earn if the same items were presented in a different form. In true-false tests particularly, some people have the habit of saying, "True" when in doubt whereas others are characteristically suspicious and respond, "False" when uncertain. If the test includes a large proportion of true statements, the acquiescent student will earn a fairly good score even if his knowledge is limited. Other response styles include leaving items unanswered when in doubt (caution), sacrificing accuracy for speed, and answering essay questions in as few words as possible. Any style, carried to an extreme, is likely to reduce a person's score.

Perhaps the most general maxim to ensure content validity is this: *no irrelevant difficulty.* Reading is irrelevant to proficiency in gunnery. Reading of long sentences is irrelevant to the task of a messenger whereas reading everyday phrases is not. Wherever a task can be simplified without making it a false example of the performance that is of interest, it should be simplified.

Statistical Properties of Items

Some test constructors try to make items harder by requiring fine discriminations or by offering alternatives that fool the test taker who does not read very closely. They believe that a good test "spreads out people." A content-valid test, however, need not discriminate among persons, and sometimes it should not. A test for applicant messengers ought to rule out those who cannot read what messengers have to read, but above that level it is improper to give preference to those who rank highest in reading skill.

The test constructor can learn something by correlating the score on each item with the total test score. Thus, those who constructed Forms S and T of TMC tried 180 items (some new; some taken from older forms). These were given to high school juniors and seniors, and item scores were correlated with the total score. Only 136 items had correlations greater than 0.2, and the final forms were chosen from these items. Unidimensional scaling is sometimes used for this item analysis instead of correlation (p. 117)

Items with low correlations should not automatically be discarded. Statistical analysis spots questionable items, but some of these will survive thoughtful review and revision. The reviewer may spot a double negative, a too-plausible alternative answer, or the like. Such items should be rewritten. The flaws confuse able students and reduce validity.

Danger arises when many items dealing with the same topic are discarded. That could *reduce* content validity by changing the way test content is distributed over the original domain. In fact, the screening of TMC items eliminated almost all the items related to electricity.

An achievement test usually samples mixed content. Dropping unusual items "purifies" the test, but the instrument then no longer represents the intended universe. A person might master the verbal portions of chemistry and still be badly confused about the quantitative parts of the course (such as balancing equations). To drop the quantitative sections just because they correlate weakly with the total makes the test a false sample of the content. On the other hand, if a question correlates poorly with the total because it requires knowledge of a certain chemical compound that few students have read about, the item is probably inappropriate and can wisely be discarded.

27. *Skill in the use of library reference materials is to be measured at the end of a how-to-study course for first-year college students. Try to specify the domain of tasks from which the test should be drawn.*
28. *The Morse code consists of a short alphabet of characters. The receiver must respond to units made up of several characters in rapid succession; the most difficult part of the task may be to separate one letter from the next.*
    a. *Describe an appropriate test for a person learning to receive ordinary nonsecret communications in English.*
    b. *Describe an appropriate test for a person learning to receive encoded messages of the form* GFVG JHBI YGTA FBSJ. . . .
29. *A test is carefully balanced to cover the kinds of knowledge and skill in high school physics that the college physics course expects of entering students. A teacher finds that her emphasis is distributed quite differently. Is the test a proper basis for grading students in high school physics? For judging the adequacy of the high school course?*
30. *For what testing purposes does the dropping of electrical content reduce the validity of TMC?*
31. *A job candidate can be observed while directing a few workers in an assembly task. If the task and the standards for judging closely resemble those of the job, content validity could be claimed. It is argued, however, that content validation is insufficient because the persons hired will be trained, and poor performance at the time of application need not forecast*

poor performance after training. What do you think? (The matter is debated by Dreyer and Sackett, 1981, and Norton, 1981.)

MORE ON CONSTRUCT VALIDATION

Construct validation is a fluid, creative process. The test constructor or any subsequent investigator works to develop an interpretation, persuade others of its soundness, and revise it as inadequacies are recognized. The interpretation has scientific aspects, but it often embodies policies and suggests practical actions. This complexity means that validation cannot be reduced to rules, and no interpretation can be considered the final word, established for all time. This has been a source of frustration and confusion.

The committee that developed the first version of the APA *Standards* had to state what constitutes adequate validation. Predictive and content validation were not hard to describe. But how should the validity of a test "of hostility" be defended? The scores might come from everyday observation, role playing, picture interpretation, or a questionnaire. No matter which, analysis of content would not guarantee that higher scores consistently indicate greater hostility. Someone might propose to count aggressive acts to measure hostility. But clinicians believe that some persons are under stress just because of strong hostile impulses that they dare not release in behavior. A count of aggressive actions would miss those cases. To get at covert hostility, many clinicians propose highly indirect assessment procedures.

The validation process is like the one for scientific concepts and measures. A concept such as "mass" takes its meaning from scientific theory. The adequacy of a measure for mass is judged by whether the numbers it provides relate to other measurements as the theory says it should. When theory changes, a new measure may be needed; thus, Freud reoriented psychology when he produced evidence that absence of hostile behavior does not prove absence of hostile impulses.

An interpretation is to be supported by putting many pieces of evidence together. Positive results validate the measure and the construct simultaneously. Failure to confirm the claim leads to a search for a new measuring procedure *or* for a concept that fits the data better (Cronbach, in Thorndike, 1971; Cronbach & Meehl, 1955; Meehl, 1977; Messick, 1981a).

Creating a long-lived theory is an unreasonably lofty aspiration for present-day testers (J. Campbell, in Dunnette, 1976). Physical scientists needed centuries to shape concepts such as the atom and the force of gravity. The eternally patient refining process of pure science sets a standard that here-and-now studies of tests can only admire wistfully. Test interpreters employ a scientific logic but—like engineers and physicians—they have to do the best they can now with comparatively primitive theory.

Many programs of research have refined the theoretical understanding of particular abilities and traits (Maslow et al., 1980)—and, of course, such research was going on long before the process was given the special name of construct validation. On the other hand, some test developers attach the term to a mere listing of ill-digested evidence. Only self-critical efforts to firm up a line of argument deserve credit as steps toward validation.

Employers defending tests whose validity is challenged in court often have to rely on indirect reasoning. Whenever their evidence departs from the ideal plan of a direct criterion-oriented or content-oriented study, interpretation brings in concepts and theoretical statements.

The Equal Employment Opportunity Commission has been reluctant to accept indirect reasoning, apparently regarding it as a verbal smokescreen (Gorham, in Maslow et al., 1980; Novick, in Wigdor & Garner, II, 1982). Lawyers and psychologists are trying—with increasing success—to work out a style of indirect validation argument that courts find persuasive (Bersoff, in Glaser & Bond, 1981).

Inquiries Contributing to Explanation

TMC scores as an example. Table 5.8 illustrates the diversity of facts brought to bear in developing and supporting an explanation. These notes based on the TMC manuals are illustrative but by no means complete; a thorough study of mechanical comprehension would consider other reports in the research literature, including evidence from tests other than Bennett's. (Whether tests with a common name measure the same variable is always a pertinent question.)

What do we mean by "explaining" performance on TMC? Essentially, we mean being able to state what influences affect the score and what influences do not. To check whether TMC measures "mechanical intelligence," we would have to ask what is meant by that phrase. If we are told that mechanical intelligence is supposed to be an inborn ability to perform all tasks involving hardware, we can begin research. TMC correlates strongly with a pencil-and-paper test of reasoning with forms, but only weakly with dexterity tests. We are inclined, therefore, to interpret it as a measure of nonverbal problem solving rather than of manipulative skill.

It is hard to believe that the ability TMC measures is inborn. TMC pictures mechanical devices that did not exist 200 years ago and that persons in a non-Western village have never seen. The test taker has to recognize common industrial devices to earn a good score, so TMC is probably not suitable for selecting factory trainees in a developing country. Even in the United States, not everyone has equal familiarity with the devices pictured. The finding that males tend to surpass females—coupled with our knowledge of traditional sex roles—leads us to suspect that experience is important. The comparatively small advantage associated with study of physics suggests that practical experience counts, not grasp of theory.

Investigators want to know how strong each influence is. I once sus-

Table 5.8. *Kinds of evidence offered to TMC interpreters*

Procedure yielding evidence	Specimen evidence or suggested conclusion
Correlations with practical criteria	(See Tables 5.2 and 5.3.)
Correlations with tests of other variables	TMC correlates 0.6 with a test of spatial reasoning and less than 0.4 with a test of dexterity in handling tools.
Demographic correlates	Scores of high school males exceed those of females on average, the difference increasing with grade level.
Content analysis	Most common content of items: hydraulics, structures, gears, pulleys.
Relationship to subjects' experience	Persons who have studied physics score, on average, modestly higher than others.
Experiment with varied testing conditions	Having taken TMC previously gives a subject little or no advantage on a new form.

SOURCES: Manual for the Bennett Mechanical Comprehension Test, 1969, and Manual supplement, 1980.

pected that much of the TMC score depended on knowledge of specific principles (e.g., gears, levers), each of which enters several items. But I found that a person good on gear problems (for example) was likely to succeed on other items. So my concept of subtypes of mechanical-comprehension aptitude was unnecessary. In an evaluation of competence as a part of job training, on the other hand, conglomerate scores mean little. Gaps in specific knowledge must be located.

Before considering research procedures further, let me point a moral. We have just convinced ourselves that TMC does not measure the "mechanical intelligence" our informant offered as an interpretation. That person might say, "TMC is invalid"; we would be wiser to say, "The proposed interpretation is invalid, and we are not persuaded that your notion of 'mechanical intelligence' is a useful construct." Validity of test and validity of construct are inseparable. When a new test is considered for a well-accepted construct, the test is at risk more than the construct. Still, the evidence could compel revision of the construct. A particularly notable example is the abandonment of traditional ideas of "feeblemindedness."

Looking into rival hypotheses. One source of confusion about construct validation is the notion that the starting point has to be a "definition." How can psychologists claim to measure intelligence when they cannot define it? The eminent journalist Walter Lippmann (1923) made that critical comment when mental tests were first introduced, and it is echoed today. But the opposite question makes better sense. How can one reasonably define a construct until one has made many pertinent observations? Definitions evolve out of reflection on experience. Physical scientists were once content to think of "uranium" as a well-defined object of inquiry; discovering the difference between U-235 and U-238 rendered the old conception obsolete for some important purposes.

Research pits hypotheses against each other. Most focused inquiries are devised to help in deciding between respected rival explanations (Cook & Campbell, 1979; Glymour, in Maslow *et al.,* 1980). What the construct validator should look into depends on the current uncertainties about a test or construct.

The range of research techniques that might be pertinent has been suggested by Table 5.8. Here is a somewhat fuller list—still not exhaustive. To add concreteness I shall suggest how each technique might be brought to bear on TMC. (These possible investigations would not be given equal priority.)

- Inspecting items. Inspection alone rules out some explanations; thus, it is easily seen that arithmetic is unlikely to affect TMC scores.
- Internal correlations (as in my study of items based on different mechanical principles).
- Stability of scores. Is mechanical comprehension a lasting, vocationally significant aptitude? Yes and no; the correlation between ninth- and twelfth-grade scores of boys is about 0.7. Ranks are far from fixed, so case histories of persons who change would be instructive.
- Administering the test to individuals who "think aloud." Perhaps some people succeed by a quick perception of answers that others reach by painstaking logic; if so, a good score means different things in different persons. The character of errors would be noted. Errors that arise from impulsive response, for example, scarcely imply inability to comprehend machines.
- Varying test procedures experimentally. If it is suggested that having to interpret pictures creates irrelevant difficulty for some subjects, one could set up a "parallel" test in which the person sees the actual machines and responds to the same questions as in the pictorial form. If this change makes items less difficult, doubt is cast on the printed test. Laboratory experimentation can lead to penetrating explanations: analysis of the roles played by perception, memory, visualization of motion, and other processes.
- Trying to improve scores. We might try to instruct low-scoring ninth-graders so that they will reason well about mechanical devices, even devices not covered in the instruction. If we succeed, that would have practical value and would suggest how mechanical comprehension develops.

- Correlation with practical criteria.
- Correlation with other tests. If TMC correlates highly with a general mental test, it need not be interpreted in terms of a specialized aptitude.
- Studies of group differences. For example, at what age does TMC performance tend to level off?

To defend a proposition about what a test measures, one looks basically for two things. The first is *convergence* of indicators. To justify a trait label, one collects two or more kinds of data that are regarded as evidence that a person is high or low on the variable. If these indicators agree, despite surface dissimilarity, the proposed theoretical interpretation is supported. The fact that Block Design correlates with a verbal reasoning test tends to support the view that both tests measure some general intellectual ability. This "multimethod" principle must be satisfied by any scientific construct (Wimsatt, 1981).

Second, scores identified with supposedly distinct aptitudes or traits should not correlate too highly. A test said to measure "ability to reason with numbers" should not rank pupils in the same order as a test of sheer computation because the computation test cannot reasonably be interpreted as a reasoning test. The interpretation would also be challenged if the correlation with a test of verbal reasoning were very high; ability to reason "with numbers" would be an unnecessary concept. This principle of *divergence* of indicators keeps a science from becoming overloaded with many names for the same thing (Campbell & Fiske, 1959). Correlation is not the whole story. The students who are best at writing French might also be best at speaking French. Despite the positive correlation, these students might communicate well to French people when writing and very badly when speaking. So having both tests makes sense.

These and other aspects of construct validation will become clearer in later chapters. On convergence and divergence, see particularly pages 256 and 312.

32. *Why would it be valuable to find out "what a test of pharmacy aptitude measures" if we already know that it predicts success in pharmacy school?*

33. *Kohs (1923, pp. 168 ff.) wished to argue that the Block Design test measured "intelligence," defined as "ability to analyze and synthesize." He then offered the following types of evidence (plus others) for his claim. How does each of these bear on construct validity? (The Stanford-Binet test was at that time regarded as the best available measure of "intelligence" but was thought possibly to depend too heavily on verbal ability and school training.)*
   a. *Logical analysis of the mental processes required by the items.*
   b. *Increase in average score with each year of age.*

    c. *Correlations as follows:*

Binet score with age	0.8
BD score with age	0.65
BD score with Binet score	0.8

    d. *Correlations:*

Binet score with teachers' estimates of intelligence	0.45
BD score with teachers' estimates of intelligence	0.25

    e. *Correlations:*

Binet score with vocabulary	0.9
BD score with vocabulary	0.8

    f. *Correlations between successive trials:*

On Binet	0.91
On BD	0.84

34. *For a test of computation given with a time limit, one significant aspect of interpretation is how "speeded" the test is. What would be learned from each of these studies?*
    a. *After the regular time expires, students continue work for 10 more minutes, using a different color of pencil. The changes in score are tabulated.*
    b. *Forms 1 and 2 are given with the regular time limit; double that time is allowed for Form 3. The investigator compares r_{13} with r_{12}.*
    c. *Having given Forms 1 and 3 described in* b, *the investigator waits for a measure* c *of success in bookkeeping and compares r_{3c} with r_{1c}.*

35. *The attempt to show that there is no irrelevant difficulty in a test amounts to a check on "rival hypotheses." Defend this statement.*

VALIDATION AS PERSUASIVE ARGUMENT

An interpretation or recommendation based on a test score requires a persuasive defense. Within an organization, one member may be persuaded that the test should be relied on. A second member, equally qualified but weighing up the risks and values differently, will prefer to rely on non-test information. The two have to argue it out. In validation, the bottom line is the collective judgment of a forum of critical users (House, 1980).

    In the defense of an inference from a score, many sentences are required. Some of these sentences are value judgments, some are appeals to common sense or prior evidence, and some are logical or legal premises. If the relevant audience finds the sentences plausible and the chain of argument coherent, it accepts the conclusion. A critic, replacing a sentence with a plausible alternative, can reach a contrary conclusion. When discussion is confined within the profession, it is fellow experts whom the interpreter must persuade. Other interpretations reach a public forum; the psychologist's view is adopted only if nonspecialistsfindherargumentmorereasonablethancompetingarguments.

Consider one of the simplest examples from early in the chapter. Students enter a law school, and their subsequent grades are crosstabulated against test scores to form an experience table. When used for prediction, the experience table is reinterpreted as an expectancy table. Asked to defend the extension, you assert that nothing much in the situation is changing from year to year. Your argument becomes more impressive when you describe next year's applicant pool, faculty, and curriculum. The example hints at what it means to defend an interpretation by combining sentences.

With student motivation, grading standards, and instructional styles all changing, it would be foolish to assert that test-criterion relations never change (Rubin & Stroud, 1977). In law schools, as a matter of fact, the validity of undergraduate grades as a predictor declined by nearly 0.1 between the 1960s and the early 1970s. (This is reported by Schrader, in Law School Admission Council, 1977, p. 530; in this same time span the validity of LSAT actually rose a bit.) Distraction of undergraduates from study during the years of student protest is a possible explanation; grade inflation may also have affected the relation.

The person investigating a test concentrates on refuting the counter-hypotheses a critic could make plausible. The job of validation is not to support an interpretation, but to find out what might be wrong with it. A proposition deserves some degree of trust only after it has survived serious challenge. In the law-school data, for example, it is important to check whether what has been true of applicants in general is true of the mature women who are being attracted to law schools in increasing numbers. A proposal to apply the test in a new site, before data are collected there, requires close comparison of the new situation with the one studied. Lacking that, only those who think all law schools are alike should believe the validity claim. And so on.

A validity coefficient supports an argument from only one corner (Figure 5.5). Other reports are needed, to answer challenges such as these:

- What justifies *this* criterion? What biases does it have?
- Does a steep regression imply that the ability measured is necessary for the course of study? Or could instructors adapt so as to make the course easier for the low scorers? High predictive validity implies bad instruction, says the egalitarian critic.
- Among the applicants who meet a reasonable standard, all of whom will probably be adequate students, what justifies creaming off the ones who scored highest? (Lerner, 1978).
- Present selection practices concentrate high scorers in prestige schools. Is this better for the nation than some mechanism that would distribute qualified law students more evenly over schools?

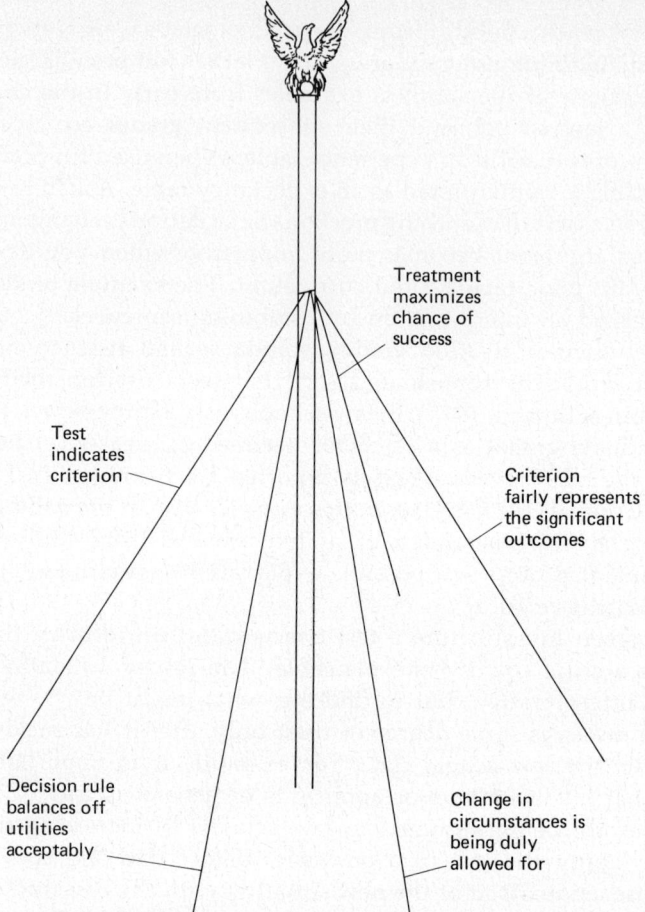

Figure 5.5. Considerations supporting validity argument for a selection program.
Source: This figure appeared in Cronbach, 1980b, and is reproduced (as adapted) by permission of Jossey-Bass, Inc.

The whole selection system is to be justified, not the test alone (Cronbach, 1980a). Empirical propositions enter the defense of the criterion, of the instruction or job requirements, and of the decision procedure, but values and prior beliefs within the audience determine what is judged reasonable.

An argument focusing on test content is likewise subject to challenges. Proof that the test samples a stated domain properly is not a complete argument. The defense must be prepared to show that the domain is relevant. A good example is the scrutiny a court gave a test for fire fighters (*Vulcan Society* v. *Commissioners*) 6 FEP 1045 [1973]). Many candidates who would otherwise have been eligible were blocked by the few arithmetic items in the

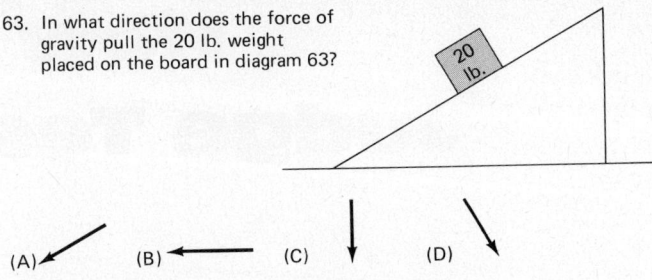

Figure 5.6. Item from a test for fire fighters.
Source: This figure appeared in Cronbach, 1980b, and is reproduced (as adapted) by permission of Jossey-Bass, Inc.

test. The court asked how critical those items were to the fire fighter's work. Not very, was its answer. Certain physics items the court scorned, not caring whether they measured what the tester intended. The judge had this to say about the item pictured in Figure 5.6: "A high school physics student would know the correct answer is (c), but the wrong answer (A) might be more useful for a fireman on the job." About another item he said: [W]hile it may be of some value for a fireman to know that 'A ball rolling along level ground will slow down and come to a stop,' we cannot appreciate the importance of his knowing whether the force that accomplishes this is called velocity, momentum, friction or equilibrium."

Whereas a test user's argument is specific to her own recommendations, a test developer is expected to lay out evidence and argument that will help the entire profession make sense of the test scores. Diverse questions come up. Users will want to know about the processes required for successful test performance, about the relation of this score to traits that are better understood, about the background factors associated with good and poor scores, and so on. Such information helps them to recognize what alternative interpretations of scores are plausible wherever they use the test. The test developer, not knowing the tester's particular subjects and local situation, cannot tell the tester what to think. The developer simply records experience with the test and brings out ideas the interpreter should consider. (Also, she shows that certain interpretations that might come to mind can be rejected in the light of that evidence.)

6
How to Judge Tests

Before discussing how to reach an integrated judgment concerning the suitability of a test, I take up one more facet of technical quality: accuracy of measurement.

CONCEPTIONS OF ERROR OF MEASUREMENT

In a 3-minute work sample, Mike types 162 words, or 54 words per minute; how well does this score represent Mike's skill? Suppose the teacher requires typing at 50 WPM before a student takes up shorthand. Is Mike truly above this level? Mike scored 45 WPM last week. Does today's score of 54 show that he has changed his technique for the better? Or is the change a chance fluctuation?

No single observation fully represents the person. To know how trustworthy a procedure is, we examine the consistency among measurements. There are many reasons for inconsistency. Attention and effort change from moment to moment. Over longer periods, score changes come from physical growth, learning, changes in health, and personality change. If we employ fresh test items for each measurement, another type of variation is introduced. The person who is lucky on one trial, finding items that are easy for him, will encounter unfamiliar items on some other trial and earn a lower score. To these factors must be added the unaccountable "chance" effects.

Decisions should not be appreciably influenced by temporary variations in performance or by the tester's choice of questions. An erroneous, favorable decision—to terminate therapy, for example—may be irreversible and damaging. An erroneous, unfavorable decision is unjust, disrupts the person's morale, and perhaps retards his development. Some purposes of testing demand greater accuracy than others: a Friday morning quiz need not be as accurate as a final examination.

True-Score Theory

As used in classical test theory, the term *error* refers to unwanted variation. The score the person earns on a particular testing, the *observed score,* differs from the thorough measurement the tester would prefer to base conclusions on. That ideal error-free measurement is traditionally called the *true score.* The difference between observed score and true score is the error of measurement. Errors can be positive or negative, and the theory assumes that over many trials they average out to zero for each person. Occasional lapses bring the observed score below the true score. An atypical success (luck? alertness? getting all the moves together?) can produce an observed score greater than the true level.

The "true" weight of a package being mailed—to use a homely example of true-score theory—is thought of as the average of the weights that would be recorded if a large number of postal clerks were to weigh the package, each using the regular postal scales where she works. Suppose that this average would turn out to be 732 grams. When Gloria Barnes reads the weight as 746 g., the error is $+14$ g. This error results from Barnes's carelessness, from a poorly adjusted postal scale, or perhaps from both.

The standard error. An inspector of postal measurements could collect evidence on errors by handing in the same package at many post offices. The many measures have a distribution; and, as with any score distribution, the mean, the variance, and the standard deviation can be calculated (pp. 98f.). In this example, the mean of the weights approximates the true score for the package. The sample s.d. approximates the *standard error of measurement* (s.e.m.) for the package. The square of the s.e.m. is called the *error variance.* A large s.e.m. implies inaccurate measurement.

Subtleties remain to be considered.

- Possibly postal clerks are especially careful when weighing packages for a businesslike customer. If the inspector herself hands in the

package every time, the inconsistency from customer to customer will not be detected.
- Possibly clerks make more errors when closing time approaches or during a rush hour. The inspector, then, ought to schedule weighings at various hours.
- Possibly inconsistencies are larger with certain types of packages. (Large ones? Clumsily wrapped ones?)
- Possibly most clerks tend to make a certain kind of error. For example, they may tend to report a borderline reading as the higher of the values it falls between. If so, the postal service takes in a bit more money than it should over the long run. The variance will not reflect this kind of consistent error. "True score" as defined in test theory is not the same as "true weight" in the engineer's sense.
- Do the errors come mostly from human error or machine error? The size of the s.e.m. does not tell what corrective approach to take.

Additional difficulties come up in psychological testing. Testing the same person many times is rarely practicable, and if it were attempted, the increase in familiarity would change what is measured. The most elementary solution is to test each person twice and subtract the smaller score from the larger one. When the s.e.m. is large, differences between the two errors tend to be large for many persons. We shall later look at formulas for estimating an s.e.m. from such data.

The reliability coefficient. The postal inspector does not ask whether clerks *rank* packages consistently. In contrast, testers' interpretations often compare people to each other or to a group average. To summarize the consistency of comparisons, it is usual to calculate a reliability coefficient.

When errors are considered to be random, this formula holds: Variance of true scores plus variance of errors equals variance of observed scores.

True-score variance = Observed-score variance − Error variance

We obtain the variance of observed scores of a group of persons and subtract the estimated error variance. That estimates the true-score variance. The reliability coefficient is this ratio:

$$r_{XX'} = \frac{\text{True-score variance}}{\text{Observed-score variance}}$$

The coefficient reaches 1.00 when all the reported score differences correspond to true differences among persons. If there is as much error as true information in the scores, the coefficient is 0.50. The symbol $r_{XX'}$ is traditional because the reliability coefficient equals the correlation of one measure X with a similar measure X'.

The coefficient and the s.e.m. are related, but they carry distinct messages. Suppose that the error variance of a test is 25. That tells how widely measures for any person are likely to spread. The s.e.m. is 5, and by the normal-distribution rule two-thirds of the cases will have errors between -5 and $+5$. If the group has a wide range of true scores, the coefficient will be large. Thus, if the true-score variance is 400 (s.d. = 20), the coefficient is above 0.95. But if the true-score variance is 25, the coefficient is only 0.50. The differences among persons are then too small for this test to rank people accurately. The fact that the s.e.m. does not change radically from group to group makes it more useful than the coefficient for most purposes.

1. *An employment interviewer asks, "How many jobs have you held since you left high school?" If we consider the response as an observed score, what is meant by "error of measurement" and "true score" in this case?*
2. *In speaking about hearing tests for children, a writer says: "Physical and psychological changes from day to day may make tests at two sittings less valid than a complete test at one sitting. We find that we get worse results on cloudy days than on sunny days."*
   In what sense is the word valid *used? Can you defend the contrary statement that scores at two sittings would be more valid than a complete test at one sitting?*
3. *In domain-referenced interpretation, why is the s.e.m. more relevant than the reliability coefficient?*

Generalizability Theory

The theory just summarized is the basis for most reports on error found in test manuals. Other procedures, more flexible and with a different terminology, are prominent in research, particularly when everyday behavior is observed. Analysis of error components by means of "generalizability (G) theory" tells more about a measuring procedure than the traditional analysis (Cronbach *et al.*, 1972).

The psychologist or educator setting out to measure a variable almost always has a domain in mind—a set of possible observations, any one of which samples the behavior that interests her. We say that she intends to generalize from a sample of behavior to the *domain* or *universe.* (The profession uses both terms.) Specifically, she generalizes from the score on the sample to the average over all the observations that could be made on the domain. If the average speed of *all* Mike's typing during May is the number she would like to know, a calculation made after observing all his typing would give the *universe score.*

Obviously, the universe score is like a true score. What is the difference? True-score theory speaks as if error variance were all of a kind and as if a person had one true score. G theory recognizes that there are several kinds of errors and alternative universes of generalization. The choice of universe depends on the purpose of the measurement as I now illustrate.

At 10:10 A.M. to 10:13 A.M. on May 5, Ms. Brown asked Mike to type a passage from a news report on the United Nations; the paper was scored by Alice Gates, Ms. Brown's student helper. No one was especially interested in how well Mike could type at 10:10; a measure at any other hour of the day would have been equally relevant. Nor did anyone wish to measure him on this news report; any similarly difficult selection would serve. Ms. Brown could accept a different tester and a different scorer. There are at least five distinguishable influences on Mike's score: tester, day, time within the day, passage typed, and scorer.

On some days Mike feels livelier. Some passages are easier for him than others, because he finds some words easier to spell and some sentences easier to carry in mind. Probably tester and scorer effects are small, but they should not be forgotten. Each of these variations in experimental conditions is a *source of variance,* because if Mike were retested under a new condition, his score would change.

Only after the universe is defined can we say which sources of variance count as "error." If Ms. Brown intends to plot day-by-day records to see which students have stabilized their skills, the universe for the May 5 observation is limited to scores on that day. Mike has up days and down days; that is a fact Ms. Brown wants the chart to represent, not "error of observation." When the test is used to decide whether Mike is proficient enough to take up shorthand, Ms. Brown wants to know Mike's typical level at this period in his development. The relevant universe extends over several weeks. Today's "up"—a departure from the average over that universe—becomes a source of error.

As a second example, consider ratings a preschool child receives on friendliness. An observer is to rate each child after observing him for 5 minutes in each of three situations: in the sandbox, on playground equipment, and at the juice break. The most evident sources of variation are:

- Observer. Some raters are generous; some, not. Some are especially generous in rating cute redheads; some, in rating children belonging to racial minorities. Observers have different concepts of "friendly" behavior, so their reports on the same event are likely to differ.
- Situation. The three situations by no means exhaust the events of the preschool day. Perhaps a certain child would be less friendly to his peers if observed in a competitive game or in a setting in which there is an adult to play up to.
- Occasion. Even in a defined situation such as the juice break, behavior varies from day to day as weather, companions and objects present, and the child's mood all change. An investigator trying to assess effects of day care would want to generalize broadly—over occasions, situations, and observers.

G theory clarifies results from classical reliability formulas by pointedly asking, "What does this procedure count as error?" G studies also help in designing measuring procedures. When we sample typing performance repeatedly, scores vary. Selections are not equally difficult, and the individual's efficiency fluctuates. One passage on one day is a tiny sample. To obtain a more accurate score, we might have the person take three passages on the same day. Or we might have each passage typed on a different day. Both observations are "three times as long" as the one-trial test, but they are not equally good bases for estimating the universe score over passages and days. The first plan samples passages three times; days, only once. Three-passages-on-three-days samples *each* source of error three times—a better basis for the intended generalization. G studies enable one to estimate how greatly scores are affected by each such change. (One application of this thinking appears at p. 532.)

Generalizability studies contribute to construct validation by showing which sources of variance are large. We find (let us say) that the extent to which a child engages in cooperative play depends on which companions are available. This finding discourages the concept of "cooperativeness" as a trait within the child's skin. We have to shift to a construct that characterizes the pair of children.

4. *Could the typewriter used for the test affect Mike's score? Can you think of further sources of variance affecting the typing test?*
5. *What sources might produce variation among several Block Design tests given to a person?*
6. *A teacher's rapport with pupils is judged by asking pupils to respond to a number of questions, such as, "Does your teacher give fair marks?" The most evident sources of variation are the questions (because other similar questions could be asked), the pupils, and the occasion. For what type of decision or investigation would one define the universe to include*
   a. *all possible pupils and questions, with observations limited to this particular semester?*
   b. *all similar questions, but only these particular pupils at this particular time?*
7. *Which sources of variance are to be regarded as "error" when a questionnaire regarding emotional problems is used for this purpose?*
   a. *To select high school pupils with whom the counselor should have an early conference.*
   b. *To identify recruits likely to break down in service.*
8. *Criteria as well as tests have error of measurement. What would be unwanted sources of variance—errors of observation—in first-year grade-point averages at a particular college? (What meaning or meanings could be given to the concept of "true grade average"?)*

ESTIMATING HOW LARGE ERRORS ARE

Simple Correlational Studies

An elementary procedure was sketched a few pages back: obtain the difference between two measures on each person; then work out the s.e.m. One efficient way to reach this result is to calculate the correlation between the two sets of scores; this is a reliability coefficient if the tests are equivalent. Equivalent ("parallel") forms have equal observed-score variances in a large group of persons. Multiplying that variance by the coefficient estimates the true-score variance as can be seen from the formula for $r_{XX'}$. Subtracting true-score variance from observed-score variance estimates the error variance; its square root is the s.e.m.

The two measurements can be collected in various ways, and different types of data answer different questions. This is illustrated here with made-up (but realistic) numbers for ninth-graders taking the TMC. To simplify, assume that the observed variance is exactly the same in every study. Here are three possible correlational studies:

1. Two forms given on the *same day*. Form S given in the morning correlates 0.92 with Form T given in the afternoon. The observed-score variance is 116.6 (s.d. = 10.8). The true-score variance is 0.92 × 116.6, or 107.2. When we subtract, the error variance is 9.3. Or, we might say, 8 percent of observed variance (1 − 0.92) is error variance; 0.08 × 116.6 = 9.3. Taking the square root, s.e.m. = 3.1.
2. Two forms given *4 weeks apart*. With 4 weeks separating the forms, the correlation drops to 0.89. Taking 11 percent of 116.6 gives the error variance as approximately 12; s.e.m. = 3.5.
3. Two forms given *1 year apart*. Greater time lapse allows more change in standings, and the correlation drops to 0.79. The error variance and s.e.m. are approximately 25 and 5, respectively.

The three studies give reliability coefficients with different meanings. To speak of "the" reliability of a test glosses over fundamentals. The first study tells about the consistency among measurements on the same day, a narrow universe. The second study samples from a broader period, but one during which the student's development remains essentially constant. The third study moves to a broader question: Will we reach the same conclusions about students' mechanical aptitude if we test in grade 9 as we will if we wait a year?

Think through the following question. Which of the following sources would Study 1 count as error variance? Study 2? Study 3?

a. Some testers give directions clearly and fully; some do not. The tester in this school changes from one year to the next.
b. A student's alertness is affected by health and anxiety.
c. The test forms are not (let us suppose) equally difficult. Scores on the second form tend to run 3 points higher for everyone.
d. One form (let us suppose) contains several items that require numerical reasoning; the other does not.

Influence d causes some persons to do better on one form than the other. In Study 1, d adds to the s.e.m., but a, b, and c do not. The tester is constant; health and mood ought not to change from morning to afternoon. Increasing everyone's score by 3 points does not affect the correlation.

Among the sources listed, b and d enter the error variance for Study 2.

In Study 3, a, b, and d count in the error variance. Differences in the students' development are a further large source of inconsistency in Study 3.

To study variation within a single day may seem trivial, but fine-grain studies of behavior look at day-to-day change. (Recall Zuckerman's study of state anxiety; p. 71.) Also, the 1-day study answers the important question, Do we have a sufficient sample of items? If two forms on the same day disagree badly, the test is inadequate.

In all the studies, the error variance includes moment-to-moment fluctuation of efficiency and luck. An immediate repetition of, say, a tennis serve will not produce the identical result though the performer has not changed in any identifiable way. Another unsystematic influence is borderline decisions of the scorer.

In a correlational study, the investigator makes two (or more) observations per person and examines how well they agree. Certain conditions vary from one observation to the next; their influence enters the reported error variance. Some other condition is held constant from one observation to the next; the analysis treats its effect on the standing of individuals as part of universe-score variance. This is incorrect unless the universe definition calls for holding that condition constant. An experiment that holds too much constant overestimates the universe-score variance, overestimates the coefficient, and underestimates the error of measurement.

If scores are obtained by having two judges score every test paper, the agreement of the scores evaluates only one source of error: that coming from the observer. The coefficient tells how well we can generalize from one scoring to the score a universe of judges would assign to that same performance. It tells, not how well we have sampled the person's behavior, but how well we have sampled judgments. The reader of a study must ask the pointed question: Are there significant sources of error that this estimate of error fails to count? When the answer is yes, he will not know how much to allow for that further source of error, but he will proceed with extra caution.

Some especially important points made in this section will be reviewed at page 172 after procedures have been examined more fully. This book rarely gives formulas or notes on computation because that is the job of texts on statistics. Some detailed information does appear in this chapter because texts on statistics usually say little about estimation of measurement error.

9. *Interpret these facts about a test measuring "liberality" of political attitudes.*

   Coefficient from two forms taken at same sitting   0.90
   Coefficient from two forms, one year apart   0.60
   Coefficient from test, and retest with same form one year later   0.65

10. *A tester presents a set of questions such as, "Do you make friends easily?" with the response alternatives* YES/NO/CANNOT SAY. *If there were two forms, each of the correlational studies described earlier could be carried out. What would contribute to error variance in each study? (Is there any counterpart of "luck" in this kind of test?)*

11. *Some studies of error examine whether two procedures for sampling behavior agree (equivalence). Other studies examine whether behavior is consistent over time (stability). Considering observations of stammering, describe a study that would primarily bring out information on equivalence and another that would primarily check on stability.*

Estimation from a Two-Way Score Table

Analysis of variance of score tables produces numbers called mean squares. These are resolved into "components of variance," which contain more information than the correlation does when the measures are not equivalent. Here only some simple, common calculations are described; for a fuller introduction to analysis of score tables, see Brennan and Kane (1979). Analysis of variance is ordinarily performed with the aid of a computer. For the theory and formulas that produce the mean squares to be discussed here, the reader should consult a text on elementary statistics.

We start with k scores for N persons. If 25 persons type five passages, each passage on a different day, N is 25 and k is 5. The observed scores can be laid out as in Table 6.1. The universe consists of selections like these and of occasions within a certain time span. In such a table it is possible to calculate error variances row by row or to correlate every pair of columns. But a statistical procedure derives three mean squares from Table 6.1, and the formulas shown in the table convert these into components of variance. The components have some meaning as they stand, and additional meaning when taken in combination.

The component for persons, 9.4, estimates the universe-score variance. The square root, approximately 3.1, estimates the s.d. for universe scores. The mean of the five column means, 51.9, estimates the mean universe score. Again applying the normal distribution rule of thumb, two-thirds of the group under study have universe scores in the range 48.8 to 55.

Table 6.1. *Analysis for five observations of typing speed*

Pupil (p)	Observed Scores X_{pi}				
	A	B	C	D	E
Mike	54	57	51	50	51
Joe	52	55	56	53	52
Carlos	50	46	49	52	50
Bruce	52	51	52	43	54
Newt	53	53	43	47	50
....					
....					
....					
Averages	52.2	53.0	51.4	51.2	51.7

Number of persons $\qquad N = 25$
Number of conditions $\qquad k = 5$

From analysis of variance:

MSp : Mean square for rows (persons) $\quad = 50$
MSi : Mean square for columns (conditions) $\quad = 10$
MSr : Mean square for residual $\quad = 3$

Estimated variance of person effects (universe scores):

$(MSp - MSr)/k = (50-3)/5 \quad = 9.40 \qquad$ [Component for persons]

Estimated variance of condition effects:

$(MSi - MSr)/N = (10-3)/25 = 0.28 \qquad$ [Component for conditions]

Estimated residual variance:

$MSr \qquad \qquad \qquad \qquad = 3.00 \qquad$ [Residual component]

The component for conditions tells how much group averages fluctuate from one selection-and-day to another. In Table 6.1 this component is small. Forms of a professionally developed ability test are likely to show a small component for conditions, as these data do. Condition variance can be large in field observations; the nurses' state-anxiety scores (p. 71) illustrate this.

The residual component (which is ordinarily large) includes all manner of unsystematic effects: Joe encountered a word he finds hard to spell several times in Selection E; Newt, between Tests B and C, lost several days of practice on account of illness; Bruce slipped into typing *h-t-e* several times on Test D. The residual component estimates the error variance that affects individual differences when everyone is observed under each condition. The corresponding s.e.m. is $\sqrt{3.00} = 1.7$.

Error variance plus true-score variance give observed-score variance: 3.0 + 9.4 = 12.4. The reliability coefficient is 9.4/12.4, or 0.76, according to the formula given earlier. This estimates the correlation to be expected if we choose two selection-and-day combinations at random, test everyone, and correlate the scores.

Return to the question. Is Mike ready to take up shorthand? This decision depends on whether his true score is above 50, not on his ranking. Because the difficulty of the selection he types affects his score, the component for conditions adds into the error. The error variance for *this* use of the test is 0.28 plus 3.00; the corresponding s.e.m. is $\sqrt{3.28} = 1.8$. The added component hardly changed the s.e.m. When it is large, applying the same standard to measures collected under different conditions is unfair. If the teacher had only the first score of 54, the conclusion would be that Mike has met the standard. He is more than 2 s.e.m. above 50. His other scores of course strengthen the conclusion.

Table 6.1 is, obviously, a two-way layout (persons "crossed with" selections). Designs can collect data to fill a three-way layout or even a more complex one. The appropriate design and computation can tease apart variances associated with observers, days, situations, and playmates in children's social interaction, for example (Cronbach *et al.*, 1972). If behavior varies from playmate to playmate, the investigator will plan in the future to collect data with several playmates (in turn) for each child. If, on the contrary, that component of variation is small, playmates can be regarded as interchangeable. One will get an adequate reading by observing the child with any available playmate.

12. *Suppose that students type the same passage every day for 5 days. The analysis could proceed as in Table 6.1. Would the findings be essentially the same as in the table? What questions would the findings answer?*
13. *Suppose that, if samples from various sections of the newspaper are used, typing tests show a large component for conditions. The tester might fix on one condition or combine conditions or narrow the universe. Just how would the tester do each of these? And for what purpose, if any, would you recommend each option?*
14. *To investigate accuracy of scoring of a test administered individually, three observers are asked to watch the testing through a one-way window, to keep independent records, and determine the test score. In this way, three scores are obtained for each of 20 children. What information is represented in each of the following?*
    a. *The variance component for persons.*
    b. *The variance component for observers.*
    c. *The residual component.*
15. *Look at Carlos's scores in Table 6.1. His average is 49.4. Do the fluctuations appear to be consistent with the calculated s.e.m. of 1.8?*

Internal-Consistency Formulas

The usual observed score is a sum or average over items, trials, raters, or occasions or a combination. The tester analyzing a composite can array the scores on the *parts*.

A remarkable number of convenient formulas, variants of the analysis just described, produce what statisticians call an intraclass correlation. This is often referred to in the measurement literature as an alpha coefficient. Using the Greek symbol for alpha (α), α_k symbolizes the coefficient for a composite of k observations.

The s.e.m. is obtained by multiplying $1 - \alpha_k$ by the variance of the composite scores and taking the square root. (The following rules develop variances for the total of the parts, not their average. Variances would be scaled down to describe average scores. The rules also assume that all scores in a column are obtained from the same item or condition—a so-called crossed design.)

You should not concern yourself with procedural details in what follows although you may find them handy for reference. The important point to be made is that these several methods of calculation produce essentially the same result when used appropriately. The many methods, then, are really one.

1. Working from variance components.
   1.1 Use mean squares as in Table 6.1 to get components.
   1.2 Multiply the component for persons by k^2 to get a.
   1.3 Multiply *MSr* by k to get b.
   1.4 Add a to b to estimate the observed-score variance c.
   1.5 The coefficient α_k is given by a/c.

Steps 1.1 to 1.5 can be carried out with k equal to some arbitrary number such as 20. That gives α_{20}, the coefficient for a composite of 20 observations. Setting k equal to 1 estimates the agreement among single observations; the discussion at the bottom of page 167 refers to α_1. Table 6.2 introduces a fresh example, with $k = 8$.

2. Working from column (item) variances.
   2.1 Start with the table of item scores. (Scores for trials or observations can be treated similarly.)
   2.2 For each column of scores, calculate the variance. Add these k values to get d.
   2.3 Total each row and calculate the variance of the totals c.
   2.4 $\alpha_k = k(1 - d/c) \div (k - 1)$.

Table 6.2. *Illustrative reliability calculations*

		Item Scores								Test Scores		
Item no.		1	2	3	4	5	6	7	8	Total	Odd	Even
Person 1		1	0	1	1	0	1	1	1	6	3	3
2		1	1	1	1	1	1	1	1	8	4	4
3		0	0	0	0	1	0	1	0	2	0	2
...										...	...	...
Variance		0.24	0.21	0.25	0.24	0.24	0.21	0.21	0.16	9.60	2.45	2.67
Proportion passing(P)		0.4	0.3	0.5	0.6	0.6	0.7	0.7	0.8			
(Q)		0.6	0.7	0.5	0.4	0.4	0.3	0.3	0.2			
											0.876	
											Correlation	

1.1   Analysis of table gives
         Component for persons   = 0.14
         Residual (MSr)   = 0.08
1.2 $(0.14) \times (8)^2 = (0.14) \times (64)$ = 8.96 = a
1.3 $(0.08) \times (8)$ = 0.64 = b
1.4   Adding,   9.60 = c
1.5   8.96/9.60   = 0.93 = α_8

2.2   The variance of each column is shown.
         $0.24 + 0.21 + \ldots$ = 1.76 = d
2.3   The variance of the Total column   9.60 = c
2.4 $8(1 - 1.76/9.60) \div 7 = 8(1 - 0.183)/7$ = 0.93 = α_8

3.1, 3.2   Use the Odd and Even score columns.
         $2.47 + 2.65$ = 5.12 = d
         From the Total column   9.60 = c
3.3 $2(1 - 5.12/9.60) = 2(1 - 0.533)$ = 0.93 = α_8

4.1, 4.2   The P value of each column is shown.
4.3 $Q = 1 - P$. PQ equals the variance.   1.76 = d
             9.60 = c
4.4   As in line 2.4,   0.93 = α_8

5.   The odd-even correlation of 0.876 applies to a half-length test. If we say that $k = 1$ and $k' = 2$, $n = 2$. For a full-length test [two halves] the coefficient is $2(.876)/1 + 0.876 = 0.93$

The name *coefficient alpha* is conventionally tied to formula 2.4 even though the other procedures also yield alpha coefficients for one or another test length.

    3. Working from test halves (split-half coefficient).
       3.1 Score test halves (usually odd items and even items).
       3.2 Enter in two columns of table. Proceed as in rule 2.2 and rule 2.3.
       3.3 Because $k = 2$ [two halves, that is], $\alpha_k = 2(1 - d/c)$.

How to Judge Tests

4. Kuder-Richardson formula: KR20. It applies when items are scored 1 for correct answers and 0 for wrong answers.
    4.1 Enter the 1 and 0 scores in the table.
    4.2 The column mean is P, the proportion of persons passing the item.
    4.3 List the values of P and Q $(= 1 - P)$. Multiply to form PQ for each item, and sum. This sum is d.
    4.4 Calculate c as in Rule 2.3, and use the formula from Rule 2.4.
5. Spearman-Brown formula. It converts a value of α_k to a value for a composite of k' items, that is, into $\alpha_{k'}$. It can convert α_1 to α_{10}, or α_{10} to α_1, α_6 to α_4, and so on.
    5.1 Suppose that α_k has already been calculated.
    5.2 Form k'/k; call this n.
    5.3 Then $\alpha_{k'} = n\alpha_k/[1 + (n - 1)\alpha_k]$.

A split-half calculation slightly different from procedure 3 is popular. A correlation between scores on odd and even halves is computed. Its value is entered in the Spearman-Brown formula (see Rule 5.3) in place of α_k, along with $n = 2$. The result rarely departs by more than 0.02 from the result procedure 3 gives.

Writers most often speak of "internal consistency" when the parts of a test (half-tests or items) are entered into the table. The method applies also to other composites. If judgments made by five raters were entered into the table, α_5 reports on the consistency across composites of five ratings. Setting k' at 1 assesses the typical variability across single raters. Observations on various occasions can also be analyzed by these procedures.

I said that the methods had to be used appropriately. The part scores have to be experimentally independent; that is, errors on one part must not be linked to errors on another. Independence is violated when a highly speeded test is scored in odd-even fashion because the person who gets stuck on an odd-numbered item will not reach the end of the test and will thereby get a lower score on *both* the odd and even parts. There is a lack of independence also if success on one problem helps the person solve the next.

Wherever such linkages are possible, it is legitimate to divide the test into physically and logically separate parts to collect data. The parts of a speed test would be given separately, each with its own prorated time limit. The part scores, not the item scores, can enter any of the formulas above. Anastasi and Drake (1954) gave half-tests with separate time limits in order to get a proper estimate for one set of speeded tests. They obtained coefficients as much as 0.15 below those calculated improperly from odd-even scoring of the intact test. (Theoretically, it is improper to apply any of the formulas to an intact speeded test, but probably only odd-even coefficients are much inflated. The theory on this point has not been worked out.)

16. *Find the s.e.m. from the information in Table 6.2.*
17. *The scores on a test have a variance of 60. The two half-tests (odd and*

even) have variances of 20 and 22. What is the reliability and error variance of the total score?

18. *For a 10-item test, the observed variance is 90. The respective items have variances 3, 1, 5, 2, 2, 4, 3, 3, 1, 4. Calculate the reliability coefficient, and say as much as you can about what it means.*

INTERPRETING FINDINGS

Some of the most popular methods of analyzing error of measurement neglect sources of variance that should concern test interpreters. Table 6.3 compares three procedures, reviewing some of what has been said earlier on this topic. The table describes correlational analysis, but it also applies to analysis of variance of the same data. In general, of course, a procedure that takes into account more sources of error will yield a larger standard error and a smaller coefficient. There is no objection to calculating an internal-consistency coefficient when a test is being used to measure a supposedly stable characteristic; if it turns out to be small, it raises serious questions. But if the coefficient is large, the user must bear in mind that consistency over occasions has not yet been investigated. (For some ability tests, a 6-month retest indicates a standard error about 40 percent larger than that obtained from two tests close together.)

19. *A chemistry teacher gives a standardized test of knowledge of scientific facts to her class. Several students make scores lower than she had expected.*
    a. *She asks, "Could it be that I gave a form of the test that included many questions these particular students happened not to know? Would their scores have changed much if they had been asked other questions of the same type?" What type of study answers this question?*
    b. *She asks, "Could the performance of these students be due to an 'off' day? Does a score on tests of this type vary much from day to day?" What type of study is most helpful in answering this question?*

Range of the Group: Effects on the Coefficient

Errors of measurement are most troublesome when we compare persons who are much alike. Then the errors are likely to mask true differences in rank.

Recall that the reliability is the ratio of true to observed variance. Given a certain error variance, the larger the true-score variance, the larger the coefficient. But this means that the reliability coefficient is higher in a wide-range group. (So is the validity coefficient; page 141). The s.e.m. is ordinarily similar in groups having different ranges unless near-chance or near-perfect scores are common.

One TMC study gave the variances for what I call here "original sam-

Table 6.3. *What error means under several procedures*

	Sources of Variation That Increase the Reported s.e.m. When the Analytic Procedure Is			
	Internal-consistency	Correlation of Test Forms Given on Same Day	Correlation of Test Forms Given on Different Days	Correlation of Test and Retest (Same Form, Different days)
Momentary inattention, luck in guessing	x	x	x	x
Choosing a particular set of items to represent the universe	x	x	x	
Health, mood, or other temporary state of the test taker			x	x
Shift in motivation from occasion to occasion			x	x
Opportunities for learning that change pupil standings as time passes			x	x

ple." A class of more select students might have the variances listed at the right.

	Original Sample	Select Sample
Observed variance	116.6	82
Error variance	12	12
True-score variance	104.6	70
Coefficient	0.90	0.85

The change in coefficient can be far more dramatic, when, for example, a test designed for representative children is administered in a remedial class. The accuracy of the information is much better described by the standard error than by the coefficient. The drop in reliability means only that the test is less able to *rank* members within the select group.

20. *For a college-entrance test, the test manual reports a reliability coefficient of 0.95 for a college applicant population where the s.d. is 20. What will the true-score, error, and observed variances and the coefficient be in a group of students actually admitted to a certain college if the s.d. in that group is 10?*

21. *A reading test is to be used in grades 4 through 6. The manual should report a coefficient calculated for each grade level separately. Why?*

Relation to the Number of Observations

A long test is generally better than a short test because every question added improves the sample of performance. Likewise, six 15-minute observations of a child's social behavior provide a better sample of typical behavior than three.

When k uncorrelated errors are averaged, the variance of the average drops to $1/k$ times the variance of a single measure. The effect is illustrated in the second column of Table 6.4. The true-score variance is constant. Therefore, as k increases, the coefficient approaches 1.0. The more observations we average, the more closely the result agrees with the true score. The change in coefficients in Table 6.4 is consistent with the Spearman-Brown formula. It is assumed that a change in length does not change the nature of the test.

This kind of analysis can indicate how much accuracy is gained by going from two scores of an essay to three, for example, and how much is lost in going from a 40-item examination to a 30-item version.

Bandwidth versus fidelity. Information from an employment interview can be recorded simply as an interviewer's summary rating on suitability. Or the interviewer can rate the applicant on half-a-dozen qualities or mark a checklist of numerous specific characteristics. Similarly, a pupil's ability in arithmetic computation can be reported as a single score, or the report can provide separate scores for many subskills.

Tests that report multiple scores are hard to evaluate. The problem is partly technical and partly one of values. A certain time is available for testing. Should the tester go after a good measure of one dimension or make

Table 6.4 *Effect on error of making additional observations*

Number of tests averaged[a] (k)	Variances			Coefficient	s.e.m.
	Error	True	Observed		
1	1.00	9.80	10.80	0.91	1.00
2	.50	9.80	10.30	0.95	.71
3	.33	9.80	10.13	0.97	.58
5	.20	9.80	10.00	0.98	.45
10	.10	9.80	9.90	0.99	.32
100	.01	9.80	9.81	0.999	.10

[a]If tests were summed, instead of averaged, the variances would be multiplied by k^2; and the s.e.m. would be multiplied by k.

several less thorough measurements? If she chooses the latter course, each score is based on a relatively small sample of behavior and is less accurate than the unitary measure. The right balance between breadth of coverage and precision is hard to strike.

This is the bandwidth-fidelity dilemma. We encounter it in debates about the proper number of aptitudes to take into account in selection and guidance, in debates about the wisdom of preparing a 10-subtest profile for the Wechsler Scale, and about the usefulness of "diagnostic" tabulations of student errors. The argument is equally vigorous in the personality domain. Some investigators settle for a simple "emotional adjustment" score; others prepare an elaborate descriptive profile.

The terms *bandwidth* and *fidelity* come from Shannon's information theory (1949), developed for the study of communication systems. Home music systems have made "high fidelity" familiar to everyone. The complementary concept of bandwidth refers to the amount or complexity of information a message tries to communicate. The fidelity of disk recording depends upon the width of the groove; crowded grooves put more music on a record, and fidelity suffers. Similarly, with a tape: with greater tape speed, greater fidelity —but less information per tape. With other things held constant, any shift in the direction of greater fidelity reduces the variety of information.

When many decisions are to be made, each requiring a different sort of information, the best solution is to allow plenty of time for gathering information. Obviously, the greatest amount of time should be given to the most important questions. When questions are of about equal importance, obtaining rough answers to most or all of them is more profitable than answering one or two precisely (Cronbach & Gleser, 1965).

In trying to help an individual, one needs fairly specific information. Psychologists and educators try to identify the particular kinds of social situations or intellectual problems where the person's functioning rises above his usual level, and the ones where his performance lags. This kind of analysis pushes bandwidth upward. When the assessor makes numerous statements, each has to be based on limited information. Critics point to the risks inherent in interpreting unreliable differences among subscores. Practitioners who remain mindful of these risks can make use of tentative leads from short tests.

The classical psychometric ideal is the instrument with high fidelity and low bandwidth. The Law School Admission Test tries to answer just one question with great accuracy. It concentrates its content in a narrow range. As its parts are highly correlated, part scores are unenlightening. At the opposite extreme, an interview can have almost unlimited bandwidth. Questions can turn in any direction, different themes being pursued with each interviewee. The report can be individualized to such an extent that no two persons are described on the same variable. A technique used as a wideband method by some testers or organizations becomes a narrowband method for others. Even the interview can concentrate on a single variable.

22. The reliability coefficient for a single testing is 0.80. If two testings are combined, what will the coefficient be? (Use the Spearman-Brown formula.)
23. A 60-word spelling test has a reliability coefficient of 0.90. What reliability would be expected for a 20-word test?
24. In World Series baseball, some pinch hitters reach batting averages as high as 0.750 whereas the best regular players rarely exceed 0.400 for seven games. How can this be explained?

Effects of Error on Correlations

Other things being equal, the more accurate a test, the stronger its correlation with other variables. The error portion of a score cannot correlate with other observations. Increasing the number of observations by increasing accuracy makes for higher validity.

Table 6.5 illustrates these important relationships, starting with a short test having a reliability coefficient of 0.40 and a validity coefficient of 0.30. The validity coefficient creeps up slowly. The *square* of the validity remains proportional to the reliability; in every column the ratio is 0.225 (= 0.09/0.40). If we extend the test until its reliability is 0.9999, the squared validity will not exceed 0.225. The limit on validity is, therefore, the square root of 0.225 or 0.47. Estimating the correlation (or regression) coefficient for an ideally accurate measure is called disattenuation or correction for attenuation. For procedures, see Cronbach *et al.*, 1972; Jöreskog & Sörbom, 1979; Lord & Novick, 1968; see also p. 394.

Under the assumptions used throughout this chapter, the reliability coefficient equals the square of the correlation between observed score and true score. And a test cannot correlate better with an external variable than it does with its own true score. Therefore, the square root of the reliability is an upper limit for the correlation of the test with a criterion. The square root of 0.40 is 0.63, so the short test in Table 6.5 might in principle have a validity coefficient above 0.6 for predicting some criterion. This is a theoretical limit; actual validity coefficients almost always fall short of it. Errors in the criterion keep the correlation from reaching the theoretical limit. Also, variables the test does not measure influence the criterion.

Table 6.5 *Effect on validity of making additional observations*

	Number of Observations for Predictor X				
	1	2	4	8	16
Reliability $r_{XX'}$	0.40	0.57	0.73	0.84	0.91
Squared validity r^2_{XY}	0.09	0.13	0.16	0.19	0.20
Validity coefficient r_{XY}	0.30	0.36	0.41	0.44	0.45

25. *Type-A behavior consists of certain reactions to stress (for example, becoming upset over small and transient inconvenience). These reactions are associated with susceptibility to heart attacks. Behavior therapy attempts to reduce the frequency of such responses, and in one study (L. Powell, personal communication) the frequency did decrease markedly. The difference (statistically significant) was found in the clients' self-reports, in the comparison of ratings given before and after treatment by their spouses, and also in ratings supplied by associates where they worked. The correlation among the three kinds of pretest was only about 0.2, and agreement among the three types of postmeasure was equally low. How can these low correlations be reconciled with the detection of a strong effect? (Hint: Powell was working only with persons who showed a considerable amount of Type A behavior.)*
26. *Two 30-item arithmetic tests for fourth-graders are studied by means of KR20. Test A has a coefficient of 0.70, and Test B has a coefficient of 0.85. Is it possible that Test A is more valid? Why?*
27. *The KR20 formula is said to report on the homogeneity of the universe the items in a test represent. What does this mean? Why would α_I be a better indicator of homogeneity?*
28. *Disattenuation formulas might be used in analyzing the relation of adolescents' educational aspirations to attitudes expressed, say at age 8, by the person and his parents. Why do disattenuated correlations answer the scientist's question better than the coefficients directly calculated from scores?*

Accuracy for Particular Individuals

Traditional procedure calculates a single s.e.m. for an age group (or some other suitable reference group). But this is no more than a convenient approximation. You will recall that a clumsily wrapped package might have a larger s.e.m. than a tidy one and also the suggestion that one student's day-to-day fluctuation is greater than another's. It is not practicable, using traditional methods, to calculate individual standard errors; that would require a large number of observations on each individual. We do know something, however, about the causes of especially large individual standard errors. After those conclusions are described, some new methods that attempt to estimate individual standard errors will be mentioned.

Accuracy as a function of score level. A test is usually designed to fit a certain level of ability, and it will measure persons at that level most accurately. Persons for whom the test is very difficult are likely to have comparatively large errors of measurement because of guessing or unstable behavior.

The scores of recruits who took a pitch-discrimination test twice are presented in Figure 6.1. If the test were accurate, the two scores for each person would be nearly the same, and all points would fall along the diagonal line. The test consists of 100 pairs of tones; in each pair, the person reports

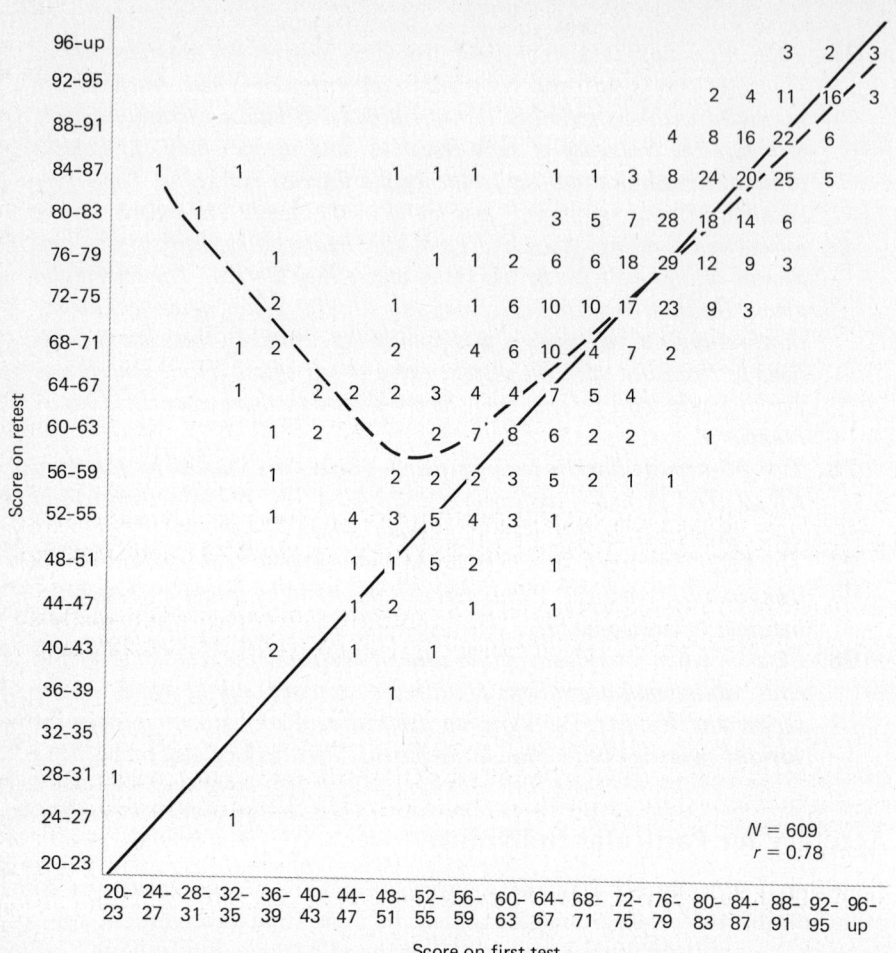

Figure 6.1. Test and retest scores on pitch discrimination.
Source: Ford et al., 1944.

whether the second tone is higher or lower than the first. A score of 50 would be obtained by pure chance. According to the scatter diagram, high scores are fairly consistent. Recruits scoring 85 on the first test fell between 72 and 95 on retest. But those scoring near the chance level (e.g., 55) scattered widely on the retest (40 to 87). The broken line shows the average score on the second test corresponding to each score level of the first test.

The upcurve at the left indicates that many men with very low scores in the first test did well on the retest. Probably those having such low scores on the first test misunderstood directions and judged the first tone instead of the second. Following directions correctly on the retest would shift their scores from 70 items wrong to 70 items right.

How to Judge Tests

A test should be appropriate in difficulty for the decision to be made. Figure 6.2 shows distributions of scores on several tests given to the same group. The very easy test A may be quite satisfactory for measuring at the lower end of the group. Test A is unsatisfactory for comparing abler persons because variation of only a few points causes a person to drop from the top of the group to the average. The test does not distinguish between the persons tying at 100 though these people probably do not have the same ability. This failure to detect differences among (and shortcomings in) superior persons is a "ceiling effect."

A score distribution that tails off to the left is appropriate for a screening test. A survey to identify persons who are at risk in some respect (or simply to obtain a count of them) ought to distinguish persons with low true scores from the general population, but there is no reason for a finely graded assessment of persons who are normal and above. Distribution A is also appropriate for "mastery tests" used in instruction and for tests used to certify competence. A checkoff test on triangles identifies geometry students ready to move ahead to theorems on parallel lines. A test where nearly everyone "hits the ceiling" is suitable (and encouraging!).

Test B is difficult. The top scores spread out, but differences at the low end of the scale are too small to distinguish individuals dependably ("floor effect"). If we need only to distinguish the best members of an applicant group, Test B is efficient. Such a test could also be used to screen out able persons who will be exempted from certain training or to award scholarships. Test C spreads out cases at both ends of the scale. Tests yielding roughly normal distributions are preferred when it is necessary to distinguish all along the scale.

Individualized standard errors. For a number of reasons, test users now have greater need for individualized standard errors than they did a few years back.

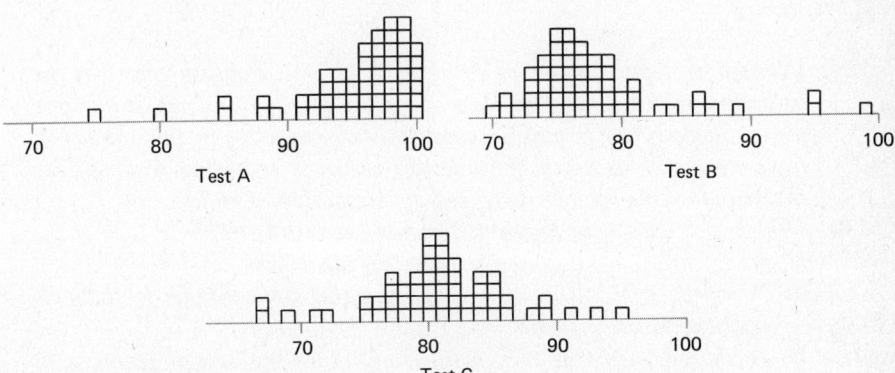

Figure 6.2. Distribution for three tests given to the same group.

Adaptive testing (p. 39) chooses different items for different persons and continues measurement of a particular variable until sufficient accuracy is obtained. This means that some people are working on hard items and some on easy items, that some are taking long tests and some are taking short tests. For example, some persons may be found well qualified on a short licensing examination whereas persons near the borderline will be given many more items. The s.e.m. is allowed to be rather large for persons well above the borderline and is kept small for persons near the minimum qualifying level.

Methods of administering tests by computer usually feed responses to a program that estimates—after each successive response—not only the person's most likely true score but also the s.e.m. that goes with the estimate at that point. When the s.e.m. is satisfactorily small, the computer stops testing the person on that variable. The stopping rule would take one form when the test is intended to rule out the incompetent, another form when the exceptionally qualified applicants are to be located.

The new tests based on unidimensional scaling may be administered in the traditional ways, individually or to a group. Scaling theory permits the estimation of a standard error that not only takes into account the number of items the individual responded to but also his degree of consistency. An unusually large s.e.m. identifies a person the test did not fit (too hard? too easy? directions not understood?). The s.e.m. is greater (other things being equal) for a child who succeeds on some hard items but misses some easy ones. Certain of the tests scaled on the basis of latent-trait or item-response theory provide a table for changing a raw score to a scaled score and indicate a "confidence interval," a range within which the true score is thought to lie.

Individualized standard errors or estimated true-score ranges are derived in many ways, and new methods are appearing. It is too early to say which methods will be most satisfactory. It should be pointed out that all these estimates refer to consistency across measurements on the same day. None of them takes into account inconsistency from day to day or month to month. They respond to the question: How good a sample of *today's* behavior did we get?

29. *When a pass-fail decision is being made, errors of measurement at the borderline matter most. The s.e.m. very likely is not uniform at all score levels. Suggest how to modify some procedure suggested in this chapter to learn about the accuracy of borderline decisions regarding readiness for shorthand. (One solution is offered by Livingston, 1982.)*
30. *Which distribution in Figure 6.2 would be most desirable in each of the following cases?*
    a. *A psychologist wishes to measure liberalness of attitudes to study its relation to voting habits.*
    b. *A college wishes to pick out freshmen needing special training in reading.*
    c. *A test for college guidance measures interest in medicine.*

d. *An employer wishes to select the best statistician from a group of applicants.*

31. *The Psychological Screening Inventory reports an Alienation score whose possible range is 0 to 22. A high score implies the desirability of an intensive psychological or psychiatric examination. Percentile ranks of males correspond to raw scores as follows:*

Score	0	2	4	6	8	10	12	14	16	18	20
Percentile rank	0	3	21	52	78	91	96	98	99	99+	99+

    a. *How would a person's percentile rank change if his score changed by 4 points?*
    b. *What is the shape of the raw-score distribution? What does this distribution imply regarding the usefulness of this test?*

32. *Assume that the range of possible scores on a test is scaled from 0 to 100. What might the rule for stopping testing be when the aim is*
    a. *To estimate each examinee's true score within 5 points?*
    b. *To rule out candidates whose true scores are probably below 50?*
    c. *To pick those few candidates whose true scores are probably above 80?*

FURTHER CONSIDERATIONS IN CHOOSING TESTS

As Chapter 5 said, the fundamental basis for choosing a test is validity. Can we interpret the test soundly? Does the information serve our purpose? Reliability is a supplementary consideration. It sometimes warns us that validity will be limited because of error of measurement, and it sometimes helps us improve the procedure. Among the additional considerations entering into the selection of a measuring procedure are costs: monetary costs of materials and tester time; burdens borne by the test taker; and convenience, time lag, and monetary cost of scoring. Norms will be an asset in some testing programs as will the availability of equivalent or equated forms. Two considerations require further discussion here. Appeal to nonspecialists—the clients, the persons who will use the report, the press and the public, and the courts—can make a world of difference in the success of a testing program. So can the assistance the publisher supplies the user.

Appeal to the lay person. The medicine a doctor prescribes loses much of its power when a patient loses faith in it. He may skip doses. In the end he may decide that doctors cannot help him and let treatment lapse altogether. For similar reasons, in selecting a test, one must consider how worthwhile it will appear to the subject who takes it and to others who will see the results.

If an applicant for a job is given an employment test that he considers unrelated to the job, he is likely to be resentful. This will make it difficult to obtain valid scores. If he is not hired, he may excuse his failure by criticizing the test; what he says to his friends damages public relations and makes it harder to obtain job applicants. Some satisfactory workers have had little schooling and are distrustful of tests that probe their weaknesses; catch questions and questions that seem childish are especially likely to arouse criticism.

If a test is interesting and "sensible," taking it is likely to be a pleasant experience. This not only tends to make the scores valid but also helps to establish good relations between the personnel worker and the subject. An Italian bus company contracted with psychological laboratories in two cities to give tests to would-be drivers. After a few months, it was found that most of the applicants were traveling to Rome—going as much as 100 miles farther than necessary—because the Rome center had elaborate testing apparatus whereas the second center used simple equipment to measure the same aptitudes. The applicants thought the elaborate tests fairer and more dependable. British experience with War Office selection boards is a second case in point. The selection board observed officer candidates during several days of field testing, apparatus tests, and discussions. Before this system was established, men from the ranks rarely applied for commissions. The tests previously used gave an advantage to applicants from good homes and good schools, they thought. The fact that they saw the selection board as a fairer system for recognizing talent made it easier to recruit candidates for commissions.

A large audience passes judgment on a testing program. British officer selection had to satisfy a Labour cabinet insistent that poor youths have a fair chance to become officers, the parents of the candidates, and the old-line officers who trained the candidates accepted. A psychologist who installs a highly valid industrial selection program will find it in the ash can a year later unless she convinces management, the union, and government regulators that the test is fair. Recall the judge's scornful analysis of the test for fire fighters (p. 157). If a group of social workers is accustomed to reports from Test A, the psychologist may be unwise to rely on Test B. Even if Test B is more accurate than A, the social worker may disregard results from B because the test does not have his confidence. So important is user acceptability that the psychologist working with teachers, industrial staffs, or physicians must often use a test that would be her second or third choice on the basis of technical qualities. The increasingly widespread practice of bringing the individuals examined or their representatives into the decision making—as in working out an instructional plan for a child who has not prospered in school —also leads the tester to select tests whose relevance is easily perceived and that can be explained in lay language. Comparatively transparent techniques are also to be favored in research uses of tests, if the findings are likely to be a subject of debate outside the profession.

A test that seems relevant to the lay person is said to have "face validity." Adopting a test just because it appears reasonable is bad practice; many a "good-looking" test has had poor validity. Civil service examiners, for example, prepared two tests to measure ability in alphabetic filing. One gave five names per item—John Meeder, James Medway, Thomas Madow, Catherine Meagan, Eleanor Meehan—and asked which name would be *third* in alphabetical order. The other test required the subject to place a name in a series; for example:

> Robert Carstens   A_____
>   Richard Carreton
>   B_____
>   Roland Casstar
>   C_____
>   Jack Corson
>   D_____
>   Edward Cranston

Though the makers were confident that the tests called on the same skill and though both tests had reliabilities above 0.8, they correlated zero (Mosier, 1947). Such evidence as this (reinforced by the whole history of phrenology, graphology, and tests of witchcraft!) warns against adopting a test solely because it is plausible. Validity of interpretations should not be compromised for the sake of face validity. Consumers accept many esoteric technical procedures, for example, the things done behind laboratory doors to the blood drawn as part of a physical examination. Confidence in those procedures whose inner workings we know little about has been painstakingly established by physicians' communications, personal and published. The psychologist who wishes to collect information that others will use, by procedures that seem mysterious to them, simply undertakes a more difficult task of explication than one who can find a method that has both technical validity and face validity.

Aids to the user. When the user is experienced or is well trained to make the decisions a test bears upon, a publisher's responsibility can stop with the presentation of the usual technical information. But when test scores will be used by persons who are not test specialists, the developer is expected to provide suggestions regarding proper interpretation and warnings regarding likely misconceptions and incorrect applications. Responsibilities for test use devolve upon many who are not trained in testing: faculty members on a college admissions committee, parole boards, homeroom teachers pressed into service as counselors. . . . The student himself belongs in the list insofar as he is using the scores for judgments of his own.

    The test producer has many ways to make professional experience and wisdom available. These range from sentences in the manual to booklets like *Taking the SAT* to computer summaries and comments on local data that have been processed centrally to whole training courses on a particular instrument. How large an effort is appropriate depends on the use to which the test is put and the subtleties (psychological, ethical, and practical) of the application.

33. *A clinical tester examines criminals from time to time to provide data bearing on their ability to distinguish right from wrong. Some of the tests will provide reports for the guidance of a hospital psychiatrist. Others will be conducted at the request of lawyers on one side of a trial. What features or characteristics of a test would make it especially suitable for one of these uses and of no particular advantage for the other use?*

34. *A certain examination for French secondary school admission was deliberately made very difficult. A skewed distribution was wanted as only a small number of places was to be filled. When the children told of the questions at home, parents organized protest meetings that ultimately brought the problem to the attention of the minister of education, who ordered a second test of those who had failed. Do you agree with this decision?*

EVALUATING A TEST

Nearly every concept used in judging the adequacy of tests has now been introduced. Subsequent chapters will apply these concepts and, in that application, explain them more completely. The concepts are summarized here and then a form useful in reviewing a test is presented in Table 6.6. Information for the review comes from materials the publisher supplies and from the research that has accumulated. (Table 6.7, illustrating the application of the form to TMC, is briefer at several places than it would be if it were to be filed by itself. To avoid repetition, crossreferences to comments in this book that the form would otherwise summarize have been inserted.)

Development of a testing program requires, first of all, a clear purpose. One searches for a test that fits the decision to be made, not just for "a good test of reading" or "a good personality test." For this reason, I suggest that any test manual be approached with a definite measurement problem in mind. The form in Table 6.6 carries a space (entry *11*) for entering this purpose, which might be specific (selecting clerks who will be trained for computer data entry) or rather general (obtaining information to be filed for subsequent use in counseling high-school students as problems arise).

The top section of the form calls for simple descriptive facts (entries *1–10*).

Date of publication (entry *7*) is not highly significant. Some older tests are excellent, and the interpreter benefits from the research that has accumulated. But some items may be obsolete, and the manual is likely to be out of date. Regarding the date of norms, see entry *23*.

The next step is to form an impression of the test by examining the items, the scoring principles, and the aims the author had in mind. Under entry *12* in the form, one can describe the items superficially and list the subtests separately scored. Attention should be given to the objectivity of scoring.

Table 6.6. *A form for evaluating tests*

1. Title.
2. Author.
3. Publisher.
4. Forms; groups to which applicable.
5. Practical features.
6. General type.
7. Date of publication.
8. Cost, booklet; answer sheet.
9. Scoring services available and cost.
10. Time required.
11. Purpose for which evaluated.
12. Description of test, items, scoring.
13. Author's purpose and basis for selecting items.
14. Adequacy of directions; training required to administer.
15. Mental functions or traits represented in each score, whether relevant or sources of invalidity.
16. Comments regarding design of test.
17. Validation against criteria: number and type of cases, criterion measure, time interval, result.
18. Other empirical evidence indicating what the test measures.
19. Comments regarding fairness.
20. Comments regarding validity for particular purposes.
21. Generalizability (procedure, cases, result).
22. Long-term stability (procedure, time interval, cases, result).
23. Norms (type of scale, selection of sample).
24. Comments regarding adequacy of above for particular purpose.
25. Aids to the user.
26. Comments of reviewers.
27. General evaluation.
28. References.

The author's stated intentions (entry *13*) help one to understand the nature of the test. The manual will usually indicate whether the author was interested in selection, guidance, clinical use, or classroom evaluation and will often tell what aptitudes, traits, or categories of behavior she had in mind when preparing items. The source of items is particularly important if the test is to be interpreted on the basis of its content.

Many test manuals report statistical studies used in selecting items. These reports are rarely significant to the test interpreter. The item-selection procedure is best judged by its fruits, namely, the evidence on validity and generalizability. When content validity is of interest, statistics are less informative than an examination of the content.

Directions (entry *14*) can be examined with regard to their clarity and the extent to which they standardize the test.

An armchair analysis of the test items (entry *15*) suggests what abilities, experiences, work habits, or personality traits influence each subscore. The comment should list irrelevant variables thought likely to distort scores.

Table 6.7. *Evaluation form for TMC*

1. *Title.* Mechanical Comprehension Test.
2. *Author.* George K. Bennett and others.
3. *Publisher.* Psychological Corporation.
4. *Forms; groups to which applicable.*
    S, T: Primarily for job applicants and trainees. Can be used with students and experienced technicians. A version appearing in the DAT battery for students is of roughly similar difficulty.
    Spanish versions available.
    Older Bennett versions ranging from easy to difficult (AA, BB, and CC) and a form W-1 consisting of items judged especially suitable for females are available, but only on special inquiry.
5. *Practical features.* Directions and items available on prerecorded tape make the test more suitable for applicants weak in verbal skills.
6. *General type.* Aptitude.
7. *Date of publication.* 1970. Earlier versions appeared from 1940 onward. Manual supplement, 1980.
8. *Cost of booklet,* 50 cents; *of answer sheet,* 12 cents (1980).
9. *Scoring services available and cost.* May be scored by hand or any automated system.
10. *Time required.* 30 minutes (plus directions).
11. *Purpose for which evaluated.* Vocational guidance of high school students.
12. *Description of test, items, scoring.* Pictures of simple apparatus. Has 3-choice questions about what will happen to an object when force is applied, which of two structures is most stable, etc. Objective scoring (number right in recent forms). No part scores.
13. *Author's purpose and basis for selecting items.* To measure an ability required in many jobs and training courses. Past experience is allowed to affect scores, but the items require understanding rather than rote knowledge. Items were put through various stages of criticism and tryout; items retained were those discriminating high scorers (on a pool of items) from low scorers.
14. *Adequacy of directions; training required to administer.* Directions are unusually clear and simple. Classroom teacher can handle.
15. *Mental functions or traits represented in each score.* General experience with machines common in Western world, understanding of simple principles of motion. Solutions can be intuitive or deductive. Unspeeded. No claim is made that the test measures an innate aptitude.
16. *Comments regarding design of test.* Highly efficient. As errors not penalized, a person who marks every item has an advantage; directions mute on this point. Any test paper with several omissions should be flagged as questionable.
17. *Validation against criteria.* Manuals refer to numerous studies in which TMC was correlated with technical-training criteria. Coefficients mostly range from 0.3 to 0.6 (Tables 5.2, 5.3). Manual often unclear about time interval separating test and criterion. A separate compilation of studies by Ghiselli (1973) confirms these validities. Results against ratings of job proficiency are poorer.
    Evidently generally useful, though the test usually must be supplemented by verbal measures. Information on usefulness of the test for prediction in high school courses and on long-range predictions from high school testing is available for DAT version.
18. *Other empirical evidence indicating what the test measures.* Correlates about 0.5 with tests of general or verbal-numerical reasoning abilities. Correlations with spatial reasoning tests reach 0.6 and above. Some investigators question whether a distinct concept of "mechanical" reasoning is necessary. (See also pages 151 and 309.)
19. *Fairness.* The tendency of females to score lower on TMC than males raises the question whether a given score has the same predictive significance for both sexes.

Table 6.7. *(Continued)*

Direct studies on that or on the comparable question about ethnic differences seem not to have been reported.
20. *Comments regarding validity for particular purposes.* Test has predictive value for nonroutine machine operation. Overlaps general and spatial tests.
21. *Generalizability.* Standard error of measurement (across forms) of 3 to 4 points on the 60-point scale. Limited data on high school students suggest form-to-form correlations close to 0.9.
22. *Long-term stability.* (See p. 309.).
23. *Norms.* Manual and supplement (1980) give percentile distributions for several specific industrial samples. High school norms come from a single city, presumably in the 1970s.
24. *Comments regarding adequacy of above for particular purpose.* Though high school norms are much poorer than those for the DAT version, norms are not highly important. Counselor should develop within-sex norms for curricular groups within her own school.

    Accuracy of test acceptable. But many a difference between TMC and other ability measures arises from error of measurement alone. Moreover, standing in mechanical comprehension changes during early years of high school.
25. *Aids to the user.* Like most older tests, TMC provides little information to assist users in deciding when and how to use the scores. This is not a drawback where the test is installed by a qualified personnel psychologist or guidance counselor.
26. *Comments of reviewers.*

    "The manuals of directions are models of conciseness and honesty.... There is little doubt that the test measures comprehension of many mechanical principles, but its value for prediction has been questioned on the ground that several items involve principles or facts which one is unlikely to encounter in everyday mechanical experience, outside of a physics course" (C. M. Harsh, in Buros, 1949, p. 720).

    "Of limited value to educational counselors and to those setting up test batteries for *differential* prediction objectives. The test may well be most useful when used alone or when used with a few clerical aptitude and manual dexterity tests to predict current performance in a few relatively simple, mechanically oriented occupations" (H. P. Bechtoldt, in Buros, 1972, p. 1049; my italics).

    "Pictures still look old-fashioned.... Unfortunate ... [no] information on degree of speededness.... [or] stability ... over various time intervals.... Very useful instrument in educational and vocational guidance" (Hambleton, 1971, pp. 55–56).
27. An exceptionally popular test; many studies show its relevance to performance in mechanical work. The concreteness of the test makes it appealing. Being unlike tests commonly encountered in school, it dramatizes for the counselee the concept of special abilities.

    Forms S and T could be helpful in bringing the ninth grader to examine his aptitudes, but the DAT battery, which includes a version of TMC, is preferable for this purpose; it gives comparable data on other aptitudes. The DAT battery is also useful later in high school, when more definite vocational and educational plans are being made. Even where a mechanical comprehension test is wanted by itself, the Bennett has no apparent advantage over the DAT version.

    TMC is a measure of understanding acquired through general exposure to tools and machines; it does not depend on training or specific technical experience. There is some question as to whether TMC information adds much of value if general and spatial abilities have been measured. TMC indicates whether the person has the concepts useful in profiting from training; it does not guarantee proficiency without training, and it has nothing to do with manual aspects of performance.

Empirical evidence of validity (entries *17* and *18*) may be of various sorts. For some tests the volume of research is so great that it can only be summarized or sampled. Under heading *18* any study might be listed that helps establish what the score measures. Here particularly it is necessary to select the most significant information from that available.

"Fairness" applies more to procedures used to make judgments and to the judgments themselves than to the test in isolation. Some aspects of fairness fall naturally under other entries (as with the reference to "Western world" in entry *15*); entry *19* provides a place for evidence or comments especially related to the purpose stated in entry *11*.

The final evaluation of validity (entry *20*) is the most important single entry. It is necessary to weigh positive and negative evidence, to decide which of several contradictory findings is most trustworthy, and to judge the body of evidence as a whole. It is important to note when evidence on some important aspect of validity is lacking. Attention should be paid to the adequacy of qualitative interpretations or decision rules if these are suggested in the manual or provided by scoring services.

Entries *21* and *22*, on error of measurement, are usually summarized from the manual. Subscores as well as totals should be discussed. Norms (entry *23*) are examined for relevance to the user's situation. If norms will be employed in interpretation, it is important to consider the adequacy of sampling and the date of the investigation. With rising educational standards, for example, adult norms rise, and old norms make a given performance look better than current norms would.

Entry *25* calls for an evaluation of the assistance given the user. This is especially important where tests will be used in planning instruction or clinical treatment and for tests that inexperienced persons are likely to misuse.

Entry *26* provides for a summary of published reviews. Entry *27* is a final summary of the advantages and limitations of the test for the particular purpose, considering both technical and practical features. It is appropriate to compare the test with others having the same general function and to mention information to be considered along with the test.

A plan is more than a list of good tests. It should minimize wasteful overlap and should get each piece of information when it will be most helpful. Testing cannot be planned by itself. In industry or the armed forces, it must be dovetailed with recruiting, training, and assignment. In the clinic, testing is part of the whole therapeutic effort. Any plan should consider how the results will be used in assigning the person or in helping him to understand himself, or, in an evaluation, how the relevant public will be informed.

PART II
TESTS OF ABILITY

7
General Ability: Appraisal Methods

Extremes of opinion about tests of mental ability and about the legitimacy of basing decisions on measured ability are found among psychologists and nonpsychologists alike (Houts, 1977; Jensen, 1980, Chap. 1; Brace and others, 1980). The accumulated evidence leaves uncertainties about factual relationships and about likely explanations. Such facts as we have leave plenty of room for debate about "human nature" and about changes that might occur if child rearing (for example) were altered. Beyond that are varying conceptions of merit: intellectual excellence is valued, but a society might value warmth and social sensitivity or eccentric creativity or evenness of temperament or charisma—or much else that tests do not measure.

Part II summarizes ideas about ability with which today's psychologists work and explains why certain other ideas have been discarded. It restates questions that, badly posed, have touched off unhelpful disputes. It describes lines of research and reasoning that begin to answer the scientific questions and that should influence judgments about educational and social policies. It describes traditional ways of using test data and emerging practices that may open greater opportunity to low-scoring individuals.

"General ability" refers to all-round effectiveness in activities directed by thought. To speak of a person's "general health" is not to deny that many ailments are specific, but good health means more than absence of disease.

It refers to the performance of the system, not to an average of scores for heart and joints and skin and so on. "General ability" likewise refers to the performance of a system. Some people perform better than others in solving problems, comprehending events and messages, and learning. They excel, then, in general ability. General ability is not fixed, even though performance rankings are fairly consistent from one year to the next. A vital question for psychologists is how growth in abilities comes about, why rankings of individuals sometimes change, and why decline sets in—at different ages for different persons and tasks.

THE EMERGENCE OF MENTAL TESTING

Measurement Before Binet

Though a history of mental testing is in large part a history of Alfred Binet's scale and its descendants, psychological measurement began a century before Binet's work.

The first systematic experimentation on individual differences in behavior arose from the discovery that astronomers differ in reaction time. In 1796, an assistant named Kinnebrook at Greenwich Observatory was engaged in recording the instant when certain stars crossed the field of the telescope. When Kinnebrook consistently reported observations 0.8 seconds later than those of his superior, the Astronomer Royal, he was thought incompetent in his work and was discharged. Twenty years later, it was realized that competent observers respond at different speeds and that the variations are more or less normally distributed. Hence astronomers cannot consider one report strictly correct and all others wrong. Such differences gradually came to be recognized as significant facts about the processing of information.

Physiologists, biologists, and anthropologists were stimulated by the scientific climate of the nineteenth century to measure a great variety of human characteristics. Notable among these workers was Francis Galton, whose interest in individuality developed from the theory of his cousin Charles Darwin. Galton invented ways of measuring physical characteristics, keenness of the senses, and mental imagery. These methods, though not developed fully by Galton, served as models for later tests. In addition, Galton demonstrated that outstanding intellectual achievement occurred unusually often in certain families. Genius, evidently, was not an accident or a gift of capricious gods, but a lawful phenomenon to be investigated scientifically.

At this time, psychology was only beginning to emerge as a science. It was suggested that mental processes—or at least their products—could be observed under standard conditions. Scientific observations, supplementing or even replacing introspection and philosophical speculation, could describe exactly the relation between the mental and physical worlds. This was the aim with which Wundt opened the pioneering psychological laboratory in Leipzig in 1879, and he and his colleagues did triumphantly establish quantitative psychological laws comparable in form to those of physics. Believing that laboratory research should analyze behavior into its simplest elements, he measured very limited functions. Wundt, trying to identify general laws governing all minds, was not concerned with individual differences. His laboratory procedures, however, had a strong influence on early tests. In the United States, as early as 1890, J. McKeen Cattell was using procedures from Wundt's and Galton's laboratories to measure sensory acuity, strength of grip, sensitivity to pain from pressure on the forehead, and memory for dictated consonants. Cattell came to the study of individual differences out of sheer curiosity, but he quickly became eager to use tests practically.

This early effort collapsed when the tests measuring elements of behavior proved to have no relation to practical affairs. The crucial study was Wissler's, on test scores of Columbia University students (1901). He correlated their marks with each of the Cattell tests, finding zero correlations for reaction time, canceling a's rapidly on a printed page, and naming colors. We now recognize that low correlations were certain to result no matter what mental functions were tested because Wissler's brief tests were inadequate samples of behavior. Moreover, the students were so highly selected that differences among them were hard to detect.

Wundt tested narrow reactions that could be precisely defined, using stimuli that could be accurately controlled. The tests had validity in the same way that a chemist's measure of the freezing point of a substance has validity; the result describes a clearly defined characteristic and is readily interpreted at a superficial level, no matter how much remains to be learned about the underlying process. Tests of elementary reactions have an obvious content validity, and continued investigation in the laboratory spins a web of theory between these measures and theoretical constructs. Their validity outside the laboratory, however, has usually been negligible (except as a defect in color vision or another sensory quality is a handicap in some task).

For practical prediction, tests constructed on quite another principle have been more successful. When a complex performance is to be predicted, a sample of complex and relevant performance will often be a good predictor. To minimize effects of specific training and to obtain a test of wide applicability, the usual test observes the general type of motor or intellectual performance required by the criterion task, not that task directly. The TMC is an example. Such a test serves as a "sign" (p. 45) of what is to be expected after some time and accumulation of experience with new machines, not simply as a sample of competence with familiar ones.

This kind of practical testing came into psychology from medicine. Clinicians dealing with mentally retarded and pathological cases needed diagnostic tests. Psychiatrists looked for tasks that would distinguish normal from abnormal subjects and distinguish among mental disorders. Kraepelin and other nineteenth-century psychiatrists observed reasoning and steadiness of effort in continuous work. Their tasks had some resemblance to requirements of life outside the laboratory. Though few tasks of this period survive in present-day diagnosis, clinical tests are still chiefly concerned with complex processes.

Binet Defines Intelligence

The person making the first mental test is in the position of hunters going into the woods to find an animal no one has ever seen. Everyone is sure the beast exists, for it has been raiding the poultry coops, but no one can describe it. Because the forest contains many animals, the hunters are going to find a variety of tracks. They can decide which tracks to follow only by means of a concept, however vague, of the nature of the quarry. If they seek a large flat-footed creature, they are more likely to bring back that sort of carcass. If they go in convinced that the damage was done by a pack of small rodents, the bag will probably consist of whatever unlucky rodents show their heads.

Binet was in just this position. He knew there must be something like intelligence because its everyday effects could be seen, but he could not describe precisely what he wished to measure. Binet was a research psychologist and not a clinician, but he spent several formative years with Charcot at a mental hospital in Paris. He studied differences among individuals, differences in the same person over the course of development, and changes within a patient from time to time. He was seeking to understand the functioning person rather than to establish laws like those of physics (Wolf, 1973).

The French system had adopted the ideal of universal education in 1881, but by the turn of the century had made none of the systematic provision for retarded children that other countries were adopting. Individuals and groups advocating more humane and suitable treatment of these children finally persuaded the government to appoint a study commission, with which Binet served.

Teachers were not trusted to decide who should receive special education. The concepts of the time were so vague that in one school a quarter of the children were called "abnormal," and not one child in the next school down the road. A teacher might so label the able child who was making no effort or the troublemaker he wished to be rid of. It was important to identify the dull from good families, whom teachers might hesitate to rate low, and the dull with pleasant personalities, whom teachers might favor. The commission said that a child thought possibly to be retarded should have a "medico-psychological examination," and Binet set to work on preparing a suitable procedure.

Having little preconception regarding the difference between brighter and duller children, he tried all sorts of measures: recall of digits, suggestibility, size of cranium, moral judgment, tactile discrimination, mental addition, graphology—even palmistry. He found most useful the tasks that required the child to make sense of objects, pictures, and stories (Binet & Henri, 1895). What such tasks (impure by Wundt's standards) measured was obscure, but scores corresponded to differences observed in everyday life.

Binet found quickly that children who were best in judgment were also superior in attention, vocabulary, and so on. If various intellectual tasks usually rank people in the same order, it is convenient to think of a general mental ability, but that ability is not a single process. Like blood pressure, a test score is a surface indication of the way in which all parts of the organism are working together. Binet gradually identified the essential features of intelligent behavior as "the *tendency to take and maintain a definite direction;* the *capacity to make adaptations* for the purpose of attaining a desired end; and the *power of auto-criticism*" (translation by Terman, 1916, p. 45; italics mine). Direction, purpose, judgment—these *together* formed the arch. Nearly one hundred years of research leave this as the ruling conception: ability is a coordinated whole. Today's analyses of subordinate processes lead to summary statements much like Binet's:

The basic skills . . . include

predicting the consequences of an action or event,
checking the results of one's own action (did it work?),
monitoring one's ongoing activity (how am I doing?),
reality testing (does this make sense?),

and a variety of other behaviors for *coordinating* and *controlling* deliberate attempts to learn and solve problems [A. L. Brown & J. S. De Loache, 1978].

To say that one person is "more intelligent" than another can only mean that he or she acts more intelligently more of the time. "Efficiency" is a concept of the same type. The efficiency of a factory is not to be located in this or that part of the operation. Rather, the purchasing division, the mechanics, the operators, the inspectors, and the shippers do their tasks with few errors and little lost time. Efficiency is a summary statement of what they accomplish as a team. Similarly, knowledge, motivation, self-questioning, and so on make up the system that produces intelligent behavior.

When, as late as 1904, he was trying to measure separate processes or faculties, Binet was pessimistic regarding the practical possibilities of testing. Binet's biographer Wolf (1973, p. 173) credits two practicing clinicians with shifting the attention of testers away from the parts and toward the whole. The right method, they said, was that of the clinic and not the dissecting table. Binet enthusiastically adopted their perspective and promptly assembled an assessment procedure guided by accumulated data. The Binet-Simon scale was published in 1905, with revisions in 1908 and 1911. Psychologists in many countries undertook studies with the Binet-Simon scale, adapting the tests as necessary. Strangely, however, the scale had negligible influence on educational practice in France.

Developments in the United States

Although Edward L. Thorndike was using experimental tests on animals, American psychological research had been dominated by introspection, anecdotes, and questionnaires, all of them as fallible as the person reporting. Educational and social research had likewise been little more than the collection of opinions until Thorndike's laboratory began to develop structured educational measures about 1905. Binet's clinical test, seemingly impartial and independent of preconceptions, was welcomed as a research technique and especially as a means of studying below-average children.

Terman's version prepared at Stanford University captured the spotlight. The acceptance of the Stanford-Binet was due to the care with which it had been prepared, its demand for complex responses, its identification of superiority as well as subnormality, and the seeming simplicity of the IQ concept.

For decades, the Stanford-Binet was central to psychological research and practice. Indeed, from 1920 to 1940 the main function of the clinical psychologist was to "give Binets" in schools and other institutions. The Stanford-Binet—modified a bit over the years, given fresh norms, and interpreted in a more sophisticated manner—has remained popular with clinical and school psychologists, but it has long since lost preeminence. The "Stanford-Binet" that Robert Thorndike and others are now preparing can be expected to depart considerably from the previous design.

Preliminary attempts at group testing had begun by the time the United States entered World War I, and it was suggested that these procedures could be used to screen the thousands of men being inducted into the army. Prospective misfits could be rejected, and the remainder could be sorted to receive training for high, low, or intermediate responsibilities. Leading psychologists quickly assembled a test whose final version became famous as Army Alpha. Alpha tested simple reasoning, ability to follow directions, arithmetic, and information.

Interest in identifying talent. Throughout the latter part of the nineteenth century, ideas about social institutions were strongly influenced by the Darwinian conception that in an ecology the species best fitted for *that* ecology is most likely to thrive. Galton, Spencer, and others in England lost sight of the specificity of fitness. They saw education as preparation for responsibility and expected the fittest persons to go furthest in *any* situation. A sound system would be one in which the ablest persons were given greatest encouragement and greatest responsibility—helping "natural selection" along. American democracy had long cherished the ideal of an open system, as we saw in Jefferson's letter to Adams (page 5f.). Hence American Social Darwinism was much interested in biological fitness *and* in improving opportunity (Hofstadter, 1944).

If some persons were naturally more "fit" intellectually than others and more likely to benefit from education, this seemed to imply that ability is unidimensional, that persons can be ranked. The influential British psychologist Charles Spearman spoke of a central, general ability, which he called g. Whereas Binet had been willing to consider personality and emotion as contributing to intellectual functioning, Spearman sought to isolate the purely intellectual element, that is, to observe "mind" at work. Spearman and his followers devised some reasoning tasks that are still in use, but their more fundamental influence was on the aims of testing and on test interpretation. In particular, their work sharply distinguished intellectual powers from acquired understandings and from emotion and temperament, ranked persons along a single dimension, and interpreted the score as a measure of native capacity. Beyond that they conveyed a sense that intellectual excellence is *the* scale on which human worth is to be judged, and influence allocated. It was this view against which Michael Young (1958) protested in his satire *The rise of the meritocracy, 1870–2033.* "How," he asked, "could men be equal in the eyes of God and yet unequal in the eyes of the Psychologist?"

Binet's tests had been designed as part of a clinical examination. American and British psychologists appreciated the value of studying how the child worked but placed far more emphasis on the score level. E. L. Thorndike defined intelligence as "the power of good responses . . . ," which pointed toward a numerical assessment of superiority or inferiority and away from Binet's attention to the full protocol. The fact that soldiers holding greater responsibility earned high scores on Army Alpha was considered to be striking evidence of the validity of tests.

The psychologists were excited by the apparent success of their new technology, and public schools were eager to adopt it (Chapman, 1979; D. Resnick, in Wigdor & Garner, II, 1982). American business had taken "scientific management" as a slogan, and school administrators were endeavoring to put schools on a businesslike basis. Providing alternative curricula at several levels of difficulty was a response to the new expectation that most adolescents would attend high school and to the new interest in fitting schooling to the learner's development. Tests were the obvious way to put each student onto the right "track." Mental tests for selecting employees were also widely accepted, but never on a scale comparable to the use of tests in schools and the military services (Hale, in Wigdor & Garner, II, 1982).

Army Alpha and most group tests that followed it did not exclude school-learned content. (Arithmetic subtests have been particularly common.) Nonetheless, these tests were generally regarded as measures of intellectual promise. Although a number of psychologists warned that the tests measure only the person's development to date and that inference about underlying capacity is hazardous, the general impression among test users during the 1920s and for some time thereafter was that the tests did indeed select those "fittest to survive" and most responsive to opportunity. The data in Figure 7.1, which tend to support this view, were widely reproduced in textbooks for psychologists and teachers. Other data from the same source (Figure 7.2) suggest that the group tests of the period were reflecting past educational opportunity rather than naked potential. Data classified in this way were much less widely reproduced than those of Figure 7.1. Psychologists making clinical interpretations, of course, tried to allow for any test taker's educational disadvantages, but only recently has the broader public become sensitive to the importance of experience in developing abilities.

It was a great mistake to adopt the words *intelligence* and *capacity* in test titles and in communications to the public. Binet and his fellow clinicians knew full well that they were examining only present performance. Binet wrote eloquently of the hope of finding new methods of cultivation that would "produce a rich harvest" from children who seemed unpromising. For him, intelligence was no more than a presently developed resource.

In British and American discourse, "intelligence" seemed usually to refer to potentiality as if the test score foretold what level the person would reach if given every educational advantage. The evidence is necessarily one-sided. Good ultimate performance proves capacity, but poor performance does not prove incapacity. The typical school-age test is best identified as a "test of general scholastic ability." It measures a set of abilities now developed and demonstrated (not a "potential"). It emphasizes abilities helpful in most schoolwork.

1. *What do the following definitions of "intelligence" include that Binet's definition does not, and vice versa?*
    a. *"The ability to do abstract thinking" (Terman).*

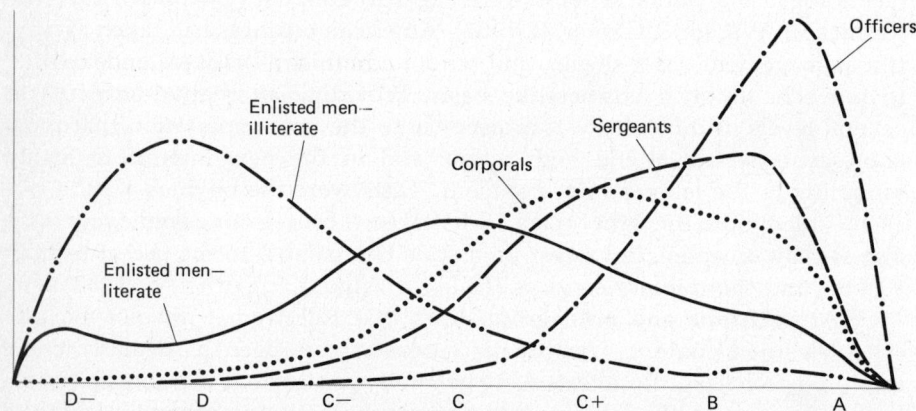

Figure 7.1. Alpha scores of Army personnel, by rank.
Source: Yoakum & Yerkes, 1920.

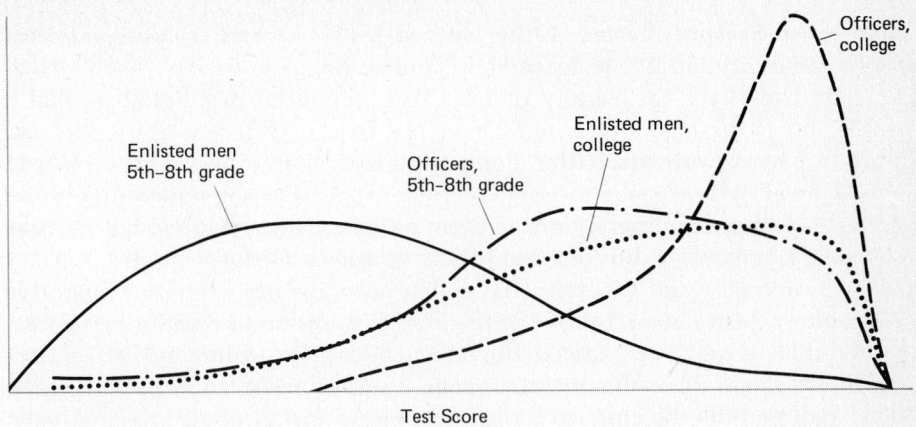

Figure 7.2. Alpha scores of U.S. Army personnel, by level of education. The divisions of the score scale do not correspond perfectly to the letter grades of Figure 7.1. *Source: Data from Yerkes, 1921, pp. 766–767.*

    b. *"The power of good responses from the point of view of truth or fact"* (E. L. Thorndike).
    c. *"The property of so recombining our behavior patterns as to act better in novel situations"* (Wells).
2. Would the same sort of test items be called for by each of these definitions?
3. Is previous learning included in intelligence by these definitions? By Binet's?
4. Critics have suggested that mental tests have measured conformity to "middle-class" ideas and values. Would the qualities listed in the Binet and Terman definitions be considered valuable in a community of poor agricultural workers? Would such a community value any qualities of thought or of coping behavior that do not appear in the definitions?

Appreciating the Diversity of Abilities

Tests of general ability are not interchangeable; each has its own emphasis and ignores what some other test includes. Some tests require command of school-taught tasks; in others, the problems are remote from school lessons. This and the following chapters will stress both the variation and the central consistency among tests of mental abilities.

    Alongside tests intended to report general ability, measures of specialized abilities sprang up. Carl Seashore, for example, produced in 1919 his "Measures of Musical Talent" *(PC)* requiring discrimination of pitch, timbre, rhythm, and the like. Although these abilities clearly are necessary to musical performance, the name of the test is unsatisfactory. It hints that these abilities are inborn and that a person who scores high on the test can be made into a brilliant performer. It is now known that these discriminations are trainable, so that a child who scores low does not have to be denied musical education. And it is certain that distinguished musicianship requires abilities subtler than those Seashore tested. Other special tests checked on perception of forms, dexterity, ability to learn code, and so on.

By the 1940s the variety of tests had convinced psychologists that a single ability dimension is insufficient. Jobs require different aptitudes, and a bright person performs better along some lines than others. During World War II, an effort was made to assign recruits to specialties in which they could do well—rather than merely rating them on one scale as Alpha had. Tests to choose a bombardier differed from those to select a pilot.

Complexity and diversity have also been themes of recent cognitive psychology. Jean Piaget, following the French tradition of examining process rather than score level, traced how the child gains command of distinct concepts such as three-dimensional space, number, and chance. Each concept, mastered, permits the child to transform objects and symbols imaginatively. He or she can say, for example, how the layout of buildings on a table looks to someone seated on the opposite side. Piaget argued that these concepts do not merely "grow," nor are they handed down from elders. Rather, the child constructs them through explorations. Herbert Simon introduced in 1956 an analysis of problem solving that compares the mind to the computer. The two perform many of the same functions: holding information in mind, restating it, identifying gaps and incongruities, retrieving needed facts, and so on. Numerous codes and skills intermesh to produce the performance. These lines of research do not discredit the concept of general ability as a *summary* description. But they—along with deeper understanding of genetics—have underlined the fact that there is no unitary endowent, strong in some persons and weak in others.

Wechsler's Scales for clinical appraisal. Wechsler's measures of general ability are the most prominent individual tests today, and they came to prominence largely because they highlight multiple facets of performance.

David Wechsler served as a clinical psychologist at Bellevue Hospital, operated by the city of New York, where adult social derelicts had to be tested. These people might be mentally subnormal, psychotic, adequately able but temporarily disturbed, or illiterate. Intellectual functioning was important to consider in decisions about disposition, and the psychological examiner was expected to appraise the disorder or handicap underlying any low score. The 1939 Wechsler-Bellevue Scale was designed to serve in such clinical evaluation. The Stanford-Binet included tasks that seemed childish to adult subjects, and proper norms for adults were lacking. Furthermore, the Stanford-Binet tasks, predominantly verbal, provided too limited a range of diagnostic clues for Wechsler's purpose.

To provide clinicians with tests of diverse functions, Wechsler reviewed tasks others had been using and organized some of them into subtests: mazes, recall of information, memory for digits, and so on. The Wechsler-Bellevue was long ago replaced by better-constructed and better-standardized forms, some of them geared to children. As with the Binet, there have been adaptations and translations throughout the world.

Wechsler's test became available at the moment when clinical psychology was emerging as a full-fledged profession. During World War II, military hospitals received great numbers of patients showing emotional disturbance or brain damage. Prompt diagnosis was wanted, and Wechsler hoped that his profile of subtest scores would help. Brain-injured patients, he postulated, were especially low on certain subtests, schizophrenics on others, and so on. His test became the standard instrument in military clinical testing; and when clinical psychologists went to work in veteran's hospitals, public mental hospitals, and child-guidance clinics after the war, the test retained its prominence.

Strange ironies attend the history of test development. Binet set out to identify subnormal children, yet the most famous piece of research with his scale was Terman's follow-up of superior children (p. 242). Wechsler designed his mental test for adults in the belief that adults and children differ in their interests and approach to work; yet today his technique is popular as a children's test. Wechsler's secondary hope in developing the test was that patterns of subtest scores would help to objectify clinical diagnosis of patients. Score profiles proved to have little diagnostic validity except when supplemented by a study of qualitative features of the responses (pp. 251, 271). Moreover, psychologists and psychiatrists have come to realize that a diagnostic label is not sufficient to guide treatment (Kaufman, 1979, pp. 11–19).

The design of Wechsler's scales rests on the experience of the first decades of modern testing, not on latter-day research; but their interpretation has moved with the times. Wechsler emphasized that performance is a complex product of biological development and experience. Like Binet, he wished to consider the complete person and was unwilling to separate intellectual from emotional processes. Emotional forces may heighten attention, persistence, and adaptability; or they may impair performance. Because anxiety, self-confidence, and desire to impress the tester are clearly learned reactions, Wechsler never saw his test as measuring potential independent of experience.

The resemblance of today's most prominent tests to those of 1905 to 1920 testifies to the pioneers' insight and ingenuity. Tests are like automobiles in this respect. The main working parts of today's machines were to be found in the cars of 1920—society is slow to supplant an invention that works. Kaufman (1979, p. 4), however, was right to say that mental testing failed to

> grow conceptually with the advent of important advances in psychology and neurology. . . . The impressive findings in the areas of cognitive development, learning theory, and neuropsychology during the past 25–50 years have not invaded the domain of the individual intelligence test. Stimulus materials have been improved and modernized; new test items and pictures have been constructed with keen awareness of the needs and feelings of both

minority-group members and women; and advances in psychometric theory have been rigorously applied to various aspects of test construction, norming, and validation. However, both the item content and the structure of the intelligence tests have remained basically unchanged.

Ash (1971) has said much the same thing about group tests for industry, blaming the standstill on the attempt to predict imprecise, nonspecific, and incomplete criteria. (See also p. 365f.) On the individual-testing scene a new generation of tests is emerging, Kaufman being author of one of them. These tests (pp. 222f., 335f.) go further than Wechsler's in emphasizing the diversity of mental processes and the need to locate specific strengths and weaknesses.

5. *Comment on this statement by Lewis (1976, p. 8): "[S]ociopolitical influences ... dictate our scientific requirements [our choice of tasks for measuring intellectual qualities].... It may be that an authoritarian ideology requires tasks of rote memory, while an ideology of personal freedom requires tasks of creativity."*
6. *An agricultural experiment station tests varieties of corn. For hybrid G, specimens yield, on the average, 47 pounds per plant.*
   a. *Does it mean anything to say that hybrid G seeds have a "potential" of 47 pounds? What is required for the "potential" to be realized?*
   b. *Might seeds of hybrid F, measured at an average of 42 pounds, have a greater "potential"?*

SCORE SCALES OF MENTAL TESTS

In this section, a review of what was said in Chapter 4 about scales for reporting scores and a comment on some obsolete score scales will pave the way for more complete descriptions of tests.

After giving almost any individual test of general ability, the tester can turn to a table that converts the score to a 100 ± 15 standard score. The Wechsler and Stanford-Binet have always called this an "intelligence quotient" or "IQ." A number of tests appearing in the 1970s, particularly group tests, have provided the same conversion but reduce misinterpretation by substituting a label like "School Ability Index." The IQ scale is anachronistic. The only justification for it is like that given for measuring in pounds and feet instead of shifting to the metric system: the older generation is used to the old scheme.

The obsolete ratio IQ. Once the IQ was truly a quotient. To understand how the quotient came into psychological tradition and why it faded from the scene, we go back to 1916. Binet had suggested describing each child in terms of the level reached on tasks of ascending difficulty. He might have attached abstract labels ("level d," for instance). But these were identified as "age levels" after norms were compiled, and the description of present status came to be called the *mental age* (MA). To describe a child's *rate* of development, Terman divided the mental age by the chronological age. (The decimal was shifted; the ratio 1.25 became the IQ 125).

A 4-year-old with mental age 5, then, had a "ratio IQ" of 125. He was said to be developing 25 per cent faster than the average. Interpreters presumed that he would continue to develop at this faster rate until adulthood. If this were true, the plot of his MAs in successive years would form an ascending straight line (but a wavering one, because of errors of measurement). A linear trend would have to break down in adulthood. The norm at age 40 is only a bit higher than the norm at 15; hence it makes no sense to speak of "mental age 40." It was for this reason that Wechsler, building a scale for adults, adopted the deviation IQ.

Standard scores. "Deviation IQs" are nothing but standard scores. Ratio IQs on the Stanford-Binet, for representative persons of any one age, had been more or less normally distributed, with a mean of 100 and an s.d. in the neighborhood of 15 (but varying from age to age). For deviation IQs, therefore, Wechsler chose a 100+15 scale. (For a few other tests, the scale is 100 +16.) The deviation IQ for the current Wechsler adult scale reports a 40-year-old's standing with reference to representative adults of age 20 to 34. This age range became the standard because average scores in the norm group were highest there.

In guidance and case analysis, most norm-referenced profiles use the 50 $\pm$ 10 standard-score scale, which does not echo the false "rate of development" theme. There is no point in continuing to report general ability on a unique scale, and there *is* a point in discarding the 100 $\pm$ 15 scale.

I am in accord with Reschly's statement (in Glaser & Bond, 1981):

> The term IQ is bound to the myths that intelligence is unitary, fixed, and predetermined. As long as the term IQ is used, these myths will complicate efforts to communicate the meaning of test results and classification decisions. . . . The solution is to abandon the term IQ and replace it with a more accurate descriptor.

Outmoded regulations in some states define degrees of subnormality in terms of the IQ. Dropping the 100+15 scale would discourage this practice. To encourage modern thinking, I shall avoid the terms *intelligence, IQ,* and *mental age* whenever possible. I usually take the liberty of substituting 50+10 standard scores (or percentiles) when summarizing data that were originally reported on the 100+15 scale.

Mental ages and raw scores. John's mental-age score indicates the age at which the average child does as well as John has done. No matter how old John may be, he is assigned a mental age of 8 if he earns as many points as the average 8-year-old. The MA is likely to be misinterpreted. Moreover, as mental ages are available only for general mental tests, the interpreter looking at a variety of tests finds them inconvenient. Wechsler dropped the mental-age concept when he introduced his test for children. (Buried in an appendix of the WISC-R manual, however, is a table that enables the traditionally minded user to calculate something much like a mental age.)

Wechsler's objections to the MA are worth quoting (1974, p. 2; originally presented in 1949):

> An MA is a definable level of test performance. If no further claims for it were made, the concept could be readily accepted as a practical method of defining levels of test performance. But much more is generally implied or subsumed. Mental age is considered to represent an absolute level of mental capacity, so that an MA of 6 means the same irrespective of whether it is obtained by a child of 6, 10 or 16. If all that is implied by this statement is that subjects of different ages can obtain the same test scores, it is true but so obvious. But if one also understands it to mean that their intelligence levels are identical, the statement is at best an assumption which has to be proved. In point of fact, both clinical and statistical evidence is clearly against such an assumption. . . .

Among those reaching the same MA, the brighter children tend to go furthest on tasks that require analysis and judgment whereas the duller children earn much of their credit on tasks for which schooling or experience gives a marked advantage (e.g., information items). Retarded (but not brain-damaged) children can use the reasoning processes that normal children of the same MA have under control and show this when the information-processing burden is reduced (Haywood *et al.*, 1975; Weisz & Yeates, 1981; see also pp. 282f.).

In some ways, the mental age serves the purpose of a raw score. Considering age and educational history alongside the score, a sophisticated interpreter would arrive at the same conclusion whether that score is given in raw units, in mental-age units, in units on a latent-trait scale, or as a standard score. Persons with limited training are least likely to misunderstand percentiles (for an appropriate reference group) or a content-referenced scale. Standard scores and percentiles, being age-adjusted, may decline when a child's performance has actually improved, if other children grew faster. This problem does not arise with content-referenced and latent-trait scales.

In research, tabulations could be made from raw scores, standard scores, or one of the other conversions. It is usually a mistake to calculate statistics from IQs or other standard scores. These summarize not ability but comparative ability. The following made-up numbers illustrate what happens when age is not uniform:

	Child A	Child B	Child C
Age	6	8	10
Raw score X	30	40	50
Standard score for X within age group[1]	58	50	42
Variable V	10	20	30

Variable V—whatever it is—increases with age. In this three-person sample, it correlates positively with X. Age differences are removed from X by the conversion to standard scores, and the correlation of V with the age-adjusted scores is negative.

7. *Three children have the following scores on an ability test:*

	MA	Raw score	Standard score
Mack, age 7 yrs., 6 mos.	10	80	70
Ray, age 10	10	80	50
Ted, age 10	13	100	70

Which boys are most similar? Can one say that any two of them are truly alike in mental ability?

8. *An investigator wants to know if rate of learning is correlated with mental-test performance. She measures learning rate by finding out how long each child requires to master a certain task. Should she correlate learning rate with the standard score or the raw score on the test?*

DESCRIPTION OF TWO INDIVIDUAL TESTS

Wechsler Test Materials and Procedure

The current scales of the Wechsler series are WPPSI—"Primary and Preschool"—for ages 4 to $6\frac{1}{2}$, WISC-R for ages 6 to 16, and WAIS-R for ages 16 to 74. The three scales have the same general pattern, with five or six subtests producing a Verbal score (hereafter denoted V) and another set generating a Performance (P) score. These combine into a Full Scale score. The subtests at different age levels are similar but not identical (Table 7.1). The table follows tradition in listing "alternate" subtests; for example, Digit Span is available if one of the "regular" verbal tests is somehow spoiled during administration. Kaufman (1979, p. 116) urges that Digit Span and Mazes be a regular part of any WISC-R administration because of the light they can shed on mental processes.

---

[1] One would reach these figures if the mean of X is 22, 40, and 58 at ages 6, 8, and 10, with s.d. 10 at each age.

Table 7.1. *Subtests of the Wechsler scales for various ages*

Young Children (WPPSI)	Children of School Age (WISC-R)	Age 16 and Up (WAIS-R)
VERBAL		
Information	Information	Information
Comprehension	Comprehension	Comprehension
Arithmetic	Arithmetic	Arithmetic
Similarities	Similarities	Similarities
Vocabulary	Vocabulary	Vocabulary
(Sentences)	(Digit Span)	Digit Span
PERFORMANCE		
Block Design	Block Design	Block Design
Picture Completion	Picture Completion	Picture Completion
	Picture Arrangement	Picture Arrangement
	Object Assembly	Object Assembly
Animal House	Coding	Digit Symbol
Mazes	(Mazes)	
Geometric Design		

NOTE: Parentheses indicate tests originally proposed as alternates or supplements. Tests with different content, format, and title are aligned horizontally when they measure approximately the same kind of behavior.

The subtests differ in length and in number of credits per item. As was explained in Chapter 4, the standard-score scale for subtests has a mean of 10 and an s.d. of 3.

The Wechsler is given by a trained examiner and requires about one hour. Verbal and Performance subtests usually are alternated. The examiner is directed to start with the easiest items or—as with Block Design—to start with intermediate items expected to be easy enough for the present subject. The examiner shifts to the next subtest when the person has clearly gone as far as he can. The stopping rule ordinarily takes such a form as "Stop after two consecutive failures," but the examiner must make rather sensitive judgments. Some practitioners, wishing to shorten the testing time, propose to substitute three or four subtests for the whole scale. It is reasonable to use a short form to confirm that a person is at a normal level. No composite score should be reported, however. A report from an abbreviated version is not comparable to a true Wechsler examination.

Verbal subtests. Table 7.2 exhibits items similar to those in Wechsler scales. For many items there are follow-up questions to elicit a fuller answer if the first one is inadequate. The items shown here represent a medium level of difficulty, compared to the range of actual questions for the same scale.

GENERAL ABILITY: APPRAISAL METHODS   207

Table 7.2.   *Wechsler verbal tasks at three levels*

INFORMATION

How many wings does a bird have?
Who was Thomas Jefferson?
Who wrote Huckleberry Finn?

COMPREHENSION

Why should we wear shoes when we go outside?
Why is it important to use zip codes when you mail letters?
Why do married people who want a divorce have to go to court?

SIMILARITIES

Puppies grow up to be dogs, and kittens grow up to be ---.
In what way are corn and macaroni alike? How are they the same?
In what way are a book and a movie alike?

VOCABULARY

What is a hammer?
What do we mean by protect?
What does formulate mean?

ARITHMETIC

(The examiner places 10 blocks in front of the child.) *Give me all of the blocks except three. Leave three of the blocks here.*
Dick had 13 pieces of candy and gave away 8. How many did he have left?
How many hours will it take to drive 240 miles at the rate of 30 miles an hour?

SENTENCES

I'm going to say something, and I want you to say it after me just the way I say it:
Karen has two dogs and a new blue wagon.

DIGIT SPAN

I am going to say some numbers. Listen carefully, and when I am through, say them right after me:
3–6–1–7–5–8.
Now I am going to say some more numbers, but this time when I stop, I want you to say them backwards:
1–9–3–2–7.

NOTE: The three rows represent, respectively, the difficulty found in WPPSI, WISC-R, and WAIS-R. Digit Span items in WISC-R and WAIS-R are similar. These items were supplied by Alan Kaufman. I thank him for this and other contributions to this section.

Performance subtests. Among the performance subtests, we have already examined Block Design (p. 52ff.). Figure 7.3 introduces some others.

These tests illustrate Wechsler's concern for variety. Block Design, for example, requires analysis of a complex whole, breaking a pattern into elements. Object Assembly gives the parts and requires the person to discover how they go together as a first step toward constructing the object. Picture Completion requires inspection of a whole to identify the essential missing part. In Picture Arrangement, cartoon panels that tell a story are laid out in

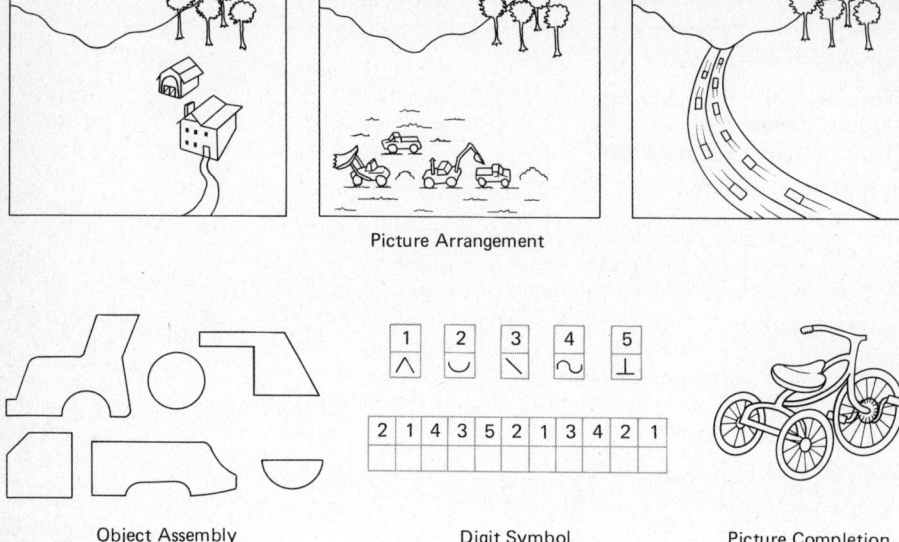

Figure 7.3. Wechsler performance tasks. The items illustrate the general form of the subtests indicated.

incorrect sequence. To arrange them, the subject must identify a complex whole from disorganized parts and reason correctly about the time sequence of events.

Digit Symbol and Coding require the person to put the proper symbol in each place, doing as much as he can in a short time. The code remains in front of the subject as he works. The illustration of Digit Symbol shows only five symbols; the actual test uses nine. Animal House requires the young child to hold a code in mind so that he can match colored houses with the animals that "live" in them.

Performance tasks are especially helpful in studying persons whose behavior or emotional responses are unstable, the mentally retarded, adults with limited education, children suspected of inefficiency in learning, persons with poor hearing, and those whose command of the tester's language is limited. Such tasks make minimal demands on verbal facility, they permit significant observations of the process of performance, and they appeal to examinees who resist schoollike tasks.

Inconsistency between Verbal and Performance standings was once considered to indicate abnormality of development or of reaction to the test. But many persons whose behavior is normal show sizable V–P differences (Kaufman, 1976). It is better to think of the two kinds of test as surveys of overlapping domains of ability, not as tests that measure "the same thing" by different methods. (See pp. 236, 250f.)

General Ability: Appraisal Methods

Mercer's multicultural system. In the 1970s, Jane Mercer, a sociologist concerned with the opportunities offered to children of minority background, introduced a System of Multicultural Pluralistic Assessment (SOMPA; PC) for ages 5 to 11. SOMPA tries to systematize a practice that has always been recommended—of interpreting a test score in the light of other information. I describe the system here because Wechsler data are central to it, first indicating the concern that inspired Mercer's work.

Dissatisfaction with past services to the handicapped has stimulated careful planning for children who have, or are expected to have, difficulty with the usual school program. Federal law now requires that schoolchildren lead lives "as little restricted as possible." Traditional practice was to shunt the handicapped child to a special class or institution for those having similar disabilities. The policy now favored is to keep the child in a classroom that enrolls a full cross section of the local child population of his age, if he can be served there. (See p. 340.)

Classes "for the retarded" have been under particular criticism because, in many localities, comparatively large numbers of children from Hispanic and black families were assigned there (Heller *et al.*, 1982). This contributed to racial segregation, and in many schools unstimulating offerings were serving these children badly. Some states adopted a rule forbidding special placement unless the mental test score fell below a certain level. But in some school systems this seemed to produce automatic assignment to special education when the test score was low, without regard to the suitability of the test for that child. To make this less likely, Mercer's SOMPA collects information on the child's background and brings norms for children of similar background into the interpretation.

From the child's parent, SOMPA collects a health history, information indicative of the child's maturity and adjustment, and information on educational, economic, and cultural characteristics of the family. The interview generates numerical indicators of family size, family structure, socioeconomic status, and urban acculturation (use of English in the home, parents' sense of efficacy, community participation, etc.). In addition, the Adaptive Behavior Inventory for Children (ABIC) covers questions such as these[2]:

> How many of the children and families living around the neighborhood (ranch or farm) does _____ know by name?
>
> 1 SOME OF THEM   2 MOST OF THEM   0 NONE OF THEM
>
> When _____ cannot have what he/she wants immediately, how often does he/she get angry and fuss about it?
>
> 0 MOST OF THE TIME   1 SOMETIMES   2 ALMOST NEVER

[2] Selections from the System of Multicultural Pluralistic Assessment Parent Interview Manual reproduced by permission. Copyright © 1977 by The Psychological Corporation. All rights reserved.

The response choices (but not the numbers) are read to the parent. The responses yield six scores: Family, Community, Peer Relations, Nonacademic School Roles, Earner/Consumer, and Self-Maintenance.

The child takes six tests of motor coordination, one of vision, and one of hearing. Weight and height are recorded. The Bender Gestalt test, in which the child copies lines of various shapes, is given as a crude check on perceptual maturity and neurological functioning (see p. 548).

Alongside the scores so far mentioned, Wechsler standard scores are considered. Significantly, they are plotted under "School Functioning Level (SFL)." This is in keeping with the view that the scores do not measure intelligence or potential. Mercer's next step is to construct an "Estimated Learning Potential (ELP)"—implicitly a claim that statistics can disclose unobserved talent. Her statistical procedure (described on p. 113) does no more than compare the child with others of somewhat similar family background. Mercer's adjustment lowers the standard score if the child's family is small, intact, and integrated with mainstream culture and raises it (perhaps by quite a lot) where the opposite is true.

Figure 7.4 displays the SFL and ELP scores of Bernice, a black 9-year-old. Bernice scored average or above on the ABIC scales, apparently being unusually able to care for herself. But her school record was very poor, and, as Mercer says, that fact plus the WISC-R scores would have led many schools to consider placing Bernice in a class for the retarded. From the ELP and background information, Mercer and Lewis (1977, p. 88) conclude that

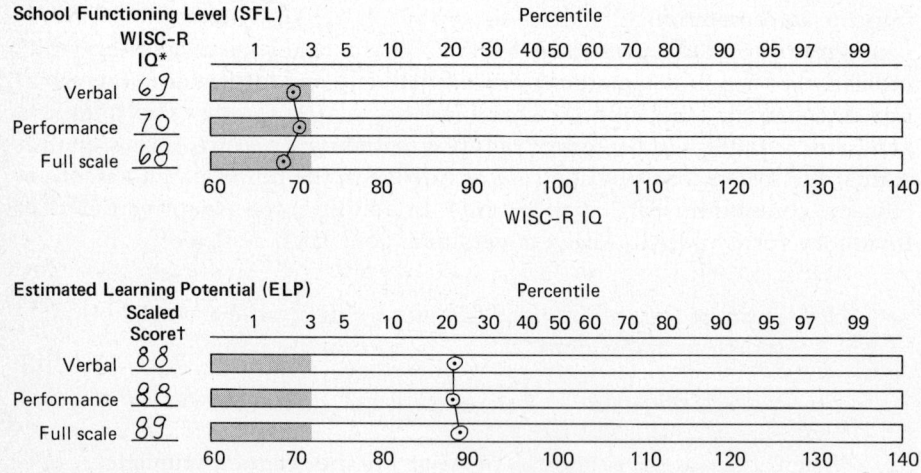

Figure 7.4. Profiles based on general and differentiated norms.
Source: Profile form and description of Bernice reproduced by permission from the System of Multicultural Assessment Parent Interview Manual (pp. 87–88). Copyright © 1977 by The Psychological Corporation. All rights reserved.

the average *WISC-R* Full Scale IQ earned by children having Bernice's configuration of scores on the *Sociocultural Scales* is 77. Her *WISC-R* Full Scale IQ of 68, therefore, is only 9 points below the mean for her normative group. This is not an important variation from the mean, and her Estimated Learning Potential, expressed as an ELP Full Scale score of 89, argues against placing Bernice in a class for the mentally retarded.

In Bernice's case, there is much to build on. She does not have a history of serious health problems, her sensory-motor abilities do not appear to be impaired, and her vision and hearing are good. As evidenced by her scores on the *ABIC,* Bernice exhibits a degree of personal independence and social responsibility greater than one ordinarily finds among children her age. Although her *WISC-R* IQs are low, her ELP scores are within the normal range. When all of these factors are considered, it seems likely that Bernice can benefit from a program of educational instruction that takes differences between her background and the culture of the school into account.

This benign interpretation is more appropriate than a prediction of school failure. The paragraph glosses over the difficulties of inventing an educational program suited to Bernice, but a test manual lacks room to develop such a theme.

Psychologists know that performance at the 2d percentile does not have the usual implications when a child demonstrates adequate functioning in home and community, so they advise considering the child's adaptation to his or her own subculture. But the ELP conversion is flawed. Mercer's Hispanic data were obtained by testing in English; testing should be in Spanish when the child has better command of that language. Mercer's samples were small and not geographically representative. At best, the formulas that fit one community would not be best for a distant community (Reschly, in Reynolds & Gutkin, 1982). Nor would a true national sample give a formula appropriate to a local clientele. Moreover, better statistical methods (Darlington, 1978) would have changed the adjustment formulas.

Mercer's techniques boost black scores by about 11 points on average and those of Hispanics by 7. Scores of a few white children are adjusted upward by similar amounts, but small downward adjustments are made for most white children. The ELP label implies that children with the same ELP are equally ready to learn and hints that proper education would bring them the same final attainment. That goes too far. The words *potential* and *capacity* again cause trouble. Mercer offered no evidence for the optimistic prediction that children like Bernice will, with appropriate nurturance, achieve as much in school as a child for whom both SFL and ELP stand at 89. (See Sattler, 1981, pp. 280–282.)

Mercer compares three models of score interpretation: "medical," "social system," and "pluralistic." Table 7.3 introduces ideas from several of her

Table 7.3 Mercer's three assessment models

Elements of Models	Medical Model	Social System Model	Pluralistic Model
Other names for models	Pathological model, Disease model, Deficit model	Social deviance model, Social adaptivity model, Social-ecological model	General intelligence model
Purposes	To screen for biological anomalies	To identify behavioral deviance	To estimate learning potential
Definition of normal/abnormal	Normal = absence of pathological signs; a residual nonsymptomatic category.	Normal = behavior that meets social norms.	Normal = scoring average for own group.
	Abnormal = presence of pathological signs.	Abnormal = behavior that violates social norms; social deviance.	Abnormal = scoring high or low on test of learning compared to own sociocultural group; a normative classification.
Assumptions of the models	1. Symptoms are caused by biological pathology.	1. Multiple definitions of "normal" behavior are role and system specific.	1. All tests measure learning and are culture specific.
	2. Sociocultural factors are not relevant to diagnosis or treatment; human organisms are similar across cultures.	2. Behavioral norms are politically, not biologically, determined; values of the dominant group are enforced.	2. Inferences regarding "intelligence" are based on comparisons among children who have had similar sociocultural experiences.

Interpretation of scores	Scores can be interpreted transculturally.	Scores measure achievement in a particular social role in a particular social system in relation to norms of the system; the person's present knowledge or skill.	Scores measure knowledge of a particular cultural heritage compared to others from the same ethclass; the person's relative knowledge or skill compared to own cultural base.
Ethical code governing interpretation	It is a more serious error in assessment to overlook a pathology that is present than to falsely suspect a pathology that is not present, since untreated pathology may lead to more serious pathology.	It is a more serious error in assessing behavior to falsely label behavior as deviant than to falsely label behavior as normal, since negative labeling may result in the placement of a child on a disabling trajectory.	It is a more serious error to underestimate than to overestimate learning potential, since underestimates may result in the placement of a child on a disabling trajectory. Overestimates may enhance educational options.

SOURCE: Abbreviated from the Technical Manual for the System of Multicultural Pluralistic Assessment and reproduced by permission. Copyright © 1979 by The Psychological Corporation. All rights reserved.

chapters. In medical diagnosis, testers locate defects (in hearing, for example). All but four of her variables, she says, seek out defects. WISC-R IQs (= SFL) and ABIC, she says, address questions posed by the "social system" model. ELP and the sociocultural scales embody a "pluralistic" conception.

The Stanford-Binet of 1960

A major redesign of the Stanford-Binet (SB) is in progress; at this time the new plan is not ready for reporting. As the old version looms large in testing history and in the research literature, some description is called for. The 1916 scale had just one form; equivalent forms, produced in 1937, were merged in 1960. In 1972 fresh norms were provided. The SB has been a single package, from tasks for 2-year-olds to those that challenge adults. In contrast with the Wechsler, the SB was not organized to provide multiple scores, and it contained few performance tasks beyond age 8.

Binet, thinking of intelligence as a steadily growing power, proposed a ladder of tasks. For each level Binet selected tasks that average children of a given age are just mastering. Young children had to display simple interpretation and recall; intellectual manipulations were required in middle childhood.

Table 7.4 lists some of the SB tasks. Ordinarily there are a number of similar items for each task, and six tasks at each level. (There are more levels than the table shows.) Save for vocabulary and digit span, the tasks are only roughly similar to the Wechsler subtests listed alongside them. As Table 7.4 suggests, the SB is less diversified than the Wechsler, the emphasis being heavily verbal. No person takes the whole test. As with Block Design, the examiner starts where she expects the person to pass, shifts downward if necessary, then works up to the highest level the person can handle.

9. *Which Wechsler subtests have the following characteristics?*
   a. *The score is affected by educational background.*
   b. *The test demands experiences common to persons in the urban American culture.*
   c. *The test requires problem solving or reorganization of knowledge rather than mere recall.*
   d. *The test measures elementary processes such as Cattell and Wissler investigated.*
10. *Have a friend prepare two strings of digits, each from 5 to 12 digits in length. Then have him give you this digit-span test, reading off each string at a steady rate, without emphasis.*
    a. *Judging from your experience, what processes are required to do well on the test?*
    b. *What might account for poor Digit Span in a high school student who performs at an average level on other Wechsler subtests?*

Table 7.4. *Representative tasks from the Stanford-Binet*

Year	Task	Correlation with test total	Comparable Wechsler task
II-6	Fits shapes to holes	0.5	(Spatial perception)[a]
	Points to object "we drink out of" (miniature)	0.55	Vocabulary
	Names pictured objects	0.7	Vocabulary
	Repeats "4–2"	0.65	Digit Span
IV	Names pictured objects	0.8	Vocabulary
	Examiner shows three toys, then hides one; child names it	0.55	(Memory)
	"Brother is a boy; sister is a. . . ."	0.55	Similarities
	Matches simple forms	0.75	(Spatial perception)
	"Why do we have houses?"	0.7	Comprehension
VI	Defines *orange, envelope*	0.65	Vocabulary
	Gives examiner 9 blocks	0.75	Arithmetic
	Maze	0.7	Mazes
	"An inch is short; a mile is. . . ."	0.65	Similarities
IX	Examiner notches folded paper; child draws how it will look unfolded	0.6	(Spatial reasoning)
	Verbal absurdities	0.85	(Verbal reasoning)
	Reproduces design from memory	0.6	(Memory)
	Repeats "6–5–2–8" backward	0.5	Digit Span
	Computes change from a purchase	0.6	Arithmetic
XII	Defines *skill, juggler*	0.8	Vocabulary
	Finds absurdity in picture	0.5	Picture Completion
	Defines *constant, courage*	0.85	Vocabulary
	Completes "The streams are dry . . . there has been little rain."	0.7	(Conceptual reasoning)
Average Adult	Defines *regard, disproportionate*	0.85	Vocabulary
	Explains how to measure 3 pints of water with a 5-pint and a 2-pint can	0.7	(Numerical reasoning)
	Explains a proverb	0.75	Comprehension
	Compares *laziness* and *idleness*	0.8	Similarities

[a]The main ability tested is identified in parentheses if no Wechsler subtest is sufficiently similar to be listed.
SOURCE: Items and correlations from Terman & Merrill, 1973, pp. 69ff. and 342ff. Items are copyright 1916 by Lewis M. Terman, 1937 by Lewis M. Terman and Maud A. Merrill, © 1960, 1973 by The Riverside Publishing Company and reproduced or adapted by permission of the publisher.

11. *Which Stanford-Binet tasks in Table 7.4 seem to require all three aspects of Binet's definition of intelligence?*
12. *Consider Mercer's models as described in Table 7.3.*
    a. *If a person drinks alcohol frequently and in large amounts, how would that behavior be described in Mercer's language? Which of the three value judgments (at the bottom of the columns) seem(s) appropriate for such a case?*
    b. *Recent immigrants from countries where English is not spoken have difficulties in the school and community. Describe them in terms of Mercer's second and third models.*
13. *What do you understand "Learning potential" to mean? Would Mercer's concept be adequately validated by a check on how well ELPs recorded 3 years ago, when children entered school, correlate with scores on a current achievement test?*
14. *Digit-span items are mixed into the SB, two or three of them being followed by items of other kinds before the next digit item is reached. Children seem to recall longer strings of digits in this format than they do in the Wechsler format (Hutton, 1964). What explanation can you offer? Does this fact suggest anything about the comparative validity of the two formats?*
15. *"The same set of items is likely to call upon different mental processes in older and younger children." What could be meant by that statement? Illustrate.*

ILLUSTRATIVE GROUP TESTS

Whereas individual tests permit an appraisal of style of performance, the group test of general ability yields only summary scores. Its impersonal administration and multiple-choice form provide little basis for qualitative interpretation. The interpreter has to assume that the person understood the nature and purpose of testing and made an effort. The examiner giving an individual test is likely to be aware when the performance does not fully reflect ability. She can sense tension or failure to understand directions. Group testing permits no similar attention to individuals. Group testing is usual, however, in routine screening of job applicants, recruits, or students, where the aim is to improve the proportion of correct institutional decisions. When one wants to understand a person, the flexibility and intimacy of the individual test have many advantages.

For ease of administration, a group test is usually given with a uniform time limit. In interpreting, therefore, one must recognize the possibility that slow response pulled down the score.

Two illustrative tests are described here at modest length. In one, all items have the same general form and in a sense measure the same ability.

The second example, with several item types, is illustrative of the group tests constructed for use in schools on a mass basis. It obtains a kind of cross section of the domain of general ability.

A Homogeneous Test: Matrices

Spearman had almost as much influence as Binet on ideas about mental ability. Spearman was not much interested in practical testing; his aim was to isolate just what made up the power of mind, apart from learned skills and associations. Abstract reasoning—the ability to perceive and apply relationships—became the center of his concept of g. Today psychologists often speak of "fluid ability" (see p. 253), distinguishing this sector of the ability domain from performances that depend more on formal learning. Piaget's theory regarding the formal reasoning of adolescents and adults is closely in line with Spearman's concept (but Piaget's analysis of the child's judgments in concrete situations is closer to Binet's).

Analogy items like those Spearman developed play important roles in current psychology (pp. 281, 337). An analogy is a set of terms in which the same relation appears between terms A and B and terms C and D: "Father is to son as mother is to ———." Analogies can be made of words, symbols, pictures, or geometric forms. The matrix item is a double figure analogy; two relationships must be identified and kept in mind.

The matrix items in Figure 7.5 illustrate the range of difficulty that is possible. The test may be speeded or unspeeded. Test takers of limited ability may be given the matrices individually. Verbal understanding plays little part; directions can be given in pantomime.

L. S. Penrose and J. C. Raven invented the matrix task, and Raven published his first version of the test in 1938. Progressive Matrices (distributed by *PC*) has versions developed at different times for somewhat different initial purposes. A single—seriously inadequate—manual now covers the procedures for and research on all of them (Raven *et al.*, 1978).

Several investigators have correlated a matrix test with the Wechsler or Binet, the results, of course, varying with the sample and the matrix test chosen. Ordinarily, the matrix test correlates at least 0.6 with the score from an individual test in a group of normal range. And it correlates about equally with Wechsler Performance and Verbal scores (see Figure 9.8). The matrix test is more purely a reasoning test than the Wechsler (or the Binet). The test requires the purposive effort and self-criticism that figured in Binet's definition. It requires the discipline that schooling teaches, but the knowledge it demands is almost universal in Western cultures.

A matrix test was the principal test for military classification in Great Britain during World War II. The test was chosen to make sure that recruits of normal ability were not rejected because of poor education. The matrix test

Figure 7.5. Matrix items at three levels of difficulty.
Source: The first matrix is an easy warmup item taken from the Variations test of the Learning Potential Assessment Device and reproduced by permission of R. Feuerstein (see p. 335). The second matrix is similar to those in the Raven test and the third, in free-response form, is at a level suitable for testing college graduates.

was most helpful in predicting performance in visual signaling and radar operating (Vernon & Parry, 1949). The homogeneity of the matrix test limited its military usefulness; tests combining analytical, verbal, and numerical abilities more accurately predicted performance in training. One reason SB and Wechsler V are successful predictors is that they call for verbal, numerical, and reasoning abilities in about the same combination that schooling itself does.

16. *Why is it not strictly correct to call the pantomimed matrix test nonverbal?*

The Cognitive Abilities Test

Representative of the tests offered to schools for group testing is the Cognitive Abilities Test (CogAT). CogAT grew out of the Lorge-Thorndike test, on which much research was reported. A multilevel edition serves grades 3 through 13; within a subtest, items are arranged according to difficulty. Figure 7.6 illustrates some item types; all of the specimens are from Level C, where a typical fifth-grade class would start work. For every starting level, there is a corresponding stopping point. In the synonyms subtest, for example, Level C begins with a word at the level of *tidy;* a class that starts there is to stop at item 35—on a word such as *gradual.* In testing fifth-graders thought to be superior, the tester would begin at Level D; if many students are expected to be below average, she would start at B. A typical tenth-grade class would start at the level of *gradual.*

Staggering the starting point has several virtues. The pupil, taking items

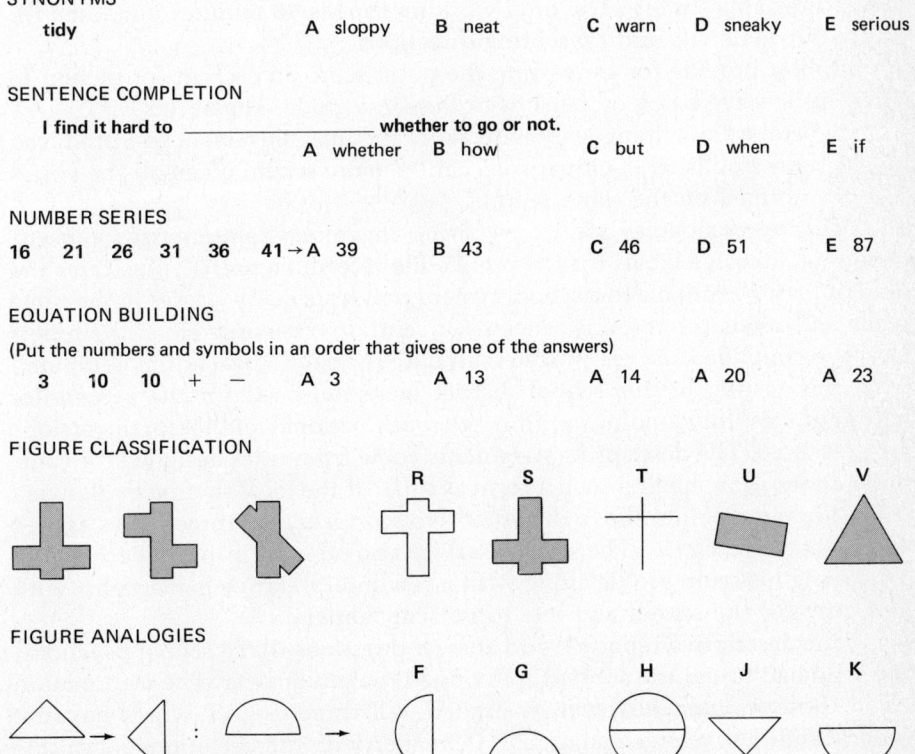

Figure 7.6. Cognitive Abilities tasks.
Source: Some of these items are copyright © 1971 or 1978 by The Riverside Publishing Company and are reproduced by permission.

suitable for his class, spends no time on items he is sure to pass. Nor does he bang his head against impossibly difficult ones where in the end he is likely to guess and so introduce random error. Furthermore, the school can test throughout the range of grades from 3 upward with the same test booklet.

The test is well suited to "out of level" testing. Very able fifth-graders will earn high scores on a test planned for the usual fifth grade; harder items would disclose more about them. Similarly, one wants a comparatively easy test for the least able fifth-graders. Those who score very high or very low on CogAT as normally administered can be started at a different level on an alternate form a few days later. More important, an adept tester can start pupils at different levels; the time allowance is the same regardless of the starting point. The several levels are calibrated onto a common scale.

There are three scores: Verbal, Quantitative, and Nonverbal (figural). Three or four subtests are provided in each category. The authors say that the items progress so steeply in difficulty that only occasionally does a child have insufficient time to attempt all the problems he is able to solve. This was verified in tryouts in which children, given extra time, could not improve their scores appreciably. The total working time is 98 minutes plus time for giving out materials and presenting directions.

Tables provide for converting the point score on each major section to a percentile score based on persons in the same grade. The norms for CogAT were developed simultaneously with those for an achievement test produced by the same publisher. Comparisons can be more secure when all the variables are normed on the same sample.

Testing companies vie in preparing ingenious computerized reports, including adhesive labels for the pupil's file record. Figure 7.7 illustrates the kind of listing available to a school system that tests many classes in the same grade and sends the response sheets for central processing. Here, the report has been simplified and rearranged to fit onto the page. Local norms computed from this testing in this school district were the basis for the percentiles within grades; for standings within age, both national and local conversions are presented. The descriptive statements come from rules designed for computer application, having such a form as this: "If the local stanine in Nonverbal is 2 or more points above the other two scores, and all three scores exceed 4, print statement 247." The scoring service also offers to print for each a page displaying his score profile along with a few interpretative paragraphs (with one copy for the school and one to be sent home).

The descriptive reports try to answer questions that a school psychologist who had tested the student individually might answer. The information given the computer, however, is limited. All three CogAT scores measure general ability to a large extent, and the validity of interpretations for profile shape is not well established.

17. *The three sections of CogAT are influenced substantially by a common or "general" factor (p. 288). Yet CogAT provides no overall score, and the*

General Ability: Appraisal Methods

Cognitive Abilities Test	STUDENT LIST REPORT	PR = Percentile Rank	S = Stanine	Teacher: MARIGOLD Grade: 5 Form: 3 Page: 1 School/District: CENTRAL School Code: Date Tested: 11/78 Norms: FALL Process No.: 000-0021-000					
PUPIL NAME ID NUMBER		NO. OF ITEMS MARKED	RAW SCORE	SCORES BY GRADE		SCORES BY AGE			
						STANDARD SCORE	NATIONAL		LOCAL
				PR	S		PR	S	PR	S
LINDHOLM, PAUL AGE 12-6	VERBAL	100	59	54	5	93	33	4	21	3
	QUANTITATIVE	60	46	76	6	101	52	5	21	3
	NONVERBAL	80	50	37	4	87	21	3	7	2
	AVERAGE IN VERBAL AND QUANTITATIVE SKILLS. BELOW AVERAGE NONVERBAL SKILLS. SHOULD BE ABLE TO MAKE ABOUT AVERAGE PROGRESS IN TYPICAL SCHOOL CURRICULUM. MAY SHOW LIMITATIONS IN SYNTHETIC AND HOLISTIC THINKING.									
MCVEY, JUDY AGE 12-7	VERBAL	100	68	74	6	100	50	5	57	5
	QUANTITATIVE	60	53	96	9	114	81	7	79	7
	NONVERBAL	80	73	96	9	120	89	8	79	7
	SOMEWHAT ABOVE AVERAGE FOR GRADE IN DEVELOPMENT OF VERBAL SKILLS. OUTSTANDING IN DEVELOPMENT OF QUANTITATIVE SKILLS. SHOULD SHOW AVERAGE ACHIEVEMENT OR BETTER IN ACADEMIC WORK, WITH SPECIAL STRENGTH IN MATHEMATICS AND QUANTITATIVELY ORIENTED SUBJECTS. FURTHER INVESTIGATION MIGHT BE WORTHWHILE TO UNDERSTAND WHY VERBAL SKILLS HAVE LAGGED BEHIND QUANTITATIVE.									

Figure 7.7. Class listing of CogAT scores for fifth-graders.
Source: The information presented was supplied by the test publishers. The form is modified here in arrangement and typographical detail; the original form is copyright © 1978 by The Riverside Publishing Company and is adapted by permission. In the original, about 12 students appear on each page.

manual recommends against forming composites for purposes of case interpretation. What risk would there be in bringing to a case conference the three part scores **plus** an overall score?

18. Discrepancies among the three CogAT scores "may reveal facts significant for vocational prospects," says the manual. Assuming that the differences interpreted are reliable and stable, what vocational implications—if any —would the following profile patterns suggest? (At what age would such an interpretation be sensible? And what facts would be valuable to supplement it?)
    a. *Verbal and Quantitative in normal range; Nonverbal superior.*
    b. *Quantitative and Nonverbal in normal range; Verbal weak.*
    c. *Verbal and Nonverbal superior; Quantitative slightly below normal.*
19. The manual describes CogAT as a measure of ability to interpret abstract concepts and symbols and to deal with their relationships. The test tasks,

it is said, do not correspond well to the notions of "mechanical intelligence," "social intelligence," and "practical intelligence." What kinds of evidence from tests or other behavior would presumably provide useful indicators for these three concepts? Is it likely that reliable differences could be found in any of these traits among persons who have equally good "abstract ability"?

20. Says the CogAT manual, "One may anticipate that a test of cognitive abilities will predict a variety of outcomes important to society, and there is no one criterion that is uniquely appropriate." Suggest some criteria that would be relevant to one or all parts of CogAT. (Specify the number of years, between the testing and the collection of criterion data, over which prediction might be hoped for.)

NOTES ON ADDITIONAL TESTS

The notes in this section introduce tests a reader might want to look into. Many tests of good quality are not listed here; the tests listed are mentioned often in the literature or have features of special interest.

New Individual Tests

Here are described two new instruments and the new form of an older one. Later another new procedure, the LPAD (p. 335), is taken up. It is more a means of clinical observation than a scored instrument.

British Ability Scales (BAS). The BAS, developed cooperatively by British psychologists and published by a British firm (*NFER*-Nelson), may soon be available from American distributors. Principal responsibility was taken by C. D. Elliott, D. J. Murray, and L. S. Pearson. The test includes 24 tasks various specialists found useful in diagnosis for ages ranging from $2\frac{1}{2}$ to 17.

Tests are fitted to age ranges. Thus the perceptual-matching tasks are restricted to ages $2\frac{1}{2}$ to 9 whereas "speed of information processing" is not tested below age 8. In the latter, each item displays five 3-digit numbers; the respondent is to mark the largest. A number of tests assess memory, and several others assess conservation or formal reasoning in the sense of Piaget. Social Reasoning was illustrated at page 85. Several tests measure basic literacy and facility with numbers.

The purpose of the test is to lay out a profile. Most users will employ some of the subtests and not others, choosing subtests to fit each case. The authors suggest that certain subtests can be averaged to produce a "General IQ," a "Visual IQ," and a "Verbal IQ." These techniques seem to have the defects that discredited so-called "short forms" of the Wechsler scales. The adequacy of the BAS measures cannot be judged on the basis of the limited

General Ability: Appraisal Methods

technical studies so far reported. Reliabilities calculated for particular scores within single age groups have ranged from 0.4 to an unbelievable 0.98. My tentative opinion is that the majority of scales have a test-retest stability as good as Wechsler subtests.

An important feature is that parts of a subtest may be given, items being chosen according to the examinee's development. Block Design, for example, has 16 patterns; a young child can be given the first 11 whereas a teenager is likely to be given items 6 through 16. The level of ability is estimated from the record of passes and failures by means of the Rasch scaling technique. Some suggestions offered by the producers of BAS regarding interpretation of this unfamiliar scale are misleading; note the cautions expressed at page 119.

The Kaufman battery. The Kaufman Assessment Battery for Children (K-ABC; *AGS*), by Alan S. and Nadeen L. Kaufman, for ages $2\frac{1}{2}$ to 12, appeared in 1983. There are 16 subtests, but, as with BAS, some subtests are designed for young children and some for older ones. The test, organized in the light of recent ideas from neuropsychology and cognitive psychology, offers four main or "global" scores.

- Sequential Processing consists of memory tasks in which the examinee is to reproduce a string of numbers after hearing them or to make a series of hand movements after seeing them or to touch easily recognized silhouettes in the order the examiner used in naming the objects pictured.
- Simultaneous Processing includes tasks that resemble Wechsler Picture Arrangement, Matrices, and Gestalt Closure (p. 292). Among the newly invented tests, one is Magic Window, in which the examiner moves a picture past a narrow window and asks the child to recognize the object pictured.
- Mental Processing Composite, an average over all subtests of the two preceding sections. The average over those subtests that can be administered by pantomime gives a Nonverbal score.
- Achievement is the name given to a score derived from tasks that depend directly on experience in the culture or the school. Tasks include reading, arithmetic, and naming pictures of well-known persons or places (information) or objects (vocabulary).

In later chapters much will be said about the distinction between "fluid" and "crystallized" abilities; these are represented respectively in the Simultaneous Processing and Achievement scores. The Sequential Processing score covers efficiency in attending and rehearsing, essentially independent of reasoning or knowledge. The Kaufmans do not emphasize scores on single subtests, as BAS does, but do propose interpretation of any marked variation within any global category.

The standard scores for the "processing" subtests are on a 10 ± 3 scale like Wechsler's. The global scores and the "achievement" subtests are placed on a 100 ± 15 scale. In addition to the usual type of national norms, scores can be converted to percentiles relative to a socioeconomic group such as black (or white) children with at least one parent who went beyond high school. Consider a 10-year-old whose national percentile on Sequential Processing is 75 and whose most-educated parent finished high school but went no further. The "sociocultural percentile" is 90 if the child is black; 75 if he is white.

The child can respond to many K-ABC tests by pointing or other nonverbal response, and no task requires more than a word or two of verbal response. For this reason, the Wechsler Comprehension subtest is suggested as a supplement. The K-ABC manual emphasizes that the test measures "current functioning," not innate abilities. Publicity for the test has suggested that it is an "intelligence" test particularly fair to children of minority background; this is open to misunderstanding. The test shows about the same black-white difference at school ages as other tests do. Across groups with similar parent education, blacks and Hispanics under age 5 and Hispanics at school age perform as well as whites. That fact is largely attributable to K-ABC's emphasis on memory and to its exclusion of verbal expression and conceptualization. Still, K-ABC demonstrates clearly that on many nonverbal reasoning tasks there is little difference across racial-ethnic lines when parent education is held constant.

Peabody Picture Vocabulary Test. Authors are Lloyd M. Dunn and Leota M. Dunn *(AGS)*. The test is for ages $2\frac{1}{2}$ to adulthood and has two parallel forms. A quick individual test requiring choice of a picture to match a word read by the examiner. The format is suitable for testing many persons with physical handicaps. The 1960 edition was widely used in research, especially with young children. Selection of items and scaling for the 1981 edition (PPVT-R) used advanced psychometric techniques. Although of some value as a screening test, for case workups PPVT-R is limited because of its narrowness and limited reliability. Two testings within the same month correlate around 0.8 after age 8, somewhat less at earlier ages. PPVT-R is a reasonable way to "match" children prior to assignment to groups in an experiment.

Conventional Group Tests

To facilitate comparison with other group tests, I repeat a few facts on CogAT.

- Cognitive Abilities Tests (CogAT); R. L. Thorndike and E. Hagen; *Riv.* Grades 3–12; the multilevel format enables one booklet to serve these grades. Three scores are reported in grade 3 and above; see pages 219ff. and 287ff. A compact booklet of simpler items forms a single-score Primary test. Norms are coordinated with the Iowa Test of Basic

Skills (grades 1–9) or the Tests of Achievement and Proficiency (9–12).
- Henmon-Nelson Test of Mental Ability; M. J. Nelson, T. A. Lamke, and J. L. French; *Riv.* Three levels spanning grades 3–12. Much like Otis-Lennon; probably more speeded. A companion Primary battery offers scores on three areas of readiness: information, vocabulary, size and number concepts.
- Otis-Lennon School Ability Test; A. S. Otis and R. T. Lennon; *PC.* Five levels spanning grades 1–12. Normed together with Metropolitan Achievement Tests. A "spiral omnibus" technique intermingles number series, matrices, verbal opposites, and other item forms in ascending order of difficulty. One total score. (Derivatives of Otis's original tests have been widely used in employment testing, the best known being the revision by Wonderlic.)
- School and College Ability Tests (SCAT); *Addison-Wesley* for *ETS.* Three levels spanning grades 3–12. Two scores, from verbal analogy and quantitative judgment items. Norms coordinated with the Sequential Tests of Educational Progress.
- Test of Cognitive Skills (TCS); *CTB.* Five levels spanning grades 2–12. Four subtests use series completion, pictorial analogies, memory, and verbal reasoning items. Some subtests mix item types; thus the series subtest includes figure series, number series, and series of letter groups. The tasks were designed to correlate with achievement but not to overlap with the *content* of achievement batteries. Apparently the main purpose of TCS is to convert scores from the publisher's California or Comprehensive achievement batteries into an overachievement/underachievement index (see p. 255).
- Wide Range Intelligence and Personality Test (WRIPT); J. F. Jastak; Guidance Associates. One form for grade 4 through adulthood; less accurate than a test whose difficulty is matched to one age or grade. Ten brief, timed subtests range from digit symbol to spelling. A preliminary screening device for guidance or other services whose potential clients range widely in age. The manual emphasizes profile interpretation, including inferences about personality; such interpretation is questionable, and inadequate technical justification is provided.

21. *The Kaufman sociocultural norms escape the technical difficulties of Mercer's regression technique. What would be appropriate ways to use these norms in interpreting the scores of a black child? What misinterpretations should users be warned against?*
22. *Would a group or an individual test be preferable*
    a. *In screening applicants for teaching positions in a large city?*
    b. *In testing juvenile delinquents prior to decisions about probation?*

c. *In research on trends in the intelligence of immigrants?*
d. *In selecting secretarial employees for a university?*
23. *The manual for the Otis-Lennon School Ability Test states that ability level is not fixed and that, though scores probably have some genetic base, they "capture the consequences of environmental limitations that affect students' ability to master schoolwork at the time of testing." Is it proper for a scholastic aptitude test to reflect environmental disadvantage?*
24. *For the Otis-Lennon test, the raw score is converted to a standard score by a table for the pupil's age. The standard score can then be converted to a percentile using a table for the pupil's* grade. *Why, for some pupils, might a school wish to consider both standing within age group and standing within grade group?*

Tests for Admission to Advanced Education

Here a few tests representative of the giant testing programs for admission to colleges and graduate training are described.

- American College Testing Program (ACT); *ACTP.* A test of English usage, math, social studies, and natural science; a composite score also is reported. ACT serves more for guidance than for college selection though it does influence admissions in some schools. Many nonselective colleges, including statewide public systems, have required or recommended that applicants take ACT. The program provides extensive statistical services; with that help, a college can build up its own experience table to identify, for example, how the several scores relate to later success in its engineering department.

    The science and social studies tests require interpretation of reading passages (usually several paragraphs long). The examinee has to draw conclusions from experiments and historical evidence, to recognize a writer's bias, and to make other inferences. It is, then, more a test of reasoning and judgment than a test of knowledge that would be acquired in particular courses. The mathematics section covers tasks from algebra and geometry courses.
- Scholastic Aptitude Test (SAT); *CEEB.* The verbal section measures verbal reasoning and comprehension of textlike materials. The Quantitative section measures reasoning with numerical materials and with the most basic principles from algebra and geometry. SAT attempts to measure skills and diligence required in college work, with minimal demand on knowledge from history, biology, and the like.

    SAT is required by most of the colleges where admission is competitive and by many that accept nearly all applicants. Copies of questions from past examinations and booklets that advise on test taking are available to the prospective test taker. A Preliminary Scholastic Aptitude Test is offered to high school juniors. It provides

Table 7.5. *Practical consequences of selective admissions*

Basis for prediction	Typical Validity Coefficient	Percentage of Admits who Reach 40th Percentile in College GPA		
		SR = 0.2	SR = 0.5	SR = 0.8
Chance	0	60	60	60
SAT-V *or* SAT-M	0.37	79	72	65
SAT-V *and* SAT-M	0.41	81	73	66
High school grade average	0.49	86	76	67
SAT-V, SAT-M, and high school grades	0.56	88	78	68

SOURCE: Adapted from Kaplan, 1982, p. 21.
Note: SR (selection ratio) is the proportion of applicants admitted.

practice, helps in decisions about which colleges to apply to, and certifies eligibility for certain scholarships.
- Law School Admission Test (LSAT); Law School Admissions Council. Measures educational skills needed in law school; intended to compare applicants who have followed different educational programs, including those not in school recently. More than 3 hours long; one total score. Covers logical reasoning, data application, interpreting graphs, mathematical reasoning, reasoning about cases, and so forth. Difficulty is achieved by requiring the person to carry reasoning through many steps. (Drawing content from legal materials serves only to add appeal.)
- Graduate Record Examination (GRE); *ETS.* Two sections resemble the more difficult items of SAT. The Analytical section is a high-level reasoning test (verbal and figural); it was added in 1977 and reports on its usefulness are only beginning to appear. GRE achievement tests are also available in several subject fields. Candidates applying to many graduate departments are required to submit GRE scores to supplement their grade records. Grading standards vary across colleges and "grade inflation" in the 1970s has caused concern; GRE provides a nearly constant yardstick.

Validity reports for tests of these kinds appear at pages 141, 247, and 370. Typical benefits from selection are described in Table 7.5; these figures are worked out on the assumption of a normal distribution plus evidence from many colleges. Combining predictors has benefits and also "diminishing returns"; see pp. 395ff.

Tests for Ages 3 to 6

Several of the group tests for school ages have simplified formats for grades K–2, and some tasks are designed especially for preschool and primary ages.

Some are individual tests, alternatives to WPPSI and K-ABC; others can be given to children in small groups. Some of the tests are used in planning instruction or developmental assistance, and some are used in research and evaluation. Here again the tests listed are selected on the basis of prominence.

- CIRCUS *(AW* for *ETS)*. Level A is for ages 4 to 6. Higher levels assess growth and learning through grade 3, after which a more conventional achievement test is provided. At Level A there are 14 tests, some developed originally for evaluating "Sesame Street" and other early childhood education. Each task examines a distinct aspect of development that might be worth a teacher's notice. The child is to tell a story about a picture or to make a tree using gummed stickers or to associate sounds (tape-recorded) with pictures. See the further examples in Figure 7.8. The user decides which sections to give and ordinarily schedules them at scattered intervals. A guide for each section carries interpretative suggestions. Norms include information on typical changes from Level A to Level B during a year of kindergarten.
- Illinois Test of Psycholinguistic Abilities (ITPA); S.A. Kirk and others; University of Illinois Press. Ages 2 to 10. Intended to diagnose language abilities, isolating a dozen functions suggested by a theoretical model. In its present form, the test seems to give clinically useful information on children who have extremely irregular profiles. To tighten up the measurement there should be *two* distinct short tasks for each process represented in the profile. The theory behind ITPA is not accepted by specialists in psycholinguistics, and the educational recommendations have not been validated. The variety of tasks, however, makes the test appealing to clinicians who are trying to shape instructional prescriptions.
- McCarthy Scales of Children's Abilities; D. McCarthy; *PC*. Ages $2\frac{1}{2}$ to $8\frac{1}{2}$; separate Verbal, Perceptual-Performance, Quantitative, Memory, and Motor scores. An individual test providing a reliable "General Cognitive" score but designed for broader diagnosis of children studied clinically. The 18 subtests range beyond knowledge and problem solving into areas indicative of neurological functioning; diagnosis requires an expert examiner-interpreter. Guidance on its use is provided by Kaufman and Kaufman (1977).

    A few of the scales may be administered by a tester with limited training, as a screening procedure at the time of school entrance. Either a low composite score or a finding of specific weaknesses warrants an extended diagnostic workup. Kaufman and Kaufman suggest that general cognitive subtests should make up the screening battery. McCarthy's publishers chose instead to package a more diversified set

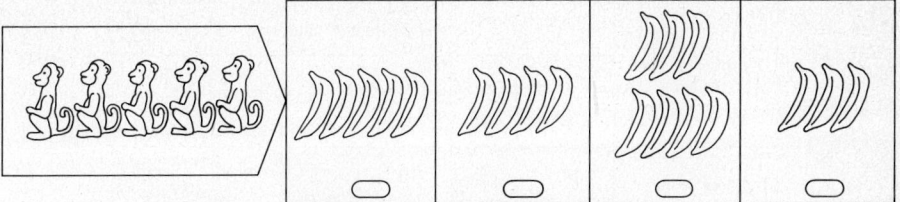

This item is from a test on quantitative concepts. The teacher says: "Which picture shows a banana for each monkey? Mark one bubble under the picture that shows a banana for each monkey."

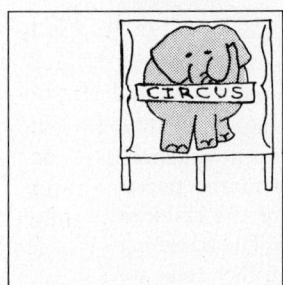  

This item is from a test of listening and recall. The teacher says: "Listen carefully. The children were excited when they saw the sign for the circus. It had a clown on it. Mark the picture that shows the sign they saw."

Figure 7.8. Items from two CIRCUS tasks.
Source: From CIRCUS. Copyright © 1976, 1979 by Educational Testing Service. All rights reserved. Reproduced by permission. (Reduced in size.)

of tasks as the "screening battery" to which Figure 7.9 refers. Children clinically diagnosed as "learning disabled" or "emotionally disturbed/behaviorally disordered" are more likely than normals to do poorly on one or more of these six tests.
- Metropolitan Readiness Tests; J. R. Nurss and M. E. McGauvran; PC. Grades K–1. "Readiness" tests, designed for administration in small groups, are intended to help teachers make short-term instructional plans. The Metropolitan has a level for school beginners and one for children with kindergarten experience; among the first-level tasks are auditory memory and comprehension, use of quantitative concepts, letter-sound matching, and form matching. The profile encourages the teacher to think in terms of improvable components of aptitude, showing what skills are available for use and which need to be developed.

Reviewers of the Metropolitan and other readiness tests (Buros, 1974, 1978) raise a variety of questions. Some object to testing at just one point in

Number of tests failed	Level defined as failure		
	10th percentile	20th percentile	30th percentile
1 or more	24 / 65	40 / 81	52 / 85
2 or more	4 / 39	13 / 55	24 / 68
3 or more	1 / 5	4 / 29	10 / 49

Figure 7.9. Experience table for a screening test. The test user may, for example, decide to examine thoroughly any child who scores at or below the 10th percentile on at least one subtest. The upper-left cell says that she should expect 24 per cent of school entrants to be flagged for examination in a representative population. This review would include 65 per cent of the children having serious intellectual or emotional problems. The screening rule would miss 35 per cent of such children. Other cells are interpreted similarly.

Source: Adapted from the *McCarthy Screening Test Manual*. Copyright © 1970, 1972, 1978 by The Psychological Corporation. Reproduced by permission. All rights reserved.

the year; readiness keeps changing, and continuing assessment is appropriate. Some reviewers believe that national norms confuse the issue in evaluating readiness and, for that reason, advise the teacher to use informal techniques rather than standardized tests. Some object to tests that reduce development to broad scores whereas others complain when, as in CIRCUS, readiness is subdivided into a dozen or more variables that no one test can assess reliably. There is agreement that (if a test is to be used) preference should go to one whose developer provides extensive advice on the instructional implications of the score pattern.

25. *One explanation offered for change in performance during early preschool experience is that the child may become more ready to interact with adults and attend to tasks. Has his mental ability, as defined by Binet, improved? Was the first test valid or invalid?*
26. *A user of a screening test wants to pick up most of the individuals needing attention while minimizing the number of diagnostic workups. Suppose that 10 per cent of the local population have serious problems. Do you agree with the McCarthy manual that an "attractive" rule is to examine thoroughly every child who falls below the 30th percentile on*

two or more tests? Would your answer be the same for a population where 3 per cent have serious problems? (The latter figure is realistic for a broad cross section of children.)
27. ITPA offers a profile of a dozen standard scores such as "Auditory Sequential Memory" (digit span) and "Auditory Association" (an analogy task similar to that in SB Year IV). Lumsden (in Buros, 1978) challenges the interpretation of differences within such profiles: "Underlying the concern with intraindividual differences seems to be the quaint categorical imperative that a well-constructed and well-instructed child ought to have a flat profile." Can the flat profile be defended as an ideal? If you say no, what principle should guide the use of profile information?
28. Some "readiness" tests provide norms for subtests or task categories. Others provide no score norms but report item-by-item norms (percentages of success). Still others are deliberately left without norms. In view of the function of readiness tests, which plan would you favor?

TESTS IN INFANCY

It is important to test infants both for research and to detect those developing abnormally. Tests sometimes disclose severe damage that experienced clinicians overlook, and sometimes they show reassuring normality in children pediatricians suspected of abnormality (Honzik, 1976). Severe pathology is hard to overcome. Lagging behind the norms, however, is not necessarily serious. Save for infants with extreme defects, measurements and observations during the first year correlate little with measures after age 3 (see p. 239). The history of infant tests and the current interpretation of the research is fully treated in books edited by Lewis (1976) and Osofsky (1979).

One cannot set a task for the infant. To study the first year of life is to study spontaneous behavior or conditioned reactions and habits. In the second year, limited tasks can be set. We may regard the child's reaching for a ring as purposive, but we credit him with visual-motor coordination rather than abstract analysis. He is perceptive when he imitates the examiner and places one block atop another, but this is scarcely problem solving. Critics make remarks such as this: "When the psychologist assesses ability by asking whether the infant follows a ball visually or uses a spoon in eating or seeks a lost toy, she looks at behavior that neither the lay person nor the psychologist would regard as integral aspects of intelligence at a later age."

The performance of the infant is unstable from day to day. A response that is just being formed is present on some days and absent on others. The age at which a response emerges may be as much a reflection of special stimulation or lack of stimulation as of the child's ability to develop the response. Twins, for instance, are slower to speak, very likely because their attention is going into nonverbal interaction when other children are practicing sounds to themselves. Mental development has many facets, and progress in sensorimotor imitation may proceed on a different schedule from that of verbal development. Indeed, enthusiastic exercise of one skill may delay emergence of another. Even when developments A and B are logically linked and achieving A is a necessary preliminary to B, the date at which the infant succeeds on B does not come a predictable number of weeks after the achievement of A. B is a new performance whose date of consolidation depends on many variables in the child's experience (Uzgiris, in Lewis, 1976).

The one prominent "standard" test is the Bayley Scales of Infant Development *(PC);* the sections assess psychomotor development and mental development from 2 to 30 months. The following items represent the "mental" content at 6 months (each item being accompanied here by Bayley's suggestion as to the function measured):

> Sustained inspection of ring (alertness of an exploratory type).
> Turn to observe moving spoon (goal-directed attention).
> Vocalizes displeasure (extrovertive responses, not goal centered).
> Smiles at image in mirror (social response).

At 12 months, the emphasis is on communication and concepts, including imitation and obedience to simple commands, though a substantial number of the items require controlled movement. Imitation, of course, is both evidence of learning and a means of further learning (McCall *et al.,* 1972).

A number of investigators sort out developmental sequences, measure them by separate unidimensional scales, and interpret them within such a theoretical framework as Piaget's. These scales are based on logic rather than on the mathematical analyses described in Chapter 4, and the emphasis is on the ordered progress from stage to stage rather than on scores. One set of such "ordinal" scales is the Infant Psychological Development Scales (Uzgiris & Hunt; University of Illinois Press). The seven scales include Visual pursuit and permanence of objects, Vocal imitation, and Development of operational causality. Each has its own strongly ordered items; an infant who fails one task is unlikely to pass an item higher on the scale. (Exceptions arise from momentary fluctuations in efficiency.)

The following paraphrase of items from the 11 stages in the scale for Construction of Object Relations in Space illustrates the unidimensional quality of the scales (but does not give an adequate impression of the testing procedure). Each item is identified here by the age at which the majority of infants "passed" the test.

> 2 months   Confronted with two objects, infant alternates glances between them.
> 3 months   In that same situation, infant alternates glances rapidly.
> 4–5 months   Presented with a graspable object, infant reaches and grasps.

7 months Tester displays an object and allows it to fall; infant directs his eyes toward its probable location on the trials when it falls out of view.

9 months Seated before an empty container and several beads or blocks, infant places objects in container and turns it over to dump them out.

Within an age group, the several scales have only modest correlations (Uzgiris, in Lewis, 1976). Such measures can trace how lines of development relate to specific elements in the infant's environment and activity. It remains useful to think of the overall level of development (as in a finding that progress across the board is inhibited by life in a bleak orphanage nursery), but it is wrong to think of development as growth of a unitary "mental ability" (McCall *et al.*, 1972).

29. *McCall* et al. *(1972) see infant tests as analogous in function to birth weights. The birth weight of a child does not predict childhood weight (even after adjustment for premature birth), yet for the pediatrician that measure is a significant signal of developmental status. How can one validate infant tests if they do not predict?*

30. *On the Bayley Scale, retests after one week showed high consistency for most items including* Lifts cup by handle, Looks for fallen spoon, *and* Imitates words. *Low consistency was found for such items as* Holds cup to drink from (in response to examiner's example), Cooperates with examiner in games, *and* Vocalizes displeasure. *How do the two sets of items appear to differ? Can you explain the variability of the second set?*

8
General Ability as a Construct

The meaning of "general mental ability"—that is, of whatever lies behind thoughtful, adaptive performance—continually evolves. Binet invested 15 years in research before arriving at his characterization of mental ability (p. 195). His ideas, though consistent with today's thinking, have been refined and extended with each passing decade.

I said earlier that "ability" is like "efficiency"; such terms refer to multiple processes being carried out in coordination. It is appropriate to assess general ability and also to identify processes within the total act. Maturing consists of more or less simultaneous advances along a broad front, accompanied by gains in an "executive" or "managerial" skill that capitalizes on the resources built up. This interpretation and its implications are the subject of Chapters 8 to 10. I seek to place familiar issues in a broad context and to clarify them, not to report all that research has learned; whole treatises have been written on the developmental psychology, the crosscultural psychology, and the experimental psychology of cognition.

Although this chapter and those that follow concentrate on data from general reasoning tests such as Chapter 7 described, *the facts and conclusions apply with almost equal force to scores on achievement tests.* Thus, when reading predictive data for the Wechsler or SAT or CogAT, you should realize that (after grade 2) a reading test or a broad measure of academic competence would show similar correlations.

234

Three styles of inquiry look into abilities: analytic research, correlational research, and clinical research. Analytic research dissects performance. It is, in a broad sense, experimental, collecting evidence under specially arranged, systematically varied conditions. A correlational study compiles scores of many persons, relating tests to each other or to external variables. The clinical investigator is concerned primarily with understanding each individual in turn. The data she collects and the themes of her interpretation are likely to change from case to case, though experience with a series of cases is sometimes summed up in statistics.

The analytic investigator typically concentrates on a specific task, to understand precisely what plans of attack, transformations of information, and attention to feedback produce good performance. Piaget thus made Binet's bead-chain task the focus of a series of studies—not because the task is especially important, but because it is easy to modify and responses are easy to observe. Processes detected in one kind of performance are presumed to be significant for many other tasks.

The statistically minded think in terms of individual differences. They concentrate on a few main streams of ability and not with all the tributaries. Various kinds of intellectual performance are strongly correlated (when each one is reliably measured). Therefore, statistical investigators ask how family background, emotional disorder, atypical experience, or other such variables relate to a general ability measure. Little more would be learned by considering a string of more specific abilities one after the other. For the clinician, however, a profile of even a dozen scores provides merely a starting point. The meaning of the scores depends on the person's background, reaction to the testing situation, and style of work. Composites such as Wechsler's Verbal and Performance scores are, as it were, the first strokes on a paper where an elaborate portrait will be developed. The first lines may be erased from view as the final portrait takes on its individual character.

Chapter 9 will discuss analytic and clinical methods of identifying processes in test performance. The present chapter looks at correlational studies of measures of general ability; correlational studies on more specialized tests come into Chapter 9. We begin here with evidence on changes in general ability from age to age after considering some preliminary facts on reliability.

CONSISTENCY AND CHANGE IN SCORES

Error of Measurement

In the interpretation of correlations from age to age and from one ability to another, allowance must be made for errors of measurement: errors in the total score, in part scores, in subtest scores, and in the differences between these.

For illustrative purposes, I concentrate on WISC-R. The reliability studies in its manual deal with split-half scoring of a single testing or with a test and retest about a month apart. Table 8.1 offers a simple, inexact summary of findings. (In some samples, the standard errors fell outside the range stated in the table. I give no coefficient for subtest differences because the coefficient changes greatly from one pair of subtests to another.)

Results for WPPSI and WAIS-R would be much like those in the table. The Stanford-Binet, with a standard error near 5 IQ points and a reliability near 0.9, is a little less accurate than WISC-R. The following conclusions are derived from the summary table and other data.

- Retests average higher than initial tests: about 0.2 s.d. higher for Verbal, 0.6 s.d. for Performance, and 0.5 s.d. for the Full Scale.
- Full Scale and Verbal scores are more reliable than the Performance score.
- The Verbal subtests are somewhat more reliable than the Performance subtests.
- Reliability below age 8 is somewhat lower than at later ages.

Some subtests are more accurate than others, but not so much as to preclude applying a common rule of thumb. The interpreter *should* operate by rule of thumb. She should think of each score as locating the person only approximately. A standard error of 5 points implies that the observed IQ may be as much as 15 points from the person's universe score. Most errors will be 5 points or less, and for practical purposes the tester probably should report an IQ scored as 90 by saying, "The IQ is estimated to fall in the range from 85 to 95." Or, with a 50±10 scale, "in the range from 40 to 46." The universe score falls outside those limits for about a third of those tested. How wide to make the band is a matter of judgment.

Kaufman (1979) suggests that the tester should try to explain any V–P difference that exceeds 12 points. Kaufman does not mean that a difference of 10 points should be regarded as a zero difference. That difference is not

Table 8.1. *Measurement error of WISC-R*

Score	Standard Error of Measurement	Reliability Coefficient (Within Age Group)
Full Scale IQ	3–4	0.95
Verbal IQ	3–5	0.94
Performance IQ	4–5	0.90
V-minus-P	6	0.76
Verbal subtests	1–1.5	0.81
Performance subtests	1.5–2	0.75
Difference between two subtests	2	(See text)

Note: Estimates are based on data in the test manual (1974, esp. pp. 32–33).

large enough to be a focus, but it remains part of the picture. A fact temporarily set aside early in the interpretative process may become meaningful in the light of other facts about the person.

Subtest standard errors of 1.5 are appreciable, considering that the standard deviation of scaled scores is 3 points. (Inaccuracy in short subtests is inevitable.) The interpreter can reasonably take notice of a subtest score that is 3 points above the person's average on subtests in the same set. She should give little attention to isolated differences among pairs of subtests. The WISC-R manual (p. 35) suggests that any pairwise difference of 3 points may be interpreted, because that difference is "significant at the 15% level." This is not a conservative standard. The Wechsler profile reports on 45 or more pairs of subtests. In a profile where every true difference is zero, chance errors ordinarily produce 3-point observed differences for six or more pairs.

Save in minor detail, what has been said about individual tests holds for group tests. The sections of CogAT have reliability coefficients near 0.9 (form-to-form correlations within a grade). The difference between two sections has a reliability of 0.75 or so.

As performance is unstable when behavior patterns are being acquired, we would expect a pencil-and-paper test score to be unstable in the earliest school years. For one first-grade test the correlation between two forms given at about the same time was 0.9—but the retest correlation over a 4-month interval was only 0.75. Once children are accustomed to school and have stabilized their work habits, group tests for successive ages give fairly stable rankings.

1. *The manual for Progressive Matrices summarizes reliabilities for Chinese, Malay, and Indian children in Singapore (from a thesis by Khatana). For Western schoolchildren in an elementary grade, the short-term retest reliability is most often near 0.8. Use principles from Chapter 6 to explain the remarkable variation among Khatana's coefficients.*

Test-retest, one-year interval, ages 7–11, 100 cases	0.71
Test-retest, one-year interval, age 7, 20 cases	0.41
Test-retest, one-year interval, age 9, 20 cases	0.44
Split-half, ages 7–8, 79 cases	0.88
Split-half, ages 8–12, 71 cases	0.99

Changes with Age

Research designs. A *longitudinal* study gives data suitable for studying the growth and decline in ability (Baltes & Nesselroade, 1979). The same persons are tested repeatedly. Few investigators can wait a generation for data to ripen, however. The most common alternative is a *cross-sectional* design: samples at several ages are tested in the same year. A cross-sectional study gives means and standard deviations for each age but not age-to-age correlations.

A compromise—the *overlapping longitudinal* design—uses several samples, following each of them for a few years. For example, one might test 3-, 6-, and 9-year-olds and retest annually for three or more years.

The longitudinal design allows comparisons over time for a fixed group of subjects. When samples are drawn for a cross-sectional comparison, the older group could be more select than the younger one (or—not so likely—less select). The overlapping design guards against this; comparing the original 6-year-old distribution with that for original-3-year-olds-turned-6 warns the investigator when the groups are not comparable.

Even if the groups are sampled from the same population, the cross-sectional comparison is ambiguous. If, in 1980, 20-year-old females do better on a math test than 30-year-old females, is aging the source of a decline? Perhaps the decline comes from failure to use the skills once schooling ends. Or the "decline" could mean that in the late 1970s more females studied math before age 20 than in the 1960s.

Level of performance. Figure 8.1 is based on a 14-year follow-up by Schaie (1979). His test score measured word knowledge and symbolic reasoning. Most other data sets confirm these main points:

- Persons born earlier and later (different "cohorts") differ notably. Because they have had more education, later-born cohorts do better than earlier generations on comprehensive tests like the Wechsler and on most subtests.
- The cross-sectional trend gives a false impression of rapid decline with age.
- Individual decline is slight on average, at least to age 60 or thereabouts. (Another study of the Wechsler finds no average decrement down to age 75; Botwinick & Siegler, 1980.)

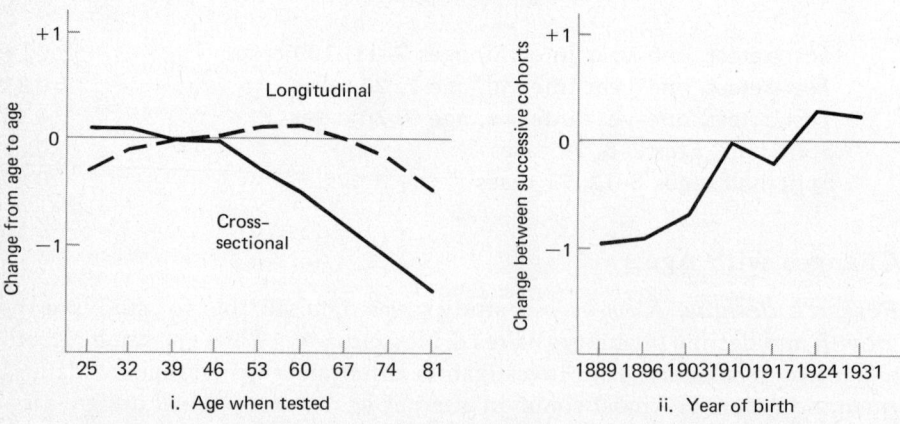

Figure 8.1. Trends over time in general ability.
Source: Calculated from a report by Schaie, 1979.
Note: Change is expressed in units of one s.d. In panel ii, the zero point is arbitrary.

One interpreter emphasizes the decline (Horn, 1979; see also an earlier debate: Baltes & Schaie, 1976; Horn & Donaldson, 1976, 1977; Schaie & Baltes, 1977). As Horn sees it, the physiological base for adaptation and learning deteriorates from infancy onwards, but this decline is offset by the steadily increasing residue from experience. Horn says that crystallized abilities (p. 254) improve into middle age and that later decline is slow. Fluid ability peaks in early adulthood, Horn says; a steady decline follows.

Comparative standing. Figure 8.2 illustrates retest correlations. Stability of scores is much greater after age 8 than before. Score at age 8 is predicted with $r = 0.6$ from a test at age 3, and less well from infant tests. Prediction from early tests is better for girls than for boys (Honzik, 1976; McCall, in Osofsky, 1979).

The increase in stability with age fits facts about development. By age 4, language functions are well established in most children. Some are exhibiting superiority that will last, and some are showing vocabulary and compre-

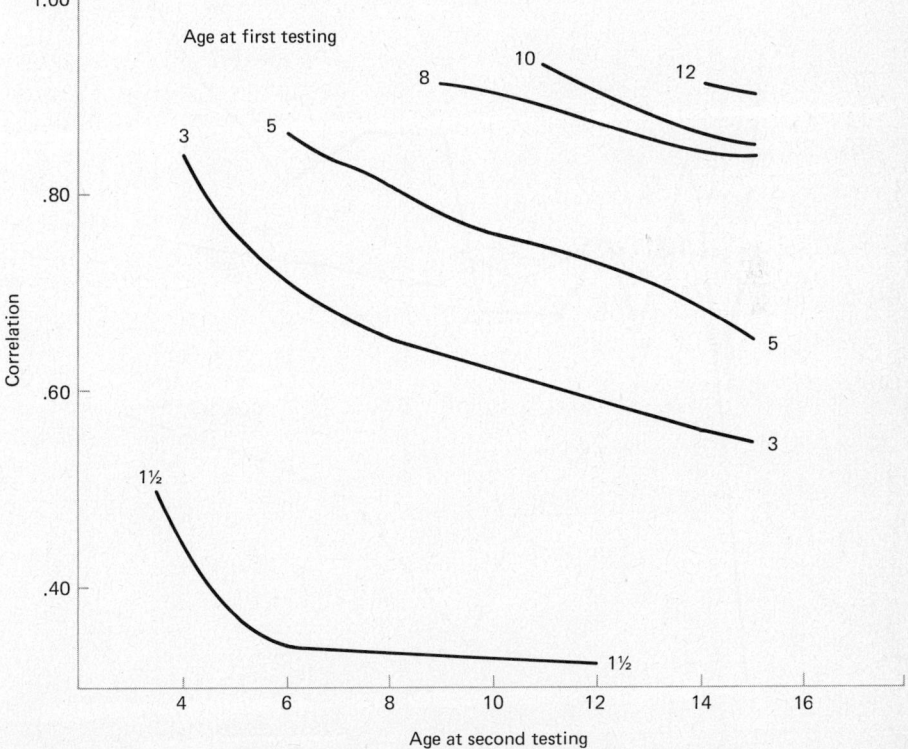

Figure 8.2. Stanford-Binet correlations from age to age.
Source: Correlations for 80 children in a longitudinal study were produced by Robert McCall and published in Jensen, 1980, p. 279. I have smoothed these values, taking into account correlations at neighboring ages, and have added values for infant tests from McCall (in Osofsky, 1979).

hension poor enough to be a serious handicap. Still, standings will change. An old mental test is not to be relied on for a critical decision. At any age, a few rankings change considerably in three years.

Simple hypotheses about causes of change are likely to be false, as the individual cases in Figure 8.3 illustrate. The standing of 783 is nearly constant, slightly above the group mean. Yet he had a history of poor health, an insecure and impoverished home background, poor grades, and symptoms such as stammering and enuresis. "There never was a time in his history when he was not confronted with extreme frustrations." Case 946 came from an unhappy home; her parents divorced when she was 7, and she appeared insecure after her mother remarried a year or so later. Her score was far below the norm during the school years, yet high in early childhood. The third case (567) shows consistent improvement. During this girl's early years there were grave illnesses in the family, and the girl was sickly and shy. After age 10, her social life expanded, and she became interested in music and sports. This blossoming is paralleled in the test scores.

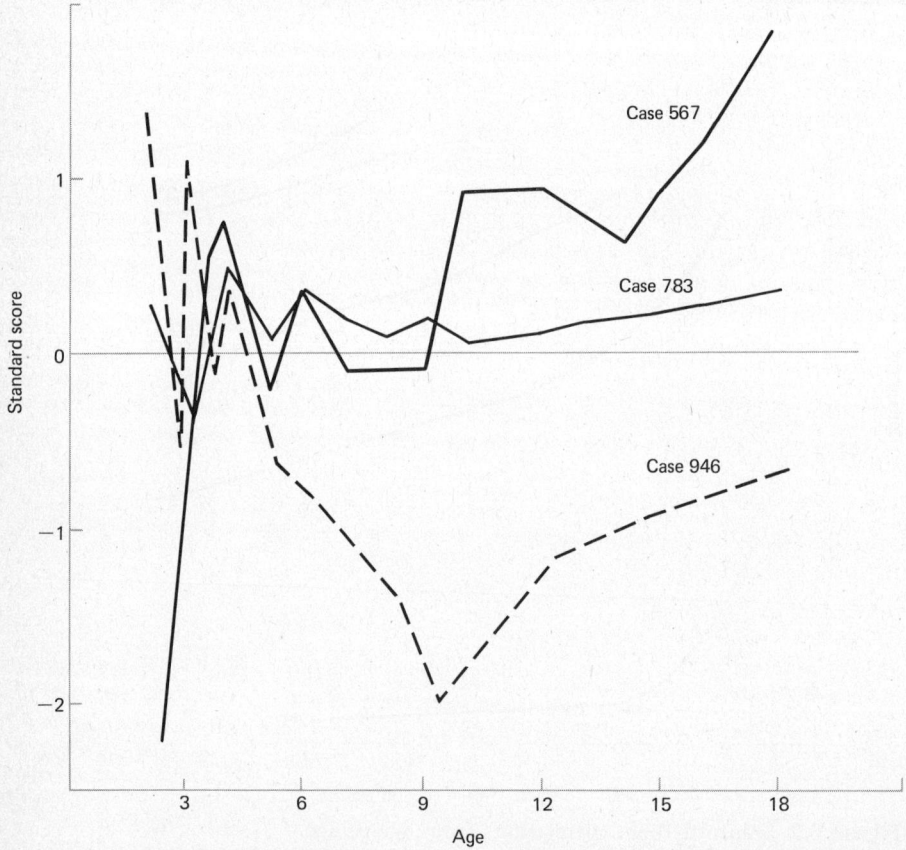

Figure 8.3. Test standings of three children from ages 2 to 18.
Source: Honzik et al., 1948.

Comparisons of those who rise in standing with those who decline are hard to summarize. In the first place, the personal characteristics are often recorded at the end of the change period and may reflect the growth rather than the antecedents. Second, the characteristics associated with rapid growth differ with age and sex. Nonetheless, one arrives at a strong impression that gains are larger among those who vigorously and independently engage in exploring their world. Gainers are described as comparatively aggressive, nonconforming, willing to work for a reward, and, of course, as having intellectual interests. The warmth and authority pattern of the home contribute complexly to development (Clarke-Stewart, 1978; Kohn & Rosman, 1972, 1974; McCall *et al.,* 1973).

In general, changes in intellectual standing seem to be associated with radical changes in the child's opportunity for learning or his emotional readiness to profit from them. These factors work together, as is illustrated by the case of Danny, who was tested when he adapted poorly to kindergarten.

Danny's low score supported a decision to keep him out of school for the year. Lowell (1941) reports a record covering the next several years. On a 50 ± 10 scale, he had these Stanford-Binet scores:

Age	5–0	6–4	8–5	11–11
Standing	39	49	57	70

Because Danny scored at the norm after his sixth birthday, he was placed in the first grade in spite of poor social adjustment. The teachers complained that Danny seemed to live in a world of his own, was poor in motor coordination, and had a worried look on his face most of the time. The mother was called in, and only then was light thrown on his peculiarities.

The mother explained that while Danny was still a baby his father had developed encephalitis. In order for the mother to work, they lived in the grandparents' home, where Danny could be cared for. Danny's high-strung, nervous old grandfather was much annoyed by the child's noise and at times expostulated so violently that Danny became petrified with fear. The grandfather's chief aim was to keep things quiet and peaceful at any cost. When Danny was excluded from kindergarten, the mother took him from the grandparents' home.

The next few years were a period of educational and emotional growth. Danny amazed teachers with his achievement. He became an inveterate reader and could solve arithmetic problems far beyond his grade level. He was under a doctor's care much of the time and was also treated by a psychiatrist because of his marked fears. He made friends with boys in spite of physical inferiority.

2. *Differences between older and younger samples in a cross-sectional study may arise from social changes. What changes other than in length of schooling might cause the test scores of 50-year-olds to average higher (or lower) in 2000 than those of similar 50-year-olds in 1980?*

3. *Danny improved markedly during the 15 months between his first and second tests, at a time when he was not yet in school. What explanations can you suggest?*

Predictive Correlations

The ultimate justification for collecting test scores is that they indicate (with some margin of error) what can be expected in the practical world. The SB and Wechsler were accepted as relevant to decisions largely on the basis of unsystematic evidence. They were supported by the consistency between test scores and clinical impressions of observers, for example, in homes for retarded children. With the passage of time, case histories of children who had been tested piled up.

Terman and his successors (see Oden, 1968; R. R. Sears, 1977) followed up some children in the top 1 per cent of their age group. Ninety per cent entered college and 70 per cent graduated. By the age of 40 or so, the 800 men had published 67 books, more than 1400 scientific and professional articles, and more than 200 short stories and plays. They had more than 150 patents to their credit. Some of Terman's bright boys—not very many—failed in college or served a prison term or had unhappy marriages and careers. As Terman's last report said (1954): "Nearly all the statistics [on achievements] of this group are from 10 to 30 times as large as would be expected for 800 men representative of the general population." The better-than-average academic, professional, marital, and financial success and adult mental health are impressive (even after allowing for the advantages of Terman's high-scoring children). The key to adult achievement seems to have been amount of education; variation in completion of college and in advanced training was strongly predicted by the early test scores. Among equally educated adults in the sample, the early test scores had no relation to the level of career achievement. For a report specifically about the women, see P. Sears and A. Barbee, 1977.

A Terman associate estimated from recorded biographical facts how some historical personages would have scored if tested in early life. "Voltaire wrote verses from his cradle; Coleridge at 3 could read a chapter from the Bible. Mozart composed a minuet at 5; Goethe, at 8, produced literary work of adult superiority" (Cox, 1926, p. 217). The IQs presumably required to account for the recorded facts: Voltaire, 180; Coleridge, 175; Mozart, 160; Goethe, 190.

Other investigators followed low-scoring children. In one study information was compiled at age 50, and some of the subjects were retested. Table 8.2 compares three groups: "very low" (more than 2 s.d. below average in early years, educated in classes for the retarded); "low"; and "average" (not more than 1 s.d. below average). Many childhood retardates performed in the normal range as adults. Low scorers supported themselves in semiskilled labor and low-level supervision. (The education of the low

Table 8.2. *Independence in adulthood of persons who scored low on mental tests in childhood*

	Very low	Low	Near Average
Institutionalized or totally dependent	11%	3%	0%
Entirely self-supporting	65%	93%	96%
Mean or median, childhood standard score	25	40	55
Mean, adult standard score	40	45	55

SOURCE: Adapted from Baller et al., 1967.

group probably was not as stimulating as the education that would be recommended today.)

Educational records. Table 8.3 gives correlations of Wechsler scores with educational criteria. The Verbal score predicted as well as Full Scale; P added nothing to prediction of marks. A third-grade SB correlates 0.65 or better with an achievement measure 2 to 5 years later; a first-grade SB correlates 0.4 with similarly distant criteria (Churchill & Smith, 1974). Group tests predict a bit less well in elementary grades than individual tests (Messé et al., 1979). The

Table 8.3 *Correlations of school marks with Wechsler scores*

	High School	College
Information	0.55	0.5
Comprehension	0.55	0.3
Arithmetic	0.45	0.2
Similarities	0.5	0.4
Digit Span	0.35	0.05
Vocabulary	0.65	0.45
Digit Symbol	0.35	0.15
Picture Completion	0.35	0.2
Block Design	0.3	0.2
Picture Arrangement	0.2	0.05
Object Assembly	0.2	0.1
Verbal	0.6	0.45
Performance	0.4	0.25
Full Scale	0.6	0.45

SOURCE: Adapted from Conry & Plant, 1965.

size of such correlations will vary with the time interval, the nature of the instruction, the criterion, and the range of the sample. The general conclusion is that after grade 1 the mental test predicts (as the past record does) with at least moderate accuracy. (Lower correlations for college students are explained by the smaller range in that sample.)

Forecasting level of academic accomplishment has some place in guidance, but planning instruction requires deeper thought. A careful study of each student's strengths and weaknesses, on tests and in the classroom, would —one hopes—suggest an instructional plan to raise him *above* the level predicted from a general experience table.

Outside school, a performance test sometimes predicts better than a verbal test. Among children classified as "borderline defective," the ones who as adults succeeded in holding down jobs outside an institution were those with Wechsler P greater than V. This observation is supported by the correlation of nearly 0.8 between a childhood maze test and a rating of adjustment to the community in adulthood. The Stanford-Binet correlated 0.6 with the rating (Appell *et al.*, 1962; see also G. D. Cooper *et al.*, 1967).

Forecasts are not very accurate. A person in the middle range of ability may do well in school and college and enter a profession, or he may drop out of school and remain in an unskilled job.

Figure 8.4 is a follow-up study of students who graduated from high school in Flint, Michigan, in 1943. Ten years later the investigator obtained information about the subsequent careers of 97 boys. The boys are divided according to a group-test IQ in grade 9. For each group, the figure charts high school grades, college history, and occupation 10 years after graduation. The data deserve detailed study; here are only a few of the relations that can be traced in the figure. Grades do correspond to test scores; practically no one in the lowest tier earned superior marks. Boys in the lowest group were more likely than others to be in unskilled jobs. A very few, with good grades, entered college. About one-third of the average-ability group entered college, and half of them graduated.

In the two upper tiers, the occupational status of persons *who went to college* averaged out the same. Regardless of test score or high school average, every student who finished college was in an upper-level occupation 10 years after high school. Among those who did not go to college, occupational level corresponded somewhat to test score. (At the time of this study, most colleges were selective. Today there are a large number of "open admissions" colleges, and we do not have comparable studies of the students who attend them. One current report [Eckland, 1980] indicates that the story remains much as Cantoni [1955] told it, save that more students enter college today.)

That adolescents who score below average can succeed in comparatively selective colleges is hard to explain in any general way, but many individual cases are understandable. A group mental test in grade 9 placed Alex at about the 30th percentile, but Alex eventually became a lawyer. (The test score was confirmed on a retest a few months later.) Alex had lived in a boarding home

Superior on mental test (30 cases)

High-school grade average:	Below 1.5		1.5–2.4			2.5+			Total		
	xxx		xxxxx xxxxx xxxxx xx			xxxxx xxxxx			30		
	No college	Entered college	No college	Entered college		No college	Entered college			College, no degree	
	xxx		xxxx xxxx	xxxxx xxxx		xxxx	xxxx xx		No college		Degree
				No degree	Degree		No degree	Degree			
				xxxx	xxxxx		x	xxxxx			
Occupational status:											
Business, professional	0		2	2	5	2	1	5	4	3	10
Skilled	0		6	1	0	2	0	0	8	1	0
Unskilled or semi-skilled	3		0	1	0	0	0	0	3	1	0
									15	5	10

Average (49 cases)

High-school grade average:	Below 1.5		1.5–2.4			2.5+			Total		
	xxxxxxxx		xxxxxxxxxx xxxxxxxxxx xxxxxxxx			xxxx			49		
	No college	Entered college	No college	Entered college		No college	Entered college		No college	College, no degree	Degree
	xxxxxx xx		xxxxxxxxxx xxxxxxxxxx x	xxxxxxxxxx xxxxxx		x	xxx				
				No degree	Degree		No degree	Degree			
				xxxx xxxx	xxxx xxxx		x	xx			
Occupational status:											
Business, professional	1		3	5	8			2	4	5	10
Skilled	6		9	2	0			0	15	2	0
Unskilled or semi-skilled	1		9	1	0	1	1	0	11	2	0
									30	9	10

Below average (18 cases)

High-school grade average:	Below 1.5		1.5–2.4			2.5+			Total		
	xxxxx		xxxxxxxxxxx			xx			18		
	No college	Entered college	No college	Entered college		No college	Entered college		No college	College, no degree	Degree
	xxxxx		xxxxxxxxxx x				xx				
				No degree	Degree		No degree	Degree			
					x		x	x			
Occupational status:											
Business, professional	1		2		1		0	1	3	0	2
Skilled	2		4		0		1	0	6	1	0
Unskilled or semi-skilled	2		4		0		0	0	6	0	0
									15	1	2

Figure 8.4. Educational and occupational histories of 97 boys.
Data supplied by L. J. Cantoni; see Cantoni, 1955.

during his early school years following the death of his mother and suffered from a sense of inadequacy that led him into aggressive, offensive behavior. A counselor felt that Alex had ability even though his tests and grades were poor. An *individual* mental test placed Alex at the 75th percentile. Under the counselor's encouragement, Alex improved his marks to the B level and transferred to a college-preparatory curriculum. His personal adjustment also improved. After war service, Alex entered college and completed his law course successfully (Cantoni, 1954).

Secondary schools and colleges with diversified programs try to route students into courses they are ready to handle, which makes good sense. Too often there are rigid barriers—as between the academic track and the commercial track in a high school, for example. A student sorted into a less demanding program has difficulty in meeting requirements for admission to a regular college program when, midway through high school, he and his teachers realize that he is capable of the heavier load. There are many "late bloomers" who seem to get the knack of academic work and develop strong motivation only belatedly. It is essential that plans for sorting students keep access open for those initially regarded as poor candidates for a tough program (Wigdor & Garner, 1982, I, p. 175).

Obviously, tests are used comparatively in admissions. Aptitude and achievement tests correlate highly. Therefore, it makes little difference which is used in comparing students who have taken the same courses. The general-ability test is more suitable for comparing the developmental level of persons coming from *different* educational backgrounds because it has little to do with lesson content.

Correlations of predictors with grade averages in 312 colleges are tabulated in Figure 8.5; see also pp. 141, 228. The variation in coefficients reflects differences among colleges and also random fluctuations. Prediction tends to be better in 4-year colleges than in 2-year colleges, better in private than in public colleges, better for women than for men (Sawyer & Maxey, 1982). High school marks alone had predictive coefficients of 0.5 on the average. Prediction improved dramatically when the score from a standard test was combined with the high school record, presumably because the test is not subject to the vagaries of local grading practices. (The coefficients for ACT considered alone had much the same range as those for high school grades alone.)

Colleges have reduced their emphasis on probable academic performance in selecting students. Two national committees have recommended against selection by formula, that is, against automatically accepting those above a certain predicted grade average and rejecting those below it (Carnegie Council, 1977; Wigdor & Garner, 1982, I, pp. 199, 202). Such a practice turns away applicants with adequate academic promise who are outstanding along other lines. A questionnaire on musical, scientific, literary, and leadership activities (e.g., Have you ever won an award in a science fair?) identifies promising cases. The self-report can, of course, be checked. Records of such

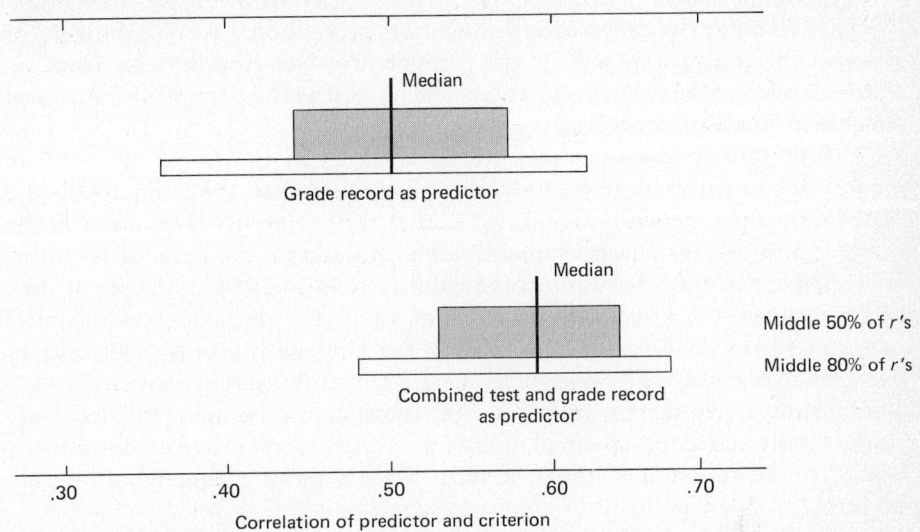

Figure 8.5. Validity with which college marks are predicted. Summary of the distribution of correlations in 312 colleges relating freshman grade average to high school grade average and to a composite predictor.
Source: Data from Linn, in Wigdor & Garner, 1982, II, p. 348.

accomplishments correlate negligibly with grade record or with test scores (Wallach, in Messick, 1976), but they do correlate with subsequent accomplishment in the same fields.

Vocational prediction. Every comparison shows higher mental-test averages in more prestigeful, more demanding occupations. For example, World War II soldiers who had been lawyers in civil life had a median on the General Classification Test of 62 (on a scale where the population median was 53); the median for general clerks was 58, and that for plumbers was 51. The lowest medians (around 45) were for farm workers, miners, and laborers. The overlap of groups is equally noteworthy. The plumbers (disregarding the extreme 10 per cent at each end of the distribution) ranged from 36 to 61. Some were far below the median for laborers, and some did as well on the test as the average lawyer.

Whereas it was once thought that the differences implied a necessary relation between mental-test score and occupational performance, it is now recognized that additional schooling explains most of these results. Children of the well-to-do have a good chance to stay in school and also to get a good position; that contributes to the correlation (McCall, 1977). We know that the person who does badly on mental tests is likely to do badly in school. One can scarcely say that poor ability causes poor learning or that poor learning causes poor ability—there is a spiral relationship. The person who gets off to a poor start fails to learn and then is ill-prepared for the next demand. Those with poor school records tend to leave school earlier. Completing college gives a license to enter the path toward executive-professional work regardless of whether the college course increases competence. The dropout who learns on a job can perform in some occupations just as well as the person who survived additional years of schooling.

A unique follow-up study traced workers in the home office of an insurance company. Nearly 700 workers hired between 1937 and 1949 were tested on a short general mental test at that time. New workers enter in the lower job categories and presumably are promoted on the basis of performance. The correlation between responsibility held in 1954 and score at time of hiring was 0.6. Fifty-four per cent of those in "decision-making jobs" had had scores of 120 and over; only 5 per cent with scores 0–99, and 19 per cent in the 100–119 range held these high-ranking jobs (Knauft, 1955). The insurance company found a high correlation because the level-of-responsibility criterion spanned many jobs. Within one job (e.g., office manager), the correlation of the test with a later merit rating would surely be lower.

The coefficients for any job title range from substantial to negligible, depending upon the range of ability in the group tested and the demands of the specific job. Ghiselli's average validities (1973) for group tests of general ability against measures or ratings of *job proficiency* fall in the following ranges:

Definitely below 0.25	Packers and wrappers, sales clerks, vehicle operators
Near 0.25	Service occupations, trade and mechanical work, some clerical work
Definitely above 0.25	Some clerical, managerial, and sales positions

Studies of the General Aptitude Test Battery (p. 303) show in addition that those who do well in technical occupations tend to be strong in general ability.

Most of the reported information on occupational validity comes from concurrent studies. The workers have been screened and accepted and often have survived for a time on the job. Allowance for reduced range must be made in interpreting the coefficients. Success in training is generally easier to predict than reports of performance on the job; the r's for training criteria run nearly 0.2 higher (Ghiselli, 1973).

To ask about the relevance of general ability to prediction is to ask too limited a question. There are many abilities, and the employer or the person seeking a vocation cannot base the decision on just one. This is clear in Figure 8.6, which describes three female applicants for an office job in terms of test scores. Obviously, the choice among them cannot be made until the employer states his requirements precisely.

General Ability as a Construct

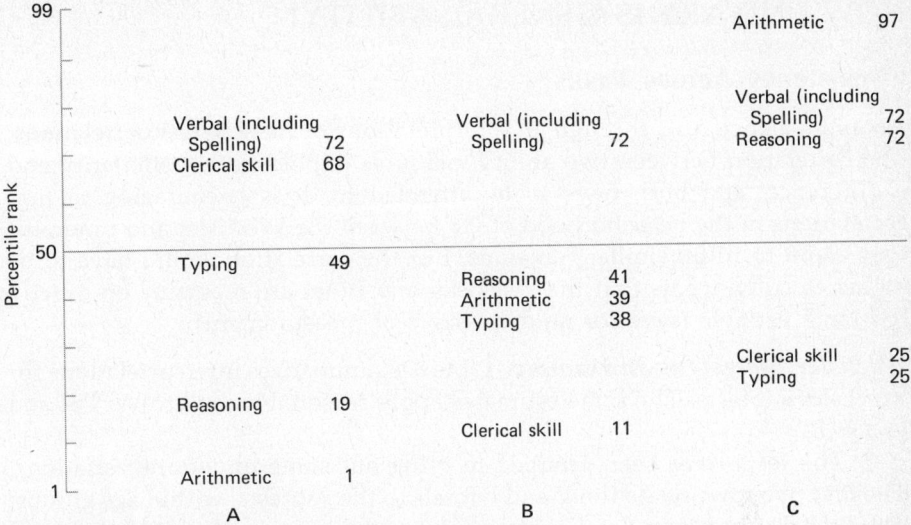

Figure 8.6. Score portraits of three job applicants.
Source: From Personnel selection by R. M. Guion, 1965, p. 10. Copyright © 1965 by McGraw-Hill Book Company and used by permission of the McGraw-Hill Book Company.

4. The correlation of scholastic aptitude with grade-point average tends to be rather low in a college that limits admission to persons with good school records and test scores. Does that imply that scholastic aptitude tests are poor bases for admission decisions in those schools?
5. One of the committees referred to earlier concluded that probable accomplishment should not be overemphasized in admissions. "When there are many applicants capable of succeeding admissions decisions should be based on social and educational values broader than . . . grade averages." Attention is drawn to "diversity" in the student body as a value, and minority representation is on the committee's mind. What other values or what other kinds of diversity should an admissions committee care about?
6. Describe an office job for which applicant A (Figure 8.6) would be an excellent prospect. Do the same for C.
7. If literary achievement in high school (e.g., publications) correlates only 0.1–0.2 with a test on English usage and with high school grades (Holland & Richards, 1965), does this imply that scholastic aptitude is unimportant for excellence in writing?
8. As in the insurance company mentioned, entry jobs are used to identify persons who can be promoted to higher levels of responsibility. A person who scores low on a general ability test may be fully qualified for the entry job and yet be unlikely to qualify for promotion. Is it fair for the company to give preference to high-scoring persons in filling vacancies in the entry job?
9. Why are training criteria easier to predict than on-the-job criteria? Consider police officers as an example.

HOW UNITARY IS GENERAL ABILITY?

Consistency Across Tasks

An ambivalence runs through all interpretations of mental-test correlations. The correlation between two ability measures implies both a similarity and a difference, and both have to be attended to. It is encouraging to find correlations in the neighborhood of 0.8 between the Wechsler and Binet, for they claim to fulfill similar functions. But the correlation would have to be higher to convince us that the Wechsler and Binet are reporting on exactly the same variable (save for random errors of measurement).

Wechsler subtests as an example. Table 8.4 summarizes intercorrelations for Wechsler subtests. The same estimates apply reasonably well to WPPSI and WAIS-R.

The tests have been grouped to bring out some important variations. The first two rows relate the V and P totals to the subtests, within age groups. The verbal subtests in Set 1 correlate only a bit more with the Verbal total than with the Performance total; that is true also of Arithmetic. At these ages, the correlation between the Verbal and Performance totals is close to 0.7.

Block Design, a performance test, correlates substantially with the Ver-

Table 8.4 *Correlations among WISC-R subscores*

	Set 1 Subtests	Set 2 Subtests	Block Design	Arithmetic	Digit Span	Coding
Verbal Scale	0.70–0.80[a]	0.40–0.55	0.55–0.60	0.60–0.65[a]	0.35–0.45[a]	0.35–0.40
Performance Scale	0.55–0.65	0.50–0.65[b]	0.65–0.75[b]	0.50–0.55	0.30–0.35	0.25–0.35[b]
Subtests singly[c] Set 1. Information, Similarities, Vocabulary, Comprehension	0.60–0.75	0.30–0.55	0.50–0.55	0.45–0.60	0.30–0.40	0.25–0.30
Set 2. Picture Completion, Picture Arrangement, Object Assembly		0.30–0.50	0.45–0.60	0.25–0.40	0.10–0.25	0.15–0.30
Block Design					←—— 0.30–0.50 ——→	
Arithmetic, Digit Span, Coding					←—— 0.30–0.40 ——→	

Notes: Estimates are based on tables in the WISC-R test manual. The range shown includes at least 60 per cent of the pertinent correlations for the six ages from 9 to 14, and often includes 90 per cent. Comparatively large correlations are shown in boldface.
[a] This is based on the correlation of each subtest with the Verbal total, excluding the subtest in question and Digit Span.
[b] This is based on the correlation of each subtest with the Performance total, excluding the subtest in question and Mazes.
[c] The lower part of the table summarizes correlations each of which relates one subtest to another subtest.

bal score; on the basis of such results, Block Design is regarded as a particularly good measure of *general* ability. The tests in Set 2 correlate about as high with verbal subtests as they do with each other, but that anomaly is accounted for by their lower reliabilities. Allowing for that, we conclude that these tests do have something special in common with each other (and with Block Design). That common element is weak.

Coding and Digit Span relate weakly to other subtests; see p. 259. Partly to simplify, I have grouped Arithmetic, Digit Span, and Coding in the last row of Table 8.4. Several writers see Arithmetic, Digit Span, and Coding as a cluster that measures "freedom from distractibility" (Kaufman, 1979); this label is a paraphrase of "maintain a mental set" (Binet). Coding and Digit Span are so simple that mobilization of attention is a main ingredient in efficiency. Slippage of attention is also bound to reduce the score in Arithmetic though that subtest demands knowledge and analysis. Weakness in this cluster is fairly common among children who have special difficulty in learning to read (Bannatyne, 1974; Rourke, in Filskov & Boll, 1982). Kaufman warns against overemphasis on the distractibility interpretation; in particular, he would look to the nature of the child's errors for supporting evidence.

Variance of scores on the typical subtest divides about as follows:

	Set 1 (Verbal)	Set 2 (Performance)
Error of measurement	20%	25%
General ability	40%	30%
Verbal ability not predicted by general	25%	—
Performance ability not predicted by general	—	10%
Ability specific to the subtest	15%	35%

The verbal set, then, has some coherence, measuring a verbal ability in addition to general ability. The concept of a "performance ability" is poorly supported. Each subtest in Set 2 is strongly influenced by ability components not required by its fellow subtests.

An improved Wechsler profile. Subtests intercorrelate, so one subtest contains information that helps in estimating the true score on another subtest. Making such estimates wipes out much of the variability that random error puts into the profile. Information from a pertinent norm group is the basis for a formula that estimates, for example, the true Comprehension score. The observed score on Comprehension is adjusted by adding in the subtests that correlate most with Comprehension. One set of data produced this formula for estimating the Comprehension true score of 8-year-olds:

$$0.24 \text{ Comp} + 0.12 \text{ Ari} + 0.29 \text{ Vocab} + 0.12 \text{ Coding} + 2.23$$

The adjustment flattens the profile, erasing deviations that probably occurred by chance. Here is an illustrative result (Cronbach, 1976a; see also Cronbach et al., 1972, pp. 314–323).

	Inf	Comp	Ari	Sim	Voc	DSp	PCom	PArr	BD	ObjA	Cod
Observed profile	10	6	6	10	10	10	12	7	10	7	6
Adjusted profile	9.2	7.9	9.9	10.0	8.4	10.2	10.3	8.6	9.3	8.9	8.2

This technique has not yet caught on. A weaker version, available since the 1920s, has also been ignored—save that *its* use is at last recommended in the 1983 manual for the British Ability Scales.

10. *In a general mental test, why is a high correlation among subtests not wholly desirable?*
11. *In my example, do the original and "improved" Wechsler profiles give the same impression of the subject?*
12. *Comment on this statement: "A person's true level of mental ability is shown by whichever IQ, verbal or performance, is higher."*
13. *Bill and John, two 15-year-olds, are referred to the school psychologist because both are failing in 9th-grade work, their courses being social studies, English, general science, and art appreciation. Bill has a Verbal IQ of 95 and a Performance IQ of 92 whereas John has a Verbal IQ of 87 and a Performance IQ of 106. What does this difference mean?*
14. *One of the subtests of an "intelligence test" developed abroad requires the subject to cross slanting lines, making X's as rapidly as he can, thus: XXXXX / / / / /. Such a subtest is rarely used in American tests measuring general ability. On what basis could the inclusion of such a test be criticized? What argument or evidence would justify including this subtest in a general mental test?*
15. *Terman and Wechsler both discarded tasks that showed a consistent difference between males and females. A fair measurement could not be made, they said, if items favored one sex or the other. Did the elimination of such items make the scale more valid or less valid*
    a. *as a predictor?*
    b. *as a measure of the intended construct?*

Fluid and Crystallized Abilities

A spectrum of general abilities. A continuum from fluid *(Gf)* to crystallized *(Gc)* abilities (Figure 8.7) provides a preliminary sorting scheme. Tests at the same level in Figure 8.7 tend to be more highly intercorrelated than tests that are distant from each other (Cattell, 1971; Guttman, 1965; Horn & Cattell, 1966; Vernon, 1979; see p. 291).

The tests at the lower end of the spectrum require information and practiced skills; a brilliant but uninformed person could not do well. When a task corresponds closely to past lessons, response can be nearly automatic.

General Ability as a Construct

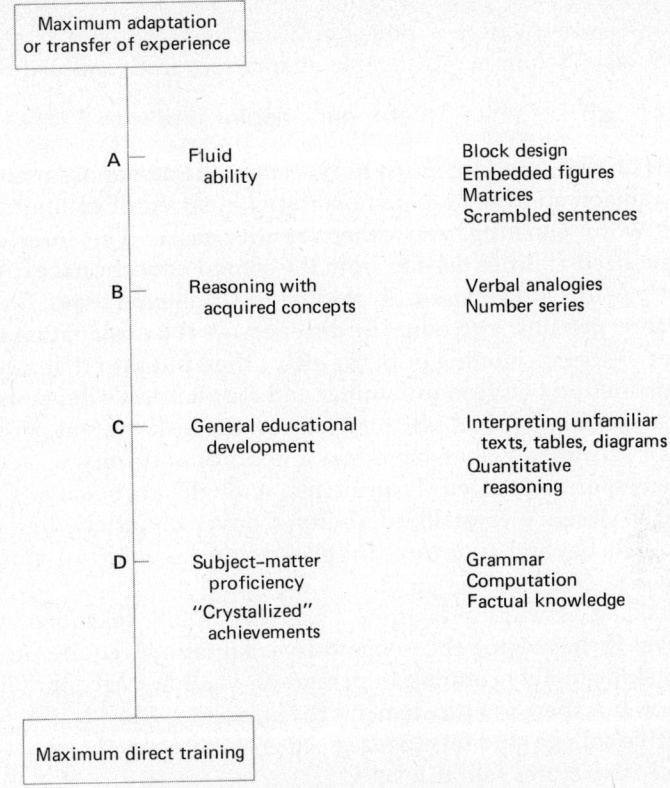

Figure 8.7. Spectrum of general abilities.

Some skills—counting, for example—are practiced so thoroughly that the person can act with almost no reflection. The test items call up practiced responses that are "in stock, nearly ready for delivery."

Tasks at the upper end of the spectrum present strange stimuli or patterns and require creation of a response on the spot (Figures 1.2, 3.2, and 7.5). Knowledge and specific skills are no more than a starting point in these tasks. The person has to extract or construct an answer. Even when a choice format is used, the answer cannot be reached by recall.

"Fluid" ability is a short label for apprehending an unfamiliar configuration and rearranging it to satisfy some requirement. This is an adaptive process. In Block Design the person must direct his attention, break up the given pattern into small squares, select and rotate blocks to match those elements, and assemble the whole, with a minimum of wasted time. One who works by trial and error will score low; one who plans ahead will be fast and accurate (see p. 273). The terms *direction, judgment,* and *self-criticism* from Binet's early thinking apply here. Fluid ability is complex, not unitary. It is convenient to speak of fluid ability in the singular simply because the several subordinate processes must function at once to produce efficient performance.

The *Gf–Gc* distinction is not simply between nonverbal and verbal. Some verbal tasks require considerable adaptation. In Scrambled Sentences,

tree   pick   an   climbed   man   our   apple   the   to

the demands on reasoning are much heavier than the demands on vocabulary.

"Crystallized abilities" are demonstrated in speed of computation, recognition of word meaning, and other familiar tasks. The intercorrelation among crystallized abilities derives from the shared educational experience to which most persons are exposed. According to Undheim (1981), *Gc* develops out of *Gf;* when persons with equal *Gf* differ on *Gc,* the explanation lies either in the extent of their schooling or in the effort they put into that schoolwork.

The distinction between unfamiliar and familiar tasks depends more on the culture and the individual's history than on the task content per se. A task may enter *Gc* if most persons have had a good opportunity to acquire and practice the responses needed. In principle, enough practice could be given to make Block Design a crystallized ability. Conversely, if children practiced no number skill beyond counting, simple addition would call mostly upon fluid ability.

The tasks at Level D in Figure 8.7 ask for familiar reactions to familiar content. Level C, increasing the demand for adaptation, requires application of practiced skills to new content. In paragraph reading, each stimulus is new to the subject, but there is little demand for ingenuity. Most of the ACT tests ask prospective college students to make sense of materials they have not seen before; these, therefore, fall at level C.

Level B demands reorganization of knowledge. A difficult verbal test at Level C or Level D introduces uncommon words or ideas; the advantage goes to the person who is well informed. At the B level, the problem is constructed of words all examinees should know well; difficulty is introduced through complexity of relationship.

Whereas some mental tests concentrate on Level A—or on A and B together—many are like the Wechsler, covering much of the spectrum. The typical group mental test for adolescents and adults is predominantly verbal, making demands on both reading and vocabulary. A poor reader's score is sure to be limited no matter how well he thinks. Some tests, like CogAT, have nonverbal sections. Conversely, a nonverbal or performance task demands ability to think of appropriate verbal concepts and make comparisons and combinations. In EFT, for example, search obviously goes faster if the person can hold in mind a good verbal description of the target figure. The tests are nonverbal in the limited sense that one does not take in words from tester or test booklet and does not give back the answer in words.

Are aptitude and achievement distinguishable? Many educators call a pupil an "underachiever" when his normed achievement score is lower than his normed general ability. A pupil who reads better than most others with the same general ability is labeled an "overachiever." It is true that a large dis-

General Ability as a Construct

crepancy suggests atypical development of abilities. But it would make equally good sense to reverse the formula. The first pupil is "superadaptive"; he solves problems better than others who have equal command of the school subjects. The second one, by the same logic, is "underadaptive." Attempts at comparison from one test to another run afoul of technical and logical difficulties. (I take up some of these in Chapters 4 and 10; but see also Thorndike, 1963, and Cronbach & Furby, 1970.)

The terminology of "over- and underachievement" should be abandoned. Teachers should do what they can to identify specific weaknesses that can be overcome whether these lie at the Gc end of the spectrum or the Gf end. The student who ranks at the same level on both types of test also is likely to have some weaknesses!

Let us look in more detail at the overlap of individual standings. The verbal score on a test like CogAT (or an overall score) correlates strongly with an achievement battery given at about the same time. For a national sample, typical within-grade correlations (grades 3 to 8) with the composite score on the Iowa Tests of Basic Skills (ITBS) are CogAT Verbal, 0.88; Quantitative (Q), 0.8; Nonverbal (NV), 0.7. The lower correlation of nonverbal (Level A) tasks is a usual finding. To interpret further, reliability coefficients are needed; I shall use the following estimates of reliability over forms and days: ITBS composite, 0.96; CogAT V, 0.91; Q, 0.88; NV, 0.90.

The variance of the V score divides into three portions. First, error of measurement accounts for 9 per cent of the variance ($= 1 - 0.91$). Second, 81 per cent would be predictable from a perfectly reliable version of ITBS. (This is slightly higher than $(0.88)^2$, the squared correlation of V with the *actual* ITBS.) Third, the remaining 10 per cent of the variance in the Verbal score arises from something the achievement test does not measure (Figure 8.8). It follows that, among children matched on achievement, about half of their apparent variation on V is due to error of measurement. Thus, reports

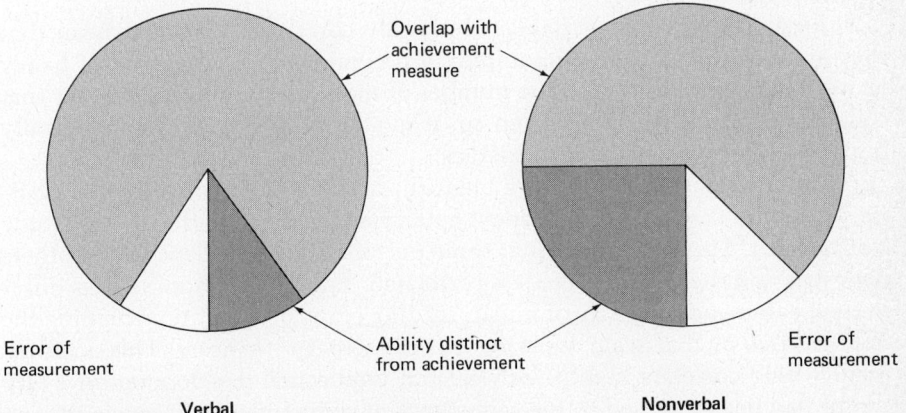

Figure 8.8. Overlap of CogAT standings with achievement standings.

of discrepancies between standing in a group test of verbal ability and measured achievement have a reliability near 0.5. Such discrepancies are most likely to be meaningful when one is comparing children who have been exposed to different curricula or who have been in different "tracks." Instructional content and pace will affect the achievement measure more than the general-ability measure.

As Figure 8.8 shows, the Nonverbal score overlaps only moderately with the achievement battery. When we compare children of equal achievement, most of their larger differences in fluid ability are due to a real difference in problem solving that the achievement test does not reflect. (Q is not as strongly related to overall achievement as V is, but would overlap greatly with a test of achievement in arithmetic.)

Failure to understand that *both* fluid and crystallized abilities are nurtured by experience and instruction has led to a peculiar asymmetry in test interpretation. This is seen in the elaborate scoring scheme for ITBS. When CogAT and ITBS are given at about the same time, an "expected" score in, for example, Computation is calculated. This is essentially the national average on Computation of pupils in this grade who matched this pupil's CogAT performance. The actual Computation score and the "expected" score are printed on the report to the teacher, and attention is drawn to the difference if it is considered too large to be explained by measurement error. (The "expected score" is determined from a regression equation, developed on a national sample, that uses CogAT performance as a "predictor.")

Experts have argued endlessly about the implications of the overlap among ability tests. Some have complained that whoever applies the label "aptitude" to one set of tests and the label "achievement" to another is a victim of the "jangle fallacy," of the illusion that things having different names must be distinct. The warning is still to be heeded, but today few experts would say that no distinction is to be made. Persons especially interested should consult a symposium on this issue (Green, 1974); I limit myself to a few basic comments.

First, the fact that variables are highly correlated does not mean that they are indistinguishable. In samples of natural water, the amount of heavy water has a correlation with the number of molecules of ordinary water that considerably exceeds 0.999. Even so, it is scientifically and technologically important to distinguish the variables.

Second, most children have plentiful opportunity to develop the abilities that enter the usual achievement battery and to develop the ones aptitude tests call for. Turn to content that some persons have experienced and others have not, and the variables are less correlated. Thus high school seniors differ in their command of theory of music: reading of musical notation, naming the notes in this or that scale, working out elementary harmony. This achievement would correlate highly with general intellectual development if every senior had been exposed to the same amount of instruction in music theory. Also, when students come new to music theory, their success can be predicted by tests of *Gf* or *Gc*. Indeed, reading rate would predict; then an achievement measure is serving as a test of aptitude.

Third, although tests of modest length are poor at assessing an aptitude-achievement difference for an individual, averages of groups are measured accurately. Differences across tests can be important in the study of developmental trends and in evaluation. Baughman and Dahlstrom (1968), for example, found that boys and girls in a certain community had about equal averages on the Stanford-Binet at each age from 7 to 14. On the Stanford Achievement Test, the sexes again tied—up to age 12. At ages 13 and 14, the boys lagged noticeably behind the girls' average. This almost certainly reflects an adolescent reaction to the schooling offered.

16. *Would it be possible for schooling to vary so that fourth-graders in one community advance in tests at both ends of the spectrum whereas in another community gains are great in crystallized abilities and small in tasks at Levels A and B?*
17. *Insofar as you can, locate the Wechsler subtests on the spectrum.*
18. *It would be possible to design lessons to train persons to solve matrix problems. If such training were regularly offered, would this change the nature of the spectrum or simply move the matrix test toward Level D?*
19. *What sort of directions and associations would have to be stored in order to enable a computer to solve problems of each of the following types? How does this relate to the classification of items on the continuum? (Assume that the computer can "read" words and drawings, call on a memory, and "hear" commands.)*
    a. *Digits Backward*
    b. *Synonyms*
    c. *Verbal Analogies*
    d. *Mazes*
    e. *Naming pictures of shop tools*
20. *In Figure 8.7, nearly all of the illustrations of Level A are figural. Is there any justification for regarding figural tests as purer measures of reasoning than others? Would the same answer apply in all cultures?*
21. *Norms for class averages are available, and it is possible to compare the achievement average of a particular class with the average over classes matching their average score on a general-ability test. What would be a reasonable conclusion or line of further questioning if, at the start of seventh grade when children come from several feeder elementary schools, class averages tell the following stories:*
    a. *Class A is at the 50th percentile of seventh-grade classes nationally in general ability and significantly below that level on achievement scores in computation and use of references.*
    b. *Class B averages at the 50th percentile in general ability and significantly higher than that on most achievement measures, including reading and mathematics.*

c. Class C averages quite high in verbal ability and only average in fluid ability.
22. Under the heading of "construct validity," the K-ABC manual reports that its Achievement score correlates about 0.8 with the Stanford-Binet and Wechsler Verbal and that the Mental Processing Composite correlates about 0.6 with those scores. With Wechsler Performance, the two K-ABC scores correlate 0.5 and 0.6. What interpretations of these three tests are given support by this evidence?

SPECIALIZED HYPOTHESES ABOUT GENERAL ABILITIES

Theorists and clinicians try to isolate segments of the general ability complex for special attention and try to assess general aptitudes that are not adequately represented in conventional tests. I introduce several of these lines of work as "hypotheses," to suggest uncertainty about whether they are distinct from Gf and Gc. The topics are miscellaneous: "adaptive behavior," ability to learn, mental speed, field independence, divergent thinking, and the left-brain/right-brain distinction.

"Adaptive Behavior"

Difficult decisions are to be made about which adults and children should be given care in an institution for their own good and that of their families. Many persons, classed as retarded in childhood by the usual mental tests, have succeeded as adults in jobs and family living. It follows that intellectual ability, narrowly defined, is not a sufficient basis for judging the seriousness of suspected retardation. Since the original Vineland Social Maturity Scale appeared in the 1920s, psychologists have taken everyday behavior into account alongside mental tests. By current standards not even the label "mildly retarded" is to be applied unless the person is far below the norm in tested general ability *and* in a measure of so-called adaptive behavior: clothing and feeding oneself, staying with a chore, and the like (Coulter & Morrow, 1978). In this usage, "adaptive behavior" is a palatable label for coping with *recurrent* everyday situations. It is not Binet's "capacity to make adaptations."

Measures of adaptive behavior are not direct tests; rather, persons who have been associated with the individual being assessed provide ratings. Instruments include the Vineland and the ABIC portion of Mercer's system (p. 209). The Adaptive Behavior Scale (American Association on Mental Deficiency; school edition distributed by *CTB*) asks about everyday competence, cooperation, language, and deviant behavior.

Nihara (in Coulter & Morrow, 1978) finds that most questions in such scales fall into three categories: personal self-sufficiency, personal-social responsibility, and community self-sufficiency. The first category has to do with elementary functioning (walking, dressing oneself, hearing, . . .). The second is more motivational and social (consideration for others, work habits, care of personal property). "Community self-sufficiency" touches on general mental ability, including concepts of time and number, and basic literacy, along with such skills as using public transportation and handling work assignments of some complexity. Adaptive behavior is adequate across the board for some people who have low scholastic ability. If it were not for institutions' obsession with categorizing clients (Reschly, in Glaser & Bond, 1981), the point of the assessment would never be to produce a summary score. Quite properly, the Adaptive Behavior Scale is designed to survey strengths and deficiencies with an eye to judgments about care and instruction.

Ability to Learn

Whether general mental tests measure "ability to learn" has been a confusing question for psychologists. The correlation of tests with later school achievement is not direct evidence, as achievement is cumulative. People superior in Gf tend also to have a head start on knowledge and academic skills. Every new lesson takes for granted a store of vocabulary and ideas. But how much knowledge one has stockpiled is scarcely the whole of "ability to learn." (On the reasoning and evidence behind this section, see Cronbach & Snow, 1981, esp. Chap. 5.)

Some psychologists have misinterpreted reports that the schoolchild's score on a mental test is negatively correlated with the change in score between that age and adulthood. The original score, they said, reflected development to date and implied nothing about probable learning in subsequent years. In truth, the negative correlations come from measurement error. In some of these data, the *true* score at age 10 correlated 0.4 with the true change during adolescence. By changing the measurement scale, however, we could change that correlation upward or downward, so it is essentially meaningless.

Ability to learn is as complex as reasoning (Estes, in Sternberg, 1982b). Digit Span increases little after age 8, so memory measures are not good indicators of intellectual development. Arthur Jensen (1973, 1980) speaks of rote learning as "Level I" ability; his "Level II" encompasses Gf and Gc. Level I performance has comparatively little relation to home background; the children of the poor perform in the normal range on rote tasks (see Table 10.3). Jensen therefore suggests making practice-and-reinforcement (sometimes called "direct instruction") the principal means of compensatory education. Drill methods do indeed succeed in teaching standardized skills (as distinct from comprehension and problem solving).

Closely related to Jensen's line of thought are J. B. Carroll's well-known "model of school learning" (1963) and Benjamin Bloom's recommendations on "mastery learning" (1976). Both take the position that any person can learn anything, given sufficient time and excellent instruction. Foreign languages may be difficult for American adolescents, but infants learn those languages easily when they grow up with them. Measures of Gf or Gc forecast how lengthy an instructional immersion the student will require to reach satisfactory competence, not whether he can reach that level. This argument asks teachers to be patient and diligent, not giving up on slow learners. And, because time for instruction is limited, the argument encourages schools to concentrate the school day of the slower learner on a few "basic" competences, to pile up the extra time-on-task he needs.

It is not surprising that memory for digit strings, resistant to meaningful interpretation, has little relation to general ability. Level I tasks, however, can easily become meaningful. For example, a resourceful learner remembers a word-pair by building a sentence around the words. Laboratory learning of unfamiliar materials (e.g., the "concept attainment" task) correlates consistently with general mental tests, and so does programmed instruction—lessons that try to supply complete and easily grasped information. Carroll (1980) has collated dozens of studies combining laboratory learning tasks and psychometric tasks. A great number of comparatively narrow learning abilities were distinguished, and, insofar as there was a "general" memory factor in the simple tasks, its relation to general ability was weak.

Persons who are intellectually efficient—as evidenced by their success in past learning and by their test scores—ordinarily learn more than others on tasks that require comprehension (Jensen, 1981, p. 31). Still, to think of a "general" learning ability—even for organized lessons—oversimplifies. Each method of instruction makes its own demands for information processing; also, there are content-specific learning abilities (for example, in foreign language). The unfinished business of educational psychology is understanding how to adapt instructional styles to individuals. (See esp. pp. 342ff.)

Industrial psychologists are beginning to explore "trainability tests"; they directly test ability to learn by means of a learning sample. To train a worker to maintain electronic switching equipment takes 6 months and costs the phone company about $25,000. For selection, a minicourse was prepared that matched in general character the main training. Time to complete the minicourse (around 20 hours) and a final exam on it predicted time to complete the main training ($r = 0.6$; Reilly & Manese, 1979). Whether the qualities that make for fast learning in a minicourse are predictable from conventional tests remains an open question (Siegel, 1978).

Learning samples may be especially suitable in employment testing of the handicapped, for whom written tests and speed tests tend to be inappropriate. One system for rehabilitation counseling (described by Sherman & Robinson, 1982, p. 59) consists of 94 work samples that take a month to work through (because time is allowed to learn each task).

Divergent Thinking

Introspective accounts from artists, mathematicians, and other creators have suggested that creativity requires intellectual fluency—adeptness in making fresh combinations of observations and ideas. The most thoughtful psychologists have not asserted that fluidity of association *is* creativity. Fluency is to be integrated with the purposiveness and critical thinking that Binet's definition emphasized and with a store of knowledge. Novel ideas are of little value if not accompanied by critical evaluation. Pouring out unrealistic, ill-considered ideas is not meritorious.

Creativity is specific to fields and subfields; composers of music are not architects. Knowledge and conceptual systems are as useful in original thinking as in other thinking—see Guilford's particularly good statements (1965) on this point. The creative producer, then, has ability in Binet's sense plus rich experience in a field plus something extra. Perhaps, say some writers, the creative person will not be found in the highest ranges of academic success: dutiful learning of school lessons may not be congenial to or conducive to a free-ranging intellect. To put the suggestion differently, rank in convergent tests corresponds to rank in creativity up to the high-average level; in the highest range, however, there seems to be a lack of correspondence between convergent tests and rank in creativity (H. J. Butcher, 1968, p. 103; Barron & Harrington, 1981).

Most of the tests suggested as measures of the special creative ingredient are "divergent." A "convergent" question has a best answer whereas there are many good answers to a divergent question. Thurstone introduced word-fluency tests (for example, "Give as many four-letter words beginning with *h* as you can in 3 minutes"); and Guilford laid out two dozen varieties of divergent tests (p. 296).

Much research has accumulated around the Torrance Tests of Creative Thinking (E. P. Torrance; Ginn), which can be applied from kindergarten to adulthood. The verbal section contains subtests such as these:

> *Product Improvement.* A picture of a stuffed animal toy is shown. The subject is to suggest changes, each of which would make the toy more fun to play with.
>
> *Unusual Uses.* This test, which originated with Guilford, asks for many possible uses for commonplace objects such as empty tin cans. (Space is provided for 50 answers!)

Torrance's figural tasks ask for drawings that tell a story or depict an object, given initial starting points. One test, for example, consists of a page of circles. The directions tell the child to make as many different pictures as possible with the circle a key part of each picture. Responses can be scored for one or more of these qualities: fluency (total acceptable responses), flexi-

Table 8.5. *Stability and consistency for convergent and divergent abilities*

Test Type, age 13	Test Type, age 15–16	Correlation[a]
Convergent	Same convergent ability	0.65
Convergent	Another convergent ability	0.5
Convergent	Divergent	0.2
Divergent	Convergent	0.2
Divergent	Divergent	0.4

[a] Approximate median, over sexes and over test-pairs.
SOURCE: Magnusson & Backteman, 1978.

bility (i.e., variety of content), originality, and elaboration. Scores on these qualities correlate highly, so perhaps the distinctions are pointless.

Torrance's data suggest that figural performance does not improve during the school years and that verbal performance improves little after grade 6. Scores on convergent tests hold up until age 50 or later. Word fluency, however, drops off steadily after about age 30 (Schaie, 1979). This, along with Torrance's evidence, suggests that the advantage from the older person's greater range of concepts and intellectual skill is neutralized by some inhibitory process. (Greater conventionality? Sterner censorship of flawed responses?) Children with high scores in divergent thinking tend to be more expansive and spontaneous in their everyday activities; children who do well on conventional tests and badly on divergent tests seem to be cautious and insecure (Getzels & Jackson, 1962; Wallach & Kogan, 1965).

Is divergent thinking distinct from convergent thinking? Table 8.5, based on a follow-up of 1000 Swedish youngsters, provides support for the distinction. The divergent score at each age was based on two or three tests, different from age to age; split-half reliabilities are high. Within either age, the convergent and divergent totals correlated about 0.25. The verbal, logical, and spatial scores from convergent tests are kept separate in my summary; thus the top line in the table is a median for verbal-with-verbal, logical-with-logical, and spatial-with-spatial scores. It can be seen that divergent tests predict other divergent tests—not well, but better than convergent tests do.

As to whether divergent tests predict genuine creativity better than convergent tests, criteria are suspect, and findings are discouragingly inconsistent. The greater instability of divergent performance (Table 8.5) implies poor predictive validity. A sympathetic review (Barron & Harrington, 1981) could not go beyond this carefully hedged conclusion:

> On the basis of those few studies [that compare predictions from divergent and conventional tests] one can say that some divergent thinking tests, administered to some samples, under some conditions and scored according to some criteria, measure facets relevant to

creativity criteria beyond those measured by indices of general intelligence.

As divergent tests are hard to score and standings are unstable, perhaps their main function is to dramatize for teachers that convergent abilities are not the whole of intellectual development.

Physiological Hypotheses

Since mental processes are carried out in the brain, individual differences must have a basis in physiological structures. In principle, information about the nervous system would provide a better indication of what the brain can do than can be inferred from behavior itself. Some form of this attractive hypothesis arises in each generation (Berger, in Eysenck, 1982). Modern electrophysiology offers increasingly sophisticated ways to measure physiological bases of mental activity (John et al., 1977).

Neural speed. Early in the century, fluid ability was thought of as a product of mental speed, specifically of speedy neural transmission. Speed of response was distinguished from the "altitude" of ability, the highest level of task the person can cope with. A contemporary version is the statement that speed, persistence, and error-checking are "major, independent aspects of the IQ, with speed the most fundamental" (Eysenck, 1979, p. 188; see chapters by Furneaux and White in Eysenck, 1973).

It is indeed possible to distinguish speed from accuracy; the two kinds of score correlate positively, negatively, or not at all, depending on conditions. A test taker can choose to work faster at the risk of a higher error rate, or vice versa. Administering items singly, with computer timing of responses, can assess speed on one run and accuracy or altitude on a second run with no time pressure. Subjects who can summon up greater speed are not generally superior in altitude. Claims have been made (for example by Jensen, in Eysenck, 1982) that choice-reaction time is strongly related to ability level. The ambiguities and inconsistencies in the data do not permit a conclusion at this time (Carroll, 1980; L. A. Cooper & D. T. Regan, in Sternberg, 1982b).

Within the general-ability domain, most makers of group tests try to set a time limit that allows at least three-fourths of the target population to reach the end of the test. Their scores would then reflect altitude and inconsistency more than speed; but differences in speed are still a factor in performance (Donlon & Angoff, in Angoff, 1971). It is true that a group of students with high test scores (verbal or nonverbal, speeded or unspeeded) will perform almost any simple recognition task faster on average than a group having poorer test scores. However, the correlation of general ability with speed on simple items is small. Speed measures correlate little from one simple task to another; for example, rotation of forms has little in common with left-right orientation. Evidently speed comes primarily from specific techniques, though Jensen and others (in Eysenck, 1982) credit part of general ability to a physiological quickness that helps with all tasks.

Altitude *(Gf)* is strongly correlated with speed when items require extensive information processing. The efficient person avoids waste motion. What counts is not sheer speed but sensitive encoding and memory search (L. A. Cooper & D. T. Regan, in Sternberg, 1982b; Horn, 1977; Lohman, 1979a, b). What can be learned by timing elementary processes in reasoning will be illustrated in the next chapter.

Electrical potentials. Electrodes on the scalp record the electrical potentials evoked by controlled stimuli; this is one way to study brain responses. Such records have not generated consistent correlations with psychometric measures (Callaway, 1975). A typical page of results lists correlations ranging from -0.1 to $+0.3$. Hendrickson (in Eysenck, 1982), however, reports correlations as high as 0.8 for one large sample; crosschecking of his methods by other laboratories is needed. Results depend on how the brain is stimulated (light flash? tone?), where electrodes are placed, which components of the response are measured, and so on. Callaway believes that the technique can someday identify persons at risk for schizophrenia, and it already serves in studying brain lesions and tumors. As an objective measure of the fine structure of attention, the brain recordings should play a role in laboratory research on information processing (Donchin & Isreal, in Snow *et al.*, 1980). A physiological measure of *Gf* is not in prospect.

Hemispheric specialization. Modern studies assign responsibility for verbal and logical processes primarily to the left brain whereas the right brain seems to handle most visual information and pictorial images or analogies. There is speculation that left-brain processes produce a well-defined, exact response whereas right-brain processes are more continuous, and their correctness is a matter of degree. The distinction is like that between digital and analog computers. The left brain, it is suggested, works with abstracted elements; the right brain, with general impressions or gestalts. Loose-coupled, intuitive machinery is needed in generating fresh ideas; possibly the right brain is best at that function.

This set of hypotheses sums up notions from a research frontier, notions that can easily be overstated (Berent, in Filskov & Boll, 1982). On many tasks the halves seem to perform interchangeably. In some persons the left brain seems to have taken over so-called right-brain functions, and vice versa.

Some test interpreters suspect that fluid processes depend on the right hemisphere whereas crystallized performances can rely on the left hemisphere. Adults and children with damaged left hemispheres usually earn better standard scores on performance tasks like Wechsler's than on the verbal tasks. The opposite is found when the damage is on the right side. Some samples fail to confirm this conclusion (small samples? difficulties of locating lesions? the confounding effect of other variables?). A V–P difference no more than hints at a possible physiological cause (Kaufman, 1979, pp. 6–7, 27–29; Matarazzo, 1972, pp. 377–398).

Field independence. For 30 years Herman Witkin and numerous collaborators and followers have investigated a set of interrelated variables, reporting on individual differences in "psychological differentiation" or "field dependence-independence" (FDI). The conceptualization and measuring procedures shifted as findings came in, and the ideas were in flux when Witkin died in 1979. My account draws on the latest writings of the Witkin group (Witkin, 1978; Witkin & Goodenough, 1981; Witkin *et al.,* 1979) and on conversation with Donald Goodenough. The Witkin-Goodenough book summarizes research on an astonishingly wide range of variables thought to be related to FDI or differentiation. For thoughtful reviews of the Witkin theses by independent scholars, see Kagan and Buriel (1977) and Laboratory of Comparative Human Cognition (in Sternberg, 1982b).

The basic phenomenon is best represented in a set of tests that pose the question, "Which way is up?" In the Rod and Frame Test (RFT), the subject sits in a room that is dark save for a luminous frame tilted perhaps 30° from the vertical and a luminous rod that the subject is to bring to an upright position by means of a remote control. To judge correctly he must disregard the frame. In the Body Adjustment Test, the subject sits in a chair mounted within a small room. The examiner has set room and chair in tilted positions; the subject is to rotate the chair to align with the gravitational vertical. Another procedure places the rod and frame against the ceiling; the person, lying flat, is to align the rod with the midline of his body. These procedures are research tools, not practical measuring devices. Scores are unreliable and subject to various fatigue and practice effects. Despite such difficulties, many findings have been replicated.

A highly FD person will place the rod many degrees away from the true vertical, more nearly in line with the frame. The FI person is little influenced by the irrelevant frame (the "field"). RFT and all other supposed measures of FDI are ability tests; there is always a right answer. During its history, however, FDI has been called a cognitive style, an aspect of personality, an indicator of a neural process, and (by Vernon, 1973) a mere synonym for fluid ability. For many years, investigators measured FDI by combinations of tests. Most of them used RFT in a portable form and not the other tests of its kind. The Embedded Figures score was almost always added in. (The figures contain a background that must be ignored, and EFT scores do correlate 0.4 with RFT.) EFT, however, is an excellent measure of *Gf,* and Witkin has even said (in Messick, 1976) that FDI is "essentially identical" to what Block Design measures. Witkin established early that perception of the vertical correlates negligibly with the verbal subtests of the Wechsler; but only recently did he make a case for distinguishing it from *Gf.*

Today's hypothesis—admittedly speculative in parts—includes the following lines of thought among others:

- The broad term *psychological differentiation* refers to a generalized tendency, of which FDI is an outgrowth or expression. A differentiator analyzes complex stimulus fields and keeps the strands of information

separate in his mind; a nondifferentiator forms a more global percept. FDI is now defined as a contrast between two tendencies in psychological functioning "to rely primarily on external referents [FD] or on the self [FI]" (Witkin *et al.*, 1979, p. 113).
- Differentiators and nondifferentiators differ (on average) in their neurophysiology.
- The tests requiring sensitivity to kinesthetic-proprioceptive-vestibular cues and disregard of visual distractions are the best measures of FDI. Superior performance may depend on separation—at a neural level—of pathways from the retina and those from the semicircular canals (Witkin & Goodenough, 1981, pp. 34 ff.).
- People who differentiate more readily are better at "cognitive restructuring." Differentiation, then, contributes to fluid ability.
- Those who differentiate less make more use of cues presented by other persons and are more effective in social relationships.

The strongest evidence for the physiological interpretation is an offshoot of the hemispheric-differentiation hypothesis. As Zoccolotti and Oltman (1978) put it, "greater psychological differentiation is expected to be associated with greater specialization of function in both hemispheres, each according to its predominant mode of information processing." They cite several relevant bits of evidence and add evidence of their own; so do Berent, in Filskov and Boll (1982), and Oltman *et al.* (1979). I take the Oltman study as an example. An extreme group of differentiators (good on both RFT and EFT) was contrasted with persons poor on both tests. Brain-wave records were analyzed, the key statistic being a correlation calculated between left-side and right-side activity for each person in turn. These correlations tended to be about 0.2 higher in the nondifferentiators, implying that the two halves of the brain were working in tandem, that is, with less specificity of function. Is the difference in brain structure or in the way subjects interpret stimuli? The question remains open.

The Witkin group (see especially Dasen, Witkin, and Berry, 1979) deny that FDI or the broader tendency to differentiate is a sign of superior development. They say that no value judgment should be attached to a person's position on the scale. What they see as a "style" (p. 270), I see as an ability.

Giving special weight to visual impressions and to cues coming from other persons is likely to impair formal reasoning, which calls for "decontextualization" (p. 328). Part of the dependents' reported tendency to lean on others may be an adaptation to their weakness in reasoning ability. "Field dependent" persons evidently tend to be more sociable, less autonomous, and more popular than others (Witkin & Goodenough, 1981). Using cues from others can be an important social aptitude (p. 329). If FD is a sign of "social competence," as Witkin says, then a group of FD persons, working together, should coordinate its work better and produce better results than a group made up of FI individuals having similar education and cultural background. Studies of the topic have barely begun (Oltman et al., 1975).

There seems to be no point in separating FDI from the concept of fluid ability at this time. Future work may show that it can be measured reliably as a distinct variable and that it has important correlates of its own. To show this, investigators would have to contrast groups matched on Gf but differing on some proposed measure of FDI. By my reasoning, EFT is a variable to match on, not to sort cases on.

23. The "field dependence" that EFT measures is often referred to as a cognitive style. Presumably a style is typical behavior, hence more easily changed than an ability. What evidence would be required to justify the interpretation of EFT as a measure of style?
24. In 1975 a federal agency said that school districts should match instructional methods to pupils' "cognitive styles." If field dependence is such a "style" and if teachers tried to devise distinct approaches for field-independent and field-dependent children, how might the two approaches differ? Would they be equally stimulating?
25. Describe some real-world tasks that would be especially likely to show an FD group superior to a group of FI persons if the Witkin hypothesis is sound.
26. Table 8.6 reports intercorrelations of K-ABC scores in one age range. Which of the subtests fit into the spectrum of Figure 8.7? Are the intercorrelations consistent with the spectrum? (The Triangles test is a variant of Block Design.)
27. Account for the fact that intercorrelations in the Simultaneous Processing category are lower than those in the other two categories. (The reliability of Triangles is slightly lower than that of other subtests, but not enough to explain the correlational differences.)

Table 8.6. *Approximate intercorrelations for subtests of K-ABC*

	Number Recall	Word Order	Gestalt Closure	Triangles	Matrix Analogies	Arithmetic	Reading/ Understanding[c]
Number Recall[a]		0.65	0.1	0.25	0.25	0.40	0.45
Word Order[a]			0.2	0.35	0.35	0.5	0.55
Gestalt Closure[b]				0.4	0.3	0.3	0.2
Triangles[b]					0.4	0.5	0.4
Matrix Analogies[b]						0.45	0.35
Arithmetic[c]							0.6

[a]Included in Sequential Processing score.
[b]Included in Simultaneous Processing score.
[c]Included in Achievement score.
SOURCE: Data from Interpretive manual of K-ABC, pp. 315–316. Correlations for ages 7 and 8 were averaged and rounded.

28. *For ages 7 and 8, the following intercorrelations and reliabilities are reported.*

	Sequential Processing	*Simultaneous Processing*	*Achievement*	*Reliability*
Sequential Processing		.45	.6	.82
Simultaneous Processing			.6	.88
Achievement				.95

What can be said for and against the decision to combine the first two sections into a Mental Processing Composite?

9
Components in Intellectual Performance

To understand the nature of ability and to assess individual strengths and weaknesses, psychologists must sort tasks into categories that call on different abilities or must resolve performance on a specific task into component processes. Clinical observation, experimental variation of tasks, and correlational analyses highlight different kinds of components or specific abilities.

I shall discuss analyses of block design and similar artificial tasks because that is where psychological research is most advanced. All these approaches are equally relevant to fundamental educational skills, as Glaser (1981) demonstrates. Even very poor performance in arithmetic or writing does not usually imply total absence of competence. A close analysis of the person's attack on different versions of the same task will show that he has knowledge of many elements and command of many processes. But crucial gaps in technique or specific misconceptions produce a high error rate. One striking example is the written composition of a college student (from Bartholomeo, 1980), which begins:

> This assignment call on chosing one of my incident making a last draft out of it. I found this very differcult because I like tham all but you said I had to pick one so the Second incident was decide.

At first glance, this student appears to be hopelessly ignorant of the rules of sentence structure. When the student was asked to read his paper aloud, he produced sentences with good structure though not without error. He inserted word endings and even added words that the structure required (e.g., "was decided on."). What this student most needed was a proofreader's skill of seeing precisely what *is* on the page rather than what he intended to put there. Once such a faulty process is identified, targeted reteaching can often produce rapid improvement.

For decades, specialists in the teaching of arithmetic, reading, speech, and writing have used informal clinical methods to pinpoint difficulties as a first step in remediation. Glaser holds out the hope that today's frontier research on modeling of components in problem solving will be extended into comparatively formal assessment of microprocesses within the tool skills in education. One such microassessment is described on page 299.

INDIVIDUAL STYLES

A person approaches a task slowly and methodically or with tentative trial responses or with brash confidence. The approach may be characteristic of the person, likely to show up elsewhere. The approach is influenced by the immediate situation (e.g., by whatever threat is implied by a pending decision). Whether we are seeing the person's *characteristic* response to intellectual challenges can be learned only by continued observation. If an inference about style can be trusted, it generates suggestions for the teacher, case worker, and other professionals. Sometimes the person can be helped to see how a style is reducing his efficiency. Clinical testers use stylistic clues in evaluating pathology (pp. 540, 547ff.).

Inferences from hesitations and errors. A tester picks up information over and above the count of successes. Indeed, the main aim of an individual examination should be to understand where the person is efficient and informed and where and why he lapses (Moriarty, 1966). This is illustrated in the notes on an 8-year-old (Biber *et al.*, 1952). Mark scored not far above average on the largely verbal Stanford-Binet. He rose to the 80th percentile or better on some performance tests.

> The most striking feature of Mark's examination was his extreme lack of confidence and his desire to do what was expected of him. This was manifested by his constant reference to the examiner. . . . to see whether the expression on the examiner's face indicated approval.
>
> In the Healy Completion [fitting small blocks into square holes to complete a picture] the examiner noticed that once when she gave him a friendly smile he was content to leave an inferior solution, as

if he were guided much more by his wish to please than by his own good intelligence. Although she busied herself with papers and tried to pay as little attention as is compatible with a test situation, it was impossible to prevent this. The directions in the Healy Completion to look the work over carefully and see if there are any changes to make seemed to imply criticism to Mark, and he removed a block which was correctly placed and substituted a blank. His first responses were all good. In this test, he placed the first three accurately; then, apparently, he began feeling anxious or uncertain, and the last three he placed were blanks. It seemed that he was using the blanks as a way of avoiding committing himself to a mistake, and that he felt that he would rather do nothing than to get the wrong result. This test was the most plainly motivated by his desire for approval, although there were indications of it throughout the other tests as well. . . .

Probably no test results on Mark are completely accurate because other factors besides ability are so definitely involved in his behavior. Difficulty . . . simply discouraged him and left him tense and uneasy. He was responsive to praise, but always with a questioning expression, as if he were trying to ferret out what one really thought of him.

Wechsler examiners learn much about the person. Earlier (p. 64) I described the testing of an executive who was masking acute depression. On the surface—good grade record, good military record, positive report on business and family affairs—the man was a fine prospect for a responsible post. His standard scores—Verbal 57, Performance 55—signaled that something was wrong in view of his educational level. The jagged profile—Comprehension and Arithmetic near 15; Digit Span, Picture Arrangement, and Digit Symbol near 7—hinted at pathology. One warning sign was the many "Don't know" responses on Information. This traveled and educated man could not identify *Genesis* or *yeast* and said that the capital of Italy is Florence. Other overcautious responses and passivity were noted.

The older research literature was filled with proposals to categorize clinical patients by adding and subtracting Wechsler subtest scores. In today's diagnosis, the Wechsler is a means of observation and not a source of scores to be treated by formula (Filskov & Leli, in Filskov & Boll, 1982; Wood, 1979). The computational approach failed because diagnostic categories are crude, and background and qualitative features of test performance were left out of account. Says Matarazzo (1972, p. 432):

> [N]o . . . Wechsler subtest pattern or . . . index has been reported which reliably differentiates "schizophrenic" patients from . . . normal individuals. . . . Using information from the Wechsler Scales, in *isolation,* to date has failed to separate patients diagnosed

schizophrenics . . . from patients diagnosed neurotic, or sociopathic, or . . . brain diseased.

Evidence from eye movements. An example of formal investigation of one style will lead into a discussion of process analysis. Confronting a multiple-choice item, a person may move "forward." He thinks about the stimuli that pose the problem (the "stem"), works out an answer for himself, and then looks for that answer among the choices offered. Another person works "backward." After glancing at the stem, this person focuses on the answers, eliminating the ones that seem not to fit and choosing among the survivors.

Snow (in Snow *et al.*, 1980) recorded eye movements of adolescents working on Paper Folding (Figure 9.1). The instructions have explained that a square paper was folded three times to produce the third shape in the row;

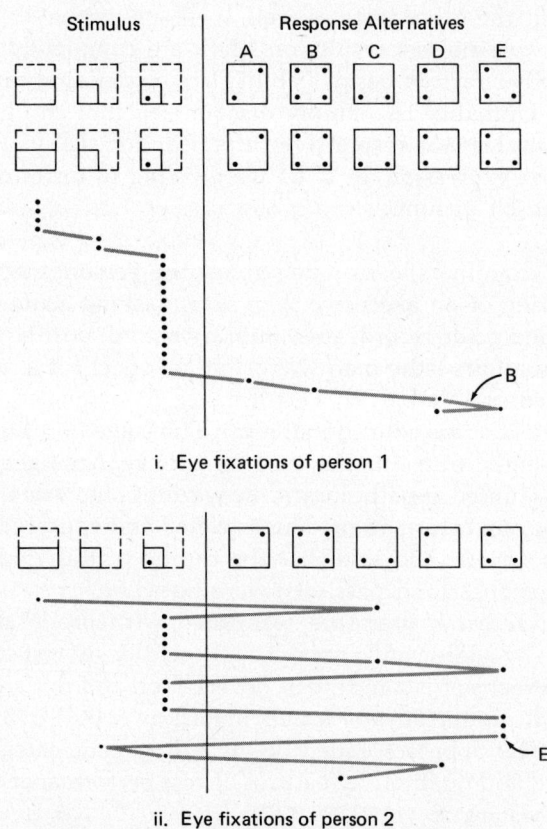

Figure 9.1. Two styles of response to a paper-folding item. Time runs down the page, and each large dot represents 0.5 seconds. The "balloon" indicates when an answer was given, and the alternative chosen.

Source: Based on Snow in Snow et al., 1980, pp. 46, 48.

then a hole was punched through all layers. Now, how will the sheet look when unfolded? This task is a good measure of Gf; spatial reasoning also counts. (A constructed-response version of the task appeared in the Binet-Simon scale.)

Person 1 moved forward. He invested 7 seconds in thinking about the folded paper, presumably imagining the unfolding. Then he marched briskly across the response options. As soon as he had glanced at the last one, he made his choice (correct). Snow calls this "constructive matching." Person 2 seemed intent on comparing response C to the folded pattern (but it is possible that, looking toward C, he was taking in its neighbors also). Next, it seems, he jumped impulsively to E, convinced himself that it could match the folded paper, and gave a wrong answer. Eliminating mismatches is not the best line of attack though some persons apply it more systematically than Person 2.

High school students of less-than-average ability are the ones most likely to attend first to the choices. (Also, they talk more to themselves and guess more.) Snow finds that abler students try constructive matching. When construction proves troublesome, they shift to response elimination or some other backup procedure.

An experimental task analysis. The person who decomposes a block design and fills one cell at a time is likely to do better than the person who holds the global pattern in mind and tries to assemble it by trial and error. Some kinds of brain damage seem to prevent patients from approaching the task analytically. Experimenters have recently been comparing block designs to determine why some are harder than others of the same size (Royer & Weitzel, 1977; Schorr *et al.*, 1982; for clinical studies, see Diller & Gordon, in Filskov & Boll, 1982).

Schorr *et al.* conducted several studies of 4- and 9-block patterns with college students (for whom these tasks are not difficult). Their basic plan is illustrated in Figure 9.2. The person was to pick the block that belongs where the asterisk appears in the target. The pattern and target were exposed on signal; the person pressed a button as soon as he made his choice. Errors were rare, and the response times were the main data. This study exemplifies the experimenter's way of investigating mental processes: comparing tasks rather

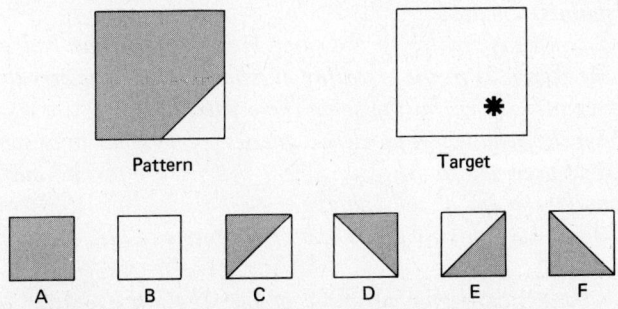

Figure 9.2. Choice format for Block-Design task.

than persons. Subjects were not "scored" on the test or questioned about their styles.

Responses tended to be most rapid when the pattern contained more single-color squares, was more symmetric, and—especially important—had fewer "interior-edge cues." An illustration will clarify this key notion. In the pictured pattern, the lower-right block has four edges: the obvious outside edges and the two interior ones that can only be imagined. The pattern has no "interior edge cues." If that block were turned to point the white triangle toward the center, the interior edges would be obvious; two cues. A checkerboard pattern, with four interior cues, is easy.

When there are few interior cues and many solid squares, the global approach is likely to work as well as the analytic approach. Thus the test developer can choose patterns that a global approach can handle fairly well or can choose patterns that demand decomposition. The contrast of scores on these two kinds of block design (administered in the traditional way) could be useful in diagnosis. Other research suggests the possible value of using the same technique to get two kinds of score for EFT (see question 5) and E. B. Hunt (1974) has applied the technique to matrix items.

1. *For a general mental test such as Wechsler's, is the influence of style of approach on a Block Design score a source of validity or invalidity? To get the best measure of Gf, should the Wechsler subtest use patterns suited to one of the styles, or should the effect be balanced out?*
2. *Suppose that the timed-choice procedure for Block Design is standardized for administration by microcomputer. If cost and convenience are disregarded, would that procedure or Wechsler's constructed-response procedure best serve the purposes for which Wechsler's test is now given?*
3. *What description of the patient's thought processes is suggested by each of these responses to "Why should we keep away from bad company?" (Schafer, 1948). (The response in a was given by an adult of average ability; the other two patients were well above average.)*
    a. *Your friends will talk about you; if we want to live in a good environment, we must choose good company.*
    b. *I don't know if that necessarily holds true. To prevent picking up their bad habits, I guess.*
    c. *It's a trend toward living the same kind of a life, get bad yourself.*
4. *Match the responses in the preceding question to these answers to "Why do we have laws?" given by the same three patients.*
    a. *Govern the behavior of people. [E queries.] There has to be some maintenance of order by which government policies are carried out as well as personal behavior of individuals.*
    b. *To have a law-abiding group of people; otherwise they would corrupt the city.*
    c. *To make good citizens out of us; to keep the unruly under control.*
5. *On a multiple-choice version of Embedded Figures, Texas schoolchildren*

outperformed a demographically similar sample from Mexico City (Holtzman et al., 1975). But the difference appeared on only half the items— the "simple" ones. In more complex items, the hidden figure is partly concealed by crisscrossing lines in the large pattern; moreover, several near-correct answer-choices confuse the child. In the simpler subset, the figure to be located has a shape that can readily be grasped as a whole. And, in the large pattern, the hidden figure is surrounded by other shapes (as in a jigsaw puzzle) but remains undivided. On such an item a global perception is sufficient; analysis is not required. The average times to solution for typical items of each type were as follows (in seconds):

	Texas	Mexico
Complex masking	107	109
Simple embedding	72	106

Interpret this result.

INFORMATION PROCESSING

As the block-design study illustrated, experimenters alter tasks or break them into parts to detect details of problem-solving technique. This section examines some of the conclusions from analytic research on cognition. A common thesis is that a problem is solved by translating sense impressions into symbols or other simple representations that can be rearranged mentally. The codes and procedures the person has at his command are important intellectual resources. This research helps explain verbal and logical processes. Cognitive psychology has had little to say about the way problem solvers use global impressions as in dealing with strongly patterned block designs. Closure (p. 292), for example, remains unexplained.

Piaget's Account of Intellectual Development

The famous Genevan psychologist Jean Piaget described judgment and reasoning as the application of mental structures. Structures of a sort are present from an early age. As the child progresses, crude and indefinite concepts are supplanted by exact and powerful ones. Some structures are of no great psychological interest—the number names that allow counting, for example. Others, however, are schemes for organizing experience and checking on arguments.

Much of Piaget's research centered on concepts of conservation of volume, shape, and so on; for example, that true shape does not change when something is viewed from a new angle, or volume when some liquid is poured into a new container. Children have to acquire these principles. In Piagetian testing, the aim is to inventory the intellectual structures the child has at his disposal.

Piaget offered an elaborate account of specific developments such as the concept of order. A concept such as "order" is at first limited to the concrete world; thus, the young child can compare bead chains laid side by side. He can compare a straight chain with one twisted into a figure eight only much later, when able to put the order into words. When the concept is sufficiently developed, he can cope with a logical problem such as "Town A is north of B, and C is south of B; what can you say about A and C?"

The remarks the child makes as he works (and as he is asked to justify his answers) are more important than the count of successes. Tasks of the same kind are varied subtly—to learn which complications the child takes in stride and which not. The conclusion that the child is following such-and-such chain of reasoning is a complex inference about events inside the child's head.

Do Piagetian tasks measure the general ability that tests measure? Yes, but—. Piagetian tasks vary. The question about towns A, B, and C calls for logic. Tasks such as these correlate strongly with conventional test scores, particularly with abstract tests such as Matrices. Command of conservation tasks is less strongly associated with mental age than is success on the logical tasks, and not closely related to school achievement (A. L. Brown, 1973; DeVries, 1974; Goodnow & Bethon, 1966).

With greater intellectual maturity, the person imposes on events a conceptual structure. He thereby detects misperceptions and so reduces overt error. A conservation principle is one such structure. The correct response can be drilled in and, in principle, could become a crystallized ability. But surface "mastery" is not mental development, as Smedslund (1961) demonstrated. He asked 5-year-olds and 8-year-olds to judge the comparative weight of two lumps of clay, originally identical, after one had been flattened. The 5-year-olds said that the two were unequal. Then Smedslund "trained" the children, using a balance so they could check their own judgments on trial after trial. After training, these children did indeed call the round lump and the flattened lump equal. But Smedslund tested the limits of their learning with "extinction" or "contradiction" trials. He secretly pinched off some of the clay or added an extra bit, so that the judgment of "equal" was contradicted by the balance. The young children accepted their errors with a sort of "you can't win 'em all" reaction; they had not truly been forming a mental representation of constancy of weight. Eight-year-olds, though, responded as the concept of weight dictated: "Something is wrong with the scales" or "Some got lost"—and scrambled down from their chairs to look on the floor for the missing clay. The training, then, served not to erase the superiority of the older children but to expose it more clearly.

It is certainly possible to teach conservation principles, by methods suited to the child's development (Siegler & Richards, in Sternberg, 1982b).

Berland (1982) reports on his experiences with Pakistani children who had been trained from infancy to play roles in a nomadic band of entertainers, adept in slight-of-hand and acrobatics. These children not only performed excellently on Piagetian tasks but would make up their own conservation tests and instruct Berland in them. They were particularly fond of pinching off a tiny bit of mud from one of the objects to fool him, and prove that he did not know how to pay close attention!

Modeling Thought Processes

How would a computer generate the same intellectual response to a problem that a human gives? Asking what the computer would need by way of storage facilities, codes, and orders for rearranging symbols leads to an imaginative construction of steps in information processing. The research is not like ordinary computer programming, which directs the computer efficiently to the right answer. The program efficient for a computer is likely not to be efficient for a person. The psychologist observes a subject at work on a certain intellectual task, infers his thought processes, and then details her conjecture in the form of a program. Her model is judged satisfactory if the computer, directed by her program, reacts to the problems as the human did, making similar errors and pausing at the same places in the sequence.

I offer as example a model for the bead-chain task (which Piaget took over from Binet). The presentation is derived from Piaget and Inhelder (1956), but includes only a fraction of their ideas and stops short of a computer program.

Assume that the child and the computer understand the directions: they are to string beads into a chain that matches a sample. Assume also that the computer has auxiliary devices to scan the bin of loose beads, pick up a bead, place it on the chain, and inspect the chain. The psychologist varies the sample chains. She increases the load on the system by adding beads or colors to the sample, by placing the sample beyond arm's reach, or by twisting the sample chain. The test taker must bring additional control processes to bear as bead-chain tasks increase in difficulty. Which complications cause failure at earlier and later ages, and what does that suggest?

Young children proceed impressionistically and make frequent errors. It is not easy to simulate a haphazard process, so I move on to about age 5, when thought is "preoperational." The child is not yet able to regulate performance adequately with abstract concepts of order and color names; instead, he picks a bead, mounts it on his chain, and then moves his chain closer to the sample to check the correspondence of colors. He does not use a representation such as "red-blue-blue." Direct sensorimotor comparison enables him to reproduce a long chain under condition *a* of Figure 9.3 (though he may eventually lose his place). When the wire on which he is to mount beads is anchored, he cannot make a direct comparison; then he is very likely to lose his place and make errors. He tries to get sensorimotor control by pointing with his

Preoperational Thought (about ages 4–5)

a. 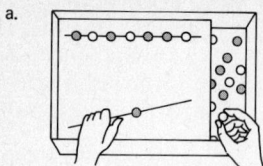 Child adds one bead at a time, putting copy alongside model to check, regulating by touch or short eye movements.

b. 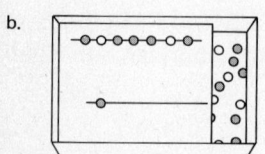 Rod is fixed by tester in offset position. Child adds one bead at a time, regulating by back-and-forth eye movements.

c. 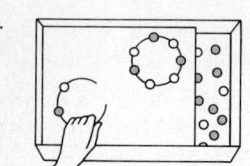 Child breaks circle into parts. Tends to lose his place and reverse direction. Has no concept of "between."

d. 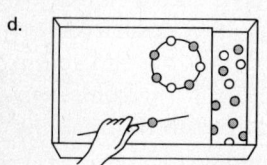 Response is mediated by image of the circle "opened out," transforming the task to one resembling that in b.

Operational Thought (about ages 6–7)

Child is told to make a chain with the order reversed. He must extract the order, neglecting appearance. The performance is regulated by verbal mediators such as "next to" and "between."

e.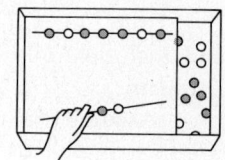

Child is told to make a chain with the order reversed from a given starting point.

f.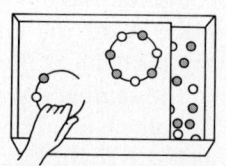

Starting point is given. Child mediates response by naming colors in order while working on each section.

g.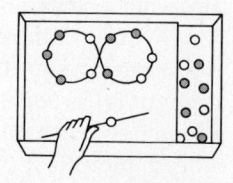

Figure 9.3. Successive stages in command of bead-chain tasks. Problems are arranged here in the order in which the child masters them, according to Piaget and Inhelder (1956). The child is to construct, on the rod he holds, a chain exactly like the model. Shadings indicate three colors of beads.
Source: Educational Psychology, Third Edition by Lee J. Cronbach, copyright © 1977 by Harcourt Brace Jovanovich, Inc. Reproduced by permission of the publisher.

finger; but this control breaks down when sample and chain are kept separated.

Figure 9.4 sketches a process that might account for the successes and failures at this stage. It is a series of steps, all of one form: try, check, and correct if necessary.

Figure 9.5 simulates (incompletely) the behavior of an older child using "operational thought." Actions are regulated by labels carried in mind, sensorimotor feedback playing little part. The simulation is a bit indefinite; we would have to learn how long a string of labels he carries in mind and how he chooses a starting point, and so on, before the program is a true simulation.

Simulations suggest types of individual differences that might be worth recognizing. A dozen skills or habits appear in Figures 9.4 and 9.5; it should

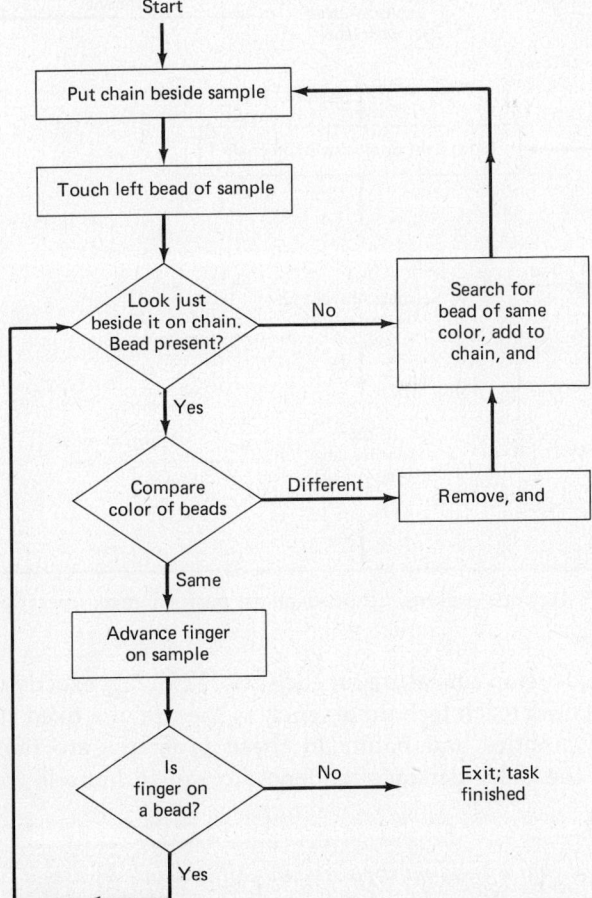

Figure 9.4. Actions making up bead-chain performance: preoperational level.

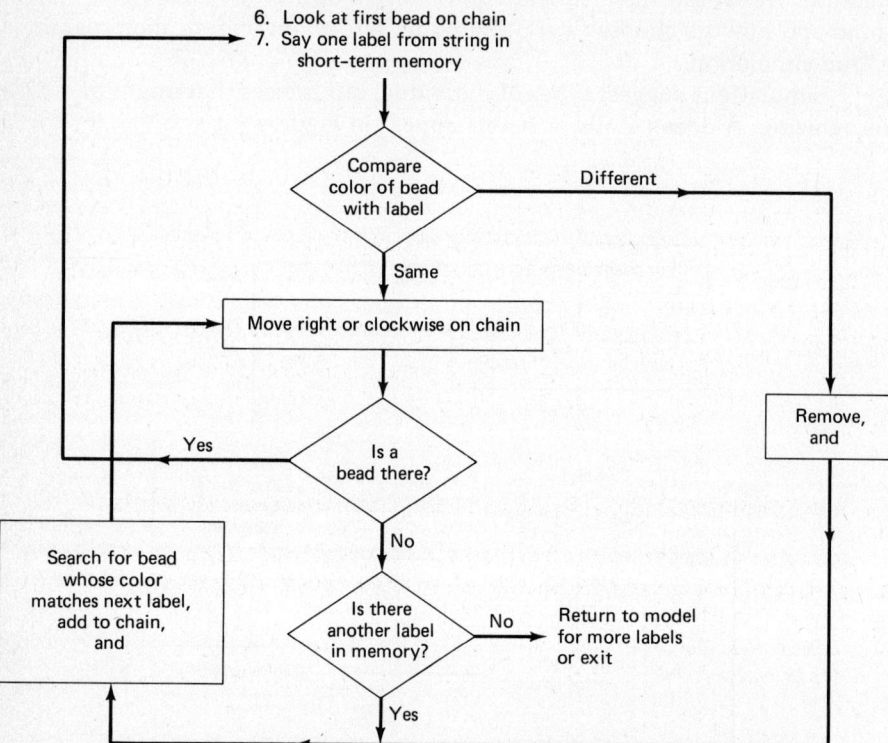

Figure 9.5. Actions making up bead-chain performance: operational level.

be possible to develop a measure for each one. Knowing exactly where a child is weak, one could teach techniques such as the use of a fixed starting point. Some of the abilities and habits in these programs are fairly general—for example, the older person's tendency to say to himself what he needs next.

6. *Logic says that a child must possess an ability before he uses it consistently. But solution of advanced bead-chain problems partly reflects typical behavior. Illustrate.*
7. *Sketch a model for block-design performance similar to that for the bead-chain task. Do the same processes enter?*

Analysis of Components

Robert Sternberg (1977) experiments with items like those in group tests. An item can be split, as in these three versions of the same item:

RED : BLOOD :: WHITE :	A. COLOR
	B. SNOW
RED : BLOOD ::	A. WHITE : SNOW
	B. BROWN : COLOR
RED:	A. BLOOD :: WHITE : SNOW
	B. BRICK :: BROWN : COLOR

Sternberg exposes the left portion of an item for study. Timing of response begins when the right portion is flashed on the screen. Each person receives some items in each form. After responses to items of all three types have been clocked, subtraction of one working time from another indicates how much time each extra step requires. Sternberg's is one among many analytic approaches. The current state of such work is represented in Snow *et al.* (1980) and Sternberg (1982a, b).

Sternberg identifies six "performance components": encoding, inference, mapping, application, justification, and response. Speaking of the preceding analogy, he would say (Sternberg & Gardner, in Eysenck, 1982, p. 238; paraphrased and abbreviated):

> According to the theory, a subject [seeing the analogy all at once]
>
> > *encodes* each term of the analogy, retrieving from semantic memory and placing in working memory attributes that are potentially relevant for analogy solution;
> > next, the subject *infers* the relation between RED and BLOOD;
> > then, the subject *maps* the higher-order relation between the first and second halves of the analogy, here recognizing that the first half deals with the color of blood and the second half deals with the whiteness of some substance;
> > next, the subject *applies* the relation to the third term, WHITE, to form ... an image of the ideal solution;
> > then the subject compares answer options, seeking the ideal among the options presented and, if none of the options fits exactly, he *justifies* one option as being closest to the ideal;
>
> finally, the subject *responds* with his answer.

The analytic experimenter tries to lay out a diagram (somewhat more detailed than Figure 9.4) describing steps a person might perform in sequence. Then, having timed each process, she determines whether the time required by the several processes matches the subject's working time on a problem of a specified complexity. Several models for the same task are needed to account for response patterns of different persons. See Sternberg and Rifkin (1979) for a succinct illustration of the techniques. Their paper also illustrates conclusions reached by these methods. For example, "second-graders appear to have used ... [incomplete] encoding, inference, and application, and either have omitted mapping or perform it at a constant rate, regardless of [item complexity]." Fourth-graders use a mapping step that does vary with item complexity and fully take stimulus features into working memory.

This kind of analysis has been reasonably successful. Speed of encoding and similar measures do correlate modestly with aptitude-test scores. Seemingly, persons efficient in one process show *that* efficiency in a variety of tasks, but are not necessarily superior in other processes.

Another important finding is that what a task measures depends on how the person attacks it. Some tasks, such as Piagetian logical problems, can be approached either by reasoning with verbal symbols or by forming a mental picture. Component measures can identify which strategy the person has adopted. It turns out that excellence of performance correlates substantially with tested verbal ability for those students who are thinking verbally and likewise with spatial ability for those students using visual imagery. Not everyone chooses the mode of analysis that is best suited to his or her aptitudes; there is much to be said for making students conscious of alternative strategies for problem solving, as choice of strategy can then become deliberate (L. A. Cooper & D. T. Regan, in Sternberg, 1982b; see also p. 335.)

Proficiency in problem solving is not accounted for very fully by timing Sternberg's six components. Sternberg attributes the large remainder to the efficiency of "executive functions," by which the person organizes and monitors elementary processes. To speak of "executive components" only translates Binet's ancient description of intelligence (p. 195) into the jargon of computers. Explaining these higher processes is a main task for the next phases of analytic research.

8. *Sternberg lists six processes in the analogy performance. Which of the processes can also be found in bead-chain performance?*
9. *Could each of the following tasks be analyzed in terms of components like Sternberg's?*
   a. *Mechanical comprehension items that present gear chains; the question is, In which direction does the final axle rotate?*
   b. *Wechsler Object Assembly.*
   c. *Pitch discrimination.*
   d. *Finding the shortest route from A to B on a map.*
10. *The traditional Similarities item asks, for example, "In what way are an orange and a banana alike?" The child has to supply a general concept, fruit. Mentally retarded children do poorly on such items. Haywood and his associates (see Haywood et al., 1975) found that, on "enriched" items, the retarded children, if not brain-damaged, do about as well as younger*

(normal) children of the same mental age. Enriched items took this form: "In what way are an orange, a banana, a peach, a plum, and a pear alike?"

What does this finding indicate about the strengths and limitations of the retarded child?

SORTING TESTS BY FACTOR ANALYSIS

I return now to correlational research. Factor analysis lives in two worlds. It and its close relatives are indispensable in reducing statistical data. A modern field study in social or behavioral science may measure hundreds of variables. The investigator has to form clusters or composites so as to make the data compact enough to think about and to smooth out sampling errors and other fluctuations. The second role of factor analysis, as an explanatory technique, concerns us here. The basic notion is that scores having high correlations "measure the same thing." Factoring a large set of tests indicates how many distinguishable kinds of individual differences enter the set of scores and how strong the influence of each such dimension is. Beyond that, it sorts tasks into sets, each supposed to measure one ability or ability-complex. Similar analyses have been made of interests, attitudes, and personality.

Factor analysis was the chief technique for studying intellectual performance from about 1925 to 1965. The first factor analyst was Spearman. He assembled tests that correlated with each other, hypothesized a "general" factor (a process required in all the tests), and calculated which tests best represented it. He assumed that a test combines a demand for general ability with its own specific demands; one could speak of Block Design as measuring the general factor plus a "Block Design specific" ability. Before long, "group" factors, present in several tests but not all, were recognized. Block Design and EFT and Verbal Analogies all intercorrelate, but the higher correlation between the first two suggests the influence in them of a shared spatial or figural ability. Burt in England and Thurstone in the United States developed procedures for identifying group factors.

Thurstone assumed at first that general ability is a mere compounding of group factors. He tried to develop tests of verbal ability that make little demand on reasoning and tests of reasoning that make little demand on word knowledge, number knowledge, or figural perception. In the end, he concluded that most group factors do interrelate; intellectual efficiency, then, extends over tasks of many kinds. But Thurstone showed that group factors can be measured reliably and advised giving attention to them in guidance and personnel selection.

Factor analysis is no longer so dominant in research on tests; many additional styles of inquiry have ripened. Today there is discontent with the assumption that tests fall into "kinds." When some persons approach a test with style A and others with style B or when a test is closely related to the experience of some persons and not others, the test is "measuring different things" in these groups. Still, testers should know how to interpret the reports and the main conceptions that come out of factor analysis.

How Factor Analysis Is Carried Out

A factor analysis starts with correlations among tests. The resulting description of any one test depends on the companion tests, the group of persons, and the technique of analysis. Despite this, accumulated research has produced consistent interpretations.

Although factor analysis is a mechanical technique carried out by computer, a large element of art or judgment enters. How to group abilities is rather like the question, "How many kinds of animals are in the zoo?" One might consider mammals as a "kind" or carnivores or hyenas or the species *Crocuta*. Some analysts favor small categories and some favor large ones; moreover, alternative category systems cut across each other. The choice derives from the purpose of a test user or theorist. From one point of view, a child's ability to tell right from left is a trivial factor within the spatial domain; from another point of view, it is a major developmental achievement.

Table 9.1 displays correlations among four tests given to job applicants. In this simple case, inspection can anticipate the findings.

Is there a general ability? No more than a trace; all the correlations are positive, but four are near zero. Therefore, no common element such as ability to understand directions plays a large role in all four tests. The absence of a general factor may seem strange because all tests have directions that must be understood. When directions are well suited to the group, however, ability to understand them will not affect score *differences*—and correlations reflect only differences among persons. These correlations come from a particular population, most of whom graduated from American high schools. Apply the tests to an applicant pool that includes a large number of newcomers from Cuba or Hong Kong, and understanding of directions would account for

Table 9.1. *Intercorrelations of four measures for adult workers*

	Arithmetic Reasoning	Turn	Assemble
Vocabulary	0.65	0.05	0.15
Arithmetic Reasoning		0.05	0.15
Turn			0.4
Assemble			

SOURCE: GATB manual, 1970, III, p. 29. (Rounded.)

Table 9.2. *Factor loadings of four tests*

	I	II	h^2
Vocabulary	0.85	0.05	0.72
Arithmetic Reasoning	0.80	0.00	0.64
Turn	0.05	0.70	0.49
Assemble	0.15	0.50	0.27
Variance[a]	1.39	0.74	2.13

[a] In columns I and II this is the sum of squares.

differences. A moderately strong general factor would appear because that source of difficulty would affect all tests.

The largest correlation in Table 9.1 implies that Vocabulary and Arithmetic Reasoning share a group factor. The factor is the crystallized ability Gc, discussed in Chapter 8, reflecting amount of schooling and success in past learning. The Turn test (placing pegs in holes) shares a second group factor with Assemble (putting rivets and washers together rapidly). (A serious study uses many more tests; with more tests, more than two factors would probably be reported.)

I use this example to demonstrate the main features of a factor-analytic report. One analysis yields the "factor loadings" in Table 9.2.

A factor is a hypothetical or "latent" variable; every person is assumed to have a true score on that variable, and each loading describes the correlation of test score with factor score. Vocabulary correlates 0.85 with Factor I, Turning correlates 0.70 with Factor II, and so on. As with other correlations, there are sampling errors in factor loadings. Because loadings will change from one sample to another, we need not take seriously the fact that (for example) Assembly loads higher than Turning on Factor I.

The brief mathematical presentation that follows assumes that the factors are uncorrelated. It is often sensible to employ correlated factors as explanatory variables. The following equations have to be modified when correlations among the factors are not zero.

The symbol h^2 stands for *communality*, the proportion of the test variance accounted for by common factors. The equation for the communality of Test i is

$$h_i^2 = r_{iI}^2 + r_{iII}^2 + \ldots$$

(The dots indicate that common factors beyond I and II might contribute to Test i. For Turning, the two-factor communality is

$$h^2 = (0.05)^2 + (0.70)^2 = 0.0025 + 0.49 = 0.49$$

Suppose now that the reliability of Turning is known to be 0.70; then 30 per cent of the variance is error variance. This carries us one step further. The variance divides into three parts:

49 per cent due to the two common factors
30 per cent due to error of measurement
21 per cent remaining, owing to the specific factor or to common factors not yet identified

In sum, 100 per cent.

Factor analysis accounts for correlations by an equation that multiplies loadings:

$$r_{ij} = r_{iI}r_{jI} + r_{iII}r_{jII} + \ldots$$

For Turning and Assembly, the numbers would be

$$(0.05)(0.15) + (0.70)(0.50) = 0.007 + 0.350 = 0.36$$

This does not quite match the original correlation of 0.38, and if you made similar calculations for other pairs of tests, you would find other small discrepancies, positive or negative. Factor analysis accounts for the data as well as possible, but not perfectly.

Table 9.2 describes the first two tests as measures of I and not II; if it were not for their specific content, they would be pure measures of I. When several such measures are combined, the specific factors tend to balance out, so that the composite score is indeed "saturated with" the factor.

11. *Confidence may be manifested in a variety of situations: making a speech to a club, taking one's car apart to repair it, piloting a jet plane, or going to a show instead of cramming for a test. Give three alternative explanations of the nature of confidence: one in which it is considered as a general factor, one in which it is divided into group factors, and one in which it is considered as a number of highly specific factors. Which theory do you think is most adequate?*
12. *Table 9.3 presents correlations among six tests given to operators in power plants. Does there appear to be a single common factor among all these tests? If so, what might be its psychological nature?*

Table 9.3. *Intercorrelations of six ability tests*

	Verbal Reasoning	Reading	Mechanical Concepts	EFT	Spatial Visualization	Mental Rotations
Verbal Reasoning		0.65	0.55	0.5	0.5	0.45
Reading			0.65	0.6	0.45	0.5
Mechanical Concepts				0.6	0.6	0.55
Embedded Figures					0.55	0.55
Spatial Visualization						0.55
Mental Rotations						

Source: Dunnette et al., 1982.

13. *A factor analysis identified four factors in the full set of 19 power-operator tests. The tests in Table 9.3 measured two of the factors. From the variation among the correlations, can you infer how this set of tests subdivided?*
14. *R. C. Gardner (1960), factoring abilities involved in using a second language in French-English Montreal, found that abilities taught in school grouped together and that abilities used outside school in interacting with speakers of the second language formed a separate factor. Explain.*

Alternative Pictures of the Makeup of CogAT

The Cognitive Abilities Test contains 10 subtests designed to represent three group factors. The manual reports test intercorrelations for 500 students in each of several grades; the pattern changes little from grade to grade. I have analyzed data from grade 7 in more than one way, primarily to show that placing the camera differently gives different pictures of the same object. I have made assumptions in the course of the analysis; another investigator would obtain slightly different numbers by modifying the assumptions. Such details are beside the point.[1]

The routine procedures print out loadings for a great number of factors. The analyst discards minor factors—those that probably reflect sampling error or that are unimportant to her. She almost always "rotates" to obtain a more interpretable pattern. Rotation substitutes new reference axes (factors) for those the computer first generated. This is much like reorienting a map on the page. In geographic maps, up-down means North-South. But some road maps of the San Francisco peninsula bring the NW-to-SE line around to vertical position, to match the way the land lies and the traffic flows.

Bringing out the general factor. My first analysis expresses the 10 CogAT scores in terms of two factors and gives some information about the residuals (Table 9.4). Four factors would surely account for all nonchance correlation among the subtests. In only a few tests (Quantitative Relations, for one) do the third and fourth factors together account for as much as 5 per cent of the variance. The last three columns in the table refer to the four-factor solution.

A strong general factor appears. A second "bipolar" factor accounts for more than 10 per cent of the variance of some subtests. (Recall that we square correlations and factor loadings to get such percentages.) A person who ranks higher on verbal tests than on figural tests has a negative score on Factor II. Factor II can be called a "Nonverbal-minus-Verbal" factor, though that is not the only plausible name. Factor II is logically rather like the V-P difference in the Wechsler. (The direction of subtraction is arbitrary.)

---

[1]Technical note. The first analysis is a centroid analysis with estimated communalities. The second analysis adapts methods from Cronbach *et al.,* 1972, to estimate the correlation of (for example) each Verbal subtest with the universe of verbal subtests these represent, and the correlations of the universe scores for the three categories. For other analyses of these data, see the 1974 CogAT manual; new item sets are analyzed in the 1982 manual. All the analyses agree save in minor detail.

Table 9.4 *Factor analysis of CogAT*

Test	Loading on Factor		h² (two factors)[a]	h² (four factors)[a]	Squared loading on specific factor[a]	Error[a]
	I	II				
1. Vocabulary	0.76	−0.37	0.71	0.72	0.15	0.13
2. Sentence Completion	0.82	−0.36	0.80	0.80	0.06	0.14
3. Verbal Classification	0.77	−0.28	0.67	0.68	0.12	0.20
4. Verbal Analogies	0.83	−0.13	0.70	0.73	0.09	0.18
5. Quantitative Relations	0.73	0.16	0.56	0.61	0.14	0.25
6. Number Series	0.79	0.12	0.65	0.68	0.16	0.16
7. Equation Building	0.77	0.15	0.62	0.67	0.14	0.19
8. Figure Classification	0.70	0.24	0.55	0.60	0.25	0.15
9. Figure Analogies	0.80	0.21	0.70	0.76	0.14	0.10
10. Figure Synthesis	0.65	0.31	0.52	0.56	0.26	0.18

[a] If the decimal were removed, these would be percentages of variance. Thus 15 per cent of Vocabulary variance is specific—not shared with other tests and not attributed to error.

Rotation. Figure 9.6 plots the loadings for the original factors (I and II) and then plots loadings for new factors (I' and II') obtained by a rotation. I chose to define I' primarily by the figural tests; it can be identified as general fluid ability *(Gf)*. Then II' represents whatever the other tests have in common that the figural tests do *not* measure; this must be mostly verbal competence. Verbal Analogies, for instance, has about equal loadings on I' and II'; it might

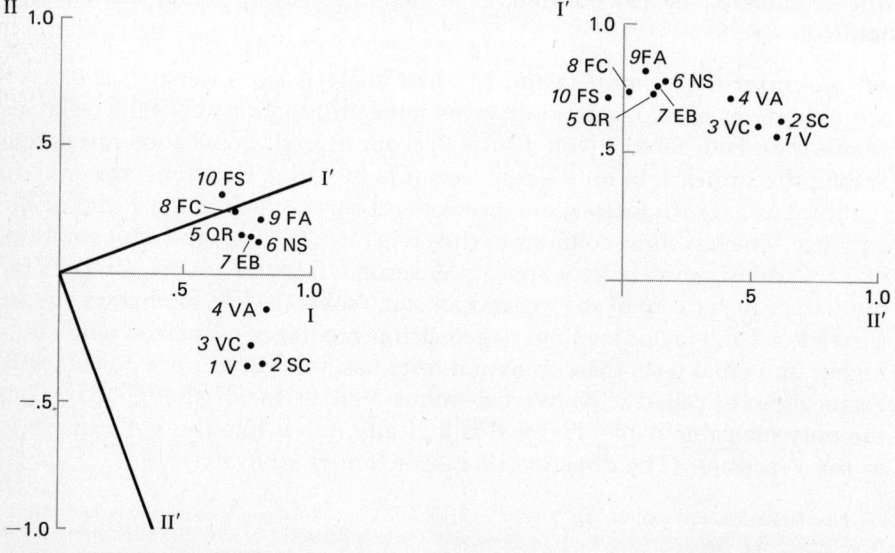

i. Unrotated loadings (and new axes)   ii. Rotated loadings

Figure 9.6. Two plots of CogAT factor loadings.

be said to place about equal weight on verbal and reasoning abilities. Figure 9.6 shows one of many legitimate rotations. The plot could place axis I" close to Vocabulary, and axis II" at right angles to I". Every rotation tells the same story, with its own slant.

Table 9.5 illustrates the option of correlated factors. I defined a verbal factor V as the common element in tests like the four verbal tasks in CogAT and calculated loadings for it. All the nonverbal subtests had loadings on the V factor, but these were far below 0.8, and to simplify, I do not show them. I developed a Q factor in the same way, and an F factor. The factors—the error-free variables—are strongly correlated, implying a general factor. (The loadings of subtests on the general factor would be similar to those in the first column of Table 9.4.)

Factor Hierarchies

Table 9.5 introduces two levels of factors, general and group. Technical methods for teasing out multilevel structures are in their infancy, but they are necessary to tell the full story. There are broadly inclusive factors; within these are narrower categories; and these can be shredded further. Within the verbal domain of CogAT, a Vocabulary specific appeared. But vocabulary items in science, for example, would form a cluster distinct from vocabulary related to art (Coffman, 1966). Marshalek (1981) demonstrates other distinct variables within vocabulary measures: abstract words vs. concrete words and choice response vs. giving definitions.

A hierarchical structure is illustrated in Figure 9.7, which draws on the work of Vernon (1965) and the CogAT analysis. No one hierarchical picture has been established as most adequate among the many arrangements that

Table 9.5 *A CogAT analysis with correlated factors*

Verbal tests		Quantitative tests		Figural tests	
No.	r_{iV}	No.	r_{iQ}	No.	r_{iF}
1	0.84	5	0.79	8	0.76
2	0.89	6	0.80	9	0.90
3	0.80	7	0.80	10	0.71
4	0.81				

Correlations Among Factors

	V	Q	F	g
V	1.00	0.86	0.75	0.91
Q		1.00	0.77	0.94
F			1.00	0.82

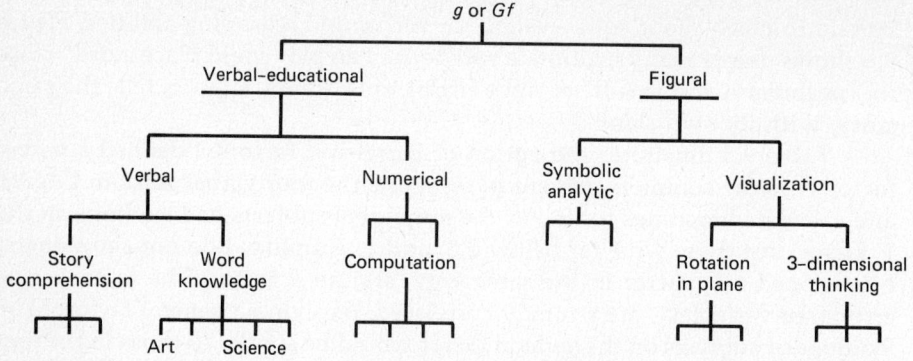

Figure 9.7. Hierarchical scheme representing relations among abilities.

fit the facts. No two-dimensional picture could do justice to all the interrelations. My picture omits many branches and leaves many twigs unlabeled; that avoids any hint of a finished structure.

We live with a paradox. Unrotated Factor I accounts for the lion's share of the non-error variance in almost any assortment of tests covering reasoning and manipulation of symbols, and Factor II accounts for much of the remainder. Yet the number of distinguishable abilities is endless. Interpreters of tests go back and forth between levels of analysis just as medical specialists shift from gross anatomy to X-ray picture to microscope to electron microscope and back. There is a time and place for every level of analysis.

Figure 9.8 conveys the message of Figure 9.7 in another way. This picture comes from a scaling procedure (which differs in detail from factor analysis; R. Shepard *et al.*, 1972). I have drawn in "constellations" to represent the groupings that appeared in a factor analysis. Such clusters are as arbitrary as constellations in a star map, and indeed Marshalek *et al.* (in press) connect up the tests in the center differently after factoring the tests in another way. The three outlying clusters are Perceptual Speed, Memory Span, and Speed of Closure. Closure, it may be explained, is a term from Gestalt psychology, referring to the detection of a strong pattern in disjointed parts (Fig. 9.9).

The tests most loaded on general ability appear near the center of the chart; outlying tests have weak general-factor loadings. Figural tests fall toward the right; verbal tests, toward the lower left; and tests that present meaningless symbols appear in the upper left. Other samples and other test sets confirm the broad picture but fill in details differently (Snow *et al.*, in press). Marshalek *et al.* point out that tests in the center require comparatively complex processing, whereas tests toward the edge are simple in their demands. Perhaps Perceptual Speed and Closure should be called "Level I" abilities along with memory. (Factor analyses of K-ABC for young children place its closure test among measures of fluid ability; this departs from findings of others based on older subjects.)

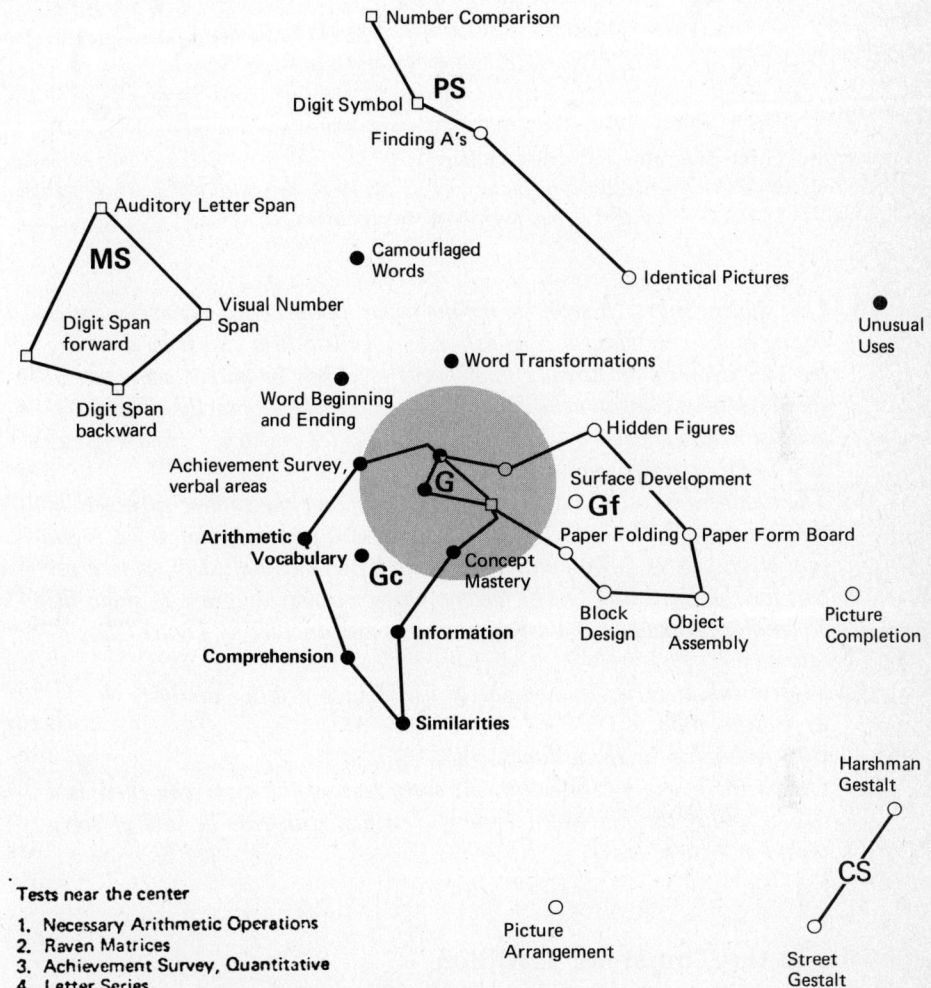

Figure 9.8. A two-dimensional mapping of diverse tests. Open circles denote figural or pictorial tests, closed circles denote verbal tests, and squares denote tests using meaningless symbols. Names in boldface identify Wechsler subtests; nearly all other tests are from the ETS Kit (p. 293). The shaded area includes tests where half the variance is attributed to the first (general) factor.
Based on data from Marshalek et al., in press.

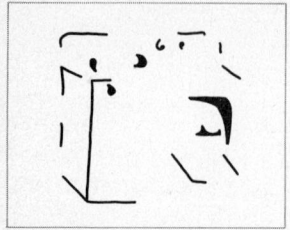 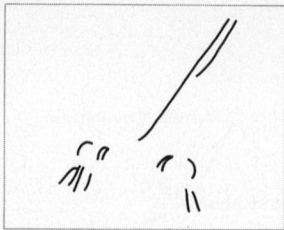 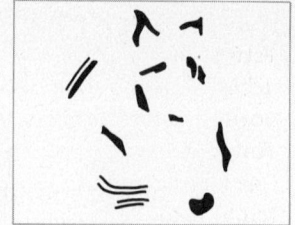

Figure 9.9. Three diagrams requiring closure.
Source: From the O-A Objective-Analytic Battery, U. I. 21, by R. B. Cattell and J. M. Scheurger, Copyright © 1955, 1971 by IPAT, Inc. Reproduced by permission.

15. One student says, "It seems to me the factor analysts are like astronomers trying to discover planets. The astronomer finds a new planet by detecting the pull it exerts on already known bodies. Then he makes more careful studies to check his conclusion and locate the planet exactly. The factor analyst locates one test against already established abilities." How satisfactory is this comparison?
16. The numbers in each row of Table 9.4 decompose the subtest variance. In the first row, $0.72 + 0.15 + 0.13 = 100$ per cent; and 0.72 is the sum of squares of 0.76 and -0.37 (with decimals adjusted), plus 1 per cent for the third and fourth factors. Prepare a bar diagram to show the percentage breakdown of Verbal Analogies and another for Figure Classification.
17. Suggest subcategories that might be useful in a detailed analysis of
    a. Computation.
    b. Visualizing in three dimensions.
18. Defend the following statement: At every level of the hierarchy there is a cell in which the Embedded Figures Test fits. Can this be said of every verbal or figural task?

Results in the Thurstone Tradition

Thurstone's research inspired hundreds of investigators and influenced the form of current test batteries. Thurstone came to accept a hierarchical conception, but his techniques generally laid out factors as if all were at the same level.

The factors that emerged in his early research Thurstone called "primary"; a by-product was the Primary Mental Abilities (PMA) tests for school children. Thurstone's seven primaries were Verbal, Reasoning, Number, Spatial, Perceptual Speed, Memory, and Word Fluency. Word Fluency first directed attention to "divergent" thinking (p. 261). Choosing the best synonym for *reconcile* measures the Verbal factor; one Fluency test calls for supplying three synonyms for an easy word, such as *house*, under time pressure.

In echoing the phrase "primary colors," Thurstone deliberately suggested that the group factors combine in various proportions to produce success in any complex intellectual performance, just as green, red, and blue spotlights can be mingled to produce any other hue or white. Thurstone's primaries have been compared also to the chemist's list of elements, but that is not a sound comparison. There is only one answer to the question: What elements make up table salt? In factor analysis there are many answers, sound but not equally appealing. The distinction between group and specific factors is not fundamental. When a psychologist becomes interested in an ability specific to one test, she can probably invent additional tasks that measure it. Then it becomes a "group" factor. The dictionary of factors can expand forever.

The ETS Kit. A factor does not become important just because several measures are invented. A list of "chief" factors has to grow out of a consensus that certain abilities deserve weight in psychological theory or practical decisions. The consensus regarding abilities significant for research is represented in the so-called ETS Kit. J. W. French, a follower of Thurstone, listed tests that had been factored and asked colleagues to judge which factors were important and what test tasks best measured them. Over the years improved tests were devised. The present Kit of Factor-Referenced Cognitive Tests (Ekstrom *et al.*, 1976, 1979) provides 72 measures—at least 3 for each of 21 factors and 2 tests for 2 more factors. The 23 factors are named to suggest a best interpretation.

An investigator wanting to measure a factor would apply at least two Kit tests for it to reduce the influence of specifics. The tests are kept short so that many factors can be included in the same investigation. The manual warns against use of the tests for purposes other than research.

In most Kit tests the subject encounters one pervasive type of difficulty and only one. Necessary Arithmetic Operations is an example of such a purified test.

> A store marked down the price of a TV set from $200 to $175. What was the per cent reduction? To solve this one would
> A. multiply and divide
> B. subtract and divide
> C. divide and add

Any American adolescent should have command of this easy reading, and of the concepts of pricing, percentage, division, and so on. The item makes no numerical demand. So differences among most subjects come from "reasoning pure and simple" (in the context of arithmetic). It should be noted that Necessary Arithmetic Operations (an indicator, say Ekstrom *et al.*, of General Reasoning) is in the center of the Marshalek chart (Figure 9.8). The multidimensional scheme of the Kit recognizes more constellations than Marshalek's flat chart (and fewer than will shortly be encountered in

Table 9.6. *Notes on the Kit of Factor-Referenced Cognitive Tests*

Factor Name and Symbol	Presumed Guilford Category	Tests Matched to the Factor and Page Where a Similar Test Is Described
Reasoning, General	CMS	Necessary Arithmetic Operations (p. 293)
Induction	CSC CSS CFC	Figure Classification (p. 219); Letter Sets
Reasoning, Logical[a]	EMR EMI	Nonsense Syllogisms
Verbal Comprehension	CMU	Vocabulary
Number Facility	MSI	Addition; Division
Spatial Orientation	CFS	Card Rotations (p. 307)
Visualization	CFT	Paper Folding (p. 272); Surface Development (p. 302)
Spatial Scanning	CFI	Maze Tracing Speed (p. 30)
Perceptual Speed	ESU EFU	Number Comparison (p. 302); Identical Figures
Closure, Flexibility of[a]	NFT[b]	Hidden Figures
Closure, Speed of[a]	CFU	Gestalt Completion (p. 292)
Memory Span (MS)	MSU	Number Span (p. 207); Letter Span
Memory, Associative	MSI	Picture-Number
Memory, Visual	MFU MFC MFR	Map Reading
Fluency, Figural	DFU DFI	Ornamentation
Fluency, Expressional	DMS	Arranging Words
Fluency, Word[a]	DSU	Word Beginnings and Endings (p. 261)
Flexibility of Use[a]	DFT NFT	Different Uses (p. 261)

[a] The Kit includes one additional reasoning factor, one additional closure factor, and two additional fluency-flexibility factors.
[b] This column is taken from Ekstrom *et al.*, 1979. This one entry I have added from Guilford and Hoepfner, 1971.

the Guilford system). The developers of the Kit settled on middling complexity.

The rubrics in Table 9.6 (Reasoning, etc.) serve to make reading easier. Not all these groupings correspond to correlations. We have previously seen strong correlations of verbal with numerical tests; and, on the other hand, the

Uses test and the Word Beginnings and Endings test (which I locate together) appear widely separated in the Marshalek analysis.

19. *Insofar as you can judge from the information presented, which Kit factors represent fluid ability and which represent crystallized abilities?*
20. *WISC-R places little emphasis on the Associative Memory, Visual Memory, and Closure Speed factors. Would the test be improved by inserting subtests involving these factors in place of some present ones?*
21. *What has happened to the traditional distinction between verbal and nonverbal tests in the listing of Table 9.6?*
22. *"Necessary Arithmetic Operations, instead of measuring 'reasoning pure and simple,' measures the extent to which a young person has accepted the conventions, values, and styles of thought of the dominant middle-class culture." What justification can you offer for that comment?*

Guilford's "Structure of Intellect"

From 1950 to about 1975, the most extensive research on individual differences was that of J. P. Guilford. Following Thurstone's lead, Guilford assumed that talent takes many forms and that a great number of factors can be distinguished. His first great success was in developing classification tests for U.S. Air Force personnel in World War II. His team developed tests for more than two dozen factors; the scores were combined to determine which airmen were best equipped to become bombardiers, for example, and which had greater aptitude for other assignments. Guilford continued the search for additional abilities after the war. Of the numerous tests his laboratory devised, some were selected for the ETS Kit, about three dozen were marketed by Sheridan, and dozens were left in research reports.

The scheme displayed in Figure 9.10 guided Guilford's search. The structure conceives of 120 abilities; Guilford hoped to produce two or three pure measures for each cell, and to explain traditional tests as composites of the 120 factors. Each cell definition is intended to suggest a combination of task characteristics that might be built into tests; Guilford ultimately "filled in" 100 of the 120 cells. In recent years he has considered auditory tests as a counterpart of the original, visual "figural" slice. Study of the 30 postulated auditory-figural factors has barely begun.

The first cell (CFU = Cognition of Figural Units) refers to tests that call for

C: recognition or simple interpretation of
F: diagrams or pictures, and
U: ask for response to well-defined elements.

The ETS Kit identifies *CFU* with Speed of Closure (Figure 9.9).

"Semantic" tasks deal with word meanings and with verbal or quantita-

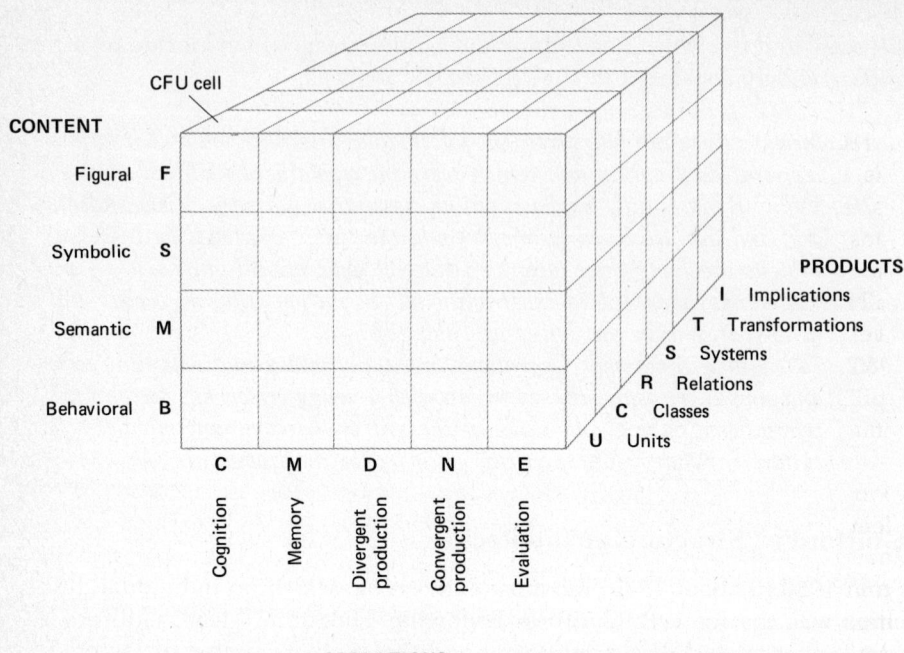

Figure 9.10. Guilford's categories for test tasks.

tive relations. "Symbolic" tasks use letters, numbers, and other symbols without regard to meanings; Digit Span and Digit Symbol are examples. The "Behavioral" category presents social scenes and communications—pictures of people, or recorded dialogue, for example.

Among the five operations, Cognition—direct apprehension of a pattern—was illustrated in Figure 9.9. And the distinction between Convergent and Divergent Production was discussed at pp. 261ff. A Memory task presents material to be studied and then immediately asks for recall. Finally, Evaluative tasks require close comparison of alternatives. For example, an Evaluative-Symbolic-Relations task presents the pair GRAND–RAN and asks which of the following pairs has most nearly the same relation:

COUNTRY–COT
RESPITE–SIT
LOVING–LOG

The second is considered correct because the letter rearrangement is most nearly like that in GRAND–RAN.

Guilford shaped and reshaped his system as he factored new sets of data. Test pairs having especially strong correlations were assigned to the same cell. Guilford formed many small constellations where others map more broadly. Whereas, for me, Matrices, EFT, and Number Series all measure

Gf, Guilford identifies Matrices with cell *CFR,* Embedded Figures with *NFT,* and Number Series with *CSS.*

Guilford rejected the traditional general factors. Among 7000 test intercorrelations that he ultimately compiled, one-sixth were at a chance level; this, he said, denies a general factor. The zeroes were produced, of course, by his reaching beyond problem solving—to memory, closure, and other functions. Currently Guilford (1981) accepts broad factors though his emphasis remains on the cells. The slice of *D* cells perhaps can be organized hierarchically with a broad *D* factor, he says, and with *DF, DS,* and so on, at the second level. The *FT* cells may fall under a "general visualization" factor (Guilford, 1980). Cell factors are said to be about equally general and equally important; Guilford expects as many tasks to fit one cell as another. No one scheme of family resemblances seems more fruitful for Guilford than other schemes.

In pressing the sorting process to an extreme, Guilford drew attention to many new variables and so enriched research. His books (1967; 1979; with Hoepfner, 1971) moved from correlational psychology toward the newer analytic hypotheses, paying particular attention to the linkage of observations on tests with observations on memory and problem solving in the laboratory. On the other hand, his classification on stimulus (task) characteristics ignores the individual's approach. Current analytic studies try to identify processes internal to the person.

Typical Guilford distinctions have limited power. The four categories in Table 9.7, said to call for diverse operations on "symbolic classifications,"

Table 9.7 *Symbolic Classification tests: Median intercorrelations for "operation" subcategories*

Category	Representative Test task	Correlation with Other Tests in Category				Approximate percentage of variance attributable to			
		CSC	MSC	DSC	NSC	Common Factor	Cell Factor	Task Specific	Form-to-Form Variation
CSC	Number classification	**0.6**	0.4	0.35	0.45	47	14	11	28
MSC	Memory for word classes	0.4	**0.7**	0.25	0.3	32	38	9	21
DSC	Multiple letter similarities	0.35	0.25	**0.35**	0.3	28	7	35	30
NSC	Letter grouping	0.45	0.3	0.3	**0.4**	38	4	30	28

NOTE: Boldface type indicates correlation for tests within same category.
SOURCE: Dunham *et al.,* 1966. I calculated the breakdown of variances before rounding correlations.

share an obvious common factor. The "cell factor" is substantial for the memory test only. The contrast among *CSC, DSC,* and *NSC* is a "trace" phenomenon. Several further evaluations of particular Guilford hypotheses appear in Cronbach and Snow (1981, pp. 155ff.).

Today's research does not rest on the Guilford "structure" in the way that earlier research rested on Thurstone's. Perhaps the conception collapsed of its own weight. Psychologists cannot spread attention over 120 dimensions, especially when told that each is as important as the next. The only virtue of distinguishing between two variables is that it leads to interpreting a score difference; but 120 cells implies 7140 differences. Many a Guilford distinction is so subtle that, according to his own data, it would take 4 hours to measure that difference reliably.

Guilford overreached in another way. Committed to study hundreds of tests and requiring a large sample for each factor analytic study, he could not stay with any research issue long enough to provide compelling evidence. His attempt to treat 120 factors as equal did not appeal to believers in general abilities; one scornfully said that Guilford had described people as "scatter-brained." The most crucial issue is whether another investigator, analyzing a selection of 50 or more tests like Guilford's, would confirm his sorting. Horn and Knapp (1973) doubt this, arguing that the methods Guilford used would "confirm" his hypotheses even if the test scores were related only by chance. Another specialist interprets the studies on which Horn and Knapp relied—and his own studies—in Guilford's favor (Elshout, 1976; Elshout, Van Hemert, & Van Hemert, 1975).

The reader not interested in this technical issue should still draw a moral about research. Guilford sought to advance his system as fast and as far as possible in the faith that the picture was basically valid. He was never careless, but his methodology did not subject the ideas to severe scrutiny. Thurstone's methods were well designed for *his* modest bandwidth of 7 to 12 factors, but it was daring of Guilford to elaborate them to 120 hypotheses. A generation of meticulous effort would have been required to determine how far these or other techniques can be trusted. Investigations that rush ahead prior to the consolidation of the methodological base are controversial. When doubts are cast on the techniques, no one can separate the good new ideas from the weak ones. Ambitious studies are more vulnerable to criticism than modest ones if only because the latter can concentrate resources and tighten their arguments. Social scientists are caught in a bind because elaborate hypotheses are required to account for behavior outside the laboratory (Cole *et al.*, 1978; Cronbach, 1975a, 1982a, b).

Possibilities in Microanalysis

For conventional applications of tests in selection, guidance, and the like, a broad-stroke picture of the individual is evidently sufficient to guide the gross choices whose detailed consequences will be worked out by events long after the date of testing. As will be seen later in this chapter and at p. 401, some investigators doubt the utility of considering separately even comprehensive group factors such as Number and Spatial. This does not deny the occasional relevance of a highly specific ability such as pitch discrimination, but it tends to discourage the study of components and elementary processes.

The elementary processes that were judged to be useless in the early days of mental measurement (p. 193) are now the focus of theoretical work on abilities. That work and the hierarchical model of factor analysis make it clear that dozens of processes can be distinguished and separately measured. Moreover, even though complex performance is more than the sum of elementary processes, defects in elementary processes can have devastating consequences. J. B. Carroll (1980), summarizing the variety of factors that can be detected in laboratory measurements of information processing, suggests that such measures will make only minor contributions to traditional predictive uses of tests.

The practical promise of microanalysis lies in the clinical domain where precise measurements of the present state of the individual can be used. Research on psychoactive drugs, for example, can take advantage of fine-grain data; if some processes are slowed and others are not, that sheds light on the physiological effect of the drug and on its clinical suitability. Moreover, microanalytic psychological measurement can be of significant help in the day-to-day management of medication for the individual patient, especially when the testing can be computerized. Most of these developments are far in the future.

One present-day example of practically useful, efficient microanalysis is the Porch Index of Communicative Ability (PICA; *CPP*), for the study of aphasia and similar disorders. This instrument grew out of a highly developed conceptualization that the concentrated effort of neuroanatomists and clinical practitioners had built up. In many ways, the design of PICA departs from the tradition of psychological testing, having more in common with physical and physiological assays. The speech clinician sometimes is asked for a one-time diagnosis, but she often monitors patient progress—either to guide case management or to evaluate a kind of treatment. PICA is, therefore, designed to be used repeatedly; it requires some adaptations that are difficult for the patient, but it has no element of novelty.

A particular commonplace object—a key, for example—is the basis for 18 items: "Point to the key." "Write the name of this [tester points to key]." "Say what I say: *key*," and so on. This permits a comparison of functions. A 16-point scoring scheme is applied to every trial. The scheme draws attention to degrees of failure and to the nature of a deficient response and, more important, is highly sensitive to tiny improvements from week to week. A score of 6, for example, is given to a response that is "intelligible but incorrect"; 11 signifies "accurate but delayed and incomplete." Ten objects (or their names), used 18 times, produce 18 subtest scores.

Certain profile shapes suggest specific kinds of brain dysfunction and their severity, others are suggestive of nonphysical disorders, and still others are characteristic of malingerers. The information is important just because decades of clinical experience indicate the likely rate of recovery from each type of disorder and the relevance of alternative treatments at each stage of recovery. (Beside the point from the standpoint of measurement but of interest nonetheless: the tasks have been programmed as automated exercises. The patient can practice on a prescribed task; he is sufficiently aware of the speed and adequacy of his response that he benefits from the trials. This not only extends treatment far beyond what the therapist's time permits, but brings help to patients in remote areas who can visit a therapist only infrequently.)

Sternberg (in Glaser & Bond, 1981) suggests that the payoff for testing from the current research on processes is likely to be a microanalytic battery adapted from laboratory measures of elements within perception, memory, and so on. If that were to come to pass, it would be belated vindication for the Wundtian approach. I do not regard such a development as likely. Tasks low in a hierarchy cover narrow domains but—even in a Porch subtest—numerous processes affect any one task. Tests of elementary processes have a role to play—in audiometry, for example, and in neurological workups. But as I see it, Porch's microanalysis pays off just because it is based on long study of the field of application. I note also that the Schorr study of Block Design grew out of an established clinical use of the test. Microanalytic tests that contribute to the teaching (for example) of mathematical reasoning will not, I think, be borrowings from the psychological laboratory. They will be invented by someone who has studied the errors learners make and has devised instructional techniques to help them.

Glaser (1977, Chap. 5) presents several examples of primary school teaching procedures in which lessons on microskills are linked to tests of highly specific processes. A test on a certain element may be given every week (or oftener) until the child demonstrates proficiency and is routed to a new mix of lessons. The tasks include aspects of fluid ability (figural analysis, for example) as well as conventional skills such as letter naming. On educational microanalysis, see also page 353.

23. *Internal-consistency coefficients for a sample of patients show that the s.e.m. for a PICA subtest score is in the neighborhood of 0.6. According to a retest study (over an interval of a week or so), the s.e.m. for such a score is about 0.8. [The subtest score is the average of the item scores, hence is on a 1-to-16 scale.] How adequate is this degree of accuracy, for the intended uses of PICA?*

MULTIFACTOR PROFILES IN GUIDANCE

Multiscore batteries generating profiles that guide career exploration did grow largely out of practical experience with prediction of vocational and educational criteria. Neither factor analysis nor theory of processes greatly influenced their design though Thurstone's writings on group factors stimulated interest in multiscore measurement.

Representative Guidance Batteries

The Differential Aptitude Tests. The profile of Robert Finchley (p. 105) came from the widely used Differential Aptitude Tests (DAT; *PC;* Fig. 9.11; for Mechanical Reasoning, see p. 51). That battery is intended primarily for high school counseling. The tests measure complex abilities that have a fairly direct relation to job families and curricula. Achievement subtests are included because of their predictive value. A composite verbal-plus-number score represents general academic abilities. The single tests require 6 to 30 minutes of working time; with the addition of time for directions, the battery requires nearly 4 hours. Except for Clerical, the tests are essentially unspeeded.

The DAT was the pioneer among integrated batteries. Prior to its publication, the counselor had to assemble her own collection of tests, which would have been normed and validated on different samples. Percentile conversions for all DAT scores were calculated on the same samples to give profile shapes as much meaning as possible. The tests are similar in difficulty.

Because little technical information on the 1982 revision (Forms V and W) has been reported to date, all findings in this book come from older forms (usually S and T). The correlations in Table 9.8 are organized to bring the tests with large correlations near each other. It is apparent that CSA (an indicator of the Perceptual Speed factor) measures something distinct from the rest of the battery. A strong general factor runs through the remaining tests. I interpret this information at page 312.

The DAT profile reports on 21 differences (considering all pairs of tests). The pairs with correlations below 0.6 provide far more reliable contrasts than the other pairs. The standard errors of all differences are about the same. However, comparatively few students will have differences large enough to consider seriously when the intercorrelation for a pair is large compared to the stability coefficients. (For precise reasoning about DAT, we would need better occasion-to-occasion correlations than are available.) As the estimated same-day, form-to-form reliabilities are above 0.9 (with minor exceptions), all the tests also contain substantial specific or group factors.

Table 9.9 goes on to report correlations of scores with marks. The modest sample sizes warn us against interpreting all the differences, but where results for boys and girls agree, the patterning can probably be taken seriously. General ability correlates with marks in all the courses and falls clearly below SR only in predicting drafting performance. In Ralston, SR predicts geometry; in the other two schools, the correlations are so low as to suggest that it is the general-ability component of the SR score that predicts. These and other data indicate that spatial ability per se has little to do with success in nontechnical courses.

VERBAL REASONING

...... is to night as breakfast is to ,,,,,

    A. supper — — — — corner
    B. gentle — — — — morning
    C. door — — — — corner
    D. flow — — — — enjoy
    E. supper — — — — morning

NUMERICAL ABILITY

$\dfrac{?}{6} = \dfrac{4}{24}$

    A. 1/6
    B. 1
    C. 4
    D. 6
    E. none of these

ABSTRACT REASONING. Which figure is next in the series?

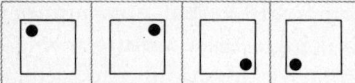 

SPACE RELATIONS. Which one of the figures can be made from the pattern?

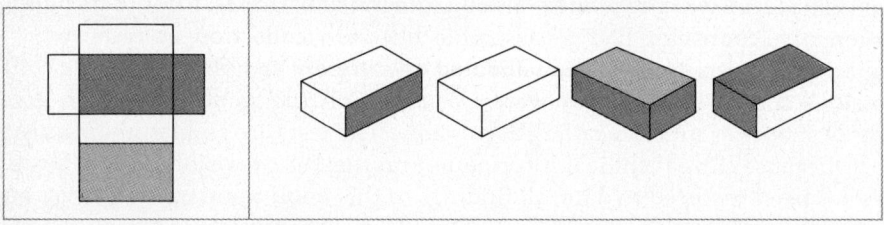

CLERICAL SPEED AND ACCURACY. Underline at right the symbol that is also underlined at left.

<u>AB</u>	AC	AD	AE	AF		AC	AE	AF	AB	AD
aA	aB	BA	ba	<u>Bb</u>		BA	Ba	Bb	aA	aB
A7	7A	B7	<u>7B</u>	AB		7B	B7	AB	7A	A7

SPELLING. Which words are incorrectly spelled?

    afirmed
    omission
    neighberhood

LANGUAGE USAGE. Which part of the sentence is incorrect in punctuation, grammar, or capitalization? Mark E if there is no error.

    Ain't we / going to / the office / next week?
        A   B   C   D

    They were / nearly starved / before they landed / somewheres in Florida.
        A   B   C   D

Figure 9.11. Items representing subtests of the DAT.
Source: The Verbal Reasoning and Abstract Reasoning items and the first Language Usage item reproduced by permission from the Differential Aptitude Tests; all other items adapted from that source and used by permission. Copyright © 1972 by The Psychological Corporation. All rights reserved.

Table 9.8. *Correlations within the DAT*

	MR	SR	AR	VR	LU	NA	Sp	CSA
Mechanical		0.6	0.6	0.6	0.6	0.6	0.4	0.2
Spatial			0.7	0.6	0.6	0.6	0.4	0.2
Abstract				0.7	0.7	0.7	0.5	0.2
Verbal					0.8	0.7	0.6	0.2
Language Usage						0.7	0.7	0.2
Numerical							0.6	0.3
Spelling								0.2
Clerical								

SOURCE: DAT manual, 1974, p. 135. Correlations calculated within grade-by-sex groups are averaged; the correlations differ negligibly from one sex to the other. Each average is based on nearly 5000 persons.

Table 9.9 *DAT correlations with course marks 9 months later*

Course	Grade	Location	Number of cases	Correlation of marks with		
				SR	VR + NA	AR
Geometry	10	Shelby County, Tenn.	74, 66	.35, .35	**.65, .55**	**.55**, .3
	10	Windsor Locks, Conn.	46, 45	.1 , .35	**.45, .55**	.0 , .3
	10	Ralston, Nebr.	33, 28	**.50, .45**	.6 , .5	.25, .35
Shop	10	Shelby County, Tenn.	86, —	**.45**, —	.6 ,—	**.5** , —
Art	10	Shelby County, Tenn.	30, 44	.3 , **.55**	**.55, .5**	.35, .3
Drafting	11	St. Louis County, Mo.	25, —	**.55**, —	.35, —	.3 , —
English	10	Shelby County, Tenn.	213, 200	.35, .4	**.55, .6**	**.45, .45**
	10	Windsor Locks, Conn.	108, 127	.0 , .2	.4 , **.45**	.25, .3

SOURCE: DAT manual, 1974.
NOTE: Data for males are listed before those for females. Correlations 0.40 and above before rounding are in boldface.

The General Aptitude Test Battery. The GATB battery was developed and published by the federal government and is applied throughout the country to adults seeking work. Versions of GATB are in use in many foreign countries. In the United States, GATB is given only in state employment services —or in job-training programs, schools, and colleges under a plan that makes results available to the school counselor and the employment service. The employment service is primarily concerned with guiding the person into suitable work. When an employer asks for referrals, he wants applicants likely to succeed. The test developers study psychological characteristics of jobs and accumulate information on the meaning of test scores. The variety of occupations studied is endless: accountant, aircraft mechanic, applicance-cord assembler, artificial breeding technician, asparagus sorter, . . . Prediction for such jobs takes us far beyond academic and reasoning abilities when the criteria measure job-specific performance.

Several of the tests are descended from research of the 1920s that produced a famous "Minnesota" series of vocational aptitude tests. A separate aptitude test for each job title is impracticable. The United States Employment Service (USES) once started to build a test for each job family, but when the number of tests passed 100, it became clear that such a collection could not be used for guidance. Guidance requires a limited number of diversified tests that can be given to everyone and that can be combined to predict in different situations. With this end in view, the current GATB contains eight pencil-paper and four apparatus tests, summed up in nine scores:

G—General (a composite of tests titled Vocabulary, Three-Dimensional Space, and Arithmetic Reasoning)
V—Verbal (Vocabulary)
N—Numerical (Computation, Arithmetic Reasoning)
S—Spatial (Three Dimensional Space)
P—Form Perception (Tool Matching, Form Matching)
Q—Clerical Perception (Name Comparison)
K—Motor Coordination (Mark Making)
F—Finger Dexterity (Assemble, Disassemble)
M—Manual Dexterity (Place, Turn)

Among the unusual features of the GATB system are these: a Spanish edition (BEAG) with its own norms; a version (NATB) for persons who do not read well; a system for testing the deaf; separate norms for handicapped persons who take the dexterity tests from a seated position; extensive orientation and practice booklets to be used where necessary; and a system linking the aptitudes to an interest battery and to elaborate occupational information (Droege & Padgett, 1982; see p. 417).

Within GATB, Vocabulary, Arithmetic Reasoning, and Computation need no description, and the Space test is much like that of DAT. Name Comparison, similar to DAT Clerical, requires quick comparison of two lists of business firms for discrepant style and spelling.

Tool Matching calls for rapid comparison of pictures of tools, alike save for differences in black-and-white markings. Picturing of tools is intended to increase the appeal of the test.

Form Matching is another speed test in which irregular shapes are to be matched up. Its evolution sheds some light on the way in which test techniques evolve. One of the original Minnesota tests was the Minnesota Spatial Relations Formboard (now published in revised form by *AGS*). The formboard version lays out before the test taker sixty pieces of wood of regular and irregular shape, with the same shape sometimes appearing in several sizes or with several proportions, together with a board with cutout holes, one matching each of the pieces. On signal, the test taker places the pieces where they fit into the board. In the USES version, the forms appear on two pages in two different arrangements. The test taker responds by writing a symbol in each shape on the first page to match it with the identical shape on the second page. By this change, the developers simplified administration and eliminated the psychomotor element from the test.

The coordination tests are likewise designed for a program that tests a million persons each year. In Mark Making, the respondent is asked only to fill squares with a simple pattern of tally marks, as many as he can make in 60 seconds. For the Place Turn test, 48 pegs are mounted in a board. A second board with holes is provided, and the test taker transfers the pegs from one board to the other as fast as possible, working with both hands. In the Turn test (single-handed), he inverts each peg while transferring it. The tests named Assemble and Disassemble call for finer coordination. A board contains 50 holes. Using both hands, the person fits a rivet and washer to each hole. In Disassemble, he replaces the rivets in their bin and puts a washer onto a rod.

GATB is efficiently designed. The working times for pencil-paper tests are close to 6 minutes each. The psychomotor tests require even less working time, but several minutes are used for demonstration and practice. The entire battery can be given in about $2\frac{1}{2}$ hours. The simple procedures allow trustworthy administration by relatively untrained testers, to subjects who have limited education or poor command of English. The psychomotor tests are so designed that each test taker leaves all the materials as he found them, ready for the next examinee. A price is paid for this efficiency. The marked speeding of nearly all GATB subtests may reduce their validity. And several scores lack the precision of DAT, which uses subtests five times as long.

GATB tests are correlated much as are those in DAT. The correlations depend on the character of the sample; the most comprehensive report (given in the manual) is for a pool of 23,000 students and adults from the validation studies. A strong "general" factor runs through the pencil-paper tests. The perception scores P and Q correlate 0.65. Because their reliability is in the neighborhood of 0.75, they measure the same thing except that reading has some influence on clerical perception. The perceptual and motor abilities intercorrelate moderately, probably reflecting their demand for speed. The dexterity tests overlap negligibly with the intellectual tests.

Probably the 9-score profile could be simplified a bit without loss of practically important information. For example, P and Q might well be collapsed into one score, and F and M into another. A proposal for radical simplification (Hunter, 1982) rests on a questionable statistical analysis. He would place chief emphasis on a $G + V + N$ composite, give minor attention to two other composites ($K + F + M$ and $S + P + Q$) in low-level jobs, and ignore more specific scores. Such a simplification could make GATB far less useful for classification and so reduce its economic contribution (p. 21).

I believe that the V/N distinction, for example, is worth retaining. Hunter correctly points out that the two scores often have similar validities, and that differences between coefficients may simply reflect sampling fluctuations. But sampling error is not a likely explanation of differences that make good sense; and when we start down the alphabet we find these jobs where N is more valid than V: accountant, audit clerk, bookkeeping-machine operator, cabinetmaker, ...

Relation of DAT to GATB. Table 9.10 sheds light on both DAT and GATB. Tests match up nicely; wherever a test has a counterpart in the other battery, it has its highest correlation with that counterpart. I simplify by omitting DAT Language Usage and Spelling; their correlations are much like those for Verbal. The motor content of GATB is, as expected, nearly unrelated to what DAT measures.

24. *Abstract reasoning can be thought of as a measure of g that is affected little by reading, vocabulary, and knowledge of arithmetic. Why is VR + NA consistently a better predictor? Is the finding that a student has AR higher than VR and NA of no importance?*
25. *Correlations of DAT scores with English grades are higher in Shelby County than in Windsor Locks. What explanations can be suggested?*
26. *If an adolescent being counseled has been tested with the Wechsler, which of the Differential Aptitude Tests would add the most useful supplementary information?*
27. *For what types of guidance does the content of GATB seem more useful than that of DAT? For what types is it less useful?*
28. *What do the correlations of DAT-Clerical with GATB tell about its meaning?*

Spatial and Mechanical Abilities

I cannot take up here the psychological and practical significance of every factor mentioned or of all the scores in DAT and GATB. After reviewing

Table 9.10 *Correlations between DAT and GATB*

DAT	\multicolumn{8}{c}{GATB Scores}
	V	N	S	P	Q	K	F	M
Verbal	.7	.5	.4	.2	.25	.0	.2	.0
Num	**.55**	**.6**	.3	.15	.2	.0	.15	.1
Abstr	.5	.5	.5	.3	.3	.0	.15	.1
Space	.45	.4	**.65**	.35	.25	.1	.25	.15
Mech	.4	.25	**.5**	.25	.2	.1	.2	.1
Cler	.3	.5	.25	**.5**	**.55**	.3	.3	.3

SOURCE: GATB manual, 1970, III, pp. 235–237.
NOTE: Each figure is the median of correlations in seven or more samples. Medians 0.5 or larger are in boldface type.

evidence on spatial and mechanical reasoning, I return to profile interpretation.

Visualization and spatial orientation. Spatial tests have played a large part in research on vocational aptitude. The DAT manual speaks of Space Relations in this way:

> The *Space Relations* test is a measure of ability to deal with concrete materials through visualization. There are many vocations in which one is required to imagine how a specified object would look if made from a given pattern, or how a specified object would appear if rotated in a given way. This ability to manipulate *things* mentally, to create a structure in one's mind from a plan, is what the test is designed to evaluate. It is an ability needed in such fields as drafting, dress designing, architecture, art, die-making, and decorating——wherever there is need to visualize objects in three dimensions.

Spatial ability is not easily distinguished from fluid ability. Some of the best tests of fluid ability, including Block Design, Embedded Figures, and Matrices, have a marked spatial component; but in assessing fluid ability the demand placed on a "vocabulary" of common forms is looked on as an impurity. Good performance might reflect ability to operate with images as distinct from symbols (L. A. Cooper & R. N. Shepard, 1973); but, as I have said, many subjects encode graphic displays in words and solve the problems in that translated form. This is one reason spatial tests overlap tests of abstract reasoning.

As the hierarchical concept of abilities implies, the spatial or figural domain can be subdivided. Spatial abilities are not strongly differentiated, but many writers distinguish Visualization from Spatial Orientation (Lohman, 1979b; McGee, 1979b). "Visualization" has to do with analysis of relatively complex forms. The spatial tests of DAT and GATB, Form Perception of GATB, EFT, Paper Folding, and Block Design all are counted in this cluster. A test of the second category, Spatial Orientation, shows a scene as viewed from (say) the cockpit of a boat and asks how the scene will appear after the boat has made a specified turn. (This may or may not be the same as the ability to maintain one's sense of direction—discussed in Liben *et al.,* 1981).

A third factor, less often separated off, is tied to speed of comparatively simple judgments about rotation. (For example, could ⌐⌐ be rotated into ⊓⊓ without turning the block over?) This was Thurstone's original Space factor; Lohman labels it Spatial Relations.

Spatial ability is more than general reasoning; one sign is that, during adolescence, males pull ahead of females on all types of spatial tasks (McGee, 1979b). The difference is not great; on DAT Spatial, for example, boys typically gain 12 points in four years whereas girls gain 8. Moreover, differences in spatial development within sexes are at least as large as the difference between sexes. Traces of the sex difference emerge early in life, and there is evidence for many explanations, including possible effects of hormones on the genetic development of left and right hemispheres, males' experiences with manipulative toys and later with tools, and girls' greater involvement in verbal and social interaction from the early years (L. Harris, in Liben *et al.*, 1981). Also, cultural and educational experience affects spatial performance (Burnett & Lane, 1980; McGee, 1979a; Segall *et al.*, 1966). More analytic studies of the processing of spatial information are needed, combined with experimental attempts to make specific processes more efficient. Then we would begin to know how spatial abilities are achieved (Wohlwill, in Liben *et al.*, 1981).

As was seen in Table 9.9, spatial ability is not particularly relevant to high school courses, not even geometry. Most of the correlation is attributable to the overlap of the spatial test with general ability. This is easy to understand insofar as the shapes to be visualized cause little difficulty for students. Drafting is the exception; the spatial test has a higher validity than the general measure. (Though N is small, other studies confirm the finding.)

A number of jobs seem to depend on spatial ability at least as much as they depend on general ability. A study of watch repairing indicates a marked correspondence between spatial ability and performance, the validity coefficient in one study being 0.7 (DAT manual, 1966). Validities depend on the precise nature of occupational duties, however; GATB data show that validities of S are negligible for watchmakers in such assignments as balance-wheel assembly and movement assembly, 0.4 in the finishing and casing departments, and 0.5 for specialized work on certain subassemblies. No doubt validities vary even for different groups having the same job title, but the general impression that S is relevant is supported.

A tremendous volume of information on vocational correlates of spatial ability is provided by research on GATB. When we start down the alphabetic list, noting samples of at least 100 cases and coefficients of 0.25 and above, these occupations are predicted by the spatial score: assembler, automobile service-station mechanic, barber, cabinetmaker, computer technical trainee, cook, dental technician, . . . Spatial ability alone rarely accounts for success, but taking aptitudes into account simultaneously improves employment decisions. Chapter 11 will discuss the combining of aptitudes in selection.

An army study with large samples found consistently high validity coefficients for vocabulary, arithmetic, spatial, and mechanical-reasoning tests in a wide variety of training courses; across-the-board ability was evidently important in the training and the course grades. In just 2 schools out of 35—for machinists and for dental technicians—was the validity coefficient for the spatial test appreciably and consistently above that for the vocabulary test. Vocabulary had greater validity than spatial ability in clerical or administrative jobs and in security work. Outside those branches, spatial and verbal abilities were equally important (Helme *et al.*, 1957). Though spatial elements were not prominant in the criteria of many schools, that may be a fault of the criteria. (See p. 365f.)

It is notorious that scholastic abilities do not predict income and other criteria of success *within* a professional group. LSAT, for example, predicts law-school grades, not earnings in midcareer. Neither tests nor grade records forecast which scientists will do distinguished work. Likewise, measures of specialized abilities fail to account for differences within a profession. But selection by institutions and self-selection operate steadily over many years to encourage the person to pursue whichever lines of work he or she handles well. In a sense, a test can only predict failure. Architects prove during their training that they can handle spatial work; if not, they drop out. The survivors have adequate spatial ability, and the differences that remain are of no great importance.

One of many studies to document this selective effect is the longitudinal Project TALENT (Flanagan *et al.,* 1973). A test of visualization in three dimensions was given (among others) to a national sample of high school sophomores. A follow-up 5 years later sorted the youths according to the jobs they were in or were preparing for. The *majority* of those within certain job categories came from the top quarter of the national distribution on the spatial test. (Likewise for other tests, in other occupations. Even with thousands of cases, there were not enough in one occupation to provide clear evidence for both sexes.) Among males, high spatial ability greatly increased the probability of gravitating into a career as architect, engineer, or physicist and, among females, of gravitating into high school mathematics teaching, physical therapy, or the visual arts.

Mechanical comprehension. Although mechanical reasoning tests predict success in many occupations, there is considerable uncertainty as to whether they measure an independent ability. It will be noted that GATB did not include a test of this type. As we saw in Table 9.10, general, verbal, and spatial abilities duplicate much of its information. Earlier (p. 152), I listed questions bearing on the construct of mechanical reasoning. Research on the construct has been limited; these tests may measure nothing beyond spatial visualization and an acquaintance with mechanical devices that makes one quick at "reading" pictures of them. Mechanical reasoning shows a much stronger sex difference than spatial tests; boys are about one s.d. ahead of girls throughout high school. A Swedish study of males shows that, during adolescence, spatial and mechanical abilities improve in proportion to the technical character of the student's training and experience (Balke-Aurell, 1982).

Tests like TMC or straightforward shop-information tests (see p. 146) are relevant to civilian and military jobs. In the army study referred to earlier, a mechanical reasoning test had validity coefficients much like those for the spatial test. In four courses—automotive mechanics, tracked vehicle repair, fuel and electrical system repair, and chassis rebuilding—the mechanical reasoning test outdid the spatial test (and most others). A car-and-truck information test had validities equal to those of the mechanical reasoning test. However, mechanical reasoning was relevant to a wider range of jobs than any one information test.

29. *Linn (in Buros, 1978, p. 659) says this:*

> Possibly the most serious nagging doubt regarding the DAT comes from the lack of empirical evidence regarding the degree of the *differential* validity of the subtests in predicting various criteria. Such evidence will not be forthcoming without the development of adequate differential criterion measures.

In this context, "differential validity" is present when each criterion is predicted by a different test or combination of tests. What academic or job criteria might bring out such validity for specialized abilities? (You might consider specialized abilities other than those in DAT and GATB.)

30. *Wallach (in Messick, 1976) notes that tests are better at forecasting failure than at forecasting outstanding achievement. He calls for "persistence forecasting" on the grounds that those who have already won races are best bets for future races. Having impressed critics on the high school stage makes one a prime candidate for a college drama department; similarly for basketball and electronics and poetry. Successful completion of research as an undergraduate indicates probable success at later stages. Is it, then, the best social policy to give opportunity to those who have used a previous opportunity well? If so, at what age should this rule take effect? (See Hudson's comment in Messick, 1976.)*

31. *GATB s correlated substantially with success of cabinetmakers, but the corresponding correlation for carpenters was low. Can you explain?*

Limitations on Interpretation of Profiles

To choose among educational and vocational options, the individual needs a sense of his strengths and weaknesses. Profiles are intended to bring differences among abilities to the surface, yet over and over we have seen that differences across scales are difficult to pin down and make sense of. The reader should keep in mind the cautions voiced earlier, alongside those this section develops.

Specificity of norms. Profiles are based on norms; PICA is a rare example where raw-score contrasts are interpretable. Insofar as a vocational decision is based on norm reference—that is, on a concept of a competitive world—it is important to compare the person with the group he will compete against, not with "people in general." The choice of reference group influences the appearance of the profile.

The GATB profile is ordinarily plotted against norms for adult workers. The profile of a student engineer plotted in the usual manner (Figure 9.12, upper profile) implies outstanding G, V, and S abilities, with several other

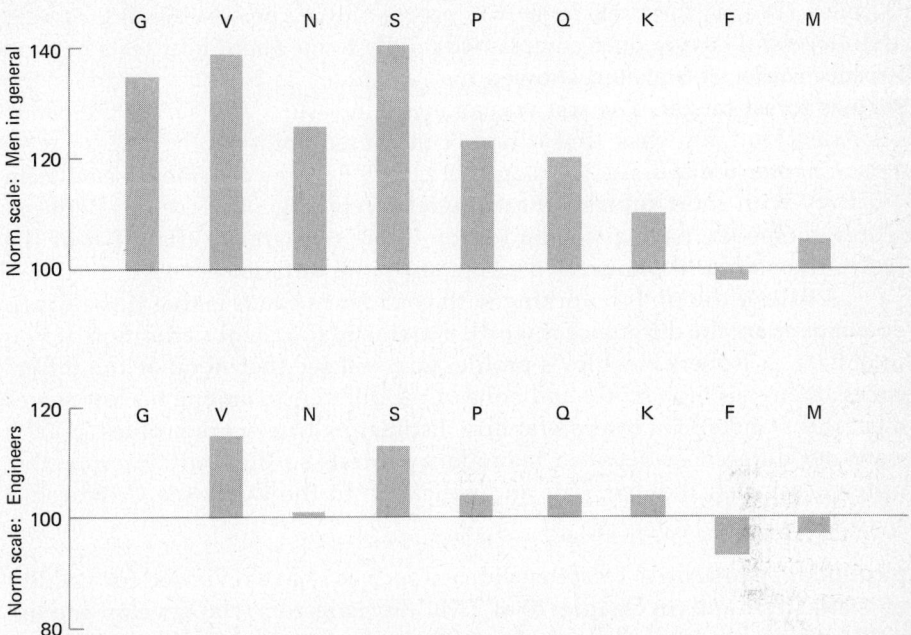

Figure 9.12. Two GATB profiles for a student engineer.

scores above average. The lower profile based on norms for engineering students is strikingly different. This student's greatest strengths, relative to other engineers, are V and S. He is only average in G and other scores.

Uncertainty in prediction. The counselor cannot make a clear prediction for Walter, with a standard score of 60, even when it is known that only 30 people out of 100 having that score fail in a certain profession. Perhaps Walter would do better if tested again. Perhaps other qualities unknown to us make Walter one of the 30 who fail rather than one of the 70 who succeed.

The counselor who is conscious of unreliability takes precautions. She starts by reporting scores as approximate rather than exact, perhaps by the "confidence band" technique illustrated in Robert Finchley's profile (p. 105). She looks to the case history to confirm the impressions the profile gives. If in doubt about a critical finding, she checks it with a second test or other sources of information. She looks for factors such as language handicaps or unusual training that might make the usual meaning of the score inapplicable.

Clients and professional workers may trust test data too much. Even when the tester's report is carefully qualified, the person receiving the report is likely to remember only portions of it. A parent, learning that his child stands at the 25th percentile in fluid ability, may forget the tester's cautions about what the test does not measure, the possibility of growth or decline in ability, and the approximate nature of predictions from it. The number may stick vividly in mind and be used as a basis for significant decisions for years to come. (Worse, the basic logic may escape the lay person. A congressman and successful lawyer once complained mildly to me about how tests he took decades earlier at Stanford showed his "aptitude" to be for an outdoor job such as forest ranger. The test was an *interest* measure, and surely the counselor said loud and clear that it hadn't measured ability.)

Chapter 6 discussed the standard error of scores considered singly. In a battery with short subtests these are relatively large. Differences between scores, moreover, have a standard error 40 per cent greater than that of the scores themselves (because two errors enter the difference).

A rule of thumb for working with confidence bands is that if the bands do not overlap, the difference is worth drawing to the client's attention. If you look back at Robert Finchley's profile, you will see that none of the differences among his high scores and none of the differences among his low scores meet this standard for interpretability. Estimating true-score profiles (p. 251) irons out differences between redundant subtests so that only interpretable differences catch the eye. (For an application to the DAT, see Cronbach *et al.*, 1972, pp. 319 ff.)

Redundancy of scores. Despite evidence such as I have reviewed for validity of spatial tests and (in Chapter 5) of TMC, investigators who develop and use multiscore instruments have been accused of picturing mountains that are really molehills. General abilities obviously do account for a great deal of variance both in school and in an occupation, and there are critics who find DAT and GATB profiles pointlessly detailed.

I have already reported Hunter's criticism of GATB. DAT scores are similarly redundant. A factor analysis (Nanda, 1967) of data like those in Table 9.8 indicates that the information dependable enough for use in guidance could be captured in four scores rather than eight:

> A verbal composite emphasizing Verbal Reasoning, Spelling, and Language Usage
> A composite emphasizing Abstract, Spatial, and Mechanical
> A numerical factor
> A clerical factor

There are weak specific factors in some tests such as Spatial and Spelling; none of the specifics is measured accurately.

In an earlier section (p. 256), I referred to the "jangle fallacy" of giving different names to similar tests and interpreting them as if they were distinct. When two tests correlate substantially, only a modest fraction of the differences in observed scores imply a meaningful difference in true scores. Among typical students, only about 20 per cent have clearly nonchance differences ($P < 0.05$) between DAT Verbal Reasoning and Language Usage.

Still, the fact that (for example) DAT Verbal, Spelling, and Language

Usage overlap does not make it inappropriate to report all three scores. Sampling three aspects of verbal abilities broadens the composite, and it reminds the counselee that verbal development has many aspects.

Humphreys (1981), reflecting on the efforts of the armed services to sort enlisted personnel for specialized training, concludes that nearly all the valid information is carried by three types of score: general-scholastic, mechanical knowledge or reasoning, and speed in arithmetic and clerical tasks. The first indicates the probability of succeeding in comparatively difficult courses and assignments involving words and ideas. The second predicts quickness in learning "dirty hands" jobs. And the third predicts for routine clerical tasks. Once these three variables have been assigned weights to match a training program, Humphreys says, other breakdowns such as those within DAT are irrelevant. (Humphreys sees a larger role for specialized tests within an academically superior group, either at the college level or in advanced military specialties. The enlisted population has generally come from a nonacademic high school track emphasizing shop *or* clerical subjects).

The critics rightly place the burden of proof in guidance and employee classification on whoever proposes a job-specific interpretation of specialized factors. The Complex Coordination test (p. 318) provides an example that cuts both ways. The designers thought they were getting at a psychomotor aptitude required by pilots, one not tapped by other tests. The test proved to be one of the best single predictors of success in pilot training (p. 396). Four-fifths of its validity, however, came from cognitive abilities tapped by pencil-paper tests (general and spatial). That does not prove that the psychomotor test was a bad idea; the fraction of the validity that did come from the multilimb-coordination component was economically significant in reducing the failure rate. (For detailed evidence, see Cronbach, 1970, p. 390.)

How early do profiles stabilize? The student is continually revising his self-concept as he goes through school, forming an impression of the fields in which he is specially strong and weak. In judgments about where a young person's talents lie, the shape of the present profile can be taken too seriously. Patterns become increasingly stable, but they are reversible even in adulthood.

Illuminating evidence on general academic abilities comes from a longitudinal study in 17 communities where several reliable tests were given in grades 5, 7, 9, and 11; 15,000 students were in the core sample for whom complete data accumulated. Table 9.11 covers a small fraction of the information, for males only. The SCAT "aptitude" battery and the STEP achievement battery overlap, but the former emphasizes reasoning, and the latter covers more specific content. The retest correlations over a 6-year interval are above 0.65; the one for SCAT-V (vocabulary and verbal reasoning) reached 0.79. Patterning is weak; most r's within the same column are of similar size. Competence in mathematics in grade 11 is predicted nearly as well by verbal abilities in grade 5 as by fifth-grade Mathematics. The person whose grade-5

Table 9.11. *Grade-11 scores predicted from grade-5 tests*

	Grade 11					
Grade 5	Verbal[a]	Reading	Social Studies	Quantitative[a]	Math	Science
Verbal tests						
Verbal[a]	**0.79**	0.69	0.70	0.58	0.58	0.62
Reading	0.76	**0.73**	0.70	0.61	0.62	0.65
Social studies	0.74	0.69	**0.70**	0.59	0.59	0.60
Quantitative tests						
Quantitative[a]	0.63	0.63	0.59	**0.70**	0.64	0.56
Mathematics	0.70	0.67	0.64	0.69	**0.66**	0.61
Science	0.73	0.68	0.67	0.61	0.61	**0.67**

[a] These two scores (from SCAT) emphasize general intellectual development and reasoning more than the ostensible achievement tests do.
SOURCE: Data supplied by T. L. Hilton. For the design of the study, see Hilton *et al.*, 1971; see also Hilton, 1980.

reasoning is superior to his achievement score in the same area tends to show a similar fluid-crystallized difference in grade 11, but the main message of the table is the stability of all-round academic-intellectual performance.

The data also show that a rolling readjustment is going on in every area. Just as we saw in Figure 8.2, correlations taper off as time elapses. Some students are rising in rank while others are dropping back. In reading, for example, the retests correlate 0.78–0.80 over a 2-year span, 0.77–0.78 over 4 years, and 0.73 over 6 years.

A profile in grade 3 will report reliable differences between verbal, numerical, spatial and other abilities for many children, but most profiles will be different a year later. Profiles become more stable during high school, probably because students scatter into distinct courses of study. Table 9.12 is based on retests of thousands of students initially tested in Grade 9. The readjustment of ranks, and of profile shapes, is drastic for the perceptual and motor tests. There is less shifting after adolescence. In a 3-year retest of adults around age 30, all the correlations were 0.75 or higher (GATB manual, p. 269).

Table 9.12 *Stability of GATB scores*

	Measures Having Coefficients in Each Range, When Grade 12 Scores are Compared with Scores Earned	
	3 Years Earlier	1 Year Earlier
0.80–0.85		G, V, N
0.70–0.79	G, V, N, S, K	S, Q, K, M
0.60–0.69	P, Q, M	P, F
0.50–0.59	F	

SOURCE: GATB manual, 1970, p. 327.

The adolescent correlations are high enough to warrant interpreting differences within a grade-9 profile. Guidance in early years of high school, however, should be concerned with helping students fill in weak spots significant for their employability and personal interests. It is one thing to say, "You will be severely handicapped in these career lines that interest you if you do not strengthen your math (or spatial reasoning, or motor coordination)"; it is quite another to say, "Don't consider those careers; let us find one that matches your profile." Emphasizing developmental experience is especially important if the student has had little exposure and encouragement in an area where his score is low—mechanical reasoning, for example. His standing is least likely to change in an area where the student has already had plentiful learning opportunities.

At any age an aptitude or achievement battery is an inventory of present competences. The scores forecast the future profile shape if the student and the school make no effort to repair shortcomings.

Ability measures and their possible instability should be explained in commonsense terms that help a counselee understand his profile and its implications. The DAT and GATB profiles are well designed for such interpretations. Labels such as Numerical Reasoning and Spelling do not sound like mysterious inborn aptitudes; they are clearly measures of a certain type of performance.

In the early days of testing, it was hoped that a test profile would permit a definite, final choice of vocation at the time the tests were given. If this were the case, the counselor and client together could reach a decision, the client relying on the counselor's interpretation of the tests. Today it is recognized that vocational choice is not a single throw of the dice; rather, it is a long-term process of development. Even after leaving school, a person has many occasions to narrow his or her field of concentration or to transfer to a new one. The engineer in a technical firm, for example, may become a manager, a salesperson, a creative designer, or an expert on specifications. Wise choice requires self-understanding; no prescription filled out by a tenth-grade or freshman-year counselor could properly anticipate later choices. On this, Chapter 12 will have more to say.

32. *The correlations below the diagonal (lower left) in Table 9.11 are usually larger than the corresponding ones toward the upper right. Thus Science 5 predicts Social Studies 11 better than Social Studies 5 predicts Science 11. What explanations can you offer?*

10
Interpreting and Fostering Individual Development

This chapter is concerned with the two-way traffic linking mental development to experience. We shall consider the role culture plays in promoting development of abilities and in shaping test performance. This raises questions about the meaning of test scores for persons of different cultural background and questions about the improvement of assessments and the improvement of abilities themselves. Much of the chapter, then, bears on such important and controversial topics as race differences and compensatory education. As the chapter proceeds, attention shifts to educational policies and educational uses of tests: pupil classification, planning of instruction, evaluation of student progress, and program evaluation. Tests serve in the management of national, state, and local school systems, as well as in planning at the schoolroom level; the chapter considers both aspects of education.

HOW NATURE AND NURTURE COMBINE

The chapter begins with the issue of "heritability." The hereditary aspect of mental development has little relevance to educational practice and social policy. Misunderstandings about it, however, generate recurrent controversy, controversy that diverts attention from matters of greater practical importance.

The Continuity of Development

Today's organism grows out of what it was yesterday. Yesterday's health, alertness, food intake, and experiences influence today's actions; these, in turn, produce tomorrow's organism. Mental processes, being carried out by physiological mechanisms, are subject to biological laws. Chemical messages lodged in the genes regulate metabolism and growth and point the way for development. Not even early effects are predetermined, however. Characteristics at birth are influenced by prenatal physical conditions and possibly by stimuli received in the womb.

Superior development cannot be attributed simply to the combination of "good" heredity with "good" environment. Environments cannot be scaled from rich to poor, good to bad. Environments differ in myriad ways. Potentially important are the presence of certain substances in the diet, the ability level of the young child's companions, the extent to which the culture stresses individual excellence, the extent to which parents press the child to take independent responsibility, the use of two languages in the child's home, and so on. Environmental factors considered advantageous to development by some psychologists are seen by others as impediments.

Darwin's message was that a successful species fits a particular ecological niche. Genes that suit a species to one environment make it unsuited to another; thus, plant species require specific soils and climates. The genes an organism received at conception leave a whole range of developmental possibilities open for that individual (B. D. Davis & P. Flaherty, 1976; Dobzhansky, 1973). Heredity could not possibly fix the level of ability the individual will attain. If—inconceivably—a set environment were imposed on everyone, some gene patterns would be especially suited to *that* environment. There is no reason to think that that same gene pattern is best for intellectual growth in all human environments. There is no reason to think that, for all gene patterns, one environment is best for intellectual development.

Controlled experiment is needed to trace the joint action of heredities and environments, but in studies of humans only gross controls are possible. Let us pause, then, for two illuminating studies of animals.

The demonstration long ago by Berkeley psychologists that rats can be bred for "maze brightness" was impressive. Generation 1 ran a maze repeatedly, and rats who had the best error records were interbred. Rats with poor records were likewise interbred. In generation 2, the two sets of offspring differed little. The same procedure—test, select, interbreed—was repeated. By generation 7, the ablest rats in the "dull strain" barely equaled the least able in the maze-bright line (R. Tryon, 1940). The difference reflected heredity, but it did not simply mean: "Rat intelligence is hereditary."

The meaning of the effect became clearer when the range of tests was widened (Searle, 1949). The "dull" rats actually outperformed the other strain when an underwater path was to be learned. Searle found the "bright" strain responsive to food as incentive, not especially eager to escape from water, and not much inclined toward exploratory wandering. The "dull" rats had just the opposite motivational pattern. A further study with a conventional maze showed that dull-strain rats were dull when trials came in quick succession, but equaled "bright" rats when practice trials were 5 minutes or more apart (McGauch *et al.*, 1962). Interbreeding had selected, then, on specific attributes advantageous in the original maze.

Freedman (1958) arrived at a similar conclusion when he contrasted indulgent and disciplined rearing of puppies. In a matched pair from a given breed, one pup was encouraged by the handler in whatever activity the pup initiated, including aggressive games. The pairmate was formally trained to sit, stay, and come on command. The test at age 8 weeks was this:

> Each time a pup ate meat from a bowl placed in the center of a [test] room, he was punished by a swat on the rump and a shout of "No." After 3 minutes the experimenter left the room and, observing through a one-way glass, recorded the time that elapsed before the pup again ate.

A dog that did not eat within 10 minutes was removed from the test room.

In Figure 10.1 each data point averages the scores of four pups with the same breed and training. Breeds differed conspicuously, sheepdogs learning quickly and basenjis refusing to learn. Indulgent rearing produced superior obedience in terriers and beagles—the breeds that, during the training, showed greatest interest in contact with the human trainer. The result is an effect of heredity *under particular conditions*—a heredity-treatment interaction.

What Kinship Correlations Do Not Mean

No scientist thinks that rank in ability is fixed at conception. Jensen (1973, p. 164), a foremost hereditarian, acknowledges that among children with the *same* genes intellectual performance at school ages spreads over about a 28-point range of IQs (2 s.d.). But tracing the sources of variation has proved difficult (Scarr, 1981).

Studies on human heredity look at similarities among close and distant kin and at the development of children reared apart from their natural parents (adopted, or in orphanages). Much is learned from the "natural experiment" that twins offer. Identical twins develop from identical genes: the test scores of twins raised in the same home correlate at the same high level as two testings of the same person. Fraternal twins, like brothers and sisters, share

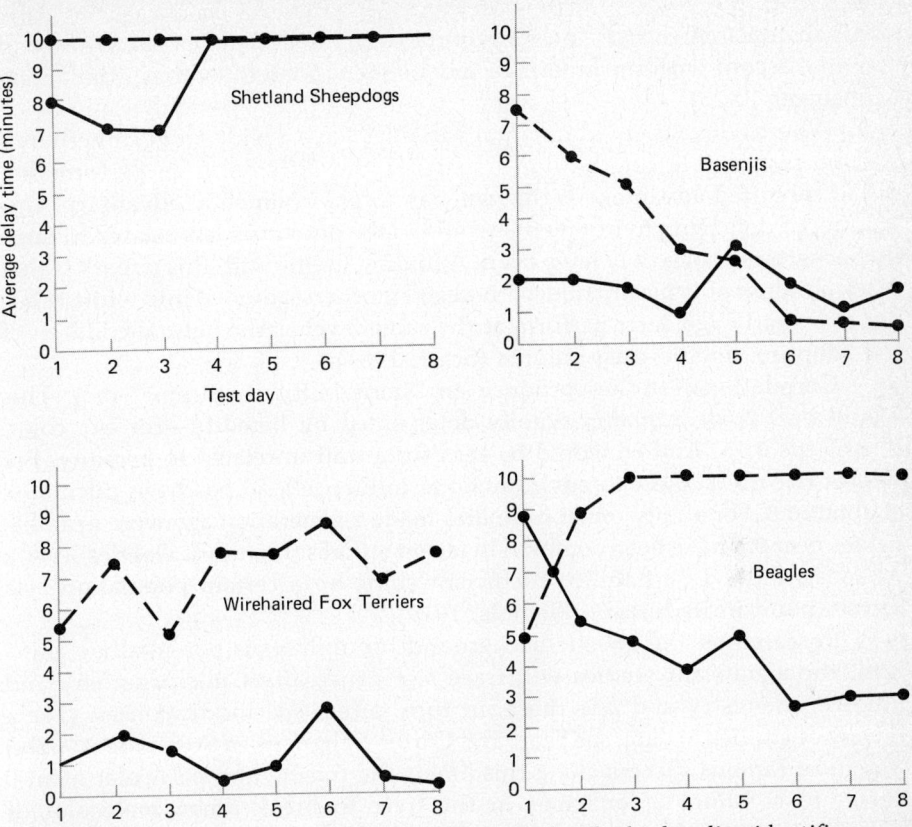

Figure 10.1. Learning curves for pups of four breeds. The broken line identifies pups who had previously been indulged, and the solid line identifies pups who had been subjected to discipline.
Source: Adapted from Freedman, 1958. Copyright © 1958 by The American Association for the Advancement of Science and reproduced by permission.

half their genes (more or less). Scores of these twins correlate no higher than do scores of brothers or sisters born separately.

A few studies located identical twins who had been separated at an early age and reared apart; despite the separate upbringing, the correlation of the twins' test scores in adulthood was high. There are good and bad reasons for discounting this as evidence of hereditary influence (Vernon, 1979). The environments of the identicals reared together must have been similar. When families were split up, the children usually moved to relatives who represented a similar culture and presumably gave the twins similar advantages. Among twins reared apart, those whose adoptive environments differed most tended to differ most in adult ability. Technical disputes about statistical procedures in research on heredity do not justify disagreement regarding the conclusions in general. (Another side issue: This line of research has been ridiculed because a main contributor, Sir Cyril Burt, in his old age made gross errors in research reports. Burt's reports over his decades of work were in essential accord with the reports of independent contemporaries; Rimland & Munsinger, 1977).

Where relevant environmental variables have a wide range, inheritance will be responsible for the lion's share of the differences in performance *only* if inherited advantage is the gateway to environmental advantage. Upgrading of deficient environments would make outcomes less related to family background than they have been. A finding in line with this remark is that black children of typically underprivileged mothers, adopted into white families at an early age, later perform at the same level as the natural children of the adopting middle-class parents (Scarr, 1981).

Correlational studies produce an "heritability coefficient" (h^2). This would be 1.0 for a quality wholly determined by heredity—for eye color, h^2 exceeds 0.95. And h^2 would be zero for a trait unrelated to heredity. For weight (clearly subject to environmental influence!), h^2 has been calculated at about 0.8. For ability, most estimates made a generation ago were near 0.8; values near 0.5 have been common in recent studies (Plomin & DeFries, 1980). At most, then, a heritability coefficient sums up a certain population at a certain point in its history (Nichols, 1979).

Research on the genetic background for abilities is potentially significant; the significant studies will trace *how* genes affect microanatomy and internal chemistry and *how* these, in turn, affect specific responses. (For a review of studies to date, see Scarr and Carter-Saltzman, in Sternberg, 1982b.) The most famous success along this line is the tracing of a particular mental defect to a failure of enzymes in the liver to break down molecules of phenylalanine (which are part of a normal diet). Subsequently, investigators devised a chemical test to detect the disorder in newborn infants and also devised a maintenance diet that enables children with the faulty gene to develop at nearly the normal rate (Willerman, 1978, pp. 216–298).

1. *Scarr (1981, p. 449) says (in part):*

    The evolutionary process virtually guarantees that genetic diversity will account for some of the intellectual differences among us.

    A just society is one that provides humane developmental environments for all of its children and thereby maximizes [the consequences of] genetic individual differences.

    Could a philosopher with a different concept of a good society defend any resource distribution other than the one that "maximizes" development of every individual?

2. *The Supreme Court ruled against the parents of Amy Rowley, who asked the school to provide an assistant who would relay to Amy in sign language what was said in class (*Board of Education v. Rowley, 50 L.W. 4925 [1982]*). Amy's hearing was impaired, but she had a satisfactory school record. When Congress voted that handicapped children were to receive*

a *"free appropriate public education,"* it did not intend, said the court, to require schools to give every handicapped child *"an opportunity to achieve his full potential."* If Congress is asked now to require that schools strive toward *"full potential,"* what arguments pro and con should it bear in mind?

3. *An athletic coach pays no attention to a player's ancestry; he does what he can with the player's muscles and skills as of the present date. No doubt, ability in sport is affected by heredity, and there is no dispute about this even though excelling in sports brings great rewards. Why does the role of inheritance in performance with words and symbols generate much more controversy than its role in performance with muscles?*

CULTURAL FACTORS

Studies of American Ethnic Groups

Score differences between culturally different groups cannot be attributed to heredity. Reasoning about "group heredity" breaks down because indefensible assumptions about environments are smuggled in (Cronbach, 1976b). If girls have a gene that helps in mechanical reasoning—one that boys lack—yet the traditional culture gives boys experience with machines and gives girls little or none, most boys will outscore most girls on TMC. Males will develop scores toward the high end of the range that their heredity permits. Females will develop scores toward the low end of their possible range. If two groups, from conception, had indistinguishable biological and social environments, we could reason simply from observed differences; otherwise, not.

Innumerable surveys, some with large and careful samples, have reported average test scores for American ethnic samples. The findings, essentially consistent, require careful interpretation. Blacks average about one s.d. below the white population on general mental tests and achievement tests (Table 10.1). This gross statistic is to be supplemented first by recognizing that members of both groups can be found at all levels of ability; at school ages about a sixth of blacks exceed the average of the white population. Every kind of test within the Gf–Gc spectrum shows about the same difference (Loehlin *et al.*, 1975, pp. 177–188; see also Table 10.2). For a review of findings on test scores of blacks, see Dreger (1973); on test scores of Hispanics see Schmidt, Pearlman, and Hunter (1980). Some ethnic groups in the U. S., notably those of Oriental descent, match or exceed the general average (Loehlin *et al.*, 1975).

Test performance reflects resources derived from parents. The race difference is greatly reduced when samples are matched on parent education, occupation, or income. The difference between blacks and white "within SES levels" is about half the original difference. The score difference is greater at higher occupational levels. (Table 10.1 should not be taken as an exact statement. The definition of socioeconomic levels was not the same in all the data

Table 10.1 *Average IQ in four demographic groups*

	Black	White	Difference Between Races Within SES Levels
Higher social status	98	107	9
Lower social status	91	94	3
Difference between SES groups within race	7	7	

SOURCE: Six studies published between 1966 and 1973 are tabulated by Loehlin *et al.*, 1975, p. 172. I have estimated the IQ that is most typical for each cell. WISC-R standardization data show about 6 points greater difference in the last column than this table does (Kaufman & Doppelt, 1976; see also Jensen, 1980, p. 43, and Reynolds & Gutkin, 1980).

sets, and my way of combining the available facts is not the only defensible one.)

The correction in Table 10.1 is incomplete. I mention three shortcomings:

- Equating years of schooling does not equate education if, by and large, black parents attended poorer schools than whites.
- Matching adults by job title does not equate groups. (For example, consider the financial and other resources for child rearing likely to be found in the group of blacks classed as "owner or manager," compared with whites so classed.) Better matching would surely assign even more of the differences to social class and the opportunities associated with it, and less to race (Deutsch, 1973).
- Home characteristics relevant to development vary when race, parent education, and economic status are held constant (Bradley *et al.*, 1977; Trotman, 1977).

Most social scientists believe that a socially important difference in mean performance of ethnic groups would remain after full adjustment. Their explanations are in conflict. Some would say that the test scores systematically underrate the true present ability of black children. Others would say that cultural traditions in some sections of the black community leave the children, on average, ill-prepared to meet demands of the school—less prepared than is the case in economically pinched households, black or white, where the child's intellectual growth is nurtured. Some say that a history of prejudice and discrimination against a group affects development of its young members in subtle ways. And, finally, some believe that a fraction of the observed difference in means is an outcropping of differences between the gene pools of the subpopulations.

How Culture Channels Motivation

When facing an ability test, children from some cultures and subcultures may be less inclined to do their best than typical Western students are. Holding oneself in is a defense many people use in alien situations. I speak of a cultural phenomenon, not shyness or withdrawal in single cases; children in an alienated group define for each other a barrier that separates them from the institution. The school and all that goes with it is alien for some children, as was suggested by Labov's anecdote regarding verbal performance (p. 67).

The failure of school observations to disclose these children's abilities is not specific to "testing." The verbal inhibitions Labov reported would impair the child's dealings with the teacher and classmates and so reduce the amount learned in school. The classroom observations of speech were a relevant indication of probable difficulty in school, but invalid as a measure of linguistic *skill*.

Motivations taken for granted in typical Western examinees run counter to the tradition of some cultural groups. Goodnow (in Resnick, 1976) notes that a culture may not value working out of complete answers or formulating general principles or doing problems in one's head. Rules by which testers formalize a question may then seem irrelevant, even absurd. The classic example is the experience of Glick in Liberia (cited in Triandis & Berry, 1980, p. 283). Adult Kpelle farmers were asked to group objects that "belong together." Theory says that intellectually mature sorters use "logical" categories: articles of clothing, containers, tools, and so on. The farmers formed "immature" functional groupings: rice with cooking pan with stirring spoon. The farmers insisted that this grouping made sense. Finally, Glick asked one of them to group the objects as a *stupid* Kpelle would. The response was a perfect logical sorting—"mature" according to Western, Piagetian theory. Berland's report from Pakistan (p. 57) is similar in its implications.

Time is not of the essence in many traditions. Wober (1972) found that advanced students in Uganda had accepted the Western idea: Quickness is a sign of intelligence. Villagers, however, typically identified intelligence with "slowness" (reflection? inhibition of impulse?).

The Zuñi teach cooperation rather than competition. Zuñi children have races. But a child who wins several races is scolded for having made others lose face. He is taught to win some races to show he is capable and then to hold back and give others an opportunity to win. White teachers sent Zuñi children to the blackboard for arithmetic drills, with instructions to do a problem and turn their backs to the board when finished. Instead, the pupils faced the board until the slowest had finished; then all turned. This was to them simple courtesy; in their eyes, the teacher had asked them to show off. Obviously, a group speed test gives misleading results among the Zuñi. An individual test fares no better. The first child tested may fail some items deliberately, because he fears the next child will be unable to answer.

Modification of Test Procedure

Psychologists studying mental development in Third World cultures started with the ideal of standardization. They learned the hard way that one should *not* keep the test operations the same in every setting (S. H. Irvine & W. K. Carroll, in Triandis & Berry, 1980). Content and procedure usually should be modified.

Consider block-design tests as an example. Ord (1971, pp. 21–22) found the traditional test useless in New Guinea.

> [M]any subjects, particularly in the Highlands, did not seem to appreciate how two-dimensional designs could be represented by three-dimensional material. They tried to use the tops and sides of blocks concurrently to make a design. There was also some manipulative difficulty. . . .

Excessive dependence on the tester was also a source of trouble; Ord's adult students responded much as Mark did (p. 270). Ord went on to revise the test. He replaced the blocks with flat tiles; he compensated for lack of dexterity by making the tiles large and by providing a tray whose sloping sides kept the tiles in place; and he had the tester construct the first patterns, so that the examinee, by imitating, could get off to a running start.

Experience with groups round the world has led to suggestions for obtaining more valid information on abilities in preliterate societies (Brislin *et al.*, 1973; Irvine & Carroll and other chapters in Triandis & Berry, 1980; Ord, 1971; Schwartz & Krug, 1972; Vernon, 1969). Not all the following suggestions can be adopted at once, and their usefulness varies with the population.

> Base test content on words, stories, and objects familiar in the culture.
> When a function such as memory or visual perception is of interest, go beyond imported tests to observe members of the community performing the function in their usual activities. Arrange standard tasks that bring controlled variation into these activities.
> Use objects rather than pictures. Pictures or diagrams made of straight lines can create an irrelevant "reading" difficulty.
> Do not set time limits or allow bonuses for fast work unless your intent is to measure speed.
> Reduce variation in style. For example, pace any timed test, so that persons who would otherwise work too hastily or too methodically do not suffer.
> To the extent possible, make the test a game—convivial, dramatic, cheerful.
> Depend as little as possible on verbal directions, even in the native language. Use visual demonstration.

Do not intermix item types. Present each type as a subtest with its own introduction.

Present instructions on film (to standardize).

Adapt all language and simplify all requirements to the point where a native can grasp the task and act as tester.

Teach every technique the examinee is expected to use (e.g., placing and turning blocks).

Teach the standards for judging a response good or bad.

Unless respondents fully command the rules of the game, their scores cannot be interpreted. In the West Indies, Uganda, and occasionally in England, children tested by Vernon were satisfied with designs they had made even though the responses had only a vague resemblance to the prescribed pattern (Figure 10.2)

Traditionally, testers introduced novelty or surprise, so as to observe adaptation rather than a practiced, specific competence. Opinion is now moving in the opposite direction. Crosscultural testers in particular recommend leading the person into the task by easy stages that amount to instruction, so that the test proper will contain no surprise beyond the particular stimuli of each item (Biesheuvel, in Cronbach & Drenth, 1972). Such testing still requires adaptive response insofar as each test item requires analysis, retrieval of knowledge, or organization of responses. But the score no longer depends on quickness in adapting to the test situation. Conventional procedure tends

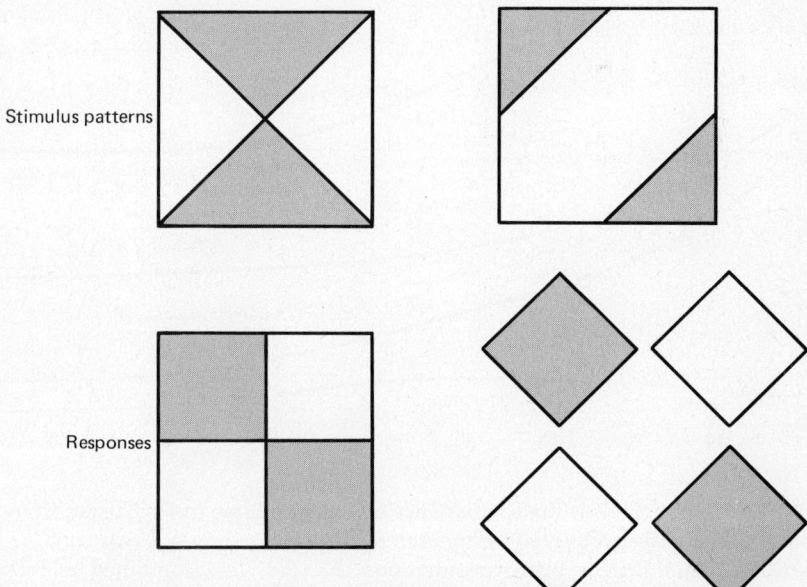

Figure 10.2. Block-Design responses accepted by non-Western subjects.
Source: Adapted from Vernon, 1969, p. 102.

to give a considerable advantage to persons who have previously faced test-like tasks or lessons.

Logically, the level a person reaches when thoroughly prepared for the test task should validly predict success in schooling or job training because weeks or months of instruction allow time for coming to understand what is wanted. In a few scattered studies, scores obtained after familiarization have shown superior predictive validity (Dague, in Cronbach & Drenth, 1972; Ombredane *et al.*, 1956). A warning must be voiced. After extended practice, standings on some tests reflect sheer speed of response or the efficiency of whatever routine the person has developed for coping with this specific task. Thus, Digit Symbol, on early trials, depends to some extent on Gf; on later trials, differences are due to motor speed.

Another example is the Complex Coordination test (p. 30). Fleishman and Hempel (1954; Fleishman, 1957) administered numerous 2-minute trials to each person; 8 minutes is the usual testing time. Figure 10.3 implies that different persons rank high at different stages of practice. In the early stages, cognitive factors—mostly spatial—dominate. When the task has become familiar, standings depend very little on Gf and S. Multilimb coordination, measured by this and several other motor tests, increases in importance during the first 40 minutes of practice but then drops back. Evidently,

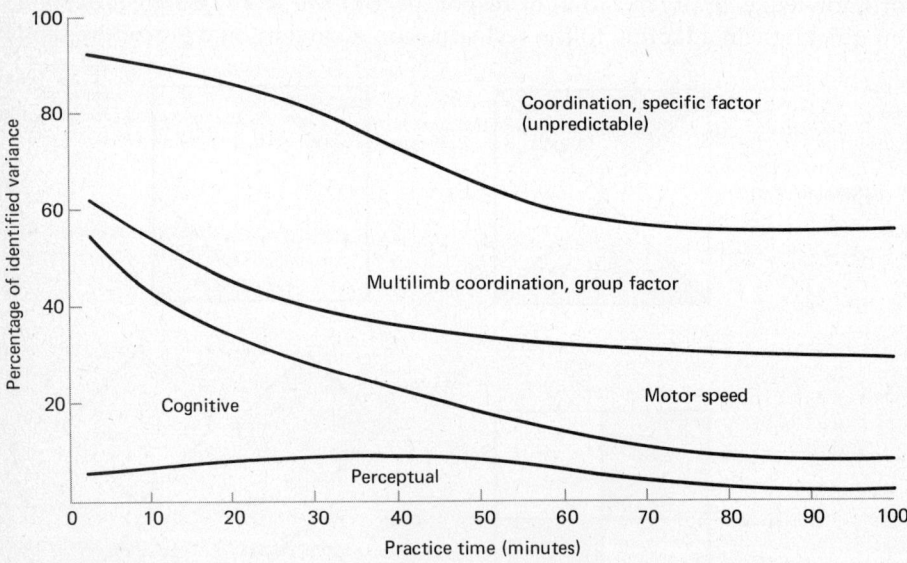

Figure 10.3. Complex Coordination variance on early and late trials. Curves show the proportion of variance accounted for by each factor (after removing error variance and unidentified minor factors from consideration. Factors were combined as follows: Cognitive includes Spatial, Visualization, and Mechanical Experience; Motor Speed includes Rate of Movement and Psychomotor Speed.
Source: Data from Fleishman & Hempel, 1954.

the early trials measure adaptation; hence standings reflect intellectual skills. At the end, sheer speed counts. A test-specific factor becomes the largest source of individual differences after the first hour of practice. This factor reflects the efficiency of the technique the person gradually fixed upon during the test.

4. *Comment on this proposition: For pilot selection, Complex Coordination gives better information during minutes 40 to 60 than in early and late blocks of trials.*
5. *In what ways, if any, might cultural experience affect performance on each of the following tests?*
    a. *Formboards (fitting blocks into variously shaped holes).*
    b. *Wechsler Picture Arrangement.*
    c. *Porteus mazes.*
6. *One could modify the Picture Arrangement test to fit other cultures by redrawing the pictures to represent scenes in each type of community. Would such adapted tests provide a suitable basis for crosscultural comparisons?*
7. *Assume that Picture Arrangement is adapted as described in the preceding question. Then would Picture Arrangement or Block Design be more nearly "culture fair"?*
8. *Irvine (cited in Triandis & Berry, 1980, p. 222) found that coaching on matrix tasks raised the correlation of such a test with concurrent school examinations and with a test of numerical ability among students in the eighth grade in Mashonaland. If admission to secondary school is selective and tests are used to compare children from different villages, does this evidence support coaching prior to testing?*
9. *Which of the suggestions for testing in Africa would be likely to improve the validity of tests for American job applicants who have attended school briefly and irregularly?*

Cultural Shaping of Profiles

By making particular activities important, providing opportunity to engage in them, and providing appropriate vocabulary and other intellectual tools, a culture promotes certain kinds of intellectual development. The same tests have been applied in many parts of the world, most often to samples of schoolchildren. Large differences appear. These studies rather often find children in more industrialized communities superior across diverse tests; but this comparison—confounded with nutrition, education, familiarity with tests, and so on—says little about cultural influences.

Groups widely separated on one set of tests are close together on others. Children of the isolated Shilluk, living on the edge of the desert in Egypt, fell far below European norms—except on a test rather like Ord's version of Block Design. On that test, the Shilluk performed above the European norm. Fahmy

(1954) attributed this to the large role played by color in ceremonies and games with which the children were familiar.

Further evidence that cultural differences cannot be summed up simply comes from a longitudinal comparison of children in Austin, Texas, and Mexico City (Holtzman *et al.*, 1975). The samples were essentially equal at the start of school on several Wechsler subtests, but the Texans steadily pulled ahead as years passed. Here are means on Block Design:

Approximate Age	Texas	Mexico
7	7.7	8.0
10	22.2	14.9
13	35.9	29.6

The averages in Arithmetic stayed close together over the years, however, and on a measure of rote associative learning the Mexican average (for boys especially) was definitely higher.

A particularly understandable example of cultural shaping of an ability is the report that Samoans are outstanding at judging whether monotone rhythmical patterns are the same or different (J. B. Ford, 1957). This almost surely is explained by the importance to Samoans of music that consists largely of rhythmic beating on tins, logs, or bundles of reeds. The U.S. Navy found Samoans exceptionally competent at sending and receiving radio code. Indeed, before tape recording was available, it was necessary to transport Samoans to Hawaii to act as receivers; no one else could keep up with the fast transmissions from Pago Pago.

Reasoning with symbols. The educated sector in most nations is accustomed to looking at systems of symbols: balance sheets, blueprints, legal syllogisms, codes, . . . A principal feature of cultural advances—many of them non-Western—has been abstract schemes like the calendar, which capture essential relations and detach them from the ever-changing context. In many cultures, children and adults who are well able to cope with village life do badly on tests that ask for analysis independent of context or for reasoning about imaginary cases. This is especially true of persons with little formal schooling (Scribner & Cole, 1973; Sharp *et al.*, 1979).

Kpelle farmers in Liberia would not produce logic on demand (Cole *et al.*, 1968, 1971). Witness the following interchange between tester and respondent (Cole *et al.*, 1971, pp. 187–188):

> EXPERIMENTER: Flumo and Yakpalo always drink cane juice [rum] together. Flumo is drinking cane juice. Is Yakpalo drinking cane juice?
>
> SUBJECT: Flumo and Yakpalo drink cane juice together, but the time Flumo was drinking the first one Yakpalo was not there on that day.

EXPERIMENTER: But I told you that Flumo and Yakpalo always drink cane juice together. One day Flumo was drinking cane juice. Was Yakpalo drinking cane juice that day?
SUBJECT: The day Flumo was drinking the cane juice Yakpalo was not there on that day.
EXPERIMENTER: What is the reason?
SUBJECT: The reason is that Yakpalo went to his farm on that day and Flumo remained in town on that day.

This evidence of lack of readiness to engage in disciplined thought is offset by other findings. Scores of Kpelle children rose according to the amount of schooling they had had. (Some villages provided more opportunity for schooling than others, so this is not a simple effect of selection.) Also, children and adults were relatively successful when, instead of having to *construct* responses about Yakpalo and his friends, they were to judge the suitability of responses the tester suggested. Finally, Cole *et al.* (1971) point to instances of "what if . . . ?" thinking in everyday Kpelle activities. The conclusion is not that the Kpelle are incapable of logic but that they find it relevant only in particular activities or settings. Note the resemblance to Labov's argument.

A natural question is whether, across the wide range of the world's cultures, abilities can be found that Westerners have not developed strongly and that Western tests neglect. One can have great respect for the Samoans' superior ability to discriminate rhythm and for ability of Bushmen to detect in their desert environment the minimal cues that make survival possible (Reuning, in Cronbach & Drenth, 1972) without regarding those abilities as resources on which alternative civilizations could be built.

Some commentators speak of the lower scores of minority groups in Western countries and of tribal groups elsewhere as signs of "difference, not deficit." They imply that, although members of these groups are not prepared to use the commonplace tools of symbolic thought, they probably are proficient in some other important kinds of thinking. We do not have evidence of these alternative abilities, so little can be said here. An example can be suggested, however, to keep the idea open.

It is reported that some cultures stress mutually supportive social relationships. Vernon (1969) quotes Jomo Kenyatta: "To the Europeans, individuality is the ideal of life, to the Africans, the ideal is right relations with, and behavior to, other people." Recall also the behavior of the Zuñi, and recall Witkin's belief that field-independent persons fall short in social skills. A group-oriented culture must develop techniques that lead to reasoned decisions; otherwise, it could not thrive in a changing world. The adaptive processes of groups makes a worthy candidate for investigation; non-Western cultures might excel in group tasks.

10. *In which of these features of modern life is "decontextualized" reasoning especially valuable?*

       Political participation   Do-it-yourself home repairs
       Investment   Child rearing   Architectural design
       Computer programming   Medical practice

11. The Russell Sage Social Relations Test (Damrin, 1959) is a block-design test in group form. The teacher remains on the sidelines as the tester distributes 20 blocks or so of several colors among the pupils, displays a comparatively large pattern that can use so many pieces, and tells the children that they are to construct it as rapidly as possible. "Before you begin, you can take as much time as you need to talk about it and to figure out a way in which the class can do it. I will not begin timing until you tell me that you are all ready to start."

    a. Can Binet's definition of intelligence (p. 195) apply to a group? Rephrase it if necessary. Does the Russell Sage test measure group intelligence in Binet's sense? If not, what?

    b. If several classes are ranked according to the average scores of their members on WISC-R Block Design, would you expect the classes to rank similarly on Damrin's test?

    c. For what purposes, if any, could this test provide more relevant information than the CogAT Non-Verbal section administered in the usual way?

CULTURAL LOADING OF ABILITY TESTS

Culture-laden test content has been challenged, particularly in recent years. For example, one WISC item asks a child what he or she should do if a smaller child starts a fight with him or her. The city streets do not value avoiding aggression as the middle class does, and "Shove him (or her) in the face" is not an unreasonable answer. Wechsler himself said a Harlem child deserves credit for responding "Fight back," but he did not modify the scoring key, which expects a response such as "Walk away." (As a matter of fact, black children do not find this item especially difficult; Miele, 1979.) A slightly different criticism is made of Wechsler's Information subtest. "Who wrote *Paradise Lost?*" asks for knowledge that not every American is likely to have encountered. Using such evidence to draw conclusions about "intelligence" has deservedly been satirized. Alternative "tests"—for example, the BITCH test of Robert Williams, 1972—have been devised on which only a person who knows the argot of the black ghetto (alternatively, of the barrio) could succeed. These tests make white college graduates look "unintelligent."

Should cultural experience count? These criticisms are sometimes shortsighted. Although some of the items challenged are indefensible, others have a legitimate function if interpreted correctly. Williams has a valid (though partial) test of familiarity with ghetto culture. The test taker who possesses garten instruction were given to children from poor families. This study, like many others set up around 1970, focused on whether the preschool experience raised Stanford-Binet scores. (The scores were adjusted according to age norms before plotting; hence year-to-year change attributable to normal development is removed from the picture.)

The experimental group was measurably superior at the end of the treatment. However, the control group "caught up" during the ensuing year. The extended period of follow-up added greatly to the value of the investigation.

The evidence in Figure 10.4 does not prove the intervention worthless. These test results strongly suggest that there was no lasting change in general ability; but that represents only one of many possible benefits (Travers & Light, 1982). Even the temporary elevation of scores the figure shows greatly reduced the chance of a child's being permanently classed as retarded because most such assignments are made during the first years of schooling.

Training in information processing. Increased understanding of processes underlying efficient performance has generated a new hopefulness (Borkowski & Cavanaugh, 1979; A. L. Brown, 1978; Campione *et al.*, in Sternberg, 1982b). I describe one of many current endeavors to improve ability, essentially by training in the "executive processes" of information management (pp. 195, 282).

Reuven Feuerstein, an Israeli psychologist trained at Geneva, has worked for decades with adolescents from a disadvantaged background. Jews whose families come from North Africa and the Middle East tend to score much lower on tests and to fare much less well in school and jobs than those of European background. Feuerstein's teachers work with apparently retarded adolescents from such families over periods as long as two years.

The Learning Potential Assessment Device (LPAD) is both a test and a vehicle for training (Feuerstein, 1979; Feuerstein *et al.*, 1982). It includes a matrix test, number series, and verbal analogies, plus several other tasks that appear to measure *Gf*. The assessment technique adopts many of the suggestions for testing in non-Western cultures. The items of each type ascend from

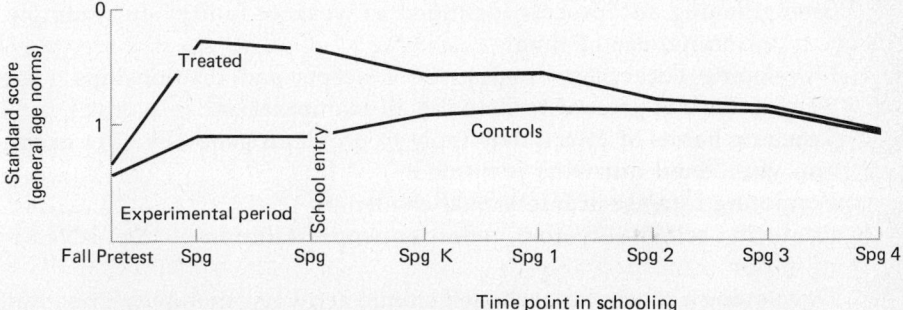

Figure 10.4. Findings in an experiment on compensatory education.
Source: Data from Weikart et al., 1978.

easy to difficult. The respondent is encouraged to concentrate and analyze, is given hints when he loses sight of the goal, and, if necessary, is guided through to the solution. Credit for success is reduced when much help has to be given. The student who profits from help on one item, making a more independent attack on the next, is judged likely to be responsive to instruction. Brown and French (1979) describe similar procedures that Russian psychologists use to assess a child's "zone of proximal development," that is, to identify specific areas where the child is ready to make a rapid advance if given focused training at this time. (See also Campione *et al.*, in Sternberg, 1982b.)

Feuerstein's matrix task (retitled "Variations") and some others can be administered to groups of students. In the group version, the teaching is more standardized than in the individual version. In the individual version the examiner is on the lookout for styles that make the person inefficient and responds accordingly.

The Israeli instructional program extends over hundreds of hours and has two aspects. General Enrichment (GE) is the instruction ordinarily given to these youths; it concentrates on arithmetic, Hebrew, history, and so on, plus field trips. For Feuerstein's trainees Instrumental Enrichment (IE) replaces 300 hours of the GE program. IE seeks to develop self-regulation—an understanding of the nature and criteria for intellectual effort plus a consciousness of, and willingness to, correct one's own procedures. (See also Brown & Campione, 1978).

Dialogue is the heart of the IE procedure—supporting, challenging, leading, recapitulating. Table 10.4 illustrates this with extracts from an 18-step interaction of tutor and beginning trainee. The first 9 steps led a child who had no conception of the task to a solution. When the right answer was given, the tester did not stop. She led the youth to explain why choice 6 was bad and then to pick the very worst response and give two reasons for rejecting it. Leading the student to be articulate about the reasons is considered highly important.

Six goals guide the teacher's effort on all the varied tasks (Feuerstein, 1980, pp. 115–144):

Strengthening any process identified as weak or faulty—for example, planning, use of time.
Developing vocabulary to describe concepts and relationships. (The student is pressed to describe all manipulations in words.)
Teaching habits of attack that apply to problems generally. (For example: "Find out what is needed!")
Promoting interest in intellectual challenges.
Producing self-observation, reflection, and inhibition of impulsive action.
Developing a concept that the self should actively generate information, not passively receive it.

Table 10.4. *Dialogue to orient a child to an easy matrix item*

Instructor's Question	Rationale	Subject's Response
1. "Look at this page. What must be done here?"	Request for definition of a problem.	"I don't know" (or incorrect or irrelevant response).
2. "Look at this rectangle. What do you see in it? Look at the bottom, and you will see 6 pieces."	Produce in the child a state of disequilibrium.	
3. "This square is gray. Is it all gray?"	Produce explicit analytic perception of a whole and a missing part.	"No. There is a white part. Some gray is missing."
4. "Yes. You are right. There is a missing part. What must you do about it?"	Orient the child toward the need to solve the problem.	"I have to color it gray."

[Steps 5 and 6 lead the subject to connect the six options to the task and say, "I can take one of these and put it here."]

7. "Yes. Right you are. Now could you show me the one that you could put in there to make it look like nothing is missing?"	Induce the child to compare on relevant dimensions (e.g., an irrelevant dimension in this task is the shape).	"Number two."
8. "It's almost good; it is the right color. But there is a better one."	Minimize the child's failure. Point to the need for a more appropriate answer.	
9. "If you want to find it, look at all the possible choices at the bottom of the page, from 1 to 6. Look at each one to see which one of them is the right one."	First attempt to produce systematic exploration, accompanied by gestural modeling.	"Four."
The examiner "models" systematic looking for the best answer among the various alternatives by pointing to each in order from 1 to 6.		

NOTE: The item is the matrix with the polka-dot pattern in Figure 7.5 (p. 218).
SOURCE: Adapted from Feuerstein, 1979, pp. 353–355.

Evidence on effects of IE was culled from files built up under field conditions. Impressive case studies of change in retarded, disturbed adolescents are offered. Those who had been school failures prior to the intervention became adult successes as manager, skilled printer, executive secretary, and so on (Feuerstein, 1979). A formal comparison of matched cases shows IE trainees ahead of GE-only trainees on several tests not used in the training. The difference on achievement tests was tiny; still, the IE trainees held their own in areas where GE trainees had many more hours of instruction. On vocabulary and verbal reasoning, IE outdid GE by very little. On EFT and spatial tests, the IE group was ahead by nearly 1 s.d. A similarly favorable result appeared on tests given during army induction, 2 years after the end of the training (Feuerstein, 1980). Ill-controlled as the studies have been, they undermine the once-popular belief that little or nothing can be done to improve mental functioning except, perhaps, by beginning in early childhood. Feuerstein's methods are now being introduced into the United States, and better evaluative reports should be forthcoming.

14. *Which elements of Feuerstein's program, if any, could reasonably be made a part of the elementary-school curriculum for average pupils in the United States, to be checked out along with what are ordinarily called "basics"?*
15. *When effects of* **Sesame Street** *were studied, it appeared that all children benefited, but that students from average homes benefited more than disadvantaged, slow developing children. Arguing that* **Sesame Street** *"widened the gap," Cook et al. (1975) questioned whether making the program freely available was in the best interest of society. What do you think?*
16. *In one of a series of behavioristic training plans, Staats and Burns (1981) trained preschool children to trace and then copy letters of the alphabet (6 hours of training). Account for each of the following results in terms of change in processes.*
    a. *The children became efficient; it took them only a few trials to learn letters introduced late in the training.*
    b. *On a WPPSI subtest where geometric shapes are to be copied, the scale score mean of controls changed from 10.7 to 11.2 from pretest to posttest; the experimentals changed from 10.6 to 13.0. (A similar gain on all subtests would raise the IQ 14 points.)*
    c. *On WPPSI mazes, the control means were 11.2 and 10.9 (a small decline). The experimental means were 10.7 and 12.7.*
17. *Do you think Staats and Burns were improving the child's "intelligence"?*

TESTING AND EDUCATIONAL DIFFERENTIATION

In a society where roles are differentiated, education is also differentiated. Sometimes the program is uniform for all students up to the age where weaker (or less wealthy) students drop out. Sometimes the program is branched long before the school-leaving age; thus, it has been common to route one fraction of adolescents into a high-level academic program and the remainder into a general or vocational track. Further differentiation occurs after high school as students sort themselves into more and less demanding postsecondary institutions and major fields. Especially in English and math, colleges and secondary schools sort students into advanced, regular, and remedial sections. In elementary schools the rates at which students are pushed along in the basic subjects depends on their performance.

Tests of general or scholastic aptitude can be used to sort entering pupils into fast and slow tracks and to identify some as handicapped. They can define eligibility for options open to "gifted" pupils, and they can count heavily in the choice among curricular options in high school. They play an obvious role in admission to college and to postgraduate training. The same decisions, of course, could be based entirely on achievement tests or on teachers' impressions. Although critics have complained about reliance on general mental tests, most of the issues—and most of the arguments in favor of systematic testing—would be the same if decisions were based on achievement tests. (Whatever test is used, information of other kinds, including the teacher's impression, should be taken into account.)

No one seems to think that the schools should hold all students to the same pace or teach them exactly the same courses. No one wants a return to the days when many students dropped out because they could not keep pace with average students of their age, and many were "held back" because they had not mastered the past year's lessons. Forcing a gangling 12-year-old into a seat in a third-grade class was disruptive for everyone. (New York City, however, is now using achievement tests to decide which pupils must "repeat a grade"; enrollments in New York are large enough to form whole classes of repeaters.)

"Tracking" or "streaming" refers especially to setting up "fast," "regular," and "slow" classrooms in each grade. Efforts to group students by readiness levels are condemned for their inflexibility and for the damage that results from labeling a person as "slow." (But children in a mainstreamed classroom are well aware that this or that classmate is "slow.")

Routing certain learners into a slow track guarantees that, after months or years have passed, the regular students will have learned far more than the "slow" group, simply because their lessons covered more ground. The slow pace of instruction offered—in all kindness—puts the student farther behind his agemates with each passing month and makes a transfer into an average class less and less practicable. The case of Alex (p. 244) and other such evidence indicates that students who at one age are not ready for brisk instruction may be fully capable at a later date.

Any sorting plan that does not provide for frequent shifts of classification, on the basis of updated judgments, should be challenged. Plans that place students in slow or fast levels for the whole school day are especially hard to reverse.

Decisions About Learners with Handicaps

The greatest sin in the treatment of the child who shows poor intellectual development is the common assumption that he is doomed forever to be substandard. This concern more than any other has produced support for "mainstreaming," for keeping the slow-learner or otherwise handicapped child with his agemates in most school activities (Hobbs, 1975; Heller *et al.*, 1982). Federal legislation (the Rehabilitation Act of 1973 and the 1974 law on handicapped children generally referred to as P.L. 94-142) has supported the concept not only of increasing the opportunities of persons with handicaps but of mainstreaming. Schools are expected to provide an "appropriate" education.

This calls for a case review using a wide range of information (often including an elaborate test battery but by no means limited to tests). Once the handicapped pupil's special needs are identified, an individual plan (IEP) is developed in cooperation with the parents and any professional advisers they bring in (Kennedy & McDaniels, in Travers & Light, 1982). Children who need a service the school cannot provide (speech therapy, for example) may be entitled to funds to support private treatment. Any diagnosis or plan is to be updated from time to time. I shall briefly discuss policies related to "learning disabilities" and "retardation." For recommendations on analysis of learners with physical, emotional, or cognitive handicaps, see the handbooks of Filskov and Boll (1982) and Reynolds and Gutkin (1982).

Learning disability. The "disability" category is essentially a residual; it makes a place for those whose difficulties are not understood. A national committee concerned with improving testing of the handicapped has this to say (Sherman & Robinson, 1982, p. 13):

> "Learning disabilities" is a very heterogeneous and ill-defined category that covers a wide range of difficulties in speaking, understanding speech, reading, and writing. The National Advisory Committee on Handicapped Children developed the following definition, which is used in the Education for All Handicapped Children Act (Wepman et al. 1976:301–302):
>
> *Children with special learning disabilities exhibit a disorder in one or more of the basic psychological processes involved in understanding or using spoken or written languages. These may be manifested in disorders of listening, thinking, talking, reading, writing, spelling, or arithmetic. They include conditions which have been referred to as perceptual handicaps, brain injury, minimal brain dysfunction, dyslexia, developmental aphasia, etc. They do not include learning problems which are due primarily to visual, hearing, or motor handicaps, to mental retardation, emotional disturbance, or to environmental disadvantages.*

There seems to be little consensus among physicians or educators about how to identify and classify learning-disabled children. The most commonly accepted indicator is a marked discrepancy between general learning ability, or "intelligence," as measured by standardized tests, and educational achievement, as measured by tests or grades. A typical working definition refers to a child of average intelligence who is about two grade levels behind in achievement. The difficulty, however, lies in determining that the achievement lag is not the result of such factors as poor motivation, emotional disturbance, environmental deficiencies, or simply poor instruction.

The confusing designation is bound to persist, if only because parents are pleased with the list of explanations for their child's lack of achievement ruled out by the Committee's definition. Children with weakness in a single subject may be classified as having a *specific* learning disability." Using, instead, a dignified label such as "dyslexia" removes none of the mystery.

Retardation. There was a time when children whose mental test performance fell below a level chosen by school officials were automatically placed in "special education." During a childhood stay in the United States, Jan Masaryk—later eminent as a Czech statesman—was classified that way. (A competent tester would have recognized his language problem and made a closer study.) We have come a long way from those practices, but no one is content with present practice.

Special classes have been called into question repeatedly, as in the case of *Larry P.* (495 F. Supp. 926 [1979]). Mental testing was the surface issue. Advocates for black children, including organizations of black psychologists, protested the use of mental testing as a part of the process whereby children were placed in classes for the "educationally mentally retarded (EMR)." The proportion of black children so classified was shockingly high. The heart of the matter was that the classification seemed to be doing harm, not good. California policy directed teachers to assume that it was "impossible" for EMR children to learn the content of regular lessons. Teachers were to develop the minimal skills for low-level employment and survival in the community. An EMR pupil was almost never returned to the regular classroom; understandably, the judge's decision said over and over that these were "dead end" classes and that a child's rights were violated if his EMR placement was invalid. The overstated directive made the state's practices hard to defend. How could one cope with "the validation burden of showing that it is impossible for those who score low to profit from the regular classes even with remedial instruction" (words from the court opinion, rearranged). Mercer, as a prosecution witness, called the regulations an instance of the conception that retarded persons suffer from an incurable disease or disorder.

The judge ruled that California could not continue to use the Wechsler and similar tests in deciding which black children were to go into EMR classes. (He did not question their use with whites.) Testing specialists called in by the state could not convince the judge that the classification was valid. Skills of retarded children do not grow faster in special classes than in regular classes, according to comparisons across school systems with different policies.

Some psychologists have criticized aspects of the ruling (Bersoff, in Reynolds & Gutkin, 1982; Lambert, in Glaser & Bond, 1981). The criticism most pertinent here is that reducing the amount of information available makes the case review less adequate. Moreover, banning tests does not, in itself, benefit black children. For several years while *Larry P.* was in the courts, California schools were enjoined from mental testing of blacks. The number of black children classified as EMR did not decline in most school districts. (The percentage of blacks among those given the EMR label, in years with and without mental testing, were 51 and 50 in Los Angeles, 85 and 84 in Oakland, 79 and 43 in San Francisco, 21 and 34 in San Diego.)

Mainstreaming is not advocated for the tiny fraction of children who, intellectually, are markedly outside the range of the school population. Figure 10.5 is representative of current thinking about those children whose limitations do not keep them out of school altogether. As you can see, the recommended plan puts a heavy burden of proof on whoever recommends special class placement.

Fitting Instruction to the Child

Many school systems give a standardized test of general ability or general achievement early in the school year. One purpose is to advise teachers so that they will demand neither too much nor too little of their pupils. It is on the basis of such expectations that a teacher paces the instruction (standing ready to give special assistance to the slow and to challenge the able). Expectations are formed by cumulative experience in daily activities and by records on teacher-made tests, as well as by standard tests of achievement and ability. There are two particular hazards in the process: teachers may have biases (for example, expecting intellectual inadequacy from unruly boys) and the expectations may not be updated as new evidence comes in.

Teacher expectancies. Standard tests given at the start of the year—and especially "intelligence" tests—have been much criticized. It is alleged that once his score labels a child as bright or dull, the teacher pitches lessons to that level even when daily performance contradicts the expectation.

Observations by Rist (1970) show how teacher expectations lead to miseducation; but an important part of his tale is that in these classes impartial tests were ignored. Testing could not prevent improper teaching, but it could have corrected some of the teachers' false impressions. Rist observed a group of black children, taught by successive black teachers, from school

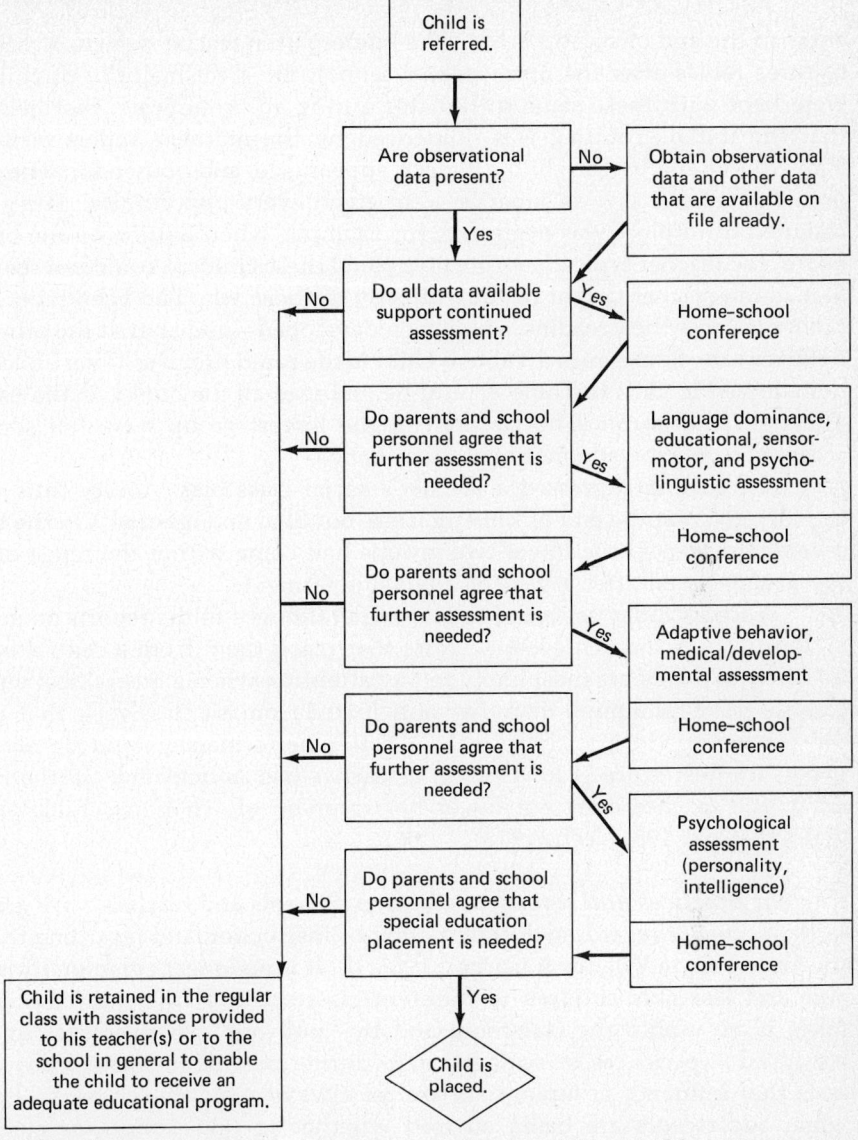

Figure 10.5. Proposed steps in evaluating a pupil referred for possible assignment to special education.
Source: Tucker, 1977, p. 96.

entry to the end of second grade. The kindergarten teacher assigned children to three tables after the first week of school; the great majority of children were kept with these same trackmates during all three years. Rist believed that the initial grouping was influenced by the mother's report on home background and by the child's dialect, appearance, and body odor. The children the teacher saw as superior were given every opportunity. The group assigned third place was neglected; for example, when writing on the blackboard, the teacher typically wrote on a panel these children could not see. The first-grade teacher taught reading directly to those who had been favored in kindergarten—their readiness had been developed—and started the others at a slower rate. Sometimes a Table B child made rapid progress. That child was not allowed to shift to Table A until he had read all the books on the list for Table B. And so on. The children in the lowest group were not socially accepted and showed emotional disturbance.

The sorting expressed a teacher's social-class bias. Ability tests were actually given at the end of kindergarten, but filed and ignored. On the tests, several children in the lower two groups had come within the range of the top group—even after a year of adverse treatment.

Teachers today seem not to give much thought to the reports on general-ability tests and achievement tests that reach them from a central office. Teachers say they are most likely to pay attention when a mental test reports a better score for a pupil than they anticipated from his classwork; that alerts the teacher to the possibility that a better performance could be elicited. When the test score is lower than a teacher had anticipated, on the other hand, the teacher does not lower her estimate of what the child can do (Salmon-Cox, 1981; Yeh, 1978).

Current practices and recommendations. Schools and teachers vary greatly in their policies regarding differentiation of instruction and regarding testing (B. Anderson, in Wigdor & Garner, 1982, II). It is no longer common to assign able and less able children to different classrooms. Rather, differentiation takes place within the classroom and by "pull-out" arrangements to give advanced experiences or remedial help during part of the school day. The tests that influence groupings are almost always achievement tests—except when adolescents are being advised whether to take college-preparatory courses.

Instructional grouping within a classroom is common. There will be groups in reading or arithmetic or groups working on science projects of varying complexity. Such grouping allows extra time for a pupil who needs a slow pace, as well as special assistance in one school subject, or allows a pupil to advance rapidly in some subjects. Moreover, frequent regrouping is possible. Such arrangements are not easy for teachers to manage; they are facilitated by team teaching, by use of more advanced students as tutors, and by availability of simplified and advanced teaching materials. Standardized tests contribute little to this kind of instructional planning. When grouping is flexible, test scores collected in September become almost irrelevant to the decisions of November; by that time the teacher has detailed information from the pupil's handling of daily assignments.

Testing for microlevel decisions is increasing. Some parts of the school curriculum can be reduced to small elements, for example, recognizing where a semicolon may properly be used and where not. A checkoff test can demonstrate that a student has "mastered" that skill (though mastery comes in many degrees). And tests of this sort can be developed in numerous forms (with or without the computer); the learner can test himself and judge his own adequacy—see 36, 299. Published tests administered once or twice a year can report scores on subsets of items; the scores for individuals are unreliable, but the teacher who finds 40 per cent of the class at a low level on punctuation and only 20 per cent at a low level on capitalization will take that into account in daily instruction (see p. 353).

General mental tests have identified many children who possessed exceptional general ability but whose school records were no more than satisfactory. Many such pupils are not challenged and do not realize that they can achieve more. Nonroutine assignments often stimulate such children.

Also, there may be a significant message in the standing of the class as a whole on a test of general ability. When last year's teacher set too easy a pace, the group will probably have a lower standing in the conventional subjects than in the abilities that develop more spontaneously. The message to step up the pace comes through clearly. But teachers ought also to try to promote fluid reasoning. (See p. 257.)

Underdeveloped skills of information processing should concern teachers just as much as underdeveloped skill in computation. No one cares about tasks such as block design, matrices, embedded figures, or scrambled sentences; they are not "subject matter" worth teaching. But skills of analysis, systematic search, self-checking, and so on, are valuable. Tests of fluid ability would remind teachers of that part of their responsibility—if we had not fallen into the habit of regarding standings on such tests as indivisible composites, somehow fixed in advance. Obviously, we want teachers to think about specific tasks and processes, not about the remote construct of "factor score Gf." This concept of information-processing abilities and habits as being plural and developable is manifest in a test such as CIRCUS (p. 227) even though it is measuring process at least as much as "subject matter."

18. *With respect to English usage, what aspects of the curriculum cannot be reduced to small elements to be checked off as "mastered" or "not mastered"?*

Evaluation of Assignment Schemes

Educators and policymakers would like hard evidence as to the effectiveness of alternative plans for differentiation. Many comparative studies have attempted to assess whether students make greater progress with or without tracking. Such studies are nearly uninterpretable because of a dilemma in measurement (Leinhardt & Seewald, 1981).

The evaluator has to decide what accomplishments to measure. Some reason that the only fair basis for comparison is an achievement test confined to the lessons covered by all the sections, fast and slow. Others favor a test over the full reach of lessons covered by *any* of the groups. The first plan—testing on what everyone studies—gives fast sections no credit for the breadth of their learning. Fast students in a fast section probably spend less time polishing elementary skills than equally fast students in a wide-range class. The first testing plan, therefore, is likely to conclude that ability grouping is bad for abler students and beneficial for weak students. The comprehensive test of the second plan tends to show that even weak students in a wide-range class have learned more than their ability-grouped counterparts because the wide-range class exposed them to more of the test content.

One solution is to build the test on the second plan but to make an analytic comparison. When students at a particular ability level are compared across treatments, some competences will have developed fastest under one condition and some under the other. These crisscrossing indicators show effects much more truthfully than any summary statistic. The summary statistic hides within it a value judgment as how heavily each specific outcome should count. The first test plan accepts the concealed value judgment that only the most elementary lessons should count; a total score on the second kind of test counts supplementary topics on the same scale as basics. If the full profile of contrasts were laid out, citizens would argue about the weightings, as they should. "Which is the better educational plan?" is as much judgmental as scientific.

A test that has predictive validity may be useless for classification. To justify teaching individuals in different ways, an aptitude-treatment interaction has to be demonstrated (or, at least, presumed). Educational psychologists conduct experiments following the plan suggested in Chapter 5 as one way of developing ideas about "aptitude." Such experiments are more a source of insight than a source of rules for teaching.

Consider the distinction between verbal and spatial abilities. One hypothesis is that "high V" students will learn more from verbal presentations and "high S" students will profit from visual presentations. The findings are mixed: some studies show that trend, and some show just the opposite. Diagrams in text materials may place a load on spatial abilities, but if they are easily perceived, they may lighten the burden of visualizing and spatial reasoning (Cronbach & Snow, 1981; Gustafsson, 1976). The same is true of words. Given a lucid verbal explanation, persons with low verbal ability can recall it; a complex explanation communicates only to high-V students, but it may leave them with a deeper understanding.

Ideally, we would be able to assess aptitude or learning styles and then teach the same school subject in different ways to fit different students' patterns. Research on aptitude-treatment interaction does not justify that kind of practical application (Cronbach & Snow, 1981). The evidence does suggest that teaching step-by-step, patiently and with regular feedback, is advantageous for less able students. Such teaching sometimes causes superior students to achieve *less* than they would from instruction that presents a greater demand for analysis. (Personality variables seem to interact with instruction more strongly than ability variables; see p. 499.)

19. *In what way can a teacher make use of the conclusion that having to organize subject matter for themselves benefits some students and handicaps others?*
20. *If a test were used formally to divide students between instructional methods A and B, would Test 1 or 2 work better? The following facts are available for equivalent groups assigned to each treatment: the s.d. of outcome Y is the same in both treatments;*

r_{Y1} is 0.4 in A and 0.0 in B.
r_{Y2} is 0.3 in A and -0.3 in B.

ACHIEVEMENT TESTS IN EDUCATIONAL MANAGEMENT

Anyone working in or with schools should be aware of the role tests play in management. Tests serve as a feedback device, that is, as a means of telling pupils and teachers how much has been learned. When someone in authority can see the test scores, tests become a means of exerting pressure. Much is said nowadays about "accountability"—of the schools to the public, of individual teachers to their superiors, and of school officials to the central governments that supply funds. When someone in authority decides that a test shall be given, one principal reason is to press persons at lower levels to strive harder to develop whatever competence the test measures. This statement is true of Regents' examinations imposed on high school seniors in New York State, of test reports that districts receiving federal funds must send to Washington, and of any teacher's quizzes and examinations.

An endless array of topics compete for time in the classroom. There are pressures to cover new subject matter (the Third World, effects of drugs) along with pressures to concentrate on so-called "basics." Authority over curriculum is divided. The United States has traditions of local control of education and of respect for the teacher's judgment, but state and federal legislators desire to set priorities. Tests are one way to influence what will receive emphasis.

For a teacher, tests are an integral part of instruction. Telling a class "what will be on the test" causes them to spend their time on those topics. Marking standards tell what level of performance is respectable, and comments on papers point out the features that make a performance excellent or inadequate. Students take in all these cues. Indeed, they go to great lengths to foresee how they will be evaluated so that they will not "waste time" on what is not to be tested. When a higher authority imposes a test on the class, the teacher plays the same game. It is common to set aside the usual curriculum during the weeks preceding the Regents' exam, to force-feed students with whatever appears in the test outline. The student who seems likely to fail a "minimum competency examination" is given a concentrated dosage of the skills that test covers. In each of these instances, "teaching (and studying) for the test" is precisely what was wanted by whoever imposed the examination.

Concentrating student and teacher effort on what will be tested is good insofar as the test content is worth the effort. Sometimes the influence of tests distorts the curriculum. The chemistry teacher may say that a main purpose of the course is to teach "scientific method," but if the examination questions are limited to technical terms, facts, and such skills as balancing equations, the students will not study whatever the reading materials have to say about the processes of science. The teacher of literature may say that she aims to help students develop their own tastes and standards of criticism—but she will discourage that development if tests give credit for parroting *her* opinions about works of literature. An experiment that set out to compare the effectiveness of several sets of teaching materials in primary arithmetic provides a further example. The test on addition included not only sets of numbers lined up vertically but also tasks in horizontal form: $3 + 2 + 3 = ?$ When, in the first year of the study, children found such items difficult, one of the competing teams rewrote its lessons to provide practice on the horizontal format. They had originally considered horizontal addition unimportant, so the change of emphasis may have been educationally unwise.

The Role of Objectives

Educators choosing tests do pay attention to content in the narrow sense of the word. They would be critical of a chemistry test that contains many items on the rare-earth elements when the instruction barely touches on them. They would be critical of a history test that emphasizes the Reconstruction period and neglects the modern Civil Rights movement. And so on. But much that the student is intended to learn cannot be identified with particular chapters of a text or particular segments of the course of study. Understanding the nature of science or of literature or of historical change—themes such as these cut across all the topics of a course, yet may not appear at all in a "content" outline.

For this reason, educational testers amplify the notion of content validity by asking how well the test tasks cover the "objectives" of instruction. Many of the most important educational objectives—intended outcomes—are generalized concepts, attitudes, and skills. Students who acquire the ability and habit of identifying the bias of a writer can apply that learning to almost anything they read, and it can be acquired as a by-product of instruction with almost any reading materials. Likewise in science or history, general concepts may be acquired by classes, each of which studies *its* local geology, for example, or *its* local community history. The evaluation of student progress ought to be concerned more with main ideas than with specific lesson content.

Ralph Tyler (1950; E. R. Smith & Tyler, 1942) was particularly responsible for the emphasis on "behavioral objectives." The function of education is to change behavior, not merely to equip the person with answers to a limited number of fixed questions. If educators and citizens say what they wish graduates to be able (and motivated) to do, mapping what graduates can do (and actually do) identifies where the educational program has succeeded. Not all the evidence can or should come from tests. What students read after they leave the course, what arguments they advance in a conversation about political matters, and how faithfully they discharge responsibilities—those kinds of evidence may contribute as much to an assessment as evidence from set questions. But here let us concentrate on knowledge and skill, which lend themselves to conventional testing.

The adjective *behavioral* forces informants to describe objectives concretely. "I want graduates to understand scientific method" is an ambiguous reply. The inquiry should be pushed further: "What would a person do or say that would indicate that his understanding is satisfactory?" The informant might say any of the following things:

- Students will express confidence in statements about the planets that are attributed to an astronomer and express doubt about statements attributed to an astrologer.
- Students, when trying to measure the solubility of a chemical in water, follow accurately the directions in the laboratory manual.
- When a student is asked to read the report of an investigation and comment on its soundness, he notes and mentions how the investigator's wishes or preconceptions may have influenced the report or mentions precautions taken against such bias which increase the credibility of the report.

You can see that each suggestion implies a different kind of test. Educators would disagree as to which gives relevant evidence on command of scientific method. Having reduced the discussion to behavioral terms was valuable just because it permits pointed disagreement about the appropriate test. No one could have disagreed about the lofty original objective.

Behavioral objectives can be subdivided finely, and then the desired responses can be directly taught. This is easiest to do for factual knowledge and tangible skills. Skill in map reading, for example, can be subdivided into specifics such as this one: "The students, given a map in Mercator projection, with marks indicating longitude at 10-degree intervals, can estimate the longitude of a point on the map to within one degree." For those aspects of learning to which it applies, listing detailed objectives can guarantee a high degree of correspondence between the description of what is to be taught and a set of test items.

Objectives having to do with subtler interpretation or with creative problem solving cannot be specified so tangibly. One test outline, for example, includes statements such as this among objectives for which items are to be written (and subscores reported): "The student will analyze the feelings, traits, or motives of characters in a passage." This is a useful reminder that reading comprehension goes beyond facts and events, but it does not "specify" themes, levels of difficulty, or standards for judging a response. It is impossible to say whether a set of items represents the objective adequately. Nor is it sensible to say that anyone reaches "mastery" of such an open-ended task. Behavioral objectives, then, help to bring the process of test planning down to earth, but they are no cure-all.

In a debate about educational evidence, a professional may ask whether a test that obviously covers basic skills in mathematics has *curricular* validity. The questioner is asking one of two things:

> Does the balance of content and difficulty in the test match what the teacher or teachers actually taught?
>
> Does the balance of content and difficulty in the test match what planners in the school system said their mathematics instruction should teach?

Educational planners in a school district may have good reasons to emphasize some topics more than schools elsewhere do—and some topics less. A test used to determine whether the plans are working out ought to have curricular validity in the second sense. Sometimes the lessons do not cover all that was planned because the plans were too ambitious or suitable teaching materials were not found. Both teachers and pupils are disturbed when the test includes what the lessons neglected. Reducing the test to what the lessons covered adequately is fair for some purposes, so long as it does not serve to hide the fact that instruction fell short of the plans.

Item banks are beginning to provide an answer to the desire to use professionally developed items while fitting the test to the local curriculum. The publisher supplies an inventory of the kinds of competence and topical knowledge for which items have been banked, and a committee of teachers or school officials decides how many items to use from each category. Although such a tailor-made test cannot have norms in the usual sense, the publisher has tried the component items on more or less representative samples of students. The record of difficulty from this tryout provides some basis for interpreting results in the local district.

Interpreting and Fostering Individual Development 351

21. *An English teacher takes up metaphors with an eighth-grade class. What might be some reasonable behavioral objectives for that instruction? Which could be investigated with choice-response questions?*
22. *Using the area of consumer economics as an example, illustrate instructional objectives concerned with maximum performance and objectives concerned with typical behavior.*
23. *Where an evaluator is to report on the performance of a group of students (not on students individually), are printed questions adequate to assess the kinds of behavior listed in response to question 22?*
24. *Three specific objectives were listed as possible aspects of understanding scientific method. Which one or more of them represents your concept of a proper aim in science courses?*
25. *"After reading a scene from* Merchant of Venice, *the student will be able to suggest two alternative answers to the question, 'How did Shylock feel during this scene?' " From the viewpoint of a test developer, how does this statement differ from the objective ". . . will analyze feelings of characters"? How could the objective be stated so that it does not press the teacher to spend time on* Merchant of Venice?

Standard Tests

Traditionally, standard achievement tests have been designed to represent the common-denominator content of school curricula across the country. The test authors examine courses of study for (say) grades 4 to 6 and identify subskills or topics that are nearly universal. Test development has generally been successful for tool skills, including language usage, spelling, reading, vocabulary, arithmetic and general mathematics, and map-reading and library skills. Although the tests cannot include all the subskills that some teachers and parents consider important, what is included is a part of almost every school's curriculum. The tests meet the needs of administrators trying to keep track of the system as a whole, of the problems of schools within a district, and of curricular areas where the district may need to make a special push.

The reports sent to each pupil's home and the reports on the district as a whole perform an important public relations function. All such reports, however, are open to misinterpretation (pp. 113, 254ff.). Moreover, the schools have responsibilities and aims that reach far beyond the basic skills, and one risk in standardized testing is that teachers will focus on the tool skills to the point of neglecting the remainder of the pupil's development. Tests covering the rest of the curriculum would provide a desirable balance of pressures.

The National Assessment of Educational Progress has attempted to provide a balanced picture of the full range of the schools' collective accomplishment. To do this, it has tested in all the following areas: reading and literature, writing, math, science, citizenship and social studies, music, art, and career planning and development of vocational skills. Questions have reached beyond facts, skills, and problem solving to questions about experiences and actions. Thus a high school senior may be asked if he has ever written a letter on any policy to an official or a newspaper and also asked whether he has visited an art museum in the past year. The assessment produces several test booklets, draws a sample of schools and a sample of students at ages 9, 13, and 17 within the schools, and has each student respond to one booklet. Instead of reporting on single students or schools, the report covers geographic regions or types of community or types of students. The public is told what proportion of students succeed on particular items. Also, it is told what proportion of items on a certain skill or topic were passed by 9-year-olds now and in a similar survey 4 years earlier. (Several reports are produced each year; the best way to locate information is through the ERIC system available in many reference libraries.) Unfortunately, policymakers and the public have been far more interested in the three or four basic skills than in the remainder of the assessment (Wirtz & Lapointe, 1982). Collecting balanced information, then, is beside the point if the public is not sensitive to the full range of school responsibilities.

Standard tests in high school subjects such as American government are available, and some teachers use them as a cross-check on their own more informal assessments. Tests of "general educational development" in particular fields have succeeded at the high school level. These tests—in social studies, literature, science, and other areas—present passages test takers are unlikely to have seen previously and ask them to make inferences, criticize arguments, and otherwise exercise the intellectual skills *any* course of study in that field should develop. Much the same strategy is seen in Advanced Placement testing, to which the next section will turn.

Some achievement tests for elementary grades and high school attempt rather unsuccessfully to survey achievement in broad fields. Understanding of the social world is surely important, for example, and is included in curricula everywhere. The curricula are not at all standard, and, therefore, a standard test fits no local curriculum. The publishers string together items on topics that appear frequently in courses of study. One of the prominent tests for the middle grades contains 60 social-studies items (multiple-choice) whose heterogeneity is illustrated by these paraphrases:

> On which continent is Spanish the language of many countries?
> A law Congress has passed can be overturned by what group?
>
> (Silhouettes of four skylines are shown.)
>
> Which shows a dead volcano?
>
> (A chart of average incomes, for 1930 through 1975, is shown.)
>
> If the trend continues, what level will income probably reach in 1990?
>
> (Four black men are named.)
>
> Which of these men won a Nobel Prize for peace?

Obviously, such a test lacks unity and must operate entirely on the sampling principle.

Many recent standard tests of tool skills shred a complex skill into narrow subskills and offer "criterion-referenced" or "mastery" scores for each of these. Such a label usually implies that the scoring service will flag any subskill on which the student's percentage-correct score falls below some specified level. Figure 10.6 displays items from two sub-subtests of Reading Yardsticks, which is one of several current instruments of this character. In all, 40 scores are reported for sub-subtests; testing time is about 5 minutes

---

Syllabication: Identify the number of syllables in a word of 1–6 syllables.

Choose the answer that tells how many syllables are in the given word.

1. spirit	(A) 1	(B) 2	(C) 3	(D) 4
3. route	(A) 1	(B) 2	(C) 3	(D) 4
6. especially	(A) 3	(B) 4	(C) 5	(D) 6
8. imaginary	(A) 3	(B) 4	(C) 5	(D) 6

Possessives: Choose the correct translation of a possessive phrase, discriminating the object owned from the owner of the object, a singular possessive from a single plural, or a singular possessive from a plural possessive.

11. The kitten's muddy paws made everyone laugh.
 What was muddy?
 (A) the paws of the kitten   (C) the kitten
 (B) the paws of the kittens   (D) the kittens

13. The trains' whistles kept Pat awake all night.
 What kept Pat awake?
 (A) the whistles of the trains   (B) the whistle of the train
 (C) the whistles of the train   (D) the whistle of the trains

15. The _____ flames flickered and died in the wind.
 Which form of the word <u>candle</u> is correct in this sentence?
 (A) candle's   (B) candles   (C) candle   (D) candles'

18. The first pitch bounced off the _____ glove.
 Which form of the word <u>catcher</u> is correct in this sentence?
 (A) catchers'   (B) catchers   (C) catcher's   (D) catcher

Figure 10.6. Items from tests of specific objectives in ability to analyze language. *Source:* These items are taken from two 8-item sections of Level 13 of Reading Yardsticks, Form 1. Copyright © 1981 by The Riverside Publishing Company and reproduced by permission. The typography has been altered in several respects; most important, in the actual test more white space separates items, and the phrases in items such as 11 and 13 are arranged vertically for easier comparison.

per objective, on average. The items are intended to be fairly easy for most students in the grade tested; the main purpose is to signal gaps that should be repaired. Prior to the scoring, the school district specifies the level below which scores are to be flagged. It might pick 40 per cent for all subtests, or a figure as high as 70 per cent. The level of this test intended for grade 7 has four main sections; the objectives in Figure 10.6 fall within the "Structural Analysis" section. For the sections, both raw scores and percentiles are reported.

Identifying the number of syllables in a word probably is a unified ability; a pupil who has learned to listen for syllables should report the right number for almost any word he can read and pronounce. The interpretation of possessives, on the other hand, is divisible—as the statement of the objective indicates. Some sub-subscores refer to broad domains, for example, ability to "interpret information given in a table." The score comes from just three questions referring to a single table. When the test has flagged a pupil as weak in an area, a large task of diagnosis remains for the teacher. And the signal system is crude; a good many pupils who get 2 items out of 3 correct are no better than those who miss 2 out of 3.

26. *If, at the end of the year, a fourth-grade class does poorly on the social-studies test described (compared to its standing on achievement in tool skills), should that information influence how the teacher covers social studies next year? If so, how?*
27. *Achievement batteries may be given either in early fall or late spring and have norms for both dates. What purposes can be served by fall testing? Spring testing? (Assume that students move to a new teacher at the end of the spring term.)*
28. *With two 8-item subtests, the standard error of measurement of the difference in percentage-correct scores is approximately 25 percentage points. Why should a teacher be mindful of this fact?*
29. *A teacher (or even a committee of students) could easily make up dozens of tests of either objective in Figure 10.6. What advantages or disadvantages does the* standardized *test for these objectives have?*

An Advanced Placement Test

Constructive use of testing in educational management is particularly well illustrated by the advanced-placement program of the College Entrance Examination Board. A student works with a teacher's help, possibly in a small group, to study some field not regularly taught in his high school. At the end of the year he takes a test set by the board. If he succeeds, the college he attends will probably exempt him from the equivalent college course and allow him to enroll directly in a more advanced course.

For each course, the board distributes a prospectus to interested schools. I shall use the European History description for 1983 and 1984 as example. Three pages describe and outline the range of topics; major events and trends from 1450 to the present will be covered, and cultural and social history will be weighted as much as political history. The remaining 25 pages consist of test questions, with brief information on how the test is graded. The student is told that passing 60 per cent of the multiple-choice items is normally considered acceptable. These items are illustrative; other items will of course make up the official test. The items in Figure 10.7 show that this test operates on a sampling principle. Most of the factual questions, however, press for comprehension of trends and concepts, not sheer recall of names and dates. Other items ask for interpretation of a map coded to show population change

---

The greatest beneficiary in the Thirty Years' War (1618–1648) was
  A. France
  B. Spain
  C. Russia
  D. Sweden
  E. the Holy Roman Empire

During the seventeenth century, developments in science served as an incentive for which of the following?
  A. The universe was perceived in increasingly mechanistic terms.
  B. Intolerance reached new heights.
  C. The Catholic Church created the Inquisition to combat new ideas.
  D. People became more religious.
  E. Major changes in industrial technology occurred.

The economist John Maynard Keynes did which of the following?
  A. He urged governments to increase mass purchasing power in times of deflation.
  B. He defended the principles of the Versailles Treaty.
  C. He helped to establish the British Labor party.
  D. He prophesied the inevitable economic decline of capitalism.
  E. He originated the concept of marginal utility to replace the labor theory of value.

All of the following statements about the Renaissance are true EXCEPT:
  A. The preeminence of medieval Scholasticism was challenged.
  B. The papacy became increasingly ascetic, promoting mystical contact with God.
  C. People looked increasingly back to the classical period for ideas and models.
  D. Wealthy merchant princes patronized the arts.
  E. There was interest in broadening the range of education.

Figure 10.7. Multiple-choice questions on European history.
Source: From Advanced Placement Course Description, History. College Entrance Examination Board, 1982. Reprinted by permission of Educational Testing Service, the copyright owner.

in France and interpretation of a political cartoon. The effect of these exhibits is to encourage wide reading with an attempt to integrate. They do not identify topics for cramming.

Essay questions are included because many college instructors are skeptical of choice-response tests and because such questions point the student's preparation in desired directions. A conventional essay test asks the student to write on one of six topics, each as broad as "European Liberalism in the Nineteenth Century." The student is to bring specific examples to bear—another encouragement to wide reading. The other essay is to respond to a "document based question" on witchcraft. The documents begin with the testimony of a midwife about an alleged confession of one Walpurga Hausmannin, progress through a quotation from Luther (". . . witches are the Devil's whores who steal milk, . . . and force people into love and immorality. . . ."), ending with a table of demographic statistics on suspected witches—over 2000 words in all. The examinee is to identify three major reasons for the persecution of individuals as witches and use the sources to justify the answer. This is a prime example of testing a generalized ability, one that students must prepare for by engaging in historical interpretation and not by digesting history others have written.

Beyond the brochure, a teacher can obtain further document-based questions from past years and a report from the reading of the previous year's examination. The report lists the main themes found in the documents, shows the rating scale used to define the several levels of adequacy of answers, and reprints a student response that received a high mark and another that was rated inadequate. The fact that a committee of high school and college teachers developed the overall plan and standards makes it likely that the plan, announcement, student-teacher collaboration, examination, grading and report will converge to serve the intended purposes. The external examination transforms the high school teacher, in the student's eyes, from a taskmaster and standard setter to a collaborator whose only responsibility is to help the student achieve. The elaborate procedure is made necessary by the fact that colleges have agreed to make an important decision about a student with whom they have no personal experience.

30. *What would be gained or lost if students and teachers were supplied a file of questions three times as long as the actual test and promised that all test questions will be taken from that file?*
31. *What features of the advanced placement plan would be appropriate when*
    a. *A state imposes an examination that all students must pass to receive a high school diploma?*
    b. *A national board in a medical specialty requires practitioners to demonstrate up-to-date knowledge before their certification is renewed?*
32. *What is to be said for and against setting up an "external examiner" for all the principal first-year courses in a college? (Some colleges have done this by establishing an examiner's office that prepares tests much as the College Board examiners do.)*

Constructed-Response vs. Choice-Response

In the discussion of advanced placement we returned to a topic introduced in Chapter 2, the adequacy of choice-response tests. The fact that mass testing programs rely on them is a recurrent complaint.

Two somewhat distinct issues are to be considered. One has to do with the role of the test in directing teaching and learning; the other, with the statistical correlates of scores. Warning students that they will be expected to organize facts to support an argument they have devised seems very likely to lead them to practice that as part of their study of history. Probably no defender of choice-response tests believes that all educational activity should consist of convergent thinking. Solving a problem requires a sharp-eyed comparison of alternatives, but generating reasonable alternatives is a distinct art, learned through another kind of practice.

The statistical question is whether persons who are identified as superior by a multiple-choice test are also the ones picked as superior by a constructed-response test. This is not necessarily the case; the preceding paragraph argued that a person might sharpen the convergent skills and neglect the divergent ones. The evidence, however, says that such discrepancies are rare. The correlation of essay test with multiple-choice test is usually about as high as the test reliabilities permit.

A particularly striking result comes from an objective test of skills used in writing (the student is to select clear expressions as well as grammatically correct ones). The choice-response test correlates well with a careful summary of the quality of writing a student shows during a course. Indeed, it correlates higher with the summary than does the mark assigned to a composition the student produces as a writing specimen (Breland, 1979a). Hogan and Mishler (1980) find similar evidence on writing in grades 3 and 8. Also relevant is an unpublished College Board report on a recent Advanced Placement test in calculus: free-response and choice-response sections correlate 0.85; that is as high as the correlation between two tests of either kind.

Psychology students have been asked to offer hypotheses to explain research results. The students who produce responses judged superior are also superior on a test in which they rate hypotheses the tester supplied. The free-response form, however, displayed the fluency with which students formed hypotheses; that divergent ability differed among students who were equally good at the convergent task (Ward *et al.*, 1980).

When the level of proficiency of a student or group is at issue, constructed responses ought to be a part of the evaluation. That is obviously true of handwriting; of artistic, musical, and literary composition; and of the ability to speak French. It is probably true of the planning of experiments, the translation of French, and the criticism of works of art. In selective admissions on the basis of general academic abilities, however, a multiple-choice test that deals with generalized intellectual skills appears to be entirely acceptable.

11
Personnel Selection

When a firm wants to fill Job X, it would be convenient if the boss could look in a test catalog, find a test labeled "Test of Aptitude for Job X," and begin using the test for selection. Establishing a sound selection program is not so easy. Tests with similar names measure different things, and sometimes the test intended to predict Job X predicts less well than a test made for another purpose. A job demands many abilities, so more than one test may be needed. And, on the other hand, it is pointless to test what all applicants can do or can learn quickly on the job.

Chapter 11 centers on selection of employees, describing older practice and also emerging developments endorsed by Division 14 in its *Principles* (Division 14, 1980) or by the Committee on Ability Tests (Wigdor & Garner, 1982). The content pertains to educational selection and planning, to decisions about clinical treatment, and to testing of military personnel, as well as to employment. The first section of the chapter includes most of the ideas that are important to nonprofessionals as well as professionals. The second section, beginning on page 394, is primarily an extension of the argument for professionals who select and classify people, but every reader should note the discussion of human judgment at the very end.

SECTION 1. BASIC CONCEPTS AND ISSUES

Personnel workers speak of the ideal system as one in which there is a match between person and job. This calls for more than a sorting process—it may call for changes in the person and in the job. Sound management integrates selection with recruitment of applicants, design of jobs, training, performance appraisal, staff development, promotion and transfer, and so on. Attracting a large group of applicants increases the contribution selection can make; improving training or reducing turnover makes selection less necessary. Another "system" aspect is the extent to which managers' misuses of predictive information can undercut validity. On this and other realities of selection practice, see Thayer's (1977) history of the Aptitude Index Battery (p. 466). Note that whereas the term *selection* suggests an accept/reject decision *by the institution*, the applicant also makes judgments about his suitability and probable satisfaction. Processes of recruitment, selection, and assignment, therefore, can profitably contain a large element of guidance ("job previews").

The developer of selection procedures is concerned with constructs that describe people and jobs, with test content, and with evidence from criteria. Although work that proceeds along only one of these lines can produce an acceptable, defensible selection plan, balanced use of all three reduces cost and generates greater understanding. This chapter gives much space to criterion-oriented methods just because there is an elaborate lore to communicate. A user of selection procedures who will not carry out follow-up studies should nonetheless know the logic of validation. Understanding how relevance is established helps her judge how much to trust a procedure and helps her defend her practices.

DEVELOPING A SELECTION PROCEDURE

In the typical empirical study, one starts by choosing a number of tests for tryout, next observes how well each of them predicts, and then devises a plan for translating scores into decisions. Psychologists are advised to devote considerable initial thought to the characteristics of the job and the criteria so as to decide what kinds of tests are promising (Division 14, 1980).

There are eight steps in traditional prediction research. (I speak of the sequence as "traditional" to hint that other procedures can be added.)

1. Analyzing the job to form hypotheses as to characteristics making for success or failure.
2. Determining that a study of reasonable cost will produce adequately persuasive evidence.

3. Choosing (or devising) tests expected to measure the listed characteristics.
4. Administering the tests to workers already on the job or to new applicants.
5. Collecting reports on the adequacy of these workers.
6. Analyzing how test scores and information on the worker's background relate to success on the job.
7. Choosing an operational selection plan.
8. Compiling later data, regularly or periodically, to check on the continuing soundness of the plan.

Step 2, important though it is, can be disposed of in a few words before we proceed. Sometimes there are so few vacancies that it would take years to compile stable statistics; sometimes no way is found to collect trustworthy criterion data (e.g., because employees are scattered); and so on. A selection procedure then has to be defended by a wholly indirect argument.

Job Analysis

Analysis of a job seeks to identify personal qualities that contribute to or limit success. The search is for KSAOs, the trade jargon says, referring to knowledge, skills, abilities, and "other characteristics" (including attitudes and habits). Job analysis can be systematic but not machinelike. The analyst brings psychological theory and her own insight to bear in developing a theory of the job. Several styles of job analysis have been developed (Dunnette, 1976; McCormick, 1979); they vary in cost and in the degree of expertise required of the analyst. Experimental comparisons do not show one technique to be consistently superior.

A first step is preliminary definition of a job category. "Salesperson," for example, is too broad; it is better to look at "representative of a drug firm who calls on physicians." Research engineers may differ from development engineers, stenographers from clerk typists (Dunnette & Kirchner, 1958). When jobs prove to be similar, the ultimate selection plan may apply to a broad category such as "general clerical tasks" (see Pearlman, 1980).

The job analyst's report should be specific. She should not state that successful workers have "mechanical ability"; she should specify to the level of "knowledge of and ability to apply principles of gears," or "speed in routine two-handed manipulation, not involving much finger dexterity or adaptation." Such definitions guide the search for a directly pertinent test.

Observing workers' motions and analyzing the cues and signals to which the worker responds suggest relevant perceptual or motor abilities. The analyst asks just what superior workers do differently and what difficulties newly hired workers have in learning the job. Reports from other firms help.

Direct observation is necessarily limited in scope, and analysts, therefore, rely on informants. But supervisors' remarks about what is important are usually vague and incomplete. Instead of asking about broad traits, job analysts ask about acts.

Analysts often employ a version of the "critical incident technique" (Flanagan, 1954; Fivars, 1980). An informant familiar with the job is asked to think of an individual who has done excellently on the job and then to recall one particular incident that showed this person's superiority. The informant then recalls a poor performer, perhaps one who had to be discharged, and the incident that led to the final verdict of unsuitability. These incidents are only one stage removed from field observation as can be seen in these examples of good and poor performance (H. Preston, 1948):

> This officer was instructed to land his P-80 on runway 15. He pedaled on the right runway but lined up to land on runway 9. He was told to go around and line up and land on runway 15 again. This time he overshot and had to go around. He was getting dangerously low on fuel so I personally talked him around the pattern, putting him on his down-wind leg, and instructed him when to turn on base. I asked him if he had runway 15 spotted and he said "Roger." After acknowledging, he flew right by runway 15 and almost "spun-in" trying to turn in on runway 9. Being low on fuel, I told him to go ahead and land. He came in hot and ran off the end of the runway.
>
> In meeting and acting as a pilot for general officers this lieutenant has brought favorable comment upon himself through the accomplishment of the mission. One specific case, when, through no fault of his own, an aircraft was allowed to depart without a retired Major General on board. Immediately upon being confronted by the general—a rather crusty old bird—he, without calling on me or any other superior, arranged for his departure to the original destination in time to overtake his original aircraft.

In one version (Dunnette, 1976, p. 490), the informants are brought together in a workshop where remarks of one participant can trigger the memory of another, and ultimately hundreds of incidents pile up. The incidents are then sorted. In summarizing incidents on performance of naval officers, 13 categories were used, including training of units and individuals, handling stressful situations, and fairness with subordinates. The incidents provide definite meaning for terms such as "fairness to subordinates."

Although recalled incidents provide richly suggestive data, the method is not truly objective. If the folklore of the business says that truck drivers must have stamina but need not be very bright, the informant is likely to bring to mind incidents where stamina counted and to forget the drivers who made themselves valuable by recognizing mix-ups in delivery orders.

1. *List aptitudes that might enter into one of the following: making pie dough; learning to use a word processor; driving a taxi.*

2. *If someone should try to define the psychological requirements for success in college faculty positions, can all such positions be analyzed together? If not, what would be an appropriately narrow category?*
3. *What practical conditions would a department-store chain consider in deciding whether a published test for salespersons in general is more suitable than a separate test for salespersons in a given department?*
4. *Skeptics have suggested that a qualified psychologist, looking into the job briefly, may do as well in devising test batteries and criteria as can be done after an expensive formal analysis (Levine et al., 1980). What are the costs of accepting this as a policy?*

Choice of Tests for Tryout

Having listed relevant characteristics, the investigator looks for ways of appraising them. If the abilities the job seems to demand are measured in published tests, such tests should be tried. Not every test with a relevant name will be suitable; for example, the investigator must consider the difficulty of the test in relation to the usual educational level of applicants. If the job calls for an ability that no test on the shelf matches, it may be better to construct a new test than to obtain a pale image of the ability from an indirect measure. When time and cost permit the development of a work sample covering important job elements, validity typically is better than that of off-the-shelf tests (Asher & Sciarrino, 1974).

Information need not come from tests. It is common to consider grade records in academic predictions and work history in decisions about employment. Tests play a particularly prominent role in selection for entry-level jobs just because past activities are not directly relevant. Work history is usually appraised informally through an interview, but it can be reduced to scorable variables. Thus Hough (1981) describes an adaptation of the critical-incident approach. Candidates for advanced responsibilities (from outside the organization or inside) are asked to describe incidents in their own work histories that illustrate their highest level of performance to date on certain dimensions. Attorneys, for example, are asked to describe incidents of "planning and organizing" and "oral communications and assertive advocacy." Asking who could confirm each such account discourages distortion. Systematic scoring of the incidents permits validating the relevance of the dimensions just as test scores are validated.

Some studies try collections of heterogeneous items. The most common example is the biographical inventory ("biodata"; Owens, in Dunnette, 1976; see also p. 466). Questions ask about work and educational experience, hobbies, athletic background, social activities, and home conditions. A "merit key" counts up the answers associated with success in that job. For example, a firm may find that its satisfactory office managers typically had 1 to 2 years of education beyond high school—not more. Then an office-manager key would assign one point to that educational level and zero to any other. In former times, weights were often based purely on statistical associations. Today not many psychologists would favor counting "played in a football league" in favor of an applicant for a police job even if (among males) that does correlate with on-the-job ratings; logical as well as empirical justification is wanted (L. A. Pace & L. F. Schoenfeldt, 1977; Wernimont & Campbell, 1968). Some life-history questions are not proper bases for selection because they introduce bias. Experiences most familiar to persons who grew up in a well-to-do family probably should not be counted even if they correlate with a criterion.

5. *If keys were to be built for the following roles, in which would it be proper to count foreign travel experience as a positive sign? (Assume that the item correlates moderately with each criterion.)*
   a. *TV newscaster*
   b. *Computer programmer*
   c. *Life-insurance salesperson*
6. *It was estimated that the direct cost of clerical turnover in a bank was $400 per case. Application blank information was scored by counting items on which long-tenure and short-tenure (female) employees differed. Applicants were assigned lower scores when they had these characteristics: between ages 20 and 25; mother worked; no family responsibilities; attended college; record of frequent job change (Robinson, 1972). Is it fair to eliminate otherwise qualified employees on these grounds?*

Experimental Trial

The tryout is crucial in verifying that the selection plan is sound and in providing legal justification. Ideally, one tests typical *applicants*, hires them, and observes the correspondence of test scores to success. When the job analyst suggests that Test X will eliminate weaker prospects, the boss would prefer to install the test and benefit from it at once, not to withhold judgment during weeks or even years of investigation. Unfortunately, in many instances tests that psychologists considered relevant proved to be of no value in selection (M. E. Parry, 1968).

A common compromise is to eliminate applicants who are poor prospects and then to check the test-criterion relation on the high scorers who are hired. Trial on an unselected group establishes more accurate critical scores and combining weights and should give sounder information on validity. A test that predicts poorly within the surviving group could, perhaps, identify the unqualified.

During World War II, U.S. Air Force psychologists thought it so important to demonstrate validity on an unselected population that they randomly sampled 1300 eligible recruits and sent them through training. They made this investment though they knew in advance that a large fraction would fail (DuBois, 1947; see also p. 394). Predictions made from the tests were sealed up until the experiment was complete; the trainees' success matched the predictions well enough to convince the generals that test scores should be taken seriously in the future. Evidence of the same kind can be obtained less expensively by hiring just a few of those who satisfy most requirements but score below the recommended cutoff on the tests (and not telling anyone the test scores). Later criterion data will make evident whether the test information is a useful early warning.

Experimental trial has practical limits. Neither the employer nor the public wants unscreened workers in responsible positions. The employer tied by seniority rules will properly refuse to hire low scorers that the firm cannot get rid of. Fortunately, within a group that has been subjected to some screening, sufficient differences remain to indicate whether scores relate to job performance.

A reasonable and relatively inexpensive first step in checking out tests is to try them on present employees though such a study must be interpreted cautiously. Under some circumstances concurrent and predictive correlations agree well (Barrett *et al.*, 1981). The manual for GATB reports that scores correlated 0.20 (on average) with job-proficiency criteria in concurrent studies and correlated 0.22 when criteria were collected some (unstated) time after testing. Such agreement is to be expected when

1. One sample is not more restricted than the other.
2. The abilities under test have matured prior to the testing.
3. *Either* the time lapse in the predictive study was not lengthy *or* no radical intervention followed the testing.

A concurrent correlation can falsely make validity look bad (Figure 11.1). Subjects are lost as time passes, and they tend to be the ones who cannot handle the job. A study carried out on survivors does not credit the test for its ability to identify dropouts. Also, higher ratings go mostly to workers with seniority. But workers out of school for a long time may score poorly on a written test, so test scores are often out of line with the ratings. The validity of the test might be fine for current applicants who are much the same in age. The person who acts on the basis of concurrent evidence, then, adopts assumptions that should be examined closely. Doing without a predictive trial on a full-range sample is easiest to justify when a test is supported by tryout studies elsewhere.

> **7.** *Suppose that an employer sets a cutting score on a test and puts the rule into use without tryout. What harm can result from this, assuming that the test has some degree of validity?*

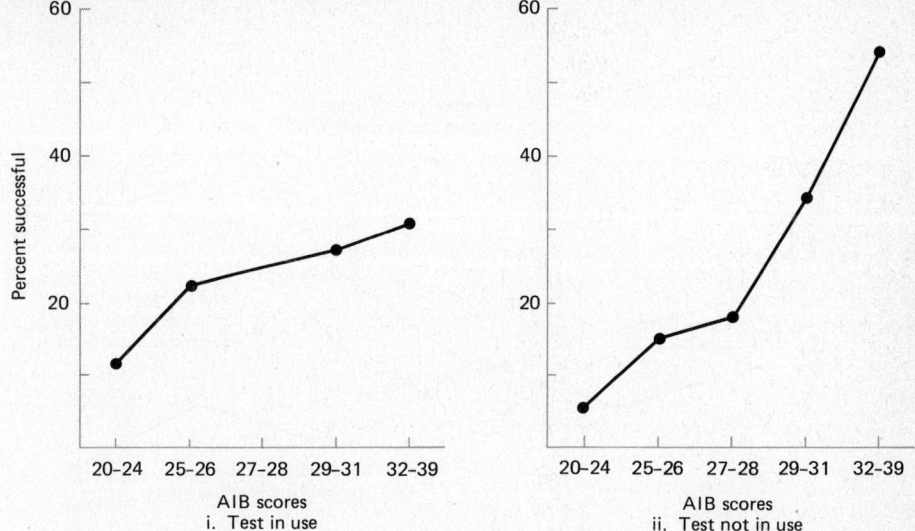

Figure 11.1. Apparent test validity under experimental and operational conditions.
Note: The Aptitude Index (see p. 466) is given considerable weight by most firms, though a few persons with low scores are hired. The relation of success to scores is usually unimpressive under these operational conditions (panel i). One firm decided to ignore the scores, selecting on the basis of an interview. A later follow-up showed a marked relationship of scores filed away prior to hiring (panel ii).
Source: Data from Peterson & Wallace, 1966.

The Criterion

After giving tests, the experimenter waits for evidence on job performance to ripen. In due time, data on success are obtained. Ideally, the criterion (or set of criteria) would cover all aspects of the job in which there are economically or socially important differences in workers' contributions. Partial criteria are acceptable, but one must guard against imbalance; history speaks badly of generals who win all their battles yet lose campaigns by reluctance to stand and fight.

A bad criterion leads to reliance on inappropriate tests. Tests that predict training criteria differ from those that best predict job performance, the former putting more stress on verbal and reasoning abilities (Ghiselli, 1973). The fault probably lies in the verbal nature of the usual training and the posttests even when the verbal load on the job is light. Norman Frederiksen (1981) calls this "the *real* test bias" because the overly verbal training criterion is a barrier for less educated applicants who could do what the job proper requires.

He refers to U.S. Navy experience; an example appears in Figure 11.2. When grades in ship's engine operation were based on instructors' judgments,

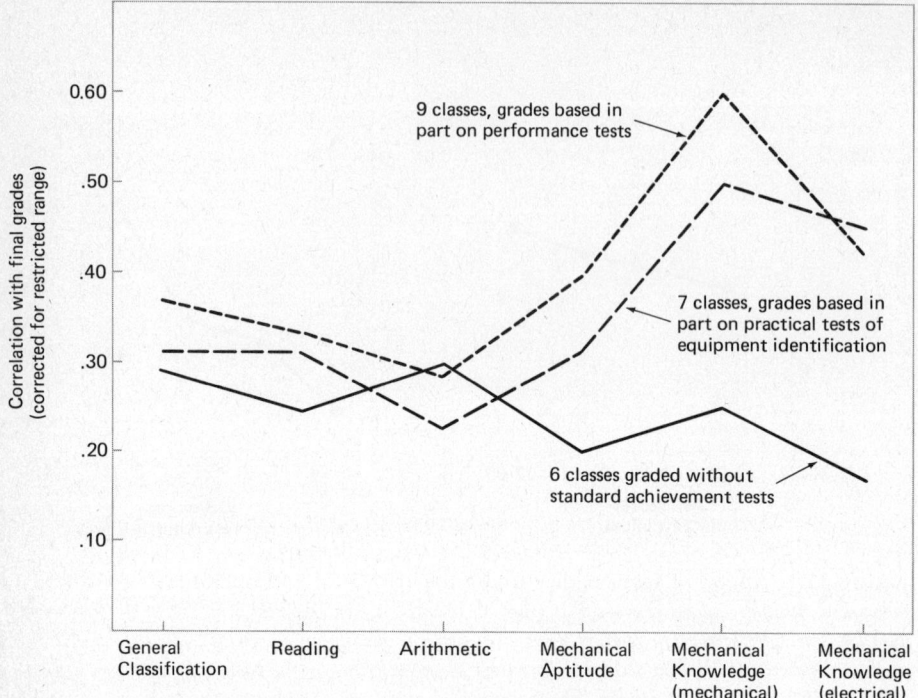

Figure 11.2. Predictive validity with three sets of criteria.
Source: Stuit, 1947, p. 307.

predictor tests did not correlate well with them. When grades were based on highly valid achievement tests, the classification tests were satisfactory predictors. The subjective judgments were most strongly related to academic and intellectual abilities. The valid criterion of job knowledge and skill was predicted best by mechanical knowledge and aptitude. The valid achievement tests asked the sailors to do what they would have to do on shipboard, handling objects and not words (see also Table 5.4). When the new criterion was made the official standard, the training itself changed. The instructors stopped lecturing on theory and set the students to practicing the shipboard tasks.

A test that can predict quality of work is likely to be discarded if it is judged against a criterion that does not adequately represent quality. Criterion error was neatly demonstrated after it was found that tests given to journeyman electricians correlated zero with supervisor ratings. By means of videotapes, the supervisors were trained to observe accurately and to communicate what they observed. The validities of the tests jumped to the range 0.4–0.6 (Pursell *et al.*, 1980). Ratings are cheaper to collect than measures of work output or observed skill, and therefore are much used. Chapter 15 discusses how to make ratings more dependable.

Judgmental criteria become contaminated if the judge knows the predictor data. A supervisor may rate a worker higher than performance warrants because the supervisor knows the worker has had considerable experience. A therapist may be quicker to note signs of progress in the patient whose intake record included a favorable test report. Such influences spuriously raise the validity coefficient and sometimes cause an irrelevant measure to appear valid. The only way to prevent contamination is to keep predictor data secret until criterion scores have been collected.

Time considerations. Correlations change in puzzling ways as the time between test and criterion measurement increases. Admission tests correlate with first-year college grades. They correlate much less with grade average in the junior and senior years, but that is because students spread out into courses that vary in difficulty and in grading standards (Humphreys & Taber, 1973). In some studies relating college success to career success, correlations increase with time. Employees entering with good school histories did no better in the first 10 years than those with middling records; subsequently, those who had done well in college pulled ahead (Roe, 1963). It seems likely that the later, fuller record is the better criterion. So there is always the possibility that good short-term predictors have limited long-run validity or vice versa.

Hypothetically, there is an "ultimate criterion" that fully represents the outcome the selector desires. The medical school would, if it could, judge the success of its students by their lifetime contribution to the health of the communities where they practice. This probably depends more on personality attributes than on intellectual abilities; it certainly is not closely related to grades in biochemistry. For practical reasons, however, medical-school grades are likely to be the criterion in selection of medical students.

One effort to get a near-ultimate criterion was made during the Korean War. Observers and interviewers went to the theater of combat to obtain information on performance; these data were supplemented by ratings from field commanders. A test battery developed to predict performance in training and in maneuvers correlated 0.27 with these peacetime criteria, but only 0.17 with the combat criterion. A battery designed to fit the combat criterion correlated 0.36 with both training and combat criteria. The important difference was that the combat-valid battery included a personality questionnaire (Willemin *et al.,* 1958).

Multiple criteria. In place of the single "ultimate criterion," it is more realistic and more illuminating to think of criteria of different kinds, becoming observable at different times (P. C. Smith in Dunnette, 1976). The more criteria the test is compared against, the more light is shed on selection policy.

There can be many patterns of success in a position. Teachers, for example, may excel in different ways: one develops into a friend and counselor for youth; one stimulates independent thinking in the few brightest students; one overcomes the blockings that cause failure among weak students. To try to score these performances on a single scale is pointless—one loses information *and* predictability.

The correlations between criteria are frequently low. Sometimes this is because one of the criteria is a bad measure. That is the only interpretation I can make of E. L. Kelly's finding (1964) that grades on a State Board examination to license physicians correlated less than 0.2 with a National Board examination in the same subject or with the grades earned in that subject the previous year. But uncorrelated criteria may reflect psychologically distinct aspects of job performance. A rating of probable success as hospital administrator might reasonably have little to do with promise as pediatrician. In Kelly's study premedical grades and aptitude measures correlated modestly with all types of criteria, but only the medical-school grade average and the national examinations were predicted well enough for decision making. The tests and premedical grades correlated low with ratings (by senior-year classmates) as to who would reach the highest income and who would be best satisfied as a family doctor in general practice. They also correlated low with ratings on diagnostic competence and sensitivity to patients' needs (made by the faculty during internship). This is a frequent finding: the closer the criterion is to book work, the better the tests predict it; the closer to the job, the more chancy the prediction.

The only solution appears to be more persistent and more analytic research, starting with the development of limited, well-measured criteria. The National Board of Medical Examiners, for example, supplements tests of book learning with a test that simulates the task of diagnosing a patient from the information available in a clinical record, bedside chart, and laboratory tests. The test of diagnostic competence measures something different from the usual test; physicians who do badly either tend to be timid, taking too few actions, or "shotgunners" who order too many procedures, including bad ones (Hubbard *et al.,* 1965; Hubbard, 1978).

With diverse and dependable criteria, it is appropriate to find out what predicts each one. That is far more instructive than combining the criteria into a single index even if it complicates decision making.

Psychological interpretation. In general, when criterion data become available, the time arrives for a serious effort to understand the nature of the job, the criteria, and the characteristics that cause applicants to succeed or fail. Far too often validation research is treated purely as a formal statistical check on a fixed hypothesis. The psychologist ought to be trying to understand the processes that generated the data, by every available means. When a worker is rated far below (or above) what was predicted, it may make sense to interview him and his supervisor or even to observe him at work. Likewise when predictions are confirmed, an effort at explanation may still improve the characterization of the job. Sometimes a variable that proved to be important was weakly measured; if so, the set of tests can be revised. A way of altering the training to overcome a weakness may emerge—or a plan for reducing the

Personnel Selection

emphasis supervisors place on qualities irrelevant to production. (Similar comments apply to clinical, correctional, and other predictions and also to evaluations of therapeutic or other treatments.)

8. *In each of the following situations, trace how contamination might occur, and suggest an improved procedure to avoid it.*
   a. *Tests for selecting salespersons are being tried experimentally. Because they are thought to be valid, the results are given to the sales manager for guidance in assigning territories to the salespersons in the experimental group. After a year of trial, each salesperson is judged by the amount of sales in relation to the normal amount for the assigned territory.*
   b. *Flight instructor's ratings are used as a basis for promotion from primary to advanced training. It is desired to check the validity of these ratings as predictors of success in advanced training. Advanced training is taken at the same field with a different instructor. This instructor's judgment supplies the criterion.*
9. *In industry, does one wish to predict an employee's maximum performance (proficiency) or typical behavior? Criteria of both types are in use; illustrate that fact.*
10. *List several independent criteria to consider in judging branch managers of an equipment firm. Branches are responsible for both sales and service.*
11. *PACE is a general-verbal ability measure formerly used as an entrance examination for the professional civil service. (Because minority applicants tended to fare badly on the test, it was forced out of use.) One validity study correlated PACE with three criteria for customs inspectors; the coefficients were 0.6, 0.6, and 0.0 (Trattner, 1979). The first two criteria were a job-information test and a work sample where the person judged what to do in situations presented by videotape. Both of these were designed in the light of a job analysis. The third criterion was the supervisor's rating. Account for the discrepant validities*
    a. *on the assumption that PACE is valid for job performance.*
    b. *on the assumption that PACE has little validity for the job.*

Translating Predictions into Decisions

The test scores, once obtained, are translated into decisions according to some plan. The plan describes how scores are to be combined if more than one measure is used, how tests are to be combined with nontest information, and what decision will be made for any given combination of facts. For the moment, we consider decisions based on a single test score.

When the number of vacancies to be filled is fixed, the obvious strategy is to rank applicants and fill vacancies from the top of the list. If there is no limit on the number to be selected, one could, in principle, set a "cut score" and reject all persons below it. In actual practice, it is usual to examine files individually rather than to let the decision rest entirely on the scores. The logic of decisions is best explained, however, by speaking as if only the scores are considered. A hire-from-the-top rule can be applied mechanically; psychologists differ about whether it is better to proceed in this strictly impersonal manner or to make individualized judgments about persons who meet minimum standards (p. 406).

The cutting score is determined from the scatter diagram or expectancy table. Considering what fraction of persons at each score level are expected to perform adequately, the interpreter sets an acceptable level of risk and fixes the critical score accordingly. Figure 11.3 shows how engineering marks at the University of Idaho in a certain year corresponded to aptitude scores. A grade average below 2.0 was regarded as unsatisfactory. The probabilities plotted in Figure 11.4 led the investigator to set the critical score at 85. In subsequent classes, applicants scoring below 85 were discouraged.

One method of examining the selection rule divides the predicted failures into "hits" (actual failures) and "false alarms." Among those above the cut score, the ones who turned out unsatisfactory are "misses." Finally, there are the "hits" who succeeded as predicted, ordinarily much the largest fraction of the sample. Among the 147 engineering students, 16 failures were predicted by a cut at 85. Two predictions were false alarms. Among the 131 persons above that cut, 32 did poorly in school (misses).

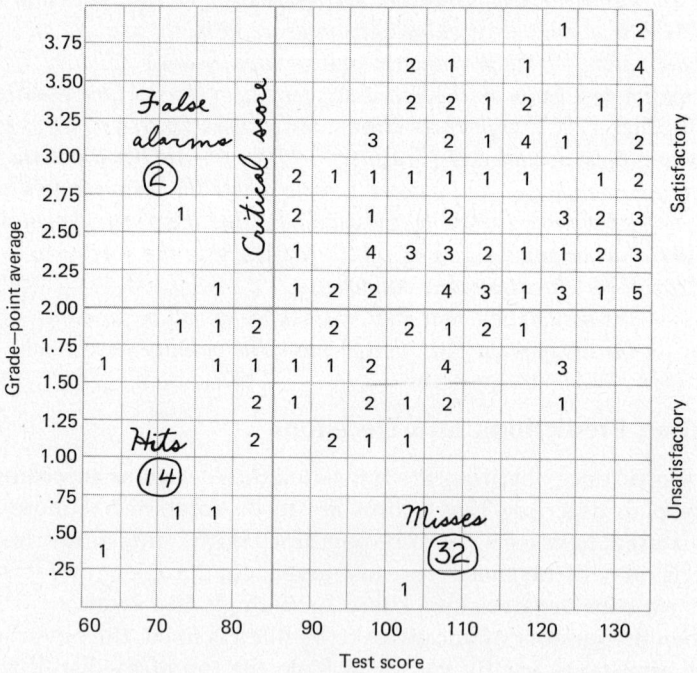

Figure 11.3. Engineering grades plotted against aptitude scores. *Sessions, 1955.*

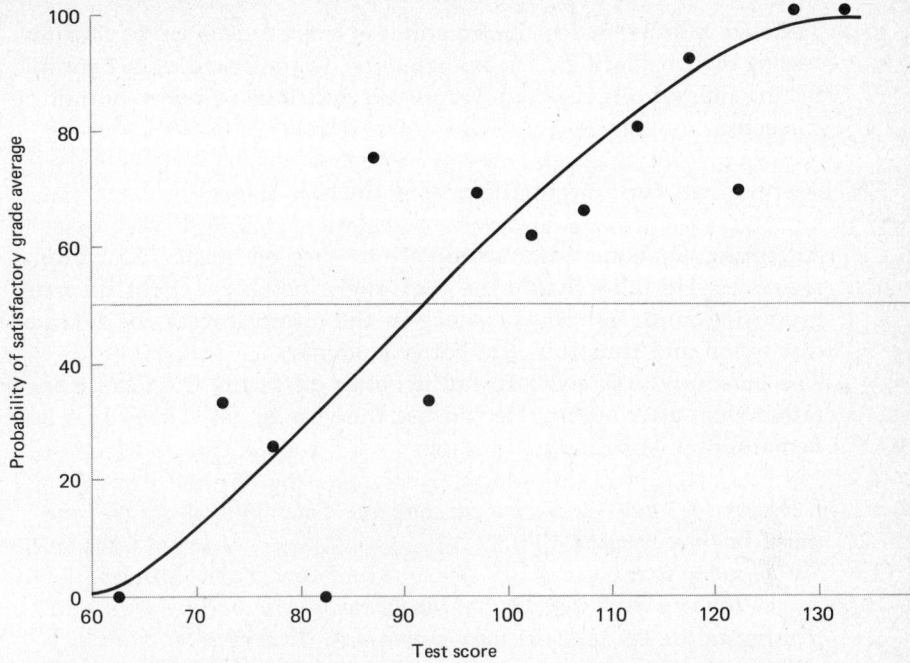

Figure 11.4. Success in engineering as a function of test score.

Setting a cut score requires a value judgment. We set it at 85 to flag applicants who have less than 38 chances in 100 of doing adequate work. If the policy is to challenge those whose chances are below 70 per cent, the cut score goes up to 105. Another policy might leave the choice to the student unless the probability of failure is very high. Then a cut score of 75 might be set to rule out those who have only one chance in five of surviving. The administrator who lowers the cut score gets fewer false alarms and more misses.

Some of the arguments that push the cut score downward (accepting more students who will fail) are these:

- A "failure" is not a total loss. The student will gain much from a year of college, even if he then drops out. If admitted, he will become worth more to society because of whatever he learns.
- An applicant refused admission may be a total loss to higher education. If he is enrolled, further investigation can perhaps identify deficiencies to be removed or help him work out a plan in which he has a greater chance of success.
- When the country needs engineers badly, it is important to process even low-grade ore to get a few extra graduates.

- Tests are fallible. A decision to admit is really a decision to continue testing by considering class performance. There is no way to continue testing one who is rejected. Erroneous decisions to reject cannot be corrected.

The arguments for a high critical score include these:

- Accepting someone who is unlikely to succeed wastes educational resources. He takes staff time that might better be spent on more promising students. His presence in the group lowers the level of discussion and thus robs the better students.
- The person who is going to fail is better off facing the fact at once rather than after a year. He can use the year to get started in a less demanding institution or in a job.

12. *In Figures 11.3 and 11.4, what cut score would identify students with one chance in three of failing?*

13. *The following is taken from a letter to* The New York Times:
"*I submit that 'slaughter on the highway' will continue until state licensing authorities recognize some simple facts: To drive a car on today's highways demands a rather complex set of sensori-motor skills. These skills are 'normally' distributed; i.e., some folks have them, some do not. Instruments are available to measure these skills. Authorities have responsibility to see that such instruments are used before licensing.*"
   a. *What degree of validity should be required before tests are used as proposed?*
   b. *If scores are normally distributed, how should the cutoff score be fixed?*

14. *A screening test is applied to school children to identify those in poor mental health so that they can be given intensive study by the school psychologist. What factors argue for a high cut score? What factors argue for a low cut score? (Consider Fig. 7.9, p. 230.)*

15. *Which is to be preferred, false alarms or misses, in each of these situations?*
   a. *Patients entering a hospital take a reasoning test that gives a rough indication that something may be physically wrong with the brain. Suspect cases are given a thorough neurological examination.*
   b. *Candidates for admission to teacher training are screened for competence in arithmetic and use of language.*
   c. *It is important to hire skilled sheet-metal workers to fill vacancies during a time of tight labor supply. Workers cannot be trained on the job.*
   d. *In inducting soldiers, a test is used to determine which recruits are too dull to be useful to the service.*
   e. *After hiring, a company puts control-room operators for a nuclear-power plant through an expensive training program; success cannot be observed until the end of the course.*

TWO EXAMPLES

Selecting Power-Plant Operators

Much of the selection research illustrated in various parts of this book comes from small and partial studies, but research in a large organization or an industry-wide project can be thorough and substantial. I describe here a study representative of the best in personnel research today (which is not to say that identical tactics would be followed in other industries or by other experts). In what is called a "cooperative study," the electric-utility industry asked the Personnel Decisions Research Institute to develop a selection system for operators at various levels in electric power plants (hydro, fossil, nuclear, and so on); data came in from more than 70 firms and thousands of individuals. Even a 3-year study with good support compromised, starting by limiting the study to present employees. I have already referred to data from this study and will return to it in later chapters; for convenience let me label it the PDRI study (for cross-references see the subject index under PDRI). The summary volume (Dunnette *et al.*, 1982) describes four phases of work.

Identifying job requirements. The following steps were taken in this phase:

- Literature review, covering "human factors" research on all process-control jobs, and studies conducted specifically in power plants (often drawn from within-company memoranda). A schematic outline identified broad functions such as "vigilance" and KSAOs were listed beneath these ("auditory acuity," "compulsivity," etc.).
- PDRI read job descriptions, then visited plants and talked with operators. Lists of tasks so identified went into a form supervisors used to describe particular jobs. Supervisors also filled out McCormick's Position Analysis Questionnaire. The importance of functions and KSAOs in each job was rated.
- A technique much like factor analysis was used to group occupations into categories with similar requirements (e.g., turbine operators were separated from boiler operators). Two dozen abilities and personal characteristics emerged as seemingly important in some or all categories.
- Because emotional stability loomed large, workshops were held to define the concept by critical-incident techniques. Experts were asked to suggest screening methods for use in hiring and in periodic check-ups (see p. 495).
- Judgments as to the dollar value of good performance. The difference in payoff between a 15th percentile worker and a 50th percentile worker is great in some jobs, modest in some others. Thus, quality in

one role in a nuclear plant was judged to be 5.6 times as important as quality in the same job in a fossil plant.

Developing predictor and criterion measures. This second phase began with an evaluation of off-the-shelf measuring procedures.

- A literature search was made with the aid of *MMY* and other sources. Fifteen diverse tests considered adequately reliable and relevant were chosen, including EFT, several tests from the Employee Aptitude Survey (Psychological Services, Inc.), and some from the ETS kit.
- Where it was desired to match more exactly the content of power-plant jobs, PDRI developed new instruments, e.g., for numerical ability and for mechanical comprehension.
- Biographical items and self-descriptive statements describing personal characteristics were borrowed from older instruments or written afresh. This became an Opinion and Attitude Questionnaire (OAQ) —over 500 items, split between two packages.
- Criteria were derived from supervisors' statements. Statements relevant to emotional stability ("willingly admits own mistakes") were assembled into a rating form that could be scored for six aspects of personality. A more elaborate rating form (see page 515) detailed specific aspects of job performance.

Field trial. After a consideration of available materials and time, a final collection was assembled: 17 ability tests, OAQ, and supplementary forms. A plan for choosing cases was drawn up, with careful attention to random sampling of nonminority males and oversampling of minorities and females to obtain more stable data on subgroups. Workshops were held to train test administrators and raters. For each person tested, ratings were filled out by two or three supervisors, working independently.

Statistical analyses covered such topics as reliability of scores and ratings, overlap among tests, and the range of workers' abilities within job categories. Factor analysis was used to reduce the ratings to a few composites, and validity coefficients were determined within jobs. Scoring scales for the OAQ were developed. Elaborate studies were made to determine which jobs differed sufficiently from the others to justify distinct selection batteries. Studies were made to learn whether test-criterion relations found in workers from the mainstream held up in minority samples. Ratings were checked for possible race bias, particularly by considering workers who had one white rater and one minority rater.

Constructing and evaluating the final plan. The staff envisioned several trial packages of tests and used the statistics to evaluate how each such package

PERSONNEL SELECTION   375

would perform, considering not only its screening effectiveness but its cost and the stability of relationships across jobs.

PDRI recommended retaining three alternative cognitive batteries that differ in length and makeup but have similar (and satisfactory) validities. Also, there is a biodata score and a score from self-reports on emotional stability.

A combining rule was selected for use in demonstrating the overall effectiveness of the battery, and this was translated into an estimate of the financial return to the industry if it were to adopt the selection procedure. Expectancy charts were produced for various kinds of plants and jobs. Recommendations were made regarding practical use of the several scores in circumstances found within one company at a given time.

16. *In what ways might the relevance of the PDRI study to future operations have benefited or suffered from the following features of the design?*
   a. *Multiple ratings on each case were collected.*
   b. *Test administrators were given a common training.*
   c. *Comparatively few poor employees were found within the group of subjects. (Many of these had survived on the job for decades.)*
   d. *The OAQ form carried the statement that replies would be held in confidence and used for research only.*

17. *Match the eight steps listed at the start of the chapter with the four phases of the PDRI outline. Do the lists overlap completely?*

An Aptitude Test for Programmers

The PDRI report said comparatively little about the content and relative usefulness of its tests. For a fuller example of test development, I turn to the Computer Programmer Aptitude Battery (J. M. Palermo; CPAB; *SRA*).

Learning to write computer programs is hard for some people, which makes it important to select good prospects for training. Routine programming is not enough. One wants programmers who can cope with novel problems and can use computer time efficiently. The original impetus for CPAB came from the desire of certain firms making computers to help their customers; a bad programmer can make the best system look bad.

The first step was a job analysis that relied in part on earlier research on success in programming. This led to a fairly long list of possibly relevant abilities. Because it was not practical to try out all of these, the list was reduced to seven kinds of task. For each task, a large set of trial items was prepared.

Experimentation began with the following:

- Verbal Meaning (fairly difficult synonyms). This sample item indicates the lowest level of difficulty in the test:[1]

RECIPIENT   donor   owner   performer   receiver   borrower

Words used were taken from material advanced programmers have to read, in fields such as business management and systems engineering. Although the programmer's own job is not primarily verbal, the programmer *does* have to communicate with specialists in these related fields.

- Letter Series, with items as difficult as this:

scagscdj——   g s c e p

This test is speeded.

- Number Series. Another reasoning task.
- Number Ability (computation). Many items ask for the answer choice that is approximately correct, so judging magnitudes is stressed rather than precise arithmetic. To encourage estimating, the test is speeded.
- Reasoning (formulating and interpreting quantitative relationships). Items are generally harder than this specimen:[2]

An office manager ordered a conference table which cost S dollars, a dozen chairs which cost P dollars each, and three book shelves which cost Y dollars apiece. The total cost of the order in dollars is

$S + P + Y$
$SP + 3Y$
$S + 12P + 3Y$
$S + \dfrac{(P + Y)}{4}$
$S + P + 3Y$

- Ingenuity. This item[3] is illustrative:

As part of a manufacturing process, the inside lip of a deep, cup-shaped casting is machine threaded. The company found that metal chips produced by the threading operation were difficult to remove from the bottom of the casting without scratching the sides. A design engineer was able to solve his problem by having the operation performed

i ___ ___ ___ ___ p   h ___ ___ h
m ___ ___ ___ ___ n   c ___ ___ e
f ___ ___ ___ ___ r   w ___ ___ l
i ___ ___ ___ ___ d   b ___ ___ k
u ___ ___ ___ ___ e   d ___ ___ n

[1] From the *Computer Programmer Aptitude Battery*. Copyright © 1964, Science Research Associates, Inc. Reprinted by permission.
[2] From the *Computer Programmer Aptitude Battery*. Copyright © 1964, Science Research Associates, Inc. Reprinted by permission.
[3] From the *Flanagan Aptitude Classification Test,* Ingenuity, Form A. Copyright © 1957 by John C. Flanagan. Reprinted by permission of the publisher, Science Research Associates, Inc. Chicago, IL.

One reaches the answer by imagining the solution and then locating the letters that identify the descriptive phrase. Most problems have to do with concrete objects and machines.

- Diagramming. To test the ability to think systematically about sequences of operation, the items employ flow diagrams similar to Figure 11.5. (Test items are more complex than this warm-up item.) The person is taught the code (e.g., Y implies a "yes" answer). He chooses an entry for each numbered cell. Cell 1, for example, requires the question: Is it in the range 3.5 to 4.4 ounces?

This summary of results intermingles data from the two forms of the test. A number of validation studies were carried out, almost invariably examining a sample of employed programmers and almost invariably using supervisor's rating as a criterion. All validations carried out during test development were concurrent, there being no opportunity to test unselected persons entering training. It was exceedingly difficult to obtain samples of reasonable size within which all persons had more or less comparable assignments. A single office or laboratory is likely to employ only a few programmers, and no supervisor knows many of them.

In one key study the set of seven tests was given to 186 programmers working at installations within the same corporation. This provided fine data for studying test intercorrelations and split-half reliabilities. A solid criterion (ratings from four or more supervisors, averaged) was available for only 46 cases. Two decisions were based on these early data. The Ingenuity subtest did not correlate with the criterion (confirmed in other samples); it was dropped. In retrospect, its subject matter seems to be more concrete than the tasks of the programmer. Number Series showed some validity, but it overlapped with other tests. Four of the remaining tests looked promising by both standards: validity and nonduplication. Verbal Meaning did not correlate with the criterion in the 46-case sample, but this was thought to reflect the use of a highly select, well-educated group. These five subtests, then, went into the further trials and eventually into the operational test.

A mixture of concurrent and predictive validity coefficients from various employers are summarized in Table 11.1. Nearly all the correlations were reduced—perhaps by 0.1 or more—as a consequence of having screened out unpromising applicants earlier. Subtest intercorrelations imply that the chief factor running through the test is measured by Reasoning and Number Ability. The Diagramming test, which to some extent simulates the programmer's work, is a specialized ability. As this appears to be a good subtest, one might wish to use more problems of this type in a future edition of the test.

Some of the criteria were seriously faulty. In one group of slightly over 40 subjects, the test did not correlate with supervisor's rating, but correlated 0.46 with grades assigned during an advanced training course. The rating criterion is suspect, as older workers received much higher ratings but had

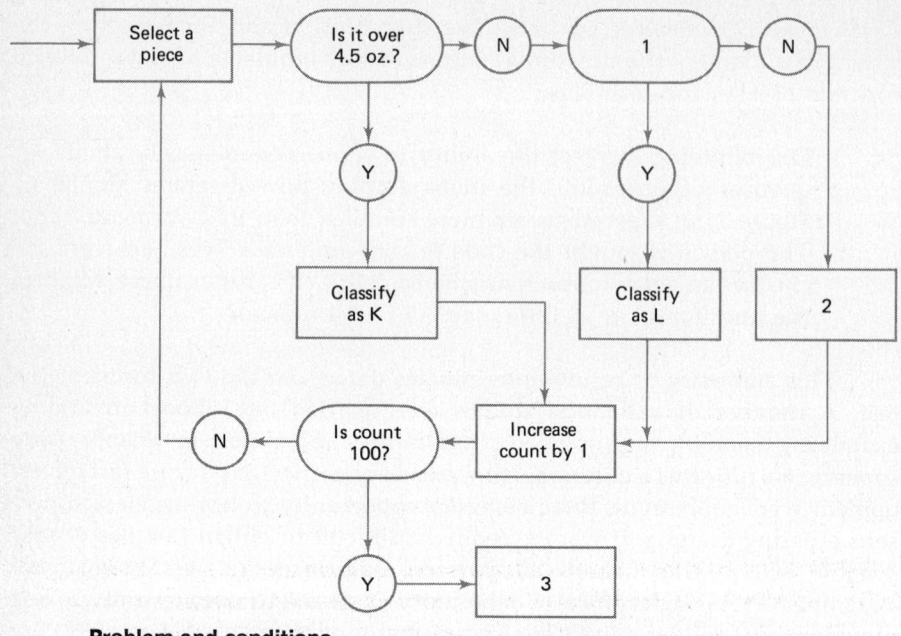

Problem and conditions

A. A company inspects and classifies its products in lots of 100.

B. It is necessary to classify the individual pieces within each lot of 100 into three classes by weight:

Class K—4.5 oz. or over
Class L—3.5 to 4.4 oz.
Class M—less than 3.5 oz.

Cell 1. A. Is it less than 3.5 oz.?
B. Select a piece.
C. Is it 3.5 to 4.4 oz.?
D. Classify as M.
E. Classify as L.

Cell 2. A. Classify as K.
B. Classification of lot complete.
C. Select a piece.
D. Classify as M.
E. Classify as L.

Cell 3. A. Select a piece.
B. Classification of lot complete.
C. Classify lot as K.
D. Classify lot as L.
E. Classify lot as M.

Figure 11.5. Diagramming task for prospective programmers.
Source: From the Computer Programmer Aptitude Battery. Copyright © 1964, Science Research Associates, Inc. Reprinted by permission.

Table 11.1. *Validity coefficients for the CPAB*

Score	Working Time (Minutes)	Split-half Reliability	Median Correlation[b] with Criteria from	
			Training	Job Performance
Verbal Meaning	8	0.86	0.3	0.2
Letter Series	10	0.67	0.2	0.25
Number Ability	6	0.85	0.3	0.2
Reasoning	20	0.88	0.5	0.35
Diagramming	35	0.94[a]	0.4	0.25
Total	79		0.5	0.4

[a] This is considered to be an overestimate, as items dealing with the same block diagram are not experimentally independent. The speeded tests were split into two separately timed parts, so the other coefficients are not overestimated.
[b] Five or six correlations per score came from training criteria, and six came from data on the job. All samples were small.
SOURCE: Manual, 1974, pp. 4, 11.

lower test scores. The older workers were highly experienced and were taking more responsibility; this did not mean that they were superior programmers.

The test manual urges continued effort toward validation, including validation by each prospective user in her own situation. The firm should determine which subtests contribute to prediction for it; for example, a firm hiring only college-educated programmers may find that the Verbal section does not contribute to prediction. A study in one firm shows how thinking might proceed.

Trainees who had passed the screening procedures normally in use ($N = 114$) were measured on 19 variables, including the Number Ability, Reasoning, and Diagramming scores of CPAB; Verbal Meaning and Letter Series were covered by somewhat similar PMA tests. Course marks in programming were the criterion. Correlations were corrected statistically to obtain validities for the unrestricted applicant population (see p. 394). Age, education, and college grades had essentially no predictive value in this firm. There were coefficients in the range 0.5–0.7 for CPAB Reasoning and Diagramming and PMA Reasoning, CPAB Number, and PMA Verbal. Several other verbal and reasoning tests (including Matrix) correlated about 0.4 with the criterion. To check on a proposed selection plan using PMA Verbal and Reasoning plus CPAB Reasoning and Diagramming, another 88 cases were studied the next year. Perry (1967) concluded that the battery would have a validity of about 0.7 for an applicant population. (Later reports on CPAB validity are not available, but readers may want to refer to reports on other tests that are basically consistent with the story told here; see DeNelsky & McKee (1974) and Schmidt, Gast-Rosenberg, & Hunter (1980).

18. *Nonwhites tend to score lower than whites on CPAB, according to limited data. The manual suggests that firms accepting whites who score above the*

60th percentile on white norms might be wise to hire nonwhites who score above the 60th percentile on nonwhite norms.
a. *What do you think? (The matter will be discussed at the end of this chapter.)*
b. *Less educated persons tend to score lower. Would you favor a similar use of percentiles for each educational level?*

WHAT LEVEL OF VALIDITY IS ACCEPTABLE?

As validity coefficients have been presented in past chapters, you have probably been classifying them mentally as "good" or "poor." Many tests, particularly those of narrow abilities, do not seem very satisfactory at first glance. But the fundamental question is, Does the test permit a better judgment than one could make without it—sufficiently better to justify its cost?

Coefficients as low as 0.3 usually imply definite practical value (see Table 11.3), and even tests with lower validities may improve decisions. One psychologist commented that the test critic who is contemptuous of low positive correlations is quite willing to accept information of no greater dependability when he plays golf or employs a physician. The correlation of golf scores between the first and second 18 holes in championship play is about 0.3, he said, and the reliability of medical diagnosis is near 0.4. The personnel psychologist can evaluate a selection device by comparing high- and low-scoring workers with respect to number of failures in training, average length of training required, rate of turnover, average production, and so on. Such analyses show that tests with validities in the range from 0.3 to 0.5 make a considerable contribution to the efficiency of the institution though they forecast wrongly for many individuals.

The significance level of the validity coefficient does *not* tell how useful the test is. Significance levels (e.g., $P < 0.05$) have to do not with worth but with certainty. A good-sized correlation that is not "significant" nonetheless argues for cumulating further experience with the test.

In evaluating a selection test, one should ask the following questions. Each question is so worded that an answer of "no" encourages consideration of tests having relatively low validity.

Are individual differences in job performance or other outcomes fairly small?
Is the number of vacancies so large that a large fraction of the applicants have to be accepted?
Does this test measure an ability that is fairly well predicted from information already taken into account in screening?

Is the reliability of the test high? (If not, lengthening the test should raise validity.)
Is the test costly to administer?
Is it feasible to discharge or transfer to other duties workers who turn out to be unsuccessful? That is, can we adapt when a predictor "misses"?

A particularly desirable approach is to screen at two or three stages rather than to promise a permanent job at the time of first hiring. Eliminating a fraction of those initially selected, after further information comes in from training sessions or work as probationer, greatly reduces the cost of initial misjudgments.

The best single rule of thumb for interpreting validity coefficients in selection is Brogden's (1949). Making certain reasonable assumptions, he showed that the benefit from a selection program increases *in proportion to the validity coefficient*. Suppose 40 applicants out of 100 are hired. Take as a baseline the average production of randomly selected workers. An ideal test would pick the 40 applicants who later earn the highest criterion scores; the average production of these workers is the maximum that any selection plan could yield. A test with validity 0.5 will select workers whose production averages halfway between the base level and the ideal. To be concrete, suppose that the average, randomly selected worker assembles 400 gadgets per day, and the perfectly selected group of workers turns out 600, on the average. Then a test with validity 0.5 will choose a group whose average production is 500 gadgets, and a test of validity 0.2 will select workers with an average production of 440 gadgets. The assumptions underlying Brogden's rule are these:

The job to be performed remains the same, whether workers of high or low ability are selected.
Production (or other measure of benefit) has a linear relation to test score.

The benefit derived from a selection plan depends on the selection ratio, as well as on the validity of the test. The *selection ratio* is the proportion of persons tested who are accepted. If there is a large labor supply, the selection ratio can be very low, but when applicants are scarce, the selection ratio is forced up toward 1.00. Even an ideal test does not raise the quality of workers when every applicant must be hired. If the employer can pick and choose, average output can be much improved. Figure 11.6 shows the relation of production to selection ratio for the gadget assemblers. It is assumed that among unselected workers the average production is 400 gadgets, and the standard deviation is 100. Tests of low validity have considerable value when the selection ratio can be very low, when individual differences in job per-

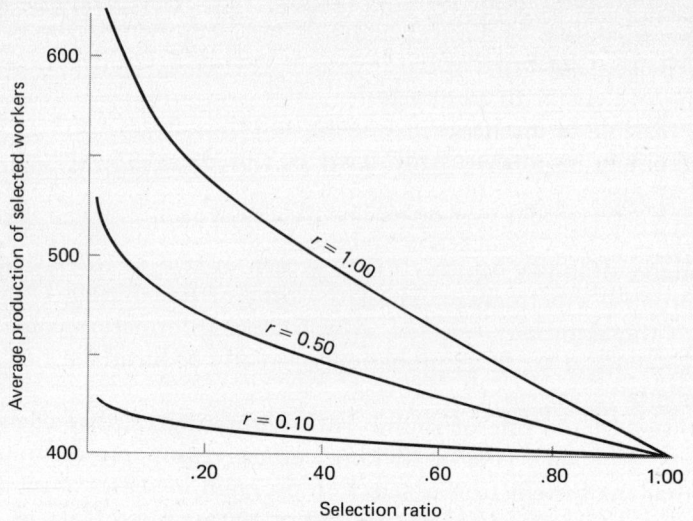

Figure 11.6. Benefit from a selection program.

formance are large, and when small increases in production have a large dollar value.

Utility analysis, a method of appraising the economic benefits from selection, is reviewed by Hunter and Schmidt (1981). Logically, in those situations where a worker's contribution can be expressed in dollars, careful accounting would determine the benefit from the selection rule. This, however, proves not to be straightforward because accounting practices embody many judgments. (See papers by Roche & van Naerssen in Cronbach & Gleser, 1965.) Current procedures follow Hunter and Schmidt in relying on estimates made by managers as in the PDRI study. The last paragraph of the PDRI report reads as follows (Dunnette et al., 1982, p. 263):

> In effect, it does not seem to be too great a stretch of the imagination to expect a potential annual gain in the neighborhood of $800,000,000 when these selection procedures are adopted by the companies participating in this research project.

Bolder projections have been made. Schmidt et al. (1979) figured that if the selection ratio were 0.2 and the validity of a programmer aptitude test appreciably higher than the validity of the selection procedure previously in use, the test would produce a benefit to the employer of $64,725 per programmer hired. Multiplying this by the number hired, they calculated that if the test had been used to select all the programmers in the American economy, the productivity gain would reach nearly $11 billion.

This projection is a fairy tale. The economy utilizes most of the persons who are trained as programmers, and only the most prestigious firm can reject

Personnel Selection

80 per cent of those who apply. If 90 per cent of the programmers are hired somewhere, the tests merely give a competitive advantage to those firms that test (when some other firms do not test). A much subtler analysis would be needed to assess the benefit to the whole economy. Essentially, that benefit would come from routing each person in the labor market into the career where he or she could make the greatest contribution, not from creaming off the best workers and discarding the others.

19. *In one study, the predictive validity of pencil-and-paper tests for selecting pilots was 0.64 against an elimination-graduation criterion. The coefficient rose to 0.69 when apparatus tests were added. Is such a small increase worthwhile?*
20. *State employment offices use tests to guide workers into appropriate positions. A very low selection ratio may be used because a particular unemployed worker may be directed into any one of hundreds of job families. In a particular insurance agency, on the other hand, it is necessary to employ about 60 per cent of those who apply for clerical jobs. Are the same tests equally suitable in both situations?*
21. *In which of these situations is there likely to be a fixed number of vacancies, and in which can the decision maker set the critical score as high or low as she judges appropriate?*
    a. *A parole board decides which prisoners may be released.*
    b. *An engineering school admits well-qualified applicants.*
    c. *A school psychologist identifies mentally handicapped children to be placed under a special teacher.*
    d. *A college counseling bureau identifies clients likely to profit from psychotherapy.*

FAIRNESS IN SELECTION

Poor, less-educated persons tend to score lower on ability tests than those with advantaged backgrounds, and women average lower than men on tests where mechanical experience helps. Tests do affect groups differently, but they also reflect real differences in qualifications. Which tests and test uses are discriminatory has had to be argued out in the courts.

Some History and Law

Title VII of the Civil Rights Act of 1964 prohibited disparate treatment of workers and job applicants from different sex, racial or ethnic, or religious groups. The Senate inserted an amendment pointedly stating that the act did not prohibit selection on the basis of "professionally developed tests," where there was no intent to discriminate. Administrative guidelines were issued and revised, charges were brought from time to time against private and public employers, and cases were settled administratively or in court. A second body of law and policy has evolved with regard to educational selection. Although much has been settled, important questions remain open. Sources on the history and legal theory include Gorham (in Maslow *et al.*, 1980), Lerner (1979), papers by Hollander and Wigdor (in Wigdor & Garner, II, 1982). Legal handbooks on employment law (Larson & Larson, 1981; Schlei & Grossman, 1976, 1979) are revised frequently, and recent rulings can be traced in the periodical *Fair Employment Practices Cases* (FEP).

Federal guidelines. The Equal Employment Opportunity Commission was set up as advocate for groups that might be discriminated against. Several other federal agencies have missions of other kinds and take conflicting positions. Their *Uniform Federal Guidelines (UFG;* EEOC *et al.*, 1978, 1979) are a compromise, open to divergent interpretations. The EEOC has pressed toward a "representative work force." Ideally, its officials have said, all groups in the community would be represented in a job category in proportion to their availability. Other agencies place greater stress on merit hiring; they oppose deliberate discrimination but not disproportion. Even the Office of Personnel Management—formerly the "Civil Service Commission," whose name was almost synonymous with merit hiring—yielded to pressure in 1981 and agreed that hereafter the percentage of blacks and Hispanics accepted into administrative and professional lines of the federal service would match the percentage of applicants from those groups. The court-approved plan discarded a test (PACE) that seemingly predicted success but on which the average minority applicant (less educated?) fell below the overall average.

In explaining the issues, I shall refer to blacks (or to "plaintiffs" as advocates for blacks) and to whites (or to employers as "defendants"). This permits brevity and recognizes that treatment of blacks has been at issue in most cases. But the rules are quite general; white males can be plaintiffs under them. Moreover, selection based on evidence other than tests must meet these standards also, say the *UFG*. An employment case turns on three successive questions:

1. Is there adverse impact? The plaintiff must show that the rejection rate of eligible blacks is greater than that of eligible whites. The rule of thumb is that a selection practice is vulnerable when the rate of black hiring is less than four-fifths the rate for whites.
2. Is the selection rule valid? If the procedure fails standard (1), the defendant has to show that the basis for selection is related to the job. According to the *UFG*, criterion, content, and construct validation are equally legitimate. Courts are impressed by criterion validation. Courts have been equally receptive to content validation if no irrelevant difficulty in the test is detected (see page 156). On construct validation, the *UFG* and the court decisions are conflicting, confusing, and not a good reflection of the relevant scholarly literature (Maslow *et al.*, 1980).

Personnel Selection

3. Can an alternative selection procedure be found that has less adverse impact? If Test X is valid but has adverse impact, the *UFG* urge the employer to seek a procedure that has validity but not adverse impact.

Court rulings. A small fraction of challenges reach the courts; very few reach the higher courts. Some employers promptly abandon or amend a plan that is challenged; sometimes the enforcement agency decides that a plan is defensible and drops the challenge. Courts take divergent positions about the cases that reach them. In one region the appeals court lays down precedents that are tough on employers; in another region the appeals court hears employers sympathetically. The Supreme Court resolves contradictions, but it tries to progress slowly, and its rulings are narrow.

The chief points in five key Supreme Court decisions were as follows:

- *Griggs* (401 U.S. 424 [1971]). A pencil-paper test given to would-be coal handlers was struck down. Employers must show "business necessity" for selection, and employment tests that have adverse impact must be validated. (The law does not require validity otherwise!)
- *Albemarle Paper Co.* v. *Moody* (422 U.S. 405 [1975]). A selection rule with adverse impact was struck down because the firm's hastily assembled validation did not meet professional standards.
- *Washington* v. *Davis*[4] (426 U.S. 229 (1976); see p. 334). A majority of the court accepted a selection rule that had adverse impact, noting that the test predicted final marks in police training and measured a logically relevant variable at a reasonable level. Two dissenters objected that the job relevance of the training criterion had not been established.
- *Bakke* (98 S. Ct. 2733 [1978]). A system that reserved a number of law-school places (a "quota") for minority applicants was struck down. But selection need not ignore race, the court said; diversity in a student body has recognized educational value.
- *Weber* (99 S. Ct. 2721 [1979]). Reserving places for blacks as trainees for supervisory positions was accepted as a remedy when a firm confessed to past discrimination.

Two later decisions in a U.S. Court of Appeals (New York) are suggestive. In *Guardians* (23 FEP 909 [1980]), a rather unsatisfactory test was upheld as of some relevance to police work. Because the measurement error was substantial, said the court, the test should be used only to eliminate definitely unqualified applicants. Above that cutoff, random selection should be considered as less discriminatory than hiring from the top. In *Kirkland* (23 FEP 1217 [1980]), the court accepted a plan that added 250 points to the score of every black applicant for police sergeant prior to ranking the eligibility list. (The

---

[4] *Washington* v. *Davis* was not judged under the Civil Rights Act, and the legal rationale differed from that of the other cases. The same was true of *Bakke*.

score difference between means of white and black applicants was near 250.) This bonus was not—the court said—a quota in disguise (!). For a similar opinion, see *Navaho Refining* (19 FEP 184 [1979]).

The psychological community has viewed this history with mixed feelings (Glaser & Bond, 1981; Wigdor & Garner, 1982). Psychologists surely supported the civil rights principles of 1964 and the demand for valid selection methods. They agree that selection rules have at times set unreasonably high and irrelevant standards that blocked competent but less-educated applicants. Many psychologists are strongly committed to the merit principle, hence to "color blind" hiring, and are opposed to quotas and special preferences. Many are distressed that employers have abandoned testing to avoid complaints and the costs of defense, when interviews should be at least as suspect as tests (Arvey, 1979). It is hard to believe that the unvalidated selection methods used by employers who do not test are fair to the applicants rejected.

22. *Explain the following statement, paraphrased from John Campbell (in Dunnette, 1976, p. 206). Public policy now stresses the reduction of false negatives, especially in disadvantaged groups, whereas the traditional emphasis was on avoiding false positives (misses). It will not be easy to judge the policy, considering who bears the implicit costs of these two kinds of errors.*

Psychometric Issues

Do regressions in subpopulations differ? When a test is valid for white male applicants, is it likely to have predictive validity for other subpopulations? Yes indeed. A formula for predicting an educational or employment criterion, worked out on a typical applicant pool, holds up for black applicants considered alone. A formula worked out on men usually holds up for women.

Bad reasoning a decade ago led to much confusion; this paragraph is intended to clear away that underbrush. (I draw especially on critiques by Hunter *et al.*, 1979, and Linn, 1978.) The standard research design is to collect data in the same setting on whites and blacks who have been accepted. Some studies reported that certain validity coefficients for blacks were "not statistically significant," implying that the tests in question were invalid for blacks. Other studies reported positive correlations in both groups, but lower ones for blacks. The small size of samples and the comparatively narrow range of black test scores (after selection) would have generated many of these findings in a population where the validity coefficients for unselected black applicants and unselected white applicants were the same. Such "differential validity" studies—comparisons of correlation coefficients—should be abandoned.

Another term, "differential prediction," refers to the true issue: Are the Y-on-X regression lines the same for blacks and whites (or other contrasted groups)? Suppose that whites who score 75 on predictor X average +1 on criterion Y. Then if blacks who score 75 on X average +2 on Y, the usual formula based mostly on white employees would seriously underrate these black applicants. Differential prediction *is* a possibility, as Figure 11.7 shows. Using a numerical predictor, the regressions for males and females are the same. With mechanical reasoning as predictor, the two regressions separate. Females are underpredicted in the sense that they do better on the criterion than statistics calculated from males and females together would predict. (In this study, the DAT was given at the start of the school year, and proficiency in arithmetic problem solving was measured in the spring. Mechanical reasoning correlated about 0.6 with the criterion in each sex group.)

When the same kind of study is carried out on blacks and whites, the picture comes out much like panel i of Figure 11.7 though the lines are rarely so neatly parallel. Sometimes there is a modest separation, smaller than that shown in panel ii. The separation, where present, shows the white regression line to be higher. See summaries by Breland (1979b) of college data, Jensen (1980), and Linn (in Wigdor & Garner, II, 1982, pp. 374–384). There are *no* studies on samples of appreciable size where the regression describing criterion performance of black workers (or students) runs above the white regression line. Thus, the white expectancy table does not underrate black applicants. (For a similar conclusion on Hispanics, see Schmidt, Pearlman, & Hunter, 1980.)

Sweeping generalizations are not warranted and indeed are not logically defensible. The disparity between regressions would change if the test were lengthened or shortened (other things being equal). Moreover, if regressions calculated on selected workers coincide, regressions in applicant populations probably would not (Cronbach & Schaeffer, 1981; Linn, 1982b).

Validators should be conscious of these complications, but it would be absurd to propose that they calculate regressions separately for old, educated,

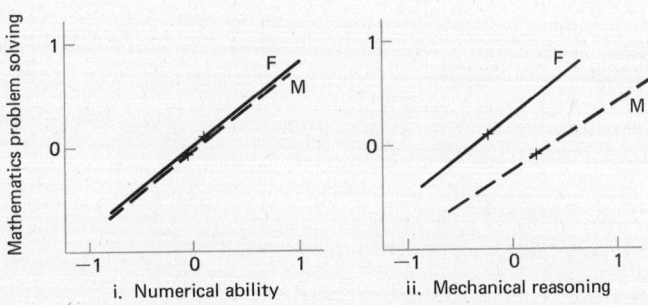

Figure 11.7. Prediction within sexes from two aptitude measures.
Source: Calculated from data in the DAT manual (1974, p. 139). Each score is expressed relative to the mean and s.d. of the sample (sexes combined).

native speakers of English, ... or young, educated, native speakers of Spanish, ... and so on ad infinitum. Such fragments of data are too small for serious statistical analysis. The properly curious, properly cautious investigator will form an overall regression equation and then examine the roster of persons for whom the formula overpredicts and those for whom the formula underpredicts. Insofar as either list seems to be unrepresentative of the pool, pointed questions can then be asked. (The finding may have nothing to do with test bias; it may turn out that a particular supervisor was the source of many instances of underprediction. In the PDRI investigation, white and black supervisors tended to rate members of their own race above other workers.)

Setting cut scores. If regressions indicate validity within each group, how should cut scores be set? Clearly, it is sensible to prefer applicants who rank appreciably above others from the same demographic group. Therefore, the traditional logic can be applied within a group. Any desire to take group membership into account can be satisfied by setting group-specific cut scores. I shall consider the propriety of treating groups differently after reviewing some theory.

Figure 11.8 is based on specific assumptions, but much the same results

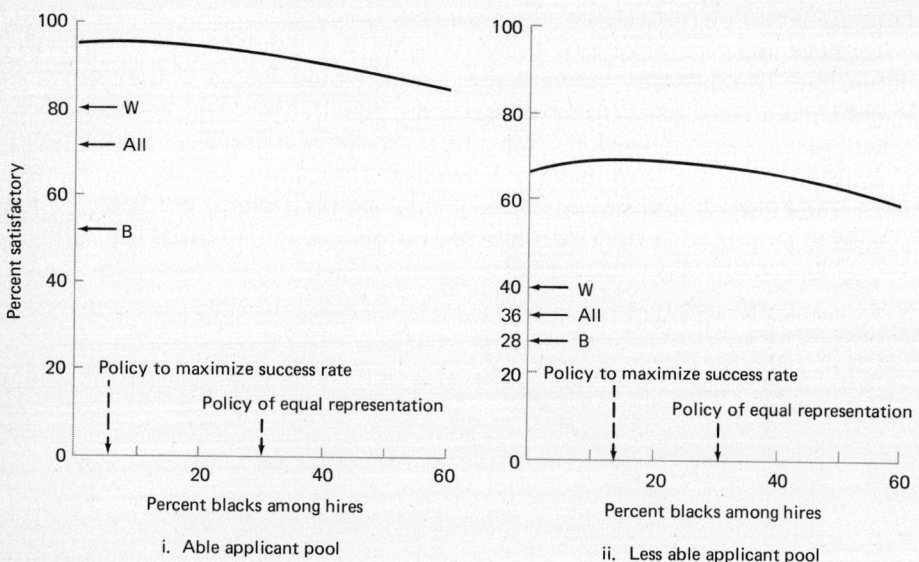

Figure 11.8. Change in work force with increase in minority hiring.
Note: In both panels it is assumed that 30 per cent of the applicants are black, that the selection test has validity 0.55, and that only 20 per cent of applicants will be hired. Cut scores will be set to choose the highest scoring members of each group, but the percentage taken from each group is allowed to shift over a wide range. The horizontal arrows indicate the assumed proportion of white (W), black (B), and all workers who would be satisfactory if selection were at random.

would be found in most real situations (Hunter *et al.*, 1977; Cronbach & Schaeffer, 1981). In both panels, use of the test greatly reduces the number of unsatisfactory workers, compared to what would occur with chance selection. Even though black applicants are assumed here to be less qualified, on average, than whites, hiring the best 20 per cent of blacks and the best 20 per cent of the whites would produce only 7 per cent failures in panel i, 32 per cent in panel ii. Compare with the peak values of 4 per cent and 31 per cent, respectively.

Certain combinations of selection ratios correspond to particular practices or "definitions of fairness," each of which has been recommended by some theorist. Rather than give extensive references, I cite Petersen and Novick (1976). Their paper and the comments published with it cover the ground.

1. *Group-blind hiring.* Traditional practice is to look at scores without regard to group membership. The same cut score is applied to both groups. If the top 20 per cent of applicants would be hired and the test-score means of the two groups differ by 1 s.d., the selection ratios for blacks and whites would be 24 and 8. The disparity would increase with a larger separation of the means.
2. *Quota hiring.* The most direct way to get a representative work force is to hire the same fraction from each group of applicants, guaranteeing zero "adverse impact."
3. *Quotas based on group merit.* One has a sense of injustice when persons who would be satisfactory are less likely to be hired if they come from a minority group. When we know what fraction of each group would be satisfactory if hired, we can adjust cut scores to equalize the chance that satisfactory applicants from each group are hired. This concept of fairness was advanced by R. L. Thorndike and by Nancy Cole.
4. *Equal marginal risk.* Another concept requires setting the cut score in each group so that the last persons hired from each group—the lowest-scoring applicants among those hired—have equal probability of success. This is "merit hiring" in the most literal sense, and it is the policy that produces the greatest number of successful workers.

As Figure 11.8 indicates, in the typical employment situation, one can move a long distance from policy (4) toward policies (2) and (3) with little loss in productivity. How policy (1) affects productivity depends on the group means, but it is bound to give worse results than policy (4)—unless the regressions coincide.

This is not the place for a long argument on the propriety of group-specific cut scores. I mention a few points that enter into policy decisions of this kind.

- The Gallup poll asked the public, in 1981, whether preferential treatment of women and minorities was justified to make up for past discrimination or whether "ability, as determined by test scores, should be the main consideration." Except among nonwhites, from 76 to 92 per cent chose the second option (with around 6 per cent undecided). Among nonwhites, the proportion was 57 (14 per cent stating no opinion). A Harris poll in 1982 reported a 3-to-1 margin in favor of affirmative action provided "that there are no rigid quotas." Tenopyr (in Glaser & Bond, 1981) believes that employers will be reluctant to act in a way that seems to treat groups differently. Linn (1982a) shows that law schools do admit many blacks whose test scores match those of white applicants rejected.
- In at least two cases (p. 385f.) appellate courts have accepted disparate cut scores for racial groups. Moreover, the *UFG* (Sec. 14B, para. 8d) appear to advise equal-marginal-risk cutoffs.
- It can be argued that, in a comparison of applicants whose scores are equal, the preference should go to the applicants who had to overcome economic and environmental disadvantage to reach those scores.
- An employer could regard having a racially mixed staff as valuable in itself for winning community or customer acceptance. Also, as Dunnette (1974) has pointed out, all members of the community share the dollar costs of social disorganization that follow when some group finds itself unable to get ahead economically.

23. *Assume, in each of these cases, that the test is reasonably valid and that the courts would accept any policy between equal marginal risk and zero adverse impact. What policy would you favor?*
    a. *A test is used to select persons for training as operators of cranes used in construction. Trainees who seem not to catch the knack or are careless are discharged before they operate the machine by themselves. Most discharges occur within the first two weeks. The discharge rate serves as the criterion for the test.*
    b. *A public-health official is expected to exercise considerable judgment and to be alert to detect unsanitary conditions and other hazards. Many persons who seem to grasp the regulations and skills used in entry-level jobs do not demonstrate the desired qualities when promoted to independent responsibility. A test is, therefore, used to screen those applying to enter the service.*
24. *Suppose that Test X has adverse impact against B's when used with a single cutting score. The adverse impact can be reduced by using a lower cutting score in group B or by using a shorter version of Test X with a single cutting score. Which policy would be better?*
25. *L. V. Jones reported to the APA convention in 1983 that since 1970 there has been a continuous reduction in the average difference between blacks and whites on achievement measures in verbal and mathematical areas.*

Most of the data come from the National Assessment of Educational Progress, and the finding is similar at age 13 and 17. Some group difference remains, however.
a. *What explanations can you suggest for the trend and for the fact that the group difference had not vanished in the early 1980s?*
b. *What questions in Table 11.2 does this finding shed light on?*

"Test bias" has received more attention from the press and from general works on testing than any other aspect of psychology. The reason for not giving it a *separate* chapter in this book should now be clear. Every aspect of testing might lead to a charge of unfair or unwise practice, and that accusation might or might not be well-grounded. Some debates are about facts, some about social policy and the law. Some are essentially about the logic of validation, as a biased interpretation lacks validity.

Table 11.2 reviews several main points made earlier. A symposium on techniques of evaluating single items (Berk, 1982), a chapter by Reynolds concerned chiefly with school psychology (in Reynolds & Gutkin, 1982), a symposium on minimum competency tests (Madaus, 1982), Jensen's (1980) massive analysis of relevant facts, and papers in the Glaser-Bond (1981) symposium—by Nancy Cole, Esteban Olmedo, Edmund Gordon and Moli-Dawn Terrell, John Garcia, and others—extend the discussion. Table 11.2 emphasizes themes that have concerned blacks and Hispanics; it would require far more space to review the concerns of women, Jews, Asiatic immigrants, the physically handicapped, and so on.

The succinct comments in the third column are intended only to remind the reader of better developed statements made on the pages referred to. Do not fix attention on these sentences out of context; they are no more than headlines to cover complex stories. If these statements were put to a vote among the dozens of psychologists who have written on bias, surely nearly every statement would be endorsed by a strong majority. Universal support for a statement, however, would be a sign that it is vague. On this topic, everything is controversial.

One further comment did not fit into the table. Whenever the suitability of using ability tests as a basis for a decision is under discussion, the debate should not focus on testing alone. As a minimum, these questions should be added:

Is this a decision that should be made (no matter on what basis)?
If yes, what will be the basis for the decision if testing is not used?
And how would questions like those in Table 11.2 be answered with regard to that alternative kind of information?

SECTION 2: SPECIALIZED TOPICS

As was explained at the start of the chapter, the following section discusses further the theory and practice of selection. These topics are "essen-

Table 11.2. *Test bias against minorities: Some questions and answers*

Central Concern	Question	Comment	Relevant Pages
Score distribution	Does one group score lower than another on average?	A common finding. Implies bias only where there is solid evidence that the groups do not differ that much on what the test is said to measure.	112f., 224, 321f., 331
Test administration	Are scores lowered when the test taker belongs to a minority group and examiner does not belong to that group?	Probably true for some test takers. Evidently not a major source of observed group differences in the United States. Scores should routinely be flagged when the tester sees the examinee's effort as weak.	60, 66f., 271, 325
	Are scores lowered when the person is not tested in his own language?	Yes, in general. But "testing in own language" is an incomplete solution.	66, 211, 324f.
	Do standard conditions bring out the best in minority test takers?	Performance may improve when conditions are altered. If conditions are modified, renorming and revalidation would be needed to support many interpretations.	39, 323–326
Test content	Does the test contain irrelevant content that holds down minority scores?	A major difficulty in crosscultural research. Not a major source of differences between groups in the United States. Review of items by minority members a potential safeguard.	323–325, 330–334
	Does the selection of items favor majority subjects?	Statistical analysis can locate items that present special	156, 259, 330–334

Table 11.2. (*Continued*)

Central Concern	Question	Comment	Relevant Pages
		difficulty for minority persons (and vice versa). Whether that difficulty is irrelevant and biasing depends on the proposed interpretation.	
Predictive validity	Do minority members tend to do better on the job or in school than majority members with the same test score?	"Underprediction" or "differential prediction" is investigated by a follow-up study in each group. It appears that discrepancies are typically small and work to the advantage of minorities.	386–388
	Does the test predict because the institution (or its criterion) in itself handicaps minority participants?	A lively possibility. Test validators should be alert to irrelevant difficulty in a treatment or bias in a criterion.	8, 342f., 365f., 368, 388, 399
Selection rule	Does the rule accept a smaller fraction of minority applicants than of other applicants?	"Adverse impact" is a preliminary consideration; it may occur when the selection rule is valid.	334, 384f.
	Does the rule accept persons from one group who are below the cutoff applied to another group?	Justification can be offered for preferential hiring of this kind.	246, 385f., 388, 390
	Does the rule neglect some valued quality on which the minority group shows to advantage?	A meaningful challenge once such a quality is pointed out and a measure of it suggested. Both law and the selector's self-interest require attention to a plausible suggestion of this kind.	246, 258f., 326, 329

tials" for those taking responsibility for selection or for clinical classification, but peripheral for other readers.

ADJUSTING VALIDITY COEFFICIENTS

In most personnel research, the validity coefficients directly calculated can mislead. The adjustment methods are dependable in some circumstances and shaky in others. Only an expert can judge, in each particular application, how near an adjusted value is to the true value of the quantity it estimates. Ordinarily, both the original coefficient and the one obtained by formula should be reported. Even though questionable, the adjustments have the important function of warning against face-value interpretations of unadjusted coefficients.

It must again be emphasized that a correlation coefficient obtained on a previously screened group will underrate the power of the test for sorting applicants. In the U.S. Air Force, the correlation with the criterion of one test composite for trainees selected by those tests was 0.37. In the completely unscreened sample sent into training for experimental purposes, the coefficient rose to 0.66. A second cause of low correlation is unreliability in the criterion (p. 176). Criteria often are unreliable because they must be collected under field conditions with limited resources and few controls.

The adjustment formulas transform an observed correlation or regression coefficient into an estimate of what would have been found if the study had been made with one or more of these ideal features:

1. Representative applicants.
2. A fully reliable criterion.
3. A fully reliable test.

The formulas most commonly used date back to the turn of the century. One, introduced by Pearson, allows for "restriction of range" (i.e., for preselection). Spearman introduced the so-called "correction for attenuation" (i.e., for unreliability). The formulas—which can be used together—appear in Lord and Novick (1968); see also Cronbach *et al.*, (1972), and Jöreskog & Sörbom (1979). The Pearson formula is strictly applicable only when one knows how persons who provided complete data differ from the applicant pool (or other population of interest). Recent work in econometrics, by adding assumptions, makes corrections possible even when unspecified judgments and self-selection caused some loss of cases (Heckman, 1979; C. Brown, 1982; Dunbar, 1983).

26. *When a selection procedure is being evaluated, it is considered legitimate to estimate a validity coefficient relating observed score on the test to true score on the criterion, but illegitimate to adjust the coefficient upward to offset the unreliability of the test. Why?*

27. *Consider the probable success in industrial jobs of graduates from an engineering school. What characteristics have a restricted range (compared to the entire population of the same age) owing to preselection? What characteristics relevant to the job probably have not been restricted?*
28. *The Flanagan Industrial Tests were validated by collecting test scores and on-the-job criteria. In the analysis for at least one job, the sample was divided into fourths on the criterion, and the two middle groups were discarded. The correlation was calculated from the remaining cases. Why does this procedure give a falsely large coefficient?*

PREDICTOR COMPOSITES

Linear Regression

Two or more scores can be combined in a weighted sum. The weighting that gives the highest correlation with the criterion is defined by a multiple-regression equation; the corresponding validity coefficient is the multiple correlation R.

Once a good predictor is available, bringing in new information of the same sort usually improves prediction only slightly. This is seen in the following correlations of predictors with elimination from flight training (DuBois, 1947, p. 194):

Pilot stanine (i.e., composite score on selection battery)	0.653
Stanine plus Qualifying examination	0.655
Stanine plus Qualifying plus General Classification Test	0.655

And, when the tests overlap, the weights matter little. The composite $X + 0.3Y$ ranks people very much as $Y + 0.3X$ does if r_{XY} is large.

Adding fresh information on a component of the job not covered by other tests in the set raises the multiple correlation. Table 7.5 displayed this increase in validity for predicting college grades: from an r of 0.37 with one score to 0.41 with two scores to 0.56 when high school marks were added in. A multiple correlation quickly reaches a ceiling; adding tests (or non-test variables) beyond the first three or four rarely is valuable.

It is of interest that in the PDRI study their mechanical comprehension test had the best validity of any measure (0.33 against rated problem-solving ability, all cases pooled) and that the validities of batteries that added in five or six more scores reached only 0.34. The reason for recommending a battery rather than the TMC alone was to obtain stable validity in various subsets of plants, jobs, and so on. (Range restriction also made it necessary to look beyond the coefficients that have been mentioned.)

Elaborate formulas can be worthwhile when each added test measures a new factor, combining weights are based on a large sample, and conditions of work are unlikely to change. Though only a few tests will enter any one prediction formula, it may be desirable to try out many more tests, especially when one wants to predict each person's success in a variety of jobs (as in guidance or military classification).

An Air Force study. Table 11.3 shows how tests were weighted to predict graduation from pilot, bombardier, and navigator training during World War II. In the selection of bombardiers, Discrimination Reaction Time and Finger Dexterity counted heavily whereas Reading and Arithmetic had very little weight. The navigator composite, on the other hand, depended primarily on intellectual abilities. The jobs have been redefined as new equipment and tactics altered crew duties; weights have changed accordingly.

Which variables pick up weights is complexly determined. Several examples can be found in a study of prediction of high school marks from

Table 11.3 *Validity data and combining weights in military classification*

Test	Correlation with Criterion			Relative Weight		
	Bomb.	Nav.	Pilot	Bomb.	Nav.	Pilot
Printed tests:						
Reading Comprehension	0.1	0.3	0.2	8	2	—
Spatial Orientation II	0.1	0.35	0.25	—	10	5
Spatial Orientation I	0.1	0.4	0.2	—	9	6
Dial and Table Reading	0.2	0.55	0.2	14	18	4
Biographical Data—pilot	—	—	0.3	—	—	15
Biographical Data—navigator	—	0.25	−0.05	—	9	—
Mechanical Principles	0.1	0.15	0.3	—	—	8
Technical Vocabulary—pilot	0.05	0.1	0.3	—	—	13
Technical Vocabulary—nav.	0.05	0.2	0.1	—	—	—
Mathematics	0.1	0.5	0.1	—	18	—
Arithmetic Reasoning	0.1	0.45	0.1	8	12	—
Instrument Comprehension I	—	—	0.15	—	—	9
Instrument Comprehension II	—	—	0.35	—	—	
Numerical Operations, front	0.15	0.25	0.0	—	—	—
Numerical Operations, back	0.1	0.3	0.0	—	—	—
Speed of Identification	0.1	0.2	0.2	—	—	—
Apparatus tests:						
Rotary Pursuit	0.15	0.1	0.2	12	—	4
Complex Coordination	0.2	0.25	0.4	12	—	17
Finger Dexterity	0.15	0.2	0.1	19	6	—
Discrimination Reaction Time	0.2	0.35	0.2	27	6	4
Two-Hand Coordination	0.1	0.25	0.3	—	11	4
Rudder Control	—	—	0.4	—	—	12

SOURCE: DuBois, 1947, pp. 99, 101.
Note: The criterion for the various validity coefficients is graduation or nongraduation from training.

GATB (Ingersoll & Peters, 1966). Marks in English are predicted ($R = 0.63$) by a combination of V, N, Q (clerical perception) and K (mark making). Since there were 1673 cases, another sample would surely give much the same result. But why no weight for G? Is it irrelevant? In the original r's, G correlated 0.55 with the criterion whereas V and N correlated 0.54 and 0.54. There is no weight for G in the formula because the formula covers the G information when it uses V and N as a pair. Although K correlates only 0.27, it gets into the formula; P, with an r of 0.31, does not. Does this mean that English requires speedy mark making? Surely not. My best guess is that K scores reflect willingness to perform an uninteresting task. Whatever relevant attribute P measures is covered in other scores, so it gets no weight. The predictor for Latin gives weights to G, Q, and N, and not to the "obviously relevant" V. But counselors keep low-V students out of Latin classes, which so restricts the range on that variable that N is a better predictor.

Crossvalidation

It may be unsafe to accept a combining rule on the basis of a satisfactory coefficient in a first sample. The particular critical score or the combining formula that gives the very best result is certain not to fit a second group as well. The investigator should be particularly skeptical of weights that make little psychological sense because they are likely to have come from sampling errors.

Although regression weights give the best prediction for the sample, the weighting best in the population (hence best for future samples) would be somewhat different. Therefore, the validity coefficient for a statistically derived formula shrinks in an independent sample. Shrinkage is relatively small when the predictors are chosen initially on the basis of substantial past experience and theory and relatively large in a "shotgun" study where miscellaneous predictors are tried with no particular rationale.

Procedures that hold shrinkage to a minimum are called "robust," and such methods are widely accepted (Darlington, 1978; Dunnette & Borman, 1979; Wainer, 1978). The simplest proposal is to apply equal weights to standard scores whenever predictors are consistently intercorrelated (Dawes, 1979; but see the objections of Remus, 1980).

Cutting scores, combining weights, and multiple correlations derived from modest samples ought to be confirmed. A rule or formula is crossvalidated by trying it on a sample not used in selecting the tests and establishing weights. Conceptually, crossvalidation requires two full-size validation studies, and the cost becomes discouraging. Fortunately, internal-consistency methods like those used to study test reliability can substitute for crossvalidation on fresh data. If the original sample is divided in half, at random, weights determined on one half can be crossvalidated on the other half—but this method underestimates the validity of weights based on the full sample. For a method that gives a more adequate estimate, see Mosteller and Tukey (1977).

When good data are available on hundreds of cases, shrinkage is not serious. Thus, an army study formed predictive composites of 10 tests, using a sample of 200 or more soldiers per job. Among electronics jobs the average validity (corrected for range restriction) was around 0.7 in both the original and the crossvalidation samples. Results were equally good in other job categories (Helme *et al.*, 1957).

29. *What is the apparent psychological meaning of each of the following regression equations? They combine standard scores on an aptitude battery somewhat like GATB to predict grades in a training course:*
    a. *Drafting grade predicted by Clerical Speed + 2 Spatial + 0.5 Arithmetic Reasoning.*
    b. *Machine Shop grade predicted by Arithmetic Reasoning + 1.5 Tool Knowledge + 1.5 Automotive Information + .01 (all other tests).*
30. *Consider the weights in Table 11.3.*
    a. *Why are different weights assigned to the first two tests, in the navigator composite, when their validity coefficients are similar?*
    b. *Consider the tasks making up each job. Which weights are open to suspicion as possible statistical flukes that would not crossvalidate?*

Classification Decisions

Let us return to predictions made in classification and guidance (pp. 20, 140, 310ff.). A test that predicts success on *many* jobs is likely to have little value for classifying applicants. The general test does not tell which job the person can do best. From a formal standpoint, classification attempts to predict a difference between two criteria. A composite predictor can be found for each of the criteria. A value comparison is required: How good a navigator must one be to be as useful (or as happy) as an average pilot? Once the scales are comparable, the predictions indicate which route is most promising for a person.

The ideal classification test has a positive correlation with performance in one job and a zero or negative correlation with performance in other jobs. For a simple example, I assume that the criterion standard deviations for pilots and navigators are about equal—that is, that the difference in value to the air force between an ace pilot and a borderline pilot is equal to that between an outstanding and a mediocre navigator. According to Table 11.3, Two-Hand Coordination has a validity close to 0.3 for *both* navigator and pilot. Therefore, it is useless for classification. Numerical Operations has a validity near 0.3 for navigator and zero for pilot. It is, therefore, a good classification test. The Mathematics test, with validities 0.5 and 0.1, is even better.

Under Brogden's assumptions, the value of a test used to assign persons to one of two treatments is proportional not to validity but to the difference between its two validities or, more exactly, to the difference in slope between

PERSONNEL SELECTION

the two criterion-on-test regressions (Brogden, 1951). Figures 1.4 and 5.4 extended this reasoning. It should be possible for employers to capitalize on differential abilities by, for example, designing two forms of training for a production task. One could be heavily verbal, and the other might rely more on concrete and visual experience. The verbal training probably would be quicker and cheaper, but the second approach could make good use of applicants who are less educated or less familiar with English. Another obvious type of differentiation is to give training in specific skills (dial reading, say, or use of calipers) to each person who appears capable of learning the job but would fail if these specific deficiencies were not repaired. An elaborate system of this type is under development for U.S. Army training.

In clinical diagnosis there is no fixed number of places to fill. Every person assessed can be called "normal," or every one can be called "schizophrenic" if such uniform classification appears correct. When the clinician is trying to identify a rare condition, uniform classification is often the best strategy—even when some test has appreciable validity. Meehl and Rosen (1955) took prediction of suicide as an example. If a test identifies a person as having a high probability of suicide, the clinician will probably recommend giving him closer attention and more intensive treatment than a probable nonsuicide. Suppose that 5 per cent of those tested in a certain clinic later attempt suicide ("base rate" probability = 0.05). A person with a low test score (on a hypothetical test) has probability 0.001 of a suicide attempt, and one can confidently place him in the nonsuicide category. With higher test scores, probability of suicide increases, so the test is valid. The highest score in the clinic sample, however, may indicate only probability 0.2 of a suicide attempt. The high-scoring person is not a "probable suicide." In labeling such persons suicide risks, we raise four false alarms for every correct decision. To put a special watch on the high scorer drains the clinic's resources. Very likely it cannot invest this effort in four false alarms in order to forestall one suicide. On the other hand, one person saved may be seen as outweighing the cost of guarding all five.

The use of valid information in classification is basically similar to that underlying the setting of cut scores in selection (p. 369). The cost of false alarms is to be weighed against the cost of misses. In general, false alarms are easily tolerated when further work with the person will disclose the error and the temporary misclassification does not significantly damage the person's interests.

31. *What tests had greatest validity for distinguishing pilots from bombardiers, according to Table 11.3?*
32. *A 20-point test for parole prediction gives these expectancies of violating parole: for a score of 20, 40 per cent; score 10, 20 per cent; score 0, 5 per cent. Can this test be used practically by a parole board, or should all prisoners be classified as likely to obey probation rules?*
33. *Could two treatments have equal test-outcome correlations, but very differ-*

ent outcome standard deviations? If so, which treatment (assignment) is advisable for a person with a high test score?

VALIDITY GENERALIZATION

Application of any validity study attempts to generalize. As Chapter 5 pointed out, a decision to select this year's law students on the basis of last year's experience requires assumptions about the stability of the local situation. A far bolder extrapolation is the claim of a new user that a test is valid for her on the basis of positive evidence collected elsewhere in allegedly similar schools or jobs. Employers would like to rely on the validations others have reported because it takes time and money to study their own workers. When the number of workers in a job category is small, firm-by-firm validation is impracticable.

An increasingly common resolution is for several firms to apply the same test or tests to their applicants, collect similar criterion data after the same lapse of time, and interpret the data all together. This procedure—seen in the PDRI study—builds up sample sizes and produces comparable data across several firms. Whoever analyzes the data does have a responsibility to dissect them, to decide whether the requirements for satisfactory performance appear to be similar from firm to firm.

"Validity generalization" refers to the working hypothesis that a selection rule found valid in one setting will be valid in the next. A firm that installs a test on the basis of experience reported in other places and makes no follow-up of its own is trusting the generalized power of the test to predict for all jobs with the same title. But no hypothesis is to be trusted blindly.

Cautious professional opinion has urged for decades that any selection plan be validated afresh in each firm. A few industrial psychologists, led by Schmidt and Hunter (1977), argue that—with rare exceptions—the validity established for a test and job will apply to all jobs in the same broad category and in all firms. Moreover (see p. 305), it is said that ability tests are more or less equally valid and that it is pointless to use different test combinations for different jobs. *Observed* validity coefficients vary from job to job within the same category. It is now recognized that much of this variation arises from the use of small samples, the restricted range in some of the samples, and similar inadequacies of the original research (Callender & Osburn, 1980; Schmidt *et al.,* 1981).

In one compilation, clerical jobs were sorted into what are ordinarily regarded as distinct families; here, I confine attention to two categories of the *Dictionary of Occupational Titles:* stenography–typing–filing and bookkeepers, accounting-machine operators, tellers. Table 11.4 shows average validity coefficients for several kinds of tests. These averages must be highly accurate because the number of coefficients is large. Though the categories seem to describe distinct kinds of work, the average coefficients are almost the same

Table 11.4 *Mean validity coefficients in two categories of clerical job*

Job family	Relation of Proficiency Criterion to Test				
	Perceptual	Quantitative	Verbal	Reasoning	Memory
Stenographic	0.22	0.23	0.19	0.18	0.18
Accounting	0.24	0.25	0.20	0.32	0.20

SOURCE: Pearlman *et al.*, 1980, p. 382. The results for regression coefficients (unpublished) were essentially similar.

for both categories. Only the reasoning tests have greater validity in one job category than the other.

Validity coefficients for 35 radically diverse military jobs had been reported by Helme *et al.* (1957). Schmidt *et al.* (1981) find that the validity coefficients for a test (after certain adjustments) typically had a standard deviation of 0.11, over jobs. Though the jobs were dissimilar (cooks, sheet-metal workers, clerks, ...), 95 per cent of a test's validities fell within ± 0.22 of the mean. Schmidt *et al.* (1981) call this variation "tiny" and conclude that evidence of validity for one job justifies using a test for jobs with *other* titles. If this position were accepted, employers would be relieved of much of the burden of validation. Critical discussions have only begun to appear (Cronbach, 1980a).

In my opinion, validities are much less generalizable than Schmidt's group suggests. Their s.d. of 0.11 means that a test with an average validity of 0.32 will have a validity below 0.21 for roughly a sixth of the jobs in the category and above 0.43 for another sixth. The initially surprising finding that quantitative tests do not correlate higher with success in bookkeeping than with success in stenography can be explained by reduced range. Persons assess their quantitative ability before they decide to become bookkeepers, employers consider it in deciding whom to hire, and it affects who stays on the job or is transferred. The restriction of range differs from category to category and from test to test. Allowing for this would break up the seeming uniformities summarized in Table 11.4.

The PDRI study established that—after appropriate adjustments—its composite of ability tests had essentially the same validity over all operator jobs and all utility companies. It did not try to establish whether the relevance of components of the battery (e.g., a reading score) was the same for different job categories. It did note, however, that its three composites—which I may call A for ability, E for experience, and S for emotional stability—behaved differently in plants of different kinds. Consequently it recommended three formulas:

$3A + 2E + S$ for fossil-fuel operators
$2A + E$ for nuclear-fuel operators
$2A + E + 2S$ for hydro operators and switchboard operators.

One generalization hypothesis, then, survived a validity check; while one did not.

McCormick *et al.* (1979), taking a more conservative position than Schmidt's group, defend the use of a test battery without tryout when a local job analysis identifies relevant dimensions *and* tests have been validated elsewhere as measures of those dimensions. McCormick speaks of "job component" validity; others have spoken of this type of informal judgment as having "synthetic validity." A limited study by Colbert and Taylor (1978) reaches conclusions about clerical workers that differ from those of Schmidt *et al.* (1981), but supports the McCormick approach.

In a stable environment, it appears safe to generalize from data analyzed in one year to applicants tested in future years. A follow-up study in many colleges shows that a regression equation developed in one year applied to at least the next four years with essentially no erosion of validity (Sawyer & Maxey, 1979). Linn *et al.* (1981) find that a predictor of law school grades has similar validities in different schools and years (after allowing for statistical fluctuations), but that, even so, coefficients are appreciably higher in some schools (and years) than in others.

34. *Tenopyr and Oeltjen (1982) suggest that, when a supervisor's rating is the criterion, validity coefficients are more likely to be similar from one job to another than when a direct measure of job performance is the criterion. Why might this be true? (Figure 11.2 may help with your answer.)*
35. *Given the PDRI rules and assuming equal importance of the jobs, what kind of applicant would be more suitable for a hydro plant than a nuclear plant?*

PATTERNS AND CONFIGURATIONS

The basic methods of combining predictors and setting cut scores assume that a linear trend relates outcome to any test score and that the employer will hire "from the top downward." Many less simple relationships are recognized in theory and sometimes in practice.

Regression of utility on a single predictor. The first matter to consider is the regression of outcome on a single test. Brogden's rule assumed that each increase in test scores implies a corresponding increase in payoff. But it would be a remarkable coincidence if the regression of utility on score were linear. Suppose, for example, that the number of gadgets produced per day *is* linearly related to Test X. The worker who produces 400 gadgets is worth more than twice as much to the firm as the worker who produces 200 because the latter's cost of equipment and overhead is much higher (per gadget produced) than that of the first worker. If the production criterion were mapped onto a utility scale, the curve would resemble panel i of Figure 11.9. This comparatively flat

Personnel Selection

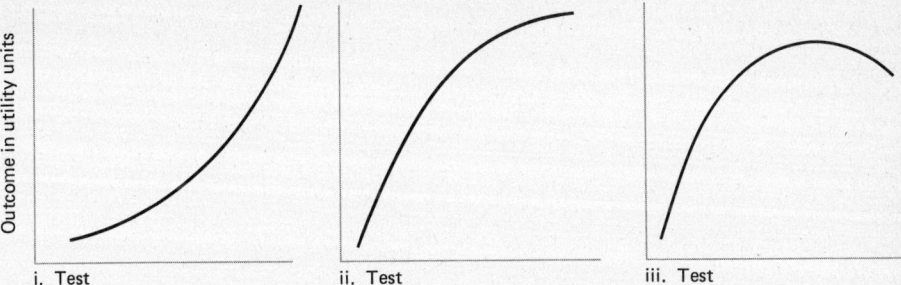

Figure 11.9. Possible nonlinear relations of outcome to test score.

trend at the left would also be seen where the failure rate during training is high for low scorers; the cost of failures being more or less uniform, utility is much the same across the high-risk region.

Panel ii describes the opposite case: utility increases with score up to a certain level, and then the rise tapers off. This occurs, for example, when a particularly fast worker on an assembly line cannot produce more because he must wait for others to supply parts. Among workers who can keep up with the standard pace with little spoilage, there is not much difference in utility. A footnote to the discussion on validity generalization is pertinent here. No doubt typing skill has general relevance over many jobs and firms, but the utility very likely tapers off as in panel ii. The cut score that eliminates inadequate workers probably varies, however; only in straight "production typing" would better-than-average speed be a worker's most important asset.

Panel iii represents the possibility that workers who are "overqualified" are poor risks. This kind of regression is most likely when turnover is weighted into the criterion; better-qualified workers leave for more rewarding jobs, and the employer benefits less from the investment in training them.

If panel iii describes the situation, the employer could logically prefer to hire persons in midrange. Where panel ii describes the facts, the employer may set a cut score at a moderate level to rule out high-risk applicants and hire at random—or on the basis of non-test characteristics—within the group who survive the cut. Where panel i tells the story, it is desirable to push the cut score as high as possible. Intensifying the effort to recruit excellent applicants would be logical.

Nonlinear Rules

Considering two variables (or more), various nonlinear trends are possible. One is illustrated in Figure 11.10, where outcome goes up as test scores W and X increase. The composite $W + X$ is the predictor suggested by conventional regression methods; it would define a cutoff line slanting from upper left to lower right. But persons along that line are not equally promis-

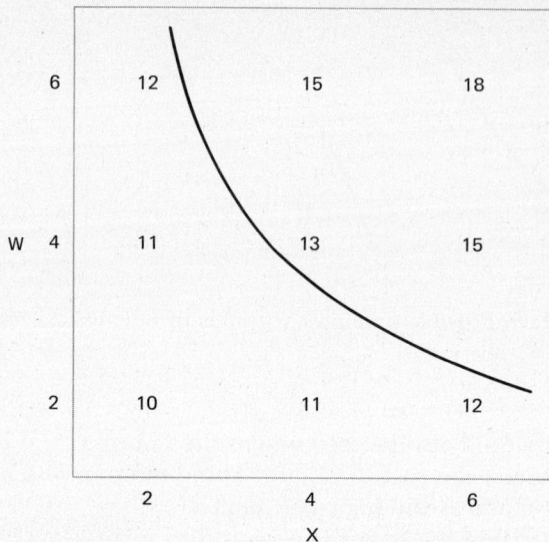

Figure 11.10. Expected outcome as a function of two predictors.

ing. The curved contour line identifies equally promising cases; for every score combination along that line, the expected outcome is 12.5. The best workers are those for whom W and X are in balance.

The term *configural prediction* refers to forecasting outcome from a pattern of scores, not a simple additive composite. Another common term is *moderator variable;* the slope of regression onto X depends on the level of W, so W "moderates" the Y-on-X regression. (And X moderates that of Y on W.) Not only may one ability influence the predictive power of a second ability, but personality variables, sex and race, and life-history variables may act as moderators.

Statistics can generate an equation for a curved line that identifies equally promising workers. A simpler approximation is to use two cutoffs. Hiring everyone whose X and W scores *both* reach 3 or better would include nearly all the persons above the curved line in the figure.

It should be added that multiple cutoff rules are sometimes used in place of linear composites, not because they are more valid, but because they are easier for clerks to apply. The USES provides rules for 400 occupations. Thus persons with scores $P = 75$, $Q = 95$, and $K = 100$ or better are considered well qualified to become electronics assemblers. (These are standard scores on a 100 ± 20 scale; GATB Manual, Sec. IV, 1980).

Configural formulas are not easy to justify. The nonlinearity in Figure 11.10 is not trivial; the regression of outcome on X is three times as steep when $W = 6$ as when $W = 2$. Yet very nearly the same persons would be hired under the $W + X$ rule as under a double-cutoff or curvilinear rule that accepts the same number of applicants. Nonlinear rules, when crossvalidated, usually turn out not to predict better than linear equations (Dunnette & Borman, 1979).

The personnel worker should nonetheless keep the possibility in mind. If strength in W compensates for weakness in X, and vice versa, a simple combination of W and X is probably a suitable predictor. If compensation is not a plausible hypothesis, linear combination may be a bad idea.

During World War II the U.S. Navy asked psychologists to select recruits suitable for training as sonar operators. All sailors whose general-ability scores qualified them for specialized training were screened. The selectors looked at a weighted sum of TMC and several tonal discrimination tests. Many of the men above the cut score were sent to sonar training. If they failed there, it was standard practice to reassign them to general sea duty. It was a serious matter when a sailor with good general ability was sent to a school for which he lacked special abilities because his general ability would not then be fully used. Many of those who failed in sonar school did so because of poor tonal judgment. They had been selected because their high mechanical comprehension raised the composite score, concealing their weakness. Such men were doomed in sonar training whereas they could have been excellent in, say, radar maintenance. (Ultimately, the composite was replaced by a multiple cutoff.)

36. *If it is unfair to reject an applicant because his ability scores are very high, what legitimate use can be made of the finding that an ability predicts length of stay on a job as shown in panel iii of Figure 11.9?*
37. *In a situation described by panel ii of Figure 11.9, what does a firm sacrifice if it sets a very high cut score?*
38. *Considering the following responsibilities, would you expect a deficit in either of the named abilities to be compensated for by superiority in the other ability?*
    a. *Baseball player: hitting, fielding.*
    b. *Opera singer: vocal range, ability to memorize roles in many languages.*
    c. *Newspaper reporter: writing skill, ability to win confidence of strangers.*

PREDICTION BY HUMAN JUDGES

The computer makes recommendations—"admit to this college," "flag as potential suicide," "label as antisocial personality"—by applying a rule to information, a rule that humans devised. The rule, even if a configural one, is applied in an unvarying fashion. Such mechanical decision making is questionable for many reasons, but it is not hard to defend the machine as superior to the human interpreter because of its consistency.

Humans looking at a file or interviewing candidates take facts into account for which there is no experience table. They consider the circumstances of the person and the institution. Colleges and universities are advised to build a diversified student body by recognizing background and interests rather than selecting mechanically the applicants with the highest predicted academic record. Ruling out all applicants who fall below a cut score has repeatedly been condemned by professional opinion; other facts in the record can alter the apparent significance of the score.

A computer cannot set a policy or rule for an institution; only humans can weigh values and decide how much risk to take. If the policy is explicit enough, a computer can carry it out. The computer can weigh up any number of facts, including exceptional ones ("lived for two years in Thailand") if the policy is clear. It can easily execute the following rule intended to increase diversity: "Among those whose predicted grade average is between 2.5 and 3.5, select 70 per cent at random for admission." Another option: ". . . . divide passable applicants into groups on the basis of interests, and pick at random with higher acceptance rates in higher categories."

This is a convenient place to mention the discouraging validity of interview data (Tenopyr, in Glaser & Bond, 1981). Repeatedly, studies have indicated that interviewers disagree in their impressions of the same candidate and that their judgments are unlikely to improve on those derived from tests and past history. The medical school at Yale reduces its pool of 3000 applicants to about 700 and interviews these; about 160 are offered places. In a validation study, 69 persons offered admission by Yale but who chose other medical schools were compared with students in those schools whom Yale had rejected following the interview. Those the interviewers favored did not differ from the rejects on the criteria: Medical Board examinations and ratings by their faculties. The interview is costly, and quite possibly personality traits irrelevant to merit as a physician enter the judgments. The investigators advised Yale to choose its 160 admits at random from applicants surviving the first screen (Milstein *et al.*, 1981). In employment practice, interviews have several functions and surely will continue to be used. The best general advice is to make sure that interviewer judgments are not given excessive weight in selection.

Are human decisions as good as those made by the computer? That question is too broad to be answered, and it is typically reduced to a simpler one: When predicting a definite criterion on the basis of a file of information, does the human reviewer do better than a statistical formula applied to all or part of that information? The answer is an emphatic no:

> Human judges are not merely worse than *optimal* regression equations; they are worse than almost any regression equation. Even if the weights in the equation are *arbitrary,* as long as they are nonzero, positive, and linear, the equation generally will outperform human judges. . . . [I]n many of the studies, the judges have had not merely expertise in the particular judgmental domain, but also

formal training in the statistical procedures necessary for prediction [Nisbett & Ross, 1980].

For the evidence see Meehl's classic analysis (1954); Dawes (1979); Dawes & Corrigan (1974); and Slovic & Lichtenstein (1971). But the answer given by this literature is overemphatic. Many of the comparative tests were unfair because the computer formula was not subjected to a crossvalidation whereas the humans were relying on *past* experience.

Also, the formula would lose much of its advantage if the judgments of half-a-dozen qualified persons were averaged; the computer is perfectly reliable whereas a single judge is inconsistent from case to case and each judge has idiosyncratic rules. As human judges are expensive, the formula still has the advantage so long as it is based on a relevant experience table. The formula makes cautious predictions when a formula has only moderate validity; it "regresses toward the mean" and rarely predicts a very good or very bad outcome. Human judges are likely to spread their predictions over the whole range of the criterion distribution. Clinicians tend to predict pathology too often whereas the computer is mindful of base rates.

The judge can beat the formula only by bringing in additional facts and weighing them correctly. Typically, judges relying on professional lore and common sense are not aware of the weights they are using. "Policy capturing" research uses various techniques to find out what weights human decision makers actually give to facts and value considerations. Their decisions often do not correspond to the policies they say they are following (Edwards *et al.*, 1975).

Figure 11.11 gives a simple example. Two interviewers rated job applicants and recommended (separately) for or against hiring. I correlated the recommendation with the ratings and arrived at the configurations by factor analysis. Each diagram locates "Intelligence" as a vertical axis and "Cooperativeness" as a second dimension. These two ratings were uncorrelated for Judge B and very slightly correlated for Judge A. The lengths of the arrows for Cooperativeness indicate that A perceived large differences in this trait whereas the ratings B gave were nearly uniform. In hiring, Judge A gave nearly equal weight to intelligence and cooperation. Judge B cared about intelligence, but gave no preference to those he saw as being creative and inquiring as well. These raters, trying to serve the same firm, were playing the game by entirely different rules, rules of which they were only half aware. Of course, they disagreed in many of their recommendations. Necessarily, one or both disagreed with whatever formula experience would have justified. (For similar evidence on a larger scale, see Forehand, 1968.)

The implication of the research on judgment is that a formula should be preferred when it truly fits the decision in hand. But what if a question extends beyond the setting, population, and criterion to which the experience table applies (Cronbach, 1982a)? Judgment *must* be brought in—if no more

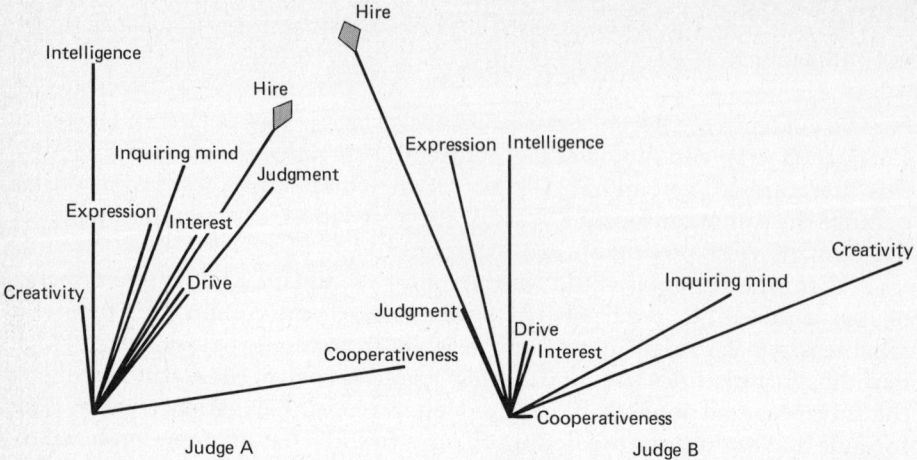

Figure 11.11. Relation among trait ratings and hiring recommendations of two industrial interviewers.
Note: The length of the arrow indicates the s.d. of ratings on the variable (ignoring any portion unrelated to intelligence and cooperativeness). The angle between two arrows is small if the correlation of the variables is high.
Source: This figure is adapted from Cronbach, 1958, p. 364; the data are from J. Sternberg, 1950.

than a judgment to *let* the computer apply a rule developed for a different situation. Facing nonstandard situations, the individual judge will find it advisable to be cautious in the "allowances" she makes for unvalidated factors, and the institution will find it advisable to call upon more than one judge and to conduct research on the policies of the judges and their validity. As Hogarth (1981) points out, humans are at their best in monitoring an evolving situation where new information trickles in. In personnel decisions, that style (if it can be arranged) is preferable to one-shot prediction.

39. *Gough (1967) found that medical school interviewers tended to favor applicants described (independently) as healthy, masculine, robust, cheerful, organized, and relaxed and* not *as individualistic, frank, unconventional, and complicated. Should a medical faculty prefer this kind of student?*
40. *I have said that much of this chapter is relevant to clinical classification though most examples have come from personnel selection. Which sections apply to such clinical decisions as screening and diagnosis?*

PART III
MEASURES OF TYPICAL PERFORMANCE

12
Interest Inventories

This third part of the book takes up investigation of habits or personal styles, attitudes, and feelings. I start with the use of self-reports to measure vocational interests. Interest inventories are important in their own right; 3,000,000 young people take them each year. Beyond that, because interest inventories and personality questionnaires are based on the same range of techniques, this chapter raises widely significant issues. Whereas personality is puzzling theoretically, interests are familiar and easy to discuss—a good starting place.

The inventory is a means of helping the person confront what he already knows about himself, for who else can say what his interests are? The inventory is more convenient than an interview and uses more questions, perhaps indirect ones. The standardized questions are objectively scored, and norms can be provided. The variety of questions and scoring scales draw attention to many vocations the student might not have considered, which is instructive in itself.

Most questions refer to commonplace activities that respondents comprehend from personal experience. Inventories also use occupational titles or abstract descriptions of work, which may not have such concrete meaning. One wonders if adolescents have a clear image of what it means to be a "juvenile delinquency expert" or to "go on expeditions to fight diseases among natives." If not, they cannot judge whether they would like the role.

Interest measurement has been controversial (Tittle & Zytowski, 1978). Because suggesting careers shapes the client's future, inventories can perpetuate cultural stereotypes—for instance, about occupations suitable for one sex or the other. Though agreeing that each individual should shape his or her own fate as fully as possible, measurement specialists disagree sharply about the best way to recognize that occupations differ in their appeal to the sexes. There are technical controversies also; methods of drawing conclusions from verbal responses seem to become less valid as the methods become subtler and more technological.

The interest profile has usually been reported back to the individual for his or her own enlightenment. Occasionally, someone proposes to use the scores in institutional decisions—in medical-school selection, for example. Even if this practice would improve prediction, it would be questionable. To favor applicants whose interest pattern matches the one most common among today's successful students or alumni makes the profession more uniform in membership and more static. Also, asking persons competing for places to testify about themselves could reward dishonesty. The interest inventory, then, is best left as an aid to self-examination.

The appropriate outcome of a counseling episode or a study of careers is growth in self-knowledge, not a definite vocational decision. It takes many years to settle into a career; successive decisions are made along the path. The adolescent should be encouraged in a wide-ranging exploration that identifies promising alternatives. Concentration comes gradually, first as choice of a broad area, then of a vocational line, and ultimately of a specialty or a personalized role.

Ideally, every inventory taken at the same time would tell much the same story about the person—but inventories constructed differently are bound to disagree. At the extreme, two scales describing "interest in a career as printer" were found to correlate *minus* 0.7 (Zytowski, 1968). Two scores from the same answer sheet can be discordant. Thus, the Artistic and Artist scales of the Strong inventory correlate only about 0.6. The items in the Artistic scale refer to liking for artistic activities. The Artist scale examines whether the person's preferences among miscellaneous activities (algebra, tennis, selling, etc.) correspond to the preferences of the majority of artists. (A summary of inventories in Table 12.1 provides details on the Strong and other inventories that will be referred to—*often by initials*—in later parts of the chapter.)

1. *A firm finds substantial turnover among its salespersons. The interest pattern of those who quit differs from the pattern of those who stay (validity coefficient 0.4). Which (if any) of these uses of the information seems appropriate?*
   a. *Use the interest pattern as an "aptitude" measure, and reject applicants for whom short tenure is predicted.*

Table 12.1 Construction patterns of selected inventories

Inventory and Publisher[a]	Item Form[b]	Type and Number of Main Keys[c]	Illustrative Scales	Norms Used in Profiling
Interest inventory (USES)	E	H(12)	Mechanical, Protective	Sexes pooled or within sex[d]
JVIS (RPP)	FC	H(34)	Engineering, Stamina	Students, within sex
OVIS (PC)	E	H(24)	Machine Work, Manual	Students, within grade and sex; the printout lists scales in order of raw score
VII (WPS)	FC	H(8)	Technical, Outdoor	Students, sexes pooled[d]
VPI (CPP)	E	H(6)	Realistic	Norms not offered
KPR (SRA)	FC	H(10)	Mechanical	Male or female students
KOIS (SRA)	FC	C(167)	Engineer(m), Nutritionist(f), English major(m or f)	Men or women in occupation[e]
SCII (CPP)	Mostly E	C(162)	Engineer(m or f)	Men or women in occupation
		H(6)	RIASEC	Adults with average of 2 years of college; sexes pooled, also within sex
		H(23)	Mechanical, Adventure	Adults with average of 2 years of college; sexes pooled, also within sex

[a] Full titles of instruments identified by initials are these: Jackson Vocational Interest Survey, Ohio Vocational Interest Survey, Kuder Preference Record (Form E, also called General Interest Survey), Vocational Interest Inventory (Lunneborg), Vocational Preference Inventory (Holland), Kuder Occupational Interest Survey (also known as Kuder DD), Strong-Campbell Interest Inventory. *Publisher abbreviations refer to Appendix B.*
[b] E = endorsement (single-stimulus) items; FC = forced choice
[c] H = homogeneous; C = criterion-keyed
[d] Items chosen to minimize sex differences.
[e] The scores are not, strictly speaking, converted to a norm scale.

b. *Give the inventory after hiring, and notify the sales manager that low tenure is predicted for applicants A and B but not for C.*
c. *Show the applicant his interest scores and the distributions for salespersons who stay and for those who quit before he commits himself to the job.*

DIMENSIONALIZING INTERESTS

An occupational choice ought to promise a harmonious fit between an individual's personal style and the work. A catalog of all a person's diverse specific interests cannot be digested; categories or dimensions are needed.

Six dimensions (*R-I-A-S-E-C;* Figure 12.1) that John Holland (1973) distilled from previous research now enter into most interpretations and have influenced the construction of several inventories. The themes are considered

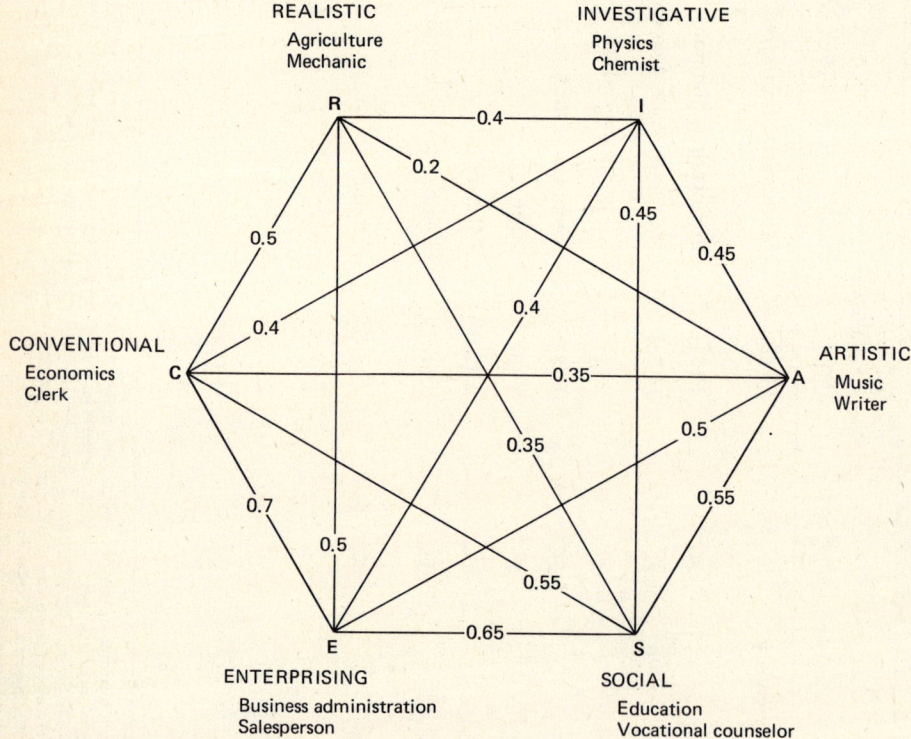

Figure 12.1. Themes in the *RIASEC* system.
Note: At each vertex is a Holland theme, a related college major, and a related occupation.
Source: This figure is adapted from the SDS manual (1979) by permission of Consulting Psychologists Press. The correlations, for interest measures on high school seniors, are from Crabtree and Hales, 1974.

singly or in pairs or triples. As artistic motivation (for example) is easily combined with scientific investigation, these are adjacent in Holland's formulation. Not often does an occupational setting encourage both artistic self-expression and conformity to conventions, so these are opposite in the diagram. Once questioning has identified the individual's salient interests, he is shown a list of occupations classified in *RIASEC* terms. For *AE* (art-and-enterprise), the list suggests these possibilities among others: advertising manager, public relations, fashion model, and lawyer.

Holland's own inventories have no indirect or disguised questions, and he brings no norms into the interpretation. These, then, are face-valid, domain-referenced procedures. His Vocational Preference Inventory (VPI) is simply a list of 160 occupations; the person responds YES/NO/UNDECIDED. The profile counts how often the person spoke favorably of each type of occupation. (Holland's early work was sponsored by the publisher ACT, and they transformed VPI into the ACT inventory [see Figure 12.2] which does use norms.) Holland's more elaborate Self-Directed Search is a teaching device as much as it is a measuring instrument. The person lists occupations he has been vaguely considering, marks which of 66 activities he would like (for example, "work on a scientific project"), checks off competences ("can use a microscope"), and rates occupations as in VPI. Each page is summarized in the *RIASEC* system. If, on several types of questions, positive responses are given to Investigative items, that is a strong indication of his self-concept.

Jackson, working from his own factor analysis, thought it appropriate to make such distinctions as Expressive/Communicative and Logical/Inquiring, and so he has 10 scales in place of Holland's 6. An unusual feature of Jackson's JVIS is a cross-cutting arrangement of the items to describe preference for jobs demanding Stamina or Planfulness or Accountability. Obviously, this complex profile is better suited for mature respondents; Holland's simple one is geared to early career exploration.

For a long time a system other than *RIASEC* was central to vocational planning. The *Dictionary of Occupational Titles (DOT),* a kind of encyclopaedia on job duties, sorted jobs according to their emphasis on data/people/things. Agriculture, for example, receives a 2-0-2 code: much to do with data; little with people; much to do with things. One interest inventory (OVIS) formed 24 scales more or less matched to the *DOT* categories.

Prediger (1976b, 1981a) amplified the three-category system into four and then factored out two dimensions: People/Things and Data/Ideas (Figure 12.2). On such a "bipolar" factor, a person can be at either extreme or intermediate. (The Verbal-minus-Nonverbal factor of CogAT was likewise a bipolar description of profile shape.) Figure 12.2 displays positions of occupational families on the two dimensions. The person's responses locate him in one or another neighborhood. As the ACT inventory yields six *RIASEC* scores also, the map reconciles the *DOT* and Holland systems—insofar as a two-dimensional picture can represent six dimensions.

The U.S. Employment Service (USES) serves persons entering the work

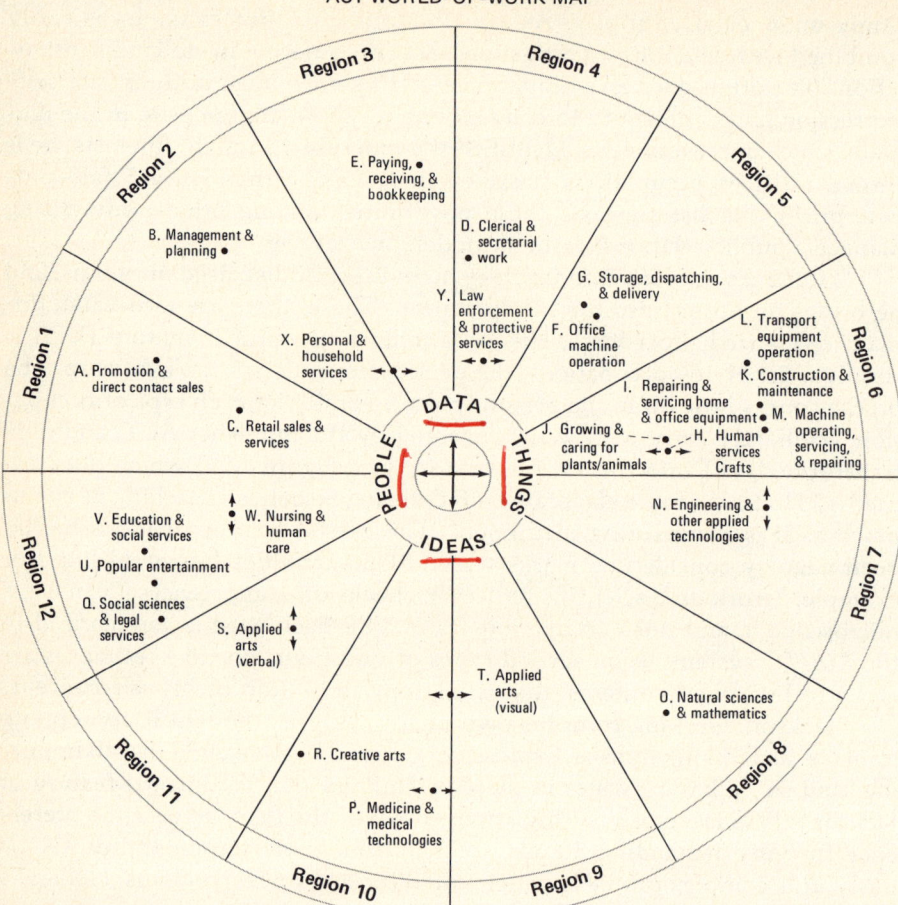

Figure 12.2. A map of the world of work.
Source: This diagram is part of an interpretative report supplied for career planning programs of the American College Testing Program (ACT). An arrow indicates that jobs within an occupational field range widely in the direction shown. Copyright © 1976 and used by permission of ACT.

force or looking for better positions. Wanting detail in its recently developed "occupational exploration system," it extracted 12 factors (Table 12.2). Most of them can be regarded as similar to or as segments within Holland categories (Droege & Padgett, 1979; L. K. Jones, 1980). Scores are taken from a simple inventory. A peak score on any dimension routes the client to certain pages in a 700-page directory. One page, for example, lists a dozen "work groups" suited to mechanical interests, and about four pages on each subfield follow. The jobs listed there are keyed to the even more massive *DOT*. The GATB will be keyed to the same categories and work groups, so that the counselor can easily bring both interests and abilities into the conversation. The mate-

Interest Inventories

Table 12.2. *Interest categories of the USES*

Category	Topics	Holland Theme
Plants and animals	Activities involving plants and animals, usually out-of-doors	R
Protective	Using authority to protect people and property	R
Mechanical	Understanding mechanical principles; using machines, hand tools, or instruments	R
Industrial	Factory work: repetitive, concrete, organized	R
Scientific	Discovering and analyzing information about the natural world; applying it to medicine	I
Artistic	Creative expression of feelings or ideas	A
Leading-Influencing	Leading and influencing others through use of high-level verbal or numerical abilities	S(I,E)[a]
Humanitarian	Helping individuals with mental, spiritual, social, physical, or vocational concerns	S
Physical performing	Physical activities performed before an audience	S
Accommodating	Catering to and serving the desires of others, usually one-on-one	S(E,R)[a]
Selling	Using persuasive and promotional techniques to bring others to a point of view	E
Business detail	Office work that is clearly defined and requires accuracy and attention to detail	C

[a]Some occupations associated with the Holland categories in parentheses were placed here by the factor analysis.

rial is laid out to facilitate self-examination, but it also is an administrative tool of government employment-referral services.

2. *What occupations seem likely to suit someone whose interests have the Holland code* AIS? *In view of the limited reliability of differences between scores, would your answer have been the same if the pattern had been* SIA *(S highest instead of A)? Would an* SIA *person like* SA *occupations?*

3. The correlations in Figure 12.1 indicate a substantial general factor among the six Holland scales. What does a high score on that factor mean?
4. Where do the six RIASEC poles seem to fall in Figure 12.2? What information does the two-dimensional representation lose?
5. Locate professional occupations and others requiring a college education in Figure 12.2. What does this suggest about the interpretation of Prediger's factors?
6. The Vocational Interest Inventory (VII) relates college majors to four bipolar interest factors:

Technical/Service   Business/Science   Outdoor/Organization   Arts/Detailed work

Interpret these findings:
   a. Engineering majors fall far to the left on the first scale (T/S) and far to the right on the second (B/Sc).
   b. On the third scale (O/Or), majors comparatively far to the left are Forestry and Art whereas those toward the right are Accounting and Political Science.
7. Do the four VII scales (question 6) have any apparent correspondence to the ACT map?

CONSTRUCTION OF INVENTORIES

Decisions in Instrument Development

Developers of interest measures have to decide how many items to include and how simple to make the scoring. Short-and-simple implies low cost and entails less thorough measurement. A form that test takers can score for themselves appeals to purchasers who want quick returns at low cost. At the opposite extreme, a client may be happy to pay for, and wait some days for, a computer printout that offers dozens of scores and several pages of "personalized" interpretation. Or perhaps the client can respond directly on a computer terminal and obtain a printout minutes after he has finished. The more elaborate the profile, the more necessary scoring by machine becomes.

Three major decisions about format have to be made. The first has to do with the kind of item: Endorsement? Or comparison? The second has to do with organizing items into a scale: Homogeneous? Or criterion-keyed? The third has to do with the basis for plotting profiles: Raw response counts (or raw percentages)? Or norm-referenced conversions? I shall argue that the advantage lies with homogeneous keying and with interpretation of a raw-score profile. As for item forms, each has advantages and disadvantages. With directly interpretable homogeneous keys, endorsement items probably serve best. Forced-choice items probably serve best where indirect criterion keys are applied. The fact that current inventories differ in all these respects makes it obvious that experts disagree on these matters.

The most vehement assertion is that domain-referenced interpretation is sexist, that only interpretations based on sex-specific norms are legitimate. A dozen years ago, whether to prepare separate inventories for males and females (as the pioneer E. K. Strong did) was also an issue. No investigator has defended sex-specific forms since separate pink and blue blanks came under attack as sexist.

Item form. Endorsement items present a single stimulus ("Repairing a bicycle") for endorsement or rejection. The person is to check what he likes or to respond LIKE/INDIFFERENT/DISLIKE or to rate on a 5-point scale (LIKE VERY MUCH, etc.). A comparison or forced-choice item presents two to four stimuli and asks the person to choose the most liked (and perhaps the least liked) as in

    Make a speech to raise funds for a cause   M L
    Write letters to raise funds for a cause   M L
    Persuade friends to volunteer as fund raisers   M L

Another forced-choice form is represented by

    I have more admiration for someone who
     A Knows a lot about astronomy
     B Can pick profitable investments

Subjects can respond faster to endorsement items than to choice items and find endorsing more comfortable than making hard choices. Forcing choices rules out the influence of yea-saying and nay-saying. With endorsement format, one person may blandly endorse nearly everything. Another may reject all but the few occupations he already had centered on. A person who usually responds LIKE or YES or AGREE is said to be "acquiescent" (Block, 1965; Cronbach, 1950). With endorsement items, his profile bumps the ceiling, and differences among his scores tend to be unreliable. Persons with many INDIFFERENT responses likewise generate uninformative profiles.

Organizing items into scales. Holland's scales—Investigative, for example—are homogeneous; responses counted within a scale refer to similar activities. The alternative technique, criterion keying, tallies responses that correlate with a criterion (usually membership/nonmembership in an occupation).

To arrive at a homogeneous set of items, the developer uses logic and correlations. Suppose that the developer's original hunch is that some work is predominantly "verbal." A checklist of verbal activities could be presented:

Writing a poem.
Persuading passersby to donate to a charity.
Translating for speakers at the UN.
Reporting a soccer match for a newspaper.

The psychological demands of these activities differ; persons who like one might dislike others. When the interitem correlations are not consistently positive, it may be possible to salvage the original category by dropping a few activities whose correlations run low. The original category could be split if, for example, "persuasive" uses of words hang together. Other coherent categories might be self-expressive writing and word processing.

Criterion keying treats the inventory as a forecasting device. The prediction-minded psychologist would prefer to try items on many young persons, later finding out which ones became aviators (say) and enjoyed the life. Those in today's generation who respond as these aviators did would be most likely to pursue and enjoy an aviation career. This key construction, like the regression-weighting procedure described in Chapter 11, is strictly empirical. Responses entering the same scale may be diverse in content.

Long-term follow-up is a slow way to develop a scale, and an enormous initial sample would be needed to finish with a suitable number of satisfied persons in aviation, business management, cabinetmaking, and so on. The shortcut is to collect responses of adults who have been in an occupation for some time and appear to be successful and satisfied. The developer locates a few hundred professional fliers and collects inventory responses from them. Whatever responses most of them share are counted as symptomatic of "aviator interests."

Criterion keys are not confined to vocational interests as items can be keyed against any external criterion. The Strong inventory offers an Academic Comfort scale, based on interests expressed by college students who have good grade records. In principle, a scale assessing accident-proneness of customers could be constructed for an insurance company (Kunce & Reeder, 1974; see also Ryan & Johnson, 1942, and Stone, 1960.)

Score reporting. Interpretation of interests has traditionally emphasized comparison across the person's scores: what does he or she like *most?* The number of positive responses depends on the number of items in a category, the attractiveness of the activities chosen to represent it, and, with forced-choice, the way pairs or triads are assembled. Scores for profiling can be expressed in several ways:

- Raw percentages: positive responses in a category as a percentage of the maximum possible. A scale for a Likes-minus-Dislikes formula can run from -100 to $+100$.
- Percentiles or standard scores based on a general reference group. An interest inventory can offer norms within sex and grade (like those for DAT) or for a broader group.
- Percentiles or standard scores based on an occupational reference group. A high school senior can be told how his interest scores compare with those of college engineering students or those of adult engineers. A manual might report the range of engineers' scores on every scale or just on the Engineer scale.

Interest norms are commonly tabulated within sexes. The USES inventory strikes an odd compromise. The profile form carries a column of percentiles using own-sex norms for a general population, but the profile bars are plotted as standard scores—not normalized—using norms for the two sexes pooled.

In my opinion, general norms should play little part in interpreting interests; if a person likes the work, it makes no difference whether 50 per cent or 90 per cent of other persons would also like it. The emphasis on norms reflects the prominence of competition in American thought, which presumes that you have a competitive advantage when you like your work better than others would—even if you hate it! On the other hand, raw scores depend on the list of items. Positive responses can be increased by adding popular items to the scale, and dropping unpopular items can conceal important aversions. If raw scores will be reported, much judgment is required in choosing items.

Norms for persons in an occupation can play a useful role, not because a high comparative standing is to be considered good but because the norms tell what the occupational world is accustomed to. If a person's interest in Realistic activities falls at an extreme of the distribution for engineers—beyond the 15th or 85th percentile, perhaps—the person is unlike most engineers. Such a signal is thought-provoking but not the final word, as outliers can fit special niches.

Terwilliger (1960) demonstrated the contrast between profiles based on counts and profiles based on norms. Job titles in four fields, with brief definitions, were sampled from the *DOT;* he had, then, a domain-referenced instrument. He defined response categories more carefully than is usual, as degrees of liking. I report on responses to the question, "Would you think quite seriously about an offer of this job and *probably accept* it?"

High school boys endorsed 17 per cent of occupations in the "artistic" field and 48 per cent of "mechanical" occupations. Mechanical and persuasive activities were popular; clerical and artistic work, unpopular. Figure 12.3 displays the responses of Jim and Nick in two ways. Jim is uniformly mild in his endorsement of all fields. Because most boys reject two of the fields, the percentiles give the mistaken impression that Jim is attracted to artistic work and clerical work. Nick's norm-referenced profile suggests that he lacks

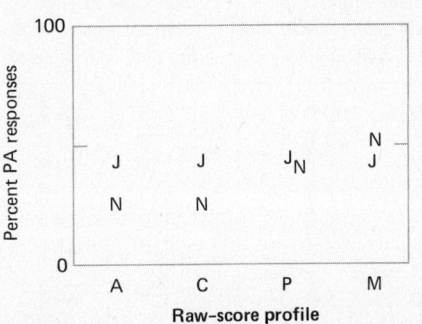 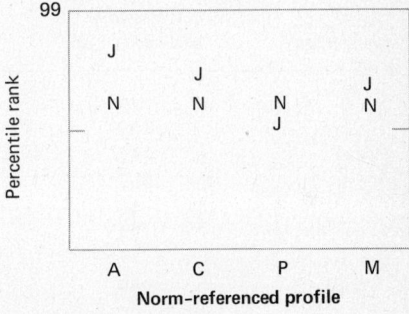

Figure 12.3. Direct and norm-referenced profiles.

any particular interest, but in fact his response to mechanical jobs was positive. (Being positive about machines is not exceptional.)

Data such as these lead me to emphasize raw scores—but among producers of inventories only Holland agrees with me. His reasoning is laid out in the manual for the Self-Directed Search. Prediger (1981b) directly challenges Holland, urging counselors to interpret norm-referenced Self-Directed Search profiles. Prediger's evidence is summarized in Table 12.3. Women who had taken SDS 1 to 3 years earlier were asked what occupation they planned to enter. Among the four women now headed for R occupations (presumably as a consequence of both counseling and satisfaction with college courses), three had given more positive responses to I items than to any other category, and one had her highest raw score in S. When percentiles were plotted instead of raw scores, three of these women had peaks in R and one in I.

8. *If the raw-score profiles J and N of Figure 12.3 were for Jane and Nelly, would you expect the norm-referenced profiles to differ from those pictured? Should that alter the interpretation?*
9. *Most scoring services resolve the problem posed by Prediger's data by printing both raw scores and norm-referenced scores on the report form (but diagramming only one profile).*
   a. *Is there any argument against presenting both diagrams (somewhat as Figure 12.3 does)?*
   b. *If you were being counseled and were given both sets of numerical scores but only one graphic profile, would you prefer to see a picture of the raw or norm-referenced profile?*
10. *A college woman has S highest in her raw-score profile and E highest in her normed profile. What does Table 12.3 imply about her decision?*
11. *Answer the same question for one whose raw-score peak is S and whose normed peak is R.*

Table 12.3 *Raw scores and normed scores as predictors for college women*

Holland Code of Occupation	Number of Women Choosing Occupation with This Code	Number of Them with That Code Highest in Raw-Score Profile, and Per cent Misclassified		Number of Them with That Code Highest in Normed Profile, and Per cent Misclassified	
R	4	0	100%	3	25%
I	139	63	55%	72	48%
A	117	57	*51%*	54	54%
S	657	481	*27%*	155	76%
E	48	2	96%	10	79%
C	24	7	71%	13	*46%*
TOTAL	989	610	*38%*	307	69%

SOURCE: Tabulated from Prediger (1981b). I have italicized the better result in each row.

12. When an inventory has norms, it is possible to display two profiles in terms of own-sex and opposite-sex percentiles. What can be said for and against this practice?

How Techniques Have Been Combined

The three decisions can be joined in any manner to produce an inventory, and most combinations have been used, as Table 12.1 has demonstrated. The descriptive information in the table and in the paragraphs here is not of great importance, save as it illustrates the diversity. The listing is not exhaustive; the *Eighth MMY* lists about 30 interest inventories on the U.S. market, and new ones continue to appear.

The homogeneously keyed Kuder Preference Record appeared in 1939. The current forms are C (older students and adults) and E (secondary schools). Criterion keying makes KOIS, also in the Kuder family, fundamentally different from KPR; more than 100 occupational scales and about 50 for college majors report how closely the person's choices match those in the criterion group. Kuder (1977) presents a book-length account of theory and research on KOIS and, incidentally, on KPR.

Strong published his famous blank for men in the 1920s and followed it with one for women. David P. Campbell and Jo-Ida Hansen later took responsibility and replaced SVIB with SCII, where both sexes answer the same questions. The last SVIB handbook (Campbell, 1971) nonetheless reports evidence of current value.

SVIB and SCII occupational keys have counted responses on which males or females in the occupational group differed from males or females in general (MIG, WIG). SCII has male and female keys for every occupation where the developers located enough cases: Dentist, Computer Programmer, Elementary Teacher, Interior Decorator, Elected Public Official, and Banker, among others.

Dozens of occupational scores presented side by side can be confusing. Therefore, SCII codes them in Holland terms (e.g., the *IR* symbol is attached to Dentist). To provide a point of entry for counseling, SCII is scored on six homogeneous *RIASEC* keys. A third set of keys—"basic interest" scales—count responses in homogeneous, comparatively narrow clusters. Thus SCII subclassifies Realistic into Agriculture, Nature, Adventure, Military, and Mechanical keys (but only Mechanical correlates highly with the SCII *R* score).

Strong's letter-grade scoring has been discarded, but it appears in important older research. Strong assigned A to a score near or above the average of the occupational group, and C to any score 2 s.d. below the average of the occupational group. A large fraction of MIG or WIG earn C's on any scale.

SVIB and SCII were keyed primarily for occupations requiring a college education. C. B. Johansson's Career Assessment Inventory *(NCS)* is keyed for occupations below the professional level; if it appeared in Table 12.1, the information would essentially match that for SCII save that CAI has fewer occupational keys.

INTEREST MEASURES IN COUNSELING

Broadening the Client's Horizon

As was pointed out earlier, counselors generally aim to promote self-understanding. The individual is to make choices as new facts become available, as he matures, or as his social circumstances and opportunities change. The student in high school may set down a definite plan to study certain subjects, to enroll in a certain college curriculum, to complete training in a certain professional school, and to seek a certain type of practice. This plan is unlikely to be carried out. Somewhere along the line instructors will open new vistas or arouse new interests. Somewhere along the line concrete experience will show that he does not enjoy some aspect of the work, and it will reveal talent in another direction. Counseling should generate plans with many branches. The significant goal in counseling is to equip the student to make later decisions. The aim in counseling should be to give the student a more sophisticated view of the world of work, of the choices open to him, and of his own range of potentialities for achievement and satisfaction.

The interest inventory can be given to entire classes, and interpretation of profiles can be carried out in group discussions rather than in individual counseling. Such a process—leading each student to list several career possibilities suggested for him by the test—is an excellent preliminary to group study of careers or to individual counseling. Some comparatively short and simple inventories for this purpose are geared to ages 12 to 14.

The interest inventory assists counselors in other ways. A promise to interpret interest scores invites students to seek out the counselor. While discussing vocations, the student will talk about family, social relations, and academic difficulties and so may touch upon problems on which the counselor can provide assistance. The conference opens a natural opportunity for the student to express desire for such help, a desire he might otherwise never have acknowledged.

Interest inventories are nonthreatening. The interpretation carries considerable force because it mirrors what the person himself has said. No psychological mysteries or esoteric constructs becloud the interest measure. The counselor hesitates to disclose scores a person will find hard to understand or to accept, but that is rarely a concern with interest measures.

Interest measures stimulate the young person to confront his future and, at first glance, seem readily interpreted. Some educators, therefore, return profiles for students to interpret on their own. I question this practice. The profiles often do not mean what they seem to mean because of the subtleties of inventory construction and of the occupational world. Even the Self-

Directed Search, a simple inventory supported by much printed comment, is less than self-interpreting; college students go astray when digesting the material without a counselor's help (R. H. Dolliver & R. N.Hansen, 1977). An increasingly prominent alternative to personal counseling is to allow the student to "converse" with the computer about career plans on his own schedule, perhaps over many months. Elaborate programs enable the computer to simulate what a commonplace but diligent counselor would say. The computer is adept at those aspects of counseling that are least "psychological," notably the retrieval of encyclopaedic facts about specific occupations and sites for training.

Nowadays homogeneous scales are generally thought to be a better starting place for counseling than criterion-keyed scales, which is why the Strong blank added basic-interest scales. A high score in verbal interests, for example, leads to follow-up questions to clarify whether the interest is in reading, writing, or speaking and whether the interest is in face-to-face communication or in writing in a quiet room. The discussion will come round to vocations that might satisfy the interest. The examples brought forward should be consistent not only with the scores but with the counselee's claimed interests, probable ultimate level of education, and abilities.

A string of scores based on homogeneous scales invites the student to think of himself as an individual rather than to concentrate on an occupational label. Mary Thomas (Figure 12.4) was majoring in child development in college at the time she filled out KPR. Her grades were mediocre, and her work with children was not especially successful. When questioned regarding her choice of major, she explained that she had set her heart on work in an orphanage. This desire arose in childhood when she read a book about a woman who helped orphan children—a "wonderful" thing to do as a lifework. The low Persuasive and Social Service scores suggest a somewhat withdrawn personality, and the high Mechanical, Computational, and Clerical scores suggest a liking for conventional, uncreative activities. When questioned about office work, Mary enthusiastically described her previous summer's work as a file clerk; her duties apparently consisted solely of alphabetizing folders; yet she had "just loved it." Moreover, she had done well in office-skills courses. Evidently both ability and interest fell in an area she had not considered as a vocational goal.

It is unwise to concentrate the interview on a few occupations. This gives the student far too narrow a description of himself and leaves too many things out of consideration. It is essential that the student go beneath occupational labels and stereotypes, that he understand the diversity of roles within the same occupation, that he understand the differences between demands of the training program and demands of the occupation, and that he recognize the shifting nature of occupations.

Darley and Hagenah (1955, p. 195) sharply criticized some common practices in vocational counseling, taking as an example a student with a high standing in the social-service category:

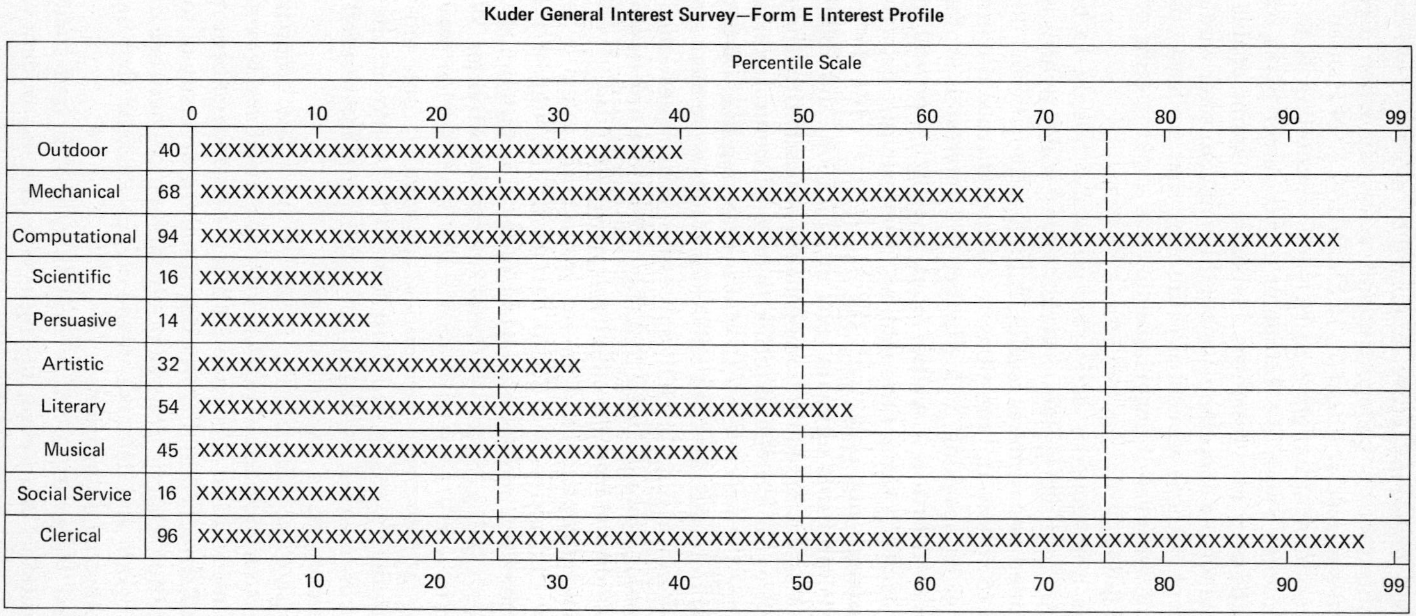

Kuder General Interest Survey—Form E Interest Profile

		0	10	20	30	40	50	60	70	80	90	99
Outdoor	40	xxxxxxxxxxxxxxxxxxxxxxxxxxxxxxxxxxxxxxxx										
Mechanical	68	xxxxxxxxxxxxxxxxxxxxxxxxxxxxxxxxxxxxxxxxxxxxxxxxxxxxxxxxxxxxxxxxxxxx										
Computational	94	xxxxxxxxxxxxxxxxxxxxxxxxxxxxxxxxxxxxxxxxxxxxxxxxxxxxxxxxxxxxxxxxxxxxxxxxxxxxxxxxxxxxxxxxxxxxxx										
Scientific	16	xxxxxxxxxxxxxxxx										
Persuasive	14	xxxxxxxxxxxxxx										
Artistic	32	xxxxxxxxxxxxxxxxxxxxxxxxxxxxxxxx										
Literary	54	xxxxxxxxxxxxxxxxxxxxxxxxxxxxxxxxxxxxxxxxxxxxxxxxxxxxxx										
Musical	45	xxxxxxxxxxxxxxxxxxxxxxxxxxxxxxxxxxxxxxxxxxxxx										
Social Service	16	xxxxxxxxxxxxxxxx										
Clerical	96	xxxxxxxxxxxxxxxxxxxxxxxxxxxxxxxxxxxxxxxxxxxxxxxxxxxxxxxxxxxxxxxxxxxxxxxxxxxxxxxxxxxxxxxxxxxxxxxx										

Percentile Scale

Figure 12.4. Interest profile of Mary Thomas.
Note: Mary took KPR Form C, but the scores are represented here in the format of the profile sheet for Form E, which is prepared by computer. The form has been simplified in minor ways.
Source: "Profile Section" from the Kuder Preference Record, Form E, by G. Frederic Kuder. Copyright © 1976, 1963, G. Frederic Kuder. Reprinted by permission of the publisher, Science Research Associates, Inc., Chicago, Ill.

At some point in the counseling interview series, the counselor [or the computer printout!] can make this bald statement: "You have the same kind of interests as successful personnel managers or . . . school superintendents." With minor modifications, this is probably the standard approach to interpretation. It is also the least effective approach and the one most likely to lead the student and counselor into ever deeper morasses of interpretive difficulties.

Agreement of profiles with claimed interests. As the case of Mary illustrates, inventories often tell a story different from the response to "What job would you like?" In one study, students were asked to estimate their standings on the KPR dimensions. The average correlation between estimated interest and inventories interest was 0.5 (Crosby & Winsor, 1941). In another investigation (Darley & Hagenah, 1955, p. 67), the inventory agreed with the estimates of roughly two-thirds of those who claimed interest in business detail, business contact, or a technical field and with only one-third of those who claimed dominant scientific, social service, and verbal-linguistic interests. (See also Super & Crites, 1962, pp. 437–441, and the JVIS manual, 1977, p. 86.)

When disagreement arises, no one can say that the profile is more valid than the self-estimate. The counselor would be unwise to dismiss the self-estimate as "wrong." She must help the counselee to an emotionally acceptable reconciliation of claimed and measured interests. To tell Mary Thomas, "You don't really want to work in child development; you want to be a secretary," would precipitate emotional conflict. No one can abandon a long-standing self-concept easily. An authority who bluntly contradicts firm beliefs invites rejection. In Mary's case, it might be best to inquire as to the reasons for her choice of child development, to ask her to envision the activities she may be engaged in 10 years hence, and to compare them with the activities rated high in the interest blank. The fact that the inventory contains only her own ratings brings her to face self-contradictions. The counselor is no longer the "authority"—she is merely holding the mirror. The counselor can go further, pointing out that agencies serving children need devoted clerical staffs. Such work is in line with Mary's ideals *and* her interests.

There are at least three explanations for apparent disagreements between scores and claimed interests. The inventory's large number of items, many of them indirectly related to the job in question, provides a reliable and penetrating sampling. Second, "strong" interest on a normed scale refers not to degree of interest but to comparative standing. It is not logically comparable to the self-estimate of strength of interest. Third, the low—sometimes scandalously low—correlations between scales bearing near-identical titles in different inventories imply that the client could not hope to predict his inventory score without knowing the peculiarities of the inventory in question.

Inconsistency among instruments. We have far too few research reports in which profiles for the same persons on two modern inventories were compared and the discrepancies explained. We do know that even inventories that are similar in construction tell divergent stories. In one study, the basic-interest scales of SVIB were scored for men who also took JVIS. The concurrent correlation of an SVIB scale with the most nearly corresponding Jackson scale does not rise above 0.5 and sometimes (Office Work vs. Office Practices) the *r* drops to 0.3. These concurrent correlations are unsatisfactory. The use of endorsement items in SVIB and forced choice in JVIS is one reason for the disagreement. Satisfactory concurrent correlations—0.6 to 0.9—are reported for corresponding *RIASEC* scales in the Strong and ACT inventories; but the same comparison of the ACT inventory with the VPI from which it descended gives *r*'s 0.35 to 0.6 (Technical report, 1981, pp. 36, 37).

Discrepancies of this magnitude imply that any instrument is just a partial indicator, which inevitably limits any kind of validity. This is a persuasive reason for looking on an inventory as a stimulus to conversation rather than as a definitive "measurement."

13. *Because school budgets are strained, little counselor time is available for most students; hence school policies should capitalize on counselors' scarce expertise. What policies would you suggest regarding which kind of inventory to use, who should be encouraged to take it and when, and what interpretative support to provide?*

Correlates of Scores

Stability. Interest inventories seek to predict satisfaction over many years to come, but interests change. Both differentiation and outright reordering of preferences occur.

Aggressiveness, bookishness, and other broad styles are shaped prior to adolescence in home and peer group. The main structure of early individual differences seems to be related to sex typing. Some boys, for example, reject activities traditional for girls, and in some cases this is a precursor of scientific interests (L. Tyler, 1964). The broadest tendencies—at the people/data/ideas/things level—are firm enough by the mid-teens to be a basis for preliminary discussion of the self-concept as it relates to occupations. Among adolescents not bound for college, interests appear to stabilize comparatively early. But teenagers, comparatively inexperienced, respond INDIFFERENT to more items than adults do; they have not yet developed some of their interests. After age 18, interest in social-service occupations is particularly likely to increase (Schletzer, 1963, 1966). For the college-bound in particular, discussion of careers should stress options to be kept open.

Files of data collected some time back have made follow-up studies possible. The SVIB manual reported stability coefficients for various samples

INTEREST INVENTORIES

(mostly college students) over short and long intervals. Profiles do have long-term meaning, especially when recorded after age 20. Here are illustrative retest correlations for three occupational keys:

Interval	Biologist	Author-Journalist	Office Worker
2 weeks	0.9	0.9	0.9
30 days	0.9	0.9	0.9
3 years	0.75	0.7	0.7
8 years	0.65	0.6	0.55
22 years	0.7	0.6	0.6

Change is appreciable in the first few years; slower thereafter. (Correlations of SCII scores at the 3-year mark were found to be higher in a small sample.)

Half—only half—of Strong's retest profiles after 18 years were similar enough to suggest essentially the same occupational advice as the originals. Just 6 per cent of A ratings changed to C; 3 per cent of C's, to A. In a few cases, however, a profile peak became a valley in the interval or vice versa (Strong, 1955, p. 64; see also Darley & Hagenah, 1955, p. 43).

Longitudinal studies of interests of females are few. Twenty years ago, one study found a hint that in a girl's development the resolution of the home-vs.-career question was central; and formation of vocational interest, secondary (Matthews & Tiedeman, 1964). In the generation for which follow-up studies have been completed, interests expressed in adolescence often faded away when the adult woman made a commitment to homemaking.

Prediction of occupational choice and satisfaction. Inventories do predict career choice. (See Harmon, 1969; Dolliver *et al.*, 1972, and Spokane, 1979, regarding SVIB or SCII; Zytowski, 1972, 1974, 1976, and McRae, 1959, regarding Kuder inventories; Gade & Soliah, 1975, regarding an inventory in the Holland family). These facts have to be set against the finding that simple questions about claimed interests predict as well or better than inventory scores (Bartling & Hood, 1981; Borgen & Seling, 1978).

About half the persons in an occupation had scored near or above the average of the relevant occupational norm group when they took SVIB or SCII in college. (Figures run lower for women if those not seeking permanent careers are included.) Likewise, men and women landed in occupations consistent with Kuder profiles recorded a dozen or more years earlier. For half the cases, a peak score matched the actual occupation; for another 30 per cent, the profile point that matched the occupation was high but not one of the peaks.

Further evidence is found in studies of men who change fields after leaving school. Strong (1943, pp. 114ff.) and Zytowski (1974, 1976) found evidence for these statements:

Those who remain in an occupation for 10 years or more average higher scores for that occupation than for any other.

Those continuing in an occupation have higher scores in that interest than those who try the occupation and change.

Those who change from one occupation to another change to one in which their interest scores were about as high as for the first choice.

Power to predict occupation entered is irrelevant to the validity of an interest measure, says Prediger (1976a), because people tend to enter occupations traditional for their sex. He objects to inventories on which, for example, more males than females have profile peaks in engineering, calling them "sex restrictive." "If Cindy's interests are compatible with engineering, one would suggest that she . . . consider engineering even if this lowers the accuracy with which occupational *entry* is predicted" (italics added).

Interest scores discriminate persons who will like a job from those who will not. A guidance service gave KPR to high school seniors and adults and a year later asked what work they were doing and how they liked it (Lipsett & Wilson, 1954). The investigators then judged whether the person's measured interests were "suitable" for the job. Interests predicted satisfaction reasonably well; interests and ability taken together gave an excellent forecast.

Prediction of success. Counselees are likely to think that the interest profile tells what they can do best, but interests tell nothing about abilities. The correlations between interests and more-or-less corresponding abilities (e.g., between KPR Clerical and DAT Clerical) are close to zero. A high interest score indicates that *if* a person survives training and enters the occupation he is likely to enjoy the work.

Few studies compare interest scores with excellence on the job. Strong's investigations of insurance agents (1943, pp. 486–500) are still notable. The value of new policies written by men with A scores in sales interest was three times that of sales by C's. A few C men reached the minimum level required to support themselves by commissions; none got much above it. The correlation is only 0.4, no doubt because most C men had dropped out of the sample during their first unproductive years. Once again we see the practical significance of a score whose correlation with a criterion is moderate.

E. L. Kelly and D. W. Fiske (1951; see also Kelly & Goldberg, 1959) tested students entering training for clinical psychology. Four years later they collected grades, scores on performance tests, ratings by training supervisors, and so forth. Particular interest attaches to the ratings on overall clinical competence and research competence. Except for a verbal-reasoning measure, no test predicted better than the Strong. Clinical ratings correlated 0.3 with SVIB Author and Lawyer keys. Ratings on research competence correlated around 0.3 with scientific interests and with lack of business or office-work interests. (These results might not hold up in crossvalidation; chance plays a large part when—with many scales and criteria—hundreds of correlations are run.)

Inventories have not been good predictors of success in vocational training. When interest scores were correlated with grades in training for 13 air-force specialties, almost all correlations were below 0.2 (Brokaw, 1956). Interests sometimes predict who stays in training and who drops out. Of those with A and B+ scores on the Strong Dentist key, 92 per cent graduated from dentistry training, compared with 67 per cent of B's and 25 per cent of C's (Strong, 1943, p. 524; see also a study on Kuder scores of teachers in training by Stewart & Roberts, 1955).

Interests are poor academic predictors. One set of results comes from academic interests: Out of 21 correlations of course mark with interest in that subject matter (expressed prior to the course), 17 were below 0.3. (Exceptions: r's just above 0.4 for females in mathematics and for males in music.) Combining information on interests with the mark in the same course from the previous year did not improve prediction above that from the mark alone. When the mark in a similar course is not available, a combination of interest and aptitude measures predicts better than aptitude does by itself (Norris & Katz, 1970).

It adds up to this: interest cannot save the incapable, and lack of interest does not spoil the chances of those with high aptitude. This is entirely consistent with the finding that the Academic Comfort scale correlates with the level of job one prepares for (a high score implying an occupation with high educational requirements). But it correlates 0.1–0.3 with grade average (SCII manual, 1981).

14. Follow-up studies on vocational choice and satisfaction almost always use persons who initially were told the implications of their score profiles. Discuss this as an example of "contamination" (p. 367).
15. There is a strong tendency for young persons to follow family tradition with respect to occupational level and, less strongly, occupation itself. For interest measures used early in high school, would it be advisable to provide separate norms for sons of professional parents and for sons of working-class parents?
16. It is possible to form occupational keys for subcategories within an occupation. What would appear to be reasonable subcategories for psychologists?
17. Barnette (1951) examined whether men who planned to enter engineering continued in such training. The Kuder Mechanical score had no relation to continuance; it was high for those who dropped out as well as for those who continued. Computational had a marked relation to continuance. Explain.
18. Several investigations have reported the following configural pattern: when students are classified as compulsive or noncompulsive, interest in science

predicts grades in engineering for the noncompulsive group only. (See Frederiksen et al., 1972, p. 5.)
   a. *Make a chart somewhat like Figure 11.10 to illustrate this finding.*
   b. *Suggest an explanation.*
   c. *Could the finding be of use in counseling or selection?*

INTERPRETING CRITERION KEYS

Criterion keying has been popular because it does not require validated theory. The counselor can make predictions without any claim that she "understands" the interests of (say) male bankers. No matter what makes for happiness in a male banker's life, the client can be advised that he (or she!) is attuned to that life if the marks on the answer sheet resemble the responses common among male bankers. Many psychologists who distrust human judgment (p. 406) favor criterion keying for interest and personality inventories.

The criterion-keying principles of Strong and Kuder differ. KOIS counts responses given frequently by members of the occupational group; I call this a commonality key. SVIB and SCII count responses where the occupational group differs from the same-sex reference group—a discriminant key. KOIS and SVIB reports on the same individual disagree fairly often; see Carek (1972). I shall question the interpretability of both types of score and point to weaknesses in techniques of criterion keying.

What Does It Mean to Be "Similar to" a Diverse Group?

Criterion keys are devised to be used one by one to pick out occupations for consideration. Homogeneous keys are devised to be considered simultaneously, to be combined into a portrait. Criterion keys can serve the same function, but only if the interpreter is prepared to say what it means (for example) to be "like an engineer." To be "like the average engineer" means little. In fact, whereas research engineers scored high on the SVIB Engineer scale, production engineers and sales engineers (engaged with people) tended to score fairly low (Dunnette, 1957).

Occupations are not homogeneous. Persons in the same occupation use it to satisfy distinctly different personal bents. I offer myself as example. Early in my career I filled out the Strong, and Campbell has rescored the blank with the 1971 scales. College Professor and Psychologist (my ostensible career lines) were among my highest scores at age 32; so were Lawyer, Journalist, Mathematician, and Political Scientist. The homogeneous scales tell a similar story: At the top are Public Speaking and Teaching, followed by Writing,

Law/Politics, and Mathematics. Science was exactly average. Either *set* of scores taken together matches my career. I probably am more at home on a platform and have gotten more into public-policy discussions than most psychologists of my generation. I have written a lot. I have analyzed data and developed mathematical theory for such analysis. I did no laboratory research and no clinical work after age 30. So the Strong gave a valid picture, not of my "similarity to psychologists," but of a role I could enjoy within that variegated profession.

Criterion-keyed scales can be "subtle" in the sense that the respondent cannot guess how some responses are going to be scored. Campbell commented, for example, that the scale Army Officer(m) is a hodgepodge (in Zytowski, 1973, p. 38, 40; edited):

> The only way to score high on the [homogeneous] Military Activities scale is to respond LIKE to "be an army officer," "drill a company of soldiers," and similar items. In contrast, the [criterion-keyed] Army Officer occupational scale . . . [includes] clusters of items; one concerns engineering and construction activities; another deals with legal power . . . ; a third has items of a general managerial nature; yet another contains straight math items. Finally, a small cluster of items deals with military activities.

The Military Activities scale is transparent; the respondent knows what responses indicate liking for an officer's job; hence the score is open to faking. On the subtle scale the respondent can make false statements, but he cannot guess the message they will convey.

19. *Under what circumstances would anyone wish to paint a false picture of himself on an inventory?*
20. *"The reason for using an interest inventory in counseling is not to rank a number of people but to rank a multitude of occupations for one person. . . . [T]he variation that is relevant to the individual is one that exists within the person" (Kuder, 1977, p. 9). What type of score best serves this purpose? Could some other purpose be stated for interest inventories?*
21. *The scoring keys for earlier editions of Strong inventories were available to the profession, but current ones are not. SCII requires machine scoring, and firms buy a license to provide that service. The publisher makes keys available only to licensees. What consequences would the policy have with regard to*
    a. *ability of psychologists to interpret the profile?*
    b. *quality of scoring and computerized interpretations?*
    c. *availability of funds to support continuing research?*

Technical Issues

Commonality keys and discriminant keys. For SCII Engineer keys, scoring weights were derived from data as shown in Tables 12.4 and 12.5. The MIG and WIG samples for the 1981 edition consist of 300 men and 300 women, evenly spread over many occupations, who responded at an average age of 33 to 35. The engineers are persons between 25 and 55 who said they liked their work and appeared to be at least adequate in it.

Table 12.4 shows response percentages for females on a series of items. On the first item the response percentages for the two groups did not differ appreciably. Therefore, it was not counted in the key for Engineer(f). WIG disliked "Machine shop supervisor" more often than women engineers did. Therefore, an L or I response counts in the Engineer(f) score and a D response counts negatively. The same scoring rule might have applied to "Machinist," but in a borderline call the key-makers decided to assign weight only to L and D. Such borderline decisions probably have little net effect on results.

As can be seen, 5 out of these 12 items picked up weights; in the entire blank, 69 items enter the Engineer(f) key. For the items in the table, the weights are unsurprising; jobs with a mechanical flavor count positively, and a traditional feminine role counts negatively. Raw scores are converted to standard scores calculated from the occupational group—here, from female engineers.

Table 12.5 presents data for men. Male engineers differ from MIG less

Table 12.4. *How Engineer(f) scoring weights were established*

	Response Distribution (%)									Scoring Weight Assigned		
	Engineers			WIG			Difference					
Item	L	I	D	L	I	D	L	I	D	L	I	D
Life insurance agent	1	11	88	2	16	82	−1	−5	6	0	0	0
Machine shop supervisor	20	35	45	3	22	75	17	13	−30	1	1	−1
Machinist	23	35	42	6	23	71	17	12	−29	1	0	−1
Manager, Chamber of Commerce	20	33	47	19	27	54	1	6	−7	0	0	0
Manager, child-care center	14	27	59	41	29	30	−27	−2	29	−1	0	1
Manager, women's style shop	15	32	53	38	30	32	−23	2	21	0	0	0
Manufacturer	40	43	17	13	42	45	27	1	−28	1	0	−1
Mechanical engineer	66	24	10	10	30	60	56	−6	−50	1	0	−1
Military officer	23	21	56	10	15	75	13	6	−19	0	0	0
Minister, priest, rabbi	8	20	72	15	23	62	−7	−3	10	0	0	0
Musician	55	26	19	64	24	12	−9	2	7	0	0	0
Newspaper reporter	39	36	25	43	35	22	−4	1	3	0	0	0

SOURCE: Data supplied by Jo-Ida C. Hansen.

Table 12.5 *How Engineer(m) scoring weights were established*

	Response Distribution (%)									Scoring Weight Assigned		
	Engineers			MIG			Difference					
Item	L	I	D	L	I	D	L	I	D	L	I	D
Life insurance agent	2	16	82	8	23	69	−6	−7	13	0	0	0
Machine shop supervisor	30	47	23	20	37	43	10	10	−20	1	1	−1
Machinist	38	43	19	22	35	43	16	8	−24	1	0	−1
Manager, Chamber of Commerce	14	43	43	27	40	33	−13	3	10	0	0	0
Manager, child-care center	4	25	71	15	31	54	−11	−6	17	0	0	0
Manager, women's style shop	2	11	87	5	20	75	−3	−9	12	0	0	0
Manufacturer	58	38	4	39	39	22	19	−1	−18	1	0	−1
Mechanical engineer	71	27	2	42	34	24	29	−7	−22	1	0	−1
Military officer	27	32	41	27	25	48	0	7	−7	0	0	0
Minister, priest, rabbi	12	29	59	16	30	54	−4	−1	5	0	0	0
Musician	46	29	25	46	29	25	0	0	0	0	0	0
Newspaper reporter	20	42	38	38	38	24	−18	4	14	−1	0	1

SOURCE: Data supplied by Jo-Ida C. Hansen.

than female engineers differ from WIG. To reach a total of 68 items, it was necessary to weight differences as small as 18 per cent. All items considered, roughly half the items keyed in the Engineer(m) scale are keyed in the corresponding (f) scale and vice versa. Suppose that Sherlock Jones responded L to the first four items, I to the next four, and D to the last. Then on the Engineer(m) key he picked up 2 points on the first four items and 1 point on the last item, for a raw score of +3 on this bit of the scale.

It would overcomplicate this discussion to describe fully the KOIS technique. Instead, I describe a procedure for keying SCII that will make Kuder's main principle apparent. Look only at the responses of the engineers in Table 12.5, and add up the percentages of engineers agreeing with Sherlock Jones: 2 per cent on the first item, 30 per cent on the second, ... 38 per cent on the last. The average is 29 per cent; to bring norms into the picture, divide by the maximum possible. 82 + 47 + . . . gives an average of 57 per cent, and Jones's ratio is close to 0.5. Note that the response L on the first item did not affect Jones's SCII score but pulled down the commonality score.

A KOIS engineer score tells how closely the person's interests resemble those of the typical engineer of like sex, and the profile highlights occupational groups the person *most* resembles. A high score on an SCII occupational key indicates that the person's interests depart markedly from those of average persons *in the direction* of the typical engineer. Two persons who depart equally from the modal response of engineers score alike on KOIS, but the SCII score is lower for the one whose interests are more commonplace.

Some technical detail will clarify this. Assume that on a certain dimension engineers have stronger interest than the average person of like sex. Figure 12.5 denotes this by putting E to the right of PIG (persons-in-general). On the discriminant key (broken line), interests definitely to the right of PIG are scored as "like engineers." The greater the distance from PIG, the higher the score. The solid line behaves like Kuder's score; persons *nearest* E are scored as most "like engineers." On the commonality key the top score goes to persons at level 2. Persons at level 1 are scored high on the discriminant key and rather low on the commonality key. If one wants a high score to represent "interests similar to engineers," commonality keying is logically superior. On the other hand, persons of radically different types earn low scores on such a key, so it has little psychological unity.

Changes from decade to decade. Over time, items change in popularity; the correlation between items changes; and the interests typical of men or women in an occupation may change. This may make it necessary to reconstruct the scales. Items found homogeneous in one generation seem likely to cohere in the next; a "realistic" item is unlikely to shift to "enterprising" or "social." Criterion keys appear to be more vulnerable, in principle.

The items in Table 12.6 (which are not necessarily typical items) illustrate change over decades. On both these items, MIG and WIG changed. Not all the movements of occupational groups were parallel. Thus, liking for regular hours distinguished male reporters from the other groups in the 1970s but not earlier.

Occupations change in some of their fundamentals—recent years have seen the advent of television journalism, poverty law, and the electronic office. This could make an occupation attractive to some who formerly disliked it and vice versa. Radical changes in interests of an occupational group from one generation to the next are rare (D. P. Campbell, 1971; J. C. Hansen, 1978). Still, there is change. Campbell compared ministers questioned in 1927,

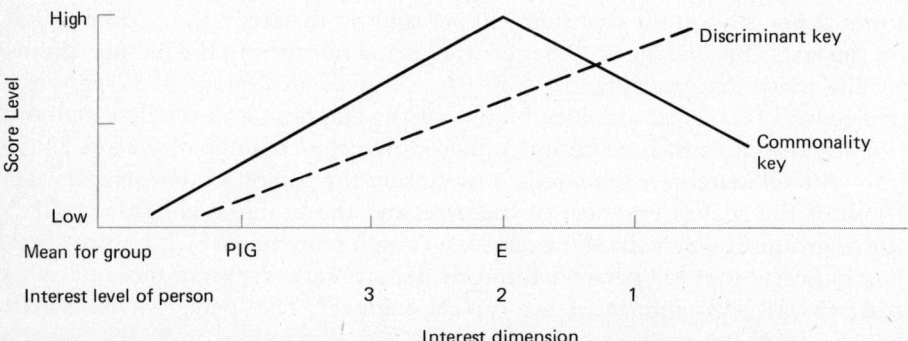

Figure 12.5. Comparison of two criterion-keying techniques.

Table 12.6 *Responses to two items in three time periods*

Item	Date of Test	Percentage Saying LIKE Among			
		Lawyers	Reporters	Life Insurance Agents	Artists
MALES					
Regular hours for work	1930s	57	47	49	39
	1960s	30	24	14	29
	1970s	27	36	14	15
Expressing judgments publicly	1930s	55	56	41	38
	1960s	66	68	56	60
	1970s	60	62	50	51
FEMALES					
Regular hours for work	1930s	59	72	56	63
	1960s	40	36	26	48
	1970s	29	38	17	25
Expressing judgments publicly	1930s	49	38	32	32
	1960s	49	49	38	40
	1970s	62	51	44	45

SOURCE: SCII manual, 1981, p. 76.

for example, with the ministers serving in the same churches in 1965. The average scores on six of the keys were:

	Minister	Social Worker	Lawyer	Rehabilitation Counselor	Psychiatrist	Chemist
1927	48	40	36	36	32	17
1965	46	48	36	42	37	13

Along with a marked consistency, there was clearly a drift toward interest in personal service. (Each s.d. among ministers is near 10.)

Sooner or later, criterion keys have to be overhauled from the ground up. The Strong Psychologist keys were revised repeatedly for good reason. Campbell (1965) displays interest profiles of certain prominent psychologists. Among 10 who were presidents of APA around 1930, just one reached a score of 52 on the *1965* Psychologist key; among the presidents for the period 1955–1965, only one scored below 52.

22. On a certain item, female engineers divide their responses evenly (33/33/33). The L/I/D distribution of WIG is 60/30/10. How would this item affect engineer scores calculated in the Strong manner? a score of the KOIS type?
23. Discuss the scoring of responses at level 3 of Figure 12.5.
24. Suppose that physicists' interests locate their average to the right of E in Figure 12.5. How would discriminant keys and commonality keys for P describe Person 2?
25. What interpretation can be given to a very low score on Investigative? On a commonality key for Chemist? A discriminant key for Chemist?

ERASING SEX DIFFERENCES

Everyone agrees that the old SVIB for Women had unfortunate social effects. Drawing the young woman's attention chiefly to occupations many women entered (librarian, psychologist, buyer, nurse) tended to narrow the options she considered. That fault has been overcome in today's instruments. Also, "fireman," "stewardess," and the like have given way to genderless job titles.

Today's question is whether interest inventories should be blind to sex or should make specific allowance for sex in selecting items, constructing keys, and interpreting profiles (Tittle & Zytowski, 1978). No doubt about it, responses of females collectively differ from those of males. One reasonable answer is blind to sex: a man and a woman who express the same likes and dislikes should be encouraged to consider the same list of occupations.

A second reasonable answer brings sex differences into the interpretation. It argues for sex-specific criterion keys and, if norms are used, for sex-specific occupational norms; Female physicians (for example) have as a group managed different kinds of practice and responsibility than male physicians. Then a criterion-keyed instrument could reasonably report whether the counselee's interests match the interests of physicians of *like* sex. This position is conservative; within many a profession, the two sexes are coming to have more nearly the same range of responsibilities.

Data in the manuals for SCII and KOIS indicate that men differ from women in the same occupation much as MIG differ from WIG. When persons are scored on the same-sex key and the opposite-sex key for the same occupation, the correlation is usually in the range 0.75–0.9. But some correlations are lower. The following detailed example shows how this comes about.

The SCII Librarian(f) and Librarian(m) scores correlate about 0.6 (across librarians, within either sex). Figure 12.6 shows means of the relevant samples on three *RIASEC* scales; corresponding differences would appear at the item level. If, for simplicity, we assume that the scoring assigns weight according to the distance of the librarian mean from WIG or MIG, Librarian(f) counts Artistic responses weakly and Librarian(m) counts them strongly. R re-

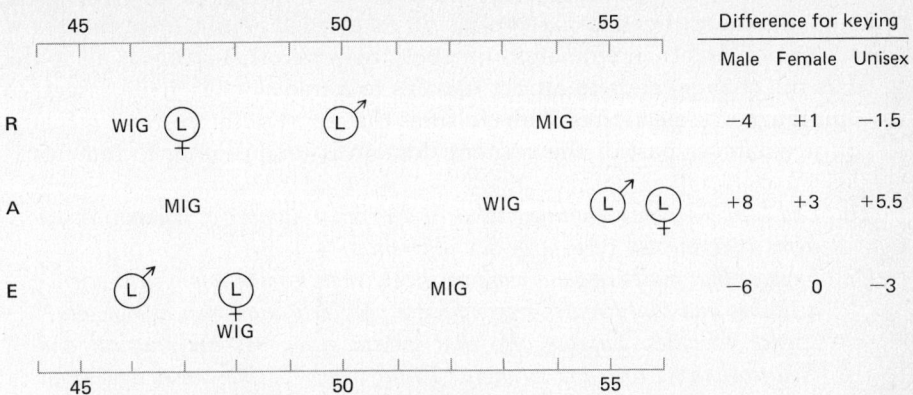

Figure 12.6. Mean scores of librarians compared with norm groups.
Source: Data from SCII manual, pp. 31, 65.

sponses add slightly to a woman's Librarian score and subtract heavily from a man's. A person with *R* at 48 and *A* at 55 resembles persons with jobs as Librarian, but the discriminant key will score a male with those responses higher than a female. The "Librarian interest" score of the woman should not be dragged down, I think, just because many women have that pattern. At the very least, those who insist on sex-specific keys should show, for example, that males with *R* at 48 and *A* at 55 like librarianship more than women with those same scores.

Some persons who accept the second answer go further, objecting to inventories on which sex differences appear. In particular, the protest is against homogeneous scales on which the sexes differ (Diamond, 1975). There is more than a hint in these statements that in an ideal society women would collectively have the same interests as men—which goes beyond the ideal of open opportunity and positive encouragement to be oneself.

To produce a seeming equality, some authors search for items that males and females like equally or items balanced so that male and female scale means are close together. The USES discarded items that were more popular with one sex than the other, but had to stop short. *After* discarding the items with the largest sex differences, the proportion of L responses to the remaining Humanitarian items was 33 for males, 60 for females (USES Manual, 1981). To erase the difference, uses would have had to abandon the attempt to measure that interest. Or perhaps uses could have reasoned as Lunneborg did to "balance" the forced-choice VII. She tried this item:

> If you were to become a teacher, which would you rather teach, history? or chemistry?

The second alternative was to be counted in a Science key and the first in a Culture (verbal-humanistic) key. Females chose the science option comparatively infrequently, so it was changed from "chemistry" to "biology." This did not eliminate the sex differential; it reversed it. Now men chose the science option less than women. Lunneborg reasoned that this was all to the good as the change tends to attract females to a traditionally male career. In my opinion, such selection of items falsifies the report of interests by refusing to count whatever part of the content domain is unappealing to females.

26. *Did USES sacrifice anything when it dropped a number of Humanitarian items that showed very large sex differences?*
27. *Suppose that males respond more positively than women to physical-science activities and that females respond more positively than men to biological-science activities. Suppose also that within either sex the physical and biological items correlate strongly. What would be the consequences, for counselee decisions and their validity, of restricting items on science to biological content?*
28. *In what ways is the proposal to construct scales on which both sexes have the same score distribution similar to (or different from) a proposal*
    a. *to use within-sex norms to interpret a* RIASEC *profile?*
    b. *to partial social background out of mental-test scores (p. 113)?*
    c. *to set hiring quotas to ensure proportionate representation in a firm (p. 389)?*
29. *Assume that the s.d. within each librarian group is 10 points. A person considering that occupation has an Enterprising score of 42. In the person's self-evaluation, what should that score, alongside the information in Figure 12.6, suggest? What if the* E *score is 60?*
30. *If the KOIS keying technique is applied to the evidence in Figure 12.6, would within-sex and unisex keys differ?*
31. *Would it be sensible to develop two criterion keys for a field such as health services, one using a college-educated criterion group (and reference group) and one using a less-educated group?*

13 General Problems in Studying Personality

Businesses assess the functioning of their staffs and size up candidates for new responsibility. Service agencies seek to help individuals and communities assess their needs and prospects. It is necessary to appraise responses to stress, to medication, and to psychotherapy; not only is change in typical behavior an important outcome, but personality influences what the outcome will be. Most lines of social and behavioral research attend to beliefs, styles, attitudes, interpretations, feelings, social interactions, and approaches to problems.

What people do depends on the situations they find themselves in. Many of the difficulties in personality theory stem from the fact that no two persons live in identical situations and that anyone's "typical" situation may change from month to month or from home to office. "Personality traits" such as dominance/submission do not exist in isolation from the stimuli that trigger response.

Early in the book a rough division was made between tests that ask what persons can do and those that ask what they typically do. This part of the book will extend the concept of typical response. Personality can be thought of as one's habits and usual style, but it also consists of abilities to play roles. Conversely, intellectual tests give clues to personality; the special value of the Porteus maze (pp. 29f., 244, 541) may come from the fact that impulsive persons do badly. To identify personality with overt behavior neglects cognitive and emotional elements.

THE RANGE OF INQUIRIES

The range of purposes, variables, and targets of inquiry is vast as the following sketchy list illustrates. The list is deliberately presented in haphazard order, and the code letters are explained at the end.

> What habits and attitudes of individual members are causing discord in this family? (S,P,L)
> Children growing up in certain cultures or subcultures are strongly motivated to achieve; how does this come about? (S,M)
> What relation is there between the duration of breast-feeding and the child's later personality? (S,P,M)
> Is this prisoner's plea of "diminished responsibility" valid? (P,L)
> Under what circumstances do citizens have a sense of political efficacy, a sense that they are capable of influencing government actions? (S,M)
> What are the effects of electroshock? And for which emotionally disturbed persons, if any, should it be used? (S,P)
> This individual, who is in continuing psychotherapy, is today expressing exceptional depression and speaks of suicide; is the risk so great that temporary hospitalization would be wise? (P, L)
> Is it true that in many cases scientific or artistic genius is an outlet for hostile feelings built up during the early years? (S)
> Is this counselee now keeping to a more regular schedule of work than before? (P)
> Does method X of teaching science reduce the extent to which students accept without question the pronouncements of "authorities"? (S,M)
> Which work crews are effective and why? (S,M)
> How can our medical school select students who as doctors will be more concerned with community welfare than with personal gain or a scientific career? (S,M)

The list could go on. S is appended where a question seems likely to interest scientists (not necessarily psychologists); P, where a question is important to practitioners helping individuals or making recommendations on them; L, where an inquiry could be relevant to legal proceedings; and M, where answers would be important to local managers or to makers of broad policy. But perhaps every question could (with slight rephrasing) qualify for every one of the codes. Recall also from Chapter 2 the categories of test use: selection and classification, promoting self-understanding, program evaluation, and scientific inquiry. Each of these emphases lies behind some items on the list.

Assessment of typical behavior by *group-* administered tests is carried out today for research purposes (including opinion surveys and program evaluations) more than for assessment of individuals as such. Personnel psychologists remain concerned with employee performance and satisfaction, but for comparatively few types of assignments do they make formal appraisals of personality. Screening instruments are sometimes used to locate students or others who are "at risk" so that they can be appraised individually.

Some clinical psychologists dealing with an individual proceed directly to work on improving his life situation and actions. Others seek to understand "the personality" and, where appropriate, to change it. Some clinicians and institutions make case workups a regular preliminary to recommendations for treatment. Retests assess progress and redirect treatment. Cerney (1978) illustrates how periodic rereading of test reports can help the therapist maintain perspective on the patient. In one case, for example, the test report was a reminder that beneath the patient's "perfect composure" were disquieting thoughts and deep-seated anxieties. It is necessary to assess how far recovery has progressed before making a decision on release from hospital. When the staff sees two patients as functioning equally well, the test may show that one has returned to emotional balance whereas the other is maintaining his demeanor only by a great effort at self-control (Schafer, 1978).

One survey (Wade & Baker, 1977) seems to indicate that a majority of clinicians use projective tests rarely or never, but that perhaps a third of the clinicians use them with most of their cases. No doubt figures for structured inventories are similar. Because many psychologists use one technique and not the other, it seems that about half of today's clinical psychologists do considerable appraisal of personality. Also among college counseling centers, approximately half use multiscore personality inventories routinely at the start of counseling to stimulate self-appraisal (Dienes, 1977).

A few questions in the preceding list refer to overt acts; others refer not only to inner feelings but to feelings the person disguises from himself. Still, either a behaviorist or a psychoanalyst could rephrase almost every question so that it would come within her sphere of interest.

Finally, look at the list in terms of the impact of the inquiry on the test taker. Is the information collected likely to be communicated to the individual assessed (hence perhaps contributing to self-direction)? Is it likely to be used by some person in authority to influence the fate of the test taker? Or is the question so general that the inquiry affects the person assessed no more than it affects others in the community? Exquisite judgment is required in evaluating the propriety and effectiveness of each application.

Suppose that we could pick adolescents "at risk" for suicide attempts (say, those for whom the chance is as high as 1 in 50). We certainly would not warn these youngsters directly, as we would warn a person at risk from diabetes. Would we alert their parents and schoolteachers to the risk? Only in rare circumstances, surely. Perhaps, however, we could encourage them to protect these youngsters from stress without saying anything about suicide. Or we might propose such a general policy as trying to help *all* adolescents to make friendships. As you see, it is easier to think of significant questions about personalities than to decide what to do with the information.

TYPES OF DATA

Inventories like those discussed in Chapter 12 are one major method of inquiry. This section surveys other alternatives to be considered more fully in Chapters 15 and 16.

Alternatives to Self-report

Observations in representative situations. The most direct inquiry observes the person. To study interests, one could observe how the person spends free time. To evaluate an adult's generosity, one could observe responses to charitable appeals, dealings with subordinates, and tipping.

Many observations are required to assess a trait or even to learn what response is typical in a specific situation. If on several occasions we see a new acquaintance engaged in quarrels, we size him up as irritable. Perhaps, however, a current worry has agitated him, and what we observed is a temporary deviation. Ups and downs ("states") are of interest in their own right.

The act of observing ordinarily ought not to affect what the person does. (For an exception, note the example of weight watchers, p. 530). An investigative procedure that itself affects behavior is said to be "reactive" or "obtrusive" (Webb *et al.*, 1981). A traffic cop at an intersection raises drivers' performance above their habitual level. Presence of the psychological observer may cause the subject to try harder even when no penalty or benefit is in prospect. Reactivity is not always a source of concern. Ratings of workers by supervisors can reasonably be regarded as reports of typical behavior in the usual situation of which the supervisor is part.

Reports from informants. Views of acquaintances and co-workers can be elicited. The rating by a supervisor is more a global impression than a record of behavior, but it is nonetheless useful. Similarly, mothers give information about children, nurses about patients, patients about ward attendants.

Reports from others shed light on corners of the person's life where the observer may never go, cover past behavior no longer observable, and take into account incidents that could not be observed directly. Self-reports have these qualities, also, but there are bound to be discrepancies between a person's report on a significant event and the report of a detached observer.

The phrase "typical behavior" directs attention to overt responses objectively described. Behaviorism can well be joined to phenomenology. Phenomenology considers how the world appears to the individual. *Self-concept, hostility, attitude toward authority,* and other such terms refer to perceptions and reactions within the individual. It can be argued that social interactions and emotional crises are shaped more by the individual's perception of events, of himself or herself, and of others than by objective reality.

A report is one individual's perception, filtered as is any perception of a fluctuating, ambiguous stimulus. When pupils describe the practices of their teacher, the reports add up to a picture of the classroom "climate." Though adult observers may not see events as the children do, the reports of pupils are significant information about the psychology of their classroom.

Performance tests. In a performance test, the measurer arranges a provocative stimulus to elicit significant behavior. The performance test permits direct comparisons across persons and times. A summary report of everyday leadership may reflect differences in opportunity to lead rather than differences in readiness, but a performance test makes opportunity uniform. The standardized situation does not observe "typical behavior." It samples response to a very special situation—namely, a leadership opportunity set up by a tester whose good opinion will have certain consequences. Such a "situational test" is usually presented as an ability measure.

Some tests simulate a social situation and ask the person to respond as he normally would—a kind of self-report! Thus, to assess assertiveness, McReynolds *et al.* (1976) use the following script in an "improvisation" technique:

> *Tester says:* "You took an expensive suede coat to the cleaners. When you pick it up, you notice some spots on the back that weren't there when you brought the coat in."
> *Actor of same sex as test taker reads:* "Does it look okay?"
> *Subject reads from script:* "No, there are two white spots here on the back."
> "Oh, yes. Those look like bleach spots. I'm afraid we can't do anything about those."
> "But they weren't here when I brought the coat in."
> "Well, it certainly couldn't have happened here. . . . There's nothing I can do about it now."

At this point the script ends. The test taker and actor are to continue the interaction, the actor having been told in general terms how to keep the conversation going. (For more on such techniques, see J. R. Hall, 1977, and McReynolds & DeVoge, 1977.)

The same situation can also be used after telling the test taker that he is to respond assertively—to show his ability to play an assertive part. Following a trial under "typical performance" directions with a trial under these "maximum performance" directions is suggested as a basis for planning for behavior modification (Nietzel & Bernstein, 1976, p. 500):

Clients who display appropriate assertion only under high-demand could then be assigned to treatment oriented toward removal of inhibitory factors. . . . Those whose assertion remains inadequate under both demand conditions could be exposed to skill-building experiences.

A much more indirect method, the *projective technique,* presents a picture or other ambiguous stimulus and asks the test taker what he sees in it or what he thinks will happen next. For example, the tester displays a picture of people at work in a hospital operating room; thoughts and feelings attributed to characters in the pictures disclose the respondent's attitudes about work roles or about surgery.

1. *Define the range, in time and situations, of the behavior one should study to answer these questions:*
   a. *How well does this supervisor handle grievances?*
   b. *Does study of philosophy make one more rational in his or her adult life?*
   c. *Does viewing a film on nutrition improve housewives' practices in menu planning?*
   d. *Do graduates of the modern elementary school write legibly?*
   e. *How anxious is this patient at this point in therapy?*

Should Methods Agree?

Chapter 5 introduced the principle that procedures claiming to assess the same variable should rank persons similarly (convergence of indicators). Chapter 12 noted discrepancies among interest scores with the same name. Discrepancies among personality measures are even more frequent. The general label *motivation to achieve* may be applied to information from a questionnaire, to a score from a projective technique, and to ratings supplied by teachers. Table 13.1 illustrates the classical "multitrait-multimethod" design (p. 153), which checks on both convergence and divergence. Raters in the same situation did not agree excellently, but the consistency of reported behavior across situations was remarkably high in view of the reliability. The traits had evidently been defined to report on distinct characteristics. If the correlations of participation with cooperation had been around 0.3, that would not prove that the data were faulty. Such overlap *would* imply that the two traits occur together and that it may not be profitable to distinguish them.

Evidence that two methods of evaluating the same trait concur is welcome when it comes. For example, a role-playing test of assertiveness was checked against a sample of behavior in everyday life. Some time after the role-playing, an experimenter posing as a salesperson telephoned each subject and tried to "hard sell" magazine subscriptions. The assertiveness of the subjects' responses correlated nearly 0.8 with the score from the laboratory

Table 13.1. *Correlations of ratings in a multitrait-multimethod design*

		Participation rated in		Cooperation rated in	
		Cottage	School	Cottage	School
Participation rated in	Cottage	0.7	0.4	0	−0.1
	School		0.5	0.1	0
Cooperation rated in	Cottage			0.7	0.5
	School				0.5

SOURCE: Koretzky et al., 1978.
NOTE: Disturbed and delinquent adolescents in a residential institution were rated by counselors in their small living groups and by teachers. Reliabilities in the diagonal report agreement among raters in the same situation, corrected by the Spearman-Brown formula. The two variables are more completely described as interest and participation vs. apathy and withdrawal, and cooperation and compliance vs. hostility and defiance.

simulation (McFall & Marston, 1970). A more complex pattern of convergence is seen in Figure 13.1. The figure displays a striking patterning among distinct methods: self-report, report of peer informant, report of teacher informant, and a situational measure (expansiveness vs. constriction in drawing). For more on this finding, see page 449. Although two examples of convergence have just been given, it is not uncommon to find disagreement when two procedures purport to measure the same construct. Similarly, when we try to match self-reports across instruments or with reports of observers we may find gratifying consistency, but that is not a universal finding (Block, in Magnusson & Endler, 1977).

Broad characteristics such as adaptiveness and morale should appear under many circumstances and should be reported by various methods. Each method, however, views the person from its own angle and filters the information in a particular way. Consequently, "method factors" raise certain correlations. Suppose that self-reports on traits A and B correlate substantially. Peer ratings on A and B are also likely to correlate. The crosscorrelations (e.g., A self-rated with B peer-rated) will be lower. The correlation of scores A and B from the same inventory will probably be higher than the crosscorrelation of score A with a measure of B from a second inventory. Likewise, A and B, judged by a single rater, will show more consistency than when one judge rates A and another rates B.

The traditional view is that when method factors appear the measurement must be defective. Something *is* wrong if speedometers in automobiles typically register lower speeds than those a radar apparatus supplies the patrol car. In the personality domain, however, what is an error for one purpose may be a significant fact for another purpose. Raters disagree because they have sampled different aspects of the person's behavior and because they feel differently about him. The interpreter can consider each rating as a report on that particular social relationship or—treating the reports as

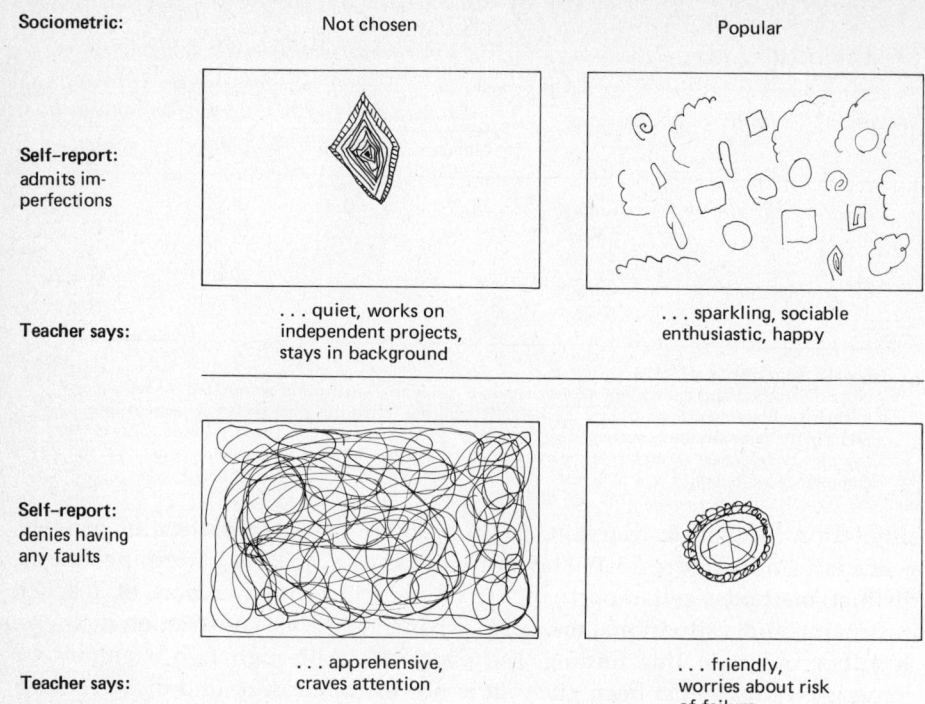

Figure 13.1. Data reflecting personalities of first-grade girls.
Source: Wallach et al., 1962, pp. 15–17. Copyright 1962 by the American Psychological Association. Adapted by permission of the publisher and author.

samples from a heterogeneous domain—can average several of them. Likewise, when a self-description departs from the person's actual behavior, such a discrepancy is a fact, not an "error."

McClelland (1981, p. 93) goes so far as to say, "Campbell and Fiske . . . were wrong in arguing that theory requires . . . consistencies across methods of measurement." Yet Campbell and Fiske were not wrong, I would say, in urging investigators to find out which variables show consistency across methods and which do not.

As cross-method validation cannot be exhaustive, two precautions are desirable, especially in research. First, testers and those who read their reports should keep in mind the method that generated the score. Second, it is advisable to measure a variable by at least two procedures. Persistence in rolling a tiny ball through a tiltable maze may or may not go with persistence on a crossword puzzle. In research on factors affecting "persistence," the investigator ought to use two or more such techniques (possibly using each with a different random subgroup of subjects). If her experimental intervention has a similar effect on each measure, she can interpret with some confidence.

Even when backed by evidence of consistency, generalization is risky.

This investigator's tests will differ in only a few respects. Someone with a new theory, introducing a new twist, may demonstrate inconsistency. Thus Feather (1961) showed that persistence is strongly dependent on the *perceived* difficulty of a problem. Increasing task difficulty increases persistence of some persons and decreases that of others.

Validation of information on personality suffers from the tendency to compile evidence on scores singly. Some research hypotheses do consider one personality variable apart from the rest of the personality. (The relation of anxiety to learning is one such problem.) Behavioral counselors may also work on a circumscribed characteristic such as assertiveness within a marital relationship. But attempts to understand personality development in general or to understand a particular person for practical purposes ought ordinarily to look at many dimensions together.

Figure 13.1 is a striking example of the "configural" character of information on personality. The meaning of one trait depends on the level of other traits. When a child says he is satisfied with himself, that may cover insecurity, or it may be part of happy and effective adjustment. Self-report, peer report, and teacher report do not correlate with drawing style when each is considered singly. The informant's report interpreted jointly with the reported self-concept yields a strong correlation.

Interpretations of score combinations and personality descriptions that integrate dimensions impressionistically can be validated. But research has not been carried out in a way that would steadily refine the theory interpreters use.

2. *How well can the four procedures—observation in representative situations, report from others, self-report, and performance tests—satisfy the following requirements? Rank the procedures from best to poorest in each respect.*
   a. *The data reflect differences in personality rather than differences in environment and opportunity.*
   b. *The data reflect the individual's behavior, undistorted by the perceptions of those who provide data.*
   c. *The data provide a summary or estimate of the individual's behavior during all moments of his current life.*
   d. *The results are the same regardless of whether the subject wishes to make a good impression on the psychologist.*
3. *Zest and Vigor of aging persons might be measured by self-report (S) and reports of observers (O). A multitrait-multimethod study produces the following correlations:*

	ZS	VS	ZO	VO
ZS		0.6	**0.1**	0.5
VS			0.1	**0.6**
ZO				0.3

a. *Do the trait scores show consistency across methods (convergence)?*
   b. *Do the persons rank differently on Z and V (divergence)?*
   c. *Internal-consistency coefficients are 0.7 for ZS and VS. Correlations between observers are 0.7 for ZO and VO. Taking all the correlations into account, how many of the reports would be worth collecting in subsequent research? (If fewer than four, which?)*

ETHICAL ISSUES

Practical personality testing has flourished in two contexts, one institutional, the other individual. Valid information about personality would presumably be of great value to employers, college admissions officers, and others who carry out institutional policies. In fact, personality questionnaires were first applied to screen out potentially neurotic soldiers. Institutional testing tries to determine the truth about the individual, whether he wants that truth known or not. In noninstitutional testing, tests are applied solely for the benefit of the person tested. Here also the tester believes that learning the truth will be valuable, but she does not feel free to violate the person's wishes. The client who comes wanting the psychologist's assistance may be quite unprepared to pay the price of unveiling his soul.

Any test invades privacy when test takers do not wish to reveal themselves. The personality test is more often regarded as invasive than the ability test. Everyone has two personalities: a social role and a "true self." If, for example, aggression and open expression of emotion are discouraged by the culture, there is certain to be some discrepancy between these two personalities. Some techniques probe into feelings and attitudes people normally conceal. Indeed, virtually all measures of personality seek information on areas that in normal social intercourse are regarded as private. The respondent is willing to admit the psychologist into these private areas only if he sees the relevance of the questions to *his* goals in working with the psychologist. The psychologist is not "invading privacy" when she is freely admitted and has a genuine need for the information.

Psychologists were shocked during the 1960s to find themselves accused of wholesale violations of human dignity (Amrine, 1965). Congressional investigators and editorial writers pilloried the psychological tester alongside the industrial spy who planted microphones in cocktail olives. At one point the Senate voted that "no [guidance] program shall provide for the conduct of any test . . . to elicit information dealing with the personality, environment, home life, parental or family relationships, economic status, or sociological and psychological problems of the pupil tested." Attacks came from those antagonistic to social services and also from civil libertarians. Pressure from critics has at times forced reputable investigators to destroy research questionnaires that had not been tabulated.

The central question is whether it is objectionable to assess personality directly when the data *are* interpreted as well as possible. But first let us dispose of contentions that are *not* central.

- "Psychologists have made indefensible claims regarding the validity of their tests." True, and important; but most test developers and users are reasonably conservative in their claims today. Many violations come from inadequately trained testers. Some come from nonprofessionals—anyone with a printing press can prepare a questionnaire and use it to tell your fortune or find you a soul mate.
- "The interpretations have low validity." In many applications this is true, but from an ethical standpoint valid appraisal could be more objectionable. A test with nearly perfect validity for forecasting treason, embezzlement, or sexual offenses would be unthinkably dangerous—a clear invitation to cast out someone who has committed no objectionable act.
- "Inventories award high scores to conformers." This is an attack on the values of decision makers in schools and business, a proper enough matter for debate. Inventories, however, are an expression of the values, not a cause. An employer who wants yes-men will get them, with or without the inventory. Personality tests find it no harder to identify the independent-minded than to pick conformers. Admittedly, some interpreters have been too quick to define "the healthy personality" as one free from emotional conflict. Conflict is a price one pays for independence.
- "Situational tests that put temptation before the person constitute improper entrapment." In some tests a child is given an opportunity to steal, not knowing—before or after—that he has been observed. Should the psychologist risk creating even transient guilt? (Kelman, 1967; Klass, 1978). This is a serious criticism, but it applies to only a few procedures.

Now to the central issues, the first of which is dignity.

Respecting the Dignity of the Persons Tested

Has an employer the right to question an applicant about matters not directly related to the work? Yes, if workers' private lives affect their usefulness as employees. It is not good for the bank when its teller is seen regularly at the racetrack (but is that *private* behavior?). At least one court (see Dahlstrom, 1980) upheld psychological evaluation of would-be firefighters because their being able to withstand stress is so much in the public interest. (The instrument under challenge was the self-report MMPI.)

Has a teacher a right to ask children about their emotions, friendships, and home life? As with any testing, the school's justification must be that the information will lead to better educational services. The public has repeatedly urged schools to develop character and promote mental health—and instruction should be guided by facts about the learners. On the opposite side is the argument that no one should be asked to testify against himself. And parents' privacy is invaded when the child is asked, "Do your parents quarrel frequently?"

Most objections to questionnaires are relevant also to observations and performance tests so long as the person is unaware of the observations or believes that he is revealing less than he is. No major issue arises when the tester requests responses, explains how they will be used, and leaves the person genuinely free not to respond. Teachers and employers have sufficient power that the person may anticipate unwelcome consequences if he does not respond; hence the consent is not always freely given. Imposing questions is difficult to justify, and the information obtained is suspect. No tester can impose questions for long unless she can convince the educated public (including advocates for the helpless) that the questioning serves the public interest and violates no recognized right of the individual. In general, the employer had better be able to demonstrate that every question has genuine relevance to ability to perform the job in question. A school board can reasonably approve an attempt to identify maladjusted individuals when there is a responsible program for helping them and can approve an unsigned inventory as part of program evaluation. It ought to be outraged by an assessment intended to detect troublemakers in advance.

The test developer can remove a good many objections simply by discarding items objectionable to her public. Employees in a manufacturing firm were asked to check items about which they would "feel personally offended" if asked to respond (Winkler & Mathews, 1967). In a typical questionnaire, the usual person objected to no more than 1 per cent of the items. Moreover, objections are reduced when the respondent understands that interpretation is based on consistent responses running through many items and that the psychologist does not draw conclusions from single responses (Fink & Butcher, 1972). The person then feels more comfortable with questions where no response choice fits him exactly. To be sure, encouraging test takers to omit items they object to makes the procedure nonstandard and scores become harder to interpret (J. Butcher & A. Tellegen, 1966).

4. *In the decision regarding firefighters, the judge gave favorable consideration to the fact that the employer saw only the psychological report, not the scores or the responses to items. Why did the judge regard this as important?*

How Permissible Is Deception?

The second issue is the acceptability of disguising the purpose of a test or of particular questions. The psychologist should ordinarily introduce procedures with as frank an account as the situation allows. The typical person seeking therapeutic help can readily understand the aim of diagnosis and that transparent diagnostic questions would invite him to choose his own diagnosis. It is harder to give a frank account of a test that observes style of work (e.g., impulsiveness); the person, knowing what is sought, will try to display that style. An investigator privileged to interview a genius about his childhood would ruin the inquiry—a difficult one at best—by explaining in advance her hypothesis about disguised hostility. Except with cooperative volunteers, the uses of disguised procedures are extremely limited.

Rules cannot define when disguise is justifiable. Universities require committee approval of plans for research on human subjects. Similar judgment by independent colleagues is advisable in clinics, prisons, advertising agencies—wherever typical behavior is investigated by standardized methods. But much is left to the judgment of the individual psychologist or counselor, especially when the data are collected by loosely structured methods such as interviews.

To keep matters open and above board in testing persons entering therapy, the psychologist can begin in this manner: "It should help to solve your problem if I collect a good deal of information. Some of the tests use straightforward questions whose purpose you will readily understand. Others dig more deeply into the personality. Sometimes they bring to light emotional conflicts that the person is not even conscious of. Few of us admit the whole truth about our feelings and ideas, even to ourselves. I think I can help you better with the aid of these tests." The client who is not ready to trust the psychologist may refuse to take disguised tests. If this is the case, the information probably could not be used constructively.

Limits on Scientific Inquiry

A third issue is freedom of research. It is important to understand why persons break under stress. Citizenship education is bound to remain impotent unless effects of various approaches on behavior are verified. Social scientists, having a high sense of social purpose, are puzzled by the public objections to some of their probings. Knowing that their intentions are pure and that the anonymity of subjects will be safeguarded, they are inclined to stress their right to inquire. If their probings threaten to expose weak spots in the society, they go further, insisting on their *duty* to inquire.

This is as it should be. On the other hand, the scientist must accept some restraints, if only to keep her study from being shot down in midflight. Patiently explaining the study to respondents and to other segments of the community is one of the costs of doing business as an investigator.

Psychologists and educators must be particularly mindful that their records are not proof against subpoena. "Good data" for a study of adolescent rebellion might be used against the respondent in a later trial for some alleged offense as an adult. Anonymity and simple coding of records is not a full safeguard. Identity can be detected by matching facts from the coded questionnaire with other facts that are openly recorded. There are enough anecdotes of malign detective work of this kind from the precomputer days of Nazi Germany to justify sober thought on the risks inherent in data banks.

Among many devices for protecting subjects (Boruch & Cecil, 1979), the virtue of random bundling should be noted. If data from individuals are coded and the records are sorted strictly at random into sets of uniform size (perhaps sets of five), average data for each bundle can be calculated (for example, average age, proportion female, proportion endorsing each item). Only these averages go into the research file; they can answer any statistical question as well as the individual data could.

5. *Can there be ethical objections to requiring newly employed engineers to fill out a questionnaire to aid the personnel manager in deciding whether to assign them to sales, research, or other responsibilities?*
6. *Discuss the following advice from an older textbook. Is it acceptable today? "Whether serving an institution or serving an individual client, the tester should not use indirect and misleading techniques unless the respondent clearly understands that anything he says may be used against him. To be sure, an employer may regard his refusal to submit to tests as grounds for denying him employment, but this is ethically preferable to obtaining deceitfully information he does not wish to give."*
7. *Investigators sometimes ask the respondent to mark a list of statements to indicate the responses the majority of people would give; that is, they present a task of social insight rather than of self-description. Scores summarizing the responses he attributes to persons-in-general may correlate with independent evidence on the respondent better than his self-description does (Goldberg & Rorer, 1966). Suppose that this indirect and disguised technique is valid. For what purposes would you consider it a proper way to measure beliefs, fears, and so forth?*
8. *To find out if questionnaires "would have utility for screening and selection decisions," an investigator gave anxiety and ego-strength questionnaires to Peace Corps volunteers during training. Correlations with criteria of performance in Nigeria were higher than correlations of ratings by the training faculty with the criteria (Mischel, 1965). He told respondents that the questionnaires were being given for research use only and would play no part in Peace Corps decisions; he adhered to this promise. Given the utility of the information, was it wise to withhold it from administrative use? Did his study warrant giving tests to future trainees without the promise of privacy?*

CONCEPTUALIZATIONS OF INDIVIDUALITY

Observations and reports are summarized in a variety of ways depending on the user's purpose and the extent to which she wishes to bring theory into the analysis. This section amplifies and restates some of the points made in Chapter 2 in describing the styles of test use. A few lines about schools of thought will tie what follows to Chapter 2 and Chapter 12.

- Behaviorists are the least "theory minded" of interpreters. Evidence is taken at face value. For them, behavior is behavior; labels such as "depression" merely block the user's view of the procedures that defined the scope of the information. They prefer to define a narrow category of situations and count responses of certain kinds.
- The "actuarial" or sign approach is psychometric; responses are reduced to numbers and—when the method is applied in its pure form—the conclusions are generated by a formula or a set of rules a computer can obey. Again, evidence is taken at face value. Actuaries see being "like engineers" as forecasting satisfaction regardless of the content of the items that entered the key. (*Some* theory is required in this approach, in selecting dimensions for criterion keys.)
- The "trait" approach is also psychometric, but its adherents think of responses in terms of samples rather than signs. The approach is illustrated by the homogeneous keys of interest inventories, where items were grouped in broad categories and responses summarized in a numerical profile. As we shall see, theories of personality have generated many trait systems.
- The phenomenological approach is radically different from that of behaviorism, being concerned with what events mean to the person more than with "facts." Though preferring direct observation, a behaviorist might ask a mother, "Does your child hang up his clothes without being prompted?" So might a phenomenologist. But whereas the behaviorist would focus on the evidence as describing the child, the phenomenologist would speak of the mother's *image* of the child. Most investigators in this school move away from objective toward impressionistic methods, but some try to handle perceptions in a strictly psychometric manner.
- The impressionistic style is seen most clearly in psychoanalytic or "dynamic" interpretations, which explain behavior in terms of motives. This is again a "sign" approach because the interpreter looks for the "significance" of an action but the meaning emerges from theory rather than from statistical tables.

These paragraphs by no means tell the full story; much will be added by examples scattered through the remainder of the book.

Trait Measures as Samples

"Measurement" of individuality is very nearly a logical impossibility because measurement implies reducing direct observations to a limited number of standard scales. Even the limited goal of measuring a single aspect of typical behavior—a trait or habit—encounters difficulties.

Defining a variable. Let us consider typical legibility of handwriting (TLH) as an example. It is reasonable to suppose that TLH changes; therefore, a definition requires a time frame. Suppose we restrict ourselves to the upcoming calendar month; whether TLH is the same from month to month and year to year (in a particular population) is left open to investigation. Suppose for the sake of the example that we invade privacy and collect, without the person's knowledge, a photocopy of everything he writes during the month. Once we assess the legibility of those specimens the median figure represents TLH. Even so, there are decisions to make.

- What is an episode of handwriting? A page? A document? (The latter counts the briefest memo and the draft of a whole essay as equals.) Let us agree to weight time slices equally, ignoring those during which the person does no writing. Perhaps, then, we settle on one score per hour.
- How to define legibility? If we collect ratings, we must choose raters. Perhaps those familiar with the person's writing read it easily but then TLH becomes a property of writer and reader jointly, not of writer alone. So let us agree to select some judges who read the papers from everyone, legibility being scored as positive for a document they can read aloud at 100 words per minute with no more than one misreading per 100 words. The readers now are standard instruments and we have an operational definition of TLH. With the same definition we may sample hours instead of evaluating all a person writes.

Our definition has neglected situational factors. Suppose Curt scores 70 (percentage of writings counted as legible) during December, but brings a new typewriter to campus after the holiday break. What he used to write for the eyes of others with careful penmanship he now types. His TLH score may well drop to 30 if his January writing consists of notes taken in class, memoranda at the telephone, and other hasty jottings. Perhaps his score on jottings alone would have been 30 in December. The change in the TLH average is real, yet we can scarcely say that there was a change in Curt. When we compare two persons or two groups on TLH, we can easily draw a wrong conclusion if their situations differ.

One significant element is the demand associated with a role. A teacher at the blackboard is constrained to do his best in a way that a student taking notes is not. Handwriting ability sets a limit on TLH, however; the teacher at his best may not be good enough.

Ordinarily, psychologists think of traits as reflecting structures within the person—that is, concepts of self, concepts of the social environment, conditioned emotional responses, and a repertoire of coping mechanisms. All this makes some responses frequent and others infrequent. Psychologists who study personality concentrate on stable differences among persons within a culture. Anthropologists are most impressed by the similarities among members of a culture. Each culture encourages its members in certain responses (or, more specifically, defines a style proper among those in a particular status—e.g., among males prior to puberty). These views are not in logical conflict, but they complicate measurement and interpretation. The same objective behavior means something different for persons in different cultures, in different statuses within the culture, and in different momentary roles.

Typical behavior cannot be defined independent of the person's life space. Our measure of TLH was based on a representative sample of Curt's life (Hammond & Wascoe, 1980). In today's jargon, Curt's ecology changed when he acquired a typewriter. The measurer who wants to come closer to what is "in the person" will have to hold situations constant in some manner (just as Ayres, to get a better measure of penmanship ability, asked everyone to write the Gettysburg Address).

During childhood and from adolescence to maturity, persons growing up normally in the community show impressive consistencies over time. Olweus (1979) inquired repeatedly about the aggressiveness of a group of boys; each rater saw the boy under somewhat different conditions, and his life situation changed in some respects. "True scores" on Aggressiveness (see p. 159) correlated 0.75 over a 1-year interval and 0.6 over 10 years.

A set of longitudinal data puts consistency and change nicely into perspective (Block, in Magnusson & Endler, 1977; Block, 1981; Bronson, 1966; Macfarlane *et al.*, 1954). Some individuals at age 40 gave impressions highly consistent with those recorded in their early teens, and others "were nearly unrecognizable" from the earlier descriptions. Psychologist's perceptions of 40-year-old adults correlated 0.4 with similar ratings made during junior high school on the following traits (among others): high aspiration level, values intellectual matters, self-defeating, and "pushes limits to see what he can get away with." The changes in males were far greater than those in females. Because status, personal resources, and social supports change over the decades, we should not expect great stability of rankings on a particular aspect of personality. Broad variables such as vigor and intellectual interests remain strong (or weak) over long periods. Some personalities evolve dramatically. Yet, as McClelland (1979, 1981) argues in describing the academic psychologist who turned to mysticism and transformed himself into Ram Dass, in many ways "the same person" shows through the new identity.

Situational domains. Our TLH measure can be improved if we divide up the life space along suitable lines. An obvious first split is between messages written for the person's own use and messages for others; it should not be difficult to sort Curt's writings and obtain two scores. Many other lines of division suggest themselves: note-taking (externally paced), academic papers turned in for a grade, drafts prepared for a typist, . . . Likewise, it is possible to subdivide domains such as stress situations or leadership opportunities.

Ordinarily, the psychologist assessing typical behavior wants a homogeneous category such that persons who respond positively to one situation within the category are likely to respond positively to others. Then the category describes a characteristic that appears in many settings. Correlations of scores based on behavioral observations in "similar" situations are characteristically low; most investigators have to settle for values of 0.3 and lower. Some persons are consistent across the category. But a person's response may be variable because of the specific significance to him of each situation (Bem & Allen, 1974). Cross-situation correlations are like correlations of single items in ability tests, which also run about 0.2–0.3. When many situations (or samples on many days) are combined in a single score, two such composites can have a high correlation (Epstein, 1979).

Whether it is better to use narrow categories (high consistency) or broader ones cannot be given a general answer. A central problem in social psychology is the extent to which actions are consistent with stated attitudes. Fishbein and Azjen (1974) found that persons who claimed religious beliefs differed very little from others on any single behavioral criterion such as saying grace before meals. But a composite score covering 70 acts—saying grace, donating money to a religious organization, and being a conscientious objector to war—correlated 0.6–0.7 with verbal attitude. It makes sense, then, to characterize persons with regard to the broad "religious actions" domain even though the composite score cannot predict any one type of action. The low correlations from one action to another have led some writers to suggest that personality lacks consistency. A better reading would be that personal style is fairly stable, and so is the ecology, but the response at any one moment is determined by many traits and states and by many features of the immediate situation. We cannot expect to predict the response on a particular occasion.

Person-situation interaction. Recent writings have debated the comparative "importance" of person, situation, and person-by-situation interaction in determining responses. No general answer can or should be given.

A specific example is a high school study. Students were asked the same questions in English, math, biology, and government classes. One of the questions was, "Do you speak out in class?" Figure 13.2 reports just a fraction of the information obtained. (The method of analysis is essentially that of generalizability theory; p. 167.)

- On participation, the average was nearly the same in every class. (Someone has to answer the teacher's questions!) The large component for persons says that some of the students spoke up more than others. The sizable interaction indicates that few pupils were equally responsive across all classes.
- On anxiety, no "person" factor appeared; that is, few pupils expressed anxiety all across their classes. Some classes elicited more anxiety than others. The size of the interaction indicates that different students were anxious in different classes.

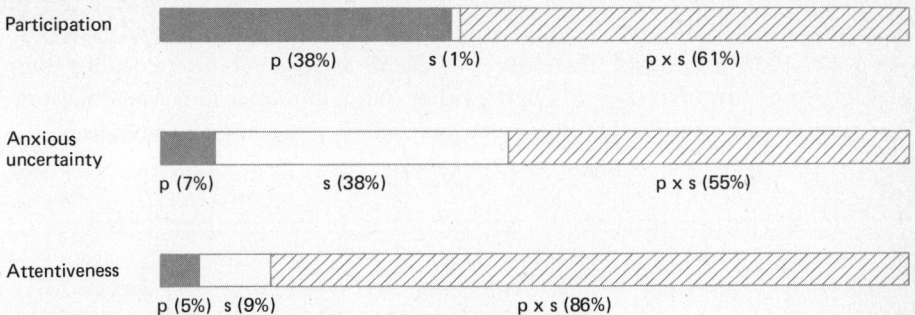

Figure 13.2. Sources of variation in student behavior.
Source: Based on an analysis by Trickett and Moos (1970). Sampling errors and errors of measurement were eliminated before adjusting totals to 100 per cent.

- On attentiveness, the interaction is overwhelmingly larger than the other components. The attentiveness of the pupil depended on the class. Average attentiveness was about the same in all classes.

A strong interaction suggests the appropriateness of developing measures for narrow categories (e.g., for anxiety in connection with mathematical tasks).

When the same response scale fits many situations and successive occasions, something akin to the content-referenced analysis of abilities becomes possible. One could map ups and downs of anxiety (or some other state) that accompany changes in conditions. The interest "is not in how people compare to others, but in how they can move closer to their own goals and ideals if they change their behavior in specific ways as they interact with the significant people in their lives" (Mischel, 1977, p. 248). In the same vein, O'Leary and Wilson (1975) wrote that behavioral assessment should "identify the environmental and self-imposed variables which are *currently* maintaining an individual's maladaptive thoughts, feelings, and behaviors" (p. 18).

Situationist criticisms warn against "typing" persons—this one as extrovert, that one as psychotic, a third as other-directed. The criticisms are much like those directed to language that suggest the existence of a fixed intelligence. Mischel (1977) makes the point that socially effective persons are *not* consistent. The person who changes from passive to aggressive, from affiliative to task-centered is discriminating one situation from another. If a person does so on the basis of role demands and considers his or her goals or resources, this fluctuation is far more adaptive than an unchanging style.

The discussion has to do with variation within an established but developing behavioral repertoire. After we have observed Sam, the best prediction is that Sam's style in the future will resemble his recent style—*and* that he will change. To say that the present personality has deep roots still allows for change in the internal system of meanings, the external coping practices, and the balance of physiological forces. As with abilities, specific aspects are easier to change than broad patterns of adaptation. It is easier to decondition fear of snakes than to modify "fearfulness," easier to teach self-scheduling than to overcome "impulsiveness." On the other hand, guidance and conversations to promote self-understanding must use broad language (R. Hogan *et al.*, 1977).

9. *What events might produce a marked increase in level of aspiration between ages 13 and 32? A marked decrease?*
10. *It is a reasonable bet that those whose level of aspiration was low at 13 and high at 43 had different profiles at age 13 from those who remained low. What traits might be precursors of adult striving?*
11. *Normal males' rankings on most personality traits at age 17 correlated 0.0 to 0.3 with rankings on the same traits at about age 35. For females the correlations ran from 0.3 to 0.6. What might explain the sex difference? (The data came from judgments of trained observers and interviewers, the early data having been collected in the 1930s; Haan, 1981.)*
12. *A person may be "stubborn" in some situations and not in others. Both actions may be typical for him. Illustrate and suggest a rational explanation for his consistency.*
13. *Criticize the trait "responsibility" from the situational standpoint. Suggest a type of inventory that might satisfy the criticism to some extent.*
14. *Define the range, in time and situations, of the behavior one should study to answer these questions:*
    a. *How well does this supervisor handle grievances?*
    b. *Does study of philosophy make one more rational in his adult life?*
    c. *Does viewing a film on nutrition improve housewives' practices in menu planning?*
    d. *How anxious is this patient at this point in therapy?*
15. *A factor analysis of legibility scores on homework papers could be carried out. If there is a large person component and little interaction, what will the factor analysis report? If there is a large interaction and a small person component, what will the factor analysis report? (Factor analysis neglects situation main effects.)*
16. *In using the Trickett-Moos questions to study how students' educational aspirations relate to their responsiveness in school, for which of the Trickett-Moos traits would you use a single overall score and for which would you keep track of class-by-class scores for each pupil?*

How Many Dimensions Should Be Distinguished?

Regarding ability, some psychologists think that one general factor tells nearly the whole story, yet a kit of tests offers to measure two dozen factors, and pictures like that of Marshalek (p. 291) represent common aspects of measures in two dimensions. In the interest domain, the general factor—

tendency to like many activities—is unexciting; the domain is described by two-dimensional and six-dimensional schemes and by profiles with two dozen scores. We have already seen that personality dimensions can be finely subdivided by categorizing situations—but how many dimensions would permit a reasonably complete description? Again, some people find a few dimensions adequate; others measure a dozen or more to pick up nuances of information (Wiggins, 1973).

Figure 13.3 starts us off with a map derived from factor analysis. There is a good/bad (evaluative, social desirability) factor and an active/passive (activity) factor. Persons judged "sociable" are typically judged active and good. (The picture is not saying that all persons with that mixture of goodness and activity are equally sociable.) Adding weakness/strength (potency) as the front-to-back dimension generates a spherical representation. Thus "deferential" combines weakness and goodness. Many other maps for children as well as adults are in basic agreement. These three dimensions, which were brought to prominence by Osgood's research on semantics, will reappear in an Osgood case study at page 504.

Goldberg (1981) tells a slightly more complex story. He sees good/bad as a general, first-impression factor and suggests that current trait theories are captured in five subordinate factors: Activity, Potency, Warmth, Conscien-

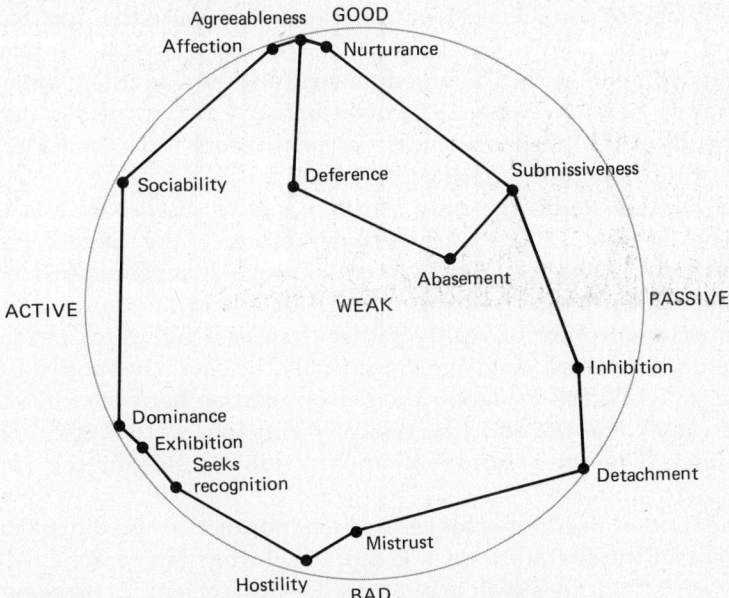

Figure 13.3. Ordered array of personality traits.
Note: Configuration derived from ratings of acquaintances. The "front-to-back" dimension of the spherical plot represents a weak-to-strong factor; all traits in this set fell on the weak side.
Source: Data from Lorr & McNair, 1965.

tiousness, and Emotional Stability. (In any such framework, rotation is possible. Figure 13.3 could be turned 45° to make warm/cold and dominant/submissive the axes instead of goodness and activity. Goldberg's list allows many other permutations [Wiggins, 1980].)

Correlations among traits reflect our language, the conceptual structure we employ in sizing up others. Ratings of strangers, based on negligible amounts of information, show the same factors as ratings of longtime acquaintances (Passini & Norman, 1966). Some theorists (Shweder & D'Andrade, 1979) contend that the dimensions are linguistic conventions and do not reflect facts about behavior. I prefer the view (Block *et al.*, 1979) that words are associated because they correspond to associations in behavior. "Kind" and "gentle" do not refer to identical behavior, but many an act has both characteristics. Moreover, a person generally tries to be consistent with a verbally framed self-concept ("I criticize gently"); the label accounts for some generality in his behavior. A further point: Experience is culturally determined. What traits are found together will change across cultures, an obvious example being components of "masculinity."

Despite the agreement among correlational studies, present terminology is chaotic; indeed, Goldberg refers to his synthesis as an attempt to "decode Babel." The emotional-stability factor appears in the literature under such aliases as anxiety, neuroticism, emotionality, lack of ego resiliency, and lack of confidence. Contrariwise, authors use the *same* word differently (Adcock, 1965; Eysenck, 1977; Guilford, 1977). "Introversion" represents for one author a brooding neurotic; for another, anyone who would rather be a clerk than a carnival barker. "Ascendance" ranges from spontaneous social responsiveness, in one theory, to inconsiderate and overbearing behavior in another.

As matters stand, the only sensible way to discuss data is to speak of "the Atkinson TAT *n* Achievement score," "the Spence-Helmreich Mastery score," "the CPI Achievement-through-Independence score," and so on according to the measure used. McClelland (1981) sees this incoherence as a reflection of reality rather than as a failure of psychologists to settle on a standard language. Specifically, he says, the motive expressed in fantasy (TAT), the valuation the person puts on hard work (a conscious ideal or value), and the effort he typically puts into work (typical behavior) are distinct. The three need not appear side by side in the same person.

Mention of need for achievement reminds us that the dimensions most prominent in the literature do not capture all that can reasonably concern psychologists. Murray's system of 35 needs—Abasement, Achievement, Affiliation, Autonomy. . . . —cuts across and goes beyond the familiar dimensions, and a test scored in those terms is not reducible to five or six dimensions (Murray *et al.*, 1938). The other complex system in most active use is that of R. B. Cattell. Having applied factor analysis to self-reports, ratings, and performance tests, he comes up with the following list of pervasive dimensions:

Warm	Impulsive	Suspicious	Radical
Intelligent	Conforming	Imaginative	Self-sufficient
Emotionally stable	Bold	Shrewd	Self-disciplined
Dominant	Sensitive	Insecure	Tense

These factor names tell Cattell's story too simply. What I list simply as "warm" is for him "Source trait A," which he unpacks as in Table 13.2.

17. Becker and Krug (1964) extracted five factors from reports on children: Calm (vs. emotional-rebellious), Submissive, Sociable, Loving (vs. distrusting), and Cooperative. Exactly what information carried in the five dimensions is not carried in the good-strong-active dimensions?
18. Name two adjectives that both would fall in the good-strong-passive sector. Do the two have distinct meanings? Could a person have one of the traits and lack the other?
19. Place the Cattell dimensions within the good-strong-active framework. Thus Dominant might be coded $-:0:+$ in the light of Figure 13.3. Do the coded descriptions carry the full meaning of the traits?
20. Harry falls at the 50th percentile (among male college students) on Sociability. What does this tell us? Is Harry sociable?
21. On a certain inventory each scale has a possible score range from zero to 30. A person who scores 15 points on Irritability falls at the 80th percentile; a person who scores 15 points on Punctuality falls at the 15th percentile. Suppose a person earns 15 points on each scale; is it correct to

Table 13.2. *Description of a Cattell factor*

SIZOTHYMIA (Reserved, Detached, Critical, Aloof, Stiff)	versus	AFFECTOTHYMIA (Warmhearted, Participating) Easygoing, Participating)
Critical	vs.	Good Natured, Easygoing
Stands by His Own Ideas	vs.	Ready to Cooperate, Likes to Participate
Cool, Aloof	vs.	Attentive to People
Precise, Objective	vs.	Softhearted, Casual
Distrustful, Skeptical	vs.	Trustful
Rigid	vs.	Adaptable, Careless, "Goes Along"
Cold	vs.	Warmhearted
Prone to Sulk	vs.	Laughs Readily

SOURCE: Cattell *et al.*, 1970, p. 80. Adapted from the Handbook for the 16 PF. Copyright © 1970 by IPAT, Inc. Reproduced by permission.

say that he is more irritable than punctual? Can any meaning be given to score-to-score differences in a personality profile?

Inferences About Internal Characteristics

Clinicians are limited in their remedial efforts if they know only the person's level of adjustment and the problems he acknowledges. Understanding the sources of behavior can point out advisable situational changes or goals for retraining. Deeper interpretations search out what Meehl (1979) calls latent entities—inner characteristics that generate interpretations, emotional reactions, and coping behavior.

Phenomenologists try to see the person's self-image and his image of other persons in his life and to grasp the meanings he puts on situations. Although phenomenologists recognize situational influences on responses, they see the respondent's perceptions of the situation as a crucial link.

Dynamic interpreters try to understand needs or motives. Psychoanalytic interpreters, in particular, expect to uncover motives of which the person is unaware. Such an interpreter assumes that acts represent an organized system of motives; she tries to construct a coherent story to resolve the contradictions and inconsistencies in behavior. She is more likely than others to think about the person's life history.

Remarks by a university counselor provide an example. Many students with distressing academic records who come for help are found to have good aptitude. Barbara Kirk (1952) characterizes many of these cases. (Her account is drastically condensed here.)

> The explanation and the excuses [given] for the academic deficiency are unrealistic, superficial, and largely implausible. The counselee demonstrates no real recognition or admission of the reasons for this deficiency, but, on the other hand, he evidences no surprise at the results of the tests. He may be surprised that he was not tense or bothered on tests administered to him during counseling because he frequently has been tense or bothered during academic examinations.
>
> [A particularly frequent MMPI pattern] is "psychoneurosis with compulsive and depressive features." Such [persons] tend to be pervasively resistant on an unconscious level to any externally imposed task. Since childhood, however, they have concealed such resistances from themselves and others by a façade of hard-workingness, meticulousness, and earnest dutifulness. In the unstructured environment of a university, the loss of the continued external pushing of teachers and parents permits the overthrow of the process of grudging achievement, and the resistances then manifest themselves in nonperformance.

The academic failure probably has meaning in terms of unconscious satisfaction of the hostility usually directed towards some member of the family who demands success, while the excellent scores on tests taken in a counseling situation may be interpreted also as hostile gestures. Because no importance is attached to these tests, the counselee is free to do with them as he wishes. It is a declaration, perhaps, of the lack of significance of his academic failure.[1]

The chief limitation of the dynamic approach is the immaturity of personality theories. Interpretation depends on two inference systems—one that runs from observations to latent characteristics and one that leads from that description to predictions or recommendations (p. 568). For many reasons, validation of either type of theory progresses slowly (Meehl, 1978, 1979).

Responses as Signs

One argument for criterion keying of personality measures is the inadequacy of psychologists' understanding. They hold some incorrect ideas about even the long-familiar category of psychoneurosis. At least, when Gough (1954) asked professional clinicians and advanced trainees to mark an inventory as neurotics would, the clinicians' responses were significantly out of line with what most neurotics said. Gough's clinicians, for example, too often expected complaints about being misunderstood and about health—and so do today's clinicians (p. 509).

The sign approach treats a test response as behavior for which interesting correlates have been identified. The correlations are established empirically (that is, "from experience"). The score on a criterion key is not a self-rating; rather, it is an index calculated from observations of verbal responses in a standard situation.

"People with this combination of age, sex, blood pressure, and heart condition have a life-expectancy of 37.2 years." Such actuarial statements, used to determine insurance premiums, are distilled from experience, and probabilities are taken seriously whether or not they have been explained. The clinical interpreter reasons similarly when she reports: "Persons with this combination of responses are likely not to control aggressive impulses."

The logical justification for making a criterion key is the intent to predict a certain criterion. It should be possible to make keys that distinguish, at better than a chance level, moderate drinkers from alcoholics and applicants for legal training who will make extended use of it from those who will leave the profession at an early age. Such a key capitalizes on the fact that a group

---

[1] Copyright 1952 by the American Psychological Association. Reprinted by permission of the publisher and author.

that has one distinctive psychological quality differs from the population on other qualities. Even small differences, cumulated over diverse clues, permit moderately accurate sorting.

The actuarial method is illustrated at its best in the Aptitude Index Battery (AIB; Thayer, 1977; S. H. Brown, 1981). As the failure rate of beginners who try to sell life insurance is high, a central agency supported by the industry has developed a screening device. Some 300 items are administered to candidates and scored at national headquarters with a key that is secret; the local manager, aided by experience tables, decides whom to accept. Thousands of persons fill out AIB each year, and an excellent bank of data for revising the instrument builds up. The validity coefficient, with amount of insurance sold as criterion, is about 0.2. (Restriction of range is partly responsible—see Fig. 11.1.) Because of the cost of failures, accepting only applicants above a certain cutoff increases profit by $10,000 per year for each agent hired. AIB seems to be far better at predicting failure than at predicting success. Few of those with low AIB scores succeed. Among those who score in the top 10 per cent, about half have poor sales records.

The items mostly have to do with personal history, so the AIB is sometimes spoken of as a "weighted application blank." Past experience shows how (within an age-sex bracket) insurance sales vary with, for example, the number of children a salesperson has. Questions on personality were part of the instrument at the beginning, but experience showed that weights for such items—valid when a test form was constructed—lost their validity within a few years, presumably because of social change. Today's AIB touches on "typical behavior" only by asking about past behavior such as participation in sports.

The soundness of a criterion key is to be judged by crossvalidation. Large and relevant keying samples are crucial. When the key is based on an inadequate sample, some items pick up weights by chance (Jackson, 1971). Also, validity of the criterion should be high; it will not do to have a predictor of delinquency that counts responses common to *all* lower-class boys just because lower-class boys made up the delinquent sample.

An actuarial key, relying on indirect information, has moderate validity at best. Unlike the insurance company, the diagnostician rarely intends to predict the original criterion. Where one is intent on predicting a criterion, multiple regression can be applied to any set of keys, of course. For predicting a diagnosis, the *item* weights derived on the basis of that criterion do not work out better (in a fresh sample) than a regression composite from homogeneous *keys* (Burisch, 1978; Goldberg, 1972; Jackson, 1975). For personality measurement, criterion keying of items may be at a dead end. (For a less pessimistic conclusion see Meehl, in J. N. Butcher, 1972.)

Any description that does not stick close to the kind of behavior observed is a "sign" interpretation. Many performance tests are given sign interpretations. The hypotheses are based on experience, but they are not backed by "actuarial tables" as SCII keys were. The graphologist tells us,

the	*the*
(a)	(b)
Lack of self-confidence	Strong will power

for example, that in these two specimens the low bar on the *t* at left shows lack of self-confidence whereas the high *t* bar in the second specimen shows strong will power. Crumbaugh (1980), after laying out the system of signs, says that it is the graphologist's integrative portrait that can be validated and not the statements based on single signs. (See also Crumbaugh & Stockholm, 1977.)

For Rorschach interpreters, *m* responses (inanimate movement; e.g., water flowing, fireworks) to the blots are a sign of a state of "stress in which the person has a sense of disruption and feels 'out of control' " (Exner, 1978, p. 104). The support for this kind of interpretation comes from a program of construct validation. Thus Exner compiles studies showing a rise in *m* responses in conjunction with impending surgery or a parachute jump. This kind of validation often stops with evidence that a relationship is present. Then two questions about inanimate movement remain unanswered: Among those who give (say) four or more *m* responses, what fraction are currently under stress? And what leads to *m* responses in persons not under stress?

22. *"In all clinical assessment procedures the validity is primarily in the clinician rather than in the technique" (Crumbaugh, 1980, p. 927).*
    a. *If this is true, how should an institution desiring to use assessments arrange to get dependable ones?*
    b. *How can the soundness of Crumbaugh's statement be investigated?*

SELF-DESCRIPTION: REPORT OF TYPICAL BEHAVIOR?

It is more reasonable to interpret the self-report as a "published" self-concept —a deliberate self-presentation—than as a factual description. Historians, examining the diary of a public figure, refuse to assume that the statements made therein are true reports of beliefs and feelings. Unless it is clear that the document was intended never to reach the eyes of others, the safest assumption is that it represents an image the person wished to write into history. The psychologist can regard questionnaire responses as a statement of the reputation the test taker would like to have or of how he requests others to regard him at this time.

This edited information may be of considerable value, especially as what is not said can be indicative. A person who presents too perfect an image may be expressing fear of losing respect. Unless the immediate situation offers a special inducement for halo-waving, the report of so perfect a self hints at a similar facade in other social relations. As a facade of control and freedom from impulse is a brittle one, maintained at considerable emotional cost, the façade itself has significance. Heaton and Pendleton (1981) point out that some persons with neurological damage or other deficits seriously overestimate or underestimate their capabilities. This is important to know: the overestimators may take on responsibilities they cannot handle and be laggard in seeking help.

Candid reporting can be hoped for when the tester is helping the test taker to solve his own problems. Also in research, the investigator can hope for an honest effort to introspect; subjects want to explain themselves. But even then it is natural to give responses that will be judged favorably insofar as respondents can guess the investigator's standards for judgment. Full candor is unlikely if certain responses will gain reward or support for the examinee's desires. Promise or threat is implicit in institutional uses of tests.

23. *Industrial workers filled out identical health questionnaires under two conditions. One questionnaire was turned in to the company medical department as a preliminary to a medical examination designed to improve the worker's health. The other questionnaire was mailed directly to a research team at a university. The workers listed far more symptoms on the research questionnaire (which would not help them) than on the other despite the fact that an honest report to the company physician might bring them medical help. Account for the discrepancy.*
24. *Distinguish in each of these cases whether the investigator is assuming that self-reports are truthful:*
    a. *The clinical symptoms of condition* x *are determined by observation. A list of symptoms (swollen feet, rash, etc.) is prepared. This list is used to determine how frequent condition* x *is in several localities. Each informant is asked to check whatever symptoms he has.*
    b. *A psychologist administers to a group of applicants a checklist in which each marks the adjectives that describe him. The success of these workers is observed, and a record is made of the characteristics checked by the successful applicants but not by the others. This checklist is then given to further applicants, and those who check the same characteristics as the previously successful workers are hired.*
25. *A questionnaire is filled out by all parents belonging to a study group as a means of identifying problems to be taken up in group discussion. Mr. Smith checks many problems having to do with developing the child's honesty, respect for the property of others, and care for his own property. The school counselor knows, however, that his son has been in difficulty several times because of aggressive fighting on the playground, window*

General Problems in Studying Personality 469

breaking, and other aggressive offenses that have been called to Mr. Smith's attention. Can the counselor draw any useful conclusion from Mr. Smith's self-report?

26. *An attitude test for first-line supervisors is given as part of a study that might lead to reorganizing the shop or to retraining the supervisors. It presents problems that might arise on the job and asks what action the respondent would take if he were supervisor. Scores are based on response patterns (e.g., "takes quick action," "seeks facts," "emphasizes morale," "emphasizes cost-cutting"). What use can be made of the responses in view of the obvious temptation to give a desirable picture?*

Limitations of Inventory Responses

Interpretations made by the respondent. Even when the test taker wants to cooperate, not all questionnaire responses are adequate communications. A first difficulty is that questions cannot be fully specified. "Do you make friends easily?" seems straightforward. But it is hard to say just what behavior the question refers to and what the tester means by "easily." The respondent is unable to count up positive and negative instances in his past. He will recall some people who became warm friends quickly and other acquaintances who remained distant for months. A try for literal interpretation bogs down. What does *friend* mean—intimate companionship? Pleasant interaction without emotional involvement? Or something in between? The respondent does not ask such fussy questions; most of his answers come from an inarticulate self-concept. If the person regards himself as the type who makes friends easily—hang niceties of definition!—he marks YES. Another equally popular respondent applying a different standard marks NO.

Questionnaires ask about the hypothetical "typical" situation, not about specific ones. "Do you seek suggestions from others?" is a fairly clear question, but most people would have to answer, "Sometimes, not always." This might be further qualified: "I do on difficult problems"; "I do if someone is around whose ideas are especially good"; "Not if I'm supposed to make the decision myself." These qualifications would have to be stated if the respondent tried seriously to report typical behavior. Since he cannot average his memories to determine what percentage of the time he has sought suggestions, the question will be answered offhand.

Response terms require interpretation. Terwilliger (1960) asked high school boys about their job interests in two ways. He asked one sample, "Would you probably accept . . . ?" (p. 421) and asked another, "Would you make a great effort to seek out . . . ?" work of each kind. On average, the "probably accept" endorsement rate was close to 27 per cent for both clerical and artistic activities, but the number of "seek out" endorsements for artistic items doubled that for clerical items (17 per cent vs. 9 per cent). The person who defines LIKE stringently rather than broadly will thereby alter the shape of his profile. Other response terms used in inventories: YES, AGREE, OFTEN, and so on are similarly equivocal (Simpson, 1944).

An instrument for assessing the quality of college experiences in different student groups used items of this form:

> How often have you had serious discussions with students having different values?
> NEVER   OCCASIONALLY   OFTEN   VERY OFTEN

As a crosscheck, C. R. Pace and J. Friedlander (1981) asked a sample to fill out this survey and, on a later page, to say how many times they had engaged in each activity during the year. Students who had marked NEVER nearly always responded "Zero" on the second version. Meanings for OFTEN, however, ranged widely. On the item above, OFTEN translated into

> Weekly or more often   41 per cent
> Once or twice a month   33 per cent
> Less than once a month   26 per cent

Moreover, students in selective liberal arts colleges tended to equate OFTEN with a high frequency. Obviously, that systematic difference in response definition confounds an evaluative survey.

Chapters 12, 13, and 14 are chiefly concerned with lengthy inventories. Considering the time and effort required, such a "test" may be less suitable than a few one-item self-ratings. The inventory does allow more precise comparisons between persons and brings norms to bear; neither of these may be of first importance in, for example, opening up counseling. Extensive research on published inventories provides a helpful background for interpretation, but of course single questions could be standardized and made the focus of research. This has been common in sociological surveys of, for example, morale of population groups. Although I concentrate on psychological data, psychologists have much to learn from the efforts of opinion pollers to identify unwanted influences on the responses they collect (Bradburn *et al.*, 1979).

Response sets. A set to say TRUE when in doubt is a nuisance when knowledge is tested with true-false items: the acquiescent respondent earns undeserved points if the test presents more true statements than false. Bias toward saying LIKE, YES, and OFTEN—or INDIFFERENT—is a nuisance to the personality tester. Similar persons reach different interest scores if they locate differently the boundary between LIKE and INDIFFERENT. A test developer who sees ambiguity of directions as the source of response biases will try to reduce that influence, as Terwilliger did.

To some degree, however, response sets express significant personal styles. The person who is submissive and conformist at heart may tend to say

YES more often. Some of those who evade questions with CANNOT SAY also are wishy-washy in daily life. Indeed, a criterion-based key gains some of its validity by capitalizing on behavioral differences between yea-sayers and nay-sayers. On SCII, auto dealers mark L rather often; male physicists do not mark L often. On questions about morale, the maladjusted mark D more often than A—even where AGREE implies positive morale on just half the items (Rundquist, 1966). Hence disagreeing is a diagnostic indicator of sorts. How much validity is enhanced or diluted by response tendencies varies with the set of items.

Faking. A structured question dealing with emotional health, responsibility, or interpersonal relations typically has one answer option that the culture considers good, and the majority of respondents are likely to pick that "socially desirable" option. The person who consistently gives desirable responses may be admirable. It is also possible that he has been less than frank or that he is deceiving himself.

A test taker may "fake bad." Draftees have been known to report impressive arrays of emotional symptoms, hoping for discharge. In an ordinary clinical test, exaggerating symptoms may be a gambit to enlist sympathy and attention. An unsuccessful student may prefer to have the tester believe that his troubles are caused by an emotional disturbance rather than to be thought of as stupid or lazy.

The "hello–goodbye" effect complicates evaluation of psychotherapy. The entering client tells a sad story. His symptoms are at such a peak that they have brought him to treatment, and full display of them bids the clinician to take his problem seriously. Just the opposite is often noted at discharge: the self-description glows, and some of the change may have come from self-deception. It would be ungrateful to dwell on symptoms the therapy did not relieve, so the exiting client gives himself and his therapist the benefit of borderline decisions. True improvement is not easily distinguished from change in test-taking attitude.

To learn how susceptible a questionnaire is to faking, one can ask some persons to fill it out honestly and ask others to give a false picture—a socially desirable report, a socially undesirable one, or one that fits a particular role. Wesman (1952) gave a personality inventory with the instructions: "I want you to pretend that you are applying for the position of salesman in a large industrial organization. You have been unemployed for some time, have a family to support, and want very much to land this position. You are being given this test by the employment manager. Please mark the answers you would give." The next week, the same inventory was filled out "as if you were applying for the position of librarian in a small town." The instrument carried a bland title, so students could only guess what variables would be scored. The scores on the two occasions differed spectacularly, as Figure 13.4 illustrates. The applicant can beat the test, and, not surprisingly, faked scores lack predictive validity (Dunnette *et al.*, 1962).

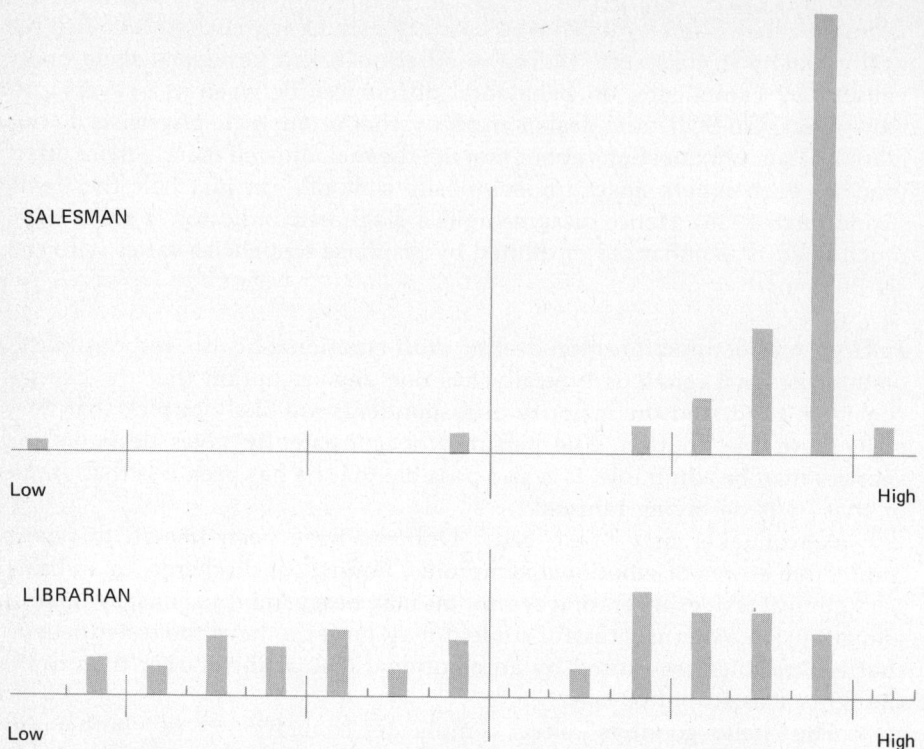

Figure 13.4. "Self-confidence" scores of students playing two roles.
Source: Wesman, 1952,

27. *Educational research is greatly concerned with tracing how teaching practices affect student gains. Hook and Rosenshine (1979) checked studies in which teachers had reported their own practices or styles and in which observers had recorded classroom practices. The two sources of information rarely agreed. There were a few negative(!) correlations, for example, between teachers' statements as to whether instruction was individualized and observers' records on the point. What explanations can you offer for the discrepancies?*

Coping with Biases and Distortions

Openness. The simplest approach is to make the purpose of the questioning and the questions themselves completely transparent. This is the usual approach in opinion polling and in the surveys of clients served or of community needs conducted to evaluate human services. Candor is encouraged by the fact that respondents are anonymous and no judgment will be passed on them.

A transparent inventory where the respondent can see what he is disclosing suits the tester who views the questionnaire as a straightforward communication. She would like the client to record no more than he would be willing to say face-to-face. She expects to start counseling or therapy by conversing on matters the client is ready to talk about, not secrets and self-delusions. "Behavioral" assessors in particular rely on openness. When a student is being helped to systematize his study habits, particular acts or patterns of behavior (for example, deliberate course-by-course allocation of each day's study time) are specified as targets for improvement. The student is asked to keep a daily record of these actions; this not only informs him and the counselor of his progress but strengthens his motivation. Of course, the student could untruthfully report actions close to the ideal; but that would not contribute to the improvement *he* is seeking.

Transparent inquiry assumes that the person's own purposes are being served by it and that he has the maturity, insight, and motivation to comply. It is easier to report on acts than on feelings. One cannot expect full disclosure on all topics or to all questioners (Chelune, 1977). The person who does not feel strongly affiliated with the counselor or other tester cannot be expected to be open with regard to matters tinged with shame or guilt.

Concealing the purpose of the test. Naturally, the tester prefers not to threaten the test taker. For this reason, the usual self-report blank carries an unrevealing title. Ordinarily, the person is told the reason for making the inquiry, but not what scores will be recorded nor what interpretations they will permit.

Sometimes the tester states a plausible but false purpose for the questions. The F scale of Adorno *et al.* (1950) was devised to study the motives underlying a world view or personal style called "authoritarian"; the inventory, however, called only for opinions about public affairs and people in general. The interpreter focused on indications that the respondent looked down on the weak and powerless and was unduly trusting of established authority. Another investigator asks children to check titles of books they have read, seemingly to learn about reading interests. Fictitious titles are in the list; the child who checks many of them is suspected of striving to make a good impression.

Forced choice. Casting items in choice format keeps most response sets from operating. Thus, in an interest inventory, the choice format requires everyone to express the same number of "likes." In a questionnaire on motives or reactions to stress, "faking good" is difficult when the choices within an item are equally "desirable." It is not difficult, however, for the person to portray himself as "like a librarian."

The "Have you stopped beating your wife?" character of forced choice arouses legitimate objection. Imagine yourself deciding what to say when someone with power over a job or parole asks which of this pair describes you better (Westin, 1967):

I feel like blaming others when things go wrong for me; or,
I feel I am inferior in most respects.

Subtle items. An item that appears irrelevant to the decision being made is said to be "subtle." Criterion keying of interests counts any answers that engineers tend to give. In that context, "Do you like ice hockey?" is a subtle item; the respondent has no way of guessing how it counts, if at all, in the Engineer score. Subtle items are difficult to fake. Indeed, on MMPI subtle items, persons asked to "fake bad" give fewer responses keyed as abnormal than do persons "faking good" (Burkhart *et al.*, 1978)! Subtle items, however, do not usually measure what the content-valid residue of the scale measures, and current practice puts little emphasis on them. Even with strict criterion keying, as in SCII and KOIS, most of the items that pick up weight have an obvious relevance to the variable scored. (Recall Campbell's remarks about the Army Officer scale, p. 433.)

Verification and correction keys. Almost all modern inventories employ one or more supplementary keys to identify test takers who respond in an unusual manner. SCII counts up the following control scores:

Total responses—If this falls far short of the possible number, scores are dubious; the person omitted many items or did not blacken spaces properly.

Infrequent responses—A person who gives many rare responses may have lost his place on the answer sheet. He may have responded in an arbitrary manner because he resented the test. Or he may be truly idiosyncratic in his interests.

Counts of L, I, *and* D *responses*—Counts far from the norm imply invalidity of the usual interpretative rules.

Nearly all the inventories to be discussed in Chapter 14 provide verification scores such as these, and some provide a count of socially desirable responses. In a personality inventory, the count of infrequent responses is increased by implausible claims to saintliness ("I never avoid people I'd prefer not to talk to") and so is sometimes called a "lie scale."

The primary use of control scores is to flag profiles that should not be taken at face value. Formal corrections can adjust for unusual response sets. Even the best researched procedure of this type, the "*K* correction" of the MMPI, is about as likely to reduce the quality of the information as to improve it (Meehl, in J. N. Butcher, 1972).

Sometimes the psychologist interprets a control score directly. Thus, the SCII manual suggests that many persons with a high L count are enthusiastic or unfocused (or both). And persons who give many socially desirable responses are seen in performance tests as comparatively conventional and persuasible (Crowne & Marlowe, 1964).

14 Personality Measurement Through Self-report

Self-report personality measures differ in many ways. Some offer a simple evaluation whereas others generate a multiscore description. Some instruments rely on homogeneous keys, and some were developed by criterion keying. A nonevaluative single-score inventory concentrates on some one trait (for example, liberalism/conservatism of political attitudes) for research purposes or for some specific practical reason; this type of inventory will not be discussed.

SPECIMEN INSTRUMENTS

Simple Evaluative Scales[1]

Single-score evaluative instruments are called measures of adjustment, anxiety, self-esteem, neurotic tendency, job satisfaction, and so on. Questions vary somewhat, but almost all of them come down to "How well are you

---

[1]Questionnaire items appearing in this chapter are copyrighted and have been reproduced by permission, as follows: Self-Esteem Inventory (School Form), Copyright 1967, published by Consulting Psychologists Press, Inc., and State-Trait Anxiety Inventory, Copyright 1968, published by Consulting Psychologists Press, Inc.; Minnesota Multiphasic Personality Inventory, University of Minnesota Press; Personal Orientation Inventory, Educational and Industrial Testing Service.

doing (or feeling)?" Broad topics can be subdivided; there are test-anxiety scales, for example, and scales for anxiety in social situations or in situations of physical threat. Shavelson and Bolus (1982) show that self-esteem subdivides, with general self-concept and academic self-concept being high-level factors under which more specific factors fall.

Galton devised the questionnaire technique in the 1880s as a standard procedure for studying mental imagery. G. Stanley Hall extended the method a bit later, using retrospective information from large samples of adults to delineate normal trends in adolescent development. (For techniques reaching back to Pythagoras and beyond, see McReynolds, 1975; for the history in the present century, see Goldberg, 1971.)

The first personality inventory primarily concerned with appraising the individual was the Woodworth Personal Data Sheet. At the beginning of World War I, the U.S. Army wanted to detect soldiers likely to break down in combat, but psychiatric interviews were not practicable when recruits were processed by the thousands. Woodworth listed some of the symptoms psychiatrists touched upon in screening interviews—"Do you daydream frequently?" "Do you wet your bed?"—and turned the list into a scored test. Men reporting many symptoms were singled out for further examination. The test detected maladjusted soldiers quickly and cheaply despite the insensitivity of mass processing.

As decades passed, instrument developers reworded Woodworth's items and shifted the content according to particular personal or institutional interests. Most items found in simple measures of adjustment reappear in multiscore inventories, sorted off into such rubrics as sociability and emotional expressiveness. The single score is a kind of synopsis, a first glance.

Various purposes are served by collecting evaluative self-reports. Surveys of morale in a community or organization, repeated periodically, alert policymakers and managers to problem areas. Self-reports can provide criteria for assessing housing arrangements for the elderly or the tone of a desegregated school. They assess incoming patients to indicate the severity of the person's difficulties and later can assess degree of improvement. Some inventories are designed like Woodworth's to serve as screening instruments, applied to incoming waves of recruits or students or prisoners. In research on motivation, group process, and the like, simple inventories identify "similar" persons; this makes it possible (for instance) to check whether anxious and nonanxious persons respond similarly to a certain teaching style. Measures in this broad category thus serve as social indicators, as evaluative criteria, as signs of individual stress (predictors of breakdown), as measures of individual improvement, and as indicators for explanatory variables.

A self-esteem scale. A 10-minute questionnaire primarily used in schools and in research on child development is the Self-Esteem Inventory (SEI; S. Coopersmith; *CPP;* one form for ages 8–15, with a second form for older persons). The child marks, as LIKE ME or UNLIKE ME, 50 statements such as

I'm popular with kids my own age.
I get upset easily at home.
I'm proud of my schoolwork.

The score is a count of desirable responses. Three brief subscales are concerned with peer relations, feelings about home and parents, and feelings about schoolwork. The profile shape is not reliably determined.

The SEI manual recommends that the school collect local norms. It also provides percentile equivalents supposedly representative of pupils in the United States, but, in fact, the cases come from two school districts in Northern Illinois. Most norms for personality measures are poorer than for tests of ability and interests.

Not surprisingly, the overall score correlates with other inventories of the same evaluative character, the median correlation being somewhere around 0.5. Nor should a correlation of about 0.3 with educational achievement and verbal ability surprise us. Most such inventories contain questions that ask in essence, "How good is your schoolwork?" Besides, abler children tend to be more popular and to receive more adult encouragement, which leads to self-assurance.

Retests 5 weeks apart correlate 0.88. This is high, but the manual rightly warns that a child may be temporarily elated or depressed as a result of some recent event, and therefore evidence of other kinds ought to be considered. If the instrument were divided into random 10-item sections to be given a week apart, the three samples would probably give a more significant self-report than 30 or more items on one day. (With another, briefer inventory, a stability coefficient of 0.45 was reported between ages 15 and 23; Bachman & O'Malley, 1977.)

SEI is an unpretentious, workaday instrument. It requires good sense on the part of the user, but little understanding of personality theory. It is deliberately unsubtle; the child is given every opportunity to send the message he chooses to the teacher. A low score, then, is a cry for help.

A state-trait inventory. In the State-Trait Anxiety Inventory (STAI; C. D. Spielberger, R. L. Gorsuch, and R. L. Luschene; *CPP*), one section is basically like SES. Though "self-esteem" and "anxiety" are not opposites, the content of the two inventories at a given age level is nearly the same. (Specific information here comes from the adult form.) STAI items are transparently evaluative:

I feel happy.
I try to avoid facing a crisis or difficulty.

To describe how he *generally* feels, the person marks a response from VERY MUCH SO to NOT AT ALL. The weighted count of unfavorable self-reports is the Trait Anxiety score.

The trait scale correlates nearly 0.8 with anxiety scales by other authors, and its test-retest reliability over 3 months is at that level. Almost no one who is not a mental patient falls outside the score range 20 to 60, and the s.e.m. of the trait measure is evidently around 4 points.

The novel feature of STAI is the roughly parallel second section in which the subject indicates how he feels *at this moment*. The "state" section can be administered by itself. In some psychological experiments—on problem solving, frustration, and the like—as few as four "state" items are given at key points in the experimental session. This monitors stress while interfering little with the intellectual task; the short scale is adequate to check the average response to experimental conditions. Another variation is to ask for recall of one's state: How did you feel generally during this exam? During this therapy session?

Research on causal links between anxiety and learning or social behavior can reasonably concentrate on state anxiety. It is hard to see how trait anxiety could affect response to a situation if the anxiety is not aroused in that place and time. In line with this expectation, stress conditions do not change trait scores greatly but do increase state anxiety. In one experiment four successive measures were taken:

Upon arrival for the session.
Following 10 minutes of relaxation exercises.
Following 10 minutes of work on a difficult test that subjects had been told was an "easy IQ test."
Following viewing of a film depicting unpleasant accidents in a workshop.

The average scores were 37, 31, 43, and 55. (This kind of evidence was originally used to select responsive items for the state scale; any tryout item whose average did not change between "relax" and "exam" conditions was discarded.)

An instrument for screening abnormality. The Psychological Screening Inventory (PSI, R. I. Lanyon; *RPP*) is intended for use by ministers, social workers, and other general practitioners in judging whether a client's difficulties are serious enough to require referral for psychological help. Though descriptive interpretation is possible, the instrument has primarily been validated as a warning device. The intercorrelations of the four scores are low, as they bear on different types of disturbance.

The author began by locating items that had shown promising validity in older instruments, put them through statistical trials and revisions, then added items to improve the balance. There are 130 true-false items; no item enters two keys. Two scales have discriminant keys and two sample broad content categories.

Negative emotional tone is the theme running through the 30-item Discomfort (*Di*) scale. Items call for reports on diverse content (headaches, confidence, appetite, . . .), half the items being worded positively. The items are said to have adequate intercorrelations despite their specific content; such mixed items have been part of many older scales labeled "neurotic tendency" or the like.

The Expression *(Ex)* scale (30 items) reports on vigor and activity of style; it taps what might elsewhere be called extroversion, dominance, and exhibition. This style is in itself considered neither desirable nor undesirable and evidently was included less because it is required for screening than because the activity-potency theme has been prominent in other instruments.

Alienation *(Al)* consists of 25 items to which hospitalized psychiatric patients (mostly schizophrenic) responded differently from normal individuals. The latter were approached in shopping malls and bus depots and asked to take home the inventory, complete it, and mail it back. After the sample was culled to improve its distribution on age and education, 200 papers remained. The abnormal sample totaled only 140 cases and would by itself be inadequate for criterion keying. Fortunately, most items had previously shown some validity in other research, and the author discarded items whose correlations did not "make sense." The content touches on emotional distress, odd thoughts, feeling ill-treated, and lacking control of one's life.

Social Nonconformity (Sn) has 25 items that discriminated the normal group from persons in a reformatory. Topics include recklessness, blaming others, having been at odds with parents, and disregard for rules and conventions.

The instrument is not trying to "predict" mental breakdown or incarceration; rather, the criterion keys signal present disturbance or deviation. The unfavorable self-report indicates that the person is likely to have bad relations with others and with institutions; still, altering his life situation or his coping mechanisms could alter the prognosis. Figure 14.1 illustrates one of the ways a professional might think about a PSI profile. The 50 ± 10 standard-score scale is for an approximate cross section of normal adults; scores above 70 are quite rare, and it is even more remarkable for a person to have extreme scores on two of the scales.

It appears that in a general population the two criterion keys have reliabilities no better than 0.60. This is not surprising; the scales are short and markedly skewed. That is proper in a screening instrument, which is not designed to assess differences among persons with average or better adjustment. The two homogeneous scales have reliabilities of 0.8 or a little less; again, skewness is partly responsible. Needed are reports on standard errors of the high scores—the ones that send important signals.

1. *In view of the cost to society of care for persons who have neglected their bodies and the cost of institutional care for mental patients, what would you think of a proposal that everyone have an annual medical checkup, one part of which would be a questionnaire more or less like PSI?*
2. *What kind of analysis would estimate a standard error of measurement for high scores on one of Lanyon's scales?*
3. *In view of its standard error, how dependable is the STAI trait score for detecting maladjusted students?*

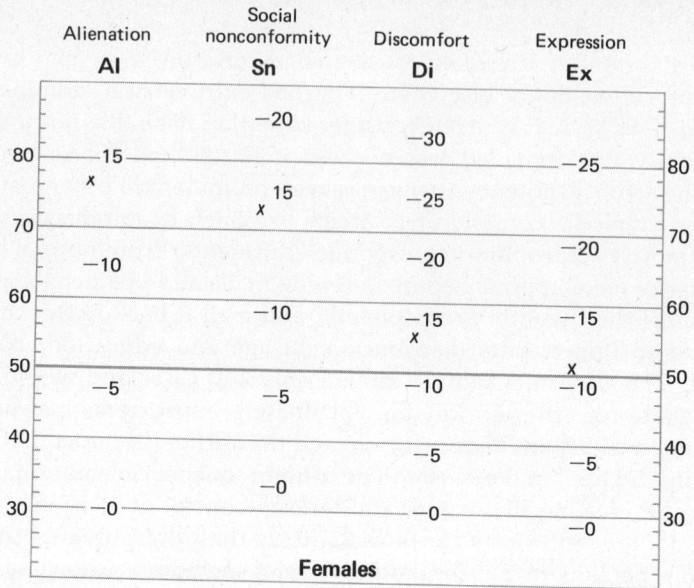

Figure 14.1. PSI profile of a rebellious adolescent girl.
Source: The score information and the case description are quoted from the PSI manual (1978, pp. 10–11). The profile form is copyright © 1968 by Richard I. Lanyon and is reproduced by permission. It has been simplified and altered in its proportions for display here.

4. *Suppose we could arrange for a student to fill out the State Anxiety form on 10 randomly scheduled occasions (different hours, different settings, over 4 months). Would you expect the average score to coincide with a score from the same items given once under trait-anxiety instructions?*

5. *Would you prefer a state or a trait measure of anxiety to investigate each of the following questions? (The measure may be limited in its situational domain.)*
    a. *Is level of stomach acidity higher in anxious persons?*
    b. *Do children from different home backgrounds differ in the anxiety they experience in school?*

c. How well is counseling overcoming a shy person's anxiety in social situations?

Multiscore Descriptions

The Jackson Personality Inventory. Jackson's JPI has been praised for painstaking construction that takes advantage of the computer and of the substantial critical literature on self-report methodology (Chapter 13). Many counselors and investigators exploring individual differences would like a multiscore profile, with dimensions describing variations within the normal range and carrying nonthreatening labels. They would like low intercorrelations between scores; repeating information under several names is inefficient and confusing. Jackson's 15 dimensions have a commonsense quality, as can be seen in Table 14.1. Although many variables resemble those of older instruments, few are closely tied to personality theory. Jackson sought to avoid overlap among scales within JPI (and of JPI with his other inventory PRF; p. 490). He also sought to minimize the good/bad factor, and succeeded. JPI Self-Esteem correlates less than 0.4 with most of the other JPI scales.

For each scale, the manual provides a description such as this one for Risk Taking:

> **High scorer:** Enjoys gambling and taking a chance; willingly exposes self to situations with uncertain outcomes; . . . . Called reckless, bold, impetuous, intrepid, enterprising, . . .

Table 14.1 *Convergent correlations for JPI scores*

	Self-Report on Short Adjective Checklist	Self-Rating[a]	Peer Rating
Anxiety	0.7	0.65	0.4
Breadth of interest	0.4	0.3	0.2
Complexity	0.65	0.4	0.35
Conformity	0.55	0.55	0.4
Energy level	0.7	0.55	0.45
Innovation	0.8	0.75	0.35
Interpersonal affect	0.65	0.6	0.3
Organization	0.8	0.6	0.35
Responsibility	0.45	0.15	0.35
Risk taking	0.75	0.7	0.5
Self-esteem	0.75	0.7	0.65
Social adroitness	0.15	0.1	0
Social participation	0.7	0.55	0.45
Tolerance	0.45	0.25	0.35
Value orthodoxy	0.7	0.55	0.55

[a] Average of two samples
SOURCE: JPI manual, 1975, pp. 28–29.

Low scorer: Cautious about unpredictable situations; unlikely to bet; avoids situations of personal risk, even those with great rewards; .... Called cautious, hesitant, careful, wary, prudent, conservative. . . .

Note that one could place a positive value on either end of the scale. All items are in true-false form; 10 of the Risk Taking items describe rashness, and 10 describe caution, hence yea-saying cannot produce an extreme score.

Figure 14.2 displays the profile of one risk taker. The peaks are Risk Taking, Complexity, Energy Level, Self-Esteem, and Social Participation; the deep valleys are Conformity and Tolerance. We are told that this young man was a leader of a peaceful demonstration on an academic-freedom issue. The low Tolerance raises a question about his liberalism: "He shows a pervasive rejection of discrepant ideas and people who disagree with him."

Jackson collected ratings from campus acquaintances to produce the correlations in Table 14.1. It is not astonishing that correlations with peer ratings are modest (see the discussion of Table 14.2). The extent to which JPI scales are useful will only be learned when experience accumulates.

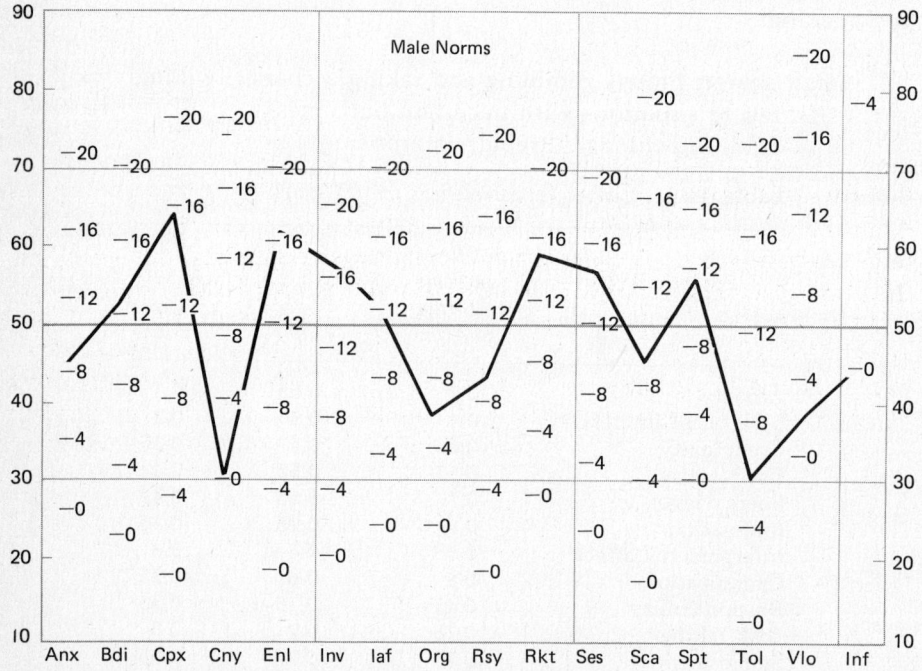

Figure 14.2. JPI profile of a 22-year-old male student.
Note: For interpretation of score abbreviations, see Table 14.1; Inf is a verification key that counts unusual responses. Norms are expressed on a 50 ± 10 standard-score scale.
Source: From the JPI manual, 1975, p. 21. Profile form copyright © 1976 by Research Psychologists Press. Adapted and reproduced by permission.

The steps in test construction included the following:

1. Deciding what dimensions to measure and defining each, much as in the description of Risk Taking.
2. Having college students write 100 or more items for each dimension.
3. Editing items and assembling several promising sets for each dimension.
4. Tryout; items were retained that had variance and that correlated with their own dimension but not (in general) with social desirability or other dimensions.
5. Assembly of two parallel forms.
6. Further tryout leading to some substitution or revision of items.

The attempt to control response bias and scale overlap succeeded. Homogeneity and match to supposedly relevant adjectives are weak for some scales (Responsibility, Tolerance, Social Adroitness). Jackson has given rather weak answers to the critics' question, "Why *these* traits?" Lykken (in Buros, 1978, p. 872) makes a plea for greater logical consistency, for tough-minded editing of items. For example, "Einstein himself might have endorsed item 103 [scored for low Complexity], 'I try to make everything as simple and easy as I can.' "

The MMPI. In clinical practice and research, the Minnesota Multiphasic Personality Inventory (S. Hathaway and J. C. McKinley, University of Minnesota Press; distributed by *NCS*) is used far more than any other inventory though its developers long ago recognized that it is unsatisfactory (J. N. Butcher, 1972; Faschingbauer, in Newmark, 1979). It is long and inefficient. A number of items are outdated, and the dimensions used in summarizing responses are—to put it kindly—relics of an antiquated psychiatry. Unlike the Wechsler and the Strong, the MMPI was not revised after 1950, nor, in all its history down to 1983, were creditable norms compiled. Koss (in Newmark, 1979) describes a number of "stopgap" supplements and shortcuts that have been tried. At best, these resemble patchwork urban renewal carried out where a new city on a modern plan would do more for the quality of life.[2]

MMPI thrives chiefly because of the experience compiled. There are thousands of published research reports and case reports on persons with various score patterns. Beyond that, many clinicians are "at home" with the test; each fresh record calls up memories of cases they have dealt with over the years.

[2] A program of "evolutionary" revision of MMPI is underway, and modifications will be introduced in 1985 and later years. The first major effort will be the preparation of new norms for a test booklet that contains most of the old items, plus additional items thought to be important in management of clinical treatment. Out-of-date items will be rephrased or dropped, but the change will be too minor to require immediate replacement of the scoring keys. Separate forms for adults and adolescents will be organized, using age-appropriate wording. After compilation of scores on the old keys with a nationally representative sample of persons, investigators with MMPI experience will be asked to cooperate in collecting clinical samples on which the original keys can be verified or altered and on which new keys can be based. The plan for revision is intended to make it possible for clinicians to rely on the accumulated experience with the original MMPI. (I thank J. N. Butcher for this information.)

MMPI was constructed 40 years ago, at a time when a primary task of clinical psychologists was to advise psychiatrists (or courts, etc.) on the severity of a patient's disorder and on a label to describe his disorder. Committed to criterion keying because they disdained available theories, the authors started with utterly miscellaneous items:

I very much like hunting.
I believe in the second coming of Christ.
I am entirely self-confident.
I am seldom troubled by constipation.

The response scale is YES, NO, CANNOT SAY.

Keying techniques much like those illustrated with Lanyon's PSI were used. The chief differences between MMPI keying and Lanyon's later keying are these: Lanyon could capitalize on the research history of items; Lanyon did not key an item whose correlation with a criterion was hard to comprehend.

MMPI criterion groups were patients that professionals in a mental hospital had assigned to particular categories of disorder. Thus, MMPI scale 4, analogous to Lanyon's Social Nonconformity, was keyed, not on miscellaneous prisoners, but on persons classed as "psychopathic deviate" by the psychiatric staff. ("Antisocial personalities" in a later jargon.) Responses in the patient group were compared with persons coming to visit patients in a city hospital, items showing a difference being counted in the key. Nine scales were constructed in this manner.

Serious abnormality was suspected when one or more of the standard scores approached 70. When MMPI was applied to students seeking counseling, to soldiers under temporary stress, and to appraisal of employees, it became obvious that many persons who function well have some high scores. Moreover, there is important descriptive information in scores that are not at all abnormal.

Though a full set of scores is usually printed out and perhaps charted, attention centers on the peaks. A code such as *49'83* . . . indicates the order of scores (*4* most elevated), the prime indicating that both *4* and *9* are above 70. (Regarding the more elaborate coding now used by clinicians, see Dahlstrom *et al.,* 1972.) This profile hints at impulsiveness, self-indulgence, and possible delinquency. It would be wrong to make a diagnosis out of context; an incoming patient and a successful actor are living in different worlds; so even if their profiles match, the meanings differ.

The MMPI was an immediate success; it became available just prior to World War II, with its great number of casualties requiring neuropsychiatric evaluation. After the war, civilian clinical psychology expanded rapidly and became steadily more independent of psychiatry, but the MMPI was the instrument the psychologists knew best. Both psychologists and psychiatrists became increasingly dissatisfied with the traditional diagnostic categories and with the very idea that the persons assigned to a category are homogeneous in the sense that patients with measles are. Descriptive interpretations were wanted. Partly for this reason hundreds of supplementary MMPI keys—covering ego strength, introversion, prejudice, and so on—appeared. Some of these served in isolated research, and only a few enter the usual clinical workup; one reviewer dismisses all but a handful as worthless (Graham, 1977). Meanwhile, the original discriminant keys acquired fresh connotations.

A vast lore built up as to what personality characteristics various scores and patterns indicated. Meehl pointed out (see Cronbach & Meehl, 1955) that scale 4 had all the following correlates:

Items discriminate patients diagnosed "Psychopathic personality, asocial and amoral type."
Delinquents, broadly defined, score in a higher range than normals.
Men who had shot a hunting companion had higher scores than other hunters.
High school students judged by their peers not to be "responsible" scored higher than those judged responsible.
Professional actors tend to score above average.
Nurses with comparatively high scores are more often rated by supervisors as "not afraid of mental patients."

A high score on 4 thus implies a certain style, in most cases not pathological.

The relation of MMPI scores in a normal population to personality as perceived by others is indicated in Table 14.2. Black (1953) asked women at Stanford to describe themselves and their dormitory acquaintances on an adjective checklist. The table shows some of the adjectives applied comparatively frequently (or—where "not" appears—infrequently) to women with particular MMPI high-point codes. The descriptions by peers are strikingly different from one category to the next and basically consistent with the interpretations clinicians suggest for the scores. Some contrasts appear between self-reports and reputations. We would expect self-reports to be comparatively favorable, but it is surprising that the "energetic" 9's see themselves as popular when others call them unpopular. The self-description of low 5's is almost the opposite of the peer description. (Responses that females in the original sample gave more often than males earn a low score on scale 5.)

In time, experience was encoded in handbooks and "atlases"; the clinician interpreting the 49'83 . . . profile could turn to the 49 page and read a summary of characteristics culled from the research literature and from clinic files. Ratings such as Black's can contribute to the bank of information. Therapists are asked to describe patients on an inventory; the Q-sort method to be described later is particularly suitable (see Marks *et al.*, 1974). Wiggins (1973) warns that although the descriptions may be based on information

Table 14.2 *Reputations and self-descriptions associated with MMPI scores of college women*

Highest score	Description by dormitory mates	Self-description
2	Shy, not energetic, not kind, not relaxed	Shy, moody, not decisive, not energetic, not relaxed
3	Many physical complaints, flattering, not partial	Trustful, friendly, not emotional, not boastful
4	Incoherent, moody, sociable, frivolous, not self-controlled	Dishonest, lively, clever, not adaptable, not friendly, not practical
5	Unrealistic, natural, not dreamy	Shiftless, unemotional, not having wide interests, not popular
5 low	Worldly, not energetic, not rough, not shy	Self-distrusting, self-dissatisfied, sensitive, shy, unrealistic
6	Shrewd, hard-hearted	Arrogant, shy, naïve, sociable
7	Dependent, kind, not self-centered	Indecisive, many physical complaints, soft-hearted, depressed, irritable
9	Shows off, boastful, selfish, energetic, not loyal, not peaceable, not popular	Enterprising, jealous, courageous, energetic, popular, peaceable, self-confident

SOURCE: Black, 1953.

independent of MMPI—from observation or therapeutic sessions—some summaries compile clinicians' descriptions derived directly if not wholly from the MMPI. The user rarely knows which statements have independent support and which merely encapsulate the clinical theory prevalent when the information was collected. For the atlas, information on the available persons with the same profile code—perhaps as few as 10 persons—is merged into a composite description. Even though their origins are actuarial, some atlases go beyond hard facts to construction of a miniature theory. Here is an extract characterizing adult patients with the *49'* pattern (Marks *et al.,* 1974, p. 119; details of wording changed):

> Whether for primarily constitutional genetic reasons or as a result of a learning history, appears to have an abnormally low capacity to experience anxiety or stress. Deficient in acquiring ego and superego controls; unlikely to learn from aversive experiences. Incapable of establishing the emotional contact and commitment that

characterizes friendship. Insecure, conflicted about emotional dependency, and harboring exaggerated needs for affection.

6. *The manual summarizes JPI Responsibility in such terms as "strong obligation to be honest," "sense of duty to others," "inflexible conscience." In Table 14.1, JPI Responsibility was correlated with ratings on "Trustworthy/Untrustworthy." Do the low correlations for this score in the table seem plausible?*
7. *The JPI profile arranges scores alphabetically. A computer printout can display scores in order from extreme to middling. For the student activist, the topmost rows would be Low Conformity, Low Tolerance, and Complexity. How suitable is this format?*

Computerized Interpretation

It was a short step from the atlas to preparing "clinical reports" by computer. There are now many services of this character, some centralized and some captured in software available to any clinician with a personal microcomputer. An illustrative fragment of computer interpretation can be taken from the published manual for one of the systems. When scores *4* and *9* reach 70, and other main scores are not in that range, the computer will print out:

> Individuals who obtain such profiles are often described as extroverted, overactive, impulsive, and rather irresponsible. When this pattern is obtained during a psychiatric evaluation, these individuals are usually seen as hostile, socially shallow and superficial, and as having fluctuating morals and poor conscience development. Though their social skills may appear quite good, they eventually display lack of judgment, poor internal controls, and neglect of obligations. They typically show flagrant excesses in their search for pleasure and self-stimulation. [Lachar, 1974, p. 131; details of wording changed].

A full printout may cover several pages, taking into account scores outside the peak area and specific items.

Computer interpretations are necessarily limited. The clinician must know a lot to make good use of the printout. Gynther and Green (1980), for instance, speak of the comparative invalidity of standard MMPI interpretation for blacks, and Golden (1979) warns that the *49'* pattern is not to be equated with "antisocial personality" unless there is a history of deviant behavior before age 15. Standard scores may be compiled within sex and age-group, but in the typical computer system the rule for interpreting the standard score is not moderated by sex, age, race, educational level, family status, or number of years in the United States. A clinician should surely consider all of these and more. Because cases with specific histories do not accumulate, it is infeasible to develop actuarial rules that acknowledge a parent's divorce, a conviction for drug possession, or an award for artistic talent. The incompleteness causes no problem when the printout is a set of suggestions, a point of departure. It is inappropriate to supply printouts directly to employers, parole boards, or admissions committees; a qualified psychologist should serve as intermediary.

Computer interpretations could be as phony as the fortunes that come out of weighing machines. The *MMY* has reviewed reports of many services; the distressed comments of one MMPI expert should be particularly noted (J. N. Butcher, in Buros, 1978).

Practitioners ought to want more information than is now available before accepting output from this software package or that. Many "validations" simply ask a clinician acquainted with the person to say whether statements in the printout fit him. Thus Lachar reports that, among patients whose profiles were interpreted by the paragraph quoted earlier, a clinician who knew the patient said that the description fitted in 44 out of 50 cases. It is impressive when a high proportion of statements are rated as sound. But this is flimsy evidence. The proportion is boosted when statements in the printout are so hedged that they apply to almost anyone and also when the clinician is disposed to accept the authority of an allegedly research-based system. One simple check would be to sprinkle statements made about superficially similar persons into the record being evaluated. A high endorsement rate for these would indicate a generous rater whose information should be discounted.

Services can be compared by sending several of them the same set of MMPI answer sheets. The contrasts in style and content would in some instances be impressive. Although some customers compare specimen interpretations before deciding which service to employ, substantial "consumer guides" have not yet been published. For one comparison of six reports on the same case, see Graham (1977).

8. *In one system, the computer program "branches" on marital status, so that when identical answer sheets from a married person and a divorced person are interpreted, about 20 per cent of the statements in the printouts differ. Recognizing that the married person may be considering divorce and that the divorced person may have achieved a stable readjustment, can such branching be justified?*
9. *Compare the descriptions of the 49 profile from Marks et al. and Lanyon. Do they cover the same ground? Where they do, do they agree?*

A Listing of Inventories

A brief account of inventories prominent in the current psychological literature is given here for reference. I shall not repeat information on the four inventories already discussed.

- Adjective Checklist (ACL); H. G. Gough and A. B. Heilbrun, Jr.; *CPP.* High school and adult. Adjectives ("arrogant," "calm," "defensive," ...) to be checked. An objective means of securing reports from acquaintances; used also for self-rating. One can explore the meaning of another instrument by seeing what adjectives its scores correlate with. Summary scores describe various styles and "needs." Apparently an ACL self-report score rarely correlates higher than 0.4 with a related score on a conventional inventory.
- California Psychological Inventory (CPI); H. G. Gough; *CPP.* High school and college. A lengthy criterion-keyed inventory with 16 principal scores: Sociability, Tolerance, Intellectual Efficiency, and so on. The instrument has been used in an extraordinary amount of research (see Megargee, 1972). The traits it measures seem significant though validity coefficients are often low. Used by trained and cautious counselors, CPI serves screening and descriptive purposes as well as any questionnaire.
- Comrey Personality Scales; A. L. Comrey; *EdITS.* Age 16 and over. This represents a particularly systematic effort to apply factor analysis to develop homogeneous scales. Each of the eight scales is defined by five subdimensions that are not scored but that sharpen the definition of the factor; for each subdimension there are four items, two scored positively and two scored negatively. Thus, Emotional Stability has subdimensions referring to inferiority feelings, depression, mood shifts, agitation, and pessimism. Other dimensions are Trust, Conformity, Activity, Extroversion, Masculinity, and Empathy. Most scale intercorrelations are low.
- Edwards Personal Preference Schedule (EPPS); A. L. Edwards; *PC.* College. To reduce opportunity to show a "good" pattern, the respondent has to choose between paired statements of equal overall desirability. Instrument is scored in terms of "needs" for achievement, affiliation, and so on. Avoidance of psychiatric constructs and of subtle keying reduces misconceptions.
- Eysenck Personality Questionnaire; H. J. and S. B. G. Eysenck; *EdITS.* Forms for age 7 through adulthood. The latest in a series of inventories identified with the names of Eysenck or Maudsley [Hospital] that have been used extensively, especially in England. The three score dimensions—psychoticism, extroversion, and neuroticism—play a central role in Eysenck's neo-Pavlovian theory of normal as well as abnormal personality. Scales are short (20–25 items per scale) and the YES/NO items transparent. Could serve as a preliminary screen; otherwise not recommended for decisions about individuals.
- Personal Orientation Dimensions; E. L. Shostrom; *EdITS.* Adults. Two-choice items. A revision and extension of the older Personal Orientation Inventory (see Knapp, 1976), which was much used in counseling research and practice. Highly evaluative, using concepts

from Maslow ("self-actualizing") and Riesman ("inner-directed"); stresses resources and flexibility rather than freedom from symptoms. Representative items from 3 of 13 subscales include

I have no objection to getting angry.
I do not feel bound by the motto "Don't waste your time."
I sometimes feel the need to withdraw from people.

- Personality Research Form (PRF); D. N. Jackson; *RPP.* Forms for ages 13 through college. Constructed in a manner like that for JPI, this somewhat earlier inventory covers different content and is not supplanted by JPI. Scales resemble those of EPPS. Jackson relies on balance of positive and negative endorsement items to control response set. Evidence on the significance of scores is scanty; followers of Murray generally deny that self-reports can measure "needs" in Murray's sense.
- Psychological Systems Questionnaire; J. H. Johnson and others; *Psych Systems.* Illustrative of emerging attempts to carry computer techniques beyond conventional testing (J. H. Johnson *et al.,* 1979). One of a set of instruments and record forms designed for tracking clients or patients in an institutional information system, as well as for immediate guidance of treatment. In any one session the terminal displays a selection from the 700 items. The items may be chosen to focus on a pending decision. An item may be modified in the light of personal facts (e.g., "Did your brother . . . ?" may be altered to "Did your older brother . . . ?"). Response sets are monitored; if a control score exceeds certain limits, the respondent is given fresh instructions to modify his set. In certain contingencies, the subject is invited to type in free responses, as with this question triggered by an extreme score: "Mr. Jones, your test responses seem to indicate that you are very depressed. Would you care to make any comments about this?" The printout provides an integrative interpretation, including predictions as to the probable outcome of this or that form of treatment.
- Sixteen Personality Factor Questionnaire (16 PF); R. B. Cattell and associates; *IPAT.* Age 16 through adult, with a special form for poor readers. Measures central factors in Cattell's system (see Table 13.2), on which he and his followers have conducted varied and extensive research. Unusual supplements include profiles for occupational groups, a handbook for clinical interpretation, and even a computerized evaluation for responses collected by marital counselors from couples. Reliability is sacrificed to bandwidth; even combining two forms yields scores with reliabilities ranging around 0.6. The other chief limitation is the claim that 16 PF meets the needs of almost any user; only a highly sophisticated reader can sort out the mass of background material and the comments of reviewers to decide for or against a particular application.

- Tennessee Self Concept Scale; W. H. Fitts; *Counselor Recordings and Tests*. Ages 12 and above. An evaluative instrument that derives an elaborate profile from 100 items (less than 20 minutes). Fourteen scores such as Self-Esteem: Physical and Self-Esteem: Moral-Ethical can be reported to the person tested. Professionals can examine another 15 scores labeled Psychoneurosis, Psychosis, Conflict, and so on. Users must discount the overelaborate report and the overemphatic score labels. Otherwise, comparable to other screening instruments.

10. *Table 14.1 lists the JPI dimensions. Table 5.6 lists many of the dimensions ("needs") for which the PRF is scored. Which description appears to be most suitable where an inventory is a starting point for college counseling intended to promote self-understanding? Would much be gained by giving both inventories?*
11. *For a multiscore instrument summarizing a 10-year-old's self-description, what is to be said for and against each of these methods of reporting to his parents and teacher?*
    a. *Profile displaying per cent of possible responses in a keyed direction (e.g., Dominance). The average profile for his sex-grade group is printed over it.*
    b. *Profile displaying percentile rank (within sex and grade) on each key. The average profile is represented by a flat line at 50.*

VALIDITY FOR EVALUATING DISORDERS

Screening

Persons who displayed symptoms in the past are more likely than others to display symptoms in the future. Lasky *et al.* (1959) found that the thickness of a mental patient's file folder correlates 0.6 with his chances of being hospitalized again after release. Self-reports are considerably less potent as predictors of deviant behavior than are records of past deviant behavior. Prediction may be enhanced by the "Give-a-dog-a-bad-name" effect. Moreover, conflict with one's environment breeds future conflict unless someone helps resolve the initial conflict. These findings are precisely like the findings in the intellectual field: the best way to predict who will do well in schooling is to find out who has been doing well in school.

This argues for rather than against the importance of tests. To predict from life history is a conservative strategy: good is expected of those good in the past, and the worst is expected of those with bad past records. The proper function of psychological methods is to locate the seemingly adjusted people for whom the risk of disturbance is high and the ones with histories of maladjustment who should respond to suitable treatment. This implies a need to measure not level of adjustment but probability of responding favorably to one or another treatment.

Apparent success in classifying cases can result from improper or inadequate analysis. This is true in validation of performance tests as well as of inventories.

> Validating a key or formula on the cases used to select items and establish weights proves nothing. Crossvalidation (p. 397) is essential to avoid placing trust in a screening rule that fits only the sample on which it was developed.
>
> To demonstrate "significant" differences (e.g., between a disturbed group and normals) is beside the point; with large samples, inaccurate predictions reach statistical significance.
>
> Comparing extreme groups can show that a relationship exists, but we ought to be told how strong the relation is over the entire population. A correlation calculated from extreme groups is exaggerated.
>
> A correlation, or a report of the percentage of correct decisions, should be augmented with a consideration of base rates.
>
> Controls for past history and for ability would reduce apparent validity for screening.

Few studies ask which tests can predict adjustment *within* a sample of persons with bad records, or within a sample with good case histories. The prediction formula ought also to be derived within a group of uniform ability. The incompetent student or recruit will have problems of adjustment, and it is no brilliant achievement for a "personality" test to predict this. Within the incompetent group, some will develop emotional symptoms and some will not; the characteristics associated with breakdown in this group might well differ from the characteristics associated with breakdowns in the high-ability group.

The screening instrument is not intended to make a final analysis of the person but to direct scarce professional time to cases meriting deeper study. A somewhat representative validity report is that for PSI. I compress details given in the manual by combining psychiatric subgroups and by discussing just one cut score, for males only. The *Al* key was originally formed by contrasting 195 college students with 71 patients (nearly all judged schizophrenic). The distributions for those two groups were studied to identify reasonable cut scores. Table 14.3 assumes that persons with standard scores of 60 or above on *Al* were flagged as possibly disturbed. The figures in the upper half of the table show that 75 per cent of the disturbed were detected at a price of 11 per cent errors on normals. The crossvalidation (lower half of table) contrasted further normal cases with mental hospital inpatients classed as having "functional psychosis." The percentages shifted, but the crossvalidation agrees with the original data.

Table 14.3 *Success of a cut score in distinguishing mental patients*

Group	N	Number Exceeding Cut Score	Error Rate (per cent)
Keying samples			
Patients	71	53	25
Normals	195	22	11
Crossvalidation			
Patients	48	40	17
Normals	305	43	14

SOURCE: Data from PSI manual, 1978, p. 20.

How adequate is this level of validity? Assume that the population has 1000 normals of whom 11 per cent have scores of 60 and over; that means 110 false alarms. Assume also that 75 per cent of disturbed persons reach a score of 60. If 200 disturbed persons were added to the basic 1000 cases, the base rate would be 200/1200 or 17 per cent; and 260 (= 110 + 150) members of the population would score 60 or over. Reviewing 260 persons is probably a good investment as the warning is confirmed in more than half the cases (150/260).

Lower base rates alter the picture:

Disturbed persons (N)	Base rate (%)	Interviews required (N)	Interviews confirming disturbance (%)
0	0	110	0
10	1	117	2
20	2	125	12
50	5	147	25
100	9	185	41
200	17	260	58

In a general community, the base rate is probably small and most of the "flags" are false alarms. The base rate will be higher among persons referred to a clinic, and the fraction of interviews "wasted" may be acceptable.

Short, undisguised questionnaires have been of distinct value for military screening. One questionnaire given 2081 recruits successfully called 525 persons suspect; 281 of them were later judged to present neuropsychiatric conditions (D. H. Harris, 1945). The test permitted psychiatrists to omit individual interviews with 1540 men—not a trifling saving. The screen missed 16 neuropsychiatric cases who got into difficulty while on duty.

Error rates may be overstated in validation of a screening procedure. The criterion is generally crude. A short interview is subject to error, and so is a fuller clinical appraisal. Moreover, some apparent false positives may be unrecognized hits. Nonpatient status is no guarantee of sound personality; many persons in the community have weaknesses that remain latent only so long as they are exposed to no exceptional stress.

12. *Callan (1972) identified MMPI items that "deviant" soldiers marked more often than others. (Deviancy included going AWOL and being punished for misconduct.) In a crossvalidation, the key and cutoff rule picked 825 out of 3328 trainees as prospective deviants. The trainees who actually got in trouble (236) included 96 of those the instrument had picked. How satisfactory is the screening instrument?*
13. *In peacetime, what use should be made of an instrument for screening recruits that identifies (with few false alarms) those from whom disciplinary violations are likely?*
14. *Assume that 20 per cent of normals and 90 per cent of disturbed persons exceed a certain cut score. Evaluate the effectiveness of this screening, assuming a base rate of 5 per cent?; of 20 per cent?*

Classification

Clinicians are often asked to distinguish one type of psychopathology from another. Classification is sometimes required for institutional bookkeeping. It is helpful in forming homogeneous groups for research (evaluation of drugs, for example), and it is used in laying initial treatment plans. By and large, attempts to classify on the basis of personality tests have worked out poorly. No more than two-thirds of the patients the test interpreter assigns to a certain category will be assigned the same label on the basis of more extended clinical analysis. Tests of *intellectual* impairment are useful for differential diagnosis where schizophrenia or brain dysfunction is suspected (Filskov & Boll, 1982; Newmark *et al.*, 1980; Phillips *et al.*, 1980).

Interest in diagnostic categorization has greatly diminished. Persons who might be given the same label differ greatly in the degree to which their lives are disrupted, and the therapist's or custodian's aim has become one of improving the quality of life for the person and those around him. One psychologist with a strong background in MMPI diagnosis expressed more than a decade ago a view that is now almost universal:

> The main difficulty with the typological, disease-oriented approach [to] human problems is simply that we are not dealing with disease types in the assessment and modification of disordered behavior. A child who strangles kittens or spits at his mother does not have a disease. He *does* have something somebody defines as a problem. . . . The therapeutic need is to get the client to change his behavior, not to cure his illness, and the vital diagnostic need is for information contributory to the behavior changing enterprise. [D. R. Peterson, 1968, pp. 4–5, 32].

Forecasting Response to Treatment

In diagnosis, a reasonable surface question is whether the person is likely to benefit from therapy. The indication that persons with the *49'* pattern change little in response to psychotherapy has a message for administrators of agencies. Apart from cases with such crystallized resistance, it is hard to believe that the person's response does not depend on which kind of treatment is undertaken.

Studying not psychopathology but participation in a weight-loss clinic, Janis (1978, 1982) and his co-workers found that, in general, it was persons with low self-esteem who stuck to the regimen through the treatment and follow-up period. When, however, Riskind (in Janis, 1982) encouraged clients with *high* self-esteem to take day-to-day responsibility for their own conduct, they adopted sound eating practices. Riskind's method did not work with clients reporting low self-esteem. Janis offers a tentative theory regarding the role of personality in response to counseling.

To date, studies of response to therapy have typically divided a panel into experimental and control groups and given members of the experimental group an essentially uniform treatment—medication, behavior modification, group discussion, or whatever. MMPI studies of this nature are reviewed by Widom (1979). Needed are studies of the validity of decision rules that assign persons to *different* treatments (p. 144). Beyond this, the need is for deeper studies of the processes of response to particular therapies, so that understanding can generate sounder decision rules (Newmark, 1979).

The situational influence on behavior was turned to advantage in a prison. From MMPI profiles it was judged that certain prisoners were especially likely to assault others and that certain others were likely to be victims of assault. The "predatory" prisoners were assigned to one dormitory; the potential victims, to a second; and intermediate cases, to a third. Prior to the reassignment, 22 assaults had been reported in nine months. Supervision was reduced in the third dormitory to permit more intensive supervision in the first two. In the subsequent nine months there were 9 reports of assault from the first dormitory, 4 from the second, and none from that with "intermediate" cases. (The study, by Bohn, is reported by Megargee & Bohn, 1979.)

Professional opinion sometimes supports the use of inventories even without direct validation. Great responsibilities are placed on operators of nuclear equipment, yet officials of power plants were able to list over 150 specific incidents of operators' disturbing behavior. Specialists in the psychometric approach to personality advised giving inventories to applicants and retesting periodically after hiring to guard against emerging pathology (Dunnette *et al.*, 1981). They recommended giving MMPI *and* CPI. (16 PF was their third choice.) Among other indicators they proposed to use, the *49'* pattern was said to signify the possibility of argumentative hostility and impulsive action. Principal reliance should be placed on two clinicians' independent examination of the information, it was said, and the reviewers should be continually mindful that statistically abnormal responses are given by some emotionally stable persons. The case report would clear many workers. The others would be studied further by means of a personal history, the Loevinger Sentence Completion Test (on ego development and self-control), and a clinical interview (its topics to include leisure pursuits, history of reactions to stress, and present life stresses). A rejected worker would have the right to appeal; this could lead to several stages of reassessment—or the worker could at any time accept the "screen out" decision. Given the unwisdom of waiting to screen workers holding these jobs until behavior turns erratic, such cautious use of inventories would probably be endorsed by most psychologists. Some would prefer performance tests or projective tests to the questionnaires.

15. *As originally conceived, the MMPI scales were to discriminate several kinds of patients from normals. Yet the traditional classification problem is to categorize a person who already is known to have social or emotional difficulty. What contrast groups will lead to relevant criterion keys for this purpose? (For an effort in this direction, see Rosen, 1966.)*
16. *Is the original keying of MMPI more like the criterion keying of SCII or that of KOIS? Which procedure would you favor for a new instrument serving the wide-ranging purposes of MMPI?*
17. *If an "ideal" predictive study of operators in nuclear power plants were carried out, as outlined in Table 5.1, what would be a suitable criterion? (Note that, in sound plant operation, cross-checks are installed to prevent an operator error from having a large effect.)*

PREDICTIONS IN THE GENERAL POPULATION

Countless studies have pursued the attractive hypothesis that data on motivation, emotional stability, and so on will predict academic and vocational success. Self-report measures have severely limited validity as selection devices. Understanding of styles and moods can be important in a teacher's or supervisor's planning, however, and some findings that fall short of practical usefulness raise stimulating questions for theory.

Occupational Predictions

The correlations for any trait measure and any job criterion range widely over samples, as was true of abilities (Ghiselli, 1973; see also Guion & Gottier, 1965). Ghiselli calculated an average coefficient in each job category for whichever personality variables seemed to have a plausible relation to the job. The validity coefficients against job performance averaged at or below 0.2 for nearly all categories. The average rose to 0.3 for executives and salespersons; in these fields, no ability measure gave a better prediction. Ghiselli does not indicate which traits entered each average, but a study by Harrell (1972) amplifies with regard to executives.

Annual earnings of Stanford MBAs in the fifth year after graduation served as Harrell's criterion. In firms with more than 1000 employees, the following characteristics (among others) correlated with the criterion: grade average in second year of course, managerial interests on SVIB, social introversion, self-assurance, energy, dominance, and initiative (as recorded on various questionnaires given when the men were in school). I estimate that the validity coefficients for these several scores hovered around 0.2. (The Stanford program is highly selective. On the other hand, correlations were run for many scores, and these highest coefficients were not crossvalidated. Data on a modest sample of men working in smaller firms confirmed some of the results.)

Among the stronger results is an analysis of practicing architects whose judged record of creativeness (*not* success!) was compared with concurrent scores on seven inventories (W. B. Hall & D. W. MacKinnon, 1969). A multiple correlation of around 0.4 (crossvalidated) was found with most instruments. The MMPI proved worthless in this application whereas the Strong blank ran well ahead of the pack ($R = 0.55$). Among the single scales with comparatively large positive correlations are these: Strong Artist and Author; and desires for Change, Exhibition, and Autonomy on Gough's ACL. The large negative correlations are equally illuminating; they include Strong Banker and Policeman; and ACL Self-control and Personal Adjustment. Other inventories tended to confirm the picture of creativity implied by these correlations. One would expect the rigid, conservative, nationalistic authoritarian to be the worst of candidates for the Peace Corps. M. B. Smith (1965) validated preinduction questionnaire measures of this trait against adaptation as a schoolteacher in Ghana, with the hunch that high scorers would make poor cultural ambassadors. The tests did not predict performance in the field. Smith tried to account for the near-zero correlations, noting first that the true authoritarian does not volunteer for the Peace Corps. Very likely the extreme Lows are too unruly and impulsive to adapt as the moderates (who within this select population rank as Highs) do. Then he notes that the Ghanaian school system is organized rigidly. Success on the job means fitting the demands of the system, even if one never gets around to making friends with the populace. As one reads Smith's postmortem on the once-lively hypothesis, the only wonder is that authoritarianism failed to correlate *positively* with success in that place and time.

A person adapts to role requirements, becoming forceful as a parent, submissive in reporting to a commanding officer, boisterous at a party, decorous in church. Personality, as commonly measured, probably has much to do with the sort of work and personal relations a person *seeks,* but little to do with his competence when thrust into a certain role. The adjusted person adapts to role demands; let Shakespeare's Kate be our reminder that sometimes one relishes the new role enough to make *it* the personality.

Personality inventories should not be directly used for employee selection though they may properly play a part when many facts are combined into a trained assessor's judgment. It is especially hazardous to evaluate nonclinic populations on tests constructed to identify pathology. Computer services have been known to interpret profiles of job applicants by means of experience tables built up in clinics, misusing pathological terms to describe individuals who are functioning in a healthy manner (J. N. Butcher, 1979). A qualified psychologist, talking over the report with the user, can minimize overinterpretation and misconceptions.

Many times I have referred to the potential importance of identifying types of situations in which a person will prosper. Such predictions on the basis of aptitude tests have been scattered and generally unimpressive; in contrast, personality inventories have produced a substantial array of interactive relationships. The suggestive findings (p. 142) on individuals' responses to more and less rigid organizational styles are one example. Fiedler (in Magnusson & Endler, 1977) has amassed evidence that whether persons who have a given style of relating to others succeed or fail as leaders depends on characteristics of the work situation. Information on personality should help in fitting work assignments to individuals.

18. *Before analyzing the relation of test scores to earnings, Harrell dropped from the sample all females, all graduates not working in business, and all graduates working in family businesses. How can these "purifications" be justified? What effects would these exclusion rules probably have on validity coefficients?*

Educational Predictions

In the academic realm, there have been many failures of prediction from inventories, along with positive reports that never get replicated. Even self-esteem or anxiety has only minimal correlation with achievement when ability is held constant (Bachman & O'Malley, 1977; Heinrich & Spielberger, 1982; Wylie, 1974, 1979). A replicated correlation for the Gordon Personal Profile (L. V. Gordon, 1978) perhaps illustrates the best that can be hoped for. Four subscores make up Gordon's self-esteem variable (which correlates well with Coopersmith's). Three of them (Ascendancy, Emotional Stability, and Sociability) have correlations with grade average that differ negligibly from zero. The fourth, Responsibility (self-report as thorough, steady, and reliable), does not correlate appreciably with ability tests and does correlate with academic success. Three studies reported correlations close to 0.2; a fourth, largest study produced a correlation of 0.1. If $r = 0.2$, adding the Responsibility score to an ability score would improve the multiple correlation by 0.04 or less. After reflection on the published literature and after sponsoring studies of its own, the College Entrance Examination Board (1963) made a noteworthy official statement warning member colleges "of very serious risks that would certainly attend the actual use of [any existing personality] tests in making admissions decisions." The problems mentioned include possible misunderstanding by the public, faking and coaching, absence of parallel forms, overemphasis on scales that correlate only slightly with marks, and inability to allow for the fact that adolescent personalities are changing.

Institutions express recurrent interest in the possible contribution of "noncognitive" measures to selection, and some may yet prove to be of practical use. Attempting to measure "strength of motivation" by questionnaire seems hopeless, but preferred styles may help in classification. The biographical inventory may be turned to advantage on the assumption that a person who previously has persisted in tasks and enterprises is a good bet; questions of this character should refer to verifiable events and not invite generalized self-advertising. Inventories might be used not to "predict success" but to increase diversity. Thus, a medical school might distribute offers of admission in some specified proportion over qualified applicants whose preferences center on administrative or scientific or personal service activities.

Cronbach and Snow (1981) review many studies on the response to instruction of different personalities. There were few studies of any one trait save anxiety, and rarely did investigators studying the same trait use the same measure of it. The summary grouped anxiety, dependency, and other indicators of inhibition under the label "defensive motivation" and confident, assertive, self-directing qualities as "constructive motivation." The broad conclusion was that students with constructive motivation benefited most from challenging instruction where there was comparatively little direction from the teacher and more opportunity for the learner to shape his activities. There were several reports that more defensive students were at their best when given orderly, firmly structured lessons. Results were inconsistent, and the outcome is expected to depend on other factors (subject matter, grade level, class ability, etc.)

One of the research programs entering the summary is that of Domino (1968, 1971). He investigated students at the high and low extremes on two CPI scores, Achievement-through-Conformity *(Ac)* and Achievement-through-Independence *(Ai)*. Both traits imply positive self-reports. The high *Ac* speaks of himself as efficient, organized, responsible, and sincere. The high *Ai* calls himself mature, foresighted, demanding, and self-reliant. Domino interviewed the students' instructors about their teaching styles. Some courses, highly structured, left students with little freedom or independent responsibility. Some encouraged initiative and self-direction. Domino calculated each student's grade average over all the courses he had had of each type. The results showed an interaction effect for *Ai* (and not for *Ac*). Low *Ai*'s did better in more structured instruction.

In the second study (a formal experiment), four sections of introductory psychology were formed, each with students of one type. The instructor encouraged student initiative in two sections and pressed for conformity in two others. Figure 14.3 shows that a match between instructor style and student style worked out best on most criteria. With regard to originality, however, only the student's styles mattered. Also, the independent students were able to rise fairly well to a demand that they conform. Several other findings reviewed by Cronbach and Snow are roughly in accord with those of Domino.

Research such as this contributes to understanding rather than to practice. Domino was comparing extremes, and relations would be weaker if the full range of student and teacher styles entered the analysis. Moreover, dozens of interest, ability, and personality variables affect response, so it would not be sensible to sort students into sections on the basis of Ai or any other such score. The finding does imply, however, that teaching different sections in different ways—and telling students in advance what style they can expect —would enable the student to sort himself into a section he expects to suit him. And, of course, an adept teacher can provide for a variety of work styles within a single class.

The potential of personality measures for research is particularly well illustrated in the research program of Atkinson and his associates (Atkinson & Raynor, 1978; Atkinson, 1981). ("Need for achievement" [$nAch$] was measured by thematic tests [p. 556] rather than by self-report in this work and in the earlier studies directed by McClelland, but Atkinson did use a questionnaire to measure anxiety.) The argument can be sketched in a few sentences.

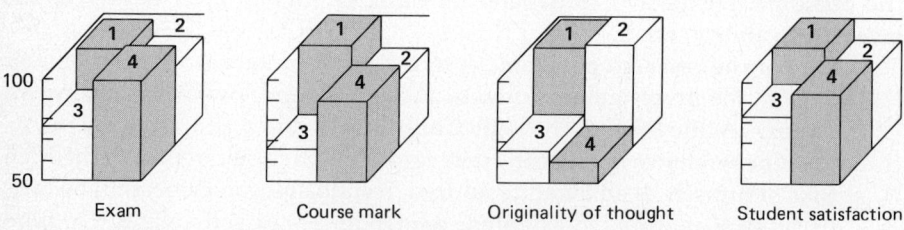

1. Students are independent (high Ai); instructor pressure is for independence.
2. Students are independent (high Ai); instructor pressure is for conformity.
3. Students are conforming (high Ac); instructor pressure is for independence.
4. Students are conforming (high Ac); instructor pressure is for conformity.

Figure 14.3. Outcomes when teacher style corresponds to student personality.
Source: Data from Domino, 1971. Shading identifies classes where student self-report matched instructor's adopted style. For each variable, the group average is expressed as a percentage of the average in whichever group ranked highest.

Anxiety expresses motivation to avoid psychological failure.

nAch expresses motivation to seek success, particularly in tasks where personal skill and effort make a difference.

The combination of the two motives defines a resultant tendency to approach or avoid a challenge (to accept a gamble, to invest effort in a problem).

The perceived difficulty of a task (or the odds against a gamble) acts as an intensifier. If probability of success is near 0.5, the tendency to approach or avoid is strong; if it is near zero or one, there is no personal challenge.

In plain words, the person with strong net constructive motivation is attracted to activities where success appears highly uncertain and makes his greatest effort on such tasks. The defensive person will prefer easy tasks—or tasks where success is so unlikely that failure implies no personal shortcoming. Predictions cannot be made simply, however; ordinarily additional motivations are aroused (e.g., affiliation, prestige, fear of rejection by peers for "showing off"); and alternative activities compete for time and attention with the task about which a prediction is made. States are of more immediate significance than traits; a motive can be temporarily satiated or heightened by recent deprivation or by situational pressures. Furthermore, learned roles seem to produce differences between the sexes in many of the laboratory and classroom situations where the theory has been tested (Farmer & Fyans, 1980).

Among the many offshoots of the theory is deCharms's (1976, 1980) educational experiment in which the motivation of inner-city youngsters was heightened by deliberately altering the self-concept. The students were taught (in grades 6 and 7) to take responsibility for initiating activities, setting goals, and monitoring their progress. Scores on a thematic test of motivation increased sharply over those of a control group, and so did school achievement; the effect could be traced down to the end of high school.

19. *What role, if any, should personality inventories play in vocational counseling?*
20. *Research such as Domino's suggests how to teach conformers so that they will tend to earn better grades. Would some other policy contribute more to their long-run educational development?*
21. *What advantages does a biographical inventory have over a personality questionnaire in employee selection?*
22. *How might lack of confidence help one student to attain high marks, yet be a drawback to another?*
23. *A leadership score identifies pupils whose responses resemble those of other pupils who have become leaders. What characteristics other than leadership ability and interest are likely to distinguish student leaders in high school from the students who take little part in student affairs?*

24. If school officials encourage pupils with high leadership scores to take leadership responsibilities, will this tend to increase or decrease the correlation between the original scores and leadership record by the end of high school?
25. Scores on certain instruments purport to identify students likely to be troublemakers and potential delinquents. Assuming that such a score has very high stability and validity, could any legitimate use be made of such a test by high schools? If, as is the case, the validity coefficients are quite low, what undesirable effects may follow if such scores are collected by principals?

STRUCTURE OF THE INDIVIDUAL

No psychologist seriously believes that a person can be adequately characterized in 3 or 5 or 16 dimensions. Investigators try, however, to bring a multitude of individuals into a single conceptual scheme. The attempt to map dissimilar individuals onto a few dimensions is an effort to achieve what the chemist does with a limited number of concepts such as molecular weight and acidity. This search for dimensions that can be woven into lawlike, universally applicable statements is referred to as *nomothetic*, in contrast to the *idiographic* portrayal of each person as unique, as in a novel. (The words come from the Greek: *nomos* for "law," *idios* for "one's own." Allport [1937], who gave the words their place in psychology, emphasized that the approaches are supplementary, not antagonistic.)

The score on a trait is a statistical summary of behavior over many situations. The person at either extreme of the possible range of a trait is well characterized. He exhibits the trait (or its absence) in unusual degree and in a large number of situations. If a man is perfectly honest, the adjective really tells us how he acts whereas a middling score on an honesty scale tells little.

A middling score implies no lack of individuality. Rather, the person's behavior is not organized along the dimension we chose to score. The description "50 per cent honest" inevitably is inadequate; *when* is the person honest? (Burton, 1963). One man acts from need; he takes money to feed his family, but will not cheat or lie. Another, prudent rather than honest, acts honestly when he might be caught. Another would never steal, but thinks it right to operate a business on the principle of "buyer beware." These men are all honest to an intermediate degree; statistically, their honesty is in the average range. A personalized description would replace the general trait dimension with dimensions that describe situations the person sees as calling for an honest act (and the opposite). The person has his own way of slicing up his world; situations one person perceives as similar are not similar for another.

Psychoanalysts—and those psychologists who probe the person's perceptual world—have written idiographic characterizations, but their work has been to a large degree artistic. How well an individual can be "characterized" through reproducible methods remains an open question.

A Semantic Differential case study. A provocative example of the possibilities is the study of Eve. The psychiatrists Thigpen and Cleckley (1953, 1957) vividly described her "split personality," and the film *Three Faces of Eve* portrayed it artistically. Osgood and Luria (1954) characterized each of Eve's personalities objectively.

They employed the Semantic Differential method, which measures connotations of words or phrases. The stimulus is rated on a scale, scales and stimuli being mixed in random order. Successive items might appear as follows:

MY FATHER soft ___:___:___:___:___:___:___ hard

FRAUD rich ___:___:___:___:___:___:___ poor

CONFUSION fair ___:___:___:___:___:___:___ unfair

MY FATHER deep ___:___:___:___:___:___:___ shallow

The scale is to be checked rapidly to capture first impressions. The method has varied uses. Items like those just listed could elicit the concepts of a patient. A study of political concepts and attitudes could use names of nations as stimuli (keeping the scales the same).

In one method of scoring, the scales are assigned to *good-bad, strong-weak,* and *active-passive* keys; for example, *soft* can be equated with *weak* and *passive.* Checkmarks are converted to numbers running from $+3$ to -3, and, for each stimulus, scales within a key are averaged. Thus, we could say that a respondent has indirectly described his father at $+1$ on good, $+2.4$ on strong, and -0.4 on active.

Eve White had three identities who "took possession" of her at various times, and her therapists were able to administer the Semantic Differential to each persona in turn. Figure 14.4 presents two of the configurations. The black ball represents the midpoint on all scales. "Good" is at the top, "active" at the left, and "weak" toward the viewer. The heavy line connecting the black ball with "doctor" (who is always good, strong, very active) helps to orient the figure.

Two psychologists interpreted these structures with no further knowledge of the case. In Eve White's record they pointed out the separation of love and sex, the meaninglessness of the spouse, the weakness of "me." Eve Black seems to place hatred and fraud in a favorable cluster with "me" and rejects spouse, love, job, and child. (The third self, Jane, is normal; love and sex are closely linked and favorable.) An impressionistic "guess" led to this summary of the first two personalities (Osgood & Luria, 1954):

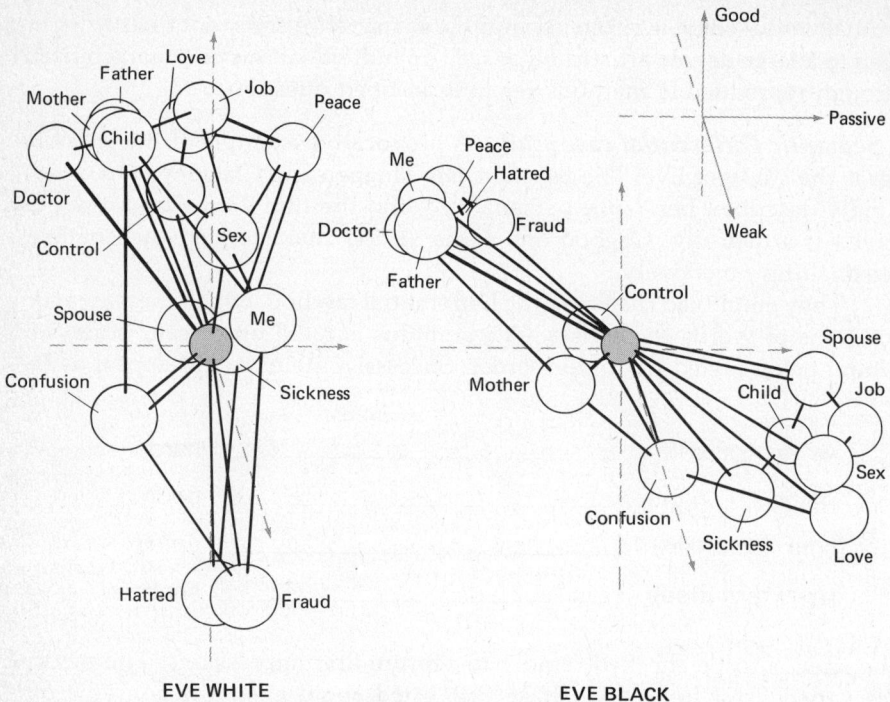

Figure 14.4. Meaning systems of the two Eves.
Source: Osgood & Luria, 1954. Copyright 1954 by the American Psychological Association. Reproduced (adapted) by permission.

Eve White is the woman who is simultaneously most in contact with social reality and under the greatest emotional stress. She is aware of both the demands of society and her own inadequacies in meeting them. She sees herself as a passive weakling and is also consciously aware of the discord in her sexual life, drawing increasingly sharp distinctions between love as an idealized notion and sex as a crude reality. She maintains the greatest diversity among the meanings of various concepts. She is concerned and ambivalent about her child, but apparently is *not* aware of her own ambivalent attitudes toward her mother. . . . Eve White [is] accepting the mores or values of others (particularly her mother) but continuously criticizing and punishing herself. . . .

Eve Black is clearly the most out of contact with social reality and simultaneously the most self-assured. To rhapsodize, Eve Black finds Peace of mind through close identification with a God-like therapist (My Doctor, probably a father symbol for her), accepting her Hatred and Fraud as perfectly legitimate aspects of the Godlike role. Naturally, she sees herself as a dominant, active

wonder-woman and is in no way self-critical. She is probably
unaware of her family situation. . . . Like a completely selfish infant,
this personality is entirely oriented around the assumption of its
own perfection.

The pattern corresponds well with the therapists' picture. They described the same personalities in these phrases, among others:

EVE WHITE: demure, almost saintly, seldom lively; tries not to blame
her husband for marital troubles; every act demonstrates sacrifice for
her little girl; meek, fragile, doomed to be overcome.
EVE BLACK: a party girl, shrewd, egocentric; rowdy wit; all attitudes
whimlike; ready for any little irresponsible adventure; provocative;
strangely secure from inner aspect of grief and tragedy.

With respect to common dimensions, Eve White has low self-esteem and is perfectionistic and unwilling to express emotion. The Semantic Differential points to specific sources of conflict: lack of acceptance of spouse and sex and also her child's weakness and need for protection. (Mrs. White's feeling that she could not give her child adequate protection was a precipitating cause of her illness.) Eve Black is shallow, uncontrolled, self-centered—extrovert on any questionnaire and on MMPI surely a *49'* or *94'*. She identifies strongly with men and rejects child and spouse. One can begin to guess what persons and treatments are likely to win her respect and cooperation and what rewards she is likely to work for. Such information goes far beyond what one can get from even the most valid description of her general style. The rewards that a therapist might ordinarily offer—opportunity to hold a job, restoration of marriage—were spurned by Eve Black. The cooperation that eventually permitted some success in therapy came only when the therapist appealed to Eve Black's fear of sickness.

The Osgood-Luria method of studying personality has unfortunately not been pursued in the quarter-century since their report, but the "personal construct" approach that the late George Kelly (1955) introduced at the same time has had followers.

Kelly's phenomenological approach. Kelly's "personal construct" theory is cognitive and phenomenological. Behavior is the result not of habit or impulse so much as it is a response to the situation as the person construes it. The data and interpretations are concerned with the individual's perceptions and the system of meanings they derive from. Kelly's approach, therefore, contrasts with the behaviorist and trait approaches that ask about typical behavior in a class of situations *the tester* considers to be similar.

Whereas most inventories ask about response to people in general or to a broad class such as persons in authority, the Kelly procedure asks about particular persons in the respondent's life. The Role Concept Repertory Test

("Rep test") can begin with a standard list of roles, for example: "Your wife or present girl friend" and "The person you feel most sorry for." Alternatively, it can be completely individualized, starting with persons the subject names. The heart of the technique is to ask (for any three roles or persons), "In what important way are two of these alike and different from the third?" Kelly thus elicits the dimensions for the analysis from the person himself, making the technique far more idiographic than Osgood's.

Mischel (a student of Kelly), in his introductory text on personality theory, uses a 25-year-old unmarried graduate student as a running example of the application of many measurement techniques, including the Rep test. Gary was selected as representative of "ordinary" people, yet, of course, was unique. The Rep test dialog went as follows, in part (Mischel, 1981, p. 288):

> List the three most important people in your life.
> —*Me, my brother, my father.*
> How are any two of these alike and different from the third?
> —*My brother and I both know how to be tough and succeed, no matter what—my father is soft, knocked out, defeated by life.*
> Think of yourself now, five years ago, and five years from now. How are any two of those alike and different from the other?
> —*Five years ago I was warmer, more open and responsive to others than I am now. Now I'm mostly a scheming brain. Five years from now I hope to have recaptured some of that feeling and to be more like I was five years ago.*

From this pair of responses we see that Gary is strongly aware of two dimensions: success and deliberate toughness. From other responses Mischel picks up two other dimensions central to Gary: security versus liberty (Gary wants both but believes they are hard to achieve within a single pattern of living) and rationality versus emotionality (Gary attaches a strong positive evaluation to what is rational). The test responses provide obvious leads for further conversation, and Mischel's two pages of summary include many sentences of this personalized character: "He generally prefers women who are stimulating and challenging though he fears all forms of domination through either authority or emotional ties."

The technique of eliciting the person's own dimensions can be applied to any kind of stimulus. Most important, it can be used to find out how the person thinks of the tasks or social situations he commonly encounters (or avoids). Such a phenomenological inquiry is a usual part of nonbehaviorist counseling, and it almost always takes the form of an informal interview. An adaptation of Kelly's structured method would extend the studies of situational variance (p. 459) that have used nomothetic (i.e., universal) categories for situations. (For a step in this direction, see Magnusson, 1971.)

Kelly approached psychotherapy by trying to modify the person's construct system. His followers, extending this style of therapy, use the basic technique of eliciting constructs in an informal manner (Landfield & Leitner,

1980). For their purposes, the standardized approach of the Rep test is cumbersome and concentrates too narrowly on constructs of persons.

Those of Kelly's followers interested in measurement and research on personality seem never to have found a convenient method of compiling individualized responses into "data." They back off to measures of *style* of construing; Fransella and Bannister (1977, esp. p. 111 ff.), after describing those techniques and some useful research based on them, warn that the summary variables lose the essence of the personal constructs. Typical nomothetic measures report the complexity of the construct system and the extent to which the person differentiates (separates) himself from others. Such scores do generate provocative findings. Carr (in Landfield & Leitner, 1980), for example, reports that therapy is more likely to be successful when the complexity indices for patient and therapist are similar.

26. *Fishbein and Azjen (see p. 458) showed that people differ reliably in the trait "tendency to act in a religious manner," but that standing on this trait did not predict behavior in particular situations.*
    a. *The actions in the list could be grouped into subsets. What subsets, if any, might account for much of the variation in behavior?*
    b. *Would it be possible to describe more of a person's religious behavior idiographically by grouping situations with respect to dimensions he considers significant? If so, illustrate.*
27. *Is idiographic analysis appropriate only to self-reports, or could it be applied to behavioral observations?*
28. *Gary's MMPI profile (Mischel, 1981, p. 147) has a 28' . . . pattern, with score 2 (originally keyed on depressed patients) reaching 80. Drawing on a standard interpretative source based on patients, Mischel notes traits commonly associated with that profile: Avoids close relations with other people; high-strung; tends to be resentful; lacking in ambition. How does this trait description differ* in character *from the description based on the Rep test?*
29. *Is the Semantic Differential fakable? Can it obtain information the person is not consciously aware of?*

15
Judgments and Systematic Observations

Reputation counts. A person who has impressed earlier teachers as imaginative is favored by a college admissions committee. Supervisors' opinions determine who gets promoted in an organization. Teachers find out what children think of each other in order to understand relationships in the classroom and to identify social misfits. Ratings provide criteria of job performance, of patients' progress in mental hospitals, and of children's development. This chapter considers techniques for eliciting the impressions of informants and then turns to systematic observations of behavior. (In this chapter and the next, female pronouns are used for raters and assessors, as well as for testers and investigators.)

RATINGS BY SUPERVISORS AND PROFESSIONAL OBSERVERS

Descriptions by industrial supervisors, teachers, or superior officers are hard to compare because their emphases and language vary. Even with trained observers, information has to be put in standard form to permit systematic analysis. Raters are usually asked to check applicable phrases or to indicate trait strength on numerical scales.

Sources of Error

Raters may define leadership (for example) in many ways. To one judge, "leadership" suggests conscious wielding of authority, crisp decisions, and general dominance. A person rated high by this judge would receive a lower rating from a judge who looks for a leader to encourage subordinates, bring out cooperative decisions, and subordinate his own views to the views of the group. Clear definition of traits reduces ambiguity.

The response alternatives may also be ambiguous. In some older scales the respondent was to rate "friendliness," for example, from 0 to 100. A particular number is used by different raters to indicate quite different behavior. *Average, excellent,* and the like, are equally indefinite.

Among errors introduced by the judge, the most serious is leniency or generosity. The teacher, asked to indicate on a report card whether the pupil is cooperative, is likely to rate all but the most troublesome pupils at the high end of the scale. Company commanders rate 98 per cent of their junior officers in the top two categories (out of five) on efficiency reports. Such ratings provide little information. There are several reasons for generosity: the rater may feel that she is admitting poor leadership if she says that subordinates are not performing well; she tends to feel kindly toward associates; she thinks she may have to justify any implied criticism; and she finds it easier to say good about everyone than to discriminate. Whereas ratings by lay persons err on the generous side, social workers, counselors, and others in the helping professions have somewhat the opposite tendency. Even rating a standard stimulus on videotape, they rate the target persons as less able and less adjusted than lay observers do (A. M. Garner & G. M. Smith, 1976; Wills, 1978).

Some judges are more generous than others. Additional constant errors or response styles are observed. One judge rarely places anyone at the extremes of the scale, whereas another describes most persons in black-and-white terms.

The observer's overall evaluation strongly influences ratings on specific traits—a "halo effect." In Table 15.1 the modest correlations in the diagonal tell us that rater-to-rater agreement on a specific trait does not often exceed the within-rater correlation for traits supposedly referring to distinct characteristics. This means that two profiles for the same worker provided by independent raters rarely agree on his or her particular strengths and weaknesses. The table, from the PDRC study, represents especially careful data collection. The correlations are held down because few of the workers were inadequate to their jobs—restriction of range, again. The data were improved by combining scales and by averaging two or three raters per worker. The

Table 15.1. *Intercorrelations of ratings on power-plant operators*

	Maintaining Standard Operations	Relationship with Co-workers	Problem-Solving Ability	Mechanical Understanding	Overall Emotional Stability	Overall Job Performance
Maintaining Standard Operations	**0.56**	0.62	0.62	0.51	0.64	0.79
Relationship with Co-workers	0.62	**0.51**	0.42	0.36	0.63	0.65
Problem Solving Ability	0.62	0.42	**0.60**	0.63	0.54	0.69
Mechanical Understanding	0.51	0.36	0.63	**0.59**	0.44	0.59
Overall Emotional Stability	0.64	0.63	0.54	0.44	**0.59**	0.72
Overall Job Performance	0.79	0.65	0.69	0.59	0.72	**0.72**

Note: Correlations are based on average ratings given by two supervisors and the interrater correlations in the diagonal describe the reliability of such averages.
SOURCE: Dunnette *et al.*, 1982, p. 128 and Appendix S.

elaborate data collection made it possible to separate two subsets of scales. The composite ratings on emotional stability and problem-solving ability correlated 0.6. This was of some importance, because each subordinate factor was predicted by different tests—making the research on selection twice as rich as most studies with ratings as criteria.

In ratings collected routinely, it is rare to have more than one reliable dimension. The dimension may not even validly represent performance. When department heads rated lower-level supervisors in one study, the rating correlated only 0.2 with an objective record of the work performance of each crew. These were supposedly ratings on productivity, but the rating correlated 0.6 with how long the department head had known the foreman, and 0.65 with her liking for the foreman (Stockford & Bissell, 1949).

Particularly discouraging is a report from the Korean War. When effectiveness of bombing teams was rated, officers and men generally agreed about which teams were most effective. But an observational study demonstrated that bombing accuracy was entirely inconsistent from day to day and so could not truly be judged. Evidently legends were built up as a consequence of random incidents; the raters could report reliably on the teams' reputations, but not on effectiveness (Hemphill & Sechrest, 1952). Such findings are particularly distressing in view of the wide use of ratings as criteria. Likewise, ratings on job knowledge correlate only about 0.35 with the knowledge measured by a formal test.

Clinical ratings suffer from the same faults. Ratings on features such as depression and anxiety are dominated by a global impression of the person's position in the range from health to sickness. Speaking particularly of ratings collected to evaluate the benefit mental patients receive from drugs, Gleser (1968) urged that trait and state labels be replaced by reports on specific symptoms. Psychiatrists, she says, assign their own meanings to traits. "Thus, one doctor might think of bound anxiety and consider certain somatic symptoms as evidence of anxiety. Another might pay attention only to anxiety manifested in the interview in the form of restlessness, tremor, perspiration, etc."

Ratings are sometimes excellent sources of data, however. A striking example is a study where ratings of "ascendance" by nursery-school teachers correlated 0.8 with a score derived from objectively recorded observations on the playground (Jack, 1934).

1. *Why might integrity and kindness be especially hard to rate reliably?*
2. *Which of the following traits would probably be hardest to rate reliably after observations: "skill in self-expression," "freedom from tension," "leadership"?*
3. *Ratings on leadership made at Officer Candidate School correlated only 0.15 with ratings on efficiency of combat leadership by superior officers observing the men in combat (Jenkins, 1947). Why is the correlation so low?*

4. *School marks may be regarded as ratings. Which sources of error discussed in this section affect marks?*

Improvement of Ratings

Efforts to improve ratings encounter the same obstacles as efforts to improve self-reports. Again, the tester must assume that the respondent will give false information if that will bring psychological rewards. Whereas the information affects the subject's future rather than the rater's, this does not mean that the rater is uninvolved. I have mentioned the rater's inclination to interpret reports on the subject as a reflection on her own teaching or supervision or therapeutic skill. Sometimes a rater gives a low rating because she wishes to retain an employee who might otherwise be promoted. Seeking to be helpful, a teacher rating a scholarship applicant may enlarge upon his merits nearly to the point of perjury.

Selecting qualified raters is the place to start. Other things being equal, those in immediate contact with the subject give superior information. One elementary precaution, often overlooked, is to ask the rater how well she knows the subject and in what kinds of situation she has observed him. Moreover, with respect to each trait rated, there should be a place where the rater can indicate "insufficient opportunity to observe." Conrad (1932) directed raters to star traits that they regarded as especially important to the child's personality. Interjudge correlations on all traits ranged from 0.7 to 0.8. But for the traits three judges agreed in starring, the ratings correlated as high as 0.96.

When the same judge is used repeatedly, it may be possible to identify her constant error. Thus, a college learns to allow for the fact that one high school has a "tough" grading or rating policy whereas another school is lenient. It is rarely practical to make exact statistical corrections for differences between raters.

Even when a scale is carefully edited, judges have to interpret the instructions. Gleser (1968) recounts an instance where two psychiatrists differed radically in rating the current degree of illness of schizophrenic patients. One psychiatrist was reporting typical behavior whereas the other was rating the most extreme deviant behavior shown by the patient. The remedy for such difficulties is to train the judges, preferably using videotape recordings. Unless the training is skillful, it may alter the judge's response set without improving accuracy (Bernardin & Pence, 1980). Therefore, expert ratings for each tape, comparatively free from halo, are used as "scoring keys" (Borman, 1979; Ivancevich, 1979).

Averaging reports of judges reduces error. Where the interjudge correlation is about 0.45, two *pairs* of independent judges will correlate 0.6, and in accord with the Spearman-Brown formula, averages of five judges correlate 0.8. The bias of one judge tends to cancel the bias of another, and each adds information the other had no opportunity to observe. It is not helpful, however, to add in a rater who is ill-informed.

Scale formats. The descriptive rating form, illustrated in Figure 15.1, is generally suitable for a routine collection of information. At each scale point a recognizable behavior pattern is described. In general, 5- to 7-point scales serve adequately.

The form shown in the figure has a "graphic" feature. The rater is allowed to mark at intermediate points if she does not find any one of the descriptions entirely suitable. Numbering the descriptions—so that decimals can represent intermediate ratings—is an alternative device.

Most course marks are essentially like ratings. Marks based on observation of the student's work or review of products may be improved by defining standards clearly. It can be advantageous to define separate aspects of good performance and prepare a rating scale for each one. A weighted combination of the scales provides an overall mark. The marks so generated often differ from the instructor's direct overall rating. Oaks *et al.* (1969) demonstrate this with data from a clinical course for medical students and discuss some of the errors that the piecemeal rating process overcomes.

The "behaviorally anchored rating scale" (BARS) pioneered by P. C. Smith and L. M. Kendall (1963) is well regarded for situations where raters are willing to give the attention it demands. The basic idea is derived from the critical incidents technique (p. 361); descriptions of acts are better media of communication than generalized phrases. Various formats have appeared. Sometimes incidents reflecting high, medium, or low degrees of a characteristic are spotted along a scale. The rater is asked to recall incidents of the

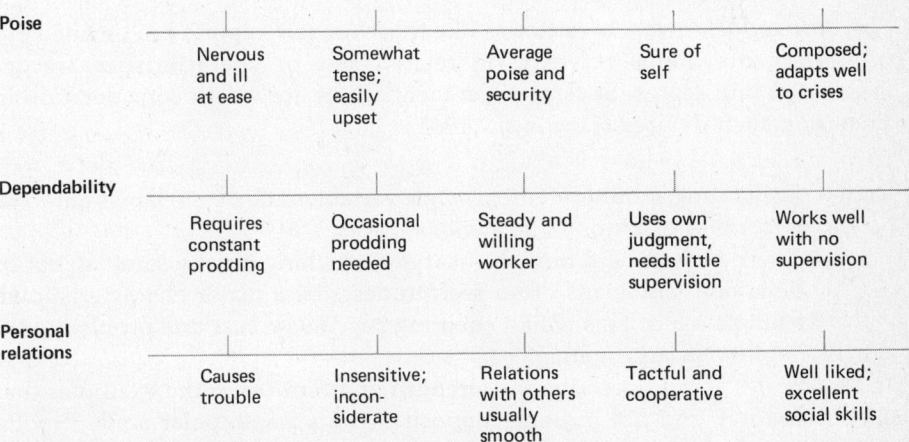

Figure 15.1. Descriptive graphic rating scales.
These scales for rating applicants or workers are adapted from the following sources: A General Foods Corporation form (National Industrial Conference Board, 1942), a Mutual Life Insurance Company of New York form (Marting, 1967), and a form from the National Retail Merchants Association (1968).

person's actual behavior and to pinpoint a scale position as most characteristic of him. An alternative technique is to ask how the person would be expected to act.

In the BARS scales illustrated in Figures 15.2 and 15.3, the rater is first to decide which of the three levels best represents her impression of the target and then to shade the meaning downward or upward, if necessary, to get a better fit. Thus, a rater who identifies a worker as superior (rating of 8) is told to shade that to 7 if she recalls occasions when the person has performed less well. The scale in Figure 15.2 was developed as part of the power-plant study discussed in Chapter 11; the agreement between two raters is represented by a correlation close to 0.4. The graphic format in Figure 15.3 assigns a precise point on the scale to each behavioral description. In development of such a scale, judges are asked to assign a scale value to each sentence. Sentences on whose placement judges agree are retained, spaced according to the average of the judgments. The rater is to think about the sentences, not the numerical equivalents. Stability coefficients over 4 months of pupil ratings in this format are near 0.75. Several scales can be combined as an overall evaluation of adjustment to school.

The BARS is troublesome to develop and use, and in comparative tests against other formats it does not consistently give better data. Borman (1979) calls it "seductively elegant." His evidence suggests that a simple numerical scale often works just as well but that each procedure is superior for some jobs and some traits. Bernardin and Smith (1981) argue that only a few varieties of BARS take advantage of some key virtues. In particular, they hope that raters in an institution who know that they will be called on to use such scales will form the habit of recording relevant incidents as these occur. Then the report comes from active observation, not dim memory.

Scorable report forms. Inventories like those for self-reports can be filled out by informants. Items referring to related acts or characteristics are accumulated into scores. Several recommendations are worth consideration in preparing such devices (Lorr *et al.*, 1963).

- Each rating should refer to a single variable. Too often, labels entangle two traits or kinds of behavior.
- There should be a number of items touching on the same aspect of behavior. Clinicians often seek to describe a major characteristic on a single scale. This is like equating success on just one problem with "ability in arithmetic."
- Scales should describe the strength of a trait (as in the examples that follow), and not present "opposite" traits as a bipolar scale. Bipolar descriptions are treacherous because logical opposites may not be psychological opposites; the opposite of "exhibitionism" could be self-effacement or indifference to attention.

MAINTAINING STANDARD OPERATIONS: MONITORING, INSPECTING, TESTING AND ADJUSTING EQUIPMENT

Inspects condition of equipment routinely, systematically, and thoroughly. Monitors equipment to confirm proper operating conditions and detects *valid* indicators of non-standard operating conditions. Recognizes situations likely to develop into problems and corrects conditions to prevent problems from occurring.

1 2 3	4 5 6	7 8 9
BELOW STANDARD	FULLY ADEQUATE	SUPERIOR
• Carries out standard inspections irregularly.	• Systematically follows all standard inspection and monitoring procedures.	• Alert at all times to indications of equipment condition and operations.
• Shows periods of inattention during monitoring.	• Shows good knowledge of most likely non-standard conditions.	• Shows unusual facility for detecting non-standard situations during routine inspections and continuing surveillance.
• Misses detection of nonstandard conditions.	• Shows good awareness of indicators of non-standard situations and what to do about them.	• Shows superior knowledge of what to do about non-standard conditions.
• Actions intended to bring operations back to standard are delayed or incorrect.		

Examples Illustrating BELOW STANDARD Maintenance of Standard Operations

- Operator fell asleep while monitoring a boiler feed pump. Unit tripped when operator did not hear low pressure and drum level alarms as load was increased.
- Operator did not make assigned round due to poor weather and did not detect vibration of deep well pump shaft bearing which had lost its oil seal. Shaft was bent and bearing destroyed.
- During start-up testing, operator silenced an oil alarm without noting its cause. A few hours later, the high head charging pump failed.

Examples Illustrating FULLY ADEQUATE Maintenance of Standard Operations

- On routine check, operator detected leaky weld on supply line to boiler feed pump and scheduled repair during low load demand period.
- Operator noted that water level showed no decrease in unit from which condensate make-up water was being transferred. Inspection showed level float had been hung. Transfer of water was stopped preventing loss of unit vacuum.
- Operator noted and corrected fan outlet temperature which had drifted to 275°F on unit designed to carry 265°F.

Examples Illustrating SUPERIOR Maintenance of Standard Operations

- Although not a part of regular inspection, operator opened a tell-tale valve and discovered water in main turbine oil tank (due to a tube leak in one of turbine lube oil coolers). He switched to alternate oil cooler, drained the water, and set up centrifuge on contaminated tank.
- Operator investigated a slight noise by opening access doors to boiler and discovered a superheat leak which he then arranged to have repaired.
- Operator noticed that a truck presumably delivering nitrogen scheduled for unloading had a flammable sticker on it. Upon checking, truck was found to be carrying hydrogen instead.

Figure 15.2. An employee-rating scale anchored in behavior.
Source: From Job Performance Appraisal Booklet for Power Plant Operators. Copyright © 1980 by Edison Electric Institute and reproduced by permission, with some modification.

This pupil is easily distracted.

―3.00―

These pupils generally have considerable difficulty disregarding even the slightest distraction in carrying out assigned tasks.

―2.75―

←This pupil flits from one thing to another. This pupil usually looks around a lot while
―2.50― ←working and has trouble concentrating on one project at a time.

―2.25― ←This pupil often talks or looks at children nearby.

―2.00―

←This pupil is easily distracted by friends and likes to distract others but will do the assigned work.

These pupils can ignore most classroom disturbances and concentrate on assigned work or activities.

―1.75―

←This pupil must be reminded occasionally to
―1.50― pay attention and to do the assigned work.

←This pupil usually pays attention but will be
―1.25― distracted if something unusual happens.

―1.00―

These pupils continue to persevere at assigned work or activities even with the most distracting situation.

―0.75― ←This pupil chooses to sit alone so as not to be distracted.

―0.50―

←This pupil wastes little time even with many distractions.
←This pupil can spend a whole hour
―0.25― concentrating.

―0.00―

Figure 15.3. A pupil-rating scale anchored in behavior.
Source: From Pupil Behavior Rating Scale by N. M. Lambert, C. S. Hartsough, and E. M. Bower. Reproduced by permission of the publisher, CTB/McGraw-Hill, Del Monte Research Park, Monterey CA 93940. Copyright © 1979 by McGraw-Hill, Inc. All Rights Reserved. Printed in the U. S. A.

- Items should be as free as possible of theoretical preconceptions. One should avoid words such as *regression, mannerisms,* and *acting out,* sticking to everyday language.
- The span of the scale should not extend beyond the range of cases. On each item, some persons should receive ratings at the highest and lowest extremes.

This last recommendation is made because extreme statements that are never checked take up space and time. However, they can play a special role as buffers. In collecting student opinions for purposes of improving college instruction, my associates and I wanted each student's response to a standard list of positive and negative comments. On the page of critical remarks that might apply to a course, we offered these response options:

YES, A SERIOUS FAULT   YES, A MINOR FAULT   NOT TRUE OF THIS COURSE.

The "serious" response was almost never given, but its presence enabled students to express discontent at the next level without seeming to condemn the instructor as a simple YES would. Likewise, for positive comments, the following scale worked well:

YES!   YES   NOT MUCH   NOT AT ALL.

Instructors worried a bit about statements that drew YES rather than YES! responses.

The Inpatient Multidimensional Rating Scale (M. Lorr and C. J. Klett; *CPP*) records the psychiatric interviewer's impressions. Each of the 75 items belongs to one of ten subsets, for example, Excitement, Hostile Belligerence, Paranoid Projection, Grandiose Expansiveness. The interviewer records her impressions from the interview, ignoring other data in the record, in response to questions such as

COMPARED TO THE NORMAL PERSON TO WHAT DEGREE DOES HE . . .
7. Express or exhibit feeling and emotions openly, impulsively, or without apparent restraint or control?
   Cues: Shows temper outbursts; weeps . . .
9. Manifest speech that is hurried, accelerated, or pushed?
40. Try to dominate, control, or direct the conduct of the interview?
   Cues: Number of times he interrupts, . . .

These items all count in the Excitement score. Responses are made on a 9-point scale:

NOT AT ALL   VERY SLIGHTLY   A LITTLE   . . .   MARKEDLY   EXTREMELY

The excitement items are scattered among items on other qualities, so that the rater is not conscious of the summary dimension. Although the use of multiple items has a clear advantage, one must not increase the rater's task to the point where she responds hastily or fails to return the rating form.

The authors' studies indicate that persons observing the same interview agree well ($r = 0.9$ for Excitement). Also, internal-consistency analysis is favorable; the coefficient for Excitement is 0.9—remarkable for a 9-item scale. What is lacking is evidence of consistency over interviews during a period of time and of stability (in the absence of radical treatment).

Q sorts. Interviewers and observers arrive at complex impressions of a person. Much of this information is lost if one collects only a few numerical ratings. A written description often includes vague remarks applicable to almost anyone and fails to touch on some important characteristics. Moreover, descriptions in essay form are hard to compare.

The Q sort is an excellent way to capture such impressions (Stephenson, 1953; Block, 1961). A standard set of phrases cover the aspects of personality or performance important to those who will use the report. The statements are written on separate cards. The California Q-Sort Deck and the California Child Q-Set *(CPP)* are standard sets for use in research on persons in the normal range. The adult cards can be used to obtain self-reports; the sensitivity of the technique makes it especially useful in studying short-term changes.

The informant is directed to sort the cards into, say, 9 piles, distributing the 100 statements in this manner:

	Most Descriptive							*Least Descriptive*	
Pile	1	2	3	4	5	6	7	8	9
Number of cards	5	8	12	16	18	16	12	8	5

The number of statements, piles, and sorting rules may, of course, be different from this. Standardizing the shape of distribution makes the report on one item dependent on the response made to other items. Experience has shown that the forcing does no great harm. Evaluative items should be few in number because a multidimensional description is wanted.

The sorting procedure has the advantage that the sorter can shift items back and forth as she proceeds. The boundaries of a category such as DEFINITELY TRUE may shift while one is working down a list, but in a Q sort we may expect the items in the same final pile to be equally descriptive of the person as the rater sees him.

Once finished, the sort may be examined impressionistically or processed formally. The median position (pile number) of relevant statements provides a score for anxiety or dominance or the like. Another approach is to treat the item placements as a column of scores and correlate one description with another. Thus, a correlation could describe the similarity of a particular wife and husband, or of the wife's self-description with the husband's description of her. This and other elaborate analyses of Q sorts can distort the data (Cronbach & Gleser, 1954; Cronbach, 1958).

Table 15.2 illustrates research with the Q sort. Women outstanding in mathematical research were interviewed and tested by psychologists who recorded their impressions. Independently, qualified mathematicians indicated the degree to which these women were original and creative (not merely competent and productive). Each Q statement was correlated with this criterion. The correlations in Table 15.2 are remarkably large, especially for single items given to a select sample. A special Q sort was used to obtain a self-description of work style. These items (among others) were rated as self-descriptive by the creative group:

> Subordinates other things to research goals.
> Is thorough and patient in approach to research issues.
> Solution to a problem often comes from an unexpected direction.

The self-characterization of the less creative group included these items:

> Enjoys instructing and working with students.
> Grasps other people's ideas quickly.
> Desire for a salary increase is an important motivating factor.
> Has an active, efficient, well-organized mind.

Criterion keying. A combination of forced choice with criterion keying has sometimes been applied when purely evaluative ratings of personnel are sought. Judgments by superiors divide a tryout sample into excellent and unsatisfactory groups. A checklist of descriptive phrases is then marked by

Table 15.2. *Characteristics associated with creativity in women mathematicians*

Correlation with criterion	Q-sort statement
+0.6	Thinks and associates ideas in unusual ways; has unconventional thought processes.
+0.55	Is an interesting, arresting person.
+0.5	Tends to be rebellious and non-conforming.
+0.5	Genuinely values intellectual and cognitive matters.
+0.4	Is self-dramatizing; histrionic.
	. . .
−0.4	Is moralistic.
−0.4	Favors conservative values in a variety of areas.
−0.4	Behaves in a sympathetic or considerate manner.
−0.45	Is a genuinely dependable and responsible person.
−0.6	Judges self and others in conventional terms like "popularity," "the correct thing to do," social pressures, etc.

SOURCE: Helson, 1971.

an acquaintance of the person. Phrases applied more often to the superior group than to the others are considered relevant. After all phrases have been rated on social desirability, pairs are made up; a criterion-related statement is paired with an equally favorable statement that did not correlate with the criterion. Thus "Wins confidence of co-workers" might be paired with "Punctual in completing reports." In one operational use of the scale, a superior is instructed to pick whichever phrase best describes her subordinate. The number of criterion-relevant phrases marked is the score. Sets of four phrases may be used instead of pairs (e.g., King et al., 1980).

Because the supervisor does not know the scoring key, her opportunity to give too favorable a report is greatly reduced. The possibly greater validity of the ratings is offset by the resistance of informants. They resent being asked to supply information whose implications they cannot foresee. Moreover, ratings in organizations usually should be fed back, to encourage self-improvement; concealed scoring rules make feedback useless (P. C. Smith, in Dunnette, 1976, p. 761).

5. *Describe a suitable rating technique for each of these purposes.*
   a. *Obtaining ratings from principals to be used in deciding which teachers should receive salary increases for special merit.*
   b. *Obtaining information for school records regarding parents' impressions of their children's personalities.*
   c. *Maintaining weekly records of ward behavior of patients as seen by attendants.*
   d. *Obtaining reports from supervisors of student teachers, to be used by campus instructors in helping the student to improve.*
6. *To what extent does the information in the California Q-set appear to go beyond the good–active–strong scheme?*

COLLECTING INFORMATION FROM ACQUAINTANCES AND ASSOCIATES

How members of a family or working group perceive each other and how students perceive their teachers can provide important data for social psychology and can be practically important. The informants cannot be given training like that given raters who will supply information repeatedly. And their communications may say as much about the rater as the ratee.

Mothers' Reports on Children

The "adaptive behavior" questionnaires discussed in Chapter 8 obtain information from parents of children who encounter difficulty in schools. Among procedures that develop more elaborate descriptions are the Child Behavior

Checklist (CBCL) and the Personality Inventory for Children (PIC). The former adopts conservative psychometric techniques—the questions are face valid and interpretations stick close to the data. The data are organized into homogeneous keys intended to facilitate classification of problem children. The second relies primarily on criterion keying to produce scores on a miscellaneous array of variables.

The Child Behavior Checklist. The CBCL is still undergoing development; the items appear in Achenbach and Edelbrock (1981), but full materials and a manual are available only from one of the authors. Three companion instruments have essentially similar content, one for obtaining the parent's report, one for eliciting reports from teachers, and one for tallying what is seen during scheduled observations. Most items ask whether during the previous 6 months the child showed a particular kind of behavior often, sometimes, or never. The wording is kept simple, and the four-page form can be filled out quickly. The same questions are used for ages 4 to 14, but the profile is based on within-sex norms for an age band (4–5, 6–11, 12–16). All items describe problems or difficulties, and therefore the median score for any category is likely to be low.

CBCL is essentially a multidimensional screening instrument, intended to detect markedly deviant behavior of any kind. As is appropriate, score distributions are severely skewed. In the Aggressive category, the maximum score is 44, but the score of the median boy is only 3. For a child below about the 70th percentile in a category, the precise magnitude of the score is unimportant; the report places him in the average-to-excellent range. The instrument spreads out those children for whom the mother reports more than the usual number of problems.

Table 15.3 illustrates the hierarchical system used in the profile. The authors hope that grouping profiles into types will enable clinicians and research workers in various places to describe children in standard terms so that their experience can be compared (Edelbrock & Achenbach, 1980). They have proposed formulas that sort, for example, most boys aged 6 to 11 among these categories:

Schizoid—Social withdrawal
Depressed—Social withdrawal—Aggressive
Schizoid
Somatic complaints
Hyperactive
Delinquent

It must be remembered that the analysis is based on a mother's report and so reflects her relations with the child and her sense of the level of behavior that can properly be described as "too neat," "loud," and so on. This is one reason for collecting information by several methods. The authors' report

Table 15.3. *Hierarchical mapping of problem behavior in children*

Broad factors	Scales within factors	Items Within Scales (Illustrative)
Internalizing	Schizoid	Auditory hallucinations Fears school
	Depressed	Feels worthless Needs to be perfect
	Uncommunicative	Secretive Shy, timid
	Obsessive-Compulsive	Strange ideas Can't sleep
	Somatic complaints	Stomach problems Headaches
(Mixed)	Social withdrawal	Unliked Likes to be alone
Externalizing	Hyperactive	Can't concentrate Acts too young
	Aggressive	Argues Cruel to others
	Delinquent	Steals outside home Vandalism

SOURCE: Based on data for boys aged 6 to 11 in Achenbach, 1978. Patterning varies slightly across age and sex groups (Achenbach & Edelbrock, 1979). Wording of actual items is less terse than in this compilation.

rather satisfactory stability of reports over time, and agreement of father and mother.

The main use of the instrument, when its interpretation has been worked out, will be to suggest how a particular child should be handled—at home, at school, or in a treatment center. Having established a standardized sorting system is the first step in a long research program. It will be necessary to amass case histories of children of each type who have been handled differently; from these, warranted policies for interpretation can be derived.

The Personality Inventory for Children (PIC). A unique inventory has been constructed to capture impressions of a child from the mother (or other informant) in scorable form. The scores form a profile as ambitious as that for the MMPI, accompanied, if desired, by a page of descriptive and evaluative prose from the computer. The PIC (R. D. Wirt, D. Lachar, J. K. Klinedinst, and P. D. Seat; *WPS*) was developed over a 20-year period by investigators at the University of Minnesota with an adaptation of the original MMPI techniques. The 600 (!) behavioral descriptions are combined into nearly three dozen (!) scales, of three kinds: control, actuarial, and content. Three short forms of PIC are available; each includes a fraction of the items and yields a less elaborate report.

The control scales alert the psychologist to any extreme response bias (e.g., the mother's wish to present the child in a glowing light).

Criterion keying produced the following scales among others:

- Adjustment *(Adj)*. Counts responses given especially often by mothers describing emotionally disturbed boys. (For this and other scales, only one keying procedure is described here; often, successive steps were taken. It is notable that *Adj* is normed on girls—separately from boys—but was not keyed on a female criterion group.)
- Achievement *(Ach)*. Counts items marked—more often than by other mothers—by mothers of second- and third-graders classed as "learning disabled" (and not "retarded").
- Intellectual Screening *(IS)*. Similar, but based on retarded children. A *single* standard-score conversion is provided (within each sex) for all ages 6 to 16. Norms for ages 3 to 5 are provided also, with a cautionary message. (Other scales offer similar conversions.)
- Delinquency *(Dlq)*. Responses used by mothers to characterize adolescents (most of them boys) who had been judged delinquent by a legal process. It is specifically noted that the score is a sign of "concurrent" delinquency.
- Ego Strength *(ES)*. The criterion group consisted of elementary school children described by teachers as good–active–sociable.
- Delinquency Prediction *(DP)*. The criterion group consisted of 191 boys tested at ages 10 to 12 and later split to distinguish the 30 who had police or traffic records from the remainder.

"Content" scales were generated chiefly by having professional judges pick out items on a certain theme, then discarding any that did not show reasonable consistency with that set as a whole. Scales are not homogeneous in the usual sense. Thus, one scale Development *(Dvl)* consists of items that judges picked as indicating poor intellectual or physical development (again, apparently making no differentiation with respect to age or sex). Here are three responses keyed in this scale:[1]

My child can [not] cut things with scissors as well as others of his (her) age.
My child has no special talents.
My child could [not] print his (her) first name by age six years.

The inserted "[not]" indicates that the response FALSE to the original item is counted. Again, one set of norms, within sex, for the wide age range. By way of illustration, a few other content scales are named: Depression, Anxiety, Family Relations (i.e., cohesion), and Social Skills.

A fair verdict on this instrument will require research reports beyond those in the manual and interpretative guide. The manual is honest and informative but sketchy. The amount of research done to date is miniscule

---
[1] Reproduced by permission of Western Psychological Services.

compared to the amount for the MMPI and for the CPI in the same tradition. Most obviously, for example, the *IS* scale should be validated by reporting the range of mental-test scores found at each *IS* score level at particular ages. Not only is the information given on the relation of *IS* to measured ability extremely superficial, but it comes from the keying sample, not from a cross-validation. Typically, keying samples are too small to be trusted (65 cases in this instance). The MMPI itself was, of course, based on similarly incomplete research and owes its reputation to accumulated experience. I conclude that PIC should have been released for research use only.

Users are encouraged to think of the instrument as measuring the child. In fact, it is summarizing the mother's perception of the child or, more precisely, the perception the mother wants the clinician to *think* she has. How family members perceive each other has been a fruitful field of research just because it is found that perceptions do not coincide with facts. The information can be of value to the clinician *if* given a phenomenological interpretation.

7. *Chapter 13 discussed many distorting factors that make the responses to a self-report inventory untrustworthy as a description of typical behavior. Which of those factors might influence a mother's response to CBCL when her child has been referred for the attention of a mental-health treatment center?*
8. *What conclusions are suggested by the following facts from 55 "normal" cases (sexes mixed, 6-year age range)?*

	Adj	Ach	Dvl	DP
Correlation of scores based on responses of father and mother	0.57	0.68	0.59	0.43
Correlation of scores based on two testings of mother (2-week interval)	0.93	0.90	0.93	0.86

9. *An advertising leaflet for PIC and its computer interpretation carries this headline: "Provides objective measures of General adjustment, Cognitive Development, Academic achievement, Emotional adjustment, Behavioral dimensions, Family function." What changes can you suggest to reduce possible misconceptions?*
10. *Criterion keys depend heavily on the adequacy of the keying sample. Can you judge the adequacy of the PIC criterion keys from what has been said here about the samples? If not, what further information would help you?*

Peer Ratings

To obtain "peer ratings" or "sociometric ratings," group members are asked to rate each other. Peers can report not only on social attributes but on any readily observed aspect of style. Black's study (p. 485) in which students rated others living in the same dormitory is one example. Whereas only one or two teachers know a student well, 10 to 30 raters give reports in a class or dormitory. As a consequence, each average rating is highly reliable. Moreover, the informants are knowledgeable and are accustomed to judging peers (Lindzey & Byrne, 1968). The same is to be said of adults who work together.

Social acceptance is a major influence on happiness and mental health. Popularity is about as stable from one year to the next as is intellectual achievement, which adds to its significance. Peers and superiors have different perceptions. A child who impresses his peers as being a leader may not be so regarded by the teacher; the peers, for example, may consider amiability whereas the teacher notices energy and initiative. The two reports gain in meaning when considered together. It is, for example, the student rated unfavorably by *both* teachers and peers who is most likely to drop out of school (Barclay, 1966).

The peer rating is an objective statement about reputation. Reputation is based to some extent on behavior, but social relationships color what the peer observers notice. Among adolescents, correlations of reputations with observations of corresponding behavior vary with the trait (0.45 to 0.7 in the study of Newman & Jones, 1946). One might suspect that fortuitous events shape reputation. But leadership ratings by fellow soldiers in one squad correlated 0.8 with ratings given to the same persons after all had been shuffled into new squads and new barracks and had worked with their new companions for 4 weeks (L. V. Gordon & F. F. Medland, 1965). This compares well with the correlation of 0.9 between ratings 4 weeks apart in squads kept intact.

We desire each peer rater to describe many individuals. An adjective checklist such as Black used can be marked quickly, can cover many aspects of behavior, and is scorable.

Nomination techniques. An alternative is to ask for nominations. Each member of the group is asked to name persons outstanding in a particular respect, such as leadership. This reduces the respondent's labor without much loss of significant information. Names of persons lacking in leadership may also be solicited, but this arouses anxiety. Subjects know that they are being considered for unfavorable nominations, and, as raters, they are reluctant to speak unfavorably of associates. In general, anyone collecting peer ratings ought to think through the legitimacy of the undertaking and ought to avoid deception.

An important distinction is to be made between unsigned and signed responses. Signed responses (more intrusive) offer information on group structure (Gronlund, 1981, Chap. 17; Lindzey & Byrne, 1968). Practitioners have used such information to form congenial work groups and living units and to study (and reduce) ethnic cleavage in a student body. Affiliations within the peer group are significant also in research on the development of motivation, values, and group morale.

Peer reports are among the most valid predictors of work criteria (Kane

& Lawler, 1978). Among officer candidates, peer reports correlate about 0.5 with ratings by superiors in later duty assignments—extremely impressive when the criterion reliability is about 0.5. The traits that predict criteria tend to be in the good–strong–active sector, but "agreeableness" and "sociability" do not predict (Kraut, 1975; Tupes, 1957). Peer judgments of colonels predict who will become generals, and ratings of management trainees forecast promotion within a corporation (R. G. Downey *et al.,* 1976; Harrell, 1972; Roadman, 1964). Moreover, patients in a ward can predict which of them will be rehospitalized as well as the professional staff can (Lasky *et al.,* 1959).

A variant of the nomination technique was worked out by Hartshorne and May (1929), who wished to compare children's reputations for honesty with their response to experimental temptations (p. 542). Their "Guess Who" format survives today in research on social acceptance (e.g., of retarded children who are mainstreamed). It is sometimes used in screening school populations for children whose maladjustment might otherwise be overlooked. The Process for Assessment of Effective Student Functioning (N. M. Lambert, C. S. Hartsough, and E. M. Bower; *CTB*) uses in combination a teacher rating (Fig. 15.3), self-rating, and peer rating. In grades 3 to 7, the peer-report form is The School Play (by Lambert and Bower). Eleven roles such as these are described:

Someone who is liked by everybody and who tries to help everybody.
A bully—someone who picks on smaller boys and girls.

The respondent is to name the class member who could best play the part. A procedure of this type can be successfully used by a teacher who is on comfortable terms with her class.

The argument for using such an intrusive instrument in mass screening is not persuasive. The validity study (Lambert, 1963) had as criterion an excellent clinical evaluation of adjustment, but reports inappropriate statistics. (Conventional correlations are unsuitable for counts of nominations because the distributions are highly skewed—like Test B of Figure 6.2 but more extreme.) The criterion was predicted (around 0.5; good enough for screening) by the summary of *teacher* responses on several scales like Figure 15.3. Maladjusted girls in grade 5 tended to receive few mentions from peers; maladjusted boys in grades 2 and 5 tended to pick up negative mentions; neither score related to the criterion among second-grade girls. It appears that no formal rule applied to the peer information improves the hit rate appreciably.

11. *Surgency (i.e., energetic, talkative, enthusiastic behavior) correlates very little with leadership behavior as rated by observers, but correlates substantially with frequency of election as leader. Explain this finding. What does it imply regarding the use of peer ratings as criteria?*
12. *When sociograms were made of squadrons of fliers on combat duty, it was found that the "administratively designated leaders" were often not the*

ones named as preferred work leaders by the men (G. Kelly, 1947, p. 133). What practical suggestions follow from this finding?
13. Love (1981) obtained peer judgments of police officers in three forms: ranking, nomination, and rating scale (BARS). The rating technique was less reliable (over sets of raters) and less correlated with supervisors' ratings and rankings. Suggest an explanation.

PARTICIPANTS' REPORTS ON SETTINGS

When trying to understand why a certain type of student persists in one college and tends to drop out of another, one wants to know how the colleges differ and, more particularly, how students *think* they differ. To investigate successful and unsuccessful teachers, one wants to know how they differ in their style and emphasis. One could send a trained observer, but it is easier to have the students or other participants record their impressions.

The usual report form is a descriptive questionnaire rather like the personality questionnaire in format. A count of TRUE responses for any item, over the sample of participants, gives a reliable report. Instruments have been prepared for several levels of schooling, for hospital wards, for work settings, and so on; a published series is the Social Climate Scales (R. H. Moos and others; *CPP*).

In a conventional test, every subject confronts the same items. Matrix sampling is often used, however, in collecting data on groups. A basic item pool is divided at random into several subsets, and each subject fills out one of these short test forms. Thus, 200 questions on college environment can be divided into 5 subsets, and each subject answers 40 questions. This saves time without serious loss in the quality of information about the situation. A far larger variety of items can be administered in a given time; hence the data are richer.

Moos (1979) finds subscales of roughly the same character applicable in the several settings:

Relationship (involvement, affiliation or cohesion, support)
Personal growth (competition or pressure, autonomy, cultural orientation, etc.)
System maintenance and change (order, clarity, innovation)

Insofar as a theory has developed around instruments of this type, it is that the personality can be described in terms of "needs"—for change, achievement, affiliation, and so on—and the situation can be described in terms of "presses" to behave in certain ways. A "press" might include formal demands from the figures in authority, subtle demands contained in the expectations of the student group, and opportunities to receive reward and attention for acts of a certain kind.

Like peer ratings and self-reports, the reports on climate are reports of perceptions rather than strictly factual reports on events. This is illustrated in Figure 15.4, based on the description of the same class by the students and the teacher (averaged over 295 classes; each scale has a range from 0 to 10). It is not too surprising that the teacher speaks a bit more favorably than the students, but there is an important message for the teacher when his perception of his clarity and emotional support so conspicuously departs from that of the students. For the same reason, Moos suggests that the counselor of adolescents and adults may find it useful to collect impressions of the home climate from each family member along with their description, on the same inventory, of the ideal home climate.

14. *Student behavior (e.g., absenteeism) and accomplishment correlates, across classrooms, with the description the classes gave of the classroom climate (Moos, 1979). Evaluate the plausibility of the following hypotheses.*
   a. *When a class is doing well, this produces desirable behavior and a favorable report on the climate.*
   b. *Certain kinds of climate stimulate cooperation and effective work.*

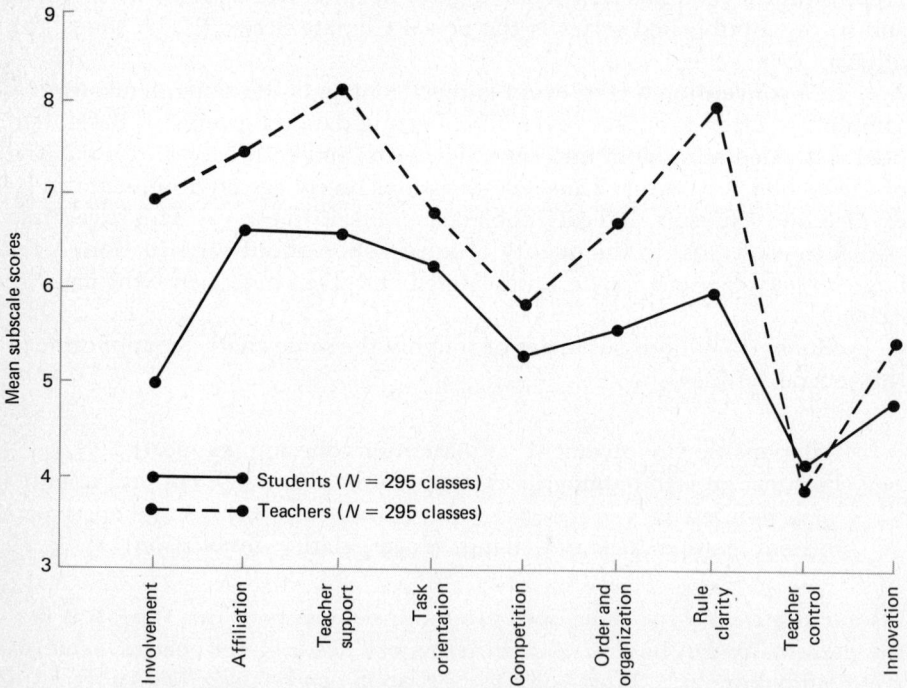

Figure 15.4. How students and teachers perceive classrooms. *Source: Moos, 1979, p. 148.*

15. *Evaluators seek to determine whether it is beneficial to use parents as volunteer aides in fourth-grade classrooms with many minority students. Explain how climate descriptions could provide one measure of the success of the change. Also, could climate descriptions clarify why the change improves learning in some classrooms and not others?*
16. *For which of these applications would you expect inventories collecting impressions of participants to be reasonably valid?*
    a. *To examine whether students from minority groups perceive the social environment of an integrated college as students of majority background do.*
    b. *To determine which prisoners have adjusted adequately to the social environment of a corrective institution.*
    c. *To collect information for a top-level administrative review of the correctional institutions of a state system.*
    d. *To distinguish elementary schools that use formal and informal methods, in a study intended to assess educational outcomes under each approach.*
17. *Figure 15.4 plots average raw scores. The manual for the scale provides norms for students and teachers, essentially consistent with the facts in Figure 15.4. Should the profile for responses of a single class and its teacher be plotted in terms of raw ratings or standard scores?*

OBSERVATION OF BEHAVIOR

The Situational Context

Reports of subjects and informants are haphazard composites. The rater did not see the individual in all situations, and selective recall operates. Systematic observations in an ecologically representative sample of times and places can come closer to typical behavior.

Comparison is inexact because one does not observe two individuals in the same situation. Even when the situation is externally constant, previous conditions affect behavior. When Jimmy fidgets more than John in the classroom, one could infer that Jimmy is "restless," "nervous," or "jumpy." If the impression is confirmed on other observations, this difference seems fundamental. But if Jimmy usually comes to school without breakfast, if he expects to be criticized by the teacher for poor work, or if he is large for the chairs provided, the difference in activity may tell nothing about restlessness per se. In fact, if conditions were reversed, Johnny might be more restless than Jimmy is now. Observations show how people typically act under their present conditions.

Some records of behavior can be nearly complete. Production of individual workers may be recorded routinely (Rothe, 1978). A mechanical device on a commercial airplane records its motion together with conversations in the cockpit. Some investigators have persuaded subjects to wear microphones and transmitters that allow all their conversations to be recorded (except when the subject throws a switch for privacy). Weight watchers may keep a diary in which they record what they eat, when, and under what circumstances. To cut back the volume of information, one has three options. Attention can focus on "significant" incidents identified by a quick scan of the record (or, in the case of the flight recorder, by external evidence that an episode was unusual). Representative samples can be extracted for coding and tabulation, or a simple numerical summary (number of eating incidents per week) can be taken off.

Ordinarily, one wants observations under conditions typical of the person. The fact that observations are being made may or may not make the situation and response atypical. The production record and the flight record are parts of the natural environment. Students are quick to accept observers in the classroom or in the schoolyard and can be expected to go about their affairs normally unless the observer conspicuously takes notes on them. What has gone onto White House tapes illustrates that a person can become habituated to a recording procedure to the point where it does not constrain him or her. The weight watcher is a different case entirely; although the diary provides data, its main function is to heighten self-consciousness and influence eating behavior. In intermediate cases—teachers, counselors, or ward attendants—it is reasonable to expect a tendency to "put on a good show." Some brief studies comparing observations made with and without the targets' awareness are summarized by Kent and Foster (in Ciminero *et al.*, 1977).

The Schedule for Sampling

The number of occasions on which the target is observed and the representativeness is critical. Responses vary because the situation changes in subtle respects and because people are inconsistent. Extreme variation in performance is illustrated by a study of navigators. The student on a mission was to compute his air speed by dead reckoning on each leg of a flight. The accuracy score had a split-half reliability of 0.77; this is an indication of leg-to-leg consistency under unchanging conditions with the same plane and so on. A day-to-day correlation was also computed; it was 0.00! (Carter & Dudek, 1947). Scores were determined almost entirely by transient conditions (e.g., wind) rather than by the individual's ability.

Despite the exceptional instances of zero and even negative correlations between observations of the same trait, an adequate sample is often meaningful. Observing on many days in many circumstances gives a score that will agree with a score collected on another series of days. Systematic scheduling improves representativeness. To study social contacts of preschool children, for example, a schedule may be drawn up. The observer watches a child for 1 minute, noting social interactions and checking a form to record what occurred. Children are watched in a predetermined order, different from day to day. Each child is observed an equal number of times during the first 5 minutes of the free-play hour, during the second 5 minutes on another day, and so on. The cumulative picture is likely to be far more typical than an equal amount of evidence obtained in a few longer observations. Moreover, errors of memory are few when the observer can make full notes during or just after observing. Observers are usually asked to record salient facts about the situation as well as the actions of the target, so that similar situations can be grouped for analysis.

Other controls are used when observing is incidental to other activities, for example, in tracking the behavior of persons undergoing behavior modification. Time sampling may be accomplished by having the person carry a signal device that goes off at irregular intervals, at which time she records that she has or has not just been engaged in the target behavior (nail-biting, for example) and what the circumstances are. Note that this is more constructive than asking the person to record each incident of nail-biting. Unscheduled recording is inaccurate and loses the opportunity to encourage the person by noting the number of times when she is not biting her nails. (One timing device is the spring-driven parking-meter reminder; each time it goes off and a record is made, the subject can ask an acquaintance to reset it for an arbitrary time lapse.)

Time samples are especially suitable for facts that can be expressed numerically (e.g., number of social contacts), but the data can also sustain judgmental interpretations. Observer-to-observer correlations, following extended sampling of children's behavior in a day camp, were near 0.9 for the following attributes, among others: instigation of physical aggression, parallel play with peers, withdrawal from the social environment, affection-seeking, attempts to master gross motor tasks (Crandall, 1966).

Applying generalizability theory. The larger the sample, the better. The theory of Chapter 6 applies: When single observations correlate only 0.1, observations in 10 situations ought to correlate 0.5 with a second set of 10 observations; 30 observations bring the correlation to 0.75. Short observations are generally advisable. Five-minute observations on each of 6 children—repeated on 12 days—use the observer's time much better than observing each child for 30 consecutive minutes on each of 2 days. A generalizability study indicates how many observations are desirable for a given purpose.

Having two or more observers look at the same target on different occasions irons out biases, but the behavior sample is narrowed if they make their records at the same time. Simultaneous observation makes sense for training observers and for getting evidence of their agreement. When error is disturbingly large, the investigator has several options. One is to sample more thoroughly—more occasions or more observers or both. Another is to reduce observer error by giving clearer instructions and more training. If scores depend heavily on the situation, breaking the domain into subdomains and sampling from each is appropriate.

Several sources of variation cause a recorded score to depart from the universe score that exhaustive observation would give. Generalizability studies play an important role in pilot work. They can assess the magnitude of multiple sources of error and so suggest how to adjust the observing schedule (Cronbach *et al.*, 1972).

A suitably simple example comes from observations of the eating behavior of adolescents (Coates & Thoresen, 1978). The counselor was trying to modify behavior that contributed to obesity; the observations provided baseline data and checked on effectiveness. It was recognized that behavior might vary from day to day, that systematic differences among observers might occur, and that some "residual" unsystematic variation was inevitable. For a G study, two observers collected data together, observing each counselee several times and making their records independently. Chiefly, they watched the client at the family dinner table.

One variable was the number of helpings the youngster took. The information from the G study is best reported in the form of variances. (I remind you that a variance is a squared s.d.; variances can be added to describe the cumulative effect of several sources.) For number of helpings, these are the key variances:

Client variation over occasions	0.00
Observer constant error	0.00
Observer-client interaction	0.00
Residual	3.5

The zeroes tell important stories. The adolescents were highly consistent from day to day; they either did or did not take seconds. Observers did not vary systematically either in the average score over all clients or in the average they would assign any one person in the long run. The residual suggests some wild random errors, however, as if one observer were recording three helpings when her companion was recording one. Faced with such a strange result, I would first check the arithmetic! Then I would look for possible causes. Maybe record sheets were illegible. Debriefing the observers shortly after they turned in discrepant reports would perhaps pinpoint the trouble. If the random disagreements continue, the only salvation is to average many observations. (As a matter of fact, the universe-score variance (between subjects) was only 0.2; these adolescents were nearly uniform, and there was little point in recording helpings.)

Time spent in eating produced these variances:

Clients	Occasions	Observers	Client-observer interaction	Residual
7.7	4.2	0.0	0.0	2.5

The observer and interaction variances of zero say that it doesn't matter which observer collects these data. Being able to regard observers as interchangeable makes it far easier to schedule data collection. The adolescents differed considerably in eating time. The residual error (haphazard variation of observers) can be reduced either by averaging two or more observers on each occasion or by observing on more days. If typical behavior during (say) the baseline period is of interest, one ought to observe on several days, so as to average out occasion-to-occasion fluctuations.

Note that my interpretation did not look at a reliability (generalizability) coefficient. The purpose of measurement here was to study systematic changes in individuals, not individual differences.

18. *Why might an unfair picture of a child's behavior be obtained if he were always observed during the first 5 minutes of the play period and never during the second 5 minutes?*
19. *As a criterion in selection research, would it be better to test every flier with repeated landings on the same day or with a similar number of landings spread over several days?*
20. *A child performed each of several tasks while raters scored the mother's behavior on a scale of 1 to 9 (Leler, 1970; summarized in Cronbach et al., 1972). Here are some of the variances calculated:*

	Task-to-task	Rater-to-rater	S-rater interaction	Residual
M reasons with child	0.7	1.2	0.6	1.1
M discourages C's talking	1.1	0.2	1.0	1.6

Note: S refers to the mother-child pair.

What interpretations or recommendations can you suggest?

Observer Error and Its Reduction

An observer notices some happenings and ignores others. Especially in social situations, the complexity of events prevents exhaustive reporting. Observers overemphasize some types of events and fail to report others.

The following reports were written by observers after seeing a preschool scene of about 10 minutes' duration. The film was shown twice without sound. The observers were directed to note everything they could about one boy, Robert, and were told to use parentheses to set apart inferences or interpretations. Numbers in these accounts, referring to scenes in the film, have been inserted to aid comparison.

> *Observer A:* (2) Robert reads word by word, using finger to follow place. (4) Observes girl in box with much preoccupation. (5) During singing, he in general doesn't participate too actively. Interest is part of time centered elsewhere. Appears to respond most actively to

sections of song involving action. Has tendency for seemingly meaningless movement. Twitching of fingers, aimless thrusts with arms.

Observer B: (1) Looked at camera upon entering (seemed perplexed and interested). Smiled at camera. (2) Reads (with apparent interest and with a fair degree of facility). (3) Active in roughhouse play with girls. (4) Upon being kicked (unintentionally) by one girl he responded (angrily). (5) Talked with girl sitting next to him between singing periods. Participated in singing. (At times appeared enthusiastic.) Didn't always sing with others. (6) Participated in a dispute in a game with others (appeared to stand up for his own rights). Aggressive behavior toward another boy. Turned pockets inside out while talking to teacher and other students. (7) Put on overshoes without assistance. Climbed to top of ladder rungs. Tried to get rung which was occupied by a girl but since she didn't give in, contented himself with another place.

Observer C: (1) Smiles into camera (curious). When group breaks up, he makes nervous gestures, throws arm out into air. (2) Attention to reading lesson. Reads with serious look on his face, has to use line marker. (3) Chases girls, teases. (4) Girl kicks when he puts hand on her leg. Robert makes face at her. (5) Singing. Sits with mouth open, knocks knees together, scratches leg, puts fingers in mouth (seems to have several nervous habits, though not emotionally overwrought or self-conscious). (6) In a dispute over parchesi, he stands up for his rights. (7) Short dispute because he wants rung on jungle gym.

Observer D: (2) Uses guide to follow words, reads slowly, fairly forced and with careful formation of sounds (perhaps unsure of self and fearful of mistakes). (3) Perhaps slightly aggressive as evidenced by pushing younger child to side when moving from a position to another. Plays with other children with obvious enjoyment, smiles, runs, seems especially associated with girls. This is noticeable in games and in seating in singing. (5) Takes little interest in singing, fidgets, moves hands and legs (perhaps shy and nervous). Seems in song to be unfamiliar with words of main part, and shows disinterest by fidgeting and twisting around. Not until chorus is reached does he pick up interest. His especial friend seems to be a particular girl, as he is always seated by her.

To reduce errors, recording should be separated from judging, to the extent practicable. The cost and inconvenience of videotaping or other automatic recording is often warranted by the opportunity it affords for scoring by several viewers and for rescoring if, as an investigation proceeds, a new code is considered desirable.

Responses to which an observer applies the same trait label may have different meanings. Newcomb (1929) observed boys in a summer camp, making daily records of cooperation in after-meal work, fighting with other boys, persistence, and so on. When these day-to-day records were studied, most boys were found to be inconsistent. As Newcomb pointed out, situations are only superficially alike. Johnny is much more likely to fight a boy he thinks he can hold his own against than another boy who seems tougher. Johnny's activity, inconsistent from an observer's frame of reference, is highly consistent to Johnny. R. Sears (1963, p. 35) showed that a concept of "dependence" in preschool children loses sight of important specifics. When Sears separately scored actions such as staying near the adult, touching the adult, seeking reassurance, and so on, the correlations across frequencies of these kinds of supposedly dependent behavior ranged from -0.2 to 0.4. One kind of dependency does not imply another kind.

The human observer's field notes, then, should stick close to behavior. Observers are unlikely to diverge when reporting that the subject's response to a question is slow; and such a record, made at specific points, allows less opportunity for judgmental error than a record of the overall impression that responses were slow. Either report of slow response, however, is more reproducible than a report that the person is "hesitant" or "uncertain." Quasi-objective field notes, free of interpretation, can be stripped of labels and intermingled if a summary judgment is to be made; this takes advantage of the fact that it is easier to "blind" judges than observers. Longabaugh (in Triandis & Berry, 1980) describes many devices to standardize field records and to encode observations for tabulation.

No general recommendation can be made as to whether the field notes should be a free description or an attempt to code, act by act, what is going on. As with other procedures, structure focuses attention and makes sure that the same variables are examined for everyone, but it impoverishes the information. Where the information summary will be highly structured—a statistical summary perhaps—then the original record will ordinarily employ a predetermined code. The more narrowly the observer is allowed to concentrate, the more closely observers are likely to agree. But relevant information that does not fit the pigeonholes is lost.

Making sure that observers know what to look for is an obvious step. But, unless the observers are co-investigators who should be developing insight while in the field, they should be left largely ignorant of the hypotheses the observations are to check. Observers are subtly motivated to support the conclusions they believe the investigator expects. (Also, their data tend to conform to their own expectations; Wildman & Erickson, in Cone & Hawkins, 1977.) Insofar as possible, neither observers nor judges should know who is in this or that experimental group, who has received therapy and who has not, who comes from "a good home" or has been diagnosed as "hyperactive."

Objectivity has its virtues, but there is much to be said for seeing through the eyes of participants. One can play back a classroom recording to a teacher, for example, stopping it periodically for the teacher's interpretation of what was happening or what she was trying to do. Some of the statements may be defensive rationalizations, but they add a dimension to the data. Anthropologists have developed a variety of techniques for understanding a culture through the eyes of its members, working on the assumption that a social group gives meanings to behavior that an outsider is unlikely to perceive (W. Goodenough, in Triandis & Berry, 1980).

21. *What do you think really happened in scene 4 of the film? Which observer came closest to adequate reporting of it?*
22. *Which of the numbered scenes appears to give the most significant information about Robert? How many of the observers reported that information?*

16
Inferences from Performance

This final chapter surveys a range of techniques, from single-score measurement of narrow aspects of behavior to summary assessments that consider ability and personality as an indivisible whole. Basically, all the methods collect information by observing in a standardized situation, but in the more comprehensive assessments information from diverse sources is considered together.

A performance test is an observation of response to a standard task, usually one designed to provoke evidence on a specific characteristic—the control and expression of aggression, for example. This is hard to observe systematically in daily life because provoking situations occur at unpredictable moments. To measure proneness to aggression, two psychologists placed classes of boys, during their sports period, in an inadequate room; about half the boys could play at any one time. The experimental arrangement doubled the amount of aggression displayed, generating plenty of data (Winder & Wiggins, 1964). Another provocative tactic is to challenge the opinions the subject voices in a standard interview. Such stress techniques of course raise ethical questions.

Performance tests differ. The test may measure numerically one narrow construct such as persistence in routine work. It may yield scores on persistence and caution and tempo simultaneously. It may try to appraise the person's whole life-style. It may sample tasks from a prospective assignment, or the task may be highly artificial.

The tasks range from highly structured to almost totally unstructured. A situation is structured if it has for all subjects a definite meaning. An unstructured situation has so little pattern that it can be given almost any meaning. The strange sound in the night is unstructured. Is it the wind? A burglar? A cat? In a structured situation, the respondent knows what he is expected to do and how he is expected to do it. Well-structured tasks are excellent for measuring ability just because they set the same target for everyone.

In the unstructured situation, one must guide oneself. The more ambiguity, the more opportunity for the individual to set his own goal. Structure is minimal when, for example, the psychologist turns the test taker loose in a studio equipped with varied art media and materials, saying no more than, "You may do anything you like with these." Projective tasks provide little structure. The test taker is free to project unconscious thoughts, wishes, and fears into the situation. The householder who interprets the creak in the dark as a burglar may be more anxious than one who interprets the same stimulus as a natural phenomenon and goes back to sleep.

PSYCHOMETRIC MEASURES

Galton compared testing to the geologist's "sinking shafts at critical points." Ratings return surface impressions. The time sample sinks its shaft at random. The performance test bores in at supposedly critical points. Most performance tests in the psychometric tradition have many or all these features:

> *Standardization.* The stimulus situation is controlled, reproducible, applicable in a nearly uniform manner to everyone.
>
> *Specificity.* The investigator is interested in a sharply defined trait. The report refers to a narrower construct than the good–strong–active dimensions of self-ratings.
>
> *Quantification.* Performance is reduced to scores, the scoring rules locating everyone on the same scale or scales.
>
> *Disguise.* The test taker is led to believe that one characteristic is being tested when the observer is looking at another. For example, "Pick the funniest jokes in this collection." In research on the individual's sense of humor, this inquiry may be disguised as a study of the jokes. The score could be based on the type of joke the person picks (e.g., hostile), not on whether he picks the ones most people consider funny.
>
> *Attention to process.* The style of performance is given more attention than the amount or quality of response.

Standard settings for observation. The simplest procedures in this category are no more than standardized observations. In research on parent-child interaction and its effects, the observer visits the home. She records, as systematically as she chooses, such variables as amount of encouragement, how closely the child clings to the mother, and so on. The data are not comparable from home to home or occasion to occasion because the ongoing activities are not comparable. Standard situations promote comparability. A task may be taken into the home, introduced into the everyday setting of the preschool, or presented at an experimental center. Standardized procedures can collect essentially the same information in different cultures.

An international team set out to study whether certain child-rearing practices of Japanese and American mothers reflect the social status and other characteristics of the family and affect the child's readiness for school similarly. The team designed situations considered to fit both cultures and developed scoring rules that can be applied in either language.

When mother and child first come to the testing center, they are taken to the test room, where pegboard materials are laid out (and a remote-controlled video camera is mounted). "Let Tommy become accustomed to the room before the day's work begins," says the experimenter; the mother is encouraged to play with the child, using the games if she wishes. The experimenter then absents herself for 10 minutes. The trays with colored pegs and pegboard are open, and the lid showing the patterns (in four colors) is in plain view (Fig. 16.1). The mother can occupy herself or interact, can lead the child or leave him free. Sound tapes are made and later transcribed for rating by as many raters as needed to obtain reliability. Additional ratings are made from the videotape.

The second procedure was structured by the requirement that the mother was to teach the child. With the child absent, the experimenter taught the mother a sorting game. From a kind of (oral) programmed instruction, the mother was to infer, demonstrate, and explain a system of the form "Tall

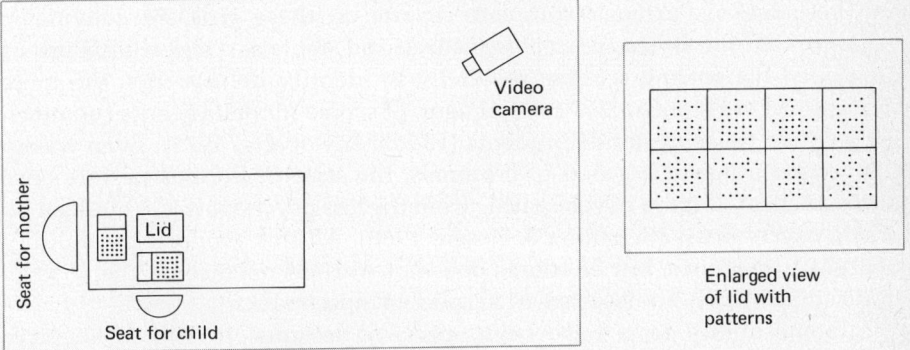

Figure 16.1. Standardized arrangement for observing mother and child.
Source: Adapted from Hess & Azuma, 1974.

blocks marked with X go together" (color and shape being ignored). When the mother had succeeded, she was told to teach the game however she liked and that after 20 minutes the examiner would return and test the child's understanding (by means of additional blocks the mother had not seen). Interest, of course, centered on the mother's teaching style and the child's responsiveness, not primarily on the child's success.

Standardized social situations have been used also at older ages, more for research in social psychology than for assessment (Carlsmith *et al.*, 1976). Behavioral assessors find controlled situations a useful supplement to self-report, particularly where research data are wanted (Cone & Hawkins, 1977). In studying phobias and treatments for them, for example, they may wire the person to apparatus that records physiological changes and then expose him to a series of pictures or objects, some neutral and some related to the phobia. Before-and-after measures on physiological response to snakes, for example, probably give more trustworthy data on the depth and breadth of change in fear than does self-report. Observed role-playing (p. 445) has advantages over self-report or everyday observation; these procedures offer rich descriptive information and are ordinarily not reduced to summary scores. On the other hand, a single role enactment—a one-item test—may be a poor sample.

Scores from ability tests. A great number of ability tests have been called objective tests of personality. Self-regulation, planfulness, and similar stylistic variables can properly be regarded as information on personality. Some psychologists regard success in detecting hidden figures as indexing field-independent style (p. 265ff.).

A better example of personality measurement based on an ability test is Porteus's measure of style in maze performance. He developed an objective Q score "intended to reveal any haphazard, impulsive, or overconfident habits of action." Two contrasting styles are displayed in Figure 16.2. Both girls solve the problem, but one proceeds painstakingly down the middle of the road through the center of every gap. The other swoops along, cutting corners and boundaries. Porteus's complete reports on these girls are convincing evidence that the styles are as personalized and stable as a signature. Porteus developed his scoring scheme especially to identify delinquents; the more reckless girl in Figure 16.2 is a delinquent. Q scores for delinquents run much higher than those of nondelinquents (Riddle & Roberts, 1977). Even within the narrow range of a group of criminals, the style of Porteus performance distinguishes the more psychopathic from the less psychopathic, as judged by prison psychiatrists (Schalling & Rosén, 1968). All this supports the validity of stylistic evidence, but of course does not warrant reliance on the Q score in deciding which adolescents to suspect of misconduct.

Some ability tests have been specially designed to stretch adaptive powers to the limit. June Downey, for example, in one of her "will-temperament tests" of the 1920s, asked subjects to copy a sentence backward (last letter first . . .) without interruption, *as slowly as possible.* In an "operational

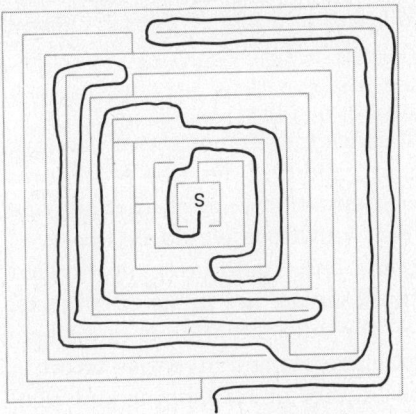 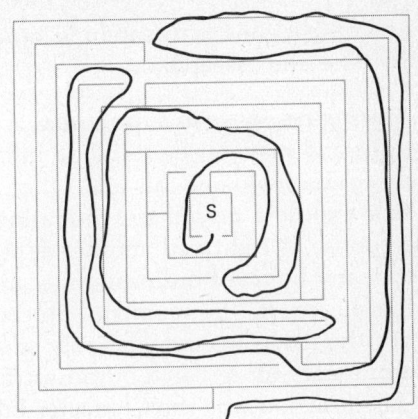

Figure 16.2. Stylistic differences in maze performance.
Source: Porteus, 1965, p. 234. Reproduced by permission of Pacific Books and The Psychological Corporation. New Series from "The Maze Test and mental differences," copyright 1933 by S. D. Porteus; and "The Porteus Maze Test and intelligence," copyright 1950 by S. D. Porteus, copyright renewed 1978 by D. Hebden Porteus and John R. Porteus. Published by The Psychological Corporation. All rights reserved.

stress test" tried with military fliers, the candidate was to throw levers as called for by signal lights while being bombarded with oral commands to work faster and to stop making errors. There are thousands of measures of adaptive abilities or preferred tempos that one or another investigator has proposed. The laboratory of R. B. Cattell alone derived more than 2000 scores from several hundred procedures, grouping them under 21 factors (Cattell & Warburton, 1967). A kit of measures of 10 factors (Extroversion, Depression, anxiety, Ego strength, . . .) has been made available (Objective-Analytic Batteries; R. B. Cattell and J. M. Schuerger; *IPAT*).

The attempt to capture information on personality by the methods of objective psychometrics has borne little fruit, despite effort by giants such as Thurstone and Cattell. There are several difficulties. First, effort has not been cumulative; with few exceptions a technique is studied only by its inventor and those he has trained. Second, considering one score at a time and trying to assess what is in the person's makeup without regard to the situation within which he acts is a feeble way to account for behavior. Third, though measures such as the Operational Stress Test correlate with important criteria, the relationship washes out when ability (as measured by ordinary tests) is held constant.

Observations of style are important in modern theory of information processing (Chapter 9), but at this time no one is reducing such measures to standard form or interpreting them as measures of a stable temperament. Later in the chapter we shall see how complex observations of style in intellectual tasks are used by clinicians; this effort is essentially independent of theory of information processing. Structured observations of social behavior and of reactions to threatening situations do play a variety of roles in current practice and research.

Testing response to temptation. A fixed situation appeals to specific motivations and may not be standard in its significance for persons tested. To lead up to discussion of this and other aspects of validity, I describe procedures that expose a person to temptation. In such situations, society defines one response as right and another as wrong. Few violations would be observed in many hours of ordinary time sampling, and few would be acknowledged in self-report. "Entrapment" procedures could violate the rights of subjects, but the risks are comparatively small when the only intention is to analyze group data for research purposes. The most elaborate and inventive effort in this direction was the Character Education Inquiry of Hartshorne and May (1928, 1929, 1930).

Honesty in a situation involving prestige was tested by a supposed ability test. The child was asked to place marks in small circles while keeping his eyes closed. It was impossible to do well. Many children turned in "successes" they could have obtained only by peeking.

Honesty with money was tested by arranging an arithmetic lesson in which each pupil had to use a boxful of coins. The box provided for each pupil was secretly identified. At the end of the lesson each pupil carried his own box to a pile in front of the room. Unaware that boxes could be identified, many pupils took advantage of the opportunity to keep some money.

The Hartshorne-May findings on character led one national agency working with youth to revise its program completely because the study showed that those who had received most recognition in the agency's character-building activities were on the average *most* likely to cheat (Maller, 1944). This is not hard to explain when we consider that striving for recognition in competition and working hard on a puzzle may stem from the same basic feeling of inadequacy. McClelland (1981) demonstrates the continuing fascination of these data by offering just the opposite interpretation: More mature children, entering adolescence, may act less morally because they are testing their own autonomy.

Motivation to put forth effort has been of particular interest because it is obviously a link between aptitude and achievement. To test how long children would persist as a task becomes difficult, Hartshorne and May had them read a story that builds to a climax: "Again the terrible piercing shriek of the whistle screamed at them. Charles could see the frightened face of the engineer. . . ." Here the examiner tells them that if they wish to learn the ending they must read the difficult printed material that follows:

CHARLESLIFTEDLUCILLETOHISBACK"PUTYOURARMSTIGHTA-ROUNDMYNECKANDHOLDON
. . . .

NoWhoWTogETBaCkoNthETREStle.HoWTOBRingTHaTTErrIFIEDB-
URDeNOFACHiLDuPtO
. . . .

fiN ALly tAp-taPC AME ARHYTH Month e BriD GeruNNing fee Tfee TcomING

The pupil separates each word with a vertical mark as he deciphers it; the amount deciphered is an index of persistence (Hartshorne and May, 1928, I, p. 292). The ambiguity of single tests is nicely illustrated by this task. Does it measure interest in adventure stories? Compulsiveness in following directions? Tolerance for annoyance? Enjoyment of an intellectual challenge? Or mostly reading skill and fluid ability?

Derivatives of the Hartshorne-May procedures are used, for example, in research concerned with the influence of models and of persuasion. Thus, Bandura and Whalen (1966) arranged for children to win coins in a game and gave them the option of depositing some of their winnings in a box as a contribution to orphans. When child models, coached to drop in some of their winnings, were used, their action stimulated other children to do the same. (For the tester, this is a reminder that what a subject does in a performance test will be altered if he can observe what other subjects are doing. These influences are probably especially strong in character tests.)

How a person thinks about moral dilemmas is an important aspect of character, especially for educators. Tests of moral judgment are intellectual tests, many of them being influenced by the research of Piaget. They correlate modestly with measures of behavior, but they do not purport to predict. Some tests for children (e.g., Selman & Lieberman, 1975) are much like Wechsler Comprehension items, with higher scores being given for responses that show full appreciation of the dilemma. Kohlberg (1973) tells a story about a painful dilemma to adolescents and adults and by Socratic questioning traces the depth of their reasoning. Basing his work on Kohlberg's thinking, Rest (1976) produced an experimental objective test in which respondents rate the importance of various value considerations in resolving a dilemma. For a critical review of recent thought and research procedure related to moral development, see Burton and Casey (1980).

1. *In each of the following enterprises, would it be preferable to employ observations in natural conditions or standardized observations where conditions are fixed in advance and identical for all subjects?*
   a. *The telephone company wishes to rate its operators on courtesy and clarity of speech. It is able to tap conversations and make recordings.*
   b. *Navy personnel are to be screened for tendency to panic under conditions of extreme noise, as in amphibious landings.*
   c. *An investigator wishes to study the habitual recklessness of 7-year-old boys in climbing and jumping.*

2. To what extent may each of the following be considered an unstructured stimulus?
   a. A teacher, during an examination, glances up from her desk and barely observes a hasty movement of one boy who is pulling his hand into his lap from the aisle.
   b. In duplicate bridge, the same set of hands is played at every table.
   c. A questionnaire is designed to obtain information about age, income, education, and so on. All possible answers are anticipated and presented on the blank in multiple-choice form.
3. To what extent could the respondent "fake good" in each of the following procedures if he knew what the tester was looking for?
   a. The tendency of a person to "repress" certain threatening ideas is measured by exposing words in a tachistoscope. Any one word is exposed very briefly and then again at increasing exposures until the person reads it. Into a list of neutral words are mixed a number of words related to sex, aggression, or some other possibly threatening topic. The score is the difference in exposure required between neutral and loaded words.
   b. Persistence is measured by determining how long a person remains at work on a college final examination when he may leave as early as he chooses.
   c. An "in-basket" test presents a person with an array of information about a job he is supposed to fill: the community, the organization he works for, his associates, his responsibilities, and so on. Then (under some time pressure) he is to work through the correspondence and memos in his basket, disposing of each by a referral, a direct reply or instruction to his staff, or by disregarding it. His performance is judged in terms of the soundness of his judgment, what priorities he assigns, and what style (e.g., buck-passing, tendency to "call a meeting," etc.) he displays.
   d. A preschool child is asked to learn to assemble a wooden gasoline station. The teacher shows him what to do, but does a number of things not included in the oral directions and not essential to the task—for example, storing the box under the table before proceeding, laying all the pumps side by side in parallel at the outset, and so on. The number of these incidental acts copied by the child when his turn comes is taken as a measure of dependency.
4. If Bill does better than Fred on the circle-dotting test of honesty, what conclusions can be drawn about Bill's character?
5. Analyze the story-completion test of persistence, identifying all the external conditions that might cause one fifth-grader to earn a higher score than another.
6. Children from homes with low socioeconomic status cheat more on achievement tests than other children: $r = 0.5$ (Hartshorne & May, 1928). How safe is it to conclude that these children are more likely to violate other standards of good conduct?

Problems of Design and Validity

With the example of character tests before us, we can discuss the evaluation of performance measures. The ultimate contribution of a procedure depends primarily on whether a theoretical explanation for it can be worked out, but that takes a long time. A theoretical advance suggests ways to refine the test, and an improvement in the test gets data that suggests ways to refine the theory. Examining a new procedure in its primitive form, one cannot say whether it will ultimately make a contribution.

Certain types of statistical research enter into the evaluation and improvement of nearly all performance tests. An ideal performance test of personality would satisfy the standards implied by this list of questions (though how close a test should come to the ideal depends on the use intended).

- Does the test obtain an accurate measure of consistent or average behavior, considering the universe of tasks like this and all occasions within this period of the subject's life?
- Are the scores stable over a reasonable period of time?
- Is there convergence between this evidence and evidence of other kinds that is thought to reflect the same trait?
- Can the scores be largely explained by well-established constructs?

In particular, does ability greatly influence the score? If so, the procedure is not giving an adequate measure of a "new" variable.

Consistency over forms and trials. The performance test is likely to be less accurate than other procedures. The test is often brief. The entire box-of-coins test of honesty consists of a single item that the subject passes or fails. The cheating-on-circles test has many "items" in the sense that we could count how many small circles have been dotted, but the decision to open one's eyes and cheat is a single decision. One critical act determines the score. This probably accounts for the low magnitude of many correlations between performance tests. Some of the tests may be highly valid, within the limits imposed by inadequate sampling.

Scores on one trial reflect temporary motivation and factors in the immediate situation. Moreover, whereas the person observed in his daily life is in a "steady state," a person tested in a strange situation is working out a fresh adaptation. Whether the person would respond similarly on further trials of the procedure is an open question. For instance, some children who did not steal coins on the one-trial test might do so if retested after some classmate says that he took coins. A conformity test puts the subject in a small group in which everyone else has been coached by the experimenter to give a bad answer. (At the simplest, everyone may be estimating the lengths of lines; when a 12-inch line is displayed, the confederates give answers close to 18 inches before the question comes round to the subject. Does he say "12" or "18"?) Not only did subjects conform less on a second test trial given a week after the first, but those who bowed to group pressure on both occasions had markedly different personalities from those who conformed on the first exposure only (Steiner & Vannoy, 1966).

To estimate the level of consistency requires a generalizability study with, as a minimum, two forms of the test given on two days by different examiners. For cheating tests there were retest correlations of 0.75 over 6 months and 0.4 between early adolescence and adulthood (Hartshorne & May, 1928, II, 88–89; V. Jones, 1946). We expect character to change; hence these results are satisfactory. Moreover, they suggest that the cheating test is reasonably accurate.

Generalization over tasks. Test interpretation ordinarily refers to a broad trait: to "cheating" rather than to "cheating in a test of two-digit multiplication." To sustain the broad interpretation, one must have reasonable consistency across measures of cheating in various school subjects and cheating in tasks not related to school. To sustain a still-broader interpretation in terms of "good character," cheating must correlate with honesty in handling money and so on.

A general measure could be built up by combining several tasks, each containing the same common element along with different specifics, but this is almost never practicable. A study evaluating character development might reduce the weight of specific content, however, by applying different tests to different subsamples. A genuine change in the desired direction should show up on all the tests.

Hartshorne and May (1930) established that a general trait cannot be measured by one or two specific behavior samples. Although each deception test was generalizable over forms and time, tasks correlated little with each other. The correlation between cheating on a classroom test and on the Circles test was only 0.5 even after correction for sampling errors. Although the positive correlations indicate a weak general-honesty factor (Burton, 1963), they contradict the notion that honesty is unified. Furthermore, honesty, cooperation, and so on intercorrelated only about 0.25, making untenable the view that a generalized "good character" accounts for desirable actions. Whatever "general factor" there may be in character has small influence on any one type of behavior.

Control for ability. One tends to think of a personality trait as independent of ability, but the two interpenetrate in perplexing ways. The child who can do his schoolwork does not need to cheat; does his failure to cheat imply honesty? One should always be aware of the possibility that ability accounts for differences in style, and sometimes it makes sense to adjust scores so as to remove the ability effect.

Thus one might pretest children on arithmetic, sort them into five ability strata, and provide for each stratum a test that causes its members considerable difficulty. Then all children are given some incentive to cheat. A separate analysis at each ability level is advisable. Cheating by a student with a good school record has a different and probably more pathological significance than cheating by an inept student; likewise for anxiety, drive to excel, and so on. Separate analyses of personality data by ability levels might explain many presently conflicting results.

When a personality test confounds a trait with other variables—and this is nearly inevitable—one wants to be sure that the *independent portion* is accurately measured and stable. How much of the 6-month stability of cheating scores results because low achievement is stable, so that the same children have an incentive to cheat? Such questions are rarely examined.

7. *What types of error in character tests do split-half correlations ignore?*
8. *For which performance tests of character would administration of half-tests on 2 days, a week apart, give adequate data on generalizability?*
9. *What would be gained in a study of child development by administering a moral-judgment test to each child in a class on a different day?*
10. *It has been suggested that the general factor running through honesty tests may be an indication, not of honesty, but of willingness to accept risk of detection and punishment. Is it possible to design unambiguous tests so as to settle this issue?*
11. *If 9-year-old boys are sorted out on general ability and moral judgment by dividing at the medians, what personalities would you expect in the High-High, Low-Low, High-Low, and Low-High groups?*

TWO STYLISTIC TESTS

Tests of perception borrowed from the laboratory have great value, especially for professionals dealing with cases of possible brain damage. Behavior disorders and learning disabilities may have organic as well as emotional roots; measures of perceptual abilities help in evaluating both the severity and locus of organic impairment. Perceptual tests are useful also with mental patients and in the studying of effects of stress on normals because perceptual distortions hint at emotional disturbances and disorders of thought processes. I shall discuss here two wide-band tests that have been especially prominent in psychological practice.

The Bender-Gestalt and the Rorschach originated in different traditions. (For the respective histories, see Hutt, 1977, and Rabin, 1981.) The former, in which simple patterns are to be copied, grew out of theories of Gestalt psychologists about how the brain processes information; pattern perception was thought to be a sensitive indicator of disturbed functioning. Rorschach, working in the tradition of Freud and Jung, wanted to penetrate to an assumed inner personality. The inkblots have little patterning; there is no "right" answer to "What do you see here?" Rorschach interpreters assume that when external structure is lacking, the response reflects mostly the person's intellectual resources, emotional state, and coping style. Although both techniques can be scored and interpreted as objectively as the Wechsler, their interpretation is usually more elaborate and impressionistic, as we shall see.

In the Bender and the Rorschach, attention centers on the subject's style. Such *stylistic* tests may be contrasted with *thematic* tests, in which the interpreter is especially concerned with the content of thoughts and fantasies. The stylistic and thematic categories are not mutually exclusive. Obsessions are sometimes revealed in the Rorschach protocol, and one can observe intellectual style in the Thematic Appercception Test (which the following section of this chapter will take up).

The Bender Gestalt

The Bender Visual Motor Gestalt Test (L. Bender; *American Orthopsychiatric Association;* or as adapted by Hutt: *GS*) displays a page of figures (Fig. 16.3), which the subject is to copy. Responses may differ in a hundred ways; the performance may be scored by rules, or the tester's observations may be interpreted clinically. Mercer included the Bender (scored by the rules of Koppitz, 1975) in SOMPA (p. 209) as a screening device, along with physical coordination tests. Deficient performance in this sample of simple sensory-motor processes is seen by many psychologists as a sign of possible neurological impairment and emotional difficulties. At school entrance, however, scores on the test are unstable (as with most pencil-paper tests). Prior to third grade, moreover, drawing is so difficult that the Koppitz score is in part a measure of general problem-solving ability. Still, one can reasonably regard poor Bender performance at any age as a signal suggesting closer study of a case.

The Bender was seen originally as a near-objective method of identifying pathology, particularly of the nervous system. Actuarial keys count features often seen in records of persons with brain damage. Though such evidence has some validity, the hit rate is too low to separate these patients from normals and neurotics.

Bigler and Ehrfurth (1981), though not denying the possible significance of poor Bender performance, demonstrate that some persons with unmistakable brain damage do well on the Bender. Such misses are costly. These authors consider other techniques (including X-ray scanning) much more dependable, and they warn especially against relying on Bender scores alone. For an extensive summary of studies on the Bender, see Buckley (1978, on children) and Tolor and Brannigan (1980).

One bit of evidence for construct validity is particularly neat. In open-heart surgery, the external heart-lung machine creates microemboli (floating particles) that can damage nerve tissues. To test experimentally a filter designed to remove microemboli, the Bender was given before and after the

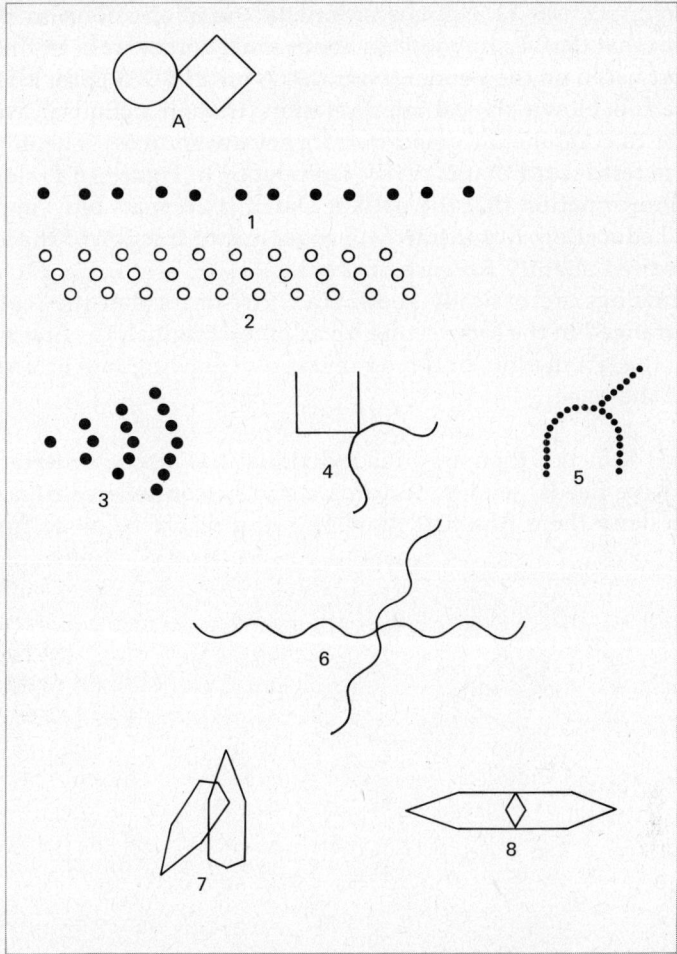

Figure 16.3. Bender-Gestalt patterns to be copied.
Note: These figures are from the Hutt adaptation. In the original Bender version, the figures are arranged differently, and the lines are heavier.

surgical operation to patients in four conditions. Objective scoring of the Bender showed which patients' performance deteriorated (perhaps only temporarily). The conditions and findings were as follows (Landis *et al.*, 1974):

1. Bubble oxygenator, no filter (18,000 emboli/min.) 57% deteriorated
2. Bubble oxygenator, with filter (1,800 emboli/min.) 21.5% deteriorated
3. Membrane oxygenator, no filter (1,500 emboli/min.) 21.5% deteriorated
4. Membrane oxygenator, with filter (100 emboli/min.) 0% deteriorated

In Chapters 2 and 13, I discussed briefly the impressionistic, dynamic interpretation that derives hypotheses about inner forces from test performance. A report based on the Bender (Hutt, 1977, pp. 211–219) provides a good example of a full-blown clinical interpretation (though a clinician would, of course, prefer to combine information from several sources). The interpreter was given the test record that is partly reproduced in Figure 16.4, along with the minimal information that the patient David is 25 years old, single, with a high school education. My extract will cover only a fraction of the analysis, and I have edited slightly for ease of reading.

The drawings are basically good. Hutt first notes that the reproduced figures are arranged in the same sequence as in the original, the first six being aligned with the left margin, but that the last two drawings are fitted into the right half of the page.

> Our first hunches then are: this individual has strong orderly, i.e., compulsive needs, tending towards a sort of compulsive ritual, but tries to deny them [the first drawing being displaced away from the

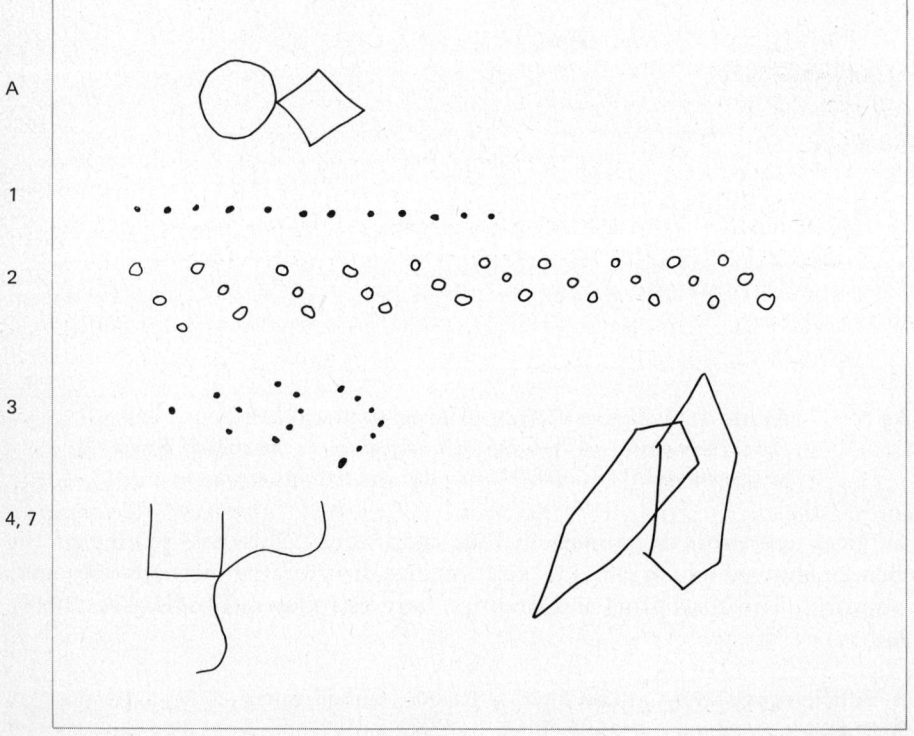

Figure 16.4. David's Bender reproductions.
Source: Reproduced by permission from Hutt, 1977, p. 212. In this illustration three figures have been omitted.

> margin and the examiner having noted that David draws fast and unhesitatingly] . . . , and he is oppressed with some (probably) generalized feelings of anxiety and (more specifically) personal inadequacy (clings to the left margin and is "constrained" to use all of the space available on this one sheet). We raise at once the question, "How strong and from what source is this anxiety and what is his defense?" We can speculate, from his use of space, that he attempts in some way to "bind" his anxiety, i.e., he cannot tolerate it for long or in large amounts, and that one of the features of this young adult's functioning is the need of control. . . . The super-ego is very strict.

Here Hutt looked at the style of performance, and then tried to infer what inner tensions and defenses could generate such a style. As Hutt said, these are initial hunches to be checked against other evidence in the protocol and against all other information about David.

Among his more detailed analyses, Hutt remarks on the reproduction of pattern 2.

> Further evidence of marked variability. The examiner notes, "Checks number of columns about two-thirds through." The angles of the columns of dots differ, becoming more slanted, with a correction towards the end. The whole figure is exaggerated in the lateral plane. Together, these findings suggest a strong need to relate to people, but difficulty in establishing such relationships. . . . We have evidence for the presence of considerable internal tension with an attempt at denial of its existence. How can we explain the apparent contradiction of the need for order and control with the speed and variability of performance? His compulsive defenses do not function effectively enough?

As Hutt goes through the remaining drawings, the following traits are mentioned (along with reminders that the interpretation, based on limited information, is tentative): suppressing conscious hostile feelings. . . . deferential, conforming. . . . depressive reactions. . . . feelings of sexual inadequacy. . . . high aspiration. . . . masochistic needs. . . . acting out, impulsivity. . . .

There are more startling things to come. Hutt turns to thematic interpretation, following certain Freudian ideas about "masculine" and "feminine" designs:

> In drawing 4, David has increased the vertical sides of the open square. . . . His reaction to authority figures can now be inferred more completely: he is hostile to such figures, unable to express this hostility directly, and reacts either symbolically or impulsively. In line with the "acting out" hypothesis, the former is more likely. The

curved portion is enlarged, flattened out in the middle and reveals an impulsive flourish at the upper end. Now we may speculate that David's major identification is with a female figure, but she is perceived as more masculine (i.e., dominant, aggressive) than feminine and is reacted to openly with antagonism. It is interesting that the upper portion of the curved figure extends well above its position on the stimulus card, and is at least as high up as the vertical lines. Here we may conjecture that David's mother (or surrogate) was stronger psychologically than his father, or at least seemed so and that David would like to use his mother (or women) to defy his father (or men).

Hutt is able to give a detailed rationale for each of his inferences. Indeed, two books (Hutt, 1977; with Gibby, 1970) lay out his principles of interpretation almost as explicitly as those that lead to MMPI computer printouts. More important, Hutt's description agrees well with the therapist's notes. Here is what the therapist (quoted by Shneidman, 1951, pp. 268–269) said about David:

> He seemed suspicious, indecisive and unable to relax. . . . There seems to be considerable guilt in relation to his own hostility. He has established some defenses against this through obsession but these defenses are cracking and he fears that his hostile impulses might become so great that he would be unable to control them. . . . The patient seemed obsessed with thoughts about death, homicide, and suicide.

Word for word, there is confirmation of hostile impulses the subject fears to express, ineffectual defense through obsession, and so on. Other remarks of the therapist support some of Hutt's most hazardous-seeming guesses: "The father seems to be a hazy person in the patient's life." "He talked of wishing to strangle his mother." "Had difficulty with authority figures." Hutt learned far more about the depths of personality than one might expect from a little task suitable for a child's drawing exercise.

Hutt's technique has not been favored by clinical psychologists who value objectivity over "insight" and who regard situational variables as more significant than inner dynamics. In 1970 Mosher called Hutt's work an anachronism:

> The unusually sensitive clinician, and Hutt is undoubtedly a good example, may well be able to keep these [situationist] assumptions in mind . . . ; but the neophyte, the hack, and perhaps even the average clinician, may be more likely to look up a test factor in Hutt's book and conclude that the increase in curvature on Figure 4

reveals overactive emotionality. While Hutt cautions against such usage, I doubt that such warnings are sufficient to prevent simplistic "dream book" interpretation.

Inkblot tests

Hermann Rorschach, a Swiss psychiatrist, showed that patients of different types respond to inkblots differently. His method, published in 1921, was altered and extended over the years (Beck, 1961–1978; Exner, 1978; Klopfer *et al.*, 1970; Rorschach, 1942). The respondent is to tell what he sees in ten inkblots, blots whose form is so irregular as to permit innumerable interpretations. The blots are calculated to arouse emotional response with their bloody reds, ominous blacks, and luminous grays and with their forms suggestive of nursery animals, overbearing giants, and sex organs. Some patients become agitated while responding to the cards, and impulsiveness or anxiety damages some responses of seemingly normal individuals.

Mischel (1981, p. 192) points out that projective techniques were seen as a "situationless situation," providing so few cues that the responses would have to be generated by forces and associations within the person. It was hoped that responses would reveal motives (guilt, hostility, etc.) the person was unwilling to admit (to others and perhaps to himself). Today it is recognized that the response is a sample of problem-solving behavior in the specific setting of the test, a self-regulated performance. "Hidden" motives may show through, but much else determines the response.

Rorschach scoring. Rorschach interpretation begins with rather objective scoring. The major scores are concerned with number of responses, location, determinants, and content. Location scores count how many responses use the whole blot *(W)*, obvious subdivisions *(D)*, or details *(Dd)*. The determinant scores consider how form, color, movement, and shading influence responses. "Movement," for example, is scored when the response describes humans in motion. *CF* is scored when the response depends on form and color, with color more significant. Form is scored + or −, according to the fit between the response and the stimulus. Finally, responses are assigned to content categories.

The scoring of four responses will illustrate the procedure. Card X is a mixture of brightly colored forms. Consider these four responses:

1. A big splashy print design for a summer dress.
2. Enlarged photograph of a snowflake [refers to a large irregularly shaped area].
3. Two little boys blowing bubbles. You just see them from the waist up.
4. Head of a rabbit.

Follow-up questions provide part of the basis for this scoring:

Response	Location	Determinant and form level	Content
1	W	CF+	Art, Clothing
2	D	F−	Nature
3	D	M+	Part of human
4	D	F+	Part of animal

The quality of responses indicates something about the respondent's intellectual level and the care he puts into his performance. Much is made of his control over impulses and emotions. Movement responses are thought to represent imagination and creative impulses arising from within. Color responses are thought to represent emotional reactions to external stimuli. Responses true to the forms in the blot imply attentiveness to reality. A person who harmonizes form and movement is said to use constructively his inner impulses; a person who rarely reports a movement response is regarded as lacking in imagination or as repressing it.

Validation of hypotheses. There has been considerably formal research on the hypotheses that enter such interpretations, but the complexity of the technique has made comprehensive research exceedingly difficult (Zubin *et al.*, 1965, pp. 193–239). Sometimes the evidence is strikingly favorable, sometimes not.

Rorschach (1942, p. 7) said that movement responses are indicative of personalities that "function more in the intellectual sphere, whose interests gravitate more towards their intrapsychic living rather than towards the world outside themselves." Support is seen in ratings made by clinical assessors using other data (Barron, 1955). Persons with strong M tendencies were described by the independent observers as inventive, having wide interests, introspective, concerned with self as object, valuing cognitive pursuits. Those giving few M responses were described as practical, stubborn, preferring action to contemplation, and inflexible in thought and action.

Hundreds of additional studies could be cited, each dealing with one bit of Rorschach lore. About half of the experimental tests of Rorschach hypotheses give results consistent with clinical theory. The interpretation certainly has "validity greater than chance." On the other hand, relationships of Rorschach indicators to particular traits are not strong. Many personality factors and abilities influence any one score, and no direct interpretation can be made with confidence.

Composites of scores have been proposed as trait measures or as predictors of criteria (of presence of organic brain damage, for example). Generally, these formulas prove valueless on crossvalidation, having no validity or too many false positives. The responses do provide a basis for judging the adequacy of thought processes. Exner (1978, pp. 339ff.) discusses how this information along with facts about the person's life situation and feelings can be the starting point for a therapeutic plan.

A psychometric version. The Holtzman Inkblot Technique (HIT; W. H. Holtzman et al., PC) is a psychometric version of the Rorschach. HIT calls for one response to each of 45 (or 90) blots. For group administration, the blots are projected onto a screen. Rules yield scores for Location (whole vs. detail), Form Appropriateness, Pathognomic Verbalization, Hostility, and so on. Test construction and standardization of high quality yielded two excellently matched forms—a rarity among personality tests. There is even a system for computer scoring of the free responses; a dictionary stored on magnetic tape that tells how "bad thunderstorm," for example, is to be coded. Although split-half coefficients are entirely satisfactory, stability coefficients are modest. In one study, the week-to-week correlations for 18 scores ranged from 0.4 to 0.8, with a median of 0.65 (Holtzman, in Rabin, 1981); no higher values should be expected from wide-band measurement. The scores evidently are somewhat sensitive to transient mental sets or moods, but even in rapidly developing schoolchildren they give information on aspects of personality and thought that can be traced through several years (Holtzman et al., 1975). Much of the stable information is captured in three composite scores:

> *Perceptual maturity.* High scores imply imagination, attentiveness to reality, and organized thinking.
>
> *Perceptual sensitivity.* High scores (often seen in schizophrenic records) would imply a dominance of emotion over objective aspects of stimuli, and extreme low scores suggest constriction of emotional response.
>
> *Psychopathology.* Indicators of anxiety and hostility, along with poor form quality and bizarre language, contribute to this factor. Moderately high scores may indicate active imagination and lack of self-criticism rather than serious disturbance.

Crosscultural and longitudinal research has amassed considerable information about correlates of HIT scores, but interpretation in terms of personality constructs is not far advanced. Rorschach theory cannot be applied to HIT unthinkingly, as similarly named variables correspond only roughly. Even after adjustment of correlations upward to allow for error of measurement, such key Rorschach variables as Color, Movement, and Shading correlate around 0.6 with their HIT counterparts (Holtzman, in Rabin, 1981).

Formal rules comparable to those developed for MMPI can distinguish clinically defined groups from normals. For example, combining two cut scores (on Anxiety and Shading) picks up a quarter of a neurotic sample and less than 2 per cent of normals or of a depressed sample. The descriptive interpretation of this pattern—"overly sensitive, fearful, and vigilant"—suggests the presence of doubts and uncertainties of which the person is little aware (Holtzman, 1975; based on the work of Hill [1972] and others). The system is incomplete, and statistics that would describe its effectiveness for screening and classification in normal and clinical populations have not been reported.

12. *Why might a "perfect" Rorschach accuracy score, 100 per cent $F+$, indicate a personality pattern undesirable for many situations?*
13. *Do the Rorschach scores related to quality of output reveal maximum ability or typical behavior? How does the Rorschach compare with the Binet test in that respect?*
14. *"Responses to ten inkblots, presented by one tester on one occasion, constitute too small a sample of behavior to measure any intellectual or emotional trait reliably." To what extent does Holtzman's instrument overcome this objection?*

THEMATIC TESTS

Thematic tests elicit open or disguised statements of beliefs, attitudes, and motives. Within that definition, nearly all self-report tests are thematic. Among unstructured thematic techniques we might count the Rep test and a request that the person write (or tell) his life story. A handful of projective tests, including sentence completion and story completion, are primarily thematic. It is hoped that the person will produce responses whose psychological significance he does not fully realize. The pictorial Thematic Apperception Test has been most used and has had the greatest influence on research.

The TAT and Its Meaning

The Thematic Apperception Test (TAT; C. Morgan and H. A. Murray; *GS*) asks the test taker to interpret a picture by telling a story—what is happening, what led up to the scene, what will be the outcome. It is presumed that the person projects himself into the scene, identifying with a character just as he vicariously takes the place of the actor when he sees a film. TAT consists of 20 pictures, some of the pictures being different for men and women. Since two 1-hour sessions are required for the full test, testers ordinarily use selected cards.

TAT, designed to cover the whole range of ideas and behavior, cannot cover any topic thoroughly. While a person obsessed with independence conflicts may bring them into story after story, most people reveal feelings about authority only on one or two cards. Any single picture is indefinite enough to bring out different types of information from different subjects. Flexibility that permits the subject to reveal almost any trait or theme prominent in his personality structure is an advantage in a free-ranging exploration of personality. It is a serious disadvantage when one wishes to answer a specific question.

Focused tests are designed to elicit thematic responses that bear on a single question. For example, Murphy and Likert (1938) carried out research on labor-management conflict with pictures of, for example, strikers in conflict with police. A focused test for fliers was based on the hypothesis that outwardly directed aggression would be associated with tolerance for high centrifugal forces. The criterion was a measure of the force required to produce blackout in a human centrifuge. In the best-designed of several validation studies, the score from the thematic test classified 18 of 25 subjects correctly as having high or low tolerance (Silverman *et al.*, 1957).

Formal scores. For a synoptic test like TAT, it is possible to develop scoring rules for dozens of variables: perception of authority, reaction to difficult tasks, originality, reliance on luck and magical intervention, the percentage of stories the outcomes of which are unhappy, the number of female characters seen as predatory, and so on. Formal TAT scoring most often emphasizes "needs"—concerns for achievement, affiliation, power, and the like. Stability coefficients over 2 months are in the range from 0.6 to 0.9 for such scores as abasement themes, giving stories with positive outcomes, and presence of words referring to relief of tension. The emphasis given a motive depends on the person's most recent experiences, which holds down the coefficient. When one recognizes the variety of scores obtained from an hour or two of testing, this quality of information is impressive.

The TAT tradition, however, is oriented to impressionistic interpretation and not formal scoring. For most users, the scores are a preliminary memorandum. One user after another developed her own pet scoring system to the point where "there would seem to be as many thematic scoring systems as there were hairs in the beard of Rasputin" (Murstein, 1963, p. 23).

Impressionistic interpretation. The stories may indicate a defeatist attitude, concern about overbearing authority figures, preoccupation with sex, and so on. The interpreter also considers such stylistic matters as fluency and concern with accuracy in fitting the story to the picture.

The interpreter looks at each story in turn, deriving hypotheses from the plot, the symbolism, and the style. The hypothesis from one story (e.g., "This man represses hostile feelings") is checked against subsequent stories. The interpreter must weigh conflicting indications and must integrate information on intellectual powers, emotional conflicts, and defense mechanisms.

A few illustrations of the impressionistic analysis can be given. Card I of TAT shows a boy, perhaps 10 years old, looking at a violin lying on a flat surface. A girl, age 14, told this story (Henry, 1956, p. 111):

> Right now the boy is looking at the violin. It looks like he might be kind of sad or mad because he has to play. Before he might have played ball with the other boys and his mother wouldn't let him. He had to go in and play. Looks like he might practice for a little while and then sneak out.

Henry commented on how clearly the story "takes into account the basic stimulus demands of the picture" and goes on to "entirely relevant elaborations of good quality . . . [which] attribute motive and action to the characters." Henry correctly placed the girl's general ability at or above the 95th percentile.

The response of a 42-year-old clerk is interpreted thematically (p. 145):

> The story behind this is that this is the son of a very well-known, a very good musician and the father has probably died. The only thing the son has left is this violin which is undoubtedly a very good one and to the son, the violin is the father and the son sits there daydreaming of the time that he will understand the music and interpret it on the violin that his father had played.

The first sentence shows preoccupation with excellence, Henry says, and a conviction that to match the example is impossible. The man dreams of things within himself, and takes no action to carry out his ambition.

A third story, told by a 29-year-old male recently come to the United States, is interpreted metaphorically (Henry, p. 178):

> A young boy sitting in front of a violin spread out on white table, or white linen. It is not clear in the expression of the face if he thinks in glorification and admiration of that what the violin and music could hold for him or if he is bored and in disgust with the lesson he has to take and doesn't want.

Note, says Henry, the emphasis on conflicting alternatives: glorification or disgust, has to take and doesn't want. This personality "may well be marked by its attraction to opposites." The core of conflict appears to be sexual, the basic issue being whether woman can be

> both the Madonna and the sexual object. . . . This is an instance of the use of the violin as a sexual symbol. The man is basically preoccupied with some strong emotional issue; hence he utilizes form details in a distorting manner [e.g., "violin spread out"]. . . . He feels impelled to make a formal heterosexual adjustment as well as a conventional social adjustment, even though both are somewhat forced and against his will.

These excerpts by no means represent the intricacy of a full interpretation in which stories are compared with each other and with background information about the subject. For examples of full interpretations see Henry (1956). Interpretations are extremely tentative if the psychologist is properly trained. They are discarded unless supporting evidence shows up elsewhere in the test or the subject's history. These illustrations do indicate the individuality of TAT responses and the variation in the interpreter's attack. No two interpreters proceed in the same way.

Correlates of Responses

Relation to other behavior. It is too simple to say that the stories describe what the person does or would like to do; people do not and should not always act in accord with their fantasies or wishes. If there were no correspondence with behavior, on the other hand, the information from fantasy would seem irrelevant. Nonchance correspondence turns up with some frequency, but relations are often puzzling (Varble, 1971).

Frequency of behavioral aggression correlated with aggression themes in stories given by problem boys, and fear of punishment judged from overt behavior correlated with frequency of mention of punishment in stories. The trait configuration matters. Every one of the seven boys with high TAT aggression and low fear of punishment behaved very aggressively; only two out of nine with high TAT aggression and high fear of punishment acted aggressively (Mussen & Naylor, 1954). In another study, a score representing *inhibition* of aggression and denial of aggressive impulses correlated as strongly with aggressive action as did presence of aggressive TAT plots (Skolnick, 1966). Olweus (1969) made a careful theoretical elaboration of the relations of aggressive tendencies and inhibitory tendencies seen in projective responses with situational factors that elicit and inhibit aggression. He obtained strong evidence for his theoretical model: among boys whose tests showed little inhibition, strength of aggressive themes correlated around 0.5 with rated overt aggression; among high inhibitors, the correlation was about -0.5. A comparable result emerged when aggressive behavior of patients in a neuropsychiatric hospital was rated by attendants (Pittluck, 1950). Aggressive behavior went with aggressive TAT stories; but the patient whose stories muffled the aggression (by introducing a plot justification or some other mechanism) was much more likely to control his aggression in the ward. To summarize: a "dimension" of response (e.g., large number of aggressive themes) cannot be interpreted except in the context of a theory that considers other variables in person and situation.

Transient situational influences. Situational factors influence TAT performance, as was neatly demonstrated by Clark (1952). He gave TAT to college men after having presented a series of slides of nude females on the pretext that rating their sexual attractiveness had something to do with studying relations of body-type to personality in a psychology course. The control group, meanwhile, had been kept busy rating landscapes. On TAT, 66 per cent of the controls gave responses high in sex imagery, compared to 27 per cent among experimentals. One might well conclude that taking sexual drives out for exercise reduces their intensity. But Clark destroys that interpretation by another experiment, essentially repeating the first one but in the context of a fraternity beer party. Sexual content was higher than in the classroom experiment, but a score that cut off the highest 26 per cent of the controls cut off 60 (!) per cent of the experimentals. Clark's interpretation is that guilt over sexual arousal in the classroom served to inhibit sexual responses on TAT. We do not know how many sexual responses came to the subjects' minds in the first experiment and were suppressed.

The sensitivity of thematic tests enhances their validity as experimental measures, but makes them less trustworthy as trait indicators. Among the most interesting of the studies is one on parachutists. Fenz and Epstein (1962) prepared pictures having high, low, or no relevance to parachuting. (See Fig. 16.5) Members of a sport parachuting club were tested on the day when they were scheduled to jump and also either two weeks before or two weeks after the jump (with a parallel set of pictures). The parachutists were much more aroused on the day of the jump. The skin conductance measure of Table 16.1 is a "sweaty palm" reaction; just showing a picture related to parachuting on the day of the jump produced a flash of tension. Whereas stories produced on the day of the jump carry a positive message about parachuting (more so than on the nonjump day), many of these stories are so exaggerated that they suggested deliberate denial of fear; e.g., "He is not afraid at all, just looks that way because of the wind that is blowing in his face. He will have a wonderful jump. It will be great, just great!"

Figure 16.5. Thematic pictures to measure reactions of parachutists.
Source: Fenz & Epstein, 1962. Copyright © 1962, Duke University Press, Durham, N.C. Reprinted by permission.

Table 16.1. *Physiological response of parachutists to thematic pictures*

Relevance of Picture to Parachuting	Mean Response of Nonparachutist Controls	Mean Response of Parachutists	
		2 Weeks from Jump	On Day of Jump
None	1.0	0.7	1.1
Low	0.8	0.8	1.3
High	0.9	1.0	2.2

SOURCE: Fenz & Epstein, 1962; see also Fenz, 1964.

15. *Harrison (1965, p. 590) says that negative evidence on TAT should be given much less credence than positive evidence:*

> Negative validity results . . . do not necessarily constitute damaging evidence, for the researchers may have employed improper methods of analysis in confounded designs against unreliable or otherwise inadequate criteria. . . . Positive results do demonstrate something, assuming that the work has been done honestly and that grievous errors have not been introduced into the design.

> *What are the merits and demerits of this position? Is it pertinent only to projective tests?*

16. *How many traits are mentioned in Henry's three interpretations?*

17. *Can one regard the frequency of punishment by authority in TAT stories as an indication of how often the respondent has been punished in life?*

INTEGRATIVE ASSESSMENT

As we have seen, a psychologist studying the nuances of performance on a single test such as the Wechsler or Bender, in the light of the person's background, can reach broad conclusions about his functioning. Typically, however, the study of an individual calls upon a variety of information.

In clinical practice with adults and children, diverse information—medical and neurological; from family members, teachers, or work associates; from interviewing the subject; possibly from observation in classroom or ward—is brought together with whatever tests seem relevant. A staff conference is commonly the means of integration, as staff members have seen the person in different settings and offer different kinds of expertise. Comprehensive assessment is wanted to evaluate the seriousness of difficulties and lay out remedial plans (environmental or therapeutic). A comparison of initial and later assessments guides further stages of case management and provides data for program evaluation. The extent and formality of analysis will differ with the problem, the resources available, and the professional theories favored by the staff. I shall not describe clinical decision making, turning instead to efforts at comprehensive assessment of persons who are functioning adequately. The issues and general conclusions to be developed are relevant to clinical practice.

History of Assessment Programs

In the United States, thinking about normal personalities during the last 40 years has evolved particularly from the base laid at the Harvard Psychological Clinic, where Henry A. Murray led or taught many who became eminent contributors. R. W. White's account (1981) of the origins of the influential *Explorations in personality* (Murray et al., 1938) reminds us that Murray's was a team approach. Orientations of team members ranged widely: Freudian, Jungian, medical, anthropological, experimental. A diverse set of investigations and novel observing procedures were put in place, each under one staff member. Approximately 50 students were enlisted to serve as subjects for *all* the investigations. The staff tried to arrive at a common understanding of the subjects and a framework for thinking about personality.

Situational forces were given almost as much weight as internal motives. Motives (conscious and unconscious), perceptions, and world views were considered more fundamental than patterns of overt action; this phenomenological emphasis is evident in the TAT, which emerged from the project. The person was viewed as an active problem solver, interpreting new social demands in the light of his needs and applying a preferred coping strategy.

The thinking was turned to practical use when the Office of Strategic Services (predecessor of the CIA) needed a thorough psychological screening of prospective employees, some of whom would be assigned to covert operations and some to unglamorous desk work. Part of the assessment staff came from the Harvard team. The assessment methods included situational tests that had been pioneered by German military assessors and extended by British officer selection boards (Wiggins, 1973, Chap. 11).

Because the assignments of most of the recruits were unforeseeable and because of the great variety of assignments, job analysis was impossible, and the secrecy of the work precluded the usual cycles of tryout and feedback. The assessors, therefore, had to appraise adaptability, vigor, and reaction to stress on the basis of unvalidated indicators.

"House party" assessments of 2 or 3 days permitted the team to observe candidates in off hours as well as in structured discussions and tasks. As many as 35 separate procedures were used to collect data, including conventional tests, peer ratings, interviews, role playing, and projective and performance tests. Some tasks were assigned to groups to permit observations on social interaction. Among several procedures designed to observe response to stress and frustration, the candidate was asked to direct two men in building a wooden structure; the helpers had been coached to be clumsy and sluggish or disrespectful. As at Harvard, the assessors came together to agree on a final report. They rejected some applicants and, for those accepted, pointed out qualities to be considered in making assignments.

Validity information from the OSS experience was necessarily sketchy, and the main report made only modest claims to success (OSS Assessment Staff, 1948). Wiggins (1973, p. 536) reworks the data considering base rate and selection ratio; he figures that the assessors judged 77 per cent of the cases correctly and that this was enough above the chance hit rate of 63 per cent to provide satisfactory payoff.

In the ensuing decade, various assessment projects were carried out, partly for practical purposes, partly to validate and improve assessment methods. Included were studies of students entering training in clinical psychology (Kelly & Fiske, 1951; Kelly & Goldberg, 1959) and psychiatry (Holt & Luborsky, 1958), of British civil servants (Vernon, 1950), of American officer candidates (Holtzman & Sells, 1954; Holmen *et al.*, 1956); and Peace Corps volunteers (see Wiggins, 1973). Particularly notable was the extended work of a diverse staff at the Institute for Personality Assessment and Research (IPAR) at Berkeley; I have referred earlier to fragments of their work on architects (p. 497) and mathematicians (p. 519). The validation reports from these several studies were not wholly negative, as we shall see; but it was discouraging to find that an expensive and elaborate technique produced validities comparable to those achieved with a few structured predictors. The impressionistic, dynamic interpretations seemed to make no contribution.

Today the principal residue of this line of effort is in assessments of executives (Finkel, in Dunnette, 1976; Moses & Byham, 1977). A program to select executive trainees for telephone companies (Bray & Grant, 1966) is regarded as a particular success, and 1000 other firms choose trainees in a similar manner. The method is also used in selecting police and military officers. These activities are far more conservative than the earlier waves of assessments, with greater reliance on face-valid work samples and little explicit attention to personality (Bray, 1982). Whereas the earlier assessments were made by assessment professionals, psychologists and managers usually serve together as assessors of executives. As we shall see, the evidence on validity is favorable.

Specialized Tests for Organizational Behavior

Before reviewing the reports on validity, I describe two further standardized test procedures; they or their close cousins play a part in most current executive assessment. The first, the in-basket technique, requires the person to play the role of manager. (It is a simplified version of the Island Story test from British house-party assessment, in which the candidate was to imagine himself appointed chief administrator of a remote island, to digest a large file of information, and then to resolve problems.) The second, the Leaderless Group Discussion, also descends from a house-party technique.

The in-basket test. An in-basket used by the Sears firm is described as follows (Lopez, 1966):

> The candidate for appointment or promotion is told to assume that he has just been assigned to replace a store manager in Exville, who is out of action with a heart attack. It is Sunday; he must go to the store today and in three hours cope with problems on the manager's desk. He cannot reach other employees on Sunday, and, because he has a trip to make, anything postponed must await his return on Thursday. He receives a chart of the store organization and a personnel list. The basket contains 37 "items"—letters, memos, policy papers for review, forms to sign, etc.—realistically done up on Sears forms. (But familiarity with company practice gives no real advantage.) Having disposed of as many items as he can by decision, referral, or whatever, the man writes down his reason for each action.

Various scores are obtained, including productivity (number of items dealt with), depth or thoughtfulness of response, and sensitivity to human relations. Scorers may also write descriptive reports on the style displayed. Frederiksen *et al.* (1972) describe several other in-baskets and reproduce 50 pages from one of them. Although our concern here is with assessment of individuals, it should be noted that in-baskets are also used for training and for checking on the effects of training. Moreover, Frederiksen *et al.* showed that, for purposes of research on organizational characteristics, the baskets could be designed to simulate alternative styles of organization (e.g., rule-bound).

Although the in-basket has appealing face validity, it is limited as a measuring device. The person's many responses are interrelated because the person is playing a consistent role. Scores on one basket generally correlate around 0.3 with scores on the same variable from another basket; thus each basket is acting like a one-item test. Reliability rises to 0.5 for a few important stylistic variables such as courtesy shown in communications (Frederiksen *et al.*, 1972, pp. 66, 154–157). Distributions on many variables are strongly skewed; that is, few respondents exhibit the characteristic often enough to pile up evidence of individual differences. (For example, the average score on "goal setting" was approximately 1 per cent of the maximum possible.) Skewness reduces correlations with criteria. For the two least skewed variables in one study, the in-basket score correlated about 0.3 with supervisor ratings (Brass & Oldham, 1976). The in-basket may gain some of its validity by duplicating information obtainable more cheaply by a conventional ability test, and it gives peers and assessors less basis for forming impressions than does observed performance in a group situation.

As with other complex assessments, the required value judgments are hard to make. Courtesy is to be appreciated, but does it contribute greatly to effectiveness? When the respondent prefers face-to-face communication to resolving a problem by a memo, is that to be regarded as a good or bad sign? In the absence of research on the job in a particular institution, the interpreter has to rely on some sterotyped theory of good management.

Group discussions. In the Leaderless Group Discussion (LGD) a group of persons are told to discuss, for example, how to increase movie attendance. The LGD is unstructured: no rules of procedure are established, the topic is left largely undefined, and the group (whose members first met at the assessment center) have no established friendships or dominance relations. Social patterns build up quickly, and the role the person plays is presumably similar to the role he is prone to adopt elsewhere.

The variables observers commonly are asked to rate have to do with prominence, goal facilitation (efficiency, suggesting useful ideas), and sociability. The LGD also provides part of the acquaintance needed to make peer ratings, which are typically part of the assessment.

The effectiveness of LGD can be evaluated in several ways. Stability over trials is fairly high; with a week between tests, the correlations range from 0.75 to 0.9. Over longer time intervals or with radical changes in the type of problem, correlations drop to about 0.5. The test is measuring some consistent and general aspect of personality. Behavior in practical situations is no doubt determined by many forces other than personality (seniority, relative prestige, specifically relevant knowledge, etc.), but LGD scores nonetheless have predictive value. Bass and Coates (1952) compared LGD scores with ratings by superiors given as much as 9 months later and found correlations of 0.4. Arbous (1955) found a validity of 0.6 for LGD against rated promise of executives in training. Suitability for the British foreign service as rated after two years on duty was predicted (validity 0.3) by LGD at the time of selection (Vernon, 1950).

LGD illustrates the advantage that can be obtained from systematic observations. Social relations are important in personnel assignment, yet difficult to judge validly from questionnaires, letters of recommendations, or interviews. LGD is an economical "worksample" of group behavior. It avoids much of the bias inherent in summary impressions. Army colonels' ratings of cadet potential were much poorer predictors of later merit ratings than were total scores recorded by these same colonels acting as observers for an LGD session (Bass, 1954).

No doubt LGD is "fakable." The applicant who wants to make an impression surely will say more and try to lead. But this only increases the validity of the technique. If he lacks social skills his ineptness will be clear to the observer. If he "puts on a good show," he is likely to put on an equally good show on a job, where he is motivated to display the same skills.

Validity, Past and Present

My review of the many reports on validity—some rudimentary and some exhaustively detailed—will be synoptic and selective; for fuller summaries, see Dunnette (1971), Finkel (in Dunnette, 1976), and Wiggins (1973).

The first wave. One finding noted early and confirmed often was that assessors obtain their best results when predicting toward a known criterion, applicable to all persons accepted. Vernon (1950), reporting on house-party assessment of executive-level civil servants, emphasizes the contribution job analysis made to the positive results. (Also, training the observers brought considerable improvement; Vernon & Parry, 1949.) The final assessment predicted grades in a training course with validity 0.8. (That, in a group with restricted range! Is it possible that the criterion raters were acquainted with the assessment ratings?) Ratings on the job were predicted with r's of 0.5 and above. Judges who observed the worksample performance provided particularly valid impressions; peer ratings were somewhat valid; written tests were next to useless.

The most noteworthy finding from the study of clinical psychologists (Kelly & Fiske, 1951, p. 169) was that clinical competence (as rated by whoever supervised a trainee's internship) was predicted with validity 0.37 on the basis of only the credentials file plus ability tests and inventories. That is not bad, considering the weakness of the criterion. More important, validity did not rise above 0.42 when the case conference also took into account reports from interviews and projective tests. Judgments based on all these data *plus* performance tests produced a validity of 0.37. Another blow to projective tests came in a study where entering aviation cadets took a group inkblot test, a sentence-completion test, a psychosomatic inventory, and so on. Authorities on projective methods could not do better than chance in identifying trainees who had to be eliminated when they developed overt personality disturbances (Holtzman & Sells, 1954).

Criterion inadequacy had sad consequences for IPAR's study of U.S. Air Force captains (Wiggins, 1973, pp. 539–543, based on unpublished technical reports by D. W. MacKinnon and others.) The several criteria of officer effectiveness supplied by the U.S. Air Force intercorrelated only 0.3. The assessors could predict these criteria with validities around 0.1 to 0.2—disappointing, but how can one hope to predict inconsistent criteria? Impressions formed by observation seemed to have some validity whereas neither objective nor projective test scores predicted better than chance.

The difficulties of assessment on the basis of inferred personality structure reflect the inadequacies of human judgment that appear even in well-structured predictions (p. 405). Beyond that, the attempt to use information of many kinds, related to many aspects of the person, presented a task beyond the reach of personality theory in this generation. Luborsky's (1954) poignant remarks about the study of psychiatrists no doubt apply to many other dynamic assessments: "Reviewing some predictions on which we erred, we were impressed with our correct assessment of many specific qualities and our inability to cast these up into proper balance so as to judge ability to develop skill as a psychiatrist."

Figure 16.6 makes evident how difficult a task the assessors undertook. Along each path from top to bottom, the chart identifies some sources of change in behavior and some limitations on inference. At the upper left, attention is drawn to the fact that the observer collects fragmentary samples of performance. Below box 2a, the left-hand branch represents impressionistic assessment, and the branch leading to the center of the chart refers to statistical-actuarial prediction. Obviously, the adequacy of prediction by formula depends on the relevance of the scores and the data from which the formula was derived, but subjectivity is not a source of error. The simplest assessment, leading to box 6b, stands or falls with the judgment of the assessor. Some of this error can be ironed out by combining observers, but invalid widely held stereotypes (e.g., of what a psychiatrist should be) survive in the average.

Complex dynamic assessment (at the far left) is more vulnerable. There is, first of all, a mapping of perceptions onto a theory of personality, from which conclusions are drawn about the person's inner motives, conflicts, and constructs. Then the assessor must draw, from observation of persons in the occupation or from her imaginings, a conception of the roles the jobholder should perform and combine this with the image of the personality in order to judge whether the person will fit into the role. Even that is not the end, for prediction of a criterion rating has to go beyond job performance to what the supervisor will think of that performance. As indicated on the right side of the chart, behavior on the job (2b) is not the criterion; the criterion is attenuated or biased by the same processes of observation and judgment that impair predictive assessments. The attempts at generalized assessments for the wide range of duties in the OSS and the wide range of roles clinical psychologists and psychiatrists play could at best point toward generalized stereotypes of job requirements. One of the clearest messages from personnel research is the contribution job analysis makes to silhouetting the predictor's target (Hunter & Hunter, 1982).

Assessment of executives. Not surprisingly, current assessment projects have taken a conservative turn. They make predictions essentially of type 6b, and they place much of the burden of judgment not on psychologists coming from a distance but on managers and supervisors who know the work demands and standards of the employing firm. The behavior sampled is largely matched to the characteristics overtly to be observed on the job—social interaction, for example. Even when projective techniques are used, the evaluation concentrates on indications of ambition and other qualities desired

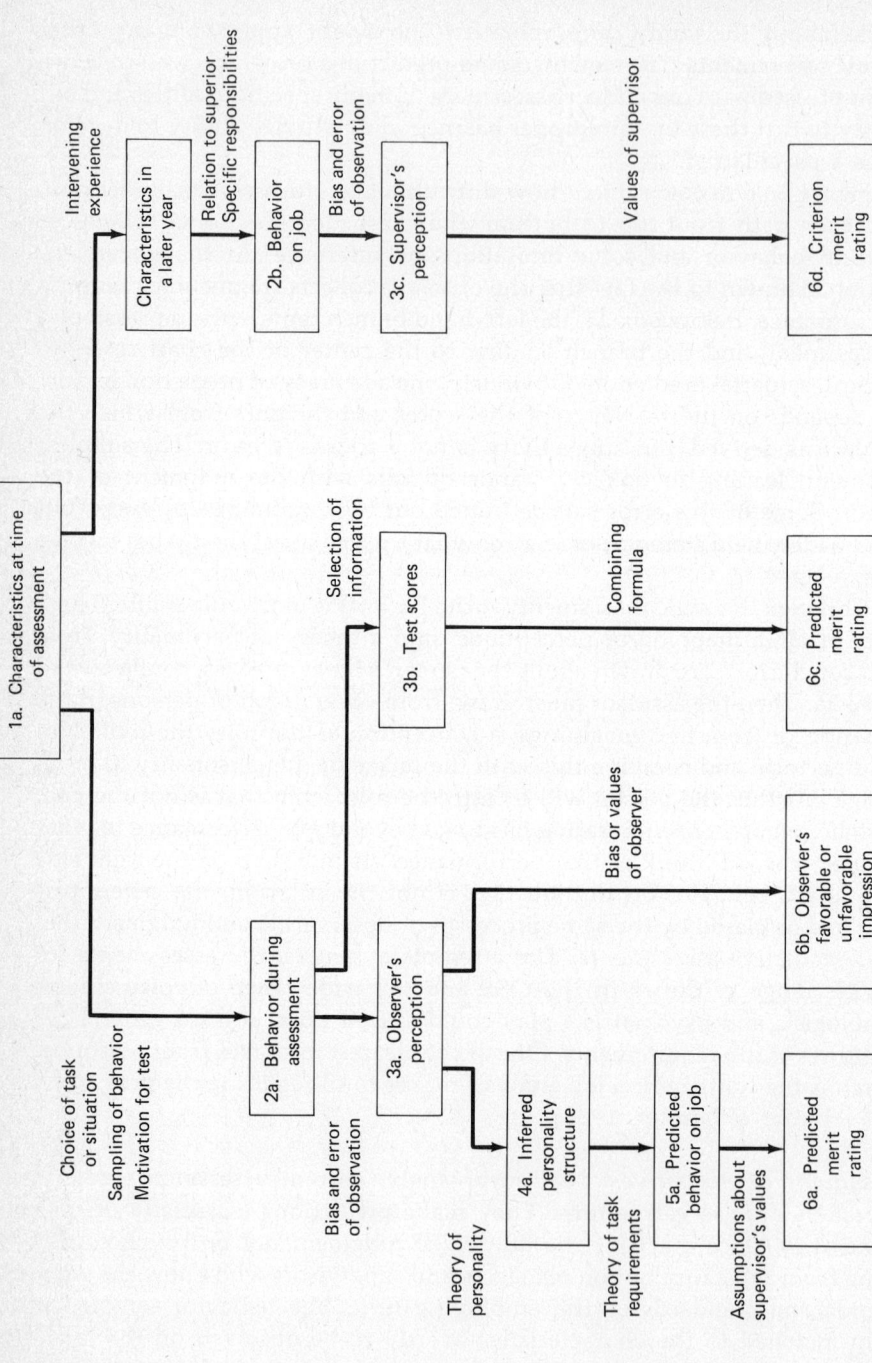

Figure 16.6. Stages in assessment and in criterion development.

Source: Permission has been granted from Lauretta Bender, M.D., and the American Orthopsychiatric Association to reproduce plate I, Page 4 from *The Visual Motor Gestalt Test and Its Clinical Use*, published by the American Orthopsychiatric Association in 1938.

in executives. The company has constructed an image of the kind of person it wants as executive, so the assessors have a good chance to recognize who will please the company. If the company stereotype is not a sound one, "valid" prediction of judgments made on the job may not be picking the executives who would do the company the most good.

Most validity coefficients with global criteria of managerial performance have ranged between 0.4 and 0.65. Some studies used rate of advancement in rank or salary as criteria, with equally satisfactory validities. Telephone-company assessors made an explicit prediction as to who would or would not reach a middle-management post within 10 years. Among college graduates, the percentage who reached middle management 6 to 8 years later was 50 for those judged favorably and 11 for those judged doubtful; for the noncollege group, the corresponding proportions were 37 and 5 (Bray & Grant, 1966; for later histories, see Bray, 1982). In this study and the one to be described next, assessments were not reported to the company, and the criteria could not have been contaminated. That is not the case in the majority of validations of assessments, according to Howard (1974).

In Table 16.2 we see that criterion rankings 2 years after an assessment tended to confirm what was originally said about strengths and weaknesses, as well as about overall merit. Although the literature taken all together suggests validity "greater than chance," I judge that the relationship of assessment profiles to criterion profiles is weak and inconsistent. Still, firms want advice on whom to promote and to what assignment. Cascio and Silbey (1979) review experience to date and argue that the cost of an assessment technique should not deter its use for positions where a firm gains many thousands of dollars by assigning the responsibility to a better-qualified person.

Many attempts have been made to determine which procedures contribute most to the assessment, but studies are too small to produce clear evidence. Every technique is supported as making an independent contribution by one research report or another. The following turn up repeatedly as

Table 16.2 *Correlation of criterion rankings with assessments of marketing managers*

Predictions of Success by Assessors	Judgments Made on the Job		
	Forecasting-Budgeting	Sales	Interpersonal Relationships
Forecasting-budgeting	**0.5**	0.15	0.35
Sales	0.0	**0.6**	0.4
Interpersonal relationships	0.0	0.25	**0.45**

Note: The intercorrelations of the three predictions ranged from 0.45 to 0.7; $N = 31$. Rankings from several informants were pooled in the criterion.
SOURCE: Albrecht *et al.*, 1964, p. 356.

showing direct validity against the criterion, influence on assessors' final ratings, and some degree of independence from the other predictors:

> Straightforward measures of academic ability.
> Interview to assess energy and motivation.
> Business simulations.
> LGD.
> Peer ratings of likability or social effectiveness.

No one can say whether objective scoring of the performance tests would have an advantage over the usual practice of rating the performances, but subjective evaluation seems natural to managers and adds to the appeal of the recommendations. Another open question is whether the integrative conference produces a final rating of overall merit that is more valid than the unweighted sum of scores or ratings from four or five procedures.

The good reputation of assessment centers illustrates the general qualities that have been associated with nearly all the more successful applications of testing. The approach is empirical, does not depend on psychological theory, and is intellectually and socially conservative.

By empiricism, I refer to the checking of test scores against other sources of evidence to determine what interpretative concepts or predictions are valid. The leaders in the development of assessment centers kept appraisals of early trials locked in files for years while they amassed case histories to determine which clues to rely on and how adequate the assessment was. The move away from assessment of personality "in depth" was dictated by follow-up findings; the state of the art in this generation clearly did not justify basing personnel decisions on dynamic interpretation. The empirical tradition goes back to Binet, who, you will recall, tried an almost endless variety of tests in order to find the ones most reflective of intellectual functioning.

Little or no theory enters into the interpretation of peer ratings or TMC or a self-report of clerical interests. Knowledge has developed around particular instruments such as the Wechsler, the MMPI, or the tests in Guilford's system; if any such body of interpreted experience constitutes "theory," it has not shaped or been much shaped by the remainder of psychological theory. Binet snatched up instruments from any source and let his own results rather than the existing theory determine his scale. Murray was equally eclectic, demonstrating his distrust of any theory by calling on all the theories simultaneously. Content-valid tests and the actuarial approach get little help from theory. One reason for the distance between the study of test data and the larger body of psychological ideas is the traditional emphasis of experimental psychology on elementary stimuli, processes, and reactions; it is hard to connect the findings with complex processes. It is perplexing that Piaget's elaborate theory, which dealt with complex processes from the outset, left so little trace on practical psychological testing. Piagetian constructs did shed light on test performance, and mental tests predicted Piagetian performances, but only with respect to moral judgment did Piaget's ideas inspire collection of information not available from conventional tests.

Empirical medicine was practiced with only modest success in the centuries before the germ theory or disease and modern pharmacology revolutionized medicine. The day will surely come when new theory revolutionizes thought about individuality and the procedures by which people are characterized. Perhaps the emergent theory of information processing will lead to a revolution in testing; if not, it will nonetheless amplify and amend test interpretations.

Current assessment is conservative. The assessors try to find out who will fit into the firm as it now operates. They take peer ratings seriously, having established that those who impress associates in one situation are likely to make a good impression on similar persons in other situations. The assessment is manifestly designed to find out who will fit into the system as it stands. So is setting up an experience table to indicate which candidates for parole are most likely to commit new crimes if released.

TOWARD AN ECOLOGICAL VIEW

A social scientist or philosopher taking a detached view of the systems where tests are applied would raise questions about the standard ways of operating. Might it be possible to modify the firm or its conception of effective management? To modify the college and its conception of success? To provide supports for the parolee that would make recidivism less likely? One can scarcely criticize those asked to provide predictions for doing that job as well as possible, but someone should be scrutinizing the criterion and all the aspects of training, supervision, and the institutional organization that lead up to the criterion. Such questions are raised at times, as in the studies of the difference between rule-bound and flexible organizations (p. 142) and in the efforts of colleges to assist individuals who would be unlikely to survive if admitted on a sink-or-swim basis. The contributions of psychological testing to the redesign of services, however, have been much less conspicuous than its contributions to organizational continuity.

Social science, including psychology, is quite good at assessing the current state of affairs, at building up experience tables, at making short inferences. Forecasts are necessarily imperfect. No problem has been studied more exhaustively than the prediction of college marks, and the predictions still contain a considerable measure of error. That is inherent in the richness of the choices available to the student (not all of them academic), the variety of accomplishments and shortcomings that are averaged into the grade record, and, of course, the unforeseeable intrusions of illness and family problems and luck-of-the-draw in roommates and teachers. The point to emphasize is not the limits of prediction—which, in this essentially static institution, have very nearly been reached—but the excellence of a conservative technology.

Regression equations relating outcome to test score hold up year after year and from one college to another even though the test items themselves are continually replaced.

The central problem for testers is that long-reach inferences have to be made. They will be made with or without the aid of tests, with or without the aid of social-science knowledge and social technology. Someone has to decide whether this youngster should be held in an institution or placed in a foster home or returned to a parent. Someone (or some bureau) must decide who shall be eligible for expensive forms of therapy that will be covered by third-party payments such as Medicare. The government of Venezuela is now entertaining a proposal to raise the educability and productivity of its next generation by dedicating the proceeds of a temporary oil bonanza to a massive effort to improve "intelligence." Results from various trials will come in before the major commitment is made. Those findings will describe only the skills developed by children within a year or two whereas the decision hinges on benefits envisioned over the whole of these citizens' working lives. Long-reach inferences are required whenever one judges whether a treatment or policy that worked for one set of cases will work well under other circumstances (Cronbach, 1982a).

As earlier chapters have said, large amounts of judgment, based on the best current understanding, are required to arrive at and defend a policy or practice. Everyone, including the tough-minded empiricist who distrusts judgment and suggests reliance on formulas, confronts problems for which there is no experience table. When empiricists do have an experience table, they must judge which cases and situations the table applies to. No one can defend mechanical rules that refuse to consider the facts about individual backgrounds and life situations. To help the individual chart his own course, the professional should do more than present odds derived from a faceless statistical aggregate. Psychology has gone far beyond folk wisdom by observing individuals over years and even decades and by closely observing persons in work settings and classrooms and during retraining intended to modify conduct and feelings. The resulting concepts suggest facts to collect in investigating particular families, schools, and factories or in identifying assets, limitations, and undeveloped strengths of an individual. The soundness of interpretations has been steadily improved by the very process of exposing oversimple and incorrect interpretations.

Perhaps the most important extension in recent years is the increased awareness that a psychology of individual organisms is inadequate. Bronfenbrenner (1979) introduces a profound book with these words: "Human abilities and their realization depend in significant degree on the larger social and institutional context of individual activity." Around each person there is an immediate social ecology created by the persons he interacts with, and these persons are part of a larger system of institutions embedded in a community embedded in a culture. Messages are transmitted all up and down the line—messages of demand, messages of reward, and subtler signals that also shape behavior. These transactions support development along some lines while neglecting or restricting abilities to play other roles.

Psychologists will have to learn from sociology and anthropology if they are to understand individuality in its context. Experimental investigations of educational, therapeutic, and other efforts designed to promote the welfare and functioning of community members have too often characterized treatments by simple labels. To try to generalize about "special education" is as senseless an act of labeling as is a generalization about "the retarded child." The identification, analysis, and objective assessment of situational differences has barely begun—but a beginning has been made in measures of group climate and in studies of situational influences on expression of personality, for example. For advancing understanding and for improving the quality of individual lives, the greatest hope lies in an intensified study of the interconnections between characteristics of persons and characteristics of social settings.

References

Achenbach, T. M. The Child Behavior Profile: I. Boys aged 6–11. *Journal of Consulting and Clinical Psychology,* 1978, *46,* 478–488.

Achenbach, T. M., & Edelbrock, C. S. The Child Behavior Profile: II. Boys aged 12–16 and girls aged 6–11 and 12–16. *Journal of Consulting and Clinical Psychology,* 1979, *47,* 223–233.

———. Behavioral problems and competencies reported by parents of normal and disturbed children aged four through sixteen. *Monographs of the Society for Research in Child Development,* 1981, *46,* No. 1.

Adcock, C. J. A comparison of the concepts of Cattell and Eysenck. *British Journal of Educational Psychology,* 1965, *35,* 90–97.

Adorno, T. W., et al. *The authoritarian personality.* New York: Harper & Row, 1950.

Albrecht, P. A., Glaser, E. M., & Marks, J. Validation of a multiple assessment procedure for managerial personnel. *Journal of Applied Psychology,* 1964, *48,* 351–360.

Allen, M. J., & Yen, W. M. *Introduction to measurement theory.* Monterey, Calif.: Brooks/Cole, 1979.

Allport, G. W. *Personality: A psychological interpretation.* New York: Holt, Rinehart and Winston, 1937.

American Personnel and Guidance Association. Responsibilities of users of standardized tests. *Guidepost,* October 5, 1978, pp. 5–8.

American Psychological Association. *Ethical principles of in the conduct of research with human participants.* Washington, D.C.: APA, 1973.

American Psychological Association, American Educational Research Association, and

National Council on Measurement in Education. *Standards for educational and psychological tests.* Washington, D.C.: APA, 1974.

American Psychological Association. Ethical principles of psychologists. *American Psychologist,* 1981, *36,* 633–638.

Amrine, M. (Ed.) [Special issue.] *American Psychologist,* 1965, *20,* No. 11.

Anastasi, A. *Psychological Testing,* 5th ed. New York: Macmillan, 1982.

Anastasi, A., & Drake, J. D. An empirical comparison of certain techniques for estimating the reliability of speeded tests. *Educational and Psychological Measurement,* 1954, *14,* 529–540.

Andrews, B. J., & Hecht, J. T. A preliminary investigation of two procedures for setting examination standards. *Educational and Psychological Measurement,* 1976, *36,* 45–50.

Andrews, J. D. W. The achievement motive and advancement in two types of organizations. *Journal of Personality and Social Psychology,* 1967, *6,* 163–168.

Angoff, W. H. (Ed.). *The College Board Admissions Testing Program.* New York: College Entrance Examination Board, 1971.

Appell, M. J., Williams, C. M., & Fishell, K. N. Significant factors in placing mental retardates from a workshop situation. *Personnel and Guidance Journal,* 1962, *41,* 260–265.

Arbous, A. G. *Selection for industrial leadership.* London: Oxford University Press, 1955.

Arvey, R. D. Unfair discrimination in the employment interview. *Psychological Bulletin,* 1979, *86,* 736–765.

Ash, P. [Review of P. H. DuBois, *A history of psychological testing.*] *Personnel Psychology,* 1971, *24,* 538–543.

Asher, J. J., & Sciarrino, J. A. Realistic work sample tests: A review. *Personnel Psychology,* 1974, *27,* 519–533.

Atkinson, J. W. Studying personality in the context of an advanced motivational psychology. *American Psychologist,* 1981, *36,* 117–128.

Atkinson, J. W., & Raynor, J. O. (Eds.). *Personality, motivation, and achievement.* Washington, D.C.: Hemisphere, 1978.

Ayres, L. P. *A scale for measuring the quality of handwriting of school children.* New York: Russell Sage Foundation, 1912.

Bachman, J. G., & O'Malley, P. M. Self-esteem in young men: A longitudinal analysis of the impact of educational and occupational attainment. *Journal of Personality and Social Psychology,* 1977, *35,* 365–380.

Balke-Aurell, G. *Changes in ability as related to educational and occupational experience.* Gothenburg: Acta Universitatis Gothoburgensis, 1982.

Baller, W. R., Charles, D. C., & Miller, E. L. Mid-life attainment of the mentally retarded: A longitudinal study. *Genetic Psychology Monographs,* 1967, *75,* 235–329.

Baltes, P. B., & Nesselroade, J. R. History and rationale of longitudinal research. In Nesselroade & Baltes (Eds.), *Longitudinal research in the study of behavior and development.* New York: Academic Press, 1979.

Baltes, P. B., & Schaie, K. W. On the plasticity of intelligence in adulthood and old age. *American Psychologist,* 1976, *31,* 720–725.

Bandura, A., & Whalen, C. K. The influence of antecedent reinforcement and divergent modeling cues on patterns of self-regard. *Journal of Personality and Social Psychology,* 1966, *3,* 373–382.

Bannatyne, A. Diagnosis: A note on recategorization of the WISC scaled scores. *Journal of Learning Disabilities,* 1974, *7,* 272–274.

Barclay, J. R. Sociometric choices and teacher ratings as predictors of school dropout. *Journal of School Psychology,* 1966, *4,* 40–44.

Barnette, W.L. An occupational aptitude pattern for engineers. *Educational and Psychological Measurement,* 1951, *11,* 52–66.

Barrett, G. V., Phillips, J. S., & Alexander, R. A. Concurrent and predictive validity designs: A critical reanalysis. *Journal of Applied Psychology,* 1981, *66,* 1–6.
Barron, F. Threshold for the perception of human movement in inkblots. *Journal of Consulting Psychology,* 1955, *19,* 33–38.
Barron, F., & Harrington, D. M. Creativity, intelligence, and personality. *Annual Review of Psychology,* 1981, *32,* 439–476.
Bartholomeo, D. The study of error. *College Composition and Communication,* 1980, *31,* 253–269.
Bartling, H. C., & Hood, A. B. An 11-year follow-up of measured interest and vocational choice. *Journal of Counseling Psychology,* 1981, *28,* 27–35.
Barzun, J. *The House of Intellect.* New York: Harper & Row, 1959.
Bass, B. M. The leaderless group discussion. *Psychological Bulletin,* 1954, *51,* 465–492.
Bass, B. M., & Coates, C. H. Forecasting officer potential using the leaderless group discussion. *Journal of Abnormal and Social Psychology,* 1952, *47,* 321–325.
Baughman, E. E., & Dahlstrom, W. G. *Negro and white children.* New York: Academic Press, 1968.
Beck, S. J. *Rorschach's test.* (3 vols.) New York: Grune & Stratton, 1961–1978.
Becker, W. C., & Krug, R. S. A circumplex model for social behavior in children. *Child Development,* 1964, *35,* 371–396.
Bem, D. J., & Allen, A. On predicting some of the people some of the time: The search for cross-situational consistencies in behavior. *Psychological Review,* 1974, *81,* 506–520.
Benjamin, M., et al. Test anxiety: Deficits in information processing. *Journal of Experimental Psychology,* 1981, *73,* 816–824.
Berk, R. A. (Ed.). *Handbook of methods for detecting test bias.* Baltimore: Johns Hopkins University Press, 1982.
Berland, J. C. Untitled remarks at Conference on human assessment and cultural factors, Queens University, Kingston, Ont., 1981.
———. *No five fingers are alike.* Cambridge, Mass.: Harvard University Press, 1982.
Bernardin, H. J., & Pence, E. C. Effects of rater training: Creating new response sets and decreasing accuracy. *Journal of Applied Psychology,* 1980, *65,* 60–66.
Bernardin, H. J., & Smith, P. C. A clarification of some issues regarding the development and use of Behaviorally Anchored Rating Scales (BARS). *Journal of Applied Psychology,* 1981, *66,* 458–463.
Betz, N. E. Prospects: New types of information. . . . In D. J. Weiss (Ed.), *Computerized adaptive trait measurement.* Minneapolis: Psychometric Methods Program, University of Minnesota, 1975.
Betz, N. E., & Weiss, D. J. Effects of immediate knowledge of results and adaptive testing on ability test performance. Research Report 76-3. Psychometric Methods Program, University of Minnesota, 1976. (a)
———. Psychological effects of immediate knowledge of results and adaptive ability testing. Research Report 76-4, Psychometric Methods Program, University of Minnesota, 1976. (b)
Biber, B., & others. *Life and ways of the seven to eight year old.* New York: Basic Books, 1952.
Bigler, E. D., & Ehrfurth, J. W. The continued inappropriate single use of the Bender Visual Motor Gestalt Test. *Professional Psychology,* 1981, *12,* 562–569.
Binet, A., & Henri, V. La psychologie individuelle. *Année psychologique,* 1895, *2,* 411–463.
Black, J. D. The interpretation of MMPI profiles of college women. Unpublished doctoral dissertation, University of Minnesota, Minneapolis, 1963.
Block, J. *The Q-sort method in personality assessment and psychiatric research.* Springfield, Ill.: Thomas, 1961.
———. *The challenge of response sets.* New York: Appleton-Century-Crofts, 1965.

———. Some enduring and consequential structures of personality. In A. I. Rabin et al. (Eds.), *Further explorations in personality.* New York: Wiley, 1981.

Block, J., Weiss, D. S., & Thorne, A. How relevant is a semantic similarity interpretation of personality ratings? *Journal of Personality and Social Psychology,* 1979, *37,* 1053–1074.

Bloom, B. S. *Human characteristics and school learning.* New York: McGraw-Hill, 1976.

Borgen, F. H., & Seling, M. J. Expressed and inventoried interests revisited: Perspicacity in the person. *Journal of Counseling Psychology,* 1978, *25,* 536–543.

Borkowski, J. G., & Cavanaugh, J. C. Maintenance and generalization of skills and strategies by the retarded. In N. R. Ellis (Ed.), *Handbook of mental deficiency,* 2d ed. Hillsdale, N. J.: Erlbaum, 1979.

Borman, W. C. Format and training effects on rater accuracy and rater errors. *Journal of Applied Psychology,* 1979, *64,* 410–421.

Boruch, R. F., & Cecil, J. S. *Assuring confidentiality of social research data.* Philadelphia: University of Pennsylvania Press, 1979.

Botwinick, J., & Siegler, I. C. Intellectual ability among the elderly: Simultaneous cross-sectional and longitudinal comparisons. *Developmental Psychology,* 1980, *16,* 49–53.

Bower, G. L., & Lewis, J. R. ASVAB expectancy tables. Technical Note. Armed Forces Vocational Testing Group, Randolph Air Force Base, Texas, 1975.

Brace, C. L., and others. [Multiple review of A. R. Jensen's *Bias in mental testing.*] *Behavioral and Brain Sciences,* 1980, *3,* 325–372.

Bradburn, N. M., Sudman, S., et al. *Improving interview method and questionnaire design.* San Francisco: Jossey-Bass, 1979.

Bradley, R., Caldwell, B., & Elardo, R. Home environment, social status, and mental test performance. *Journal of Educational Psychology,* 1977, *69,* 697–701.

Brass, D. J., & Oldham, G. R. Validating an in-basket test using an alternative set of leadership scoring dimensions. *Journal of Applied Psychology,* 1976, *61,* 652–657.

Bray, D. W. The assessment center and the study of lives. *American Psychologist,* 1982, *37,* 180–189.

Bray, D. W., & Grant, D. L. The Assessment Center in the measurement of potential for business management. *Psychological Monographs,* 1966, *80,* No. 17.

Breland, H. M. *Can multiple-choice tests measure writing skills?* New York: College Entrance Examination Board, 1979. (a)

———. *Population validity and college entrance measures.* New York: College Entrance Examination Board, 1979. (b)

Brennan, R. L., & Kane, M. T. Generalizability theory: A review. *New Directions in Testing and Measurement,* 1979, *4,* 33–51.

Brislin, R. W., Lonner, W. J., & Thorndike, R. M. (Eds.). *Cross-cultural research methods.* New York: Wiley, 1974.

Brogden, H. E. A new coefficient: Application to biserial correlation and to estimation of selective efficiency. *Psychometrika,* 1949, *14,* 169–182.

———. Increased efficiency of selection resulting from replacement of a single predictor with several differential predictors. *Educational and Psychological Measurement,* 1951, *11,* 173–196.

Brokaw, L. D. Technical school validity of the Airman Activity Inventory. *AFPTRC Development Report* 56–109, 1956.

Bronfenbrenner, U. *The ecology of human development.* Cambridge: Harvard University Press, 1979.

Bronson, W. C. Central orientations: A study of behavior organization from childhood to adolescence. *Child Development,* 1966, *37,* 125–155.

Brown, A. L. Conservation of number and continuous quantity in normal, bright, and retarded children. *Child Development,* 1973, *44,* 376–379.

———. Knowing when, where, and how to remember: A problem of metacognition. In R. Glaser (Ed.), *Advances in instructional psychology.* Hillsdale, N.J.: Erlbaum, 1978.
Brown, A. L., & Campione, J. C. Permissible inferences from the outcome of training studies in cognitive development research. *Quarterly Newsletter, Institute for Comparative Human Development,* 1978, *2,* 46–53.
Brown, A. L., & De Loache, J. S. Skills, plans, and self-regulation. In R. S. Siegler (Ed.), *Children's thinking: What develops.* Hillsdale, N. J.: Erlbaum, 1978.
Brown, A. L., & French, L. A. The zone of potential development: Implications for intelligence testing in the Year 2000. *Intelligence,* 1979, *3,* 255–273.
Brown, C. Estimating the determinants of employee performance. *Journal of Human Resources,* 1982, *17,* 182–194.
Brown, S. H. Validity generalization and situational moderation in the life insurance industry. *Journal of Applied Psychology,* 1981, *66,* 664–670.
Buckley, P. D. The Bender Gestalt Test: A review of reported research with school age subjects. *Psychology in the Schools,* 1978, *15,* 327–338.
Burisch, M. Construction strategies for multivariate personality inventories. *Applied Psychological Measurement,* 1978, *2,* 97–111.
Burkhart, B. R., Christian, W. L., & Gynther, M. D. Item subtlety and faking on the MMPI: A paradoxical relationship. *Journal of Personality Assessment,* 1978, *42,* 76–80.
Burnett, S. A., & Lane, D. M. Effects of academic instruction on spatial visualization. *Intelligence,* 1980, *4,* 233–242.
Buros, O. K. (Ed.). *The Mental Measurements Yearbooks.* Highland Park, N.J.: Gryphon Press, 1941–1978 (irregular).
Burton, R. V. Generality of honesty reconsidered. *Psychological Review,* 1963, *70,* 481–499.
Burton, R. V., & Casey, W. M. Moral development. In R. H. Woody (Ed.), *Encyclopaedia of clinical assessment.* San Francisco: Jossey-Bass, 1980.
Butcher, H. J. *Human intelligence.* London: Methuen, 1968.
Butcher, J. N. (Ed.), *Objective personality assessment: Changing perspectives.* New York: Academic Press, 1972.
Butcher, J. N. (Ed.). *New developments in the use of the MMPI.* Minneapolis: University of Minnesota Press, 1979.
Butcher, J. N., & Tellegen, A. Objections to MMPI items. *Journal of Consulting Psychology,* 1966, *30,* 527–534.
California Assessment Program. *Technical report.* Sacramento: California State Department of Education, 1977.
Callan, J. P. An attempt to use the MMPI as a predictor of failure in military training. *British Journal of Psychiatry,* 1972, *121,* 553–557.
Callaway, E. *Brain electrical potentials and individual psychological differences.* New York: Grune & Stratton, 1975.
Callender, J. C., & Osburn, H. G. Development and test of a new model of validity generalization. *Journal of Applied Psychology,* 1980, *65,* 543–558.
Campbell, D. P. The vocational interests of APA presidents. *American Psychologist,* 1965, *20,* 636–644.
———. *Handbook for the Strong Vocational Interest Blank.* Stanford, Calif.: Stanford University Press, 1971.
Campbell, D. T., & Fiske, D. W. Convergent and discriminant validation by the multitrait-multimethod matrix. *Psychological Bulletin,* 1959, *56,* 81–105.
Cantoni, L. J. Guidance: 4 students 10 years later. *Clearing House,* 1954, *28,* 474–478.
———. High school tests and measurements as predictors of occupational status. *Journal of Applied Psychology,* 1955, *39,* 253–255.
Carek, R. Another look at the relationships between similar scales on the Strong

Vocational Interest Blank and the Kuder Occupational Interest Survey. *Journal of Counseling Psychology,* 1972, *19,* 218–223.
Carlsmith, M., Ellsworth, P., & Aronson, E. *Methods of research in social psychology.* Reading, Mass.: Addison-Wesley, 1976.
Carnegie Council on Policy Studies in Higher Education. *Selective admissions in higher education.* San Francisco: Jossey-Bass, 1977.
Carroll, J. B. A model of school learning. *Teachers College Record,* 1963, *64,* 723–733.
———. Individual difference relations in psychometric and experimental cognitive tasks. Report No. 163, The L. L. Thurstone Psychometric Laboratory, University of North Carolina, Chapel Hill, 1980.
Carter, L. F., & Dudek, F. J. The use of psychological techniques in measuring and critically analyzing navigators' flight performance. *Psychometrika,* 1947, *12,* 31–42.
Cascio, W. F., & Silbey, V. Utility of the assessment center as a selection device. *Journal of Applied Psychology,* 1979, *64,* 107–118.
Cattell, R. B. *Abilities: Their structure, growth, and action.* Boston: Houghton Mifflin, 1971.
Cattell, R. B., Eber, H. W., & Tatsuoka, M. M. *Handbook for the Sixteen Personality Factor Questionnaire (16 PF).* Champaign, Ill.: Institute for Personality and Ability Testing, 1970.
Cattell, R. B., & Warburton, F. W. *Objective personality and motivation tests.* Urbana: University of Illinois Press, 1967.
Cerney, M. S. Using the psychological test report in the course of pshchotherapy. *Journal of Personality Assessment,* 1978, *42,* 457–463.
Chapman, P. Lewis M. Terman and the intelligence testing movement, 1890–1930. Unpublished doctoral dissertation, Stanford University, Calif., 1979.
Charters, W. W., Jr. Social class and intelligence tests. In W. W. Charters, Jr. & N. L. Gage (Eds.), *Readings in the social psychology of education.* Boston: Allyn & Bacon, 1963.
Chelune, G. J. Nature and assessment of self-disclosing behavior. In P. McReynolds (Ed.), *Advances in psychological assessment,* vol. 4. San Francisco: Jossey-Bass, 1977.
Churchill, W. D., & Smith, S. E. Relationships between the 1960 Stanford-Binet Scale and group measures of intelligence and achievement. *Measurement and Evaluation in Guidance,* 1974, *7,* 40–45.
Ciminero, A. R., et al. (Eds.). *Handbook of behavioral assessment.* New York: Wiley, 1977.
Clancey, W. J., Shortliffe, E. H., & Buchanan, B. G. Intelligent computer-aided instruction for medical diagnosis. In R. A. Dunn (Ed.), *Symposium [3d] on computer applications in medical care: Proceedings.* New York: Institute of Electrical and Electronic Engineers, 1979.
Clark, R. A. The projective measurement of experimentally induced levels of sexual motivation. *Journal of Experimental Psychology,* 1952, *44,* 391–399.
Clarke-Stewart, K. A. Evaluating parental effects on child development. *Review of Research in Education,* 1978, *6,* 47–119.
Coates, T. J., & Thoresen, C. E. Using generalizability theory in behavior observation. *Behavior Therapy,* 1978, *9,* 605–613.
Coffman, W. E. A factor analysis of the Verbal section of the Scholastic Aptitude Test. Research Bulletin 66–30, Educational Testing Service, 1966.
Colbert, G. A., & Taylor, L. R. Empirically derived job families as a foundation for the study of validity generalization. Study III. Generalization of selection test validity. *Personnel Psychology,* 1978, *31,* 355–364.
Cole, M., Gay, J., & Glick, J. Some experimental studies of Kpelle quantitative behavior. *Psychonomic Monograph Supplements,* 1968, *2* (10), 173–190.
Cole, M., Hood, L., & McDermott, R. *Ecological niche-picking: Ecological invalidity as an axiom of experimental cognitive psychology.* New York: Laboratory of Comparative Human Cognition, Rockefeller University, 1978.

Cole, M., et al. *The cultural basis of learning and thinking.* New York: Basic Books, 1971.
College Entrance Examination Board. A statement on personality testing. *College Board Review,* 1963, *51,* 11–13.
―――. *Reports of the Commission on Tests* (2 vols.) New York: CEEB, 1970.
―――. *On further examination: Report of the Advisory Panel on the Scholastic Aptitude Test score decline.* New York: CEEB, 1977.
Cone, J. D., & Hawkins, R. P. (Eds.). *Behavioral assessment: New directions in clinical psychology.* New York: Brunner/Mazel, 1977.
Conrad, H. S. The validity of personality ratings of nursery-school children. *Journal of Educational Psychology,* 1932, *23,* 671–680.
―――. "Statistical analysis for the Mechanical Knowledge Test." Princeton, N.J.: College Entrance Examination Board, 1944.
Conry, R., & Plant, W. T. WAIS and group test predictions of an academic success criterion: high school and college. *Educational and Psychological Measurement,* 1965, *25,* 493–500.
Cook, T. D., & Campbell, D. T. *Quasi-experimentation: Design and analysis issues for field settings.* Chicago: Rand McNally, 1979.
Cook, T. D., et al. *"Sesame Street" revisited: A case study in evaluation research.* New York: Russell Sage Foundation, 1975.
Cooper, G. D., et al. The Porteus maze test and various measures of intelligence with southern Negro adolescents, *American Journal of Deficiency,* 1967, *71,* 787–792.
Cooper, L. A., & Regan, D. T. Attention, perception, and intelligence. In R. Sternberg (Ed.), *Handbook of human intelligence.* New York: Cambridge University Press, 1982.
Cooper, L. A., & Shepard, R. N. Chronometric studies of the rotation of mental images. In W. G. Chase (Ed.), *Visual information processing.* New York: Academic Press, 1973.
Coulter, W. A., & Morrow, H. W. (Eds.) *Adaptive behavior: Concepts and measurements.* New York: Grune & Stratton, 1978.
Counseling from profiles: A casebook for the Differential Aptitude Tests. New York: Psychological Corporation, 1977.
Cox, C. M. *Genetic studies of genius: II. The early mental traits of three hundred geniuses.* Stanford, Calif.: Stanford University Press, 1926.
Crabtree, P. D., & Hales, L. W. Holland's hexagonal model applied to rural youth. *Vocational Guidance Quarterly,* 1974, *22,* 218–223.
Crandall, V. C. Personality characteristics and social and achievement behaviors associated with children's social desirability response tendencies. *Journal of Personality and Social Psychology,* 1966, *4,* 477–486.
Cronbach, L. J. Further evidence on response sets and test design. *Educational and Psychological Measurement,* 1950, *10,* 3–31.
―――. A validation design for qualitative studies of personality. *Journal of Consulting Psychology,* 1948, *12,* 365–374.
―――. Proposals leading to analytic treatment of social perception scores. In R. Tagiuri & L. Petrullo (Eds.), *Person perception and interpersonal behavior.* Stanford, Calif.: Stanford University Press, 1958.
―――. *Essentials of psychological testing.* (3d ed.) New York: Harper & Row, 1970.
―――. Beyond the two disciplines of scientific psychology. *American Psychologist,* 1975, *30,* 116–127. (a)
―――. Five decades of public controversy over mental testing. *American Psychologist,* 1975, *30,* 1–13. (b)
―――. On the design of educational measures. In D. N. M. De Gruijter & L. J. Th. van der Kamp (Eds.), *Advances in psychological and educational measurement.* New York: Wiley, 1976. (a)

———. [Review of *Race differences in intelligence.*] *Contemporary Psychology,* 1976, *21,* 389–390. (b)

———. *Educational psychology.* (3d ed.) New York: Harcourt Brace Jovanovich, 1977.

———. The Armed Services Vocational Aptitude Battery—A test battery in transition. *Personnel and Guidance Journal,* 1979, *58,* 232–237.

———. Selection theory for a political world. *Public Personnel Management,* 1980, *9* (1), 37–50. (a)

———. Validity on parole: How can we go straight? *New Directions for Testing and Measurement,* 1980, *5,* 99–108. (b)

———. *Designing evaluations of educational and social programs.* San Francisco: Jossey-Bass, 1982. (a)

———. Prudent aspirations for social inquiry. In W. H. Kruskal (Ed.), *The social sciences: Their nature and uses.* Chicago: University of Chicago Press, 1982. (b)

Cronbach, L. J. & Drenth, P. J. D. (Eds.) *Mental tests and cultural adaptation,* The Hague: Mouton, 1972.

Cronbach, L. J., & Furby, L. How should we measure "change"—or should we? *Psychological Bulletin,* 1970, *74,* 66–80.

Cronbach, L. J., & Gleser, G. C. [Review of *The study of behavior.*] *Psychometrika,* 1954, *19,* 327–333.

———. *Psychological tests and personnel decisions.* (2d ed.) Urbana: University of Illinois Press, 1965.

Cronbach, L. J., & Meehl, P. E. Construct validity in psychological tests. *Psychological Bulletin,* 1955, *52,* 281–302.

Cronbach, L. J., & Schaeffer, G. A. Extensions of personnel selection theory to aspects of minority hiring. Report 81-A2, Institute for Educational Finance and Governance, Stanford University, Calif., 1981.

Cronbach, L. J., & Snow, R. E. *Aptitudes and instructional methods.* New York: Irvington, 1977. [Paperback edition, 1981.]

Cronbach, L. J., et al. *The dependability of behavioral measurements.* New York: Wiley, 1972.

———. *Toward reform of program evaluation.* San Francisco: Jossey-Bass, 1980.

Crosby, R. C., & Winsor, A. L. The validity of students' estimates of their own interests. *Journal of Applied Psychology,* 1941, *25,* 408–414.

Crowne, D. P., & Marlowe, D. *The approval motive.* New York: Wiley, 1964.

Crumbaugh, J. C. Graphoanalytic cues. In R. H. Woody (Ed.), *Encyclopaedia of clinical assessment,* vol. 2. San Francisco: Jossey-Bass, 1980.

Crumbaugh, J. C., & Stockholm, E. Validation of graphoanalysis by "global" or "holistic" method. *Perceptual and Motor Skills,* 1977, *44,* 403–410.

Dahlstrom, W. G. Screening for emotional fitness: The New Jersey case. In W. G. Dahlstrom & L. E. Dahlstrom (Eds.), *Basic readings on the MMPI.* Minneapolis: University of Minnesota Press, 1980.

Dahlstrom, W. G., Welsh, G. F., & Dahlstrom, L. E. *An MMPI handbook* (rev. ed.) (2 vols.). Minneapolis: University of Minnesota Press, 1972, 1975.

Damrin, D. E. The Russell Sage Social Relations Test: A technique for measuring group problem solving skills in elementary school children. *Journal of Experimental Education,* 1959, *28,* 85–99.

Darley, J. G., & Hagenah, T. *Vocational interest measurement: Theory and practice.* Minneapolis: University of Minnesota Press, 1955.

Darlington, R. B. "Reduced-variance regression." *Psychological Bulletin,* 1978, *85,* 1238–1255.

Dasen, P. R., Berry, J. W., & Witkin, H. A. The use of developmental theories cross-culturally. In L. H. Eckensburger *et al.* (Eds.), *Cross-cultural contributions to psychology.* Amsterdam: Swets and Zeitlinger, 1979.

Dauterman, W. L., & Suinn, R. M. "Stanford-Ohwaki-Kohs Tactile Block Design Intelligence Test for the Blind: Final report." Washington, D.C.: Vocational Rehabilitation Administration, 1966.
Davis, B. D., & Flaherty, P. (Eds.). *Human diversity: Its causes and social significance.* Cambridge, Mass.: Ballinger, 1976.
Davis, W. A. Socio-economic influences upon children's learning. *Understanding the Child,* 1951, *20,* 10–16.
Dawes, R. M. The robust beauty of improper linear models in decision making. *American Psychologist,* 1979, *34,* 571–582.
Dawes, R. M., & Corrigan, B. Linear models in decision making. *Psychological Bulletin,* 1974, *81,* 95–106.
deCharms, R. *Enhancing motivation: Change in the classroom.* New York: Irvington, 1976.
———. The origins of competence and achievement motivation in personal causation. In L. J. Fyans Jr., (Ed.), *Achievement motivation.* New York: Plenum, 1980.
DeNelsky, G. Y., & McKee, M. G. Prediction of computer programmer training and job performance using the AABP test. *Personnel Psychology,* 1974, *27,* 129–137.
Deutsch, C. Social class and child development. In B. M. Caldwell & H. N. Ricciuti (Eds.), *Review of Child Development Research,* vol. 3. Chicago: University of Chicago Press, 1973.
DeVries, R. Relationships among Piagetian, IQ, and achievement assessments. *Child Development,* 1974, *45,* 746–756.
Diamond, E. E. (Ed.). *Issues of sex bias and sex fairness in career interest measurement.* Washington, D.C.: National Institute of Education, 1975.
Dienes, J. T. Testing programs. In B. M. Schoenberg (Ed.), *A handbook and guide for the college and university counseling center.* Westport, Conn.: Greenwood, 1977.
Division 14, American Psychological Association. *Principles for the validation and use of personnel selection procedures* (2d ed.). Berkeley, Calif.: Division of Industrial-Organizational Psychology, 1980.
Dobzhansky, T. *Genetic diversity and human equality.* New York: Basic Books, 1973.
Docter, R. F., & Winder, C. L. Delinquent vs. nondelinquent performance on the Porteus Qualitative Maze Test. *Journal of Consulting Psychology,* 1954, *18,* 71–73.
Dolliver, R. H., & Hansen, R. N. [Review of the Self-Directed Search.] *Measurement and Evaluation in Guidance,* 1977, *10,* 120–123.
Dolliver, R. H., Irvin, J. A., & Bigley, S. S. Twelve-year follow-up of the Strong Vocational Interest Blank. *Journal of Counseling Psychology,* 1972, *19,* 212–217.
Domino, G. Differential predictions of academic achievement in conforming and independent settings. *Journal of Educational Psychology,* 1968, *59,* 256–260.
———. Interactive effects of achievement motivation and teaching style on academic achievement. *Journal of Educational Psychology,* 1971, *62,* 427–431.
Downey, R. G., Medland, F. F., & Yates, L. G. Evaluation of a peer rating system for predicting subsequent promotion of senior military officers. *Journal of Applied Psychology,* 1976, *61,* 206–209.
Dreger, R. M. Intellectual functioning. In K. S. Miller & R. M. Dreger (Eds.), *Comparative studies of blacks and whites in the United States.* New York: Seminar Press, 1973.
Dreyer, G. F., & Sackett, P. R. Some problems with applying content validity to assessment center procedures. *Academy of Management Review,* 1981, *6,* 551–560, 567–568.
Droege, R. C., & Padgett, A. Development of an interest-oriented occupational classification system. *Vocational Guidance Quarterly,* 1979, *27,* 302–310.
———. A new counselee assessment–occupational exploration system and its interest and aptitude dimensions. *School Counselor,* 1982, *30,* 61–67.
DuBois, P. H. (Ed.). *The classification program.* Washington, D.C.: Government Printing Office, 1947.

Dunbar, S. B. Corrections for sample selection bias. *Dissertation Abstracts,* 1983, *43*, entry 2872-A. (Unpublished octoral dissertation, University od Illinois, Urbana, 1982).
Duncan, A. K. Some comments on the Army General Classification Test. *Journal of Applied Psychology,* 1947, *31,* 143–149.
Dunham, J. L., Guilford, J. P., & Hoepfner, R. Abilities pertaining to classes and the learning of concepts. Report No. 39, *Psychological Laboratory, University of Southern California,* Los Angeles, 1966.
Dunnette, M. D. Vocational interest differences among engineers employed in different functions. *Journal of Applied Psychology,* 1957, *41,* 273–278.
Dunnette, M. D. Personnel selection and job placement of disadvantaged and minority persons: Problems, issues, and suggestions. In H. L. Fromkin & J. J. Sherwood (Eds), *Integrating the organization.* New York: Free Press, 1974.
———. The assessment of managerial talent. In P. McReynolds (Ed.), *Advances in psychological assessment,* vol. 2. Palo Alto, Calif.: Science and Behavior Books, 1971.
Dunnette, M. D. (Ed.). *Handbook of industrial and organizational psychology.* Chicago: Rand McNally, 1976.
Dunnette, M. D., & Borman, W. C. Personnel selection and classification systems. *Annual Review of Psychology,* 1979, *30,* 477–525.
Dunnette, M. D., Bownas, D. A., & Bosshardt, M. J. Prediction of inappropriate, unreliable, or aberrant job behavior in nuclear power plant settings. Minneapolis: Personnel Decisions Research Institute, 1981.
Dunnette, M. D., & Kirchner, W. K. Validation of psychological tests in industry. *Personnel Administration,* 1958, *21,* 20–27.
Dunnette, M. D., *et al.* A study of faking behavior on a forced-choice self-description checklist. *Personnel Psychology,* 1962, *15,* 13–24.
Dunnette, M. D., *et al. Development and validation of an industry-wide electric power plant operator selection system.* Minneapolis: Personnel Decisions Research Institute, 1982.
EEOC *et al.* Adoption by four agencies of Uniform Federal Guidelines on Employee Selection Procedures. *Federal Register,* 1978, *43,* 38290–38315.
EEOC *et al.* Adoption of questions and answers. . . . *Federal Register,* 1979, *44,* 11996–12009.
Eckland, B. K. Competent teachers and competent students. *Behavioral and Brain Sciences,* 1980, *3,* 341–342.
Edelbrock, C. S. & Achenbach, T. M. A typology of Child Behavior Profile patterns: Distribution and correlates for disturbed children aged 6–16. *Journal of Abnormal Child Psychology,* 1980, *8,* 441–470.
Edwards, W., Guttentag, M., & Snapper, K. A decision-theoretic approach to evaluation research. In E. L. Streuning & M. Guttentag (Eds.), *Handbook of evaluation research,* vol. 1. Beverly Hills, Calif.: Sage, 1975.
Eells, K., *et al. Intelligence and cultural differences.* Chicago: University of Chicago Press, 1951.
Ekstrom, R. B., French, J. W., & Harman, H. H. *Kit of factor-referenced cognitive tests.* Princeton, N. J.: Educational Testing Service, 1976.
———. Cognitive factors: Their identification and replication. *Multivariate Behavioral Research Monographs,* 1979, *79–*2.
Elliott, C. D., Murray, D. J., & Pearson, L. S. *British Ability Scales. Manual 3: Directions for administering and scoring.* Windsor, England: NFER Publishing Company, 1978.
Elshout, J. J. Karakteristic Moeilijkheden in het Denken. Doctoral dissertation, University of Amsterdam, 1976.
Elshout, J. A., Van Hemert, N. A., & Van Hemert, M. Comment on Horn and Knapp: On the subjective character of the empirical base of Guilford's Structure of Intellect model. *Tijdschrift voor Onderwijsresearch,* 1975, *1,* 15–25.

Epstein, S. The stability of behavior: On predicting most of the people much of the time. *Journal of Personality and Social Psychology,* 1979, *37,* 1097–1126.
Epstein, S. The Stability of behavior. II. Implications for psychological research. *American Psychologist,* 1980, *35,* 790–806.
Evans, F. R., & Pike, L. W. The effects of instruction for three mathematics item formats. *Journal of Educational Measurement,* 1973, *10,* 257–272.
Exner, J. E., Jr. *The Rorschach: A comprehensive system.* New York: Wiley, 1978.
Eysenck, H. J. (Ed.). *The measurement of intelligence.* Lancaster, England: Medical and Technical Publishing Co., 1973.
Eysenck, H. J. Personality and factor analysis: A reply to Guilford. *Psychological Bulletin,* 1977, *84,* 405–411.
———. *The structure and measurement of intelligence.* New York: Springer, 1979.
Eysenck, H. J. (Ed.). *A model for intelligence.* Berlin: Springer, 1982.
Fahmy, M. *Initial exploring of the Shilluk intelligence.* Cairo: Dar Misr Printing Co., 1954.
Farmer, H. S., & Fyans, L. J., Jr. Women's achievement and career motivation: Their risk taking patterns, home-career conflict, sex role orientation, fear of success, and self-concept. In L. J. Fyans, Jr. (Ed.), *Achievement motivation.* New York: Plenum, 1980.
Feather, N. T. The relationship of persistence at a task to expectation of success and achievement related stories. *Journal of Abnormal and Social Psychology,* 1961, *63,* 552–561.
Fenz, W. D. Conflict and stress as related to physiological activation and sensory, perceptual, and cognitive functioning. *Psychological Monographs,* 1964, *78,* No. 8.
Fenz, W. D., & Epstein, S. Measurement of approach-avoidance conflict along a stimulus dimension by a thematic apperception test. *Journal of Personality,* 1962, *30,* 613–632.
Feuerstein, R. *The dynamic assessment of retarded performers.* Baltimore: University Park Press, 1979.
———. *Instrumental enrichment.* Baltimore: University Park Press, 1980.
Feuerstein, R., Haywood, [H.] C., & Rand, Y. *Examiner manuals for the Learning Potential Assessment Device.* Jerusalem: Hadassah-Wizo-Canada Research Institute, 1982. [Preliminary version]
Filskov, S. B., & Boll, T. J. (Eds.). *Handbook of clinical neuropsychology.* New York: Wiley, 1982.
Fink, A. M., & Butcher, J. N. Reducing objections to personality inventories with special instructions. *Educational and Psychological Measurement,* 1972, *32,* 631–639.
Fishbein, M., & Azjen, I. Attitudes toward objects as predictors of single and multiple behavioral criteria. *Psychological Review,* 1974, *81,* 59–74.
Fivars, G. *The critical incident technique: A bibliography* (2d ed.) Palo Alto, Calif.: American Institutes for Research, 1980.
Flanagan, J. C. The critical incidents technique. *Psychological Bulletin,* 1954, *51,* 327–358.
———. The development of an index of examinee motivation. *Educational and Psychological Measurement,* 1955, *15,* 144–151.
Flanagan, J. C., et al. *The career data book: Results from Project TALENT's five-year follow-up study.* Palo Alto, Calif.: American Institutes for Research, 1973.
Flaugher, R. The many definitions of test bias. *American Psychologist,* 1978, *33,* 671–679.
Fleishman, E. A. A comparative study of aptitude patterns in unskilled and skilled motor performances. *Journal of Applied Psychology,* 1957, *41,* 263–272.
Fleishman, E. A., & Hempel, W. E., Jr. Changes in factor structure of a complex psychomotor test as a function of practice. *Psychometrika,* 1954, *19,* 239–252.
Ford, A., et al. *The sonar pitch-memory test: A report on design standards.* San Diego, University of California Division of War Research, 1944.
Ford, J. B. Some more on the Samoans. *American Psychologist,* 1957, *12,* 151.
Forehand, G. A. On the interaction of persons and organizations. In R. Tagiuri & G.

H. Litwin (Eds.), *Organizational climate: Explorations of a concept.* Boston: Graduate School of Business Administration, Harvard University, 1968.

Fransella, F., & Bannister, D. *A manual for repertory grid technique.* London: Academic Press, 1977.

Frederiksen, N. R. The real test bias. *Research Report* 81-40. Princeton, N. J.: Educational Testing Service, 1981.

Frederiksen, N. R., et al. *Prediction of organizational behavior.* New York: Pergamon, 1972.

Freedman, D. G. Constitutional and environmental interactions in rearing of four breeds of dogs. *Science,* March 14, 1958, *127,* 585-586.

French, J. W. The relationship of problem-solving styles to the factor composition of tests. *Educational and Psychological Measurement,* 1965, *25,* 9-28.

Gade, E. M., & Soliah, D. Vocational Preference Inventory high point codes versus expressed choices as predictors of college major and career entry. *Journal of Counseling Psychology,* 1975, *22,* 117-121.

Galassi, J. P. et al. The College Self-Expression Scale: a measure of assertiveness. *Behavior Therapy,* 1974, *5,* 165-171.

Gardner, J. W. *Excellence: Can we be equal and excellent too?* New York: Harper & Row, 1961.

Gardner, R. C. Motivational variables in second-language acquisition. Unpublished doctoral dissertation, McGill University, 1960.

Garner, A. M., & Smith, G. M. An experimental videotape technique for evaluating trainee approaches to clinical judging. *Journal of Consulting and Clinical Psychology,* 1976, *44,* 945-950.

Getzels, J. W., & Jackson, P. W. *Creativity and intelligence.* New York: Wiley, 1962.

Ghiselli, E. E. The validity of aptitude tests in personnel selection. *Personnel Psychology,* 1973, *26,* 461-477.

Glaser, R. *Adaptive education: Individual diversity and learning.* New York: Holt, Rinehart and Winston, 1977.

―――. The future of testing. *American Psychologist,* 1981, *36,* 923-936.

Glaser, R., & Bond, L. (Eds.). Testing: Concepts, policy, practice, and research. *American Psychologist,* 1981, *36,* No. 10.

Gleser, G. C. Psychometric contributions to the assessment of patients. In D. H. Efron et al. (Eds.), *Psychopharmacology: Review of progress, 1957-1967.* Washington, D.C.: Government Printing Office, 1968.

Goldberg, L. R. A historical survey of personality scales and inventories. In P. McReynolds (Ed.), *Advances in psychological assessment,* vol. 2. Palo Alto, Calif.: Science and Behavior Books, 1971.

―――. Parameters of personality inventory construction and utilization: A comparison of predictive strategies and tactics. *Multivariate Behavioral Research Monographs,* 1972, *72*-2.

―――. Language and individual differences. In L. Wheeler (Ed.), *Review of personality and social psychology,* vol. 2. Beverly Hills, Calif.: Sage, 1981.

Goldberg, L. R., & Rorer, L. G. Use of two different response modes and repeated testings to predict social conformity. *Journal of Personality and Social Psychology,* 1966, *3,* 28-37.

Golden, C. J. *Clinical interpretation of objective psychological tests.* New York: Grune & Stratton, 1979.

Goodnow, J. J., & Bethon, G. Piaget's tasks: The effects of schooling and intelligence. *Child Development,* 1966, *37,* 573-582.

Gordon, L. V. *Gordon Personal Profile Inventory manual.* New York: Psychological Corporation, 1978.

Gordon, L. V., & Medland, F. F. The cross-group stability of peer ratings of leadership potential. *Personnel Psychology,* 1965, *18,* 173-177.

Gough, H. G. Some common misconceptions about neuroticism. *Journal of Consulting Psychology*, 1954, *18*, 287–292.
———. Nonintellectual factors in the selection and evaluation of medical students. *Journal of Medical Education*, 1967, *42*, 642–650.
Graham, J. R. *The MMPI: A practical guide.* New York: Oxford University Press, 1977.
———. Review of Minnesota Multiphasic Personality Inventory special scales. In P. McReynolds (Ed.), *Advances in personality assessment,* vol. 4. San Francisco: Jossey-Bass, 1977.
Green, D. R. *The aptitude-achievement distinction.* Monterey, Calif.: CTB/McGraw-Hill, 1974.
Gronlund, N. *Measurement and evaluation in teaching* (4th ed.) New York: Macmillan, 1981.
Guilford, J. P. Intellectual factors in productive thinking. In M. J. Aschner & C. E. Bish (Eds.), *Productive thinking in education.* Washington, D. C.: National Education Association, 1965.
———. *The nature of human intelligence.* New York: McGraw-Hill, 1967.
———. Will the real factor of Extraversion-Introversion please stand up? Reply to Eysenck. *Psychological Bulletin*, 1977, *84*, 412–416.
———. *Cognitive psychology with a frame of reference.* San Diego: EdITS, 1979.
———. Fluid and crystallized intelligence: Two fanciful concepts. *Psychological Bulletin*, 1980, *88*, 406–412.
Guilford, J. P. Higher-order structure-of-intellect abilities. *Multivariate Behavioral Research*, 1981, *16*, 411–435.
Guilford, J. P., & Hoepfner, R. *The analysis of intelligence.* New York: McGraw-Hill, 1971.
Guion, R. M. *Personnel testing.* New York: McGraw-Hill, 1965.
———. On trinitarian doctrines of validity. *Professional Psychology*, 1980, *11*, 385–398.
Guion, R. M., & Gottier, R. F. Validity of personality measures in personnel selection. *Personnel Psychology*, 1965, *18*, 135–164.
Gustafsson, J.-E. *Verbal and figural aptitudes in relation to instructional methods.* Gothenburg: Acta Universitatis Gothoburgensis, 1976.
Guttman, L. The structure of relations among intelligence tests. *Proceedings, Invitational Conference on Testing Problems, 1964.* Princeton, N. J.: Educational Testing Service, 1965.
Gynther, M. D., & Green, S. B. Accuracy may make a difference, but does a difference make for accuracy? *Journal of Clinical and Consulting psychology*, 1980, *48*, 268–272.
Haan, N. Common dimensions of personality development: Early adolescence to middle life. In D. H. Eichhorn *et al.* (Eds.), *Present and past in middle life.* New York: Academic Press, 1981.
Hall, B. W., Tocco, T. S., & Schwartz, L. S. Effect of stress and relax instructions on the predictive validity of a test device. *Measurement and Evaluation in Guidance*, 1974, *7*, 46–50.
Hall, J. R. Assessment of assertiveness. In P. McReynolds (Ed.), *Advances in psychological assessment,* vol. 4. San Francisco: Jossey-Bass, 1977.
Hall, W. B., & MacKinnon, D. W. Personality inventory correlates among architects. *Journal of Applied Psychology*, 1969, *53*, 322–326.
Hambleton, R. K. [Review of Bennett Mechanical Comprehension Test.] *Journal of Educational Measurement*, 1971, *8*, 55–56.
———. Latent trait models and their application. *New Directions in Testing and Measurement*, 1979, *4*, 13–32.
Hammond, K. R., & Wascoe, N. E. (Eds.). *Realizations of Brunswik's representative design.* San Francisco: Jossey-Bass, 1980.
Hansen, J. C. Age differences and empirical scale construction. *Measurement and Evaluation in Guidance*, 1978, *11*, 78–87.

Harmon, L. W. The predictive power over 10 years of measured social service and scientific interests among women. *Journal of Applied Psychology,* 1969, *53,* 193–198.

Harrell, T. W. High earning MBA's. *Personnel Psychology,* 1972, *25,* 523–530.

Harrington, D. M. Effects of explicit instructions to "be creative" on the psychological meanings of divergent thinking test scores. *Journal of Personality,* 1975, *43,* 434–454.

Harris, D. H. Questionnaire and interview in neuropsychiatric screening. *Journal of Applied Psychology,* 1945, *30,* 644–648.

Harrison, R. Thematic apperception methods. In B. B. Wolman (Ed.), *Handbook of clinical psychology.* New York: McGraw-Hill, 1965. Pp. 562–620.

Hartshorne, H., & May, M. A. *Studies in deceit.* (2 vols.) New York: Macmillan, 1928.

———. *Studies in service and self-control.* New York: Macmillan, 1929.

———. *Studies in the organization of character.* New York: Macmillan, 1930.

Haywood, H. C. *et al.* Behavioral assessment in mental retardation. In P. McReynolds (Ed.), *Advances in psychological assessment,* vol. 3. San Francisco: Jossey-Bass, 1975.

Heaton, R. K., & Pendleton, M. G. Use of neuropsychological tests to predict adult patients' everyday functioning. *Journal of Abnormal Psychology,* 1981, *49,* 807–821.

Hebb, D. O., & Williams, K. A. method of rating animal intelligence. *Journal of Genetic Psychology,* 1946, *34,* 59–65.

Heckman, J. J. Sample selection bias as a specification error. *Econometrica,* 1979, *47,* 153–161.

Heinrich, D. L., & Spielberger, C. D. Anxiety and complex learning. In H. W. Krohne & L. Laux (Eds.), *Achievement, stress, and anxiety.* Washington, D.C.: Hemisphere, 1982.

Heller, K. A., Holtzman, W. H., & Messick, S. (Eds.). *Placing children in special education: A strategy for equity.* Washington, D. C.: National Academy Press, 1982.

Helme, William H., Gibson, Wilfred A. & Brogden, H. E. An empirical test of shrinkage problems in personnel classification research. Personnel Research Branch Technical Research Note 84. Washington, D.C.: Adjutant General's Office, 1957.

Helson, R. Women mathematicians and the creative personality. *Journal of Consulting and Clinical Psychology,* 1971, *36,* 210–220.

Hemphill, J. K., & Sechrest, L. B. A comparison of three criteria of air crew effectiveness in combat over Korea. *Journal of Applied Psychology,* 1952, *36,* 323–327.

Henry, W. E. *The analysis of fantasy.* New York: Wiley, 1956.

Hess, R. D., & Azuma, H. Unpublished manual. School of Education, Stanford University, 1973.

Hill, E. F. *The Holtzman Inkblot Technique: A handbook for clinical application.* San Francisco: Jossey-Bass, 1972.

Hilton, T. L. Annotated bibliography of Growth Study papers. *Research Report* 80-2. Princeton, N.J.: Educational Testing Service, 1980.

Hilton, T. L., Beaton, A. E., & Bower, C. P. "Stability and instability in academic growth—A compilation of longitudinal data." *Research Report* 0–0140. Princeton, N. J.: Educational Testing Service, 1971.

Hobbs, N. *The futures of children.* San Francisco: Jossey-Bass, 1975.

Hofstadter, R. *Social Darwinism in American thought.* Philadelphia: University of Pennsylvania Press, 1944.

Hogan, R., DeSoto, C. B., & Solano, C. Traits, tests, and personality research. *American Psychologist,* 1977, *32,* 255–264.

Hogan, T. P., & Mishler, C. Relationships between essay tests and objective tests of language skills for elementary school students. *Journal of Educational Measurement,* 1980, *17,* 219–227.

Hogarth, R. M. Beyond discrete biases: Functional and dysfunctional aspects of judgmental heuristics. *Psychological Bulletin,* 1981, *90,* 197–217.
Holden, C. Health records and privacy: What would Hippocrates say? *Science,* Oct. 28, 1977, *198,* 382.
Holland, J. L. *Making vocational choices: A theory of careers.* Englewood Cliffs, N. J.: Prentice-Hall, 1973.
Holland, J. L., & Richards, J. M., Jr. Academic and nonacademic accomplishment: Correlated or uncorrelated? *Journal of Educational Psychology,* 1965, *45,* 165–174.
Holmen, M. G., & Docter, R. *Educational and psychological testing.* New York: Russell Sage Foundation, 1972.
Holmen, M. G., et al. An assessment program for OCS applicants. *HumRRO Technical Report,* No. 26, 1956.
Holt, R. R., & Luborsky, L. *Personality patterns of psychiatrists.* New York: Basic Books, 1958.
Holtzman, W. H. New developments in Holtzman Inkblot Technique. In P. McReynolds (Ed.), *Advances in psychological assessment,* vol. 3. San Francisco: Jossey-Bass, 1975.
Holtzman, W. H., Diaz-Guerrero, R., & Swartz, J. *Personality development in two cultures: A cross-cultural longitudinal study of school children in Mexico and the United States.* Austin: University of Texas Press, 1975.
Holtzman, W. H., & Sells, S. B. Prediction of flying success by clinical analysis of test protocols. *Journal of Abnormal and Social Psychology,* 1954, *49,* 485–490.
Honzik, M. P. Value and limitations of infant tests: An overview. In M. Lewis (Ed.), *Origins of intelligence.* New York: Plenum, 1976.
Honzik, M. P., Macfarlane, J. W., & Allen, L. The stability of mental test performance between two and eighteen years. *Journal of Experimental Education,* 1948, *17,* 309–324.
Hook, C. M., & Rosenshine, B. V. Accuracy of teacher reports of their classroom behavior. *Review of Educational Research,* 1979, *49,* 1–12.
Horn, J. L. The rise and fall of human abilities. *Journal of Research and Development in Education,* 1979, *12,* 59–78.
Horn, J. L., & Cattell, R. B. Refinement and test of the theory of fluid and crystallized intelligence. *Journal of Educational Psychology,* 1966, *57,* 253–276.
Horn, J. L., & Donaldson, G. On the myth of intellectual decline in adulthood. *American Psychologist,* 1976, *31,* 701–719.
———. Faith is not enough. *American Psychologist,* 1977, *32,* 369–373.
Horn, J. L., & Knapp, J. R. On the subjective character of the empirical basis for Guilford's Structure-of-Intellect model. *Psychological Bulletin,* 1973, *80,* 33–43.
Horne, L. V., & Garty, M. K. What the test score really reflects: Observations of teacher behavior during standardized test administration. Unpublished paper, American Educational Research Association, 1981.
Hough, L. Development and evaluation of an accomplishment based method of selecting and promoting professionals. Unpublished doctoral dissertation, University of Minnesota, 1981.
House, E. R. *Evaluating with validity.* Beverly Hills, Calif.: Sage, 1980.
Houts, P. L. (Ed.). *The myth of measurability.* New York: Hart, 1977.
Howard, A. An assessment of assessment centers. *Academy of Management Journal,* 1974, *17,* 115–134.
Hubbard, J. P. *Measuring medical education* (2d ed.) Philadelphia: Lea and Febiger, 1978.
Hubbard, J. P., et al. An objective evaluation of clinical competence. *New England Journal of Medicine,* 1965, *272,* 1321–1328.
Humphreys, L. G. The primary mental ability. In M. P. Friedman et al. (Eds.), *Intelligence and learning.* New York: Plenum, 1981.

Humphreys, L. G., & Taber, T. Postdiction study of the Graduate Record Examination and eight semesters of college grades. *Journal of Educational Measurement,* 1973, *10,* 179–184.

Hunt, E. B. Quote the Raven? Nevermore! In L. W. Gregg (Ed.), *Knowledge and cognition.* Potomac, Md.: Erlbaum, 1974.

Hunt, J. McV. *Intelligence and experience.* New York: Ronald Press, 1961.

Hunter, J. E. The dimensionality of the General Aptitude Test Battery (GATB) and the dominance of general factors over specific factors in the prediction of job performance. Paper presented to American Psychological Association, 1982.

Hunter, J. E., & Hunter, R. F. The validity and utility of alternate predictors of job performance. Paper presented to American Psychological Association, 1982.

Hunter, J. E., & Schmidt, F. L. Fitting people to jobs: The impact of personnel selection on national productivity. In E. A. Fleishman (Ed.), *Human performance and productivity.* Hillsdale, N. J.: Erlbaum, 1981.

Hunter, J. E., Schmidt, F. L., & Hunter, R. Differential validity of employment tests by race: A comprehensive review and analysis. *Psychological Bulletin,* 1979, *86,* 721–735.

Hunter, J. E., Schmidt, F. L., & Rauschenberger, J. M. Fairness of psychological tests: Implications of four definitions for selection utility and minority hiring. *Journal of Applied Psychology,* 1977, *62,* 245–260.

Hutt, M. L. *The Hutt Adaptation of the Bender-Gestalt Test,* 3d ed. New York: Grune & Stratton, 1977.

Hutt, M. L., & Gibby, R. G. *An atlas for the Hutt Adaptation of the Bender-Gestalt Test.* New York: Grune & Stratton, 1970.

Hutton, J. B. A comparison of digit repetition scores on the WISC and the Revised Binet, Form L-M. *Journal of Clinical Psychology,* 1964, *20,* 364–366.

Ingersoll, R. W., & Peters, H. J. Predictive indices of the GATB. *Personnel and Guidance Journal,* 1966, *44,* 931–937.

Ivancevich, J. M. Longitudinal study of the effects of rater training on psychometric errors in rating. *Journal of Applied Psychology,* 1979, *64,* 502–508.

Jack, L. M. An experimental study of ascendant behavior in preschool children. *University of Iowa Studies on Child Welfare,* 1934, *9,* No. 3.

Jackson, D. N. The dynamics of structured personality tests. *Psychological Review,* 1971, *78,* 239–248.

———. The relative validity of scales prepared by naive item writers and those prepared by empirical methods of personality scale construction. *Educational and Psychological Measurement,* 1975, *35,* 361–370.

Jaeger, R. M. The national test-equating study in reading (The Anchor Test Study). *Journal of Educational Measurement,* 1973, *4*(4), 1–8.

Jaeger, R. M., et al. An iterative structured judgmental process for setting passing scores on competency tests, applied to the North Carolina High School Competency Tests in reading and mathematics. University of North Carolina, Greensboro, 1980.

Janis, I. L. Personality differences in decision making under stress. In K. R. Blankstein et al. (Eds.), *Advances in the study of communication and affect,* vol. 6. New York: Plenum, 1978.

Janis, I. L. (Ed.). *Counseling on personal decisions: Theory and research on short-term helping relationships.* New Haven: Yale University Press, 1982.

Jenkins, W. O. A review of leadership studies with particular reference to military problems. *Psychological Bulletin,* 1947, *44,* 54–79.

Jensen, A. R. *Educability and group differences.* New York: Harper & Row, 1973.

———. *g:* Outmoded theory or unconquered frontier? *Creative Science and Technology,* 1979, *2,* 16–29.

———. *Bias in mental testing.* New York: Free Press, 1980.
———. *Straight talk about mental tests.* New York: Free Press, 1981.
Jensen, A. R., & Reynolds, C. R. Race, social class, and ability patterns on the WISC-R. *Personality and Individual Differences,* 1982, *3,* 423–438.
John, E. R., *et. al.* Neurometrics. *Science,* 1977, *196,* 1393–1410.
Johnson, E. S., & Baker, R. F. Some effects of computerizing an experiment in human problem solving. Report 105, the L. L. Thurstone Psychometric Laboratory, University of North Carolina, Chapel Hill, 1972.
———. Computers in behavioral science: The computer as experimenter: New results. *Behavioral Science,* 1973, *18,* 377–385.
Johnson, J. H., Giannetti, R. A., & Williams, T. A. Psychological systems questionnaire: An objective personality test designed for on-line computer presentation, scoring, and interpretation. *Behavior Research Methods and Instrumentation,* 1979, *11,* 257–260.
Jones, L. K. Holland's typology and the new *Guide for occupational exploration:* Bridging the gap. *Vocational Guidance Quarterly,* 1980, *29,* 70–76.
Jones, V. A comparison of measures of honesty at early adolescence with honesty in adulthood—a follow-up study. *American Psychologist,* 1946, *1,* 261.
Jöreskog, K. G., & Sörbom, D. *Advances in factor analysis and structural equation models.* Cambridge, Mass.: Abt Books, 1979.
Kagan, S., & Buriel, R. Field dependence-independence and Mexican-American culture and education. In J. L. Martinez, Jr. (Ed.), *Chicano psychology.* New York: Academic Press, 1977.
Kane, J. S., & Lawler, E. E. III. Methods of peer assessment. *Psychological Bulletin,* 1978, *85,* 555–586.
Kaplan, R. M. Nader's raid on the testing industry. *American Psychologist,* 1982, *37,* 15–23.
Kaufman, A. S. Verbal-Performance IQ discrepancies on the WISC-R. *Journal of Consulting and Clinical Psychology,* 1976, *44,* 739–744.
———. *Intelligent testing with the WISC-R.* New York: Wiley, 1979.
Kaufman, A. S., & Doppelt, J. E. Analysis of the WISC-R standardization data in terms of stratification variables. *Child Development,* 1976, *47,* 165–171.
Kaufman, A. S., & Kaufman, N. L. *Clinical evaluation of young children with the McCarthy scales.* New York: Grune & Stratton, 1977.
Kelly, E. L. Alternative criteria in medical education and their correlates. *Proceedings, Invitational Conference on Testing Problems, 1963.* Princeton, N. J.: Educational Testing Service, 1964.
Kelly, E. L., & Fiske, D. W. *The prediction of performance in clinical psychology.* Ann Arbor: University of Michigan Press, 1951.
Kelly, E. L., & Goldberg, L. R. Correlates of later performance and specialization in psychology. *Psychological Monographs,* 1959, *73,* No. 12.
Kelly, G. A. *The psychology of personal constructs.* (2 vols) New York: Norton, 1955.
Kelly, G. A. (Ed.). *New methods in applied psychology.* College Park: University of Maryland, 1947.
Kelman, H. C. Human use of human subjects: The problem of deception in social psychological experiments. *Psychological Bulletin,* 1967, *67,* 1–11.
Kent, G. H. Suggestions for the next revision of the Binet-Simon Scale. *Psychological Record,* 1937, *1,* 409–433.
King, L. M., Hunter, J. E., & Schmidt, F. L. Halo in a multidimensional forced-choice performance evaluation scale. *Journal of Applied Psychology,* 1980, *65,* 507–516.
Kirk, B. A. Test versus academic performance in malfunctioning students. *Journal of Consulting Psychology,* 1952, *16,* 213–216.

Klass, E. T. Psychological effects of immoral actions: The experimental evidence. *Psychological Bulletin,* 1978, *85,* 756–771.
Klopfer, B., et al. *Developments in the Rorschach technique.* (3 vols.) New York: Harcourt Brace Jovanovich, 1970.
Knapp, R. R. *Handbook for the Personal Orientation Inventory.* San Diego: EdITS, 1976.
Knauft, E. G. Test validity over a seventeen-year period. *Journal of Applied Psychology,* 1955, *39,* 382–383.
Kohlberg, L. (Ed.) *Collected papers on moral development and moral education.* Cambridge, Mass.: Harvard University Press, 1973.
Kohn, M., & Rosman, B. L. Relationship of preschool social-emotional functioning to later intellectual achievement. *Developmental Psychology,* 1972, *6,* 445–452.
———. Social-emotional, cognitive, and demographic determinants of poor school achievement: Implications for a strategy of intervention. *Journal of Educational Psychology,* 1974, *66,* 267–276.
Kohs, S. C. *Intelligence measurement.* New York: Macmillan, 1923.
Koppitz, E. M. *The Bender Gestalt test for young children.* (2d ed.) New York: Grune & Stratton, 1975.
Koretzky, M. B., Kohn, M., & Jeger, A. M. Cross-situational consistency among problem adolescents: An application of the two-factor model. *Journal of Personality and Social Psychology,* 1978, *36,* 1054–1059.
Kraut, A. I. Prediction of managerial success by peer and training staff ratings. *Journal of Applied Psychology,* 1975, *60,* 14–19.
Kuder, G. F. *Activity, interests, and occupational choice.* Chicago: Science Research Associates, 1977.
Kunce, J. R., & Reeder, C. W. SVIB scores and accident proneness. *Measurement and Evaluation in Guidance,* 1974, *7,* 118–121.
Labov, W. The logic of nonstandard English. In F. Williams (Ed.), *Language and poverty.* Chicago: Markham, 1970.
Lachar, D. *The MMPI: Clinical assessment and automated interpretation.* Los Angeles: Western Psychological Services, 1974.
Lambert, N. M. The development and validation of a process for screening emotionally disturbed children in school. Sacramento, Calif.: California State Department of Education, 1963.
Landfield, A. W., & Leitner, L. M. (Eds.). *Personal construct psychology: Psychotherapy and personality.* New York: Wiley, 1980.
Landis, B., et al. Bender-Gestalt evaluation of brain dysfunction following open heart surgery. *Journal of Personality Assessment,* 1974, *38,* 556–562.
Larson, A., & Larson, L. K. *Employment discrimination.* New York: Matthew Bender, 1981.
Lasky, J. J., et al. Post-hospital adjustment as predicted by psychiatric patients and by their staffs. *Journal of Consulting Psychology,* 1959, *23,* 213–218.
Law School Admission Council. *Reports of LSAC sponsored research: Volume III, 1975–1977.* Princeton: Law School Admission Council, 1977.
Leinhardt, G., & Seewald, A. M. Overlap: What's tested, what's taught. *Journal of Educational Measurement,* 1981, *18,* 85–96.
Leler, H. O. Mother-child interaction and language performance in young disadvantaged Negro children. Unpublished doctoral dissertation, Stanford University, Calif. 1970.
Lerner, B. Employment discrimination: Adverse impact, validity, and equality. In P. B. Kurland & G. Casper (Eds.), *Supreme Court Review, 1979.* Chicago: University of Chicago Press, 1979.
———. Washington v. Davis: Quantity, quality and equality in employment testing. In P. Kurland (Ed.), *Supreme Court Review, 1976.* Chicago: University of Chicago Press, 1977.

Lerner, B. Equal protection and external screening: Davis, DeFunis, and Bakke. In *Proceedings of the Invitational Conference on Testing Problems, 1977*. Princeton, N.J.: Educational Testing Service, 1978.

Levine, E., Ash, R. A., & Bennett, N. Exploratory comparative study of four job analysis methods. *Journal of Applied Psychology*, 1980, *65*, 524–525.

Lewis, M. (Ed.) *Origins of intelligence: Infancy and early childhood*. New York: Plenum, 1976.

Liben, L. S., Patterson, A. H., & Newcombe, N. (Eds.). *Spatial representation and behavior across the life span*. New York: Academic Press, 1981.

Lindzey, G., & Byrne, D. Measurement of social choice and interpersonal attraction. In G. Lindzey & E. Aronson (Eds.), *The handbook of social psychology* (2d ed.), vol. 2. Reading, Mass.: Addison-Wesley, 1968.

Linn, R. L. Single-group validity, differential validity, and differential prediction. *Journal of Applied Psychology*, 1978, *63*, 507–512.

———. Admissions testing on trial. *American Psychologist*, 1982, *37*, 279–291. (a)

———. Predictive bias as an artifact of selection procedures. In H. Wainer (Ed.), *Advances in psychometric theory: Festschrift for Frederic M. Lord*. Princeton, N.J.: Educational Testing Service, 1982. (b)

Linn, R. L., Harnisch, D. L., & Dunbar, S. B. Validity generalization and situational specificity: An analysis of the prediction of first-year grades in law school. *Applied Psychological Measurement*, 1981, *5*, 281–289.

Lippman, W. A defense of education. *The Century*, 1923, *106*, 95–103.

Lipsett, L., & Wilson, J. W. Do "suitable" interests and mental ability lead to job satisfaction? *Educational and Psychological Measurement*, 1954, *14*, 373–380.

Livingston, S. A. Estimation of the conditional standard error of measurement for stratified tests. *Journal of Educational Measurement*, 1982, *19*, 135–138.

Loehlin, J. C., Lindzey, G., & Spuhler, J. N. *Race differences in intelligence*. San Francisco: Freeman, 1975.

Lohman, D. F. Spatial ability: Individual differences in speed and level. Technical Report No. 9, Aptitude Research Project, Stanford University, Calif. 1979. (a)

———. Spatial ability: A review and reanalysis of the correlational literature. Technical Report No. 8, Aptitude Research Project, Stanford University, Calif. 1979. (b)

London, M., & Bray, D. W. Ethical issues in testing and evaluation for personnel decisions. *American Psychologist*, 1980, *35*, 890–901.

Lopez, F. M., Jr. *Evaluating executive decision making*. New York: American Management Association, 1966.

Lord, F. M. *Applications of item response theory to practical testing problems*. Hillsdale, N. J.: Erlbaum, 1980.

Lord, F. M., & Novick, M. *Statistical theories of mental test scores*. Reading, Mass.: Addison-Wesley, 1968.

Loret, P. G., et al. *Anchor Test Study: Equivalence and norms tables for selected reading achievement tests*. Washington, D.C.: Government Printing Office, 1974.

Lorr, M., Klett, C. J., & McNair, D. M. *Syndromes of psychosis*. New York: Pergamon, 1963.

Lorr, M., & McNair, D. M. Expansion of the interpersonal behavior circle. *Journal of Personality and Social Psychology*, 1965, *2*, 823–830.

Love, K. G. Comparison of peer assessment methods: Reliability, validity, friendship bias, and user reaction. *Journal of Applied Psychology*, 1981, *66*, 451–457.

Lowell, F. E. A study of the variability of IQ's in retest. *Journal of Applied Psychology*, 1941, *25*, 341–356.

Luborsky, L. Selecting psychiatric residents: survey of the Topeka research. *Bulletin of the Menninger Clinic*, 1954, *18*, 252–259.

McCall, R. B. Childhood IQ's as predictors of adult educational and social status. *Science*, 1977, *197*, 482–483.

McCall, R. B., Appelbaum, M. I., & Hogarty, P. S. Developmental changes in mental performance. *Monographs, Society for Research in Child Development,* 1973, *38,* No. 3.

McCall, R. B., Hogarty, P. S., & Hurlburt, N. Transitions in infant sensorimotor development and the prediction of childhood IQ. *American Psychologist,* 1972, *27,* 728–748.

McClelland, D. C. Testing for competence rather than "intelligence." *American Psychologist,* 1973, *28,* 1–14.

———. Is personality consistent? In A. I. Rabin *et al.* (Eds.), *Further explorations in personality.* New York: Wiley, 1981.

———. *Power: The inner experience.* New York: Irvington, 1979.

McCormick, E. J. *Job analysis: Methods and applications.* New York: Amacom, 1979.

McCormick, E. J., Denisi, A. S., & Shaw, J. B. Use of the Position Analysis Questionnaire for establishing the job component validity of tests. *Journal of Applied Psychology,* 1979, *64,* 51–56.

McFall, R. M., & Marston, A. R. An experimental investigation of behavior rehearsal in assertive training. *Journal of Abnormal Psychology,* 1970, *76,* 295–303.

Macfarlane, J. W., Allen, L., & Honzik, M. P. *A developmental study of the behavior problems of normal children between twenty-one months and fourteen years.* Berkeley: University of California Press, 1954.

McGauch, J. L., Jennings, R. D., & Thomson, C. V. Effect of distribution of practice on the maze learning of descendants of the Tryon maze bright and maze dull strains. *Psychological Reports,* 1962, *10,* 147–150.

McGee, M. G. Human spatial abilities: Psychometric studies and environmental, genetic, hormonal, and neurological influences. *Psychological Bulletin,* 1979, *86,* 889–918. (a)

———. *Human spatial abilities: Sources of sex differences.* New York: Praeger, 1979. (b).

McRae, G. G. The relationship of job satisfaction and earlier measured interests. Unpublished doctoral dissertation, University of Florida, Tallahassee, 1959.

McReynolds, P. Historical antecedents of personality assessment. In P. McReynolds (Ed.), *Advances in personality assessment,* vol. 3. San Francisco: Jossey-Bass, 1975.

McReynolds, P., & DeVoge, S. Use of improvisational techniques in assessment. In P. McReynolds (Ed.), *Advances in psychological assessment,* vol. 4. San Francisco: Jossey-Bass, 1977.

McReynolds, P., *et al.* Manual for the Impro-I. Mimeographed. Department of Psychology, University of Nevada, Reno, Nev., 1976.

Madaus, G. F. (Ed.) *The courts, validity, and minimum competency testing.* Boston: Kluwer-Nijhoff, 1982.

Magnusson, D. An analysis of situational dimensions. *Perceptual and Motor Skills,* 1971, *32,* 851–867.

Magnusson, D., & Backteman, G. Longitudinal stability of person characteristics: Intelligence and creativity. *Applied Psychological Measurement,* 1978, *2,* 481–490.

Magnusson, D., & Endler, N. S. (Eds.). *Personality at the crossroads: Current issues in interactional psychology.* Hillsdale, N. J.: Erlbaum, 1977.

Maller, J. B. Personality tests. In J. McV. Hunt (Ed.), *Personality and the behavior disorders.* New York: Ronald, 1944.

Marks, P. A., Seeman, W., & Haller, D. L. *The actuarial use of the MMPI with adolescents and adults.* Baltimore: Williams and Wilkins, 1974.

Marshalek, B. Trait and process aspects of vocabulary knowledge and verbal ability. Unpublished doctoral dissertation, Stanford University, Calif., 1981.

Marshalek, B., Lohman, D. F., & Snow, R. E. The complexity continuum in the radex and hierarchical models of intelligence. *Intelligence,* in press.

Marting, E. (Ed.). *AMA book of employment forms.* New York: American Management Association, 1967.

Maslow, A. P., et al. (Eds.). *Construct validity in psychological measurement.* Princeton: Educational Testing Service, 1980.

Matarazzo, J. D. *Wechsler's Measurement and appraisal of adult intelligence.* (5th ed.). New York: Oxford University Press, 1972.

Matthews, E., & Tiedeman, D. V. Attitudes toward career and marriage and the development of life style in young women. *Journal of Counseling Psychology,* 1964, *11,* 375–384.

Meehl, P. E. *Clinical versus statistical prediction.* Minneapolis: University of Minnesota Press, 1954.

———. Specific etiology and other forms of strong influence: Some quantitative meanings. *Journal of Medicine and Philosophy,* 1977, *2,* 33–53.

———. Theoretical risks and tabular asterisks. Sir Karl, Sir Ronald, and the slow progress of soft psychology. *Journal of Consulting and Clinical Psychology,* 1978, *46,* 806–834.

———. A funny thing happened on the way to the latent entities. *Journal of Personality Assessment,* 1979, *43,* 564–577.

Meehl, P. E., & Rosen, A. Antecedent probability and the efficiency of psychometric signs, patterns or cutting scores. *Psychological Bulletin,* 1955, *52,* 194–216.

Megargee, E. I. *The California Psychological Inventory handbook.* San Francisco: Jossey-Bass, 1972.

Megargee, E. I., & Bohn, M. J., Jr. *Classifying criminal offenders.* Beverly Hills, Calif.: Sage Publications, 1979.

Mercer, J. R. *Technical manual, System of Multicultural Pluralistic Assessment.* New York: Psychological Corporation, 1979.

Mercer, J. R., & Lewis, J. E. *Parent interview manual, System of Multicultural Pluralistic Assessment.* New York: Psychological Corporation, 1977.

Messé, L. A., et al. Evaluation of the predictive validity of testing of mental ability for classroom performance in elementary grades. *Journal of Educational Psychology,* 1979, *71,* 233–241.

Messick, S. The standard problem: Meaning and values in measurement and evaluation. *American Psychologist,* 1975, *30,* 955–966.

Messick, S. *The effectiveness of coaching for the SAT: Review and reanalysis of research from the fifties to the FTC.* Princeton: Educational Testing Service, 1980.

Messick, S. (Ed.). *Individuality and learning.* San Francisco: Jossey-Bass, 1976.

Messick, S. Constructs and their vicissitudes in educational and psychological measurement. *Psychological Bulletin,* 1981, *90,* 575–585.

Messick, S., & Jungeblut, A. Time and method in coaching for the SAT. *Psychological Bulletin,* 1981, *89,* 191–216.

Miele, F. Cultural bias in the WISC. *Intelligence,* 1979, *3,* 149–164.

Mill, J. S. *Collected works.* (J. M. Robson, Ed.) Toronto, University of Toronto Press, 1977.

Millman, J., Bishop, C. H., & Ebel, R. An analysis of test-wiseness. *Educational and Psychological Measurement,* 1965, *25,* 707–726.

Millman, J., & Outlaw, S. Testing by computer. Ithaca, N.Y.: Extension Service, Cornell University, 1977. (Reprinted in *AEDS Journal,* 1978, *11,* 57–72.)

Milstein, R. M., et al. Admission decisions and performance during medical school. *Journal of Medical Education,* 1981, *56,* 77–82.

Mischel, W. Predicting the success of Peace Corps volunteers in Nigeria. *Journal of Personality and Social Psychology,* 1965, *1,* 510–517.

———. *Personality and assessment.* New York: Wiley, 1968.

———. On the future of personality measurement. *American Psychologist,* 1977, *32,* 246–254.

———. *Introduction to personality.* (3d ed.) New York: Holt, Rinehart and Winston, 1981.

Moos, R. H. *Evaluating educational environments.* San Francisco: Jossey-Bass, 1979.
Moriarty, A. E. *Constancy and IQ change: A clinical view of relationships between tested intelligence and personality.* Springfield, Ill.: Thomas, 1966.
Moses, J. L., & Byham, W. C. *Applying the assessment center method.* New York: Pergamon, 1977.
Mosher, D. L. Optimist and pessimist. *Contemporary Psychology,* 1970, *15,* 373–374.
Mosier, C. I. A critical examination of the concepts of face validity. *Educational and Psychological Measurement,* 1947, *7,* 191–205.
Mosteller, F., & Tukey, J. W. *Data analysis and regression.* Reading, Mass.: Addison-Wesley, 1977.
Murphy, G., & Likert, R. *Public opinion and the individual.* New York: Harper & Row, 1938.
Murray, H. A., et al. *Explorations in personality.* Cambridge, Mass.: Harvard University Press, 1938.
Murstein, B. I. *Theory and research in projective techniques (emphasizing the TAT).* New York: Wiley, 1963.
Mussen, P. H., & Naylor, H. K. The relationships between overt and fantasy aggression. *Journal of Abnormal and Social Psychology,* 1954, *49,* 235–240.
Nanda, H. Factor analytic techniques for interbattery comparison and their application to some psychometric problems. Unpublished doctoral dissertation, Stanford University, Calif., 1967.
National Industrial Conference Board. Employee rating. *Studies in Personnel Policy,* No. 39. New York: the Board, 1942.
National Retail Merchants Association. *Appraising retail executive and employee performance.* New York: the Association, 1968.
Nedelsky, L. Absolute grading standards for objective tests. *Educational and Psychological Measurement,* 1954, *14,* 3–19.
Newcomb, T. M. *The consistency of certain extrovert-introvert behavior patterns in 51 problem boys.* New York: Teachers College, Columbia University, 1929.
Newman, F. B., & Jones, H. E. The adolescent in social groups. *Applied Psychological Monographs,* 1946, No. 9.
Newmark, C. S. (Ed.). *MMPI: Clinical and research trends.* New York: Praeger, 1979.
Newmark, C. S., et al. Using discriminant function analysis with clinical, demographic and historical variables to diagnose schizophrenia. *British Journal of Medical Psychology,* 1980, *53,* 365–373.
Nichols, R. C. Policy implications of the IQ controversy. *Review of Research in Education,* 1978, *6,* 3–46.
Nietzel, M., & Bernstein, D. Effects of instructionally mediated demand on the behavioral assessment of assertiveness. *Journal of Consulting and Clinical Psychology,* 1976, *44,* 500.
Nisbett, R. E., & Ross, L. *Human inference: Strategies and shortcomings of human judgment.* Englewood Cliffs, N. J.: Prentice-Hall, 1980.
Nitko, A. J. Distinguishing the many varieties of criterion-referenced tests. *Review of Educational Research,* 1980, *50,* 461–485.
Norris, L., & Katz, M. R. The measurement of academic interests. Part II. The predictive validities of academic interest measures. *Research Bulletin* 70–67. Princeton: Educational Testing Service, 1970.
Norton, S. D. The assessment center process and content validity: A reply to Dreyer and Sackett. *Academy of Management Review,* 1981, *6,* 561–566.
Oakland, T. Research on the Adaptive Behavior Inventory for Children and the Estimated Learning Potential. *School Psychology Digest,* 1979, *8,* 63–70.
Oaks, W. W., Scheink, P. A., & Husted, F. L. Objective evaluation of a method of assessing student performance in a clinical clerkship. *Journal of Medical Education,* 1969, *44,* 207–213.

References

Oden, M. H. The fulfillment of promise: 40-year follow-up of the Terman gifted group. *Genetic Psychology Monographs,* 1968, *77,* No. 1, 3–93.

O'Leary, K. D., & Wilson, G. T. *Behavior therapy: Application and outcome.* Englewood Cliffs, N. J.: Prentice-Hall, 1975.

Oles, H. J., & Davis, G. D. Publishers violate APA standards on test distribution. *Psychological Reports,* 1977, *41,* 713–714.

Oltman, P. K., Semple, C., & Goldstein, L. Cognitive style and interhemispheric differentiation in the EEG. *Neuropsychologia,* 1979, *17,* 699–702.

Oltman, P. K., et al. Psychological differentiation as a factor in conflict resolution. *Journal of Personality and Social Psychology,* 1975, *32,* 730–736.

Olweus, D. *Prediction of aggression.* Stockholm: Scandinavian Test Corporation, 1969.

Olweus, D. Stability of aggressive reaction patterns in males: a review. *Psychological Bulletin,* 1979, *86,* 852–875.

Ombredane, A., Robaye, F., & Plumail, H. Résultats d'une application répétée du matrix-couleur à une population de Noirs Congolais. *Bulletin, Centre d'Études et Recherches Psychotechniques,* 1956, *6,* 129–147.

Ord, I. G. *Mental tests for pre-literates.* London: Ginn, 1971.

Osgood, C. E., & Luria, Z. A blind analysis of a case of multiple personality using the Semantic Differential. *Journal of Abnormal and Social Psychology,* 1954, *49,* 579–591.

Osofsky, J. D. (Ed.). *Handbook of infant development.* New York: Wiley, 1979.

OSS Assessment Staff. *Assessment of men.* New York: Holt, Rinehart and Winston, 1948.

Pace, C. R., & Friedlander, J. The meaning of response categories: How often is "Occasionally", "Often," and "Very often"? Paper presented to American Educational Research Association, 1981.

Pace, L. A., & Schoenfeldt, L. F. Legal concerns in the use of weighted applications. *Personnel Psychology,* 1977, *30,* 159–166.

Parry, M. E. Ability of psychologists to estimate validity of personnel tests. *Personnel Psychology,* 1968, *21,* 139–147.

Passini, F. T., & Norman, W. T. A universal conception of personality structure? *Journal of Personality and Social Psychology,* 1966, *4,* 44–49.

Pearlman, K. Job families: A review and discussion of their implications for personnel selection. *Psychological Bulletin,* 1980, *87,* 1–28.

Pearlman, K., Schmidt, F. L., & Hunter, J. E. Validity generalization results for tests used to predict job proficiency and training success in clerical occupations. *Journal of Applied Psychology,* 1980, *65,* 373–406.

Perry, D. K. Evaluation of tests for improvement of programmer trainee selection. SDC Technical memorandum 3570, System Development Corporation, Santa Monica, Calif.: 1967.

Personnel classification tests. War Department Technical Manual 12-260. Washington, D. C.: War Department, 1946.

Pervin, L. A., & Lewis, M. (Eds.). *Perspectives in interactional psychology.* New York: Plenum, 1978.

Petersen, N. S., & Novick, M. R. An evaluation of some models for culture-fair selection. *Journal of Educational Measurement,* 1976, *13,* 3–29.

Peterson, D. A., & Wallace, S. R. Validation and revision of a test in use. *Journal of Applied Psychology,* 1966, *50,* 13–17.

Peterson, D. R. *The clinical study of social behavior.* New York: Appleton-Century-Crofts, 1968.

Phillips, W. M., Phillips, A. M., & Shearn, C. R. Objective assessment of schizophrenic thought. *Journal of Clinical Psychology,* 1980, *36,* 79–89.

Piaget, J., & Inhelder, B. *The child's conception of space.* London: Routledge & Kegan Paul, 1956.

Pike, L. W. Short-term instruction, testwiseness, and the Scholastic Aptitude Test: A

literature review with research recommendations. *Research Bulletin* 78-2. Princeton: Educational Testing Service, 1978.
Pittluck, P. The relation between aggressive fantasy and overt behavior. Unpublished doctoral dissertation, Yale University, New Haven, 1950.
Plomin, R., & DeFries, J. C. Genetics and intelligence: Recent data. *Intelligence*, 1980, *4*, 15–24.
Porteus, S. D. *Porteus maze test—fifty years application.* Palo Alto, Calif.: Pacific Books, 1965.
Prediger, D. J. *Alternatives for validating interest inventories against group membership criteria. ACT Research Report* No. 76. Iowa City: American College Testing Program, 1976. (a)
———. A world-of-work map for career exploration. *Vocational Guidance Quarterly*, 1976, *24*, 198–208. (b)
———. Getting "ideas" out of the *DOT* and into vocational guidance. *Vocational Guidance Quarterly*, 1981, *29*, 293–305. (a)
———. A note on Self-Directed Search validity for females. *Vocational Guidance Quarterly*, 1981, *30*, 117–129. (b)
Preston, C. E. Psychological testing with Northwest Coast Alaskan Eskimos. *Genetic Psychology Monographs*, 1964, *69*, 323–419.
Preston, H. O. *The development of a procedure for evaluating officers in the United States Air Force.* Pittsburgh: American Institute for Research, 1948.
Prestwood, J. S., & Weiss, D. J. The effects of knowledge of results and test difficulty on ability test performance and psychological reactions to testing. Research Report 78-2, Psychometric Methods Program, University of Minnesota, Minneapolis, 1978.
Pursell, E. D., Dossett, D. L., & Latham, G. P. Obtaining valid predictors by minimizing rating errors in the criterion. *Personnel Psychology*, 1980, *33*, 91–96.
Quay, L. C. Language dialect, age, and intelligence-test performance in disadvantaged black children. *Child Development*, 1974, *45*, 463–468.
Rabin, A. I. (Ed.). *Assessment with projective techniques: A concise introduction.* New York: Springer, 1981.
Ragosta, M. Handicapped students and the SAT. *College Board Research and Development Report* 80-12. Princeton: Educational Testing Service, 1980.
Rasch, G. *Probabilistic models for some intelligence and attainment tests.* (2d ed.). Chicago: University of Chicago Press, 1980.
Raven, J. C., Court, J. H., & Raven, J. *Manual for Raven's Progressive Matrices and Vocabulary Scales.* London: H. K. Lewis, 1978.
Redick, R. L. A compilation of measurement devices compendia. *Measurement and Evaluation in Guidance*, 1975, *8*, 193–202.
Reilly, R. R., & Manese, W. R. The validation of a minicourse for telephone company switching technicians. *Personnel Psychology*, 1979, *32*, 83–90.
Remus, W. E. Measures of fit for unit rules. *American Psychologist*, 1980, *35*, 678–680.
Resnick, L. B. (Ed.) *The nature of intelligence.* Hillsdale, N. J.: Erlbaum, 1976.
Rest, J. New approaches to the assessment of moral judgment. In T. Lickona (Ed.), *Moral development and behavior.* New York: Holt, Rinehart and Winston, 1976.
Reynolds, C. R. Differential construct validity of intelligence as popularly measured. *Intelligence*, 1980, *4*, 371–379.
Reynolds, C. R., & Gutkin, T. B. A multivariate comparison of the intellectual performance of black and white children matched on four demographic variables. *Personality and Individual Differences*, 1980, *2*, 175–180.
———. *The handbook of school psychology.* New York: Wiley, 1982.
Reynolds, C. R., & Jensen, A. R. WISC-R subscale patterns of abilities of blacks and whites matched on Full Scale IQ. *Journal of Educational Psychology*, 1983, *75*, 207–214.

Riddle, M., & Roberts, A. H. Delinquency, delay of gratification, recidivism, and Porteus Maze Tests. *Psychological Bulletin,* 1977, *84,* 417–425.

Rimland, B., & Munsinger, H. Burt's IQ data. *Science,* 1977, *195,* 248.

Rist, R. C. Student social class and teacher expectations: The self-fulfilling prophecy in ghetto education. *Harvard Educational Review,* 1970, *40,* 411–451.

Roadman, H. C. An industrial use of peer ratings. *Journal of Applied Psychology,* 1964, *48,* 211–214.

Robinson, D. D. Prediction of clerical turnover in banks by means of a weighted application blank. *Journal of Applied Psychology,* 1972, *56,* 282.

Roe, A. An adaptive decision structure for educational systems. Report 63-63. Los Angeles: Department of Engineering, University of Southern California, 1963.

Rorschach, H. *Psychodiagnostics.* P. Lemkau & B. Kronenberg (trans.) (2nd ed.) Bern: Huber, 1942.

Rosen, A. Development of MMPI scales based on a reference group of psychiatric patients. *Psychological Monographs,* 1966, *70,* No. 8.

Rosenthal, R. *Experimenter effects in behavioral research.* New York: Appleton-Century-Crofts, 1966.

Roskind, W. L. *Detroit Edison Co.* v. *N.L.R.B.,* and the consequences of open testing in industry. *Personnel Psychology,* 1980, *33,* 3–9.

Rothe, H. F. Output rates among industrial employees. *Journal of Applied Psychology,* 1978, *63,* 40–46.

Royer, F. L., & Weitzel, K. E. Effect of perceptual cohesiveness on pattern recording in the block design task. *Perception and Psychophysics,* 1977, *21,* 39–46.

Rubin, D. C., & Stroud, T. W. F. Comparing high schools with respect to student performance in university. *Journal of Educational Statistics,* 1977, *2,* 139–155.

Rundquist, E. A. Item and response characteristics in attitude and personality measurement. *Psychological Bulletin,* 1966, *66,* 166–177.

Ryan, T. A., & Johnson, B. R. Interest scores in the selection of salesmen and servicemen: Occupational vs. ability-group scoring keys. *Journal of Applied Psychology,* 1942, *26,* 543–562.

Salmon-Cox, L. Teachers and standardized achievement tests: What's really happening. *Phi Delta Kappan,* 1981, *62,* 631–634.

Sarason, I. G. (Ed.) *Test anxiety: Theory, research, and applications.* Hillsdale, N. J.: Erlbaum, 1980.

Sarason, S. B., Mandler, G., & Craighill, P. G. The effect of differential instructions on anxiety and learning. *Journal of Abnormal and Social Psychology,* 1952, *47,* 561–565.

Sarnacki, R. E. An examination of test-wiseness in the cognitive test domain. *Review of Educational Research,* 1979, *49,* 252–279.

Sattler, J. M. Racial "experimenter effects" in experimentation, testing, interviewing, and psychotherapy. *Psychological Bulletin,* 1970, *73,* 137–160.

———. *Assessment of children's intelligence.* Philadelphia: Saunders, 1974.

———. *Assessment of children's intelligence and special abilities* (2d ed.) Boston: Allyn & Bacon, 1981.

Sawyer, R., & Maxey, E. J. The validity over time of college freshman grade prediction equations. *Research Report* 80. Iowa City: American College Testing Program, 1979.

Sawyer, R., & Maxey, E. J. The relationship between college freshman class size and other institutional characteristics and the accuracy of freshman grade predictions. *Research Report* 82. Iowa City: American College Testing Program, 1982.

Scarr, S. *IQ: Race, social class and individual differences, new studies of old problems.* Hillsdale, N. J.: Erlbaum, 1981.

Schafer, R. *Psychoanalytic interpretation in Rorschach testing.* New York: Grune & Stratton, 1954.

———. Psychological test responses manifesting the struggle against decompensation. *Journal of Personality Assessment,* 1978, *42,* 562–571.

Schaie, K. W. The Primary Mental Abilities in adulthood: An exploration in the development of psychometric intelligence. In P. B. Baltes & O. G. Brim, Jr. (Eds.), *Life-span development and behavior,* vol. 2. New York: Academic Press, 1979.

Schaie, K. W., & Baltes, P. B. Some faith helps to see the forest. *American Psychologist,* 1977, *32,* 1118–1120.

Schalling, D., & Rosén, A.-S. Porteus maze differences between psychopathic and non-psychopathic criminals. *British Journal of Social and Clinical Psychology,* 1968, *7,* 224–228.

Schlei, B. L., & Grossman, P. *Employment discrimination law.* Washington, D. C.: Bureau of National Affairs, 1976.

———. *Employment discrimination law; 1979 supplement.* Washington, D. C.: Bureau of National Affairs, 1979.

Schletzer, V. M. A study of the predictive effectiveness of the Strong Vocational Interest Blank for job satisfaction. Unpublished doctoral dissertation, University of Minnesota, Minneapolis, 1963.

———. SVIB as a predictor of job satisfaction. *Journal of Applied Psychology,* 1966, *50,* 5–8.

Schmidt, F. L., Gast-Rosenberg, I., & Hunter, J. E. Validity generalization results for computer programmers. *Journal of Applied Psychology,* 1980, *65,* 643–661.

Schmidt, F. L., & Hunter, J. E. Development of a general solution to the problem of validity generalization. *Journal of Applied Psychology,* 1977, *62,* 529–540.

Schmidt, F. L., Hunter, J. E., & Pearlman, K. Task differences and validity of aptitude tests in selection: A red herring. *Journal of Applied Psychology,* 1981, *66,* 166–185.

Schmidt, F. L., Pearlman, K., & Hunter, J. E. The validity and fairness of employment and educational tests for Hispanic Americans. *Personnel Psychology,* 1980, *33,* 705–724.

Schmidt, F. L., *et al.* The impact of valid selection procedures on workforce productivity. *Journal of Applied Psychology,* 1979, *64,* 609–626.

Schneider, B. Person-situation selection: A review of some ability-situation interaction research. *Personnel Psychology,* 1978, *31,* 281–297.

Schorr, D., Bower, G. N., & Kiernan, R. Stimulus variables in the block design task. *Journal of Clinical and Consulting Psychology,* 1982, *50,* 479–488.

Schrader, W. B., & Pitcher, B. Relation of mean and standard deviation of LSAT scores to validity coefficients. Unpublished report to Law School Admission Council from Educational Testing Service, Princeton, 1969.

Schwartz, P. A., & Krug, R. E. *Ability testing in developing countries: A handbook of principles and techniques.* Palo Alto, Calif.: American Institutes for Research, 1972.

Scribner, S., & Cole, M. Cognitive consequences of formal and informal schooling. *Science,* 1973, *182,* 553–559.

Searle, L. V. The organization of hereditary maze-brightness and maze-dullness. *Genetic Psychology Monographs,* 1949, *39,* 279–325.

Sears, P. S., & Barbee, A. H. Career and life satisfaction among Terman's gifted women. In J. Stanley *et al.* (Eds.), *The gifted and the creative: Fifty-year perspective.* Baltimore: Johns Hopkins University Press, 1977.

Sears, R. R. Dependency motivation. In M. R. Jones (Ed.), *Nebraska symposium on motivation.* Lincoln: University of Nebraska Press, 1963.

———. Sources of life satisfactions of the Terman gifted men. *American Psychologist,* 1977, *32,* 119–128.

Seashore, H. G., & Ricks, J. H., Jr. Norms must be relevant. *Test Service Bulletin* 39. New York: Psychological Corporation, 1950.

Segall, M. H., Campbell, D. T., & Herskovits, M. J. *The influence of culture on visual perception.* Indianapolis: Bobbs-Merrill, 1966.
Selman, R. L., & Lieberman, M. Moral education in the primary grades: An evaluation of a developmental curriculum. *Journal of Educational Psychology,* 1975, *67,* 131–142.
Sessions, F. Q. An analysis of the predictive value of the Pre-Engineering Ability Test. *Journal of Applied Psychology,* 1955, *39,* 119–122.
Shannon, C., & Weaver, W. *The mathematical theory of communication.* Urbana, Ill.: University of Illinois Press, 1949.
Shapiro, M. B. Experimental method in the psychological description of the individual psychiatric patient. *International Journal of Social Psychiatry,* 1957, *3,* 89–103.
Sharp, D., Cole, M., & Lave, C. Education and cognitive development: The evidence from experimental research. *Monographs of the Society for Research in Child Development,* 1979, *44,* Nos. 1–2.
Shavelson, R. J., & Bolus, R. Self-concept: The interplay of theory and methods. *Journal of Educational Psychology,* 1982, *74,* 3–17.
Shepard, R. N., Romney, A. K., & Nerlove, S. B. *Multidimensional scaling.* New York: Seminar Press, 1972.
Sherman, S. W., & Robinson, N. M. (Eds.). *Ability testing of handicapped people: Dilemma for government, science, and the public.* Washington, D.C.: National Academy Press, 1982.
Shneidman, E. S. (Ed.) *Thematic test analysis.* New York: Grune & Stratton, 1951.
Shweder, R. A., & D'Andrade, R. G. Accurate reflection or systematic distortion? A reply to Block, Weiss, and Thorne. *Journal of Personality and Social Psychology,* 1979, *37,* 1075–1084.
Siegel, A. I. Miniature job training and evaluation as a selection/classification device. *Human Factors,* 1978, *20,* 189–200.
Silverman, A. J., *et al.* Prediction of physiological stress tolerance from projective tests. *Journal of Projective Techniques,* 1957, *21,* 189–193.
Simpson, R. H. The specific meanings of certain terms indicating different degrees of frequency. *Quarterly Journal of Speech,* 1944, *30,* 328–330.
Skolnick, A. Motivational imagery and behavior. *Journal of Consulting Psychology,* 1966, *30,* 463–478.
Slack, W. V., & Porter, D. The Scholastic Aptitude Test: A critical appraisal. *Harvard Educational Review,* 1980, *50,* 154–175.
Slinde, J. A., & Linn, R. L. Vertically equated tests: Fact or phantom? *Journal of Educational Measurement,* 1977, *14,* 23–32.
Slovic, P., & Lichtenstein, S. Comparison of Bayesian and regression approaches to the study of information processing in judgment. *Organizational Behavior and Human Performance,* 1971, *6,* 649–744.
Smedslund, J. The acquisition of conservation of substance and weight in children. *Scandinavian Journal of Psychology,* 1961, *2,* 1–10, 71–84, 85–87, 153–160, 203–210.
Smith, E. R., & Tyler, R. W. *Appraising and recording student progress.* New York: Harper, 1942.
Smith, M. B. An analysis of two measures of "authoritarianism" among Peace Corps teachers. *Journal of Personality,* 1965, *33,* 513–535.
Smith, P. C., & Kendall, L. M. Retranslation of expectations: An approach to the construction of unambiguous anchors for rating scales. *Journal of Applied Psychology,* 1963, *47,* 149–155.
Snow, R. E., Federico, P.-A., Montague, W. E. (Eds.). *Aptitude, learning, and instruction.* (2 vols.). Hillsdale, N.J.: Erlbaum, 1980.
Snow, R. E., Kyllonen, P. C., & Marshalek, B. The topography of ability and learning

correlations. In R. J. Sternberg (Ed.), *Advances in the psychology of human intelligence.* Hillsdale, N. J.: Erlbaum, 1982.

Spielberger, C. D., Anton, W. D., & Bedell, J. The nature and treatment of test anxiety. In M. Zuckerman & C. D. Spielberger (Eds.), *Emotion and anxiety: New concepts, methods and applications.* Hillsdale, N.J.: Erlbaum, 1976.

Spielberger, C. D., et al. Examination stress and test anxiety. In C. D. Spielberger & I. G. Sarason, (Eds.), *Stress and anxiety,* vol. 5. Washington: Hemisphere, 1978.

Spokane, A. R. Occupational preference and the validity of the Strong-Campbell Interest Inventory for college women and men. *Journal of Counseling Psychology,* 1979, *26,* 312–318.

Staats, A. W., & Burns, G. L. Intelligence and child development: What intelligence is and how it is learned and functions. *Genetic Psychology Monographs,* 1981, *104,* 237–301.

Starch, D., & Elliott, E. C. Reliability of grading high school work in English. *School Review,* 1912, *20,* 442–457.

Starch, D. & Elliott, E. C. Reliability of grading high school work in mathematics. *School Review,* 1913, *21,* 254–259.

Steiner, I. D., & Vannoy, J. S. Personality correlates of two types of conformity behavior. *Journal of Personality and Social Psychology,* 1966, *4,* 307–315.

Stephenson, W. *The study of behavior.* Chicago: University of Chicago Press, 1953.

Sternberg, J. An analytical study of a selection interview procedure. Unpublished master's thesis. Syracuse University, 1950.

Sternberg, R. J. *Intelligence, information processing, and analogical reasoning.* Hillsdale, N.J.: Erlbaum, 1977.

Sternberg, R. J. (Ed.). *Advances in the psychology of human intelligence,* vol. 1. Hillsdale, N.J.: Erlbaum, 1982. (a)

———. *Handbook of human intelligence.* New York: Cambridge University Press, 1982(b)

Sternberg, R. J., & Rifkin, B. The development of analogical reasoning processes. *Journal of Experimental Child Psychology,* 1979, *27,* 195–232.

Stewart, L. H., & Roberts, J. P. The relationship of Kuder profiles to remaining in a teachers college and to occupational choice. *Educational and Psychological Measurement,* 1955, *15,* 416–421.

Stockford, L., & Bissell, H. W. Factors involved in establishing a merit rating scale. *Personnel,* 1949, *26,* 94–116.

Stone, V. W. Measured vocational interests in relation to intraoccupational proficiency. *Journal of Applied Psychology,* 1960, *44,* 78–82.

Strong, E. K., Jr. *Vocational interests of men and women.* Stanford, Calif.: Stanford University Press, 1943.

———. *Vocational interests 18 years after college.* Minneapolis: University of Minnesota Press, 1955.

Stuit, D. B. (Ed.) *Personnel research and test development in the Bureau of Naval Personnel.* Princeton, N.J.: Princeton University Press, 1947.

Super, D. E., & Crites, J. O. *Appraising vocational fitness.* (2d ed.) New York: Harper & Row, 1962.

Swets, J. A., & Feurzig, W. Computer-aided instruction. *Science,* 29 October 1965, *150,* 572–576.

Tenopyr, M. L., & Oeltjen, P. D. Personnel selection and classification. *Annual Review of Psychology,* 1982, *33,* 581–618.

Terman, L. M. *The measurement of intelligence.* Boston: Houghton Mifflin, 1916.

———. The discovery and encouragement of exceptional talent. *American Psychologist,* 1954, *9,* 221–230.

Terman, L. M., & Merrill, M. A. *Stanford-Binet Intelligence Scale* (1972 norms ed.). Boston: Houghton-Mifflin, 1973. (Now published by Riverside Publishing Company, Iowa City.)

Terwilliger, J. S. Representation of vocational interests on an absolute scale. Unpublished master's thesis, University of Illinois, 1960.
Thayer, P. W. "Somethings old, somethings new." *Personnel Psychology,* 1977, *30,* 523–524.
Thigpen, C. H., & Cleckley, H. A case of multiple personality. *Journal of Abnormal and Social Psychology,* 1953, *49,* 135–151.
Thigpen, C. H. & Cleckley, H. A. *The three faces of Eve.* New York: McGraw-Hill, 1957.
Thissen, D. M. Information in wrong responses to the Raven Progressive Matrices. *Journal of Educational Measurement,* 1976, *13,* 201–214.
Thorndike, R. L. *The concepts of over- and under-achievement.* New York: Teachers College, Columbia University, 1963. (a)
Thorndike, R. L. (Ed.), *Educational measurement.* Washington, D.C.: American Council on Education, 1971.
Tittle, C. K., & Zytowski, D. G. (Eds.). *Sex-fair interest measurement: Research and implications.* Washington, D.C.: National Institute of Education, 1978.
Tolor, A., & Brannigan, G. G. *Research and clinical applications of the Bender-Gestalt Test.* Springfield, Ill.: C. C. Thomas, 1980.
Training Aids Section. A comparative study of verbalized and projected pictorial materials. Ninth Naval District Headquarters, Great Lakes, Ill., 1945.
Trattner, M. H. Task analysis in the design of three concurrent validity studies of the Professional and Administrative Career Examination. *Personnel Psychology,* 1979, *32,* 109–119.
Travers, J. R., & Light, R. L. *Learning form experience: Evaluating early childhood demonstration programs.* Washington, D.C.: National Academy Press, 1982.
Triandis, H. C., & Berry, J. *Handbook of cross-cultural psychology, Vol. 2: Methodology.* Boston: Allyn & Bacon, 1980.
Trickett, E. J. & Moos, R. H. Generality and specificity of student reactions in high school classrooms. *Adolescence,* 1970, *5,* 373–390.
Trotman, F. K. Race, IQ, and the middle class. *Journal of Educational Psychology,* 1977, *69,* 266–273.
Tryon, G. S. The measurement and treatment of test anxiety. *Review of Educational Research,* 1980, *50,* 343–372.
Tryon, R. C. Genetic differences in learning ability in rats. *Yearbook of the National Society for the Study of Education,* 1940, *39,* 111–119.
Tucker, J. A. Operationalizing the diagnostic-intervention process. In T. Oakland (Ed.), *Psychological and educational assessment of minority children.* New York: Brunner/Mazel, 1977.
Tupes, E. C. Relationships between behavior trait ratings by peers and later officer performance of USAF Officer Candidate School graduates. *AFPTRC Research Bulletin* 57–125, 1957.
Tyler, L. E. Antecedents of two varieties of vocational interests. *Genetic Psychology Monographs,* 1964, *70,* 177–277.
Tyler, R. W. *Basic principles of curriculum and instruction.* Chicago: University of Chicago Press, 1950.
Undheim, J. O. On intelligence IV: Toward a restoration of general intelligence. *Scandinavian Journal of Psychology,* 1981, *22,* 251–266.
Urry, V. W. Tailored testing: A successful application of latent trait theory. *Journal of Educational Measurement,* 1977, *14,* 181–196.
Varble, D. L. Current status of the Thematic Apperception Test. In P. McReynolds (Ed.), *Advances in psychological assessment,* vol. 2. Palo Alto, Calif.: Science and Behavior Books, 1971.
Vernon, P. E. The validation of civil service selection board procedures. *Occupational Psychology,* 1950, *24,* 75–95.

———. Ability factors and environmental influences. *American Psychologist,* 1965, *20,* 723–733.
———. Intelligence and cultural environment. London: Methuen, 1969.
———. Multivariate approaches to the study of cognitive styles. In J. R. Royce (Ed.), *Multivariate analysis and psychological theory.* New York: Academic Press, 1973.
———. *Intelligence: Heredity and environment.* San Francisco: W. H. Freeman, 1979.
Vernon, P. E., & Parry, J. B. *Personnel selection in the British forces.* London: University of London Press, 1949.
Wade, T. C., & Baker, T. B. Opinions and use of psychological tests: A survey of clinical psychologists. *American Psychologist,* 1977, *32,* 874–882.
Wainer, H. On the sensitivity of regression and regressors. *Psychological Bulletin,* 1978, *85,* 267–273.
Wallach, M. A., & Kogan, N. *Modes of thinking in young children.* New York: Holt, Rinehart and Winston, 1965.
Wallach, M. A., et al. Contradiction between overt and projective personality indicators as a function of defensiveness. *Psychological Monographs,* 1962, *76,* No. 1.
Ward, W. C., Frederiksen, N., & Carlson, S. B. Construct validity of free-response and machine-scorable forms of a test. *Journal of Educational Measurement,* 1980, *17,* 11–30.
Webb, E. J., et al. *Nonreactive measures in the social sciences.* (2d ed.) Boston: Houghton Mifflin, 1981.
Wechsler, D. *Manual for the Wechsler Intelligence Scale for Children—Revised.* New York: Psychological Corporation, 1974.
Weikart, D. P., Bond, J. T. & McNeil, J. *Ypsilanti preschool project: Preschool years and longitudinal results through fourth grade.* Monograph No. 3. Ypsilanti, Mich.: High/Scope Research Foundation, 1978.
Weisz, J. R., & Yeates, K. O. Cognitive development in retarded and nonretarded persons. *PSychological Bulletin,* 1981, *90,* 153–178.
Wepman, J., et al. Learning disabilities. In N. Hobbs (Ed.), *Issues in the classification of children,* vol. 1. San Francisco: Jossey-Bass, 1976.
Wernimont, P. F., & Campbell, J. P. Signs, samples, and criteria. *Journal of Applied Psychology,* 1968, *52,* 372–376.
Wesman, A. G. Faking personality test scores in a simulated employment situation. *Journal of Applied Psychology,* 1952, *36,* 112–113.
Westin, A. F. *Privacy and freedom.* New York: Athenaeum, 1967.
White, R. W. Exploring personality the long way: The study of lives. in A. I. Rabin et al. (Eds.), *Further explorations in personality.* New York: Wiley, 1981.
Widom, C. S. MMPI profiles and the longitudinal prediction of adult social outcome. In C. S. Newmark (Ed.), *MMPI: Clinical and research trends.* New York: Praeger, 1979.
Wiener, G. The effect of distrust on some aspects of intelligence test behavior. *Journal of Consulting Psychology,* 1957, *21,* 127–130.
Wigdor, A. K., & Garner, W. R. *Ability testing: Uses, consequences, and controversies.* (2 vols.). Washington, D.C.: National Academy Press, 1982.
Wiggins, J. S. *Personality and prediction: Principles of personality assessment.* Reading, Mass.: Addison-Wesley, 1973.
Wiggins, J. S. Circumplex models of interpersonal behavior. In L. Wheeler (Ed.), *Review of Personality and Social Psychology,* vol. 1. Beverly Hills, Calif.: Sage Publications, 1980.
Willemin, L. P., Mellinger, J. J., & Karcher, E. K., Jr. Identifying fighters for combat. *Personnel Research Branch, Technical Research Report* 1112, 1958.
Willerman, L. *The psychology of individual and group differences.* San Francisco: Freeman, 1978.
Williams, R. L. The BITCH Test (Black Intelligence Test of Cultural Homogeneity). St. Louis, Mo.: Williams and Associates, 1972.

Wills, T. A. Perception of clients by professional helpers. *Psychological Bulletin,* 1978, *85,* 968–1000.
Wilson, D. P. *My six convicts.* New York: Holt, Rinehart and Winston, 1951.
Wilson, J. W., & Carpenter, K. E. The need for restandardizing altered tests. *American Psychologist,* 1948, *3,* 172f.
Wimsatt, W. C. Robustness, reliability and overdetermination. In M. B. Brewer & B. E. Collins (Eds.), *Scientific inquiry and the social sciences.* San Francisco: Jossey-Bass, 1981.
Winder, C. L., & Wiggins, J. S. Social reputation and social behavior: A further validation of the peer nomination theory. *Journal of Abnormal and Social Psychology,* 1964, *68,* 441–448.
Winkler, R. C., & Mathews, T. S. How employees feel about personality tests. *Personnel Journal,* 1967, *46,* 490–492.
Wirtz, W., & Lapointe, A. *Measuring the quality of education: A report on assessing educational progress.* Washington, D.C.: Wirtz & Lapointe, 1982.
Wissler, C. *The correlation of mental and physical tests.* New York: Columbia University, 1901.
Witkin, H. A. *Cognitive styles in personal and cultural adaptation.* Worcester, Mass.: Clark University Press, 1978.
Witkin, H. A., & Goodenough, D. R. *Cognitive styles: Essence and origins.* Psychological Issues Monograph 51. New York: International Universities Press, 1981.
Witkin, H. A., Goodenough, D. R., & Oltman, P. K. Psychological differentiation: Current status. *Journal of Personality and Social Psychology,* 1979, 37, 1127–1145.
Wober, M. Culture and the concept of intelligence: A case in Uganda. *Journal of Cross-cultural Psychology,* 1972, *3,* 327–328.
Wolf, T. H. *Alfred Binet.* Chicago: University of Chicago Press, 1973.
Wood, R. L. The relationship of brain damage . . . to quantitative intellectual impairment. In D. J. Oborne *et al.* (Eds.), *Research in psychology and medicine,* vol. 1. London: Academic Press, 1979.
Wylie, R. C. *The self-concept: Theory and research on selected topics.* (2 vols.). Lincoln: University of Nebraska Press, 1974, 1979.
Yeh, J. Test use in the schools. Center for the Study of Evaluation, University of California, Los Angeles, 1978.
Yerkes, R. M. (Ed.). Psychological examining in the United States Army. *Memoirs of the National Academy of Sciences,* 1921, No. 15.
Yoakum, C. S., & Yerkes, R. M. *Army mental tests.* New York: Holt, 1920.
Young, M. *The rise of the meritocracy, 1870–2033.* London: Thames and Hudson, 1958.
Zoccolotti, P., & Oltman, P. K. Field independence and lateralization of verbal and configurational processing. *Cortex,* 1978, *14,* 155–163.
Zubin, J., Eron, L. D., & Schumer, F. *An experimental approach to projective techniques.* New York: Wiley, 1965.
Zuckerman, M. General and situation-specific traits and states: New approaches to assessment of anxiety and other constructs. In M. Zuckerman & C. D. Spielberger (Eds.), *Emotions and anxiety.* Hillsdale, N. J.: Erlbaum, 1976.
Zytowski, D. G. Relationship of equivalent scales on three interest inventories. *Personnel and Guidance Journal,* 1968, *47,* 44–49.
Zytowski, D. G. A concurrent test of accuracy-of-classification of the Strong Vocational Interest Blank and the Kuder Occupational Interest Survey. *Journal of Vocational Behavior,* 1972, *56,* 183–185.
Zytowski, D. G. Predictive validity of the Kuder Preference Record, Form B, over a 25-year span. *Measurement and Evaluation in Guidance,* 1974, *1,* 122–129.
———. Predictive validity of the Kuder Occupational Interest Survey: A 12- to 19-year follow-up. *Journal of Counseling Psychology,* 1976, *22,* 221–223.
Zytowski, D. G. (Ed.). *Contemporary approaches to interest measurement.* Minneapolis: University of Minnesota Press, 1973.

Appendix A

Sources Listing Specialized Tests and Measurement Devices

Note: This list amplifies and updates a compilation by Redick (1975). Redick supplies about 200 words of description for the sources he covers.

Beatty, W. H. (Ed.). *Improving educational assessment and an inventory of measures of affective behavior.* Washington, D.C.: National Education Association, 1969.

Beere, C. A. (Ed.). *Women and women's issues: A handbook of tests and measures.* San Francisco: Jossey-Bass, 1979.

Biesheuvel, S. (Ed.). *Methods for the measurement of psychological performance.* International Biological Program Handbook Number 10. Oxford: Blackwell, 1969.

Bolton, B. (Ed.). *Handbook of measurement and evaluation in rehabilitation.* Baltimore: University Park Press, 1976.

Bonjean, C. M., Hill, R. J., & McLemore, S. D. *Sociological measurement: An inventory of scales and indices.* San Francisco: Chandler, 1967.

Boyer, E. G., Simon, A., & Karafin, G. (Eds.). *Measures of maturation: An anthology of early childhood observation instruments.* Philadelphia: Research for Better Schools, Inc., 1973.

Brislin, R. W., Lonner, W. J., and Thorndike, R. M. (Eds.). *Cross-cultural research methods.* New York: Wiley, 1974.

Cattell, R. B., & Warburton, F. W. *Objective personality and motivation tests.* Urbana: University of Illinois Press, 1967.

Chun, K.-T., Cobb, S., & French, J. R. P., Jr. *Measures for psychological assessment: a guide to 3,000 original sources . . . [on mental health].* Ann Arbor: Institute for Social Research, University of Michican, 1975.

Comrey, A. L., Backer, T. E., and Glaser, E. M. *A sourcebook for mental health measures.* Los Angeles: Human Interaction Research Institute, 1973.

Feshbach, Norma D. *Manual of individual difference variables [aggression through suggestibility] and measures.* Los Angeles: Center for the Study of Evaluation, University of California, 1968.

Frankenburg, W. K., & Camp, B. W. (Eds.). *Pediatric screening tests.* Springfield, Ill.: Thomas, 1975.

Hoepfner, R., *et al.* (Eds.). *CSE school test evaluations.* Los Angeles: Center for the Study of Evaluation, University of California. Various levels and dates: Preschool/kindergarten, elementary, Grades 7–8, Grades 9–10, Grades 11–12; 1970–.

Hoepfner, R., *et al. CSE-RBS test evaluations: Tests of higher order cognitive, affective, and interpersonal skills.* Los Angeles: Center for the Study of Evaluation, University of California, 1972.

Johnson, O. G. (Ed.). *Tests and measurements in child development: Handbook II.* (2 vols.). San Francisco: Jossey-Bass, 1976.

Kapes, J. F., & Mastie, M. M. (Eds.). *A counselor's guide to vocational guidance instruments.* Falls Church, Va.: American Personnel and Guidance Association, 1982.

Kiesler, D. J. *The process of psychotherapy: . . . systems of analysis.* [Scales for coding behavior and interview processes.] Chicago: Aldine, 1975.

Lake, D. G., Miles, M. B., & Earle, R. B., Jr. (Eds.). *Measuring human behavior: Tools for the assessment of social functioning.* New York: Teachers College Press, 1973.

Lyerly, S. B. *Handbook of psychiatric rating scales.* Rockville, Md.: National Institute of Mental Health, 1973.

Pfeiffer, J. W., & Heslin, R. *Instrumentation in human relations training.* La Jolla: University Associates Consultants, Inc., 1974.

Robinson, J. P. [and various coauthors]. *Measures of . . . attitudes.* Ann Arbor: Institute for Social Research, University of Michigan. Three listings: Political, 1968; occupational, 1969; social-psychological, 1973.

Rosen, P. (Ed.). *Test collection bulletin.* Issued quarterly by Educational Testing Service, Princeton, N.J.

Shaw, M. E, & Wright, J. M. *Scales for the measurement of attitudes.* New York: McGraw-Hill, 1967.

Simon, A., & Boyer, E. G. (Eds.). *Mirrors for behavior: An anthology of observation instruments.* (24 vols.). Wyncote, Pa.: Communications Materials Center, 1967–1974.

Walker, D. K. *Socioemotional measures for preschool and kindergarten children.* San Francisco: Jossey-Bass, 1973.

Wylie, R. C. *The self-concept.* (2 vols.) Lincoln, Nebr.: University of Nebraska Press, 1974; 1979.

Appendix B

Selected Publishers and Test Distributors

American College Testing Program; P. O. Box 168; Iowa City, Iowa, 52240. *(ACTP)*
American Guidance Service; Circle Pines, Minn., 55014. *(AGS)*
CTB/McGraw-Hill; Del Monte Research Park; Monterey, Calif., 93940. *(CTB)*
Consulting Psychologists Press, Inc.; 577 College Ave.; Palo Alto, Calif., 94306. *(CPP)*
Educational and Industrial Testing Service; P. O. Box 7234; San Diego, Calif., 92107. *(EdITS)*
Educational Testing Service; Princeton, New Jersey, 08540. *(ETS)*
Grune & Stratton, Inc.; 111 Fifth Ave.; New York, N.Y., 10003. *(GS)*
Institute for Personality and Ability Testing; 1602 Coronado Drive; Champaign, Ill., 61820. *(IPAT)*
National Computer Systems; P. O. Box 1416; Minneapolis, Minn., 55440. *(NCS)*
NFER-Nelson Publishing Co., Ltd.; 2 Oxford Road East; Windsor, Berks, SL4 1DF, England. *(NFER)*
Psych Systems; 600 Reisterstown Road; Baltimore, Md., 21208.

Psychological Corporation; 7500 Old Orchard Road, Cleveland, Ohio, 44130. *(PC)*

Publishers Test Service; 2500 Garden Road; Monterey, Calif., 93940.

Research Psychologists Press; P. O. Box 984; Port Huron, Mich., 48060. *(RPP)*

Riverside Publishing Co.; 1919 S. Highland Ave.; Lombard, Ill., 60148. *(Riv)*

Scholastic Testing Service, Inc.; 480 Meyer Rd.; Bensenville, Ill., 60106.

Science Research Associates; 155 N. Wacker Drive; Chicago, Ill., 60606. *(SRA)*

Sheridan Psychological Services; P. O. Box 6101; Orange, Calif., 92667.

Western Psychological Services; 12031 Wilshire Blvd.; Los Angeles, Calif., 90025. *(WPS)*

Subject Index

Ability, 29, 45. *See also* Clerical abilities; General mental ability; Performance, etc.
  crystallized, 239, 252–257, 291
  fluid, 217, 239, 252–257, 265ff., 291
  improvement of, 276, 309, 334–338
Ability grouping. *See* Instruction
Ability to learn, 259f., 317. *See also* Educational success; Instruction; Memory
Ability-personality complex, 241, 262, 266, 441, 540
Absolute score, 86
Achieve, motivation to, 323, 446, 457, 462, 499–501
Achievement tests, 31, 131, 234, 345, 351–357. *See also* Evaluation
  as administrative controls, 6, 23, 68, 107, 113f., 146, 331, 347–356.
  construction, 36f., 145f., 346, 348–350
  overlap with general ability, 31–32, 254ff.
Acquiescence, 147, 419, 470
Actuarial keying. *See* Criterion keying; Clinical interpretation versus statistical; Experience table
Adaptive behavior, 209, 258f.
Adaptive testing. *See* Computer in test preparation
Adjustment. *See* Anxiety; Neurotic; Pathology
Administering tests, 37–40, 49–74, 206, 324f.
Adverse impact, 384f., 393. *See also* Fairness
Age changes in ability, 203, 237–241, 262. *See also* Development
Age-equivalent score, 101
Aggression, 59, 246, 457, 494, 521, 537, 559
Air Force. *See* Aviators; Military personnel
Alpha coefficients, 169–171
Ambiguity in test items. *See* Structure
Analytic research, 235
Anchor test, 115
Anxiety
  as construct, 45, 458, 476, 511
  effect on performance, 70–73, 271, 498, 501, 551
  measurement, 70, 111, 477f.
  situational factors, 458, 560
Aptitude, 31, 254. *See also* Clerical abilities

Aptitude-treatment interaction. *See* Interaction
Arithmetic. *See* Mathematics; Numerical ability; Tests and techniques, K-ABC, Wechsler
Army. *See* Military personnel
Assertive behavior, 46, 445, 446. *See also* Aggression
Assessment
  behavioral, 47f., 459, 473, 540
  integrative, 561ff.
  state and national, 5, 113f., 351
Attenuation. *See* Disattenuation
Attitudes, testing of, 35, 458, 473, 557
Auditory abilities, 37–39, 119, 177f., 200, 328, 405
Aviators, 29–31, 57, 361, 363f., 395, 396–398, 511, 526, 560

Bandwidth, 174
Base rate, 399, 407, 465, 492f.
Bead-chain task, 277ff.
Behavioral assessment, 47f., 459, 473, 540
Behaviorally anchored rating scale, 513ff.
Behaviorism, 46, 455
Behavior modification or behavior therapy, 47, 70, 177, 444, 445, 495, 530–532
Bias in rating, 388, 393, 509ff., 535
Bias in test use, 7, 9, 67f. *See also* Culture; Fairness
Biographical data, 41, 246, 362f., 374, 396, 406, 466
Blacks. *See also* Court decisions, *Larry P.*; Culture; Ethnic; Fairness; Social class
  educational provisions for, 209–214, 341f.
  influences on test performance of, 39, 66f., 320–322, 330, 331f., 392
  criterion-related studies, 386f., 393, 487
  score distributions, 224, 321f., 332, 392
Blind scoring, 69, 535
Brain dysfunction, 468, 494, 548, 553
Brain functions, 264, 266

Calibration, 114, 118, 220
Capacity, 198, 211
Catalog, test, 13–14
Ceiling effect, 179
Certification, 21, 91, 180, 347

Character tests, 7, 451, 473, 526, 542–547.
  See also Delinquency; Honesty,
  measurement of
Children, procedures for studying, 33, 34,
  58, 162, 514ff., 530f. *See also* Infancy;
  General mental ability, etc.
Choice response, 27, 42, 78, 272f., 329, 357
  in inventories, 418f., 517
  scoring of, 61, 82
Civil service, 6, 36, 182, 369, 384
Classification decisions, 20–22, 140–144,
  345ff., 396, 398ff., 494
Classroom environment, 458f., 499–501,
  527f.
Clerical abilities, 158, 166ff., 182f., 301, 304,
  313
Clerical workers, 248, 360, 400f.
Clinical interpretation, 235, 464ff., 485–488,
  502–507
  versus statistical, 406f.
Clinical practice, 46–48, 63–65, 76, 399,
  442f., 506, 561
Clinical research, 235, 442f.
Closure, 291f.
Coaching, 78–80, 325f., 326
College. *See also* Engineering; Mathematics;
  Professional schools, etc.
  admission policies and practices, 6, 11, 22,
  78–80, 91, 155, 246, 402, 406, 499,
  512
  information for applicants, 22
  prediction or explanation of success, 193,
  226f., 246f., 367, 387, 464, 500
Combining scores, 395–399, 406ff. *See also*
  Clinical interpretation
Commonality key, 432ff.
Comparability of tests, 105f., 108, 114f.
Compensatory education, 259, 334ff.
Competence, 5. *See also* Minimum
  competency
Competition as social policy, 8, 80, 88, 329,
  542
Components of ability. *See* Factor;
  Information processing
Computer
  as model of information processing, 200,
  277
  in test preparation and administration,
  35–41, 118
  in test scoring, reporting, and
  interpretation, 38, 39, 82f., 118, 180,
  220, 405–408, 425, 487f., 490, 555
Confidence band, 106, 180, 236
Confidentiality, 75–76
Configural interpretation. *See* Pattern
Conformity, 408, 451, 500, 545
Conservation (Piaget), 57, 257f.
Construct validation. *See* Validation
Constructed response, 41–42, 356f.
  scoring of, 81–85

Construction of tests from content
  specifications, 145, 348–350, 483
Contamination, 367, 535
Content-referenced interpretation, 88f., 92,
  353f.
Content validation. *See* Validation
Control keys, 474
Convergence of indicators, 153, 446f.
Coordination. *See* Psychomotor, Tests and
  techniques: Complex Coordination
Correlation, 136–141
  adjustment for measurement error, 176,
  259, 379, 394
  adjustment for restricted range, 379, 394
  between ability measures, 250, 254ff., 262,
  267f., 314. *See also* Factor
  intraclass, 169
  multiple, 395
Correlational research, 204, 235ff., 442
Costs of testing, 83
Counseling, use of tests in, 22, 88, 89, 106,
  246, 260, 311, 412, 424–428, 443, 464f.,
  473. *See also* Guidance
Court decisions, 125, 182, 385, 451
  Albemarle Paper Co. v. *Moody,* 385
  Bakke, 385
  Debra P., 146, 331
  Detroit Edison, 75
  Griggs v. *Duke Power,* 385
  Guardians, 385
  Kirkland, 385
  Larry P. v. *Riles,* 144, 341
  Navaho Refining, 385
  Rowley, v. *Board of Education,* 320
  Vulcan, 156
  Washington v. *Davis,* 334, 385
  Weber, 385
Creativity, 142, 261ff., 497, 519
Criterion, 127, 134, 248, 364–369, 394, 486,
  511, 566
Criterion keying, 147, 362f., 406, 419f.,
  432ff., 465ff., 479, 484, 519, 523
Criterion reference, 87ff. *See also* Domain
  reference
Critical incidents technique, 361, 362, 373,
  513
Crosscultural comparisons, 275, 328, 536,
  539. *See also* Culture
Cross-sectional design, 337
Crossvalidation, 397, 466, 492
Crystallized abilities, 239, 252–257, 291. *See
  also* Achievement, Mathematics, Reading
Culture. *See also* Crosscultural, Social class
  adapting test procedures, 66, 324, 331
  influences on development and test
  performance, 119, 323, 327ff.
  non-Western, testing in, 57, 66, 323, 328f.,
  497
Cut score, 91, 180, 246, 369ff., 381, 385,
  388ff., 393, 397, 403ff.

Subject Index

Decisions, 19–24, 91f., 175, 338–345, 369ff., 380ff., 398f., 402–408
Decontextualization, 266, 328f.
Delinquency, 447, 479, 485, 523, 540
Design
  of developmental research, 237f.
  of experiments, 68, 168, 345f.
Development
  intellectual, 237–247, 254, 275–280, 282, 317–329, 334f.
  personal characteristics, 428f., 457, 460
Dexterity. *See* Psychomotor
Diagnosis, 22, 47, 126f., 175, 201, 264, 271, 298ff., 340ff., 484, 494
Dictionary of Occupational Titles, 400, 415, 421
Differences within the person, 86, 96f., 105f., 251, 255, 310–315, 398, 421. *See also* Diagnosis; Profile
  reliability, 106, 237, 312–314
  Verbal-minus-Performance, 208, 236f., 251, 264
Differential prediction, 386f. *See also* Classification; Interaction; Profile
Difficulty of test or item, 39, 117, 179, 220, 354, 501
Directions, 41f., 51–57, 61, 178, 324f., 469f., 512
Disadvantaged children, 259, 322, 331–338, 501
Disattenuation, 176, 251, 259, 394
Disclosure of tests, 73. *See also* Privacy; Security
Discriminant key, 432ff.
Disguise of test procedure, 33, 451, 452f., 473, 538
Distractibility, 251, 332. *See also* Rapport
Distribution of scores, 94, 99, 102f., 179
Divergence of indicators, 153, 256, 446ff.
Divergent thinking, 142, 261ff., 296ff., 357, 376, 418
Domain reference, 87ff., 119, 161, 353f. *See also* Trait, conceptualization; Validation, content
Drawing, style of, 447ff., 548ff.
Drivers, tests for, 26, 182, 372
Drugs, research on, 299, 511
Dynamic interpretation, 45–48, 455, 464f., 550ff., 562f., 566f.

Ecological validity, 457
Education. *See* Instruction; School
Educational success, prediction of, 242–247, 303, 431, 498ff. *See also* College; Instruction; Law-school; Training
Efficiency, intellectual, 195, 234. *See also* Information processing
Electrophysiology, 263f.
Employment testing, 15–18, 64, 97, 142, 156, 181ff., 197, 202, 260, 303–310, 326, 358–408, 495–498. *See also* Fairness; Managerial; Vocational

Endorsement items, 418f.
Engineering careers, prediction, 360, 371, 431, 432, 434ff.
English usage and composition, 81, 301ff., 312f., 353, 357, 397
Entrapment, 451
Equal Employment Opportunity Commission (EEOC), 150, 384
Equating of tests, 100, 114–116, 118
Equivalent forms, 164
Error of measurement, 106, 114, 158–180, 235ff., 251, 311, 509ff.
Essay test. *See* Constructed response
Ethical issues and standards, 17, 33f., 74–77, 412, 450–454, 525, 537. *See also* Fairness; Privacy; Standards
Ethnic and racial correlates, 321f., 386f. *See also* Blacks; Culture; Fairness; Social class; Tester characteristics
Evaluation of programs and treatments, 23, 56, 69, 79, 107, 113f., 257, 334f., 338, 341, 345–354, 446f., 476, 495, 535, 540, 549
Executive processes, 234, 253, 335f.
Expectancy of teacher or tester, 67–69, 342, 535. *See also* Experience table
Experience table, 89f., 112, 370, 571
Experimentation as validation method, 152

Face validity, 76, 182, 363
Factor analysis, 283ff.
  ability, 283–298, 312, 326
  interests, 414ff.
  personality, 460ff.
Fairness, 7–9, 155–157, 182, 188
  issues in education and guidance, 331, 334, 341f., 438ff.
  issues in employment, 75, 334, 363, 383–394
  issues in student selection, 8, 79
Faking, 70, 467ff., 530, 565
False alarm, 370, 399, 492f.
Fatigue, 55
Field dependence, 265ff., 540
Fire fighters, 156, 451
Fluency. *See* Divergent thinking
Fluid ability, 217, 239, 252–257, 265ff., 291
Forced choice, 418f., 473, 519. *See also* Choice response
Free-response tests. *See* Constructed response

q, 197, 217, 283
Gains, measuring, 102, 119f., 255, 259, 345f.
General factor, 283ff.
General mental ability, 30, 103, 191–233, 234–268, 269–292, 316–345
  group tests, 196ff., 216–221, 224ff., 237, 243
  historical background, 192–202

General mental ability (*Continued*)
  individual tests, 52–54, 194–196, 200–202, 205–218, 222–224, 235–237, 323ff., 335ff.
  overlap with achievement, 31–32, 254ff.
  predictive validity, 242–249. *See also* Educational; College; Vocational
  stability, 237–241, 314
Generalizability, 161ff., 458f., 531ff.
Gifted persons, 192, 242
Grade-equivalent score, 101, 125
Groups, performance of, 142, 266f., 329f., 458f., 527f. *See also* Peer ratings
Group tests, 27. *See also* General mental ability
Guessing, 57, 61f., 78
Guidance, 300–315, 450. *See also* Counseling

Handicapped test takers, 62f., 209, 260, 340. *See also* Retarded
Handwriting, 82, 455f., 466f.
Hearing. *See* Auditory
Heredity, 316–321
Hispanic test takers, 66, 101, 111–113, 209–211, 224, 321, 328, 387
History of testing, 4–12, 192–202, 476
Home background, 7–10, 112–114, 209, 241, 247, 318–322
Homogeneity of test items, 119, 148, 177, 354
Homogeneous keying, 418, 425, 433, 466
Honesty, measurement of, 502, 542ff. *See also* Faking
Hostility, 45, 149

Idiographic approach, 502
Impressionistic assessment, 41–48, 65, 455, 464f., 518, 550ff.
Incentives and test performance, 70
Individualized instructional plan, 209, 340
Industrial applications of tests. *See* Employment testing
Infancy, testing in, 231ff., 239, 320
Inference from test scores, 44–48, 154–157, 464–467, 571ff. *See also* Decisions; Policy; Validation
Information processing, 272–282, 336ff., 345
Information, tests of, 309, 330f., 366
Informed consent, 33f., 74, 450ff., 472
Inkblots, 68, 467, 547, 553ff.
Institutional decisions, 450ff.
Instruction
  adaptation to fit ability, 6, 75, 209–214, 259f., 338–345, 399
  classroom use of tests, 36, 342–348, 353f.
  effect on general ability, 257, 276f., 334ff.
  grouping, tracking, 5–7, 143, 246, 338–347, 500
  influence of tests on, 342, 347ff.
Intelligence, 31, 203. *See also* Ability; Capacity; General mental ability; Information processing
  definition, 151, 194f., 198f.
Intelligence quotient, 100, 202–204, 236ff.
Interaction, 140–144
  among traits, 403ff., 449
  heredity and environment, 318
  person with situation, 71f., 142, 458ff., 498, 535
  personal factors with instruction, 143, 259f., 346, 399, 499ff.
  personality with therapeutic method, 495
Interest measures, 109, 129, 411–440, 469
  change over time, 428f., 436f.
  consistency among procedures, 412, 427f., 438
  dimensions, 414–417, 419, 423
  prediction of criteria, 420, 422, 427–431, 497
Internal consistency, 169ff., 397. *See also* Homogeneity
Interpretation, dynamic, 45–48, 455, 464f.
  to test taker, 75, 182
Intervals, equal, 83f., 119
Interview, 405ff.
Inventory. *See* Interest; Personality; Self-report
Item characteristic curve, 116
Item response theory, 117
Items. *See also* Choice response; Constructed response; Criterion keying; Endorsement; Forced choice
  banks of, 36, 118, 350
  critical review, 92, 330ff., 392, 452
  statistical analysis, 116ff., 147f., 185, 333, 392

Job analysis, 359ff., 373, 402
Job performance. *See* Employment; Ratings
Judgment. *See also* Clinical interpretation; Impressionistic assessment; Ratings
  errors of, 81, 122, 405–408, 465, 509ff., 533ff.
  policies underlying, 92, 407f.

Knowledge of results, 39
Kuder-Richardson formulas, 171

Labeling, 22, 47, 76, 201, 339–342, 459, 494, 535, 573
Language used in testing, 66, 392
Latent trait theory, 117
Laws and legal actions related to testing, 17, 19, 73, 75–76, 209, 383ff., 450. *See also* Court decisions
Law-school admission, 11, 127, 141, 155, 390, 400, 402. *See also* Tests and techniques, LSAT
Lay person, appeal to, 181ff., 332. *See also* Face validity

Subject Index

Leadership, 498, 509, 511, 525, 526, 565
Learning ability, 259ff., 317. *See also* Educational success; Instruction; Memory
Learning disability, 22, 340
Length of test or number of observers, 174–176, 458
Logical abstraction, 328f.
Longitudinal design, 237, 335

Managerial positions, selection for, 248, 362f., 497, 526, 563–570
Manual for test, 13, 110f., 123
Mastery, 31, 179, 260, 345, 353
Mathematics. *See also* Numerical ability
  success in, 314
  tests of, 79, 81, 291, 348, 357, 376, 396, 398
Matrix sampling, 352, 527
Maximum performance, 28–32, 58–59, 445
Maze performance, 29–30, 45, 68, 317, 540
Mean, 98
Mechanical comprehension, 50–52, 90, 98, 146, 150f., 309–314, 366, 387, 395. *See also* Tests and techniques, Bennett, DAT
Median, 93
Medicine
  prediction and selection, 129, 367, 406, 408, 438, 499
  proficiency, 40, 368, 513
Memory, 259f., 290f. *See also* Tests and techniques, Digit Span
Mental age, 203–205
Mental deficiency. *See* Retarded
Mental Measurements Yearbook, 13, 122, 124, 374, 423
Merit key, 362f., 420, 466, 520
Metacognition, 195, 336ff.
Method factors, 447
Military personnel, 55, 65, 72, 90, 146f., 182, 196ff., 217, 247, 308, 313, 363, 365ff., 398f., 401, 405, 431, 433, 476, 493, 494, 509, 511, 525, 526, 562ff.
Minimum competency test, 31, 92, 146, 331, 348, 391
Moderator variable, 404. *See also* Interaction
Moral judgment, 82–85, 543
Motivation of persons tested, 29, 38, 39, 58–60, 64–67, 69–73, 181f., 323, 336, 471
Multiple choice. *See* Choice response
Multiple correlation and regression, 395–398, 403
Multimethod design, 153, 183, 446f.
Musical abilities, 45, 199, 256

Navy. *See* Military
Needs, 462, 489, 490, 527, 557
Neurotic tendencies, 462, 464, 471, 476, 478f., 489, 555

Nomothetic approach, 502
Nonlinear relations, 402–405
Nonverbal tests, 221, 254, 255f. *See also* Fluid ability; Performance; Pictorial
Norm reference, 87f., 92, 310f., 418
Normal curve equivalent, 101
Normal distribution, 102f.
Normalized scores, 104
Norms, 27, 90, 93–120, 124
  differentiated, 107, 111–114, 210, 214, 224
  in interest measurement, 418, 420ff., 438f.
  local, 91,108
Numerical ability, 90, 118, 305f., 396, 401. *See also* Mathematics; Tests and techniques, CogAT, DAT, Wechsler, etc.

Objectives of instruction, 348ff.
Objectivity, 27, 43, 65, 81
Observation, 33f., 529–536. *See also* Ratings; Sampling of behavior
  during tests of ability, 269–271
  errors and inconsistency, 159f., 162f., 168, 171, 174, 458, 529ff.
  in field situation, 444, 529ff., 535
  in standard situation, 445, 538ff.
Obsolescence of test information, 75, 101, 155, 240, 436f., 466, 483
Occupational. *See* Vocational
Out-of-level testing, 220

Parent behavior and perception, 520ff., 533
Pathology, detection of, 271, 373, 475–479, 484, 492ff., 526, 539f., 548, 555. *See also* Brain dysfunction; Diagnosis; Screening
Patients
  procedures for testing, 39, 64, 201, 264
  tests and ratings, 271, 461, 503ff., 511, 512, 517, 559
Pattern interpretation, 403–405, 449. *See also* Differences within the person; Profile
PDRI, 286, 373ff., 382, 388, 395, 400f., 495, 510, 515
Peace Corps, 454, 497
Peer ratings, 447f., 481ff., 524ff., 566, 570
Percentage score, 83f., 354
Percentiles, 93ff., 103f.
Perception
  of other persons, 407f., 505ff.
  of situation, 448, 449, 458ff., 527f., 536
  speed and accuracy, 19, 29ff., 301–306, 329, 547ff.
Performance tests, 27
  of mental ability, 52–54, 207, 250–251, 324ff.
  of personality, 33, 445ff., 537–565
Persistence, 448, 542
Personality
  as component of ability, 201, 262

Personality (*Continued*)
  conceptualization 32, 45–46, 149, 441, 455–463, 502, 535
  stability, 457, 546
Personality measures, 29–34, 441–571. *See also* Assessment
  as predictors of success, 142, 367, 401, 454, 496–500
  consistency across procedures, 446–449, 454, 462, 472, 477, 511, 555
  performance tests, 33, 445ff., 537–565
  ratings, 444, 508–527
  self-report, 34, 443, 475–507
Phenomenological interpretation, 444, 455, 464, 505f.
Piagetian tasks, 57, 200, 222, 275–280, 282
Pictorial items, 146, 324
Placement, 21
Police, testing of, 334, 527
Policy capturing, 407
Policy issues, 4–10, 23–24, 75–76, 92, 182, 197, 338–350, 371f., 383–391
Power-plant operators. *See* PDRI
Prediction, 19, 44. *See also* Assessment; Clerical; College; Correlation; Validation, etc.
Preparation of the test taker, 73–80, 183, 324–326, 336ff., 453, 472f.
Preschool tests, 205f., 227–230
Primary mental abilities, 292
Prisoners, 67, 399, 495, 540
Privacy, 33, 76, 450–454
Problem solving. *See* General mental ability; Process
Process of test performance, 42f., 195, 251, 253, 269–283, 299, 336ff.
Professional schools, 8, 11, 18. *See also* Law; Medicine
Proficiency test, 31, 38, 128f., 131f., 366. *See also* Achievement tests; Criterion
Profile, 104–106, 175, 420ff.
  estimate for true scores, 251
  interpretation, 105f., 237, 250ff., 271, 300–315, 484ff., 521
Program evaluation, 23, 68f. *See also* Evaluation
Program tests, 18, 54, 226f., 354ff.
Programmer aptitude, 375–379, 382
Projective techniques, 42, 443, 538, 553–561, 566
Proximal development, zone of, 336
Psychologists and psychiatrists, selection and guidance, 430ff., 437, 563, 566
Psychometric testing, 41–43, 57, 175, 502, 538ff. *See also* Clinical interpretation versus statistical
Psychomotor abilities, 60, 90, 304–306, 312–314, 326, 396
Psychotherapy, 47, 443, 471, 495, 506, 555. *See also* Evaluation

Publishing of tests, 10–18, 83
Purchasing of tests, 15–19

Q sort, 485, 518f.
Quantitative reasoning. *See* Mathematics; Numerical
Questionnaires. *See* Self-report
Quota hiring, 385f., 389f.

Range, effect of restricting, 127, 140f., 161, 172f., 363ff., 394, 397, 401, 509
Rapport, 58, 63–65, 67, 324
Ratings, 82, 127, 366f., 402, 444–447, 508–514
  as reflection of rater's concepts and style, 409, 445, 503–506
  behaviorally anchored, 513ff.
  bias in, 377, 388, 509ff.
Raw score, 83–86
Reaction time, 192, 193, 263, 396. *See also* Speed
Reactive measurement, 34, 444, 530
Reading, 89, 114, 143, 251
  tests of, 115, 350, 353
Reasoning. *See* General mental ability; Information processing; Logical abstraction
Regression, 112–114, 138, 143, 386ff., 394–399, 402–407
Reinforcement. *See* Incentive; Knowledge of results
Release of questions. *See* Preparation of the test taker; Security
Reliability, 160–180, 301, 312–315, 459. *See also* Generalizability; Ratings, etc.
Reporting of test scores, 74, 220f., 351, 488
Reports of informants, 444, 508–528. *See also* Job analysis
Research
  freedom of, 453
  use of tests in, 4, 24, 75, 77, 192f., 442, 453, 540
Response sets and styles, 147, 419, 469–474, 483, 490, 509. *See also* Style
Retarded persons, 4, 204, 209, 242–244, 258, 282, 320, 338–342
Reviews of tests, 124, 187, 488
RIASEC system, 414
Role playing, 29, 445f., 450, 497

Salespersons, 134–138, 248, 360, 430, 437, 466, 497, 569
Sampling of behavior, 33, 45, 162f., 221, 455ff., 477, 529–533
Scales for test scores, 85f., 89, 93–106, 420ff.
  unidimensional, 116ff., 180
Scatter diagram, 137, 139, 370. *See also* Experience table
Scholastic aptitude. *See* Educational success; General mental ability

Subject Index

School testing programs, 113, 343–345, 350, 451ff. *See also* College; Instruction
Science, tests of knowledge or reasoning, 145, 148, 314, 348, 349, 357
Scoring, 69, 81–120, 456, 534f. *See also* Empirical keying; Ratings; Scales; Standard score, etc.
  correction for guessing, 61
  errors in, 74, 75, 82, 165
Screening, 21, 179, 230, 476, 478f., 491, 495, 521, 526, 535
Security, 19, 36, 54, 75f., 453
Selection, 8, 21, 155ff., 358–408. *See also* Assessment; College; Employment; Engineering careers; Screening, etc.
Selection ratio, 380ff.
Self-concept, 22, 70, 462, 475ff., 481f., 486, 491ff.
Self-esteem. *See* Self-concept
Self-monitoring, 34, 336, 530, 532
Self-report, 34, 411–507. *See also* Interest; Personality
  as self-description, 427, 467ff.
  use in selection, 412, 430, 451f., 466, 495–500
Self-understanding, 22, 412, 415, 424–428
Set. *See* Response set; Style
Sex differences, 98, 257, 308, 387, 501
  in interest measurement, 411, 419, 430, 438ff.
Shopwork. *See* Trade
Shrinkage, 397
Sign versus sample, 45, 87, 193, 455, 465ff.
Situation
  description by participants, 527ff.
  influence on behavior, 33, 46, 142, 162, 447, 456–460, 478, 495, 497, 529, 559ff., 572
Situational test, 445, 562–565
Social class as correlate of test performance and interpretation, 7, 8, 111–114, 321f., 330ff.
Social interactions. *See also* Groups, performance of; Peer ratings
  observations of, 162f., 445, 539f.
Social judgment, 82–85
Sociometric rating. *See* Peer ratings
Spatial ability, 90, 108, 151, 302–309, 312, 346, 396
Spearman-Brown formula, 170f., 174, 512
Special education, 4, 144, 194, 209, 335, 341–343. *See also* Retarded
Spectrum of general ability tests, 253
Speech, 67, 231, 299
Speed of response, 263f., 323, 326. *See also* Motor speed; Perceptual speed; Reaction time; Time limits
Spelling, 23, 301ff.
Split-half procedure, 170f., 397

Stability, 79, 114, 164, 237–241, 313ff., 428ff., 457, 491, 525
Standard deviation, 98f.
Standard error, 159ff., 164, 167, 177–180
Standard score, 99ff., 203
Standardization, 4, 27, 49, 54–57, 445, 538ff. *See also* Norms
Standards for tests and testing, 17, 18, 33, 74, 124f., 149
Standards of performance, 91–93, 107f., 354
Stanine, 100f.
State of persons tested, 45, 70, 459, 477f., 559f.
Statistical procedures, 93–104, 492
Strategy, 273f., 282
Structure in situations and tasks, 42, 538
Style, 42, 266, 270–274, 323f., 368, 507, 540
Stylistic tests, 547ff.
Subtle items, 433, 474
Suicide, 399, 443
Synthetic validity, 402

Tailored tests. *See* Computer in test preparation
Talent, search for, 5f., 196ff.
Teachers
  judgments by, 194, 342–344, 509ff., 526, 528
  judgments or observations on, 342–344, 458f., 472, 528, 536
  tests given to, 431, 497
Technical courses. *See* Trade
Test(s). *See also* Essay test; Standardized, etc.
  choosing, 13–15, 49, 122, 181–188, 358–369, 374ff.
  classification of, 26–48
  critical review, 121–125
  definition, 3–4, 26
  functions, 3, 19–24, 347f., 442
  sources of information, 13–15, 123f., 183
  title of, 34, 198
Test standards. *See* Standards
Tester
  interaction with subject, 58–60, 63–65, 67, 270f., 324, 452f.
  motives of, 58, 66–69
  personal characteristics, 66f., 325, 392
  qualifications, 16
Testing industry, 10–12
Tests and techniques, specific
  ACT Interest Inventory, 415f., 428
  Adaptive Behavior Inventory for Children, 209, 258
  Adaptive Behavior Scale, 258
  Adjective Checklist (ACL), 408, 489, 497, 499
  Advanced Placement in European History, 354ff.
  American College Testing (ACT), 226, 246, 415f., 428

Tests and techniques (*Continued*)
  Analogies, 217, 219, 281, 288. *See also* Tests and techniques, Matrix
  Aptitude Index Battery, 365, 466
  Armed Services Vocational Aptitude (ASVAB), 89–90, 122
  Army Alpha, 196–199
  Ayres Handwriting, 81–82
  Bayley scales, 231
  Bead chain, 277ff.
  Bender Gestalt, 547ff.
  Bennett Mechanical Comprehension (TMC), 50–52, 62, 68, 86, 94, 97, 98, 115, 116, 129ff., 147, 150–153, 172, 186–187, 395. *See also* Tests and techniques, Differential Aptitude
  BITCH, 330
  Block Design, 28, 52–54, 62, 100, 134, 153f., 250, 253, 265, 273, 324, 325–330. *See also* Tests and techniques, Wechsler
  British Ability Scales, 82–85, 118, 223f., 252
  California Achievement Tests, 107
  California Psychological Inventory (CPI), 462, 489, 495, 499
  California Q-Sort, 518
  Career Assessment (Johansson CAI), 424
  Child Behavior Checklist, 521
  Child Behavior Profile, 759
  Cognitive Abilities Test (CogAT), 219f., 224, 237, 255f., 287ff.
  CIRCUS, 228ff.
  Complex Coordination, 29–31, 83, 313, 326, 396
  Computer Programmer Aptitude Battery, 375ff.
  Comrey Personality, 489
  Davis-Eells, 331ff.
  Differential Aptitude (DAT), 50, 104–108, 115, 186–187, 216, 301ff., 306, 308, 310, 312, 387, 430
  Digit Span, 116, 205, 250, 259. *See also* Tests and techniques, K-ABC, Wechsler
  Downey Will-Temperament, 540
  Edwards Personal Preference (EPPS), 142, 489
  Embedded Figures (EFT), 4, 13–15, 30, 265ff., 274f., 286, 374, 540
  ETS Kit, 291, 293ff., 374
  Eysenck Personality, 489
  F scale, 473
  Flanagan Aptitude Classification, 376
  General Aptitude (GATB), 248, 284, 303–311, 314, 364, 397, 404, 416
  Gordon Personal Profile, 498
  Graduate Record, 227
  Hand-Tool Dexterity, 60
  Henmon-Nelson, 225
  Holtzman Inkblot, 555
  Illinois Psycholinguistic (ITPA), 228, 231
  Improvisations, 445
  In-basket, 564
  Infant Psychological Development Scales, 232
  Inpatient Multidimensional Rating Scale, 517
  Iowa Test of Basic Skills (ITBS), 101, 102, 224, 256
  Jackson Vocational Interest (JVIS), 109, 413, 415, 428
  Jackson Personality, 481–483
  Kaufman Ability Battery for Children (K-ABC), 223f., 258, 267f., 290
  Kit of Factor-Referenced Cognitive Tests, 291, 293ff., 374
  Kuder Occupational Interest Survey (KOIS), 413, 423, 429, 432, 435f., 438, 474
  Kuder Preference Record (KPR), 413, 423, 425ff., 429ff.
  Law School Admissions Test (LSAT), 4, 11, 140, 155, 175, 227, 309
  Leaderless Group Discussion, 565
  Learning Potential Assessment Device, 335ff.
  Matrix, 217f., 274, 237, 327, 337, 379
  Maze, 30, 45, 66, 68, 72, 73, 205, 294, 317, 441, 540f. *See also* Tests and techniques, Wechsler
  McCarthy Scales of Children's Abilities, 229f.
  Medical College Admissions, 104
  Metropolitan Achievement, 60, 115
  Metropolitan Readiness, 229
  Minnesota Multiphasic (MMPI), 464, 474, 483–488, 494ff., 497, 507
  Multiple Affect Adjective Checklist, 71
  Objective-Analytic Batteries, 292, 541
  Ohio Vocational Interest, 413
  Otis-Lennon, 225
  PACE, 369, 384
  Paper folding, 272, 291, 294
  Peabody Picture Vocabulary, 224
  Personal Orientation Dimensions, 489
  Personality Inventory for Children, 522
  Personality Research Form, 490
  Porch Index of Communicative Abilities, 299
  Porteus Mazes, 29f., 441, 541. *See also* Tests and techniques, Mazes
  Position Analysis Questionnaire, 360, 373
  Primary Mental Abilities, 292, 379
  Process for Assessment of Effective Student Functioning, 526
  Progressive Matrices, 217, 237, 291
  Psychological Screening, 181, 478ff., 484, 492f.
  Psychological Systems Questionnaire, 490
  Pupil Behavior Rating Scale, 516
  Reading Yardsticks, 353

Subject Index

Rod and Frame, 265
Role Concept Repertory (Rep), 505
Rorschach, 467, 547, 553ff.
Russell Sage Social Relations, 330
Scholastic Aptitude (SAT), 6, 11, 54, 79–80, 100, 114, 226–228. *See also* College Entrance Examination Board
School and College Ability (SCAT), 225, 313
Seashore Measures of Musical Talent, 199
Self-Directed Search, 414f., 422, 425
Self-Esteem (Coopersmith), 476
Semantic Differential, 503ff.
Sixteen Personality Factor (16 PF), 462f., 490, 495
Social Climate Scales, 527
Stanford Achievement, 257
Stanford-Binet, 58, 195–196, 214f., 236, 239, 241, 243, 244, 250, 257
State-Trait Anxiety (STAI), 477f.
Strong and Strong-Campbell inventories, 129, 412f., 419f., 423, 425, 428–439, 471, 474, 497
System of Multicultural Pluralistic Assessment (SOMPA), 112f., 209f., 258, 548
Tennessee Self-Concept, 491
Test Anxiety, 70
Tests of Cognitive Skills, 225
Thematic Apperception (TAT), 17, 462, 500, 556ff., 562
Torrance Tests of Creative Thinking, 261
Unusual Uses, 261, 291, 294, 334
USES Interest Inventory, 114, 413, 415, 417, 439
Vineland Social Maturity, 258
Vocational Interest Inventory (Lunneborg), 413, 418, 439
Vocational Preference Inventory (Holland VPI), 413, 415, 428
Wechsler (WAIS, WISC, WPPSI), 53, 64, 72, 99–101, 200, 214, 235ff., 238, 243f., 250ff., 258, 264, 271, 291, 322, 332, 338. *See also* Tests and techniques, Block Design, Digit Span
Wide Range Intelligence and Personality Test, 225
Wonderlic, 225
Test-wiseness, 61, 78
Thematic test, 548, 556ff.
Therapy. *See* Behavior modification; Drugs; Psychotherapy
Time limits, 55, 147, 171, 263, 324
Time sampling
Trade and technical work, prediction for, 89–90, 248, 260, 303–310, 313, 365f., 398, 405. *See also* PDRI
Trainability tests, 260

Training, prediction, 248, 365f., 379. *See also* Instruction
Trait, 45f., 441
  conceptualization, 455–463, 502ff., 535, 546
  versus state, 45, 477f.
True score, 159–162
Typical behavior, tests of, 28–29, 32–35, 441–571

Underachievement, 255, 341
Unidimensional scaling, 116ff., 180, 223
Units of measurement. *See* Intervals
Universe score, 161f. *See also* Domain
Unobtrusive measures. *See* Reactive
U. S. Employment Service, 11, 101, 108, 303f., 404, 415, 439. *See also* Tests and techniques, GATB
Utility, 86, 373, 388–390, 402f., 569

Validation, 43, 125–157, 384f. *See also* Assessment; College; Engineering; Screening, etc.
  concurrent, 127–129, 363ff.
  construct, 126, 131, 149–154, 163, 384
  content, 108, 126, 131–134, 145–148, 156f., 348–351
  criterion-oriented, 126–131, 134–144, 359f., 363–383, 385–388, 394–408, 492
  for personality descriptions, 488, 505
  predictive. *See* Validation, criterion-oriented
  relation to reliability, 176, 394
  synthetic, 402
Validity coefficient, 136
  acceptable, 140, 380ff.
  effect of test length, 176
Validity generalization, 400ff., 407f.
Variance, 99. *See also* Factor
  analysis of, 166–170
  of errors, 159f.
  sources of, 162f., 172f., 459, 532f.
Verbal ability, 79, 206, 238, 251, 255, 346, 396, 401. *See also* General mental ability, etc.
Verification key, 474, 522
Vocational choice and success, prediction, 242–249, 303–308, 313, 367, 429–433, 496ff., 566ff. *See also* Clerical; Employment; Trade, etc.

Weighting of scores, 395–398. *See also* Actuarial
Work sample, 131, 260, 362, 366, 368, 564f.
Writing, tests of, 42, 81, 357

z-score, 99f.

Name Index

Achenbach, T. M., 521f., 575, 584
Adams, J., 6
Adcock, C. J., 462, 575
Adorno, T. W., 7, 473, 575
Albrecht, P. A., 569, 575
Alexander, R. A., 577
Allen, A., 577
Allen, L., 458, 589, 594
Allen, M. J., 117, 575
Allport, G., 502, 575
American Educational Research Association, 575
American Personnel and Guidance Association, 74, 575
American Psychological Association, 33, 74, 124, 575f., 583
Amrine, M., 450, 576
Anastasi, A., 48, 78, 171, 576
Anderson, B., 344
Andrews, B. J., 93, 576
Andrews, J. D. W., 142, 576
Angoff, W. H., 100, 114, 263, 576
Anton, W. D., 602
Appelbaum, M. I., 594
Appell, M. J., 244, 576
Arbous, A. J., 565, 576
Aronson, E., 580, 593
Arvey, R. D., 386, 576
Aschner, M. J., 587
Ash, P., 202, 596
Ash, R. A., 593
Asher, J. J., 362, 576
Atkinson, J. W., 462, 500f., 576
Ayres, L. P., 81, 576
Azjen, I., 458, 585
Azuma, H., 539, 588

Bachman, J. G., 477, 498, 576
Backer, T. E., 606
Backteman, G., 262, 594
Baker, R. F., 38, 73, 591
Baker, T. B., 443, 604
Balke-Aurell, G., 309, 596
Baller, W. R., 243, 576
Baltes, P. B., 237, 239, 576, 600
Bandura, A., 543, 576
Bannatyne, A., 251, 576
Bannister, D., 507, 586
Barbee, A. H., 242, 600

Barclay, J. R., 525, 576
Barnette, W. L., 431, 576
Barrett, G. V., 364, 577
Barron, F., 261, 262, 554, 577
Bartholoomeo, D., 269, 577
Bartling, H. C., 429, 577
Barzun, J., 8, 577
Bass, B. M., 565, 577
Baughman, E. E., 257, 577
Bayley, N., 232
Beaton, A. E., 588
Beatty, W. H., 606
Bechtoldt, H. P., 187
Beck, S. J., 553, 577
Becker, W. C., 463, 577
Bedell, J., 602
Beere, C. A., 606
Bem, D. J., 458, 577
Bender, L., 548
Benjamin, M., 72, 577
Bennett, G. K., 50, 186
Bennett, N., 593
Berent, S., 264, 266
Berger, M., 263
Berk, R. A., 221, 334, 391, 577
Berland, J. C., 57, 277, 323, 577
Bernardin, H. J., 512, 514, 577
Bernstein, D., 445, 596
Berry, J. W., 266, 323–327, 535f., 582, 603
Bersoff, D. N., 74, 125, 144, 150, 342
Bethon, G., 276, 586
Betz, N. E., 39, 577
Biber, B., 270, 577
Biesheuvel, S., 325, 606
Bigler, E. D., 548, 577
Bigley, S. S., 583
Binet, A., 192ff., 577
Bish, C. E., 587
Bishop, C. H., 595
Bissell, H. W., 511, 602
Black, J. D., 485f., 524, 577
Blankstein, K. R., 590
Block, J., 419, 447, 457, 462, 518, 577, 578
Bloom, B. S., 259, 578
Bohn, M. J., Jr., 495, 595
Boll, T. J., 70, 251, 264, 266, 271, 273, 340, 494, 585
Bolton, B., 606
Bolus, R., 476, 601

621

Bond, J. T., 604
Bond, L., 4, 5, 7, 9, 74, 78, 125, 150, 203, 259, 300, 342, 386, 390, 406, 586
Bonjean, C. M., 606
Borgen, F. H., 429, 578
Borkowski, J. G., 335, 578
Borman, W. C., 397, 405, 512, 514, 578, 584
Boruch, R. F., 76, 454, 578
Bosshardt, M. J., 584
Botwinick, J., 238, 578
Bower, C. P., 588
Bower, E. M., 516, 526
Bower, G. L., 90, 600
Bower, G. N., 578
Bownas, D. A., 584
Boyer, E. G., 606, 607
Brace, C. L., 191, 578
Bradburn, N. M., 470, 578
Bradley, R., 322, 578
Brannigan, G. G., 548, 603
Brass, D. J., 564, 578
Bray, D. W., 74, 563, 569, 578, 593
Breland, H. M., 357, 387, 578
Brennan, R. L., 166, 578
Brewer, M. B., 605
Brim, O. G., Jr., 600
Brislin, R. W., 324, 578, 606
Brogden, H. E., 21, 381, 398f., 578, 588
Brokaw, L. D., 431, 578
Bronfenbrenner, U., 572, 578
Bronson, W. C., 457, 578
Brown, A. L., 195, 276, 335f., 578
Brown, C., 394, 579
Brown, S. H., 466, 579
Buchanan, B. G., 580
Buckley, P. D., 548, 579
Buriel, R., 265, 591
Burisch, M., 476, 579
Burkhart, B. R., 474, 579
Burnett, S. A., 308, 579
Burns, G. L., 338, 602
Buros, O. K., 13, 122, 124, 187, 231, 310, 483, 488, 579
Burt, C., 283, 319
Burton, R. V., 502, 543, 546, 579
Butcher, H. J., 261, 579
Butcher, J. N., 452, 466, 474, 483, 488, 498, 579, 585
Byham, W. C., 563, 596
Byrne, D., 525, 593

Caldwell, B. M., 578, 583
California Assessment Program, 114, 579
Callan, J. P., 494, 579
Callaway, E., 264, 579
Callender, J. C., 400, 579
Camp, B. W., 607
Campbell, D. P., 423, 432f., 436f., 579
Campbell, D. T., 152, 153, 448, 579, 581, 601

Campbell, J. P., 44, 149, 363, 386, 604
Campione, J. C., 335f., 579
Cantoni, L. J., 244ff., 579
Carek, R., 432, 579
Carlsmith, J. M., 540, 580
Carlson, S. B., 604
Carnegie Council, 246, 580
Carpenter, K. E., 108, 605
Carr, J. E., 507
Carroll, J. B., 259, 260, 263, 299, 437, 580
Carroll, W. K., 324
Carter, L. F., 530, 580
Carter-Saltzman, L., 320
Cascio, W. F., 569, 580
Casey, W. M., 543, 579
Casper, G., 592
Cattell, J. McK., 193
Cattell, R. B., 252, 292, 462, 490, 541, 580, 589, 606
Cavanaugh, J. C., 335, 578
Cecil, J. S., 76, 454, 578
Cerney, M. S., 443, 580
Chapman, P., 197, 580
Charles, D. C., 576
Charters, W. W., Jr., 332, 580
Chase, W. G., 581
Chelune, G. J., 473, 580
Christian, W. L., 579
Chun, K.-T., 606
Churchill, W. D., 243, 580
Ciminero, A. R., 47, 530, 580
Clancey, W., 40, 580
Clark, R. A., 559, 580
Clarke-Stewart, K. A., 241, 580
Cleckley, H., 503, 603
Coates, C. H., 565, 577
Coates, T. J., 532, 580
Cobb, S., 606
Coffman, W. E., 289, 580
Colbert, G. A., 402, 580
Cole, M., 248, 328, 580, 600, 601
Cole, N., 389, 391, 581
College Entrance Examination Board, 22, 61, 101, 499, 581
Collins, B. E., 605
Comrey, A. L., 489, 606
Cone, J. D., 535, 540, 581
Conrad, H. S., 146, 572, 581
Conry, R., 243, 581
Cook, T. D., 152, 338, 581
Cooper, G. D., 244, 581
Cooper, L. A., 263, 264, 282, 307, 581
Coopersmith, S., 476
Copeland, E. P., 66, 70
Corrigan, B., 407, 583
Coulter, W. A., 258, 581
Court, J. H., 598
Cox, C. M., 242, 581
Crabtree, P. D., 414, 581
Craighill, P. G., 599

NAME INDEX

Crandall, V., 531, 581
Crites, J. O., 427, 602
Cronbach, L. J., iv, 4, 23, 123, 126, 142, 143, 149, 156–157, 161, 168, 175, 176, 251, 255, 259, 278, 287, 298, 312, 313, 321, 325f., 329, 346, 382, 387, 389, 394, 401, 407, 408, 419, 485, 499, 519, 532f., 572, 581f.
Crosby, R. C., 427, 582
Crowne, D. P., 474, 582
Crumbaugh, J. C., 467, 582

Dague, P., 326
Dahlstrom, L. E., 582
Dahlstrom, W. G., 257, 451, 484, 577, 582
Damrin, D. E., 330, 582
d'Andrade, R. G., 462, 601
Darley, J. G., 425, 427, 429, 582
Darlington, R. B., 211, 397, 582
Darwin, C., 192
Dasen, P. R., 266, 582
Dauterman, W. L., 63, 583
Davis, B. D., 317, 583
Davis, G. D., 18, 597
Davis, W. A., 331, 583
Dawes, R. M., 397, 407, 583
deCharms, R., 501, 583
DeFries, J. C., 320, 598
de Gruijter, D. N. M., 581
De Loache, J. S., 195, 579
DeNelsky, G. Y., 379, 583
Denisi, A. S., 594
DeSoto, C. B., 588
Deutsch, C., 322, 583
DeVoge, S., 445, 594
DeVries, R., 276, 583
Diamond, E. E., 439, 583
Diaz-Guerrero, R., 589
Dienes, J. T., 443, 583
Diller, L., 273
Division, 14, 124, 358, 359, 583
Dobzhansky, T., 317, 583
Docter, R. F., 11, 17, 583, 589
Dolliver, R. H., 425, 429, 583
Domino, G., 499f., 583
Donaldson, G., 237, 589
Donchin, E. M., 264
Donlon, T., 263
Doppelt, J. E., 322, 591
Dossett, D. L., 598
Downey, J., 540
Downey, R. G., 526, 583
Drake, J. D., 171, 576
Dreger, R. M., 321, 583
Drenth, P. J. D., 325f., 329, 582
Dreyer, G. F., 149, 583
Droege, R. G., 304, 416, 583
DuBois, P. H., 364, 395f., 576, 583
Dudek, F. J., 530, 580
Dunbar, S. B., 394, 584, 593

Duncan, A. K., 55, 584
Dunham, J. L., 299, 584
Dunn, Leona M., 224
Dunn, Lloyd M., 224
Dunn, R. A., 580
Dunnette, M. D., 149, 286, 360, 361, 362, 367, 373, 382, 386, 390, 397, 405, 432, 471, 495, 510, 520, 563, 567, 584

EEOC, 584
Earle, R. B., Jr., 607
Ebel, R. L., 126, 595
Eber, H. W., 580
Eckensberger, L. H., 400, 582
Eckland, B. K., 244, 584
Edelbrock, C., 521f., 575, 584
Edwards, A. L., 489
Edwards, W., 407, 584
Eells, K., 332, 584
Efron, D. H., 586
Ehrfurth, J. W., 548, 577
Eichhorn, D. H., 587
Ekstrom, R. B., 293, 584
Elardo, R., 578
Elliott, C. D., 84, 222, 584
Elliott, E. C., 81, 602
Ellis, N. R., 578
Ellsworth, P., 580
Elshout, J. A., 298, 584
Endler, N. H., 143, 447, 457, 498, 594
Epstein, S., 458, 560, 585
Erickson, M. T., 535
Eron, L. S., 605
Evans, F. R., 79, 585
Exner, J. E., Jr., 467, 553, 554, 585
Eysenck, H. J., 263f., 462, 489, 585
Eysenck, S. B. G., 489

Fahmy, M., 327, 585
Farmer, H. S., 501, 585
Faschingbauer, T. R., 483
Feather, N. T., 449, 585
Fechner, G., 119
Federico, P.-A., 601
Fenz, W. D., 560, 585
Feshbach, N. D., 607
Feuerstein, R., 218, 335ff., 385
Feurzig, W., 40, 602
Fiedler, F. E., 498
Filskov, S. B., 70, 251, 264, 266, 271, 273, 340, 494, 585
Fink, A. M., 452, 585
Finkle, R. B., 563, 566
Fishbein, M., 458, 585
Fishell, K. N., 576
Fiske, D. W., 153, 430, 448, 563, 566, 579, 591
Fitts, W. H., 491
Fivars, G., 361, 585
Flaherty, P., 317, 583

Flanagan, J. C., 70, 309, 361, 376, 585
Flaugher, R. L., 32, 585
Fleishman, E. A., 326, 585, 590
Ford, A., 178
Ford, J. B., 328, 585
Forehand, G. A., 142, 407, 585
Foster, S. L., 530
Frankenburg, W. K., 607
Fransella, F., 507, 586
Frederiksen, N. R., 143, 365, 432, 564, 586, 604
Freedman, D. G., 318, 586
French, J. L., 225
French, J. R. P., Jr., 606
French, J. W., 293, 584, 586
French, L. A., 336, 579
Friedlander, J., 470, 597
Friedman, M. P., 589
Fromkin, H. L., 584
Furby, L., 255, 582
Furneaux, W. D., 263
Fyans, L. J., Jr., 501, 583, 585

Gade, E. M., 429, 586
Gage, N. L., 580
Galassi, J. P., 46, 586
Galton, F., 7, 192, 196, 476
Garcia, J., 391
Gardner, J. W., 7, 586
Gardner, M. K., 281
Gardner, R. C., 287, 586
Garner, A. M., 509, 586
Garner, W. R., 8, 10, 74, 80, 125, 150, 197, 246, 247, 344, 358, 384, 386, 387, 586, 604
Garty, M. K., 60, 68, 589
Gast-Rosenberg, I., 379, 600
Gay, J., 580
Getzels, J., 262, 586
Ghiselli, E. E., 18, 248, 365, 496, 586
Gianetti, R. A., 591
Gibby, R. G., 552, 590
Gibson, W. A., 588
Glaser, E. M., 575, 606
Glaser, R., 4, 5, 7, 9, 74, 78, 80, 125, 150, 203, 259, 269, 300, 342, 386, 390, 406, 579, 586
Gleser, G. C., 175, 382, 511f., 519, 582, 586
Glick, J., 323, 580
Glymour, C., 152
Goldberg, L. R., 59, 430, 454, 461, 462, 466, 476, 563, 586, 591
Golden, C. J., 487, 586
Goldstein, L., 597
Goodenough, D. R., 265f., 605
Goodenough, W., 536
Goodnow, J. J., 276, 323, 586
Gordon, E., 391
Gordon, L. V., 498, 525, 586
Gordon, W. A., 273

Gorham, W., 150, 384
Gorsuch, R. L., 477
Gottier, R. F., 496, 587
Gough, H. G., 408, 465, 489, 587
Graham, J., 485, 488, 587
Grant, D. L., 569, 587
Green, D. R., 256, 587
Green, S. B., 487, 587
Gronlund, N. E., 525, 587
Grossman, P., 384, 600
Guilford, J. P., 261, 294, 295ff., 462, 584, 587
Guion, R. M., 126, 249, 496, 587
Gustafsson, J.-E., 346, 587
Gutkin, T. B., 66, 70, 113, 126, 144, 211, 322, 332, 340, 342, 391, 598
Guttentag, M., 584
Guttman, L., 252, 587
Gynther, M. D., 487, 579, 587

Haan, N., 460, 587
Hagenah, T., 425, 427, 429, 582
Hagen, E., 224
Hale, M., 197
Hales, L. W., 414, 581
Hall, B. W., 70, 587
Hall, G. S., 476
Hall, J. R., 445, 587
Hall, W. B., 497, 587
Haller, D. L., 594
Hambleton, R. K., 117, 187, 587
Hammond, K. R., 457, 587
Haney, W., 4
Hansen, J. C., 423, 434ff., 587
Hansen, R. N., 425, 583
Harman, H. H., 584
Harmon, L. W., 429, 588
Harnisch, D. L., 593
Harrell, T. W., 497, 526, 588
Harrington, D. M., 261, 262, 577, 588
Harris, D. H., 493, 588
Harris, L., 308
Harrison, R., 561, 588
Harsh, C., 187
Hartshorne, H., 526, 542–547, 588
Hartsough, C., 516, 526
Hathaway, S., 483
Haywood, H. C., 204, 282, 585, 588
Hawkins, R. P., 535, 540, 581
Heaton, R. K., 70, 467, 588
Heaton, S. K., 70
Hebb, D. O., 73, 588
Hecht, J. T., 93, 576
Heckman, J., 394, 588
Heilbron, A. B., Jr., 489
Heinrich, D. L., 498, 588
Heller, K. A., 9, 209, 340, 588
Helme, W. H., 308, 398, 401, 588
Helson, R., 519, 588
Hempel, W. E., Jr., 326, 585
Hemphill, J. K., 511, 588

Name Index

Hendrickson, D. E., 264
Henri, V., 195, 577
Henry, W. E., 557ff., 588
Herskovits, M. J., 601
Heslin, R., 607
Hess, R. D., 539, 588
Hill, E. F., 556, 588
Hill, R. J., 606
Hilton, T. L., 314, 588
Hobbs, N. L., 340, 588, 604
Hoepfner, R., 294, 297, 584, 587, 607
Hofstadter, R., 197, 588
Hogan, R., 460, 588
Hogan, T. P., 357, 588
Hogarth, R. M., 408, 589
Hogarty, P. S., 594
Holden, C., 76, 77, 589
Holland, J. L., 249, 414–418, 422, 589
Hollander, P., 384
Holmen, M. G., 11, 17, 563, 589
Holt, R. R., 563, 589
Holtzman, W. H., 275, 328, 555, 563, 566, 588, 589
Honzik, M. P., 231, 239f., 589, 594
Hood, A. B., 429, 577
Hood, L., 580
Hook, C. M., 472, 589
Horn, J. L., 239, 252, 264, 298, 589
Horne, L. V., 60, 68, 589
Hough, L., 362, 589
House, E. R., 154, 589
Houts, P. L., 191, 589
Howard, A., 569, 589
Hubbard, J. C., 368, 589
Hudson, L., 310
Humphreys, L. G., 313, 367, 589, 590
Hunt, E. B., 274, 590
Hunt, J. McV., 232, 590, 594
Hunter, J. E., 305, 321, 379, 382, 386, 387, 389, 400, 567, 590, 591, 597, 600
Hunter, R., 567, 590
Hurlburt, N., 594
Husted, F. L., 596
Hutt, M., 547–553, 590
Hutton, J. B., 216, 590

Ingersoll, R. W., 397, 590
Inhelder, B., 277, 597
Irvin, J. A., 583
Irvine, S. B., 324
Isreal, J. B., 264
Ivancevich, J. M., 512, 590

Jack, L., 511, 590
Jackson, D. N., 109, 415, 466, 481ff., 490, 590
Jackson, P. W., 262, 586
Jaeger, R. M., 93, 115, 590
James, W., 140
Janis, I., 495, 590

Jastak, J. F., 225
Jefferson, T., 5–6, 197
Jeger, A. M., 592
Jenkins, W. O., 511, 590
Jensen, A. R., 66, 67, 103, 191, 239, 259, 260, 318, 322, 332, 387, 391, 578, 590f., 598
Johansson, C. B., 423
John, E. R., 263, 591
Johnson, B. R., 420, 599
Johnson, E. S., 38, 73, 591
Johnson, J. H., 490, 591
Johnson, O. G., 607
Jones, H. E., 525, 596
Jones, L. K., 416, 591
Jones, L. V., 120, 591
Jones, M. R., 600
Jones, V., 546, 591
Jöreskog, K. G., 176, 394, 591
Jungeblut, A., 79, 595

Kagan, S., 265, 591
Kane, J. S., 525, 591
Kane, M., 166, 578
Kapes, J. F., 607
Kaplan, R. M., 227, 591
Karafin, G., 606
Karcher, E. K., Jr., 604
Karp, S. A., 14
Katz, M. R., 431, 596
Kaufman, A. S., 201f., 205, 207, 208, 223, 228, 236, 251, 264, 322, 591
Kaufman, N., 223, 228, 591
Kelly, E. L., 368, 430, 563, 566, 591
Kelly, G. A., 505ff., 527, 591
Kelman, H. C., 451, 591
Kendall, L. M., 513, 601
Kennedy, M. M., 340
Kent, G., 133, 591
Kent, R. N., 530, 591
Kenyatta, J., 329
Khatana, J. A., 237
Kiernan, R., 600
Kiesler, D. J., 607
King, L. M., 520, 591
Kirchner, W. K., 360, 584
Kirk, B. A., 464, 591
Kirk, S. A., 228
Klass, E. T., 451, 592
Klett, C. J., 517, 593
Klinedinst, J. K., 522
Klopfer, B., 553, 592
Knapp, J. R., 298, 589
Knapp, R. R., 489, 592
Knauft, E. G., 248, 592
Kogan, N., 262, 604
Kohlberg, L., 82, 543, 592
Kohn, M., 241, 592
Kohs, S. C., 52, 134, 153, 592
Koppitz, E. M., 548, 592

Koretzky, M. B., 447, 592
Koss, M. P., 483
Kraut, A., 526, 592
Krohne, H. W., 588
Krug, R. E., 324, 600
Krug, R. S., 463, 577
Kuder, G. F., 423, 433, 592
Kunce, J. R., 420, 592
Kurland, P. B., 592
Kyllonen, P. C., 601

Laboratory of Comparative Human Development, 265
Labov, W., 67, 323, 592
Lachar, D., 487, 522, 592
Lake, D. G., 607
Lambert, N., 5, 342, 516, 526, 592
Lamke, T. A., 225
Landfield, A. W., 506f., 592
Landis, B., 549, 592
Lane, D. M., 308, 579
Lanyon, R. I., 478, 484
Lapointe, A., 352, 605
Larson, A., 384, 592
Larson, L. K., 384, 592
Lasky, J. J., 491, 526, 592
Latham, G. P., 598
Laux, L., 588
Lave, C., 601
Law School Admission Council, 592
Lawler, E. E., III, 526, 591
Leinhardt, G., 346, 592
Leitner, L. M., 506f., 592
Leler, H. O., 553, 592
Leli, D. O., 271
Lennon, R. T., 225
Lerner, B., 155, 334, 384, 592f.
Levine, E., 362, 593
Lewis, J. E., 90, 210, 578, 589, 595
Lewis, M., 143, 202, 231, 232f., 593, 597
Liben, L. S., 307f., 593
Lichtenstein, S., 407, 601
Lickona, T., 598
Lieberman, M., 543, 601
Light, R. J., 335, 340, 603
Likert, R., 557, 596
Lindzey, G., 525, 593
Linn, R. L., 114, 118, 247, 310, 386, 387, 402, 593, 601
Lippmann, W., 151, 593
Lipsett, L., 430, 593
Livingston, S., 80, 593
Loehlin, J. C., 321f., 593
Loevinger, J., 496
Lohman, D. F., 264, 307, 593, 594
London, M., 74, 593
Longabaugh, R., 535
Lonner, W. J., 578
Lopez, F. M., Jr., 593, 594
Lord, F. M., 117, 119, 176, 394, 593

Loret, P. G., 115, 593
Lorr, M., 461, 514, 517, 593
Love, K. G., 527, 593
Lowell, F. E., 241, 593
Luborsky, L., 563, 566, 589, 593
Lumsden, J., 231
Lunneborg, P. W., 439
Luria, Z., 503ff., 597
Luschene, R. L., 477
Lutey, C., 66, 70
Lyerly, S. B., 607
Lykken, D., 483

McCall, R. B., 232, 233, 239, 241, 247, 593f.
McCarthy, D., 228
McClelland, D. C., 44, 448, 457, 462, 500, 542, 594
McCormick, E. J., 360, 402, 594
McDaniels, G. L., 340
McDermott, R., 580
McFall, R. M., 447, 594
Macfarlane, J. W., 457, 589
McGauch, J. L., 318, 594
McGauvran, M. E., 229
McGee, M. G., 307f., 594
McKee, M. G., 379, 583
McKinley, J. C., 483
MacKinnon, D. W., 497, 566, 587
McLemore, S. D., 606
McMahon, E. A., 70
McNair, D. M., 461, 593
McNeil, J., 604
McRae, G. G., 429, 594
McReynolds, P., 445, 476, 580, 584, 586, 587, 588, 589, 594, 603
Madaus, G. F., 391, 594
Magnusson, D., 143, 262, 447, 457, 498, 506, 594
Maller, J. B., 542, 594
Mandler, G., 599
Manese, W. R., 260, 598
Marks, J., 575
Marks, P. A., 485, 594
Marlowe, D., 474, 582
Marshalek, B., 289, 291, 594, 601
Marston, A. R., 447, 594
Martinez, J. L., 591
Marting, E., 513, 594
Masaryk, J., 341
Maslow, A. P., 150, 152, 384, 595
Mastie, M. M., 607
Matarazzo, J. D., 64, 264, 271, 595
Mathews, T. S., 452, 605
Matthews, E., 429, 595
Maxey, E. J., 246, 402, 599
May, M., 526, 542–547, 588
Medland, F. F., 525, 583, 586
Meehl, P. E., 149, 399, 407, 464ff., 474, 485, 582, 595
Megargee, E. I., 489, 495, 595

Mellinger, J. J., 604
Mercer, J., 112f., 209–214, 216, 258, 341, 548, 595
Merrill, M. A., 58, 69, 215, 602
Messé, L. A., 243, 595
Messick, S., 79, 93, 126, 149, 247, 265, 310, 588, 595
Miele, F., 330, 595
Miles, M. B., 607
Mill, J. S., 6, 595
Miller, E. L., 576
Miller, K. S., 583
Millman, J., 36, 78, 595
Milstein, R. M., 406, 595
Mischel, W., 47, 454, 459, 506f., 553, 595
Mishler, C., 357, 588
Montague, W. E., 601
Moos, R. H., 459, 527ff., 596, 603
Morgan, C., 556
Moriarty, A. E., 270, 596
Morrow, H. W., 258, 581
Moses, J. L., 563, 596
Mosher, D. L., 552, 596
Mosier, C., 183, 596
Mosteller, F., 397, 596
Munsinger, H., 320, 599
Murphy, G., 557, 596
Murray, D. J., 222, 584
Murray, H. A., 462, 556, 562, 596
Murstein, B., 557, 596
Mussen, P. H., 559, 596

Nanda, H., 312, 596
National Council on Measurement in Education, 576
National Industrial Conference Board, 513, 596
National Retail Merchants Association, 513, 596
Naylor, H. K., 559, 596
Nedelsky, L., 93, 596
Nelson, M. J., 225
Nerlove, S. B., 601
Nesselroade, J., 237, 576
Newcomb, T. M., 535, 596
Newcombe, N., 535, 593
Newman, F. B., 525, 596
Newmark, C. S., 483, 494, 495, 596, 604
Nichols, R. C., 320, 469, 596
Nietzel, M., 445, 596
Nihara, K., 258
Nisbett, R., 407, 596
Nitko, A. J., 88, 596
Norman, W. T., 462, 596
Norris, L., 431, 596
Norton, S. D., 149, 596
Novick, M. R., 125, 150, 176, 389, 394, 593, 596
Nurss, J. R., 229

Oakland, T., 596, 603
Oaks, W. W., 513, 596
Oborne, D. J., 605
Oden, M. J., 242, 597
Oeltjen, P., 402, 602
Oldham, G. R., 564, 578
O'Leary, K. J., 459, 597
Oles, H. J., 18, 597
Olmedo, E., 391
Oltman, P. K., 14, 266f., 597, 605
Olweus, D., 457, 559, 597
O'Malley, P. M., 477, 498, 576
Ombredane, A., 326, 597
Ord, I. G., 324, 597
Osburn, H. G., 400, 579
Osgood, C. E., 461, 503ff., 597
Osofsky, J., 231, 239, 597
OSS Assessment Staff, 563, 597
Otis, A. S., 225
Outlaw, S., 36, 595
Owens, W. A., 362

Pace, C. R., 470, 597
Pace, L. A., 363, 597
Padgett, A., 304, 416, 583
Palermo, J. M., 375
Parry, J. B., 217, 566, 604
Parry, M. E., 363, 597
Passini, F. T., 462, 597
Patterson, A. H., 593
Pearlman, K., 321, 360, 387, 597, 600
Pearson, K., 394
Pearson, L. S., 222, 584
Pence, E. C., 512, 577
Pendleton, M. G., 468, 588
Penrose, L. S., 217
Perry, D. K., 379, 597
Pervin, L. A., 143, 597
Peters, H. J., 397, 590
Petersen, N. S., 389, 597
Peterson, D. A., 365, 597
Peterson, D. R., 494, 597
Petrullo, L., 581
Pfeiffer, J. W., 607
Phillips, A. M., 597
Phillips, J. S., 577
Phillips, W. M., 497, 597
Piaget, J., 57, 82, 200, 276ff., 543, 597
Pike, L. W., 79, 585, 597
Pitcher, B., 141, 600
Pittluck, P., 559, 598
Plant, T., 243, 581
Plomin, R., 320, 598
Plumail, H., 597
Porch, B. R., 299
Porter, D., 79, 601
Porteus, S. D., 541, 598
Powell, L., 177
Prediger, D. J., 415, 422, 430, 598
Preston, C., 66, 598

Preston, H. O., 361, 598
Prestwood, J. S., 39, 598
Pursell, E. D., 366, 598

Quay, L. C., 66, 598

Rabin, A., 547, 555, 578, 594, 598, 604
Ragosta, M., 63, 598
Rand, Y., 585
Rasch, G., 117, 598
Raskin, E., 14
Rauschenberger, J. M., 590
Raven, J. B., 217, 598
Raven, J. C., 217, 598
Raynor, J. O., 500, 576
Redick, R. L., 598, 606
Reeder, C. W., 420, 592
Regan, D. T., 263, 264, 282, 581
Reilly, R. R., 260, 598
Remus, W. E., 397, 598
Reschly, D. J., 113, 203, 211, 259
Resnick, D., 10, 197
Resnick, L., 323, 598
Rest, J., 543, 598
Reuning, H., 329
Reynolds, C. R., 66, 70, 113, 126, 144, 211, 322, 332, 340, 342, 591, 598
Ricciuti, H. N., 583
Rice, J. M., 23
Richards, D. D., 276
Richards, J. M., Jr., 249, 589
Ricks, J. H., Jr., 111, 600
Riddle, M., 540, 599
Rifkin, B., 282, 602
Rimland, B., 320, 599
Riskind, J. H., 495
Rist, R., 342, 599
Roadman, H. C., 526, 599
Robaye, F., 597
Roberts, A. H., 540
Roberts, J. P., 431, 599, 602
Robinson, D. D., 363, 599
Robinson, J. P., 607
Robinson, N. M., 63, 144, 260, 340, 601
Roche, W. F., Jr., 382
Roe, A., 367, 599
Romney, A. K., 601
Rorer, L., 454, 586
Rorschach, H., 547, 553ff., 599
Rosen, A., 399, 496, 599
Rosen, A.-S., 540, 600
Rosen, P., 607
Rosenshine, B. V., 472, 589
Rosenthal, R. M., 67, 599
Roskind, W. L., 75, 599
Rosman, B. L., 241, 592
Ross, L., 407, 596
Rothe, H., 529, 599
Rourke, B. P., 251
Royce, J. R., 604

Royer, F. L., 273, 599
Rubin, D., 155, 599
Rundquist, E. A., 471, 599
Ryan, T. A., 420, 599

Sackett, P. R., 149, 583
Salmon-Cox, L., 344, 599
Sarason, I. G., 70–72, 599, 602
Sarason, S., 71–72, 599
Sarnacki, R. E., 78, 599
Sattler, J. M., 66, 67, 599
Satz, P., 70
Sawyer, R., 246, 402, 599
Scarr, S., 7, 318ff., 599
Schaeffer, G., 387, 389, 582
Schafer, R., 63, 65, 274, 443, 599
Schaie, K. W., 238, 239, 262, 576, 600
Schalling, D., 540, 600
Scheink, P. A., 596
Schlei, B. L., 384, 600
Schletzer, V. M., 428, 600
Schmidt, F. L., 321, 379, 382, 387, 400–402, 590, 591, 597, 600
Schneider, B., 142, 600
Schoenberg, B. M., 583
Schoenfeldt, L., 363, 597
Schorr, D., 273, 300, 600
Schrader, W. B., 141, 155, 600
Schuerger, J. M., 292, 541
Schwartz, L. S., 587, 600
Schwartz, P. A., 324, 600
Sciarrino, J. A., 362, 576
Scribner, S., 328, 600
Searle, L. V., 318, 600
Sears, P. S., 242, 600
Sears, R. R., 242, 535, 600
Seashore, C. E., 199
Seashore, H. G., 111, 600
Seat, P. D., 522
Sechrest, L. B., 511, 588
Seeman, W., 594
Seewald, A. M., 346, 592
Segall, M., 308, 601
Seling, M. J., 429, 579
Sells, S. B., 563, 566, 589
Selman, R. L., 543, 601
Sempel, C., 597
Sessions, F. Q., 370, 601
Shannon, C. E., 175, 601
Shapiro, M. B., 59, 601
Sharp, D., 328, 601
Shavelson, R. J., 476, 601
Shaw, J. B., 594
Shaw, M. E., 607
Shearn, C. R., 597
Shepard, L., 334
Shepard, R. N., 290, 307, 581, 601
Sherman, S. W., 63, 144, 260, 340, 601
Sherwood, J. J., 584
Shneidman, E. S., 552, 601

Shortliffe, E. H., 580
Shostrom, E. L., 489
Shweder, R. A., 462, 601
Siegel, A. I., 260, 601
Siegler, I. C., 238, 578
Siegler, R. S., 276
Silverman, A. J., 557, 601
Silbey, V., 569, 580
Simon, A., 607
Simon, H. A., 200
Simon, T., 195
Simpson, R. H., 470, 601
Skolnick, A. A., 559, 601
Slack, W. V., 79, 601
Slinde, J. A., 114, 118, 601
Slovic, P., 407, 601
Smedslund, J., 276, 601
Smith, E. R., 349, 601
Smith, G. M., 509, 586
Smith, M. B., 497, 601
Smith, P. C., 367, 513f., 520, 577, 601
Smith, S. E., 243, 580
Snapper, K., 584
Snow, R. E., 142, 259, 264, 272, 281, 298, 346, 499, 582, 594, 601
Solano, C., 588
Soliah, D., 429, 586
Sörbom, D., 176, 394, 591
Spearman, C., 197, 201, 217, 283, 394
Spielberger, C. D., 70, 72, 477, 498, 588, 602, 605
Spokane, A. R., 429, 602
Spuhler, J. N., 593
Staats, A., 338, 602
Stanley, J. C., 602
Starch, D., 81, 602
Steiner, I. D., 546, 602
Stephenson, W., 518, 602
Sternberg, J., 408, 602
Sternberg, R. J., 263, 264, 265, 276, 281f., 300, 320, 335, 581, 602
Stewart, L. H., 431, 602
Stockford, L., 511, 602
Stockholm, E., 467, 582
Stone, V. W., 420, 602
Streuning, E. L., 584
Strong, E. K., Jr., 129, 419, 429ff., 602
Stroud, T. W. F., 155, 599
Stuit, D. B., 366, 602
Sudman, S., 578
Suinn, R. M., 63, 583
Super, D. E., 427, 602
Swartz, J. D., 589
Swets, J. A., 40, 602

Taber, T., 367, 590
Tagiuri, R., 581, 585
Tatsuoka, M. M., 580
Taylor, L. R., 402, 580
Tellegen, A., 452, 579

Tenopyr, M., 390, 402, 406, 602
Terman, L. M., 58, 69, 195f., 198, 201, 215, 242, 602
Terrell, M., 391
Terwilliger, J. S., 421, 469, 603
Thayer, P. W., 359, 466, 603
Thigpen, C. H., 503, 603
Thissen, D. M., 119, 603
Thomson, C. W., 594
Thoresen, C. E., 532, 580
Thorndike, E. L., 196f., 199
Thorndike, R. L., 114, 120, 149, 196, 219, 224, 255, 389, 603
Thorndike, R. M., 578, 606
Thorne, A., 578
Thurstone, L. L., 11, 283, 292f.
Tiedeman, D. V., 429, 595
Tittle, C. K., 412, 438, 603
Tocco, T. S., 587
Tolor, A., 548, 603
Torrance, E. P., 261
Training Aids Section, 147, 603
Trattner, M. H., 369, 603
Travers, J. R., 335, 340, 603
Triandis, H. C., 323–327, 535f., 603
Trickett, E. J., 459, 603
Trotman, F. K., 322, 603
Tryon, G. S., 72, 603
Tryon, R. M., 317, 603
Tucker, J. A., 343, 603
Tukey, J. W., 397, 596
Tupes, E. C., 526, 603
Tyler, L. E., 428, 603
Tyler, R. W., 349, 601, 603

Undheim, J. O., 254, 603
Urry, V. W., 36, 603
Uzgiris, I. C., 232f.

van der Kamp, L. J. Th., 581
Van Hemert, M., 298, 584
Van Hemert, N. A., 298, 584
van Naerssen, R. F., 382
Vannoy, J. S., 546, 602
Varble, D. L., 559, 603
Vernon, P. E., 217, 252, 265, 289, 319, 324f., 329, 565f., 604

Wade, T. C., 443, 604
Wainer, H., 397, 593, 604
Walker, D. K., 607
Wallace, S. R., 365, 597
Wallach, M. A., 247, 262, 310, 448, 604
Warburton, F., 541, 606
Ward, W. C., 357, 604
Wascoe, N. E., 457, 587
Weaver, W., 601
Webb, E. J., 444, 604
Wechsler, D., 53, 200f., 204, 330f., 604
Weikart, D., 335, 604

Weiss, D. J., 39, 577
Weiss, D. S., 578, 598
Weisz, J. R., 204, 604
Weitzel, K. E., 273, 599
Wells, F. L., 199
Welsh, G. S., 582
Wepman, J., 340, 604
Wernimont, P. F., 363, 604
Wesman, A. G., 471f., 604
Westin, A. F., 473, 604
Whalen, C. K., 576
Wheeler, L., 586, 604
White, P. O., 263
White, R. W., 562, 604
Widom, C. S., 495, 604
Wiener, G., 71, 604
Wigdor, A. K., 8, 10, 74, 80, 125, 150, 197, 246, 247, 344, 358, 384, 387, 604
Wiggins, J. S., 461f., 485, 537, 562f., 566, 604, 605
Wildman, B. G., 535
Willemin, L. P., 367, 604
Willerman, L., 320, 604
Williams, C. M., 576
Williams, F., 592
Williams, K. A., 73, 588
Williams, R. L., 330, 605
Williams, T. A., 591
Wills, T. A., 509, 605
Wilson, D. P., 67, 605
Wilson, J. W., 108, 430, 593, 605
Wilson, G. T., 459, 597

Wimsatt, W. C., 153, 605
Winder, C. L., 537, 583, 605
Winkler, R. C., 452, 605
Winsor, A. L., 427, 582
Wirt, R., 522
Wirtz, W., 352, 605
Wissler, C., 193, 605
Witkin, H. A., 14, 15, 265ff., 582, 685
Wober, M., 323, 605
Wohlwill, J. F., 308
Wolf, T. H., 194f., 605
Wolman, B., 588
Wood, R. L., 271, 605
Woodworth, R. S., 476
Woody, R. H., 579, 582
Wright, J. M., 607
Wundt, W., 193
Wylie, R. C., 498, 605, 607

Yates, L. G., 583
Yeates, K. O., 204, 604
Yeh, J., 344, 605
Yen, W. M., 117, 575
Yerkes, R. M., 198f., 605
Yoakum, C. S., 198, 605
Young, M., 9, 197, 605

Zocolotti, P., 267, 605
Zubin, J., 554, 605
Zuckerman, M., 71, 165, 602, 605
Zytowski, D. G., 412, 429, 433, 438, 603, 605

83 84 85 9 8 7 6 5 4 3 2 1